Engaging the Reader

Activities that are tied to each skill level offer students multiple opportunities to engage with the reading and receive immediate feedback.

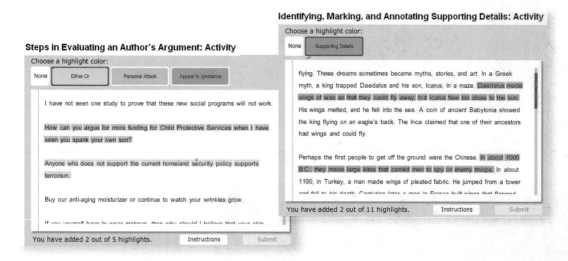

"Connect Reading gives [students] more study options and a fresh perspective to listen and learn from."
–Yvette Daniel, Central Georgia Tech.

Reading Critically

LiveInk, a research-based technology, increases the reader's comprehension, which leads to improved synthesis and understanding of information, the foundation of critical reading and critical thinking.

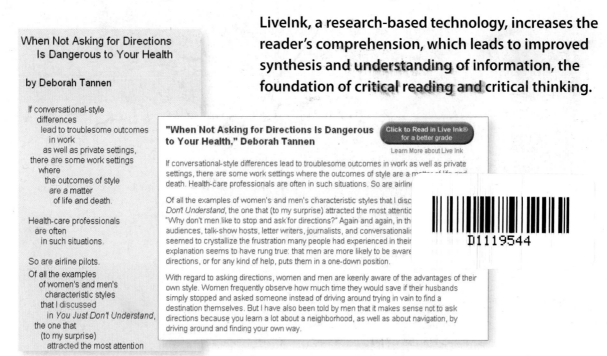

The Art of Critical Reading

Brushing Up on Your Reading, Thinking, and Study Skills

THIRD EDITION

Peter Mather
retired from
Glendale Community College
Glendale, Arizona

Rita McCarthy
Glendale Community College
Glendale, Arizona

McGraw Hill

Connect
Learn
Succeed™

The McGraw·Hill Companies

Connect
Learn
Succeed™

Published by McGraw-Hill, an imprint of The McGraw-Hill Companies, Inc., 1221 Avenue of the Americas, New York, NY 10020. Copyright © 2012, 2009, 2005. All rights reserved. No part of this publication may be reproduced or distributed in any form or by any means, or stored in a database or retrieval system, without the prior written consent of The McGraw-Hill Companies, Inc., including, but not limited to, in any network or other electronic storage or transmission, or broadcast for distance learning.

This book is printed on acid-free paper.

2 3 4 5 6 7 8 9 0 RJE/RJE 1 0 9 8 7 6 5 4 3 2

ISBN: 978-0-07-340721-0 (student edition)
MHID: 0-07-340721-6 (student edition)
ISBN: 978-0-07-741143-5 (instructor's edition)
MHID: 0-07-741143-9 (instructor's edition)

Senior Sponsoring Editor: *John Kindler*
Senior Marketing Manager: *Jaclyn Elkins*
Developmental Editor: *Merryl Maleska Wilbur*
Production Editor: *Jasmin Tokatlian*
Manuscript Editor: *Margaret Hines*
Design Manager: *Allister Fein*
Text Designer: *Pam Verros*
Cover Designer: *Brian Salisbury*
Photo Research: *Sonia Brown*
Buyer: *Tandra Jorgensen*
Media Project Manager: *Jennifer Barrick*
Composition: *10/13 Palatino by Aptara®, Inc.*
Printing: *45# New Era Matte Thin, R. R. Donnelley & Sons*

Vice President Editorial: *Michael Ryan*
Publisher: *David Patterson*
Senior Director of Development: *Dawn Groundwater*

Cover: *The Book*, 1913 (oil on canvas), Gris, Juan (1887–1927) / Musee d'Art Moderne de la Ville de Paris, Paris, France / Giraudon / The Bridgeman Art Library/Getty Images.

Credits: The credits section for this book begins on page C-1 and is considered an extension of the copyright page.

Library of Congress Cataloging-in-Publication Data

Mather, Peter.
   The art of critical reading : brushing up on your reading, thinking, and study skills / Peter Mather, Rita McCarthy.—3rd ed.
      p. cm.
   Includes bibliographical references and index.
   ISBN-13: 978-0-07-340721-0 (acid-free paper)
   ISBN-10: 0-07-340721-6 (acid-free paper) 1. Reading (Higher education)
   2. Critical thinking. 3. Study skills. I. McCarthy, Rita. II. Title.
   LB2395.3.M27 2011
   428.4071'1—dc23
                                                          2011037356

The Internet addresses listed in the text were accurate at the time of publication. The inclusion of a website does not indicate an endorsement by the authors or McGraw-Hill, and McGraw-Hill does not guarantee the accuracy of the information presented at these sites.
www.mhhe.com

Peter dedicates this book to his late parents,
Carl and Dorothy; and his brother and sister-in-law,
John and Peggy.

Rita dedicates this book to her sons, Ryan and Steve; her
daughters-in-law, Bonnie and Raquel; her grandchildren,
Zachary, Kate, and Dylan; and especially her husband,
Greg.

Letter from the Authors

Dear Colleagues,

Thank you for taking the time to consider *The Art of Critical Reading* for your course. We wrote this book with the goal of helping students become better at reading, understanding, and evaluating college-level materials. With this in mind we considered the things that we felt were important for students to have in order to be successful in this course and beyond. This is how we arrived at our title for the book. We wanted to show students that as is the case with Art, reading involves critical thinking and reflection. It drives students to discover and understand the meaning of the artist—and writer. We want students to see that becoming a better reader will allow them to do so much more.

We wrote this text focusing on three things that we believe will help students become better readers. First, we have made sure there are many high interest and engaging readings throughout the text. We wanted to expose students to the types of readings they will encounter in other college courses, including excerpts from college textbooks, literature, newspapers, and popular fiction and nonfiction. Second, we have given the students multiple opportunities to practice and develop their reading skills. With the multiple mastery tests and quizzes throughout the book, students have ample opportunities to assess what they know and don't know. Lastly, we focused on giving the students more access to vocabulary, especially vocabulary in context. While most vocabulary activities come directly from the readings, students also receive instruction on the basics, including Latin and Greek roots, prefixes, and suffixes, giving the students a better understanding of word meanings.

Students are more likely to read when they think of themselves as readers and when they see reading as a way to achieve more. By making reading fun and rewarding, students will engage in it. Our hope is that we've succeeded and that you will find the readings and exercises in our textbook interesting, imaginative, and enriching.

Rita McCarthy

About the Authors

Dr. Peter Mather—Dr. Mather earned his B.A. in government from the University of Redlands, his first M.A. in African studies from the University of California, Los Angeles, his second M.A. in reading from California State University, Los Angeles, and his Ed.D. in curriculum and instruction from the University of Southern California. Before recently retiring, he taught reading at the secondary, adult education, and community college levels for close to 30 years. While at Glendale Community College, he taught both developmental and critical and evaluative reading. He also taught American government and was the college director of the America Reads/Counts program. In addition to being the coauthor of *Reading and All That Jazz*, now in its fifth edition, and *Racing Ahead with Reading*, he has published articles in the *Journal of Reading*.

Ms. Rita Romero McCarthy—Ms. McCarthy earned her B.A. in sociology and history from the University of California, Berkeley, and her M.A. in education from Arizona State University. She has taught at the elementary, secondary, and college levels. For the past 23 years, she has taught English as a second language, developmental reading, and critical and evaluative reading at Glendale Community College. She is the coauthor of *Reading and All That Jazz* and *Racing Ahead with Reading*. Ms. McCarthy has also published articles in professional journals and other media; most of these have been concerned with the use of bibliotherapy. She has also published reading lists for beginning and remedial readers.

Brief Contents

Contents

APPENDICES A-1

Preface

The Art of Critical Reading provides multiple assessment opportunities, engaging and diverse reading selections, and in-context and essential vocabulary content in an integrated print and digital program designed to prepare students for reading in college and beyond.

MULTIPLE ASSESSEMENTS

Multiple assessment opportunities in the book and online help students test their knowledge to understand what their next steps will be in advancing their reading skills. Assessments are placed after each reading and throughout the chapters giving students the opportunity to understand what they know and don't know. Modules also promote vocabulary enhancement through the integration of vocabulary exercises.

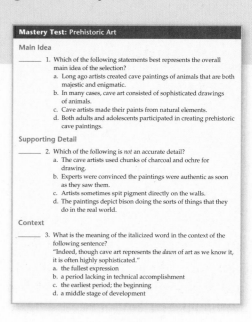

Mastery Test: Prehistoric Art

Main Idea

_____ 1. Which of the following statements best represents the overall main idea of the selection?
  a. Long ago artists created cave paintings of animals that are both majestic and enigmatic.
  b. In many cases, cave art consisted of sophisticated drawings of animals.
  c. Cave artists made their paints from natural elements.
  d. Both adults and adolescents participated in creating prehistoric cave paintings.

Supporting Detail

_____ 2. Which of the following is *not* an accurate detail?
  a. The cave artists used chunks of charcoal and ochre for drawing.
  b. Experts were convinced the paintings were authentic as soon as they saw them.
  c. Artists sometimes spit pigment directly on the walls.
  d. The paintings depict bison doing the sorts of things that they do in the real world.

Context

_____ 3. What is the meaning of the italicized word in the context of the following sentence?
  "Indeed, though cave art represents the *dawn* of art as we know it, it is often highly sophisticated."
  a. the fullest expression
  b. a period lacking in technical accomplishment
  c. the earliest period; the beginning
  d. a middle stage of development

New to this edition, **Mastery Tests** feature the type of questions that appear on standardized tests. Mastery Tests are interspersed throughout the text to reinforce skills and remind students that while individual skills may be practiced in isolation, the reading process is cumulative.

CONNECT READING DIAGNOSTIC

| 1: Vocabulary Skills | 2: Understanding | 3: Interpreting | 4: Reading Critically | 5: Study Skills |

McGraw Hill **connect** | READING

Connect Reading places reading in the hands of the students, giving them the opportunity to judge for themselves what they know and what they still need to learn.

ENGAGING AND DIVERSE READING SELECTIONS

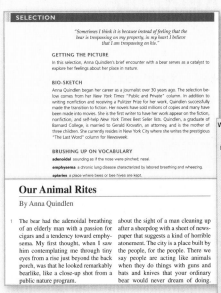

Reading selections were chosen for their excellence, their contemporary relevance and interest, and their overall diversity.

Powered by Connect, The Art of Critical Reading uses the research-based LiveInk technology to increase the student's reading comprehension which leads to improved synthesis of information.

The third edition of The Art of Critical Reading includes **eight new reading selections** with accompanying exercises.

IN-CONTEXT AND ESSENTIAL VOCABULARY

Two units present key vocabulary development techniques and provide context practice. Ten additional units introduce a set of Latin or Greek word parts or homonyms. Students learn college-level words associated with these word parts and then practice the key words and solve crossword puzzles.

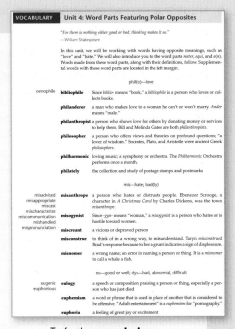

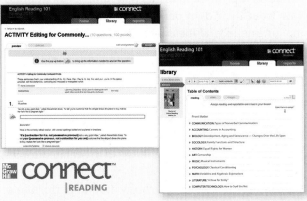

Connect Reading brings 3 levels of Vocabulary to the students.

To further **vocabulary development,** each end-of-chapter vocabulary unit now includes additional college-level words, listed in the margins, that draw on the unit's word parts.

Hallmarks of *The Art of Critical Reading*

> *"Everyone who knows how to read has it in their power to magnify themselves, to multiply the ways in which they exist, to make their lives full, significant, and interesting."*
>
> —ALDOUS HUXLEY

In 2005, we published the first edition of *The Art of Critical Reading*, a textbook that uses the theme of art to highlight an exciting and engaged approach to reading and learning. This year we are proud to present the third edition.

The Art of Critical Reading was designed as a higher-level sequel to our popular *Reading and All That Jazz*, now in its fifth edition. Like *Jazz*, *The Art of Critical Reading* is designed to draw readers in with its engaging exercises and its reading selections, which are taken from a variety of sources: college textbooks, newspapers, magazines, and classic and contemporary literature. As with *Jazz*, the purpose of this book is to assist college students in developing the skills they need for reading, understanding, and critically evaluating textbooks and other college-level reading. While *Art* may be appropriate for a more advanced audience than is *Jazz*, it is still a book that will motivate and engage readers through its theme, its exciting reading selections, and its stimulating visuals and exercises.

Theme and Title

We chose art as the theme of this book because, like written texts, art is a form of communication. Like works of literature, works of art range from the easily understood to the enigmatic and thought provoking. In art, the viewer may dislike the unfamiliar, at least at first, but when he or she understands the "language" of art and its structure, the visual experience becomes richer. So, too, with written works. In the case both of written texts and art, the better a person understands the purpose and structure of the material, the more likely it is that that person will be able to interpret it accurately and enjoy it.

Art, like literature, sharpens our perceptions of life and requires us to re-examine our thoughts. Both artists and writers compose their works with a purpose in mind. And both artists and writers draw from their own personal experiences and backgrounds to convey their emotional or intellectual messages. Both viewers of art and readers of literature must bring their own perspectives to bear when engaged in evaluation and interpretation.

We emphasize the theme by introducing each chapter with a major work of art so that students may reach a deeper understanding of it. To enhance students' experience of the works of art, we include journal prompts to encourage students to form their own opinions and share them with their instructors and classmates. Throughout the text, we have included provocative selections on a range of art-related topics, such as public art, Egyptian artifacts, prehistoric cave art, art theft, the *Mona Lisa*, and the Vietnam War Memorial. We conclude with a section on body art and performance art from a popular cultural anthropology textbook. Our hope is that students will find much material in this book, both visual and written, to stimulate and enrich.

Reading Selections and the Questions That Follow

The reading selections in this book were chosen, first, for their excellence. Many of the authors are famous or award winning. We also chose readings with contemporary relevance and interest. We tried to find selections that would broaden students' general knowledge about current events and be otherwise informative and useful. Finally, we sought readings that would appeal to a diverse audience. The selections address a wide variety of disciplines, from art to psychology to ethics to science. They also come from a wide variety of sources: while *The Art of Critical Reading* emphasizes textbook selections, it also presents other kinds of material students are likely to encounter in their college classes—works of literature as well as selections from magazines and newspapers.

While most of the selections are nonfiction, we also include poetry, fables, and cartoons. And although we emphasize contemporary material, we also include some classics. The one trait all the selections share is that they will enable students to clarify their own values as they experience events through someone else's eyes. Although many of the selections have not previously appeared in a reading textbook, instructors can use them with confidence, as they have been tested in our classes and in those of our colleagues.

The questions following the reading selections require students to engage in recalling, understanding, interpreting, and evaluating. They come in various formats—multiple-choice, true-or-false, fill-in-the-blank, matching, discussion, and written-response. The objective questions are written in the style of questions asked on standardized tests. The open-ended questions for discussion and writing are included to give students practice in analyzing, synthesizing, and evaluating. Such questions give students the opportunity to bring their personal experiences to bear, and they are organized in such a way as to lead students to a greater understanding of the selections. These questions rarely have a right or wrong answer; instead, they are meant to provoke discussion and encourage debate.

Organization of the Text

This book is organized along two dimensions. First, each successive part of the book focuses on different skills that an effective critical reader must master. Second, the book begins with a narrow perspective, focusing on students' personal experience, and then moves to increasingly broader perspectives, focusing in turn on interpersonal, social, national, and international issues. The book becomes increasingly challenging as it progresses, both in the selections presented and the critical reading skills taught:

- **Part 1 explores the skills likely to lead to a successful college experience.** Material presented in this section includes an overview of creative and critical thinking skills, an introduction to study skills, discussions about stress, and computer and Internet skills. The Introduction in Part 1 is meant to be completed in the first week of class. The objective questions and short written assignments that follow the selections will allow instructors to assess the skills of individual students and the class as a whole.

- **Part 2 reviews the basic skills needed for effective critical reading.** Focusing on the processes and structures of reading, Part 2 reviews skills that include identifying the topic, identifying the main idea and supporting details, and determining the author's purpose. Students practice recognizing and using transition words and patterns of organization. They also have the opportunity to apply multiple study techniques and study skills in conjunction with their work on patterns of organization. Vocabulary activities focus in part on identifying homonyms and other confusing words. The selections, which include fables, poems, and anecdotes, touch on themes of perception, motivation, risk taking, and ethics.

- **Part 3 emphasizes reading as an interpretive and analytical process.** The goal of Part 3 is to enable students to become proficient at reading between the lines. Part 3 topics include inference, figurative language, and author's tone. Themes include animals, nature, and overcoming adversity. Selections include material from such noted authors as Michael J. Fox, Bill Bryson, Rosa Castillo Guilbault, Farley Mowat, and Hayden Herrera.

- **Part 4 concentrates on developing critical reading and thinking skills.** Topics discussed include fact and opinion, the author's point of view, bias, propaganda techniques, logical fallacies, and the structure and parts of an argument. Selections cover such varied topics as astrology, nutrition, prehistoric art, animal rights, media literacy, the Vietnam War Memorial, and the Declaration of Independence and Bill of Rights. In Part 4, students are given an opportunity to evaluate evidence with material that covers the theme of death and dying, from various perspectives.

- **Part 5 is devoted to improving study skills.** Throughout earlier chapters, we introduce students to study skills such as SQ3R, outlining, mapping, and annotating. Part 5 asks students to apply these skills to part of a chapter about body and performance art taken from a popular college anthropology textbook.

- **The Appendices address the skills needed to use a thesaurus and to interpret visual aids effectively.** The section on visual aids—tables, charts, graphs, maps—is designed to be used as an independent unit or in conjunction with specific reading selections. The Appendices now include tips for taking objective and essay exams. We also include a section on coping with test-taking anxiety.

Organization of the Chapters

Each chapter begins with an overview of the chapter topic and a discussion of the key terms needed for understanding the topic, followed by short exercises designed to help students understand and master the topic, and then by longer reading selections that further develop the topic. Introducing each of the longer reading selections are several pre-reading activities. A section titled "Getting the Picture" seeks to engage students with the subject of the upcoming selection. It is followed by a "Bio-sketch" of the author, which in turn is followed by a section entitled "Brushing Up on Vocabulary," which offers a discussion of unusual words that appear in the selection.

Following the selections are a variety of post-reading exercises, including "Comprehension Checkup" questions and "Vocabulary in Context" exercises. There is also a section entitled "In Your Own Words," which provides a series of open-ended questions designed to encourage critical thinking and analysis on the part of the students. "The Art of Writing" follows next. This section often includes directions for longer written assignments, some of which will call for research by students. Finally, the section called "Internet Activity" asks students to research on the Internet interesting or unusual topics covered in the selection.

The exercises in each chapter are sequential, progressing from relatively easy to quite difficult. These exercises use many different formats in order to maintain student interest. The instructor should feel free to pick and choose among the exercises in accord with the needs of particular students or classes. The exercises are designed so that the instructor can have the students work individually or in groups.

Special Features of *The Art of Critical Reading*

One thing you'll notice immediately is the beautiful, full-color design, which adds interest to the art works, cartoons, and other visuals throughout the text.

You'll also notice that the reading selections are designed to look similar to how they appeared in their original media contexts. In other words, reading selections taken from newspapers and magazines are set to look like news and magazine articles; selections taken from popular books and literature are set to look like excerpts from books; and textbook material is designed to appear as it would in an authentic textbook.

Throughout the text, emphasis has been placed on vocabulary development. The vocabulary units are integrated into the chapters, and each reading selection has a section on vocabulary-in-context featuring the words from the selection. Unlike many reading textbooks, the vocabulary exercises are varied and include creative exercises as well as matching, fill-in-the blank, and crossword puzzles.

Because this textbook is meant to encourage critical and evaluative reading, we have included selections discussing creativity and critical thinking. We have also provided numerous opportunities for students to practice analytical reasoning by comparing and contrasting reading selections and art works. And more opportunities are provided to deal with issues that are of real concern to today's students, such as cheating, Internet use, food and health safety, relationships, and school and community. Authors from diverse backgrounds are represented.

In addition to the wide range of readings and challenging questions that test and reinforce student learning, we've included several features especially aimed at reinforcing skills crucial to success in college:

- **Quotations in the margins that prompt student journal writing and discussion.** These quotations respond in provocative ways to reading selections and encourage students to reflect on the implications of what they have read.
- **Study Techniques.** We've included coverage of a variety of study techniques—from annotating and summarizing to outlining and mapping—to reinforce the basic skills students need to succeed in college. These study techniques are not only interspersed throughout the book but they are also a point of focus in Part 5, where they are applied to a partial textbook chapter.
- **Developing a college-level vocabulary.** There are 10 vocabulary units, each of which introduces students to a set of Latin or Greek words parts or homonyms. Students learn college-level words associated with these word parts and then practice the key words by means of exercises and crossword puzzles.

New to This Edition

The third edition of *The Art of Critical Reading* includes eight new reading selections with accompanying exercises:

Chapter 1: "All-Nighter?" by Sharon LaFraniere

Chapter 1: "Analyzing Internet Sites" by Hamilton Gregory

Chapter 3: "Impulse Control: The Marshmallow Test" by Daniel Goleman

Chapter 6: *A Walk in the Woods* by Bill Bryson

Chapter 6: "Book of Dreams" by Rosa Castillo Guilbault

Chapter 9: "Our Animal Rites" by Anna Quindlen

Chapter 10: "Somebody's Baby" by Barbara Kingsolver

Chapter 10: "Media Literacy" by Mary-Lou Galician

The new edition also includes two new poems:

Chapter 6: "Introduction to Poetry" by Billy Collins

Chapter 9: "The Vietnam Wall" by Albert Ríos

Among the many changes made to strengthen and improve the text, the most substantial are as follows:

- **Chapter 2, Topics, Main Ideas, and Details:** This chapter has updated information on "The Look of a Victim" and "Public Art." It includes a new chart and special tips for deciding the appropriate use of the homonyms *lie* and *lay*.

- **Chapter 4, Transition Words and Patterns of Organization:** This chapter has been completely revised to include additional writing patterns such as spatial organization. It also has new material on transition words that signal the relationship of ideas within sentences and between sentences. Five new exercises to practice these skills have been included. The chapter also better integrates the multiple study techniques with the patterns of organization presented.

- **Chapter 5, Inference:** In this chapter, the introduction to the key concepts has been completely revised.

- **Chapter 8, Fact and Opinion:** This chapter features a new skimming and scanning activity for the Prehistoric Art selection. It also has new fact-and-opinion exercises calling for more critical thinking on the part of the student.

- Propaganda techniques in **Chapter 9, Point of View** and logical fallacies in **Chapter 10, Bias** have been completely redone. There are also new exercises on point of view and bias.

- **Chapter 11, Analyzing and Evaluating Arguments:** This chapter has been completely revised. It now includes the Structure of an Argument, the Parts of an Argument, Evaluating Arguments, and Applying Critical Thinking to Arguments. There are three new exercises on evaluating arguments and a completely redone section on inductive and deductive reasoning.

- **New to this edition are MASTERY TESTS on five art-related selections.** These feature the type of questions that appear on standardized tests. Mastery tests are interspersed throughout the text to reinforce skills and remind students that while individual skills may be practiced in isolation, the reading process is cumulative.

- **REVIEW TESTS are interspersed throughout the text.** All of the review tests from the previous edition have been updated. Two new review tests on the high-interest topics of cheating and debt have been added.

- **To further vocabulary development,** each end-of-chapter vocabulary unit now includes additional college-level words, listed in the margins, that draw on and exemplify the unit's word parts.

- **To further stimulate logical, creative, and critical thinking,** a new section entitled "Brain Teasers" calls on students to solve a variety of puzzles. The

Brain Teasers appear toward the end of each chapter. These can be fun group activities.

- **Finally, the Appendix now features a dedicated section on Test-Taking Tips.** These tips provide helpful hints for mastering objective and subjective exam questions.

Teaching and Learning Aids Accompanying the Book

Supplements for Instructors

- **Annotated Instructor's Edition (ISBN: 0-07-741143-9).** The Annotated Instructor's Edition contains the full text of the Student Edition plus answers to the objective exercises and some suggested answers to open-ended questions.

- **Online Learning Center (www.mhhe.com/mather).** This password-protected site houses many resources for instructors, including:
  - *Instructor's Manual and Test Bank.* Available online for easy downloading, the Instructor's Manual and Test Bank, written by the authors of the textbook, are a robust resource providing innovative teaching tips, vocabulary quizzes, unit tests, supplementary activities, and useful connections to other resources, such as poems, movies, and political and cultural events.
  - *PowerPoint Slides.* Also available on the instructor's site are PowerPoint slides on which the instructional content of each chapter is summarized for overhead projection.

Supplements for Students

- **Online Learning Center (www.mhhe.com/mather).** Our companion Web site offers journal prompts for each chapter, links to direct students to reliable Web sources, search exercises to give students practice at finding reliable sites on their own, and much, much more.

- **Study Smart (www.mhhe.com/studysmart).** This innovative study-skills tutorial for students is an excellent resource for the learning lab or for students working on their own at home. Teaching students strategies for note taking, test taking, and time management, Study Smart operates with a sophisticated answer analysis that students will find motivating. Available on CD-ROM or online, Study Smart is free when packaged with a McGraw-Hill text.

- **Word Works.** These Merriam-Webster and Random House reference works are available at low cost when ordered with *The Art of Critical Reading*:
  - *Merriam-Webster's Notebook Dictionary.* A compact word resource conveniently designed for 3-ring binders, *Merriam-Webster's Notebook Dictionary* includes 40,000 entries for widely used words with concise, easy-to-understand definitions and pronunciations.
  - *The Merriam-Webster Dictionary.* This handy paperback dictionary contains over 70,000 definitions yet is small enough to carry around in a backpack, so it's always there when it's needed.
  - *Random House Webster's College Dictionary.* This authoritative dictionary includes over 160,000 entries and 175,000 definitions—more than any other college dictionary—and the most commonly used definitions are always listed first, so students can find what they need quickly.

- *Merriam-Webster's Collegiate Dictionary & Thesaurus CD-ROM.* This up-to-the-minute electronic dictionary and thesaurus offers 225,000 definitions, 340,000 synonyms and related words, and 1,300 illustrations.
- *Merriam-Webster's Notebook Thesaurus.* Conveniently designed for 3-ring binders, *Merriam-Webster's Notebook Thesaurus* provides concise, clear guidance for over 157,000 word choices.
- *Merriam-Webster Thesaurus.* This compact thesaurus offers over 157,000 word choices and includes concise definitions and examples to help students choose the correct word for the context.
- *Merriam-Webster's Vocabulary Builder.* *Merriam-Webster's Vocabulary Builder* focuses on more than 1,000 words, introduces nearly 2,000 more, and includes quizzes to test the student's progress.
- **Novel Ideas.** These Random House and HarperCollins paperbacks are available at a low cost when packaged with the text:

  The Monkey Wrench Gang **(Abbey)**; *Things Fall Apart* **(Achebe)**; *The Lone Ranger and Tonto* **(Alexie)**; *Integrity* **(Carter)**; *The House on Mango Street* **(Cisneros)**; *Heart of Darkness* **(Conrad)**; *Pilgrim at Tinker Creek* **(Dillard)**; *Love Medicine* **(Erdrich)**; *Their Eyes Were Watching God* **(Hurston)**; *Boys of Summer* **(Kahn)**; *Woman Warrior* **(Kingston)**; *One Hundred Years of Solitude* **(Marquez)**; *Clear Springs* **(Mason)**; *All the Pretty Horses* **(McCarthy)**; *House Made of Dawn* **(Momaday)**; *Joy Luck Club* **(Tan)**; *Essays of E. B. White* **(White)**.

For more information or to request copies of any of the above supplementary materials for instructor review, please contact your local McGraw-Hill representative at 1-800-338–3987 or send an e-mail message to **english@mcgraw-hill.com.**

Acknowledgments

No textbook can be created without the assistance of many people. First, we relied on the thoughtful reactions and suggestions of our colleagues across the country who reviewed this project at various stages:

Jesus Adame, *El Paso Community College*

Taddese Addo, *Community College of Denver*

Karin S. Alderfer, *Miami Dade College*

Edy Alderson, *Joliet Junior College*

Bonnie Arnett, *Washtenaw Community College*

Heidi Beck, *Seattle University*

Julia Bickel, *Indian Wesleyan University*

Shawn Bixler, *The University of Akron*

Doralee Brooks, *Community College of Allegheny County*

Marta Brown, *Community College of Denver*

Helen Carr, *San Antonio College*

Gertrude Coleman, *Middlesex College*

Susan Dalton, *Alamance Community College*

Marion Duckworth, *Valdosta State College*

Desiree F. Dumas, *Greenville Technical College*

Jan Eveler, *El Paso Community College*

Amy Girone, *Arizona Western College*

Suzanne Gripenstraw, *Butte College*

John Grether, *St. Cloud State University*

Joan Hellman, *Community College of Baltimore*

Rita L. Higgins, *Essex County College*

Sue M. Hightower, *Tallahassee Community College*

Suzanne Hughes, *Florida Community College*

Lorna Keebaugh, *Taft College*

Julie Kelly, *St. Johns River Community College*

Sandi Komarow, *Montgomery College*

Leon Lanzbom, *San Diego Mesa College*

Monique Mannering, *Brookhaven College*

Mary D. Mears, *Macon State College*

Ronald Mossler, *Los Angeles Valley Community College*

Elizabeth Nelson, *Tidewater Community College*

Mary Nielsen, *Dalton State College*

Cindy Ortega, *Phoenix College*

Paul J. Quinn, *Houston Community College*

Kathleen Riehle, *Sinclair Community College*

Michelle Riley, *Miami Dade College*

Jackie Roberts, *Richland Community College*

Carol Saunders, *Chipola College*

Susan Silva, *El Paso Community College*

Margaret Sims, *Midlands Technical College*

Marsha Stowe, *Ivy Tech Community College*

Peggy Strickland, *Gainesville Junior College*

Margaret Triplet, *Central Oregon Community College*

Michael Vensel, *Miami Dade College–Kendall*

Danya D. Wahlberg, *Santa Barbara City College*

Richard S. Wilson, *Community College of Baltimore County*

Lynda Wolverton, *Polk Community College*

Cynthia Ybanez, *College of Southern Maryland*

In addition to our reviewers, our friends and colleagues at Glendale Community College offered their thoughts and supported our efforts: Dave Gallet, Darlene Goto, R.J. Merrill, Mary Jane Onnen, Brendan Regan, David Rodriguez, Linda Smith, Scott Kozak, and Russ Sears. A special thanks to Pam Hall, who loaned us so many art books and provided invaluable advice. Others who helped us were Marilyn Brophy, Roberta Delaney, Nancy Edwards, Cindy Gilbert, Tom Mather, Mary Holden, Lynda Svendsen, and Gwen Worthington.

We'd also like to thank the people at McGraw-Hill who worked to produce this text. First, there were our editors at McGraw-Hill. John Kindler, our sponsoring editor, has kept the process of creating a third edition running smoothly and has always been willing to discuss our ideas. Our developmental editor, Merryl Maleska Wilbur, has made the creation of the third edition a true pleasure. Thanks also to Peggy

Hines, manuscript editor, Sonia Brown, photo editor, Jasmin Tokatlian, production editor, and Tandra Jorgensen, buyer.

To all the people who participated with us in creating this book, we offer our sincerest thanks.

Peter Mather
Rita McCarthy

We hope that your experience using *The Art of Critical Reading* will be entirely successful. If you have comments or suggestions for improving the way this textbook works, we'd like to hear from you. Send an email to **english@mcgraw-hill.com,** and our editors will gladly pass it along.

Introductory Puzzle

At right you will find a crossword puzzle that will introduce you to the material covered in this book. The answers to some of the clues can be found in the Table of Contents and the Index. The Table of Contents shows you the major divisions of the book. The Index, found at the back of the book, is an alphabetical listing of many important topics and the page numbers on which the information is located. For a few answers, you may have to search through the book itself. Happy Hunting!

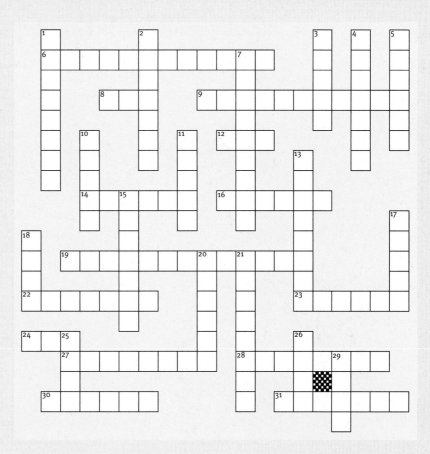

ACROSS CLUES

6. Chapter 4 discusses patterns of _____.

8. The first word in the title of the selection in Chapter 13 is _____ and the Aesthetic.

9. Charles Finney's selection discusses the western diamondback _____.

12. A discussion of similes, metaphors, and personification is found in Chapter _____.

14. The last name of the coauthor of this book who attended the University of Redlands.

16. An author whose purpose is to _____ will provide readers with knowledge or information.

19. Marian Wright Edelman was born in the state of _____.

22. Chapter 2 discusses topics, main ideas, and _____.

23. One type of pattern of organization is called cause and _____.

24. According to Vocabulary Unit 3, the prefix for nine is _____.

27. One type of pattern of organization is called _____ and illustration.

28. The last name of the coauthor of this book who has taught ESL classes.

30. Figurative language compares two or more _____ things.

31. Study Technique 6 is titled _____.

DOWN CLUES

1. In the Introduction, Dr. Seuss discusses the art of eating _____.

2. Most reading selections begin with a section titled "Getting the _____."

3. One type of logical fallacy is called _____ analogy.

4. The Introduction features a painting by well-known artist Pablo _____.

5. Frida Kahlo was married to Diego _____.

7. Study Technique 4 is titled _____.

10. Dave Barry wrote for the _____ Herald.

11. Study Technique 3 will teach you how to write summaries of _____ articles.

13. An author's purpose may be to _____ a reader or to try to change the reader's opinion.

15. If you learn by doing, your learning style would be called _____.

17. Chapter _____ discusses the difference between fact and opinion.

18. _____ stacking is one type of propaganda technique.

20. "The Bill of _____" is a selection in Chapter 11.

21. Michael J. Fox wrote the book _____.

25. Study Technique 9 will teach you how to make a _____ Diagram.

26. _____ Ying Lin designed the Vietnam Veterans Memorial.

29. Test-taking _____ are found in the Appendices.

Life in College and Beyond

Chapters in Part 1

The School of Athens (1510)

by Raphael

Scala/Art Resource, NY

Applying Creative and Critical Thinking

Three Musicians (1921) BY PABLO PICASSO

View and Reflect

1. This painting by Picasso is quite large. In fact, the three musicians, which include a Harlequin and a monk, are approximately life-size. What instruments are recognizable in the painting?

2. What animal is depicted on the left? Although the animal's body parts are disconnected, what parts can you clearly recognize?

3. What is the overall mood of the painting? Is it a solemn or happy occasion?

4. The painting is done in the cubist style, which tries to portray three-dimensional objects in a two-dimensional space. The result is a flat jigsaw puzzle effect. Which parts of the painting give the feeling of something being cut out or pasted on paper?

Oe of the desired outcomes of a college education is the ability to think critically. But it's important to be able to think creatively as well. A creative thinker can generate many solutions to a problem, and a critical thinker can determine which solution is the best.

The selections that follow will explain the processes of creative and critical thinking.

SELECTION

Bull's Head
(1942) BY PABLO PICASSO

Réunion des Musées Nationaux/Art Resource, NY/ ARS © 2011 Estate of Pablo Picasso/Artists Rights Society (ARS), New York

"Intelligence and creativity are not the same thing."

GETTING THE PICTURE

The influential artist Pablo Picasso once said, "Every child is an artist. The problem is how to remain an artist once he grows up." Picasso, noted for his creativity, meant that children are unafraid to try new things even at the risk of feeling foolish or experiencing failure. As we age, many of us place more emphasis on saving face, being practical, and thinking inside the box.

Picasso, as the story goes, took a walk around his yard one day and saw an old, rusted bicycle. He took the seat and the handlebars back to his studio and welded them together to create his famous sculpture of the head of a bull. The selection below explains the creative process and the characteristics of creative thinkers like Picasso who don't just think of a bicycle seat as something to sit on. Perhaps, after reading the selection, you'll be able to unleash some of your own creative energy.

BIO-SKETCH

John Santrock is a professor of psychology and human development at the University of Texas. He is the author of many popular, well-regarded textbooks.

BRUSHING UP ON VOCABULARY

divergent differing; deviating; having no finite limits

convergent coming together; merging

Excerpt from
PSYCHOLOGY

by John Santrock

CREATIVITY

What does it mean to be creative? **Creativity** is the ability to think about 1 something in novel and unusual ways and to come up with unconventional solutions to problems. Intelligence and creativity are not the same things. Many highly intelligent people produce large numbers of products, but the products are not necessarily novel. Highly creative people defy the crowd, whereas people who are highly intelligent but not creative often try simply to please the crowd.

Creative people tend to be divergent thinkers. **Divergent thinking** produces 2 many answers to the same question. In contrast, the kind of thinking required on conventional intelligence tests is **convergent thinking.** For example, a typical item on an intelligence test is "How many quarters will you get in return for 60 dimes?" There is only one correct answer to this question. However, the following question has many possible answers: what image comes to mind when you hear the phrase "sitting alone in a dark room"?

Thinking further about intelligence and creativity, most creative people are 3 quite intelligent, but the reverse is not necessarily true. Many highly intelligent people are not very creative.

Steps in the Creative Process

The creative process has often been described as a five-step sequence: 4

1. *Preparation.* You become immersed in a problem or an issue that interests you and arouses your curiosity.

2. *Incubation.* You churn ideas around in your head. This is the point at which you are likely to make some unusual connections in your thinking.

3. *Insight.* At this point, you experience the "Aha!" moment when all the pieces of the puzzle seem to fit together.

4. *Evaluation.* Now you must decide whether the idea is valuable and worth pursuing. Is the idea really novel, or is it obvious?

5. *Elaboration.* This final step often covers the longest span of time and the hardest work. This is what the famous twentieth-century American inventor Thomas Edison was talking about when he said that creativity is 1 percent inspiration and 99 percent perspiration. Elaboration may require a great deal of perspiration.

Characteristics of Creative Thinkers

Creative thinkers tend to have the following characteristics: 5

- *Flexibility and playful thinking.* Creative thinkers are flexible and play with   6 problems, which gives rise to a paradox. Although creativity takes hard work, the work goes more smoothly if it is taken lightly. In a way humor greases the wheels of creativity. When you are joking around, you are more likely to consider any possibility. Having fun helps to disarm the inner censor that can condemn your ideas as off base.

- *Inner motivation.* Creative people often are motivated by the joy of   7 creating. They tend to be less inspired by grades, money, or favorable feedback from others. Thus creative people are motivated more internally than externally.

- *Willingness to risk.* Creative people make more mistakes than their less imag- 8 inative counterparts. It's not that they are less proficient but that they come up with more ideas, more possibilities. They win some, they lose some. For example, the twentieth-century Spanish artist Pablo Picasso created more than 20,000 paintings. Not all of them were masterpieces. Creative thinkers learn to cope with unsuccessful projects and see failure as an opportunity to learn.

"Creativity requires the courage to let go of certainties."

—Erich Fromm

- *Objective evaluation of work.* Despite the stereotype that creative people are   9
eccentric and highly subjective, most creative thinkers strive to evaluate
their work objectively. They may use an established set of criteria to make
judgments or rely on the judgments of respected, trusted others.

Living a More Creative Life

*"The world is but
a canvas to the
imagination."*
—Henry David Thoreau

Here are recommendations for achieving a more creative life: 10

- *Try to be surprised by something every day.* Maybe it is something you see,   11
hear, or read about. Become absorbed in a lecture or a book. Be open to
what the world is telling you. Life is a stream of experiences. Swim widely
and deeply in it, and your life will be richer.

- *Try to surprise at least one person every day.* In a lot of things you do, you   12
have to be predictable and patterned. Do something different. Ask a question you normally would not ask. Invite someone to go to a show or a museum you have never visited.

- *Write down every day what surprised you and how you surprised others.* Most   13
creative people keep a diary, notes, or lab records to ensure that experiences are not fleeting or forgotten.

- *When something sparks your interest, follow it.* The world is our business. We   14
can't know which parts are more interesting until we make a serious effort
to learn as much about as many aspects of it as possible.

- *Take charge of your schedule.* Figure out which time of the day is your most   15
creative time. Carve out time for yourself when your creative energy is at
its best.

*"The best way to
have a good idea is
to have lots of ideas."*
—Linus Pauling

- *Spend time in settings that stimulate your creativity.* Many report their highest 16
levels of creativity occur when they are walking, jogging, driving, or swimming. These activities are semiautomatic in that they take only a certain
amount of attention while leaving some free to make connection among
ideas. Highly creative people also report coming up with novel ideas in the
deeply relaxed state we are in when we are half-asleep, half-awake.

To evaluate the extent to which you engage in creative thinking complete the   17
following chart.

How Creative Is Your Thinking?

Rate each of the following items as they apply to you on a scale from 1 = not like me at all,
2 = somewhat unlike me, 3 = somewhat like me, 4 = very much like me.

1. I am good at coming up with lots of new and unique ideas.   _____

2. I like to brainstorm with others to creatively find solutions
   to problems.   _____

3. I'm a flexible person and like to play with my thinking.   _____

4. I like to be around creative people, and I learn from how they think.   _____

continued

How Creative Is Your Thinking? *(continued)*

5. I like to be surprised by something every day.   _____

6. I wake up in the morning with a mission.   _____

7. I search for alternative solutions to problems rather than giving a
   pat answer.   _____

8. I know which settings stimulate me to be creative, and I try to
   spend time in those settings.   _____

9. I tend to be internally motivated.   _____

Total your scores for all 9 items. Your creativity score is _____. If you scored 32–36 points, you likely are a creative thinker. If you scored 27–31 points, you are inclined to be creative, but could benefit from thinking about some ways to get more creativity in your life. If you scored 26 or below, seriously think about ways to become more creative.

_____

(John Santrock, *Psychology*, 7/e, 2003)

✓ COMPREHENSION CHECKUP

True or False

Indicate whether the statement is true or false by writing **T** or **F** in the blank provided.

_____ 1. Intelligence and creativity are precisely the same thing.

_____ 2. Many highly intelligent people are not very creative.

_____ 3. In the creative process, evaluation takes the most time and requires the hardest work.

_____ 4. Humor is an asset in the creative process.

_____ 5. External motivation plays a large part in the creative process.

_____ 6. Creative people have a positive attitude toward failure.

_____ 7. Most creative thinkers are highly eccentric.

_____ 8. To live a creative life, the author recommends being open to new experiences.

_____ 9. Predictability is an essential characteristic of the creative life.

_____ 10. People sometimes come up with creative ideas when they are doing a physical activity that requires little mental energy.

Vocabulary Practice

Answer the following in the blank provided.

1. You put your car in *reverse*. Are you are going forward or backward?

   _____

2. Your cousin is *proficient* at typing. Is she skilled or unskilled?

   _____

3. If you come up with a *novel* way to travel, are you coming up with something that is new or something that has been done before? _____

4. If you are *striving* for an A in class, are you making a strong effort or a weak one? _____

5. If you got a *fleeting* glimpse of a friend at a basketball game, did you see a great deal of her or very little? _____

6. If you *defied* your commander, are you being obedient or disobedient? _____

7. If your thinking is *flexible,* can you change your mind about something, or must you "stick to your guns"? _____

8. If you take a test with all multiple-choice questions, are you taking an *objective* test or a *subjective* one? _____

9. If you *disarm* an alarm system, are you turning it on or off? _____

10. If the label on the medicine bottle says, "For *external* use only," should you swallow the medicine? _____

11. Give an example of something that is completely *predictable*. _____

12. What is wrong with using *stereotypes*? _____
_____

In Your Own Words

1. Give your own definition of *creativity*.

2. What does the author mean when he says, "Humor greases the wheels of creativity"?

3. Study the following problems to determine how creative you are.
   a. What objects can you think of that begin with the letters "br"?
   b. How could discarded aluminum cans be put to use?
   c. How many uses can you think of for a newspaper?
   d. What would happen if everyone suddenly lost the sense of balance and could no longer stay upright?

4. How is Garfield illustrating creative problem solving in the cartoon below?

GARFIELD ®

5. Which of the following is more likely an example of creative thinking? Explain the reasons for your choice.
   a. A 16-year-old trying to come up with as many reasons as she can to explain her poor grades to avoid being grounded.
   b. A 16-year-old taking a multiple-choice test.

6. When a group tries to come up with as many solutions to a problem as possible, it's called *brainstorming*. Why is this technique considered a creative thinking strategy?

The Art of Writing

It has been suggested by various creativity experts that the testing process could be improved to allow for more creative responses. For instance, professors might give more points for the most unusual correct answers to a question. Or professors might ask questions that have more than one correct answer and then give credit based on the number of correct answers a student gives. What do you think about these suggestions? Should test-makers be encouraged to allow for more creative responses? Write a few paragraphs giving your opinion.

Internet Activity

At the end of many reading selections, you will find one or more suggested Internet activities. Although we have checked each site, Web sites do come and go, and URLs change frequently. If the Internet site mentioned in the activity is no longer available, then use a search engine like Google <www.google.com> or Yahoo! <www.yahoo.com> to find a similar site.

Check out the following Web site to try out some creative thinking activities. Can activities like these help you become a more creative individual?

www.mycoted.com/Category:Creativity_Techniques

Brain Teasers

Study the following test of divergent thinking. How could you complete each figure?

*"Nampeyo's success became a pattern that other Indian
artists would follow."*

GETTING THE PICTURE

The craft of ceramics involves making objects from clay, a naturally occurring earth substance. Nearly every known culture has practiced the craft of ceramics, and civilizations in the Middle East understood the basic techniques as early as 5000 B.C.E. One method for creating ceramic pots is known as *coiling*. The ceramist rolls out ropelike strands of clay, then coils them upon one another and joins them together. The coils can then be smoothed to produce a uniform, flat wall. The early Native American peoples of the southwestern United States made extraordinarily fine pots by this method. In the twentieth century, their craft was revived by a few supremely talented and creative individuals, including the famous Nampeyo, whose work is described in the selection below.

(Mark Getlein, *Gilbert's Living with Art*, 2005)

BIO-SKETCH

Now retired, Duane Preble was a professor of art at the University of Hawaii from 1961 to 1991. Preble currently serves on the Board of Trustees of Hawaii's major art museum, the Honolulu Academy of Arts.

BRUSHING UP ON VOCABULARY

abstract emphasizing line and color in a nonrepresentational design.

curator the person in charge of a museum or art collection.

shards fragments of broken earthenware.

Excerpt from

ARTFORMS

by Duane Preble

SHAPING HER PEOPLE'S HERITAGE: NAMPEYO (1857?–1942)

Traditional Native American ceramic arts had fallen into decline when Nampeyo 1 first learned the trade from her grandmother. Most Indians in the Hopi region of Arizona, and even the Pueblo peoples of New Mexico, made very little pottery. The encroachment of mass produced goods, coupled with the severe poverty of both regions, led most Native families in the late nineteenth century to buy low-priced dishes and cooking utensils from white traders rather than pursue the ancient and time-consuming art of ceramics. Nampeyo's fusion of artistic talent and interest in the past sparked a pottery revival that spread throughout the Southwest and continues to this day.

The date of her birth is uncertain, since no one kept close records of such 2 things in the village of Hano on land that the Hopis called First Mesa. She was born into the Snake Clan, and was given the name Nampeyo, which means

"Snake That Does Not Bite." There were no paved roads leading to the village, and the nearest city—Winslow, Arizona—was three days' journey away. In that isolated environment, Nampeyo grew up. Her family responded to her early artistic interests by sending her to a neighboring village to learn pottery-making from her grandmother, one of the few who still made pots. Her grandmother's large water jars were rather simply decorated, with only one or two designs on the face of each one.

Sometime in the middle 1890s, Nampeyo began picking up broken shards of 3 pottery from the near-by site of an ancient Hopi village called Sikyatki. This village had been abandoned well before the Spanish Conquest. The ancient pottery fragments were more ornate and abstract than the basic symbols that Nampeyo had been painting; she was fascinated by the ancient designs and began to incorporate them into her own pots.

In 1895, the anthropologist Jesse Walter Fewkes arrived to dig and study the 4 ruins of Sikyatki, and his presence transformed Nampeyo's work. Her husband was one of several assistants to Fewkes; he helped with the digging and told the anthropologist what he knew about the ancestral customs of the Hopi peoples. Fewkes and his assistants and students unearthed hundreds of burials, finding many more examples of ancient Hopi pottery in excellent condition. It was traditional to bury the dead with a seed jar, a low container with a narrow opening at the top, as a symbol of spiritual rebirth. These jars had abstract designs in brown or black over a rich yellow body. Her husband brought pieces home for Nampeyo, and soon she met Fewkes and accompanied him on digs.

Nampeyo invigorated her pottery by her sustained exposure to the work of 5 her ancestors. She copied, studied, and practiced the ancient symbols. She mastered the shape of the traditional seed jar. Because the clay in the ancient pots was of finer quality than she was used to making, she sought new places to dig better clay from the earth. Fewkes, keenly interested in this revival of ancient techniques, took Nampeyo to Chicago so that she could demonstrate her knowledge to the curators of the Field Museum of Natural History. She also demonstrated her skills to tourists and archaeologists at the Grand Canyon.

"All acts performed in the world begin with imagination."

—Barbara Grizzuti Harrison

Once she learned the vocabulary of symbols, she found that she could freely 6 adapt and combine them, rather than merely copy ancient models. She told an anthropologist, "When I first began to paint, I used to go to the ancient village and pick up pieces of pottery and copy the designs. That is how I learned to paint. But now I just close my eyes and see designs and I paint them." Fewkes referred to her as a "thorough artist."

Probably Nampeyo's biggest surprise was that nonnative Americans were in- 7 terested in buying her pots. She discovered that there was a ready market for pottery with the ancient designs. In this effort she was a pioneer. The relatively rare ancient pottery had always found buyers among a few select collectors; however, when Nampeyo began making pots in that style, to her delight she found that she could easily sell her entire production. She used the new income to support her entire extended family, and alleviate some of the poverty on First Mesa.

Nampeyo's success became a pattern that other Indian artists would follow. 8 In the Pueblo of San Ildefonso, Maria Martinez and her husband, in collaboration with anthropologist Edgar Hewitt, soon reintroduced ancient black pottery from that Pueblo. Lucy Lewis of Acoma was similarly inspired by ancient designs. The revival of Pueblo and Hopi pottery contributed to the creation, in 1932, of the Native American Arts and Crafts Board, the first government attempt to encourage Native creators to practice their traditional art forms.

Nampeyo continued to produce work herself until she began to lose her eyesight in the 1920s. Her husband painted some of her designs until his death in 1932. Today her great-granddaughters continue the tradition. 9

_____

(Duane Preble, et al., *Artforms*, 7/e, 2008)

✓ COMPREHENSION CHECKUP

True or False

Indicate whether the statement is true or false by writing **T** or **F** in the blank provided.

_____ 1. Nampeyo learned the art of pottery making from her aunt and cousins.

_____ 2. Nampeyo had obtained samples of pottery from the ruins of Sityaki before the arrival of Fewkes.

_____ 3. Nampeyo's art began with basic symbols and gradually evolved into more complex designs.

_____ 4. Nampeyo's skill in making pots lives on in her sons.

_____ 5. Nampeyo began to lose her sight in the 1930s.

_____ 6. Nampeyo's work was largely derivative in the beginning of her career but became more original as time passed.

_____ 7. The clay used in the ancient pots was of a superior quality to that in Nampeyo's early work.

_____ 8. When Nampeyo began making money from her pots, she shared the proceeds with her family.

_____ 9. Before Nampeyo, no one was interested in collecting ancient pottery.

_____ 10. Nampeyo's pot designs were more ornate than her grandmother's.

Multiple Choice

Write the letter of the correct choice in the blank provided.

_____ 11. Which of the following best states the main idea of the selection?
   a. Probably Nampeyo's biggest surprise was that nonnative Americans were interested in buying her pots.
   b. Fewkes referred to her as a "thorough artist."
   c. Nampeyo invigorated her pottery by her sustained exposure to the work of her ancestors.
   d. Nampeyo's fusion of artistic talent and interest in the past sparked a pottery revival that spread throughout the Southwest and continues to this day.

_____ 12. The author wrote this selection to
   a. persuade the reader to support the art of indigenous peoples
   b. describe in detail the beautiful pots created by Nampeyo
   c. explain how a gifted artist revived a Native American art form
   d. tell the story of the ancient Hopi

_____ 13. In paragraph 8, the examples of Maria Martinez and Lucy Lewis
illustrated
   a. that other Native American artists followed in the footsteps
      of Nampeyo
   b. the rivalry between fellow artists
   c. the importance of excavating ancient sites
   d. the usefulness of seed jars

_____ 14. The tradition of pottery making had fallen into decline because of
   a. the amount of time required to make a pot
   b. the availability of cheap dishes
   c. the lack of appropriate clay
   d. both a and b

_____ 15. The seed jars of the early Hopi had all of the following characteristics
except
   a. they were decorated with abstract designs.
   b. they were a symbol of spiritual rebirth.
   c. they were always completely white.
   d. they were low with a narrow opening.

_____ 16. Nampeyo visited all of the following places _except_
   a. the Field Museum of Natural History in Chicago
   b. the Grand Canyon
   c. the Pueblo of San Ildefonso
   d. the ruins of Sikyatki

_____ 17. All of the following were mentioned as being instrumental in
Nampeyo's success _except_
   a. her grandmother, who introduced her to the art of pottery making
   b. the late Senator Barry Goldwater, who was an avid collector of her pots
   c. her husband, who brought ancient pottery shards home to her
   d. the anthropologist Jesse Walter Fewkes, who allowed her to
      accompany him on digs

_____ 18. The village of Hano
   a. is located on the First Mesa
   b. is largely isolated
   c. is on Hopi land
   d. all of the above

_____ 19. If something is relatively rare, it means that it
   a. can be found readily
   b. is somewhat hard to find
   c. has been cooked too much
   d. is commonplace

_____ 20. Nampeyo is considered to be a pioneer. This means that she
   a. helped settle the West
   b. initiated something
   c. guided the way for others to follow
   d. both b and c

Vocabulary Practice

Fill in the blanks with a word from the list below. Not all of the words will be used.

alleviate	encroachment	incorporate	ornate	sparked
collaboration	extended	invigorated	pioneer	sustained
coupled	fusion	isolated	revival	

1. The _____ Palace of Versailles, home to the kings of France, welcomes thousands of visitors each year.

2. Many people take medication to _____ the painful symptoms of arthritis.

3. Amelia Earhart, the first woman to pilot an airplane across the Atlantic Ocean, was a _____ in the field of aviation.

4. There has been a _____ of interest in the music of the sixties.

5. Realizing that everyone had forgotten to invite Brittany to the office party, Caroline hurriedly _____ an invitation.

6. After a workout at the gym and a long swim in the heated pool, Greg felt _____.

7. After the blizzard, the people in the small village were left completely _____ from emergency services and supplies.

8. In many places along the coast, the _____ of the sea on the land is causing concern.

9. In the three-car crash, many observers were surprised that no one _____ any injuries.

10. Their close _____ on the project resulted in many gains for the company.

In Your Own Words

1. What characteristics do you think innovators possess? What makes someone decide to attempt something that hasn't been done before?

2. In what ways did Nampeyo's family encourage her artistic talent? How can we encourage more people to participate in the arts?

3. Many of the great painters spent years copying the masters before developing their own distinct styles. Is it necessary to copy others before you can develop your own vision?

4. Do you think anthropologists would be able to investigate digs today the way Fewkes did in 1895? What is likely to happen today if an anthropologist proposes to dig in ancient burial grounds?

Written Assignment

Give a detailed description of a piece of pottery. Try to make your description so vivid that someone could draw a picture of it based on your words.

Internet Activity

Visit one of the following Web sites to learn more about Nampeyo. Write a few short paragraphs giving additional biographical information about her that was not included in the reading selection.

www.statemuseum.arizona.edu/nampeyo   www.meyna.com/nampeyo.html

SELECTION

"Critical thinkers analyze the evidence supporting their
beliefs and probe for weaknesses in their reasoning."

GETTING THE PICTURE

To succeed as a college student, you will need to be able to read, write, and think critically. The following selection from a popular introductory psychology textbook defines the process of critical thinking.

BIO-SKETCH

After earning a doctorate in psychology from the University of Arizona, Dennis Coon taught for 22 years at Santa Barbara City College in California. He recently returned to Tucson, Arizona, to teach, write, edit, and consult. Although he has written two college textbooks that have been used by 2 million students, his real passion is teaching introductory psychology classes.

BRUSHING UP ON VOCABULARY

empirical testing gathering verifiable information from experience or experiments.

guru a leader or person with some authority and respect. Originally, a *guru* was a Hindu spiritual leader or guide.

anecdotal evidence information gathered about a person through a series of observations rather than through systematic research. Teachers often collect *anecdotal* information about their students through firsthand observation.

Excerpt from

APPROACH TO MIND AND BEHAVIOR

by Dennis Coon

CRITICAL THINKING—UNCOMMON SENSE

Most of us would be skeptical when buying a used car. But all too often, we may be tempted to "buy" outrageous claims about topics such as "channeling," dowsing, the occult, the Bermuda Triangle, hypnosis, UFOs, numerology, and so forth. Likewise, most of us easily accept our ignorance of subatomic physics. But because we deal with human behavior every day, we tend to think that we already know what is true and what is false.

For these, and many more reasons, learning to think critically is one of the lasting benefits of getting an education. Facts and theories may change. Thinking and problem-solving skills last a lifetime.

In the broadest terms, *critical thinking refers to an ability to evaluate, compare, analyze, critique, and synthesize critical thinking information.* Critical thinkers are willing to ask hard questions and challenge conventional wisdom. For example, many people believe that punishment (such as a spanking) is a good way to reinforce learning in children. Actually, nothing could be farther from the truth.

"Thought is the strongest thing we have. Work done by true and profound thought—that is a real force."

—Albert Schweitzer

That's why a critical thinker would immediately ask: "Does punishment work? If so, when? Under what conditions does it not work? What are its drawbacks? Are there better ways to guide learning?"

The core of critical thinking is a willingness to actively evaluate ideas. It is, in a 4 sense, the ability to stand outside yourself and reflect on the quality of your own thoughts. Critical thinkers analyze the evidence supporting their beliefs and probe for weaknesses in their reasoning. They question assumptions and look for alternate conclusions. True knowledge, they recognize, comes from constantly revising and enlarging our understanding of the world.

Critical thinking is built upon four basic principles: 5

1. *Few "truths" transcend the need for empirical testing.* It is true that religious be- 6 liefs and personal values may be held without supporting evidence. But most other ideas can be evaluated by applying the rules of logic and evidence.

2. *Evidence varies in quality.* Judging the quality of evidence is crucial. Imagine 7 that you are a juror in a courtroom, judging claims made by two battling lawyers. To judge correctly, you can't just weigh the evidence. You must also critically evaluate the quality of the evidence. Then you can give greater weight to the most credible facts.

3. *Authority or claimed expertise does not automatically make an idea true.* Just be- 8 cause a teacher, guru, celebrity, or authority is convinced or sincere doesn't mean you should automatically believe them. It is unscientific and self-demeaning to just take the word of an "expert" without asking, "What evidence convinced him or her? How good is it? Is there a better explanation?" This is especially true of information on the Internet, which is often inaccurate.

4. *Critical thinking requires an open mind.* Be prepared to consider daring depar- 9 tures and go wherever the evidence leads. However, it is possible to be so "open-minded" that you simply become gullible. Critical thinkers try to strike a balance between open-mindedness and healthy skepticism. Being open-minded means that you consider all possibilities before drawing a conclusion; it is the ability to change your views under the impact of new and more convincing evidence.

A CASE STUDY OF CRITICAL THINKING

An anxious mother watches her son eat a candy bar and says, "Watch, it's like light- 10 ing a fuse on a firecracker. He'll be bouncing off the walls in a few minutes." Is she right? Will a "sugar buzz" make her son "hyper"? Does eating excessive amounts of sugar adversely affect children's behavior? What are the implications of this claim? If it is true, children who eat sugar should display measurable changes in behavior.

Anecdotal Evidence.   What evidence is there to support the claim? It should 11 be easy to find parents who will attest that their children become high-strung, inattentive, or unruly after eating sugar. However, parents are not likely to be objective observers. Beliefs about "sugar highs" are common and could easily color parents' views.

Casual Observations.   Perhaps it would help to observe children directly. Let's 12 say you decide to watch children at a birthday party, where you know large amounts of sugary foods will be consumed. As predicted by the claim, children at the party become loud and boisterous after eating cake, ice cream, and candy. How persuasive is this evidence? Actually, it is seriously flawed. Birthday parties expose children to bright lights, loud noises, and unfamiliar situations. Any of these conditions, and others as well, could easily explain the children's "hyper" activity.

Authority. For nearly 50 years, many doctors, teachers, nutritionists, and other "experts" have emphatically stated that sugar causes childhood misbehavior. Should you believe them? Unfortunately, most of these "expert" opinions are based on anecdotes and casual observations that are little better than those we have already reviewed.

Formal Evidence. The truth is, parents, casual observers, and many authorities have been wrong. Dr. Mark Wolraich and his colleagues recently reviewed 23 scientific studies on sugar and children. In each study, children consumed known amounts of sugar and were then observed or tested. The clear-cut conclusion in all of the studies was that sugar does not affect aggression, mood, motor skills, or cognitive skills.

Studies like those we just reviewed tend to be convincing because they are based on systematic, controlled observation. But don't just accept the investigators' conclusions. It is important to review the evidence yourself and decide if it is convincing.

_____

(Dennis Coon, *Approach to Mind and Behavior,* 10/e)

✓ COMPREHENSION CHECKUP

Fill in the Blanks

Fill in the blanks with details from the selection.

1. Critical thinking refers to an ability to evaluate, compare, analyze, _____, and synthesize information.

2. The core of critical thinking is a willingness to actively _____ ideas.

3. _____ testing is needed to evaluate most ideas.

4. The quality of the _____ must be critically evaluated.

5. Even the evidence of an _____ must be evaluated.

6. Critical thinkers must keep an open _____.

7. The problem with anecdotal evidence is that people are not _____ observers.

8. Casual _____ is not always reliable.

9. An authority might want to offer an expert _____.

10. You should _____ the evidence yourself to determine if it is convincing.

Vocabulary Practice

Using a dictionary, define the following words. Then use ten of the words in a sentence. You may change or add endings. The paragraph number in parentheses tells you where the word is located in the selection.

1. skeptical (1) _____

2. conventional (3) _____

3. reinforce (3) _____

4. drawbacks (3) _____

5. probe (4) _____

6. transcend (6) _____

7. crucial (7) _____

8. credible (7) _____

9. demeaning (8) _____

10. gullible (9) _____

11. open-minded (9) _____

12. adversely (10) _____

13. attest (11) _____

14. unruly (11) _____

15. color (11) _____

16. boisterous (12) _____

17. flawed (12) _____

18. anecdotes (13) _____

In Your Own Words

1. Many advertisers claim that you can increase your ability to think critically by doing mental exercises. Do you think these exercises are likely to work?

2. What is the difference between critical thinking and negative thinking?

The Art of Writing

1. In a few paragraphs, explain the following: To think critically, you must be willing to think creatively.

2. Pick one of the following real-life situations, and explain how you arrived at your solution.
   a. You are no longer getting along with your live-in girlfriend/boyfriend. You want her/him to move out, but you'd still like to remain friends.
   b. Your neighbor's new puppy barks for large parts of the night, and as a result, you're not getting enough sleep. You're close friends with the neighbor, who has done you a lot of favors in the past. How do you solve the problem?
   c. Your girlfriend/boyfriend has resumed smoking after quitting for two years. You can't stand to be around second-hand smoke. What do you do?

Internet Activity

Consult the following Web site on the topic of creative thinking.

www.virtualsalt.com/crebook1.htm

Evaluate the author's suggestions. Which ones do you think might work for you?

Brain Teasers

Several problems are given below. They are meant to test your critical thinking and problem-solving abilities. To solve them, you need to look at each problem in a different way. Be cautious about making assumptions.

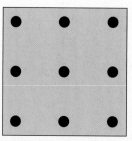

The nine-dot problem.
The answer is found
on page 29.

1. Nine dots are arranged in a square. Can you connect them by drawing four continuous straight lines without lifting your pencil from the paper?

2. Unscramble each set of letters to make a word that uses all the letters:

    MEST   _____

    LFAE   _____

    DUB   _____

    STKAL   _____

    OTOR   _____

    LTEPA   _____

    Now try a new list:

    FINEK   _____

    OPONS   _____

    KROF   _____

    PUC   _____

    SDIH   _____

    LTEPA   _____

3. See how many of the following questions you can answer correctly.

    a. Argentinians do not have a fourth of July. T or F? _____

    b. How many birthdays does the average person have? _____

    c. A farmer had 19 sheep. All but 9 died. How many sheep did the farmer have left?
        _____

    d. Some months have 30 days, some have 31. How many months have 28 days? _____

    e. I have two coins that together total 30 cents. One of the coins is not a nickel. What are the two coins? _____

    f. If there are twelve one-cent candies in a dozen, how many two-cent candies are there in a dozen? _____

SELECTION

"And do not ever stop learning and improving your mind,
because if you do, you are going to be left behind."

GETTING THE PICTURE

The following selection is from a college commencement speech delivered by Marian Wright Edelman at Washington University in St. Louis, Missouri, on May 15, 1992. The eight lessons she mentions in the speech were meant to serve as "road maps" for graduating seniors. Because Edelman does not feel that she "has all the answers," students were urged to "ignore, revise, or use all or any of the lessons as they see fit." Edelman, who considers her life a testament to the American Dream, hopes that her words of advice might aid some in "developing a positive passion in life."

BIO-SKETCH

Marian Wright Edelman, the youngest of five children, was born in 1939 in Bennettsville, South Carolina. In the days when African-Americans were not allowed in city parks, Edelman's father built a park for them behind his church. Edelman graduated from Spelman College, a historically African-American college in Atlanta, went on to graduate from Yale Law School, and became the first African-American admitted to the Mississippi Bar. She has written many articles and books, including her autobiographical bestseller, *The Measure of Our Success: A Letter to My Children and Yours.* She is the founder and president of the Children's Defense Fund, has served on many boards, and has received numerous honorary awards. She is married to Peter Edelman, a professor at Georgetown Law School. They have three sons and two granddaughters.

BRUSHING UP ON VOCABULARY

free lunch something acquired without due effort or cost. The term originated in the 1800s from the custom of taverns offering free food to their patrons to encourage them to buy drinks. Today *free lunch* is often used in a pejorative way.

cut corners do something in the easiest or least expensive way; act illegally. The term was first used in the late 1800s. It originally meant to go around a corner as closely as possible so as to reduce the distance traveled, thereby saving time.

expediency regard for what is advantageous rather than for what is right or just. The word *expediency* is derived from the Latin *expedire*, meaning "to free one caught by the foot."

illiterate *illiterate* is derived from the Latin word *litera*, meaning "letter." So an *illiterate* is someone who does not know letters—that is, someone who lacks the ability to read.

integrity adherence to moral and ethical principles; honesty. The word *integrity* is derived from the Latin *integer*, meaning "a whole number." The word later came to mean "in one piece."

Excerpt from

Commencement Address

BY MARIAN WRIGHT EDELMAN

Washington University
St. Louis, Missouri
May 15, 1992

I want to share a few lessons of life taken from a letter that I wrote to my own three 1 wonderful sons. I recognize that you can take or leave these lessons, but you won't be able to say that you were never told them. Let me give you a few of them.

"The lust for comfort, that stealthy thing that enters the house a guest and then becomes a host, and then a master."

—Kahlil Gibran

The first lesson is, there is no free lunch. Do not feel entitled to anything you do 2 not sweat or struggle for. Your degree will get you in the door, but it will not get you to the top of the career ladder or keep you there. You have got to work your way up hard and continuously.

Remember not to be lazy. Do your homework. Pay attention to detail. Take care 3 and pride in your work. Take the initiative in creating your own opportunity and do not wait around for other people to discover you or do you a favor. Do not assume a door is closed; push on it. Do not assume if it was closed yesterday that it is closed today. And do not ever stop learning and improving your mind, because if you do, you are going to be left behind.

Lesson two is, assign yourself. Daddy used to ask us whether the teacher gave us 4 any homework and if we said no, he said, well, assign yourself some. Do not wait around for somebody else to direct you to do what you are able to figure out and do for yourself. Do not do just as little as you can to get by.

Do not be a political bystander or grumbler. Vote. Democracy is not a spectator 5 sport. Run for political office. But when you do run and when you do win, don't begin to think that you or your reelection are the only point. If you see a need, do not ask, "Why doesn't somebody do something?" Ask, "Why don't I do something?" Hard work and persistence and initiative are still the non-magic carpets to success for most of us.

Lesson three: Never work just for money. Money will not save your soul or build 6 a decent family or help you sleep at night. We are the richest nation on earth with the highest incarceration rate and also with some of the highest drug addiction and child poverty rates in the world.

Do not confuse wealth or fame with character. Do not tolerate or condone 7 moral corruption or violence, whether it is found in high or low places, whatever its color or class. It is not okay to push drugs or to use them even if every person in America is doing it. It is not okay to cheat or to lie even if every public- and private-sector official you know does. Be honest and demand that those who represent you be honest. Do not confuse morality with legality. Dr. King once noted that everything Hitler did in Nazi Germany was legal. Do not give anyone the proxy for your conscience.

Lesson four: Do not be afraid of taking risks or being criticized. If you do not 8 want to be criticized, do not do anything, do not say anything, and do not be anything. Do not be afraid of failing. It is the way you learn to do things right. It doesn't matter how many times you fall down. All that matters is how many times you get up. Do not wait for everybody to come along to get something done. It is always a few people who get things done and keep things going.

"To bring up a child in a way he should go, travel that way yourself once in a while."

—Josh Billings

This country desperately needs more wise and courageous shepherds and fewer 9 sheep who do not borrow from integrity to fund expediency.

Lesson five: Take parenting and family life seriously, and insist that those you 10 work for and who represent you also do so. Our nation mouths family values that we do not practice or honor in our policies.

I hope that your generation will raise your sons to be fair to other people's daugh- 11 ters and share parenting responsibilities. I am the mother of three sons, so I have told them to "share," and not just help with, family life.

I hope that you will stress family rituals and be moral examples for your children, 12 because if you cut corners, they will too. If you lie, they will too. If you spend all of your money on yourself and tithe no portion of it for your university or civic causes or religious life, they will not either.

Lesson six is please remember and help America remember that the fellowship of 13 human beings is more important than the fellowship of race and class and gender in a democratic society. Be decent and fair and insist that others do so in your presence. Do not tell, do not laugh at or acquiesce in racial, ethnic, religious, or gender jokes or any practice intended to demean rather than enhance another human being. Walk away from such jokes. Make them unacceptable in your presence.

And let us not spend a lot of time uselessly pinning and denying blame rather than 14 healing our divisions. Rabbi Abraham Heschel put it aptly when he said, "We are not all equally guilty, but we are all equally responsible for building a decent and just America."

Lesson seven: Listen for the "sound of the genuine" within yourself. Einstein said, 15 "Small is the number of them that see with their own eyes and feel with their own heart." Try to be one of them.

Howard Thurman, the great black theologian, said to my Spelman colleagues in 16 Atlanta, Georgia, "There is in every one of us something that waits and listens for the sound of the genuine in ourselves, and it is the only true guide you'll ever have. And if you cannot hear it, you will all of your life spend your days on the ends of strings that somebody else pulls."

"Knock the 't' off of the 'can't'."

—George Reeves

You will find as you go out from this place so many noises and competing de- 17 mands in your lives that many of you may never find out who you are. I hope that you will learn to be quiet enough to hear the sound of the genuine within yourself so that you can then hear it in other people.

Lesson eight: Never think life is not worth living or that you cannot make a dif- 18 ference. Never give up. I do not care how hard it gets; and it will get very hard sometimes. An old proverb reminds us that when you get to your wit's end, remember that is where God lives.

Harriet Beecher Stowe said that when you get into a tight place and everything 19 goes against you, till it seems as though you cannot hang on for another minute, never give up then, for that is just the place and the time the tide will turn.

I do not care how bad the job market is. I do not care how hard the challenges 20 seem to be. Hang in with life. And do not think you have to win or win immediately or even at all to make a difference. Sometimes it is important to lose for things that matter. And do not think you have to make a big difference to make America different.

My role model was an illiterate slave woman, Sojourner Truth, who could not 21 read or write, but she could not stand second-class treatment of women and she hated slavery. My favorite Sojourner story came one day when she was making a speech against slavery, and she got heckled by a man who stood up in the audience and said, "Old slave woman, I don't care any more about your antislavery talk than for an old fleabite." And she snapped back and said, "That's all right. The Lord willing, I'm going to keep you scratching."

So often we think we have got to make a big difference and be a big dog. Let us just try to be little fleas biting. Enough fleas biting strategically can make very big dogs very uncomfortable. I am convinced that together fleas for justice, and fleas in schools and religious congregations, and fleas in homes as parents committed to a decent American society are going to transform our nation and make it un-American for any child to be poor or without health care in our rich land.

Finally, let me just hope that you will understand that you cannot save your own children without trying to help save other people's children. They have got to walk the same streets. We have got to pass on to them a country that was better than the one that we inherited.

What do you think would happen if every American, if every one of you, reached out and grabbed the hand of a child and committed yourself to seeing that no child is left behind? I hope that you will think about doing that, because everything that we hold dear as a people with faith depends on each of us committing to leaving no American child behind.

(Marian Wright Edelman, *The Measure of Our Success*, 1992)

✓ COMPREHENSION CHECKUP

Multiple Choice

Write the letter of the correct answer in the blank provided.

_____ 1. Which of the following does Edelman consider key to career success?
   a. If you are special, someone will "discover" you.
   b. A good degree is all you need.
   c. Look at the big picture and ignore the details.
   d. Keep working hard.

_____ 2. Edelman would agree with which of the following?
   a. If someone asks you to do a task, and another task needs to be done as well, do both tasks without waiting to be asked.
   b. If you see a need, try to fill it.
   c. Don't do any more homework than you have to.
   d. Both a and b

_____ 3. With respect to parents and their children, Edelman would agree with which of the following statements?
   a. Parents should serve as moral role models for their children.
   b. Our nation takes family values seriously.
   c. Good parenting is not as important today as it was 50 years ago.
   d. Children are not likely to emulate their parents' attitudes and beliefs.

_____ 4. Edelman is passionate about
   a. trying hard and taking initiative
   b. the importance of leading a moral life
   c. protecting and helping children
   d. all of the above

_____ 5. Edelman mentioned in the excerpt that failure
   a. is to be avoided at all costs
   b. is the way that you learn to do things right
   c. is something you should be ashamed of
   d. is rarely experienced by successful people

_____ 6. Edelman would agree with which of the following?
   a. We should care only about our own children.
   b. How children are raised doesn't matter much for society.
   c. Our society should make a commitment to protecting and nurturing all of its children.
   d. How parents' behave doesn't have much effect on how their children behave.

_____ 7. Edelman is likely to admire those who
   a. spend all of their money on themselves
   b. donate money to charitable causes
   c. marry into money
   d. work hard to become powerful and famous

_____ 8. Edelman is likely to agree with which of the following?
   a. It's every person for her- or himself.
   b. The end justifies the means.
   c. If corporate CEOs are lying, it's okay for you to lie as well.
   d. Lying and cheating to succeed are not acceptable.

True or False

Indicate whether the statement is true or false by writing **T** or **F** in the blank provided.

_____ 9. Edelman's role model was Sojourner Truth.

_____ 10. Edelman likely feels that one vote is relatively insignificant in the scheme of things.

_____ 11. Edelman agrees that people should try to avoid being criticized.

_____ 12. Edelman believes that something can be legal and still not be moral.

_____ 13. Edelman believes that it is important to listen to yourself.

_____ 14. Edelman believes that the easy path is the best one.

_____ 15. Edelman believes that the little contributions people make over time can make a big difference.

Vocabulary in Context

Look through the paragraph indicated in parentheses to find a word that matches the definition given below.

1. having a right or claim to something (paragraph 2) _____

2. confinement; imprisonment (6) _____

3. disregard; overlook; excuse (7) _____

4. power or agency to act for another (7) _____

5. just right; fittingly; appropriately (14) _____

6. a person who specializes in the study of divine things or religious truth (16)

   _____

7. associates; fellow members of a profession (16) _____

8. harassed with impertinent questions; shouted insults (21) _____

Choose one of the following words to complete the sentences below. Use each word only once. Be sure to pay close attention to the context clues provided.

continuously	corruption	initiative	persistence	pinned
rituals	snickered	strategic	tide	tithe

1. Despite many obstacles to her academic success, Estella refused to give in, and finally her _____ paid off with a $10,000 scholarship to the college of her choice.

2. Ruben took the _____ in collecting 10,000 signatures to get the proposal for a light-rail system on the ballot.

3. When Carrie got an F in English, she _____ the blame on everyone but herself.

4. Because she was _____ in pain from her leukemia, her doctor decided to try radiation as a palliative treatment.

5. Even though Marcus was on a fixed income, he was able to _____ a portion of his salary to his new church.

6. The audience _____ when the microphone went dead, but the politician continued with his speech completely unaware.

7. One of my daily _____ is a 45-minute walk with my friend Marilyn.

8. In many reality television shows, the players form _____ alliances in order to win.

9. The _____ turned against him, and he lost the election.

10. The new mayor's biggest job is to weed out _____ in governmental agencies.

Vocabulary in Context

Without using a dictionary, define the following phrases.

1. political bystander (paragraph 5) _____

2. spectator sport (5) _____

3. mouths family values (10) _____

4. wit's end (18) _____

5. tight place (19) _____

6. hang in (20) _____

7. second-class treatment (21) _____

In Your Own Words

1. What is your personal reaction to each of Edelman's lessons? What do Edelman's lessons say about her as a person? What are Edelman's priorities in life?

2. What does Edelman have to say about being a creative or critical thinker?

3. The following is an excerpt from a speech given by President Theodore Roosevelt.

It is not the critic who counts;
Not the man who points out
Where the strong man stumbled,
Or where the doer of great deeds
Could have done them better.
The credit belongs to the man
Who is actually in the arena;
Whose face is marred
By dust and sweat and blood;
Who strives valiantly;
Who errs and comes up short
Again and again;
And who, while daring greatly;
Spends himself in a worthy cause;
So that his place may not be
Among those cold and timid souls
Who know neither victory nor defeat.

Which of Edelman's lessons does Roosevelt's speech support? In what ways is their advice the same?

The Art of Writing

Create a top-five list of suggestions of your own by drawing on knowledge that you learned the hard way. Include a short explanation for each of your choices. Try to give a personal anecdote illustrating each suggestion.

Internet Activity

1. The Web site below gives you additional information about Marian Wright Edelman's background:

   www.womenshistory.about.com

   Visit this site, and then write a short paragraph about what you find interesting about Edelman's life.

2. Use a search engine like <www.google.com> or <www.yahoo.com> to locate information about one of the following individuals mentioned in Edelman's commencement speech: Sojourner Truth, Howard Thurman, Harriet Beecher Stowe, Dr. Martin Luther King, Jr., Albert Einstein, or Rabbi Abraham Heschel. What contributions did the individual you selected make to American society?

Thinking Critically About a Poem

"Life is the sum of all your choices."

—Albert Camus

The late Theodore Seuss Geisel (1904–1991) was known to millions of readers (adult as well as children) as Dr. Seuss. In his lifetime, he wrote and illustrated over 40 books, many of which are children's classics. Among the best known are *Horton Hears a Who, Hop on Pop, How the Grinch Stole Christmas,* and, of course, *The Cat in the Hat.* Critics praised his books, saying that he dispensed "nonsense with sense."

My Uncle Terwilliger on the Art of Eating Popovers

BY DR. SEUSS

My uncle ordered popovers
from the restaurant's bill of fare.
And, when they were served,
   he regarded them
with a penetrating stare . . .
Then he spoke great Words of Wisdom
as he sat there on that chair:
"To eat these things," said my uncle,
"you must exercise great care.
You may swallow down what's solid . . .
BUT . . . you must spit out the air!"
And . . . as you partake of the world's
   bill of fare,
that's darned good advice to follow.
Do a lot of spitting out the hot air.
And be careful what you swallow.

(Dr. Seuss, *Seuss-isms*, 1997)

Directions: Dr. Seuss is dispensing his advice on the subject of critical thinking in a very creative way. Briefly explain what he means when he recommends: "Do a lot of spitting out the hot air. And be careful what you swallow."

_____

_____

_____

_____

_____

VOCABULARY	Introduction: Developing a College-Level Vocabulary

"The investigation of the meaning of words is the beginning of education."
—Antisthenes

To be a successful college student, you need a college-level vocabulary. Improving your vocabulary will make you a better reader, speaker, and writer. Is there a painless way to improve your vocabulary? The answer is "No." Developing a college-level vocabulary requires effort. But there are some effective techniques that can help. These techniques are described below.

Context

When you come across an unfamiliar word in your reading, the first step you should take toward discovering its meaning is to look for context clues. The context of a word is what surrounds it and includes the sentence it appears in, other nearby sentences, and even the whole article. Try placing your finger over the unfamiliar word, and see if you can supply another word or phrase that gives the sentence meaning.

For example, see if you can figure out the meaning of the italicized word from the context of the sentence:

> Ellen's multiple sclerosis became increasingly *debilitating* to the point that she could no longer walk unaided and had to consider using a wheelchair.

You could go to the dictionary to look up the definition of *debilitating*, but you can probably guess from context clues that *debilitating*, at least as it appears in this sentence, means "to make feeble or weak."

Remember that if you are reading a light novel for enjoyment, the exact meaning of a word may not be as important as when you are reading a textbook.

Structure

The Greeks and Romans devised a system for creating words by putting together smaller word parts. To the main part of the word, which is called the root, they attached prefixes, which come before the root, and suffixes, which come after it.

This way of building words allows you to discover the meaning of a word by breaking it down into its parts. Knowing the meaning of the word's parts should help you decipher the word's meaning. Let's try an example:

> As a confirmed *misogamist,* it was unlikely Barry would be making a trip to the altar anytime soon.

The word *misogamist* has in it the word parts *mis* and *gam. Mis* means "hate" and *gam* means "marriage." So a *misogamist* is someone who hates marriage, or matrimony. In this book, we have included eight vocabulary units that familiarize you with more than a hundred word parts.

Dictionary

Often when people come across a word they don't know, their first impulse is to look it up in the dictionary. But this should be your last recourse for determining the meaning of a word. It's best first to try to determine a general meaning of the word by paying attention to context clues and word structure. If these techniques don't give you a sure enough sense of what the word means, then go to the dictionary to confirm or clarify the meaning. In the dictionary, you may find several different definitions for a particular word. You need to pick the one that fits the word in its sentence. Context clues will help you pick the right definition. For example, suppose in your reading you come across the following sentence, and you don't know what the word *steep* means:

> To make good sun tea, you need to *steep* several tea bags in a large jar of water out in the sun for several hours.

You look *steep* up in your dictionary and find several definitions. The first definition may be "having an almost vertical slope." The second definition may be "unduly high; exorbitant." But it is the third definition, "to soak in a liquid," that seems to fit. So now you know that to make sun tea, you must let the tea bags soak in water.

Combination

In trying to determine the meaning of an unfamiliar word, you may need to employ all of these techniques in combination. Take the following example:

> Because of his *premonition* that he would not live to see his eighty-third birthday, he made the effort to say good-bye to all of his loved ones.

Look at the context, which suggests that the word has something to do with thoughts or feelings about the future. Now look at the word parts. *Pre* means "before" and *mon* means "warn." Now you are getting closer to the meaning in this sentence. The word *premonition* as used here has a meaning similar to "forewarning." Now go to the dictionary. You will find the definitions "impression that something evil is about to happen" and "strong feeling or prediction." Now you have a better grasp of what the word means. The man had a strong feeling warning him that he would be dead before his eighty-third birthday.

Homonyms

As part of our vocabulary study, we will also learn about homonyms. Although homonyms are not a technique for discovering the meaning of an unfamiliar word, we discuss them because misuse of homonyms is common. *Homo* means "same" and *nym* means "name." So homonyms are words or phrases with the same "name" or pronunciation but different spellings or meanings.

Look at the following sentence:

> Because Tomoko *already* knows all of her colors and shapes and most of the letters of the alphabet, I'd say she's *all ready* for kindergarten.

In this example, *already* means "previously," and *all ready* means "completely prepared." People often confuse these two homonyms, as they do other homonyms. In the two sections on homonyms, you will learn how to use many homonyms correctly.

Thesaurus

"What's another word for thesaurus?"

—Steven Wright

A thesaurus, a special kind of word book organized by categories, enables you to refine your writing by helping you select precisely the right word for any given situation. Many of us use the same word over and over because we cannot think of an appropriate synonym. A thesaurus gives synonyms for the most common nouns, verbs, adjectives, and adverbs in the English language. In the following sentence, you can choose from any of the italicized synonyms to convey your meaning more precisely:

> As the famous fashion model made her way down the runway, the audience noted that she was extremely *slender, slim, svelte, lithe, skinny, lean, thin.*

You will learn about using a thesaurus in the Appendix.

Answer to Nine-Dot Problem

The nine-dot problem can be solved by extending the lines beyond the square formed by the dots.

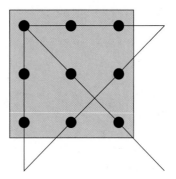

Learning How to Be a Successful Student

The Scream (1893) BY EDVARD MUNCH

Erich Lessing/Art Resource, NY/© 2011 The Munch Museum/The Munch-Ellingsen Group/
Artists Rights Society (ARS), NY

View and Reflect

1. What is your initial response to the painting? What overall impression does it convey?
2. What do you think the landscape is meant to represent? The receding figures on the bridge? The two ships in the background? What does the combination of elements in the painting suggest?
3. What do you think the figure in the foreground is meant to represent? What does the face resemble as it screams? Use one word to describe the overall feeling of the painting.

Doing What Successful Students Do

As you work through this book (and as you proceed through college), you will be introduced to a wide variety of reading selections. Underlining (or highlighting) and annotating the material will help you remember the authors' key points.

STUDY TECHNIQUE 1

Underlining, Highlighting, Annotating

When **underlining** or **highlighting** important words or phrases in reading selections, be careful not to overdo it. The goal is to mark just the important points to save you from having to reread. **Annotating**, another technique for helping you remember what you're reading, is particularly useful when reading textbook material. When you annotate, you write notes to yourself, often in the margins of the book. You might write down abbreviations or symbols to identify key ideas or terms. To the right is a list of things you might want to identify, with suggested abbreviations.

MI (main idea)

T (thesis)

S (summary)

Ex (example)

Def (definition)

? (questions, needs clarification)

* (important point)

KV (key vocabulary)

SELECTION

"Respond ineffectively to stress, and eventually it will take a toll on your sense of wellness."

GETTING THE PICTURE

In this selection from a popular health textbook, you will learn about stress and how you can lower it. After reading the bio-sketch and vocabulary sections, you will practice marking and annotating a section of a textbook. Look at the sample margin notes and underlining in the first section of the reading selection below, and follow this example in marking and annotating the remainder of the textbook material on stress.

BIO-SKETCH

Both writers of this textbook teach at the Stanford University Medical School. Paul M. Insel is an adjunct clinical associate professor in the Department of Psychiatry and Behavioral Sciences, and Walton T. Roth is a professor of psychiatry and behavioral medicine. Roth is also the chief of psychiatric consultation services at the Veterans Administration Medical Center in Palo Alto.

BRUSHING UP ON VOCABULARY

hippocampus a lower portion of the brain that consolidates short-term memories into long-term memories.

biological predispositions tendencies or inclinations based on biology rather than background or experiences.

Excerpt from

CORE CONCEPTS IN HEALTH

by Paul M. Insel and Walton T. Roth

STRESS: THE CONSTANT CHALLENGE

Ex
Ex
Ex
Ex

MI

As a <u>college student</u>, you may be in one of the <u>most stressful periods of your</u> <u>life</u>. You may be <u>on your own</u> for the first time, or you may be <u>juggling the</u> <u>demands of college</u> with the responsibilities of a job, a family, or both. <u>Financial</u> <u>pressures</u> may be intense. <u>Housing and transportation</u> may be sources of additional hassles. You're also <u>meeting new people</u>, engaging in <u>new activities,</u> <u>learning new information</u> and skills, and setting a new course for your life. Good and bad, all these changes and challenges are likely to have a powerful effect on you both physically and psychologically. <u>Respond ineffectively</u> to stress, and eventually it will <u>take a toll</u> on your sense of wellness. <u>Learn effective</u> <u>responses</u>, however, and you will <u>enhance your health</u> and <u>gain a feeling of</u> <u>control over your life</u>.

Test Your Knowledge

_____ 1. Which of the following events can cause stress?
   a. taking out a loan
   b. failing a test
   c. graduating from college

_____ 2. High levels of stress can impair memory and cause physical changes in the brain. True or false?

_____ 3. Which of the following can result from chronic stress?
   a. violence
   b. heart attack
   c. stroke

_____ 4. Because eating induces relaxation, it is an excellent means of coping with stress. True or false?

Answers

1. *All three.* Stress-producing factors can be pleasant or unpleasant and can include physical challenges and goal achievement as well as events that are perceived as negative.

2. *True.* Low levels of stress may improve memory, but high stress levels impair learning and memory and, over the long term, may shrink an area of the brain called the hippocampus.

3. *All three.* Chronic—ongoing—stress can last for years. People who suffer from long-term stress may ultimately become violent toward themselves or others. They also run a greater than normal risk for certain ailments, especially cardiovascular disease.

4. *False.* Eating as a means of coping with stress may lead to weight gain and to binge eating, a risky behavior associated with eating disorders.

Everybody talks about stress. People say they're "overstressed" or "stressed out." They may blame stress for headaches or ulcers, and they may try to combat stress with aerobic classes—or drugs. But what is stress? And why is it important to manage it wisely?

MI—Stress usually associated with negative events

<u>Most people associate stress with negative events</u>: the death of a close relative or friend, financial problems, or other unpleasant life changes that create nervous tension. But stress isn't merely nervous tension. And it isn't something to be avoided at all costs. In fact, only death brings complete freedom from stress. Consider this list of common stressful situations or events.

- Interviewing for a job
- Running in a race
- Being accepted to college
- Going out on a date
- Watching a baseball game
- Getting a promotion

MI—Can be related to physical challenges, personal goals

Can modify your behavior

Obviously <u>stress doesn't arise just from unpleasant situations</u>. Stress can also be <u>associated with physical challenges and the achievement of personal goals</u>. Physical and psychological stress-producing factors can be pleasant or unpleasant. The actions you take in response to stress are influenced by your biological predispositions, past experiences, and current circumstances. While you cannot change who you are or what you've been through in the past, <u>you *can* modify your</u> current <u>behavior</u> and seek out people, places, and experiences that will improve your ability to deal with stress. In other words, what is crucial is how you respond, whether in positive, life-enhancing ways or in negative, counterproductive ways.

What Is Stress?

Just what is stress, if such vastly different situations can cause it? In common usage, "stress" refers to two different things: situations that trigger physical and emotional reactions *and* the reactions themselves. We'll be using the more precise term **stressor** for situations that trigger physical and emotional reactions and the term **stress response** for those reactions. A date and a final exam, then, are stressors; sweaty palms and a pounding heart are symptoms of the stress response. We'll use the term **stress** to describe the general physical and emotional state that accompanies the stress response. A person on a date or taking a final exam experiences stress.

Each individual's experience of stress depends on many factors, including the nature of the stressor and how the stressor is perceived. Responses to stressors include physical changes and emotional and behavioral responses.

How High Is Your Stress Level?

Many symptoms of excess stress are easy to self-diagnose. To help determine how much stress you experience on a daily basis, answer the following questions:

1. Are you easily startled or irritated?
2. Are you increasingly forgetful?

3. Do you have trouble falling or staying asleep?

4. Do you continually worry about events in your future?

5. Do you feel as if you are constantly under pressure to produce?

6. Do you frequently use tobacco, alcohol, or other drugs to help you relax?

7. Do you often feel as if you have less energy than you need to finish the day?

8. Do you have recurrent stomachaches or headaches?

9. Is it difficult for you to find satisfaction in simple life pleasures?

10. Are you often disappointed in yourself and others?

11. Are you overly concerned with being liked or accepted by others?

12. Are you concerned that you do not have enough money?

Experiencing some of the stress-related symptoms or answering "yes" to a few questions is normal. However, if you experience a large number of stress symptoms or you answered "yes" to a majority of the questions, you are likely experiencing a high level of stress. Take time out to develop effective stress-management techniques. Your school's counseling center can provide valuable support.

SYMPTOMS OF EXCESS STRESS

Physical Symptoms	Emotional Symptoms	Behavioral Symptoms
Dry mouth	Anxiety or edginess	Crying
Excessive perspiration	Depression	Disrupted eating habits
Frequent illnesses	Fatigue	Disrupted sleeping habits
Gastrointestinal problems	Hypervigilance	Harsh treatment of others
Grinding of teeth	Impulsiveness	Increased use of tobacco, alcohol, or other drugs
Headaches	Inability to concentrate	
High blood pressure	Irritability	Problems communicating
Pounding heart	Trouble remembering things	Social isolation

Mind/Body/Spirit: Healthy Connections

Meaningful connections with others can play a key role in stress management and overall wellness. A sense of isolation can lead to chronic stress, which in turn can increase one's susceptibility to temporary illnesses like colds and to chronic illnesses like heart disease. Although the mechanism isn't clear, social isolation can be as significant to mortality rates as factors like smoking, high blood pressure, and obesity.

There is no single best pattern of social support that works for everyone. However, research suggests that having a variety of types of relationships may be

TOP 20 STRESSFUL LIFE EVENTS

Death of a spouse
Divorce
Marital separation
Jail term
Death of a close family
  member
Personal injury or illness
Marriage
Fired at work
Marital reconciliation
Retirement
Change in health of family
  member
Pregnancy
Sex difficulties
New family member
Business readjustment
Change in financial status
Death of a close friend
Change to a different line
  of work
Change in number of
  arguments with spouse
Mortgage or loan for
  major purchase
  (home, etc.)
(Thomas H. Holmes and
  Richard H. Rahe, *Journal
  of Psychosomatic
  Research*, 1967)

important for wellness. To help determine whether your social network measures up, circle whether each of the following statements is true or false for you.

T F   1. If I needed an emergency loan of $100, there is someone I could get it from.

T F   2. There is someone who takes pride in my accomplishments.

T F   3. I often meet or talk with family or friends.

T F   4. Most people I know think highly of me.

T F   5. If I needed an early morning ride to the airport, there's no one I would feel comfortable asking to take me.

T F   6. I feel there is no one with whom I can share my most private worries and fears.

T F   7. Most of my friends are more successful making changes in their lives than I am.

T F   8. I would have a hard time finding someone to go with me on a day trip to the beach or country.

To calculate your score, add the number of true answers to questions 1–4 and the number of false answers to questions 5–8. If your score is 4 or more, you should have enough support to protect your health. If your score is 3 or less, you may need to reach out. There are a variety of things you can do to strengthen your social ties:

- Foster friendships. Keep in regular contact with your friends.

- Keep your family ties strong. Participate in family activities and celebrations.

- Get involved with a group. Choose activities that are meaningful to you and that include direct involvement with other people.

- Build your communication skills. The more you share your feelings with others, the closer the bonds between you will become.

(Paul Insel, *Core Concepts in Health*, 11/e, 2010)

✓ COMPREHENSION CHECKUP

Multiple Choice

Write the letter of the correct answer in the blank provided.

_____ 1. An event that triggers stress is called a
    a. response
    b. stressor
    c. headache
    d. none of the above

_____ 2. Stress is best described as
    a. something completely under your control
    b. something rarely experienced by college students
    c. a physical and emotional response to a stressor
    d. a realistic and positive outlook on life

_____ 3. Which of the following could be a potential stressor?
   a. having to visit a relative you dislike
   b. failing a final exam
   c. the unexpected death of a relative
   d. all of the above

_____ 4. High levels of stress can
   a. aggravate high blood pressure
   b. contribute to insomnia
   c. both a and b
   d. improve memory

_____ 5. All of the following are correlated with high mortality rates except
   a. smoking
   b. social isolation
   c. marriage
   d. high blood pressure

True or False

Indicate whether the statement is true or false by writing **T** or **F** in the blank provided.

_____ 6. Stress arises only from unpleasant situations.

_____ 7. Excessive sweating may be a physical symptom of stress.

_____ 8. Chronic stress can lead to heart disease.

_____ 9. Healthy connections with others may play a role in the management of stress.

_____ 10. Having good relationships with others is unlikely to contribute to wellness.

Vocabulary Practice

Choose the word from the following list that best completes each sentence.

chronic	isolation	overly	temporary
counter- productive	juggling	overwhelmed	triggered
crucial	mortality obesity	recurrent susceptible	
impair			

1. People who have too many problems that they can't solve may feel

   _____.

2. A smoker is likely to have a higher _____ rate than a nonsmoker.

3. Because many young children have unhealthy diets and fail to get enough exercise, _____ has become a problem of national concern.

4. The refusal of the airline to discuss improving employee benefits _____ a walkout by baggage handlers and flight attendants.

5. The prisoner was deemed a threat to others and so was placed in

   _____.

6. In winter, people are more _____ to colds and flu.

7. Working parents today are so busy because they are _____ many roles.

8. It is of _____ importance that you come to each class session prepared.

9. The substitute teacher was _____ until the regular teacher returned from maternity leave.

10. Exposure to loud noises at an early age may _____ the ability to hear later in life.

11. He had the same _____ dream about flying every night. Unfortunately, he woke up only after he had fallen out of bed.

12. If a parent is _____ protective, a young child might not develop a sense of self-sufficiency.

13. If you have _____ throat infections, your doctor might recommend having your tonsils removed.

14. It might be _____ to work long hours at a job if your grades in school suffer as a result.

In Your Own Words

1. What is the difference between a stressor and stress? What are some of your stressors?

2. In what ways does the college experience contribute to the stress level of students?

3. Can stress be positive? Give an example of positive stress in your life.

4. What physical reactions does stress cause in the body?

5. Describe some healthy ways to deal with stress.

The Art of Writing

In a brief essay, respond to one of the items below.

1. Keep track of your own stress for several days. Try to determine what events are likely to trigger a stress response in you. Is your home life, work life, or school life the most stressful? Is your life more or less stressful than you expected?

2. Interview a friend or family member who seems to handle stress well. What strategies does this person use to successfully cope with stress?

Internet Activity

1. Stress has been linked to many illnesses. To find a list of the negative effects of stress on people's health, go to: www.stress.about.com/

   Write a paragraph describing what you learned about stress and disease.

   Use what you learn to evaluate how well you are handling your personal stressors.

2. To find information on stress management, click "work and school" on the American Psychological Associations's Help Center:

   http://helping.apa.org

STRESS AT WORK

Most Stressful Jobs

Inner-city high school teacher	Stockbroker
Police officer	Journalist
Miner	Customer service representative
Air traffic controller	Secretary
Medical intern	Waiter

(The American Institute of Stress, 2010)

VOCABULARY   Words in Context

One technique for discovering the meaning of an unfamiliar word is to examine its context, the words surrounding it. Suppose you didn't know the meaning of the word *craven*. Would you be able to decipher the meaning of the word more easily from Example 1 or Example 2?

EXAMPLE 1
When their young are threatened, even the most *craven* animals will become courageous.

EXAMPLE 2
Craven means which of the following?
   a.   contrite
   b.   churlish
   c.   cowardly
   d.   crotchety

Most people are more likely to decipher the meaning of a word by using context as in Example 1. In many instances, the neighboring words provide clues to help decipher the meaning. As readers, we also call on our own backgrounds and experiences to help us determine the meanings of unfamiliar words. As a result, a sentence containing the word, as in Example 1, would be more helpful to most people.

There are several different kinds of context clues you can use, and it is worthwhile to become familiar with all of them. Familiarizing yourself with these techniques will go a long way to helping you study your college textbooks without having to interrupt your reading to look up a specific word. When having a precise definition is not necessary, the use of context clues can be sufficient and save you time. Of course, if a precise definition is necessary, consulting a dictionary is essential.

Definition

Sometimes a writer provides us with a definition of a word somewhere within the sentence or nearby sentences, especially if the word is one that we are likely to be unfamiliar with.

> Every year many people buy self-help audio tapes containing *subliminal* messages to help them relieve stress. These tapes contain messages that are supposedly below the level of human consciousness.

Subliminal here is simply defined as "below the level of consciousness."

Synonym

A synonym, which is another word with a similar meaning, may be used elsewhere in the sentence.

> Massages are thought to provide *therapeutic* benefits by relieving stress; however, their curative powers do not extend to all patients.

You can infer from this sentence that *therapeutic* and *curative* have similar meanings.

Antonym

Sometimes you can determine the meaning of a word by finding an antonym, a word with an opposite meaning, somewhere in the sentence.

> Juana's house was very well-maintained, but her sister's house was *dilapidated.*

You can see that the writer is making a contrast, and that *well-maintained* is the opposite of *dilapidated.*

Examples

Sometimes examples illustrate the meaning of a word.

> Terry has such *boundless* energy that even after working a full shift and taking care of her two small children, she still wants to go out dancing with her husband at night.

This example suggests to you that *boundless* means "infinite or vast."

Explanation

Sometimes a writer simply gives the reader an explanation of what a word means.

> The Russian gymnastic team was *disconsolate* after its loss to the Romanians. No amount of comfort or kind words from coaches and fans could raise the spirits of the young athletes.

The writer is telling you that the word *disconsolate* means "persistently sad or unhappy."

Experience or Knowledge of Subject

This way of discovering the meaning of a word draws on your personal experience or familiarity with the subject.

> Have you ever been seated next to someone in a restaurant whose *loquaciousness* on a cell phone made you ask to be moved to another table?

Perhaps you have experienced this or a similar situation, and you can infer that *loquaciousness* means "talkativeness."

Combination

You can use a number of these strategies at the same time to decipher the meaning of a word.

> The man at the party was a real *introvert.* He sat quietly in a corner of the room by himself working a crossword puzzle.

Here you probably used explanation, experience, and familiarity with the subject to determine that *introverts* are persons who are much more focused on their own inner thoughts and feelings than on the social environment.

Exercise 1: Context Clues

Now define the following words, without consulting your dictionary. First, give your own definition for the italicized word, and then, indicate the method(s) you used to arrive at the definition. The first example is done for you.

1. Because Americans are eating better and have access to better medical care, their *longevity* is increasing.

   Definition: <u>length of life</u>

   Method(s) used: <u>example, knowledge of subject, explanation, maybe experience</u>

2. Nudists claim it is a *liberating* experience to be without the restrictions of clothes.

   Definition: _____

   Method(s) used: _____

3. Pictures of *emaciated* and starving children filled the news as the famine in the war-torn country continued.

   Definition: _____

   Method(s) used: _____

4. *Badgered* by her children's constant pleas for a big-screen TV, the young mother finally gave in.

   Definition: _____

   Method(s) used: _____

5. Walter's *obeisance* to his brother was a source of irritation to Nancy, who couldn't figure out why Walter always deferred to him.

   Definition: _____

   Method(s) used: _____

6. After her divorce, Reyna tried to *obliterate* all evidence of her former husband by throwing out his clothes, pictures, and CDs.

    Definition: _____

    Method(s) used: _____

7. Jonathan Swift, author of *Gulliver's Travels*, did not like people in the *aggregate*, but he could tolerate them as individuals.

    Definition: _____

    Method(s) used: _____

Exercise 2: Context Clues

Use context clues to determine the meaning of the italicized words. Circle the clue word(s).

1. Tomoko tried to *pacify* her young son by giving him a lollipop, but her efforts to calm him failed.

2. John Lennon of the Beatles had an *innate* talent for music, but despite his natural ability, he still had to work hard to achieve success.

3. We have taken to calling our *inquisitive* neighbor "Mrs. Nosy Parker."

4. At his death, his property was distributed to his children in a just and *equitable* manner.

5. The doctor determined that constant ear infections had robbed the elderly woman of her *equilibrium*, so he prescribed a walker to help her maintain her balance.

6. Just as muscles can *atrophy* from lack of exercise, so too the mind can waste away from lack of use.

7. The *flippant* remark to his teacher earned Joel a detention. The teacher did not like Joel's joking attitude.

8. Many remarked about his *ostentatious* life style, but he refused to modify his showy ways.

9. Vincent was in a *pensive* mood, and he remained quietly thoughtful even while sitting in a noisy cafeteria.

10. Scientists have offered many explanations for why dinosaurs became *extinct*, but none of these explanations can fully explain their disappearance.

11. Venus Williams is an *agile* tennis player. Her coordination has saved many a shot.

Exercise 3: Context Clues with Nonsense Words

Try to determine the meaning of each made-up word by noting context clues.

1. Your dog or cat *donahs* by means of barks and meows. Do you think barking and meowing is a real language?

    donahs: _____ Comunicates _____

2. In most of the rock videos produced in the United States, females are generally irrelevant, presented simply as *feruna,* or ornaments, for the male performers.

   feruna: _____

3. Many American parents use television as an electronic *rennoo,* sitting their children down in front of it while they go off to do other things.

   rennoo: _____

4. Many youngsters at an increasingly early age are being exposed to a great deal of *zantun* on television, such as people being stabbed, poisoned, run over, or strangled.

   zantun: _____

5. As introverts age, they tend to become more introspective. On the other hand, people who were *metix* when they were young tend to remain just as outgoing and interested in other people as they age.

   metix: _____

6. Each of us has an area around us called our personal bubble. We may open that bubble to those we perceive as friendly, but we are careful to keep people we perceive as *sistos* away.

   sistos: _____

7. Throughout history, some form of patriarchy, a system in which men dominate women, has been the norm. There are no records of a true *kikitus,* a social system in which women dominate men.

   kikitus: _____

8. Arlie Hochschild pointed out that in the typical American home with both spouses working, the wife after putting in eight hours comes home and does a second shift of cooking, cleaning, and child care. Many men get out of performing tasks at home by demonstrating *ibil.* When it's their turn to cook, they burn the food. When they go to the grocery store, they forget the shopping list. They don't pick up an object unless they fall over it. Some even forget where they left the kids.

   ibil: _____

Exercise 4: Context Clues

Use the context to determine the missing words. Briefly describe the clue or clues that you found.

1. Some students have a strong fear of success. They often "play dumb" with their friends or back away from winning in sports or school. Because success is perceived as stressful, they are more comfortable with __failure__.

   Clue: _____

2. Both men and women are prone to fear of success. But women have an additional burden. If women define success as masculine, they are more likely to avoid it in order to be perceived as _____ by their peers.

   Clue: _____

3. Avoiding success is not always undesirable. An overemphasis on achievement can be just as bad. In the United States, there are many successful but unhappy workaholics. A truly successful life strikes a _____ between achievement and other needs. A happy medium is sometimes best.

   Clue: _____

4. What does it take to achieve great success? Many great Olympic athletes began with quite ordinary skills. It was their drive and determination that made them truly _____.

   Clue: _____

5. Parents can raise high achievers by nurturing dedication and hard work. The parents of Olympic athletes supported their child's interest and emphasized doing one's _____ at all times.

   Clue: _____

6. Most of us cannot achieve elite performance, but all of us can improve our everyday motivation. If you fail, regard it as a sign that you need to work _____ , not that you lack ability.

   Clue: _____

SELECTION

"For this test, some Chinese cram all year."

GETTING THE PICTURE

The current gao kao is a descendant of the imperial civil service exam that dates from about 600 A.D. In those days, the grueling exams lasted days and covered a range of topics from arithmetic to horsemanship. The gao kao exams were reinstated in 1977 after a decade-long suspension during China's Cultural Revolution. A good score on the exam is a requirement for admission into China's universities.

BIO-SKETCH

Sharon LaFraniere is an American journalist who has covered southern Africa for the *New York Times* since 2003. She has also served as an investigative reporter. In 2006, LaFraniere received the Michael Kelly Award for "the fearless pursuit and expression of truth."

BRUSHING UP ON VOCABULARY

SAT a trademark used for a set of standardized college entrance examinations, which are divided into two principal sections, verbal and mathematical. The tests are taken by U.S. high school students applying for college admission. Many colleges consider the SAT exams to be a gauge of an applicant's ability and likely success in college.

above the notch (a notch above) superior to

holed up taken refuge or shelter; hidden. The idiom originally referred to animals hibernating in winter or hiding from attack in caves or holes.

make the cut-off qualify; succeed

All-Nighter?

By Sharon LaFraniere

1 TIANJIN, CHINA—For the past year, Liu Qichao has focused on one thing, and only one thing: the gao kao, or the high test.

2   Fourteen to 16 hours a day, he studied for the college entrance examination, which this year will determine the fate of more than 10 million Chinese students. He took one day off every three weeks.

3   He was still carrying his textbook from room to room last Sunday morning before leaving for the exam site, still reviewing materials during the lunch break, still hard at work Sunday night, preparing for Part 2 of the exam that Monday.

4   "I want to study until the last minute," he said. "I really hope to be successful."

5   China may be changing at head-twirling speed, but the ritual of the gao kao (pronounced *gow kow*) remains as immutable as chopsticks. One Chinese saying compares the exam to a stampede of "a thousand soldiers and 10 horses across a single log bridge."

6   The Chinese test is in some ways like the American SAT, except that it lasts more than twice as long. The nine-hour test is offered just once a year and is the sole determinant for admission to virtually all Chinese colleges and universities. About three in five students make the cut.

7   Families pull out all the stops to optimize their children's scores. In Sichuan Province in southwestern China, students studied in a hospital, hooked up to oxygen containers, in hopes of improving their concentration.

8 Some girls take contraceptives so they will not get their periods during the exam. Some well-off parents dangle the promise of fabulous rewards for offspring whose scores get them into a top-ranked university: parties, 100,000 renminbi in cash, or about $14,600, or better.

9   "My father even promised me, if I get into a college like Nankai University in Tianjin, 'I'll give you a prize, an Audi,'" said Chen Qiong, a 17-year-old girl taking the exam in Beijing.

10   Outside the exam sites, parents keep vigil for hours, as anxious as husbands waiting for their wives to give birth. A tardy arrival is disastrous. One student who arrived four minutes late in 2007 was turned away, even though she and her mother knelt before the exam proctor, begging for leniency.

11   Cheating is increasingly sophisticated. One group of parents last year outfitted their children with tiny earpieces, persuaded a teacher to fax them the questions and then transmitted the answers by cellphone. Another father equipped a student with a miniscanner and had nine teachers on standby to provide the answers. In all, 2,645 cheaters were caught last year.

12   Critics complain that the gao kao illustrates the flaws in an education system that stresses memorization over independent thinking and creativity. Educators also say that rural students are at a disadvantage and that the quality of higher education has been sacrificed for quantity.

13   But the national obsession with the test also indicates progress.

Despite a slight drop in registration this year—the first decline in seven years—five million more students signed up for the test than did so in 2002.

14   China now has more than 1,900 institutions of higher learning, nearly double the number in 2000. Close to 19 million students are enrolled, a sixfold jump in one decade.

15   Liu Qichao, 19, a big-boned student with careful habits, plans to be the first in his family to go to college. "There just were not a lot of universities then," said his father, Liu Jie, who graduated from high school in 1980 and sells textile machinery. His son harbors hopes of getting into one of China's top universities.

16   But the whole family was shaken by the results of his first try at the gao kao last June.

17   The night before the exam, he lingered at his parents' bedside, unable to sleep for hours. "I was so nervous during the exam my mind went blank," he said. He scored 432 points out of a possible 750, too low to be admitted even to a second-tier institution.

18   Silence reigned in the house for days afterward. "My mother was very angry," he said. "She said, 'All these years of raising you and washing your clothes and cooking for you, and you earn such a bad score.'"

19   "I cried for half a month."

20   Then the family arrived at a new plan: He would enroll in a military-style boarding school in Tianjin, devoting himself exclusively to test preparation, and retake the test this June.

21   Despite the annual school fee of 38,500 renminbi (about $5,640)—well above the average annual income for a Chinese family—he had plenty of company.

22   One of his classmates, Li Yiran, a cheerful 18-year-old, estimated that more than one-fourth of the seniors at their secondary school, Yangcun No. 1 Middle School, were "restudy" students.

23   Ms. Li said she learned the hard way about the school's strict regimen. When her cell phone rang in class one day, the teacher smashed it against the radiator. Classes continue for three weeks straight, barely interrupted by a one-day break.

24   Days after most of their classmates left for home, Mr. Liu and Ms. Li were still holed up last week in their classrooms. Mr. Liu's wrist was bruised from pressing the edge of his blue metal desk, piled with a foot-high stack of textbooks.

25   Ms. Li's breakfast was a favorite among test-takers: a bread stick next to two eggs, symbolizing a 100 percent score.

26   Hours after they finished the test on Monday, both students had collected the answers from the district education bureau and begun the laborious process, with the help of their teachers, of estimating their scores.

27   Mr. Liu calculated that his score leaped by more than 100 points over last year's dismal performance. But he was still downcast, uncertain whether he would make the cutoff to apply to top-tier universities. The cutoff mark can vary by an applicant's place of residence and ethnicity.

28   Ms. Li, on the other hand, was exhilarated by her estimate of 482.5, figuring it was probably high enough for admittance to a college of the second rank.

29   By Wednesday evening, both were buoyed by news of the cutoff scores for their district. His estimated mark was well above the one needed to apply to first-tier schools, and hers was a solid five points above the notch for the second tier.

30   Before the test, Ms. Li's aunt warned her that this was her last

chance for a college degree. Even if she knelt before her mother and begged, her aunt said, her mother would refuse to let her take the test again.

But Ms. Li, a hardened veteran of not one but two gao kao ordeals, had a ready retort: "Come on. Even if my mother kneels down before me, I will refuse to take this test again." ₃₁

(Huang Yuanxi contributed research.)
(Sharon LaFraniere, "All-Nighter?," the *New York Times*, 2009)

✓ COMPREHENSION CHECKUP

The Main Idea

What is the main idea of this selection?

_____

_____

True or False

Indicate whether the statement is true or false by writing **T** or **F** in the blank provided.

_____ 1. The gao kao determines who enters China's colleges and universities.

_____ 2. A country changing at "head-twirling speed" is changing rapidly.

_____ 3. The Chinese educational system places the emphasis on thinking "outside the box."

_____ 4. China has increased the number of institutions of higher learning since the year 2000.

_____ 5. In China, parents are reluctant to put pressure on their offspring to succeed.

_____ 6. There have been instances of hi-tech cheating on the gao kao.

_____ 7. The cutoff mark on the score varies according to location and ethnicity.

_____ 8. Competition is stiff to get into the top tier Chinese universities.

_____ 9. Rules are strictly enforced by officials administering the gao kao.

_____ 10. Because of stiff penalties, cheating is virtually nonexistent on the gao kao.

_____ 11. Students are able to take the gao kao more than once.

_____ 12. The gao kao is held every two years.

_____ 13. Students have no way of estimating their scores on the test.

_____ 14. Students living in rural areas have many advantages over their urban peers on the gao kao.

Vocabulary in Context

Fill in the blanks with a word from the list below. Not all of the words will be used.

buoyed	flaws	lingered	regimen
determinant	harbors	obsession	retort
downcast	hardened	optimize	sole
exhilarated	immutable	proctor	tardy
	laborious	reigned	vigil

1. It is an _____ law of nature that night follows day.

2. In June 2009, a little girl was the _____ survivor of a plane crash that killed 152 people.

3. A student was _____ for class three times in a row.

4. The mother kept a _____ by the bed of her seriously ill son.

5. The last guest at the party _____ for 30 minutes after everyone else had left.

6. Her specific health _____ consisted of a vigorous swim every day and eating only fruits, vegetables, and lean protein.

7. Years of _____ study are required to become a physician.

8. Sara was _____ when she wasn't able to attend her best friend's wedding.

9. It was a good thing Michelle held back her angry _____ or I think her boss would have fired her for insolence.

10. Graduating from college with an "A" average has become an all-consuming _____ with him.

Vocabulary in Context

Without using a dictionary, define the following phrases.

1. as immutable as chopsticks (paragraph 5) _____

2. pull out all the stops (7) _____

3. begging for leniency (10) _____

4. my mind went blank (17) _____

5. silence reigned (18) _____

6. dismal performance (27) _____

7. buoyed by news (29) _____

8. hardened veteran (31) _____

In Your Own Words

1. Explain the meaning of the following analogy: The gao kao is like a stampede of a thousand soldiers and 10 horses across a single log bridge.

2. What do you see as the problems with a test such as the gao kao? What are the advantages?

3. Are Chinese universities simply accepting those students who are good at taking tests?

4. "The *gao kao* is about the most pressure-packed examination in the world," says Ari Wolfe, an English teacher in Guangzhou, "given the numbers, the repercussions, and the stress involved." Do you think it's a good idea to subject teenagers to such a high-pressure exam?

The Art of Writing

The acceptance system for universities in China has become increasingly controversial. Female students complain that they are being discriminated against because of their gender. Urban students complain that rural students, who were slighted in the past, are routinely admitted with lower test scores. And many educators feel the test itself is no longer valid because of its emphasis on rote learning and its lack of emphasis on creativity.

In a short essay, discuss the following: How do the issues raised by university acceptance in China compare to those in the United States? The U.S. system has granted educational preferences to minorities in order to redress past grievances. Is this similar to what China is trying to do with students from rural areas? What are the difficulties in trying to redress past wrongs to specific communities by granting preferences? What are the problems with replacing an objective test with one that calls for answers that are more subjective?

Internet Activity

How would you fare on the Gao Kao? Do an Internet search for "sample gao kao questions" and try your luck.

SELECTION

"Charles Schwab was very strong in math, science, and sports (especially golf), which helped him get into Stanford. But anything involving English 'was a disconnect.'"

GETTING THE PICTURE

The article excerpted below describes individuals who used creative problem-solving techniques to overcome their personal limitations.

BIO-SKETCH

Betsy Morris, senior writer for *Fortune,* has firsthand experience with dyslexia. Her son Johnny was diagnosed with dyslexia at age 7. Over the years, Morris learned a lot from watching Johnny deal with dyslexia. In particular, she came to admire his "patience, perseverance, and his ability not to give up when things don't come easily."

BRUSHING UP ON VOCABULARY

dead-end a situation with no escape or solution. The term originated in the late 1800s and referred specifically to a passageway that has no exit, and so halts all progress.

perilously involving great risk; dangerous. The word *perilous* originated from the Latin *periculum,* which referred to the danger of going on a trip. Historically, travel was dangerous and uncomfortable, and as a result was "full of peril."

trivia matters or things that are unimportant or inconsequential. In Latin, *tri* means "three" and *via* means "way." In ancient Rome, at the point where three roads crossed, the women would meet to talk and gossip on the way back from the market.

late-bloomer someone who matures after the usual or expected time. The term originally referred to roses that failed to bloom when they were expected to do so.

humility the quality or state of being humble or modest. The word comes from the Latin *humus,* or earth, and originally referred to people who prostrated themselves on the ground because they didn't think much of themselves.

Overcoming Dyslexia

By Betsy Morris

1 CONSIDER THE FOLLOWING four dead-end kids.

2 One was spanked by his teachers for bad grades and a poor attitude. He dropped out of school at 16. Another failed remedial English and came perilously close to flunking out of college. The third feared he'd never make it through school—and might not have without a tutor. The last finally learned to read in third grade, devouring Marvel comics, whose pictures provided clues to help him untangle the words.

3 These four losers are, respectively, Richard Branson, Charles Schwab, John Chambers, and David Boies. Billionaire Branson developed one of Britain's top brands with Virgin Records and Virgin Atlantic Airways. Schwab virtually created the discount brokerage business. Chambers is CEO of Cisco systems. Boies is a celebrated trial attorney, best known as the guy who beat Microsoft.

4 In one of the stranger bits of business trivia, they have something in common: They are all dyslexic. So is billionaire Craig McCaw, who pioneered the cellular phone industry; John Reed, who led Citibank to the top of banking; Donald Winkler, who until recently headed Ford Financial; Gaston Caperton, former governor of West Virginia and now head of the College Board; Paul Orfalea, founder of Kinko's; and Diane Swonk, chief economist of Bank One. The list goes on. Many of these adults seemed pretty hopeless as kids. All have been wildly successful in business. Most have now begun to talk about their dyslexia as a way to help children and parents cope with a condition that is still widely misunderstood.

5 What exactly is dyslexia? The everyman definition calls it a reading disorder in which people jumble letters, confusing *dog* with *god,* say, or *box* with *pox.* The exact cause is unclear; scientists believe it has to do with the way a developing brain is wired. Difficulty reading, spelling, and writing are typical symptoms. But dyslexia often comes with one or more other learning problems, as well, including trouble with math, auditory processing, organizational skills, and memory. No two dyslexics are alike—each has his own set of weaknesses and strengths. About 5 percent to 6 percent of American public school children have been diagnosed with a learning disability. 80 percent of the diagnoses are dyslexia-related. But some studies indicate that up to 20 percent of the population may have some degree of dyslexia.

6 A generation ago this was a problem with no name. Boies, Schwab, and Bill Samuels Jr., the president of Maker's Mark, did not realize they were dyslexic until some of their own children were diagnosed with the disorder, which is often inherited. Samuels says he was sitting in a school office, listening to a description of his son's problems, when it dawned on him: "Oh, shit. that's me." Most of the adults had diagnosed themselves. Says Branson: "At some point, I think I decided that being dyslexic was better than being stupid."

7 Stupid. Dumb. Retard. Dyslexic kids have heard it all. According to a

"You must have long-range goals to keep you from being frustrated by short-range failures."

—Charles C. Noble

March 2000 Roper poll, almost two-thirds of Americans still associate learning disabilities with mental retardation. That's probably because dyslexics find it so difficult to learn through conventional methods. "It is a disability in learning," says Boies. "It is not an intelligence disability. It doesn't mean you can't think."

8   He's right. Dyslexia has nothing to do with IQ; many smart, accomplished people have it, or are thought to have had it, including Winston Churchill and Albert Einstein. Sally Shaywitz, a leading dyslexia neuroscientist at Yale, believes the disorder can carry surprising talents along with its well-known disadvantages. "Dyslexics are over represented in the top ranks of people who are unusually insightful, who bring a new perspective, who think out of the box," says Shaywitz, codirector of the Center for Learning and Attention at Yale.

9   Dyslexics don't outgrow their problems—reading and writing usually remain hard work for life—but with patient teaching and deft tutoring, they do learn to manage. Absent that, dyslexia can snuff out dreams at an early age, as children lose their way in school, then lose their self-esteem and drive. "The prisons are filled with kids who can't read," says Caperton. "I suspect a lot of them have learning disabilities."

10   Dyslexia is a crucible, particularly in a high-pressure society that allows so little room for late-bloomers. "People are either defeated by it or they become much more tenacious," says McCaw. Don Winkler, a top financial services executive at Bank One and then at Ford Motor, remembers coming home from school bloodied by fights he'd had with kids who called him dumb. Kinko's founder, Paul Orfalea, failed second grade and spent part of third in a class of mentally retarded children. He could not learn to read, despite the best efforts of parents who took him to testers, tutors, therapists, special reading groups, and eye doctors. As young classmates read aloud, Orfalea says it was as if "angels whispered words in their ears."

11   In his unpublished autobiography, Orfalea says that to a dyslexic, a sentence is worse than Egyptian hieroglyphics. "It's more like a road map with mouse holes or coffee stains in critical places. You're always turning into blind alleys and ending up on the wrong side of town." He finally graduated but not before being "invited to leave . . . practically every high school in Los Angeles." One principal counseled his mother to enroll him in trade school, suggesting that Orfalea could become a carpet layer. His mother went home and tearfully told her husband, "I just know he can do more than lay carpet."

12   Charles Schwab was very strong in math, science, and sports (especially golf), which helped him get into Stanford. But anything involving English "was a disconnect." He couldn't write quickly enough to capture his thoughts. He couldn't listen to a lecture and take legible notes. He couldn't memorize four words in a row. He doesn't think he ever read a novel all the way through in high school. He was within one unit of flunking out of Stanford his freshman year. "God, I must be really dumb in this stuff," he used to tell himself. "It was horrible, a real drag on me." So horrible that Schwab and his wife, Helen, created a foundation to help parents of children with learning disorders.

13 It was as if Schwab and the others were wearing a scarlet letter: "D" for dumb. Until about five years ago Chambers kept his dyslexia a secret. As CEO, he says, "you don't want people to see your weaknesses." One day a little girl at Cisco's Bring Your Children to Work Day forced him out of the closet. Chambers had called on her, and she was trying to ask a question before a crowd of 500 kids and parents. But she couldn't get the words out. "I have a learning disability," she said tearfully.

14 Chambers cannot tell this story without choking up himself. "You could immediately identify with what that was like," he says. "You know that pain. She started to leave, and you knew how hurt she was in front of the group and her parents." Chambers threw her a lifeline. "I have a learning disability too," he said. In front of the crowd, he began talking to her as if they were the only two people in the room. "You've just got to learn your way through it," Chambers told her. "Because there are some things you can do that others cannot, and there are some things others can do you're just not going to be able to do, ever. Now my experience has been that what works is to go a little bit slower. . . ."

15 It was the kind of coaching that proved crucial to nearly everybody we talked to: mentors who took a genuine interest, parents who refused to give up, tutors who didn't even know what dyslexia was. Winkler recalls that his parents refused to let their fear of electrocution stand in the way of his fixing every iron and toaster in the neighborhood. "I wired every teacher's house," he says. "I got shocked all the time." His parents owned a mom-and-pop shop in Phillipsburg, N.J. His mother cleaned houses to pay for his tutoring. Chambers, who read right to left and up and down the page, says his parents, both doctors, claim they never once doubted his abilities, even though he says, "I absolutely did." His parents' faith was important to him. So was his tutor, Mrs. Anderson. Even today Chambers remembers tutoring as excruciating. "It might have been once or twice a week," he says, "but it felt like every day." Nonetheless, he adds, "Mrs. Anderson had an influence on my life far bigger than she might have ever realized."

16 If you could survive childhood, dyslexia was a pretty good business boot camp. It fostered risk taking, problem solving, resilience. School was a chess game that required tactical brilliance. Schwab sat mostly in the back of the room. But he was conscientious and charming, and gutsy enough to ask for extra help. Boies took a minimum of math and avoided foreign languages and anything involving spatial skills. Orfalea worked out a symbiotic relationship with classmates on a group project at USC's Marshall Business School; they did the writing, he did the photocopying (and got the germ of the idea that led to Kinko's).

17 At Vanderbilt Law School, Samuels spent a lot of time in study-group discussions. "That's how I learned the cases," he says. His friends helped with the reading; he paid for the beer. Better than most people, dyslexics learn humility and how to get along with others. It's probably no accident that Kinko's, Cisco, and Schwab have all been on *Fortune's* list of the best places to work. "I never put people down, because I know what that feels like," says Branson, who seldom asks for a résumé either "because I haven't got one myself."

18   By the time these guys got into business, they had picked themselves up so many times that risk taking was second nature. "We're always expecting a curve ball," says Samuels. Schwab remembers how hard it was to watch his friends receive awards and become General Motors Scholars, Merit Scholars, Baker Scholars. "I was so jealous," he says. Later on, he thought, some of the prizewinners had trouble dealing with adversity.

If as kids, the dyslexic executives 19 had learned the downside of their disorder inside out, as adults they began to see its upside: a distinctly different way of processing information that gave them an edge in a volatile, fast-moving world. "Many times in business, different is better than better," says Samuels. "And we dyslexics do different without blinking an eye."

✓ COMPREHENSION CHECKUP

Multiple Choice

Write the letter of the correct answer in the space provided.

_____ 1. Morris suggests all of the following about dyslexia *except*
   a. dyslexia has nothing to do with IQ
   b. typical symptoms of dyslexia are difficulty reading, writing, and spelling
   c. dyslexia is the same in all individuals
   d. dyslexia is not likely to be outgrown

_____ 2. What is the meaning of the word *devouring* as used in paragraph 2?
   a. scrutinizing
   b. collecting
   c. tearing apart
   d. taking in greedily with the senses or intellect

_____ 3. In paragraph 3, when the author refers to Charles Schwab, Richard Bronson, John Chambers, and David Boies as losers, she is being
   a. serious
   b. facetious
   c. cheerful
   d. optimistic

_____ 4. As described in paragraph 4, a *pioneer* is a person who
   a. first settled a region, opening it up for occupation by others
   b. a soldier detailed to make roads in advance of the main body
   c. a person who is among the earliest in any field of inquiry, enterprise, or progress
   d. an organism that successfully establishes itself in a barren area

_____ 5. When the author refers to an *everyman definition* in paragraph 5, she means
   a. a definition commonly used by the typical or average person
   b. a definition used by people who are not in the medical or scientific field
   c. both a and b
   d. none of the above

_____ 6. In paragraph 6, the expression *dawned on* means
  a. became clear; registered
  b. sank in, came as a realization
  c. began to be perceived or understood
  d. all of the above

_____ 7. What is the meaning of the word *snuff* as used in paragraph 9?
  a. extinguish
  b. suppress
  c. crush
  d. all of the above

_____ 8. *Crucible* in paragraph 10 refers to
  a. a short-term effect
  b. a temporary setback
  c. a severe test or trial having a lasting influence
  d. a momentous undertaking

_____ 9. As described in paragraph 10, a *tenacious* person is likely to be
  a. persistent
  b. capricious
  c. infallible
  d. disenchanted

True or False

Indicate whether the statement is true or false by writing **T** or **F** in the blank provided.

_____ 10. Chambers kept his dyslexia secret because as CEO he felt that it was inadvisable to reveal his weaknesses.

_____ 11. One reason Chambers revealed his secret was because he felt a great deal of empathy for the little girl with the learning disability.

_____ 12. A relationship that is mutually beneficial to two parties could be called *symbiotic.*

_____ 13. As children, dyslexics can see the benefits of having dyslexia, but adults can see only the liabilities.

_____ 14. Fully 60 percent of the male population is prone to dyslexia to varying degrees.

_____ 15. Dyslexia does not have a genetic component.

_____ 16. Dyslexics may have difficulty learning things in a conventional manner.

_____ 17. Dyslexia is usually outgrown by the time of puberty.

_____ 18. If something is excruciating, it causes great physical or mental suffering.

In Your Own Words

1. Dr. Mel Levine (professor of pediatrics at the University of North Carolina Medical School and an expert on learning differences) says, "Schools reward well-roundedness, but so many of the most successful people have brains that are

rather specialized." The dyslexic business leaders profiled in the *Fortune* magazine article by Betsy Morris all say that children should be allowed to specialize.
For instance, Charles Schwab suggests that foreign language requirements
should be abandoned, and Paul Orfalea says the same about trigonometry.
What do you think? How much of the basic school curriculum should be modified to suit individual learners' needs?

2. Paul Orfaela recalls that as he was growing up his mother used to console him
   by saying that in the long run "the A students work for the B students, the C
   students run the businesses, and the D students dedicate the buildings." What
   is your opinion about the relationship between grades and business success?

3. Our current educational system places a great deal of emphasis on good grades
   and high test scores to the disadvantage of the dyslexic. Do you think the emphasis should be changed?

The Art of Writing

In a brief essay, respond to the item below.

David Boies, in addition to being dyslexic himself, has two dyslexic sons. One
graduated from Yale Law School despite childhood testing that indicated he
would not be able to accomplish very much. Boies thinks our current educational climate does not allow for late-bloomers. "In this environment," he says,
"you get children who think they are masters of the universe, and children who
think they are failures, when they're 10 years old. They're both wrong. And neither is well served by that misconception."

Vocabulary Puzzle

Directions: Use the vocabulary words to complete the puzzle.

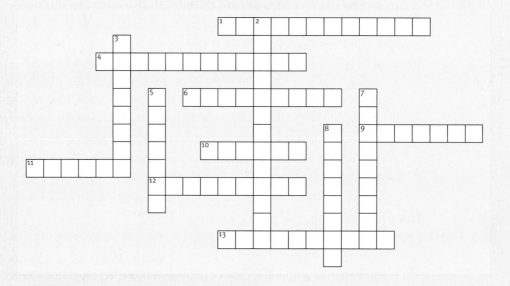

adversity	dawned	jumble	symbiotic
conscientious	excruciating	mentors	tenacious
conventional	fostered	resilience	volatile
crucial			

ACROSS CLUES

1. Causing intense suffering
4. Conforming to established practice
6. Persistent
9. Wise and trusted counselors or teachers
10. Began to be perceived
11. To confuse mentally
12. Misfortune; unfavorable circumstance
13. Ability to recover readily from adversity

DOWN CLUES

2. Meticulous; careful
3. Characterized by sudden changes
5. Of vital importance
7. Mutually beneficial relationship between two persons
8. Promoted the growth and development of

SQ3R Study Method

SQ3R is a technique for reading and studying text-book material that was developed by Dr. Francis P. Robinson over 50 years ago. SQ3R stands for survey, question, read, recite, and review. Research shows that using the SQ3R method can help you improve both your reading comprehension and your grades.

A. **Survey** (Orient yourself to the assignment)

1. Read introductory and summary paragraphs.

2. Read headings and subheadings.

3. Look at illustrations and tables.

At this stage, look at key parts of the article to achieve a general idea of how the article is structured and what it is all about.

B. **Question** (Find the main points)

1. Ask who, what, where, when, why, and how.

2. Contrast the material in front of you to previous material and to your background knowledge.

3. Turn headings and subheadings into questions.

At this stage, you will formulate questions about the material you would like to have answered.

C. **Read** (Read actively instead of passively)

1. Look for answers to your questions.

2. Underline or highlight key words or phrases.

3. Make notes in margins.

4. Summarize key points in your own words.

The goal of this stage is to read the material in an active, questioning, purposeful way. While you are reading, keep in mind the questions you have already formulated. Don't hesitate to read the material a second or third time. How often you should read something depends on how difficult it is. Reading something a second or third time is like seeing a movie over again—new details and meanings begin to appear.

D. **Recite** (Demonstrate your understanding of the material)

1. Put the information you have learned into your own words.

2. Recite the main points from memory.

3. Organize the material through outlining, mapping, diagraming, or similar techniques.

Say the answers to your original questions either to yourself or out loud. Be sure you can recite the answers to the who, what, where, when, why, and how questions you orignally posed.

E. **Review** (Memory is improved by repetition)

1. Review material frequently.

2. Practice giving answers.

Just as you shouldn't hesitate to read material more than once, you shouldn't hesitate to test yourself on it more than once. Continual review is the key to learning material and remembering it.

Computer and Internet Skills

To do well in college today, you need to have a basic proficiency with computers and the Internet. The Internet is a powerful tool for communicating with others, doing research for papers, and completing other classroom projects. As one expert has said, "Don't let that little glowing screen become an adversary. If you plan correctly, the computer can become your most useful tool at college—next to your brain." And of course your computer and Internet skills also will serve you well in the workforce. More and more jobs require at least minimal computer skills, and many jobs are going to require higher levels of computer skills. Therefore, your mastery of basic computer skills is important for achieving both college and occupational success.

However, it is important to keep in mind that all Internet Web sites do not provide accurate and reliable information. The Internet is also a source of error, falsehood, and even fraud. You need to be careful to select Web sites that will provide you with sound and helpful information. The following selection gives advice on evaluating Web sites.

SELECTION

*"To avoid being manipulated, weigh web advice carefully
and verify that the information is corroborated by sources
that you know you can trust."*

GETTING THE PICTURE

Practice your SQ3R techniques with this reading selection. Read the first paragraphs, the first sentence of subsequent paragraphs, the subheadings, the information in bold type, and the graphic material. Then read the questions at the end. What do you already know about this topic? Before you start reading, come up with some questions of your own. As you are reading the selection, highlight (or underline) the definitions for each of the key terms. Use the margins for any notes you wish to make.

BIO-SKETCH

Hamilton Gregory teaches public speaking at Asheville-Buncombe Technical Community College in North Carolina. He is the author of *Public Speaking for College and Career,* which is used by over 300 schools in the U.S. and Canada. A native of Tennessee, Gregory earned his bachelor's degree at the University of Tennessee at Chattanooga, and his master's at the University of Texas at El Paso. Before beginning his teaching career, he was a writer and photographer for the Associated Press. He lives with his wife and their three children in Asheville, North Carolina.

BRUSHING UP ON VOCABULARY

reliability consistency and dependability over a period of time. The *reliability* of a car is determined by whether or not it operates consistently well. What is the *reliability* of your car?

validity soundness; logical correctness. Copernicus and Galileo both believed that the sun was the center of the universe as opposed to the earth being the center. The *validity* of their belief was proven by later research.

Excerpt from

PUBLIC SPEAKING FOR COLLEGE AND CAREER

by Hamilton Gregory

ANALYZING INTERNET SITES

Because information on the Internet ranges from extremely useful to totally use- 1
less, how can you sort out the good from the bad? Here are some suggestions.

Don't Be Swayed by Widespread Dissemination

When some people make preposterous claims and their "facts" are challenged, 2
they defend themselves by saying, "It must be true—it's all over the Internet."
But widespread appearance on the Internet is no proof of accuracy. Unfortunately, misinformation can be spread to all parts of the planet in the twinkling of
an eye.

Millions of people have received the following e-mail: 3

Urgent Alert!
    If you are driving after dark and see an oncoming car with no headlights on, DO NOT flash your lights at them! This is a common gang member "initiation game." Here is how the game works: The new gang member under initiation drives along with no headlights, and the first car to flash their headlights at him is now his "target." He is now required to turn around and chase that car, and shoot at or into the car in order to complete his initiation requirements. Make sure you share this information with all the drivers in your family!

This alert is a hoax, but it has been widely distributed on the Internet in arti- 4 cles as well as e-mails. Newspaper reporters and police investigators have discovered that it is considered to be true by many people, who say they will no longer engage in headlight flashing.

Some widespread information on the Internet can be deadly. Many cancer 5 patients avoiding medical treatment that might save their lives, try (unsuccessfully) to cure themselves by using miracle cures that various Internet sites tout as guaranteed to eliminate cancer.

Watch Out for Web Manipulation

When you watch TV, you can easily spot an infomercial—a show that tries to look 6 like an information report but really is a scripted commercial. For example, you see five people chatting about how the Fabulous Flat-Tummy Machine chiseled their torsos and made them live happily ever after.

The Internet equivalent of infomercials is harder to detect. Let's say you are 7 searching for information on how to take care of an automobile, and you come across a Web page with 12 tips on maintaining a car's exterior. The suggestions look like objective, reliable material. One of the tips ("Use high-quality wax") has a link that, when clicked, takes you to a page that is openly commercial—it sells exterior wax. Unknown to you, the original page and the wax page are both operated by the same source—a company that sells wax. The company has done nothing illegal, but it has acted unethically in leaving you with the impression that the tips page was written by impartial researchers who are honestly recommending the best product. You have been manipulated.

To avoid being manipulated, weigh Web advice carefully and verify that the 8 information is corroborated by sources that you know you can trust.

Don't Be Dazzled by High-Tech Design

News stories often tell the sad story of Internet users—including highly intelligent, 9 college-educated men and women—who are lured into buying worthless merchandise or nonexistent services. How can so many bright people be fooled by con artists? One of the thieves' techniques is to create a Web site that has beautiful graphic design. The high-tech sparkle gives the Web site an aura of professionalism, wealth, and respectability.

A study by Stanford University psychologist B. J. Fogg found that people usu- 10 ally judge the reliability of a Web site by its appearance—not by an investigation into who sponsors it. Even the BBC (British Broadcasting Company) was duped by a handsome but fake Web site into broadcasting an interview with a man who claimed to represent Dow Chemical but really was an opponent that wanted to make Dow look bad.

Look at the following advertisement, which purports to offer a vacation to China. Does it look legitimate to you? In fact, it is a fraud! It was created on my home computer to demonstrate how easy it is for Internet crooks to create impressive-looking graphics.

If you apply a bit of skepticism, you can detect that the vacation package is a rip-off because of the ridiculously low price. A company that charged so little would quickly go out of business.

As you search for information, remember that high tech design is no indicator of honesty and reliability.

Investigate Sponsors and Authors

Who is behind a Web site? Are the owners and writers honest and unbiased? To help you evaluate a site, use these strategies.

Look for Author Credentials

Is the author of a Web page qualified to write authoritatively on the subject at hand? Look for some mention of his or her credentials or achievements. If none are listed, look for an e-mail link and send a message like this: "I am gathering material for a _____, and I need to evaluate the credibility of your Web page. Could you please tell me about your qualifications and experience on this subject?"

Get Background Information on Sponsors

Who is funding or sponsoring a Web site? If the site does not display this information on the opening screen, sometimes you can get details by clicking on a button (such as "About Us"). Or, if there is an e-mail link, you can send a message requesting background information.

Designed by Hamilton Gregory (author of selection) on his home computer to replicate a computer ad for a cheap vacation to China. Page 132 of *Public Speaking for College and Career*, 9/e, McGraw-Hill, 2010. Courtesy of Hamilton Gregory.

Try investigating the Web site by feeding the keywords of its name into a 17
search engine such as Google. Evaluate what supporters and opponents of the
Web site are saying about it.

Examine Internet Domain Names

An Internet address is known as a domain name. The suffix at the end of the name 18
signifies the "top-level domain," indicating whether the address belongs to a business, an educational institution, or one of the other broad categories shown in
Table 1. These top-level domains can give you clues about a source's objectivity and
motivations. For example, the address www.npr.org is the domain name for National
Public Radio. The suffix ".org" (pronounced dot.org) denotes a nonprofit organization.

Commercial Web pages (.com) tend to be the least objective of all the do- 19
mains. The Web site for Bayer aspirin (bayer.com) is obviously biased in favor of
using aspirin for pain relief. You are more likely to find research that is objective
and accurate if you visit an educational address (.edu)—for example, the Harvard
Medical School (hms.harvard.edu).

But don't jump to the conclusion that all ".com" addresses are untrustworthy. 20
Many businesses offer excellent information. For example, the Mayo Clinic (www
.mayoclinic.com) supplies valuable information about first aid. Some ".com" sites
are operated by magazines and newspapers that provide reliable reporting. For
example, the online *Christian Science Monitor* (www.csmonitor.com) is a business
enterprise, but it has a reputation for honest, careful journalism.

Though ".edu" sites tend to be more objective and accurate than ".com" sites, 21
this is not always the case. Some university research projects are funded by corpora-
tions that have a vested interest in a certain outcome. A professor at the University
of Wisconsin recently announced on an ".edu" site that he had discovered that
purple grape juice can help prevent heart attacks. A few days later, Reuters news

TABLE 1   TOP LEVEL DOMAINS

Original

.com	commercial (business)
.org	nonprofit organization
.net	networks
.gov	government nonmilitary organization
.mil	U.S. military branches
.edu	educational and research institutions

Additional

.biz	businesses
.info	informational
.name	individuals

agency revealed that the professor's study was funded by a juice manufacturer. The professor's findings may prove accurate, but until they are confirmed by researchers who are not paid by juice companies, we should remain skeptical.

We should also retain skepticism when considering other noncommercial 22 domains. For example, nonprofit organizations (.org) are often reliable sources but they, too, have biases. The United Nations (www.un.org) can provide trustworthy international statistics, but it obviously has a bias in reporting U.N. peacekeeping operations.

The vast majority of sites on the Web are ".com," and they can create a lot of 23 clutter when you are trying to find purely educational material. To overcome this problem, several search engines, such as Google's Advanced Search (www. google.com and click on "Advanced Search"), allow you to search by domain. In other words, you can specify that you want returns only from ".edu" sites.

Look for Country of Origin

Gathering information from throughout the world can be rewarding. If you are 24 researching ways to combat soil erosion and find a Web page on an innovative program in Costa Rica, you have broadened your knowledge base.

Beware, however, of using such material incorrectly. Suppose you come across 25 an appealing Web page that lists major prescription drugs and the ailments they treat. If you notice that the page originates in another country, you would be wise to use the information carefully, if at all. Other countries have different trade names and different rules on which drugs are permissible. A prescription drug that is available in England may not be FDA-approved for the United States.

Most Web sites display an address or give some indication of the place of 26 origin. For those that do not, you will have to look for clues:

1. **Investigate place names that do not sound familiar.** If you are looking for 27 articles on criminal law and you find a Web page about legal cases in New South Wales, you should find out just where New South Wales is located. When you discover that it is a state in Australia, you should explore whether the information applies to the United States.

2. **Look for abbreviations in the Internet address.** Web sites in various countries 28 may use the same identifiers used by American sites—.org, .net, and so on. But sometimes their addresses include two-letter international abbreviations. For example, www.cite-sciences.fr is the address for a French science site.

   You can find a list of international abbreviations at one of these sites: 29

   www.wap.org/info/techstuff/domains.html

   www.ics.uci.edu/pub/websoft/wwwstat/country-codes.txt

Examine Date

Most Web pages will give the date on which the information was created or up- 30 dated. If the page is old, you may need to find another, more recent source.

Look at Evaluations of Web Sites

If you are investigating the reliability or validity of a Web site, the best strategy is 31 what we've already suggested: Look for other sources, especially opposing views.

TABLE 2   EVALUATIONS OF WEB SITES

Directory with Related Sites	**Misinformation Alerts**
These directories provide links to Web sites that are ranked according to quality.	These services try to expose scams, quackery, and phony news not only in Web sites and e-mail, but with more historical urban legends.
Librarians' Index to the Internet (www.lii.org) selects only reliable sites and often appends an evaluation, which you can reach by clicking on the "More info" icon.	*Snopes.com*–(www.snopes.com)
	Urban Legends–(www .urbanlegendsabout.com)
	TruthorFiction.com–(www .truthorfiction.com)
	The Skeptic's Dictionary– (www.skepdic.com)

Another good strategy is to see how other people rate a particular Web site. Table 2 provides links to services that evaluate Web sites for reliability.

Bear in mind that these services do not pretend to rate all Web sites. Also, 32 don't accept the reviews as indisputable. Just as a movie reviewer's good rating does not guarantee you a movie that you will enjoy, a Web reviewer's good rating does not guarantee you a reliable source.

Summary

(1) When you evaluate material, look for high-quality information that is fac- 33 tual, reliable, well supported, current, verifiable, fair, and comprehensive.

(2) Apply healthy skepticism, probing for erroneous or unreliable data. Reject 34 claims that are based solely on anecdotes, testimonials, or opinions. Don't use just one source, because it might turn out to be wrong. Examine opposing viewpoints in an effort to find truth and to anticipate possible objections.

(3) Be cautious in using polls because some people don't respond honestly, 35 and results often depend upon how a question is asked.

(4) Recognize the fallibility of experts. Don't assume that a PhD or MD is al- 36 ways trustworthy. Don't assume that affiliation with a prestigious university is assurance of credibility.

(5) Watch out for groups with names that can mislead the public into think- 37 ing they are unbiased. Find out who is financially backing the group.

(6) In analyzing Internet sites, watch out for subtle manipulation on Web pages. 38 Examine domain names for clues on a source's objectivity and motivation. See if the material comes from a foreign country. If a Web site has a beautiful, sophisticated design, don't assume that it is reliable and highly professional. Investigate its sponsors and authors to see if they are legitimate authorities on their subject matter.

(Hamilton Gregory, *Public Speaking for College and Career, 7/e,* 2010)

✓ COMPREHENSION CHECKUP

Multiple Choice

Write the letter of the correct answer in the blank provided.

_____ 1. The author suggests that the Internet
   a. contains only accurate information
   b. contains only misleading information
   c. can be a useful tool
   d. should be used by everybody

_____ 2. According to the author, commercial Web sites
   a. are designed to manipulate the public
   b. can contain useful information
   c. should never be trusted
   d. none of the above

_____ 3. Which of the following statements would apply to the word *hoax* as used in the selection?
   a. Hoaxes present false information.
   b. Many are fooled by the hoaxes they have found on the Internet.
   c. There isn't any way to determine the truthfulness of Internet hoaxes.
   d. both a and b

_____ 4. Which of the following are used to manipulate visitors to Web sites?
   a. high-tech graphic design
   b. not giving complete background information related to sponsors and authors
   c. using links to other Web pages that are sponsored by the same company or organization as the original Web page
   d. all of the above

True or False

Indicate whether the statement is true or false by writing **T** or **F** in the blank provided.

_____ 5. Each Web site has a domain name with a suffix indicating the kind of Web site it is.

_____ 6. One must be qualified in a particular subject to be able to post a Web page on the Internet.

_____ 7. All ".com" addresses are untrustworthy.

_____ 8. High tech does not necessarily equal high value.

_____ 9. The funding of a Web site may indicate its possible bias.

_____ 10. The word *corroborated* in paragraph 8 means "contradicted."

Vocabulary in Context

Directions: Look through the given paragraph and find a word that matches the definition.

1. varies within certain limits (paragraph 1)   _____

2. senseless; foolish (2)   _____

3. praise extravagantly (5)   _____

4. unbiased; fair; just (7)   _____

5. influenced skillfully and often unfairly (8)   _____

6. tempted; enticed; attracted (9)   _____

7. doubt or unbelief (12)   _____

8. trustworthiness (15)   _____

9. covering much; inclusive (33)   _____

10. short accounts of incidents (34)   _____

11. difficult to detect (38)   _____

12. appealing to cultivated tastes (38)   _____

Matching

Match the following organizations and businesses with an Internet address (or domain). Write the letter for the correct address in the blank.

_____ 1. Microsoft   a. www.u.s.c.edu

_____ 2. National Public Radio   b. www.dot.state.az.us

_____ 3. The White House   c. www.kantei.go.jp/foreign

_____ 4. U.S. Army   d. www.spain.info

_____ 5. University of Southern California   e. www.microsoft.com

_____ 6. Arizona Department of Transportation f. www.whitehouse.gov

_____ 7. Spanish Tourist Offices worldwide   g. www.npr.org

_____ 8. Prime Minister of Japan   h. www.army.mil

In Your Own Words

1. Do you believe the U.S. government should take action against writers of Web sites that present false or misleading information? Explain your answer.

2. Do you think the Internet needs to be regulated? Some people think computers should be registered and users should have to get a license to drive on the "information highway." What do you think?

3. What are your thoughts about censorship on the Internet? Should certain kinds of sites be "policed"?

The Art of Writing

Keeping in mind what you have learned from the selection, respond to one of the following:

> "You can fool too many of the people too much of the time."
> —James Thurber

> "A fool and his money are soon parted."

Internet Activity

1. Many colleges have a Web site. Go to a search engine and type in the name of your college. If your college has a Web site, you should now see its name and be able to "click" your way to it. Once you have brought up your college's Web site, see if you can find the academic calendar for your present term. Are the dates for final exams listed? What are those dates? What dates are listed as academic holidays? When does registration for the next term open and end? Can you find anything else of interest or help to you in your college's Web site? What suggestions could you make to your college to improve the Web site? Write a paragraph about what you learned about your college.

2. Table 2 from the article lists four Web sites that broadcast misinformation alerts about Web pages and e-mail messages. Find a message of interest to you from two of these sites. Print out the Web pages you read and briefly explain what you learned about the possible hoaxes or urban legends.

Brain Teasers

Can you solve these?

1. As I was going to St. Ives,

   I met a man with seven wives.

   Each wife had seven sacks.

   Each sack had seven cats.

   Each cat had seven kits.

   Kits, cats, sacks, wives.

   How many are going to St. Ives?

   _____

2. A man and his son are in a car accident. The man dies at the scene, but the son is rushed to the hospital. When he gets there the surgeon on duty says, "I can't operate on this boy. He's my son." How is this possible?

   _____

3. If a plane crashes exactly on a border, where are the survivors buried?

   _____

4. Two friends are walking in the forest. Suddenly, one of them spots a tiger that looks both hungry and angry. The other friend sits down, and puts on his running shoes. Seeing this, the first guy says, "Do you really think that those shoes will help you outrun the tiger?" How will the running shoes help save his life?

   _____

Discovering Meaning Through Structure

Chapters in Part 2

Heroes for Wheels (1985)
by Jane Wooster Scott
© Jane Wooster Scott/SuperStock

Topics, Main Ideas, and Details

Carte Blanche (1965) *BY RENÉ MAGRITTE*

Banque d'Images, ADAGP/Art Resource, N.Y./© 2011 C. Herscovici,
London/Artists Rights Society (ARS), New York

View and Reflect

1. *Carte Blanche* was created by the highly imaginative painter René Magritte. What does the painting illustrate about perception, which is the theme of this chapter? Is the scene you are viewing physically possible?
2. Do the trees hide or reveal the woman and the horse? Can you see the woman and the horse in the open spaces in the painting?
3. What is the topic of the painting? The main idea?
4. What is the definition of *carte blanche*? In what way does the definition apply to the painting?

Identifying Topics, Main Ideas, and Details

Most paragraphs are about a particular **topic** or **subject.** The topic is usually a single word or phrase and is often the noun that is mentioned most frequently in a paragraph. We can identify the topic by asking ourselves, "What is this all about?" or "Who is this all about?"

Paragraphs are typically organized around a main idea with all sentences supporting this **main idea,** or key point, of the paragraph. The main idea can be identified by asking, "What key point does the author want me to know about the topic?"

The main idea may be directly stated in a paragraph—usually, but not always, in the first or last sentence—or it can be implied. When trying to find a main idea that is directly stated, it helps to remember that you are looking for a general statement, not a specific one. When main ideas are implied, you, the reader, are responsible for coming up with a general statement that unites the author's key details. This general statement should be no more than one sentence long.

Details are supporting sentences that reinforce the main idea. While the main idea is a general statement, supporting details provide specific information, such as facts, examples, or reasons, that explain or elaborate on the main idea.

As an illustration of the difference between main ideas and details, study the invitation below. The main idea of the invitation is the fact that a reception is going to be held. The details tell us who the reception is for and when and where it will occur.

El telar de las mariposas (2009) *BY CLAUDIA P. MARTINEZ*

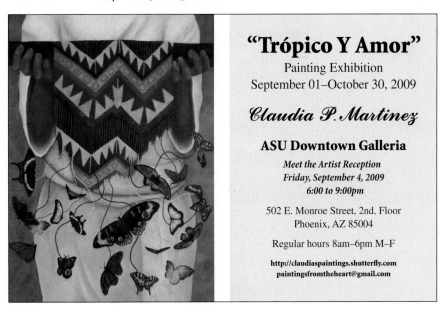

© Claudia P. Martinez

Those supporting sentences that directly reinforce the main idea are called **major** supporting details, and those sentences that serve only to reinforce the major supporting details are called **minor** supporting details.

Read the following paragraph from *Gilbert's Living with Art* by Mark Getlein. The topic of the paragraph is perception.

1. In visual perception, our eyes take in info-rmation in the form of light patterns; the brain processes these patterns to give them meaning. The mechanics of perception work much the same way for everyone, yet in a given situation

we do not all perceive the same things. The human eye cannot take in all available visual information. Our world is too complex, and we are constantly bombarded with an incredible range of visual images. To avoid overloading our mental circuits, the brain responds only to that visual information required to meet our needs at one moment.

The next paragraph contains a main idea sentence and a series of examples that support it. The topic of this paragraph, and the others that follow, is also perception.

"The field of consciousness is tiny. It accepts only one problem at a time."

—Antoine de Saint-Exupéry

2. It is easier to cope with our complex visual world if we simplify our perceptions and see according to our immediate needs. Suppose you are motoring along a busy street. Your eyes "see" everything, but what does your brain register? If you are the car's driver, you will see the traffic signs and lights, because awareness of such details is necessary. If you are hungry, your attention may be attracted by fast-food signs. If you are looking for a specific address, you will focus on building numbers and block out nearly everything else.

Identify the main idea sentence in paragraph 3 below.

3. Studies indicate that the brain is often more important than the eyes in determining what each of us sees as we move through the world. The brain's ability to control perception is obvious when we study ambiguous figures, such as the classic one reproduced here. When you first look at this drawing, you may see a white vase. Or you may see two dark profiles. Even after you have been made aware of the two images, you must consciously work at going back and forth between them. You can feel your brain shifting as it organizes the visual information into first one image and then the other.

Vase-profile illusion

"Facts as facts do not always create a spirit of reality because reality is a spirit."

—G. K. Chesterton

Paragraph 3 expresses the main idea in the first sentence and then gives us an example that illustrates it.

To gain understanding of how main ideas and major and minor supporting details work together in a paragraph, read the following paragraph and study the outline that follows.

4. While perception can cause us to miss seeing what is actually present in the visual field, it can also do the reverse: cause us to "see" what is not present. The brain supplies information to create a kind of order it requires, even though that information may not be recorded by the eyes. In the illustration of wavy forms you may see a perfect white circle, but there is no circle. There is only the

illusion of a white circle created by breaks in the wavy forms. This is just another trick our brains play on us as part of the phenomenon of perception.

(Mark Getlein, *Gilbert's Living with Art*, 6/e, 2002)

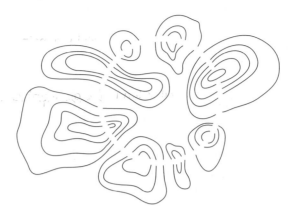

Wavy Forms
"Wavy Forms," from Mark Getlein, *Gilbert's Living with Art*, 6th ed., New York: McGraw-Hill, 2002, p. 274. Copyright © 2002 McGraw-Hill. Reprinted by permission of The McGraw-Hill Companies, Inc.

Key: MI (main idea), MSD (major supporting detail), msd (minor supporting detail)

I. Perception can cause us to miss seeing what is there and can cause us to "see" what is not there. (MI)

  A. The brain supplies information to create order in what our eyes see. (MSD)

    1. You see a perfect white circle in the wavy forms. (msd)

    2. In this way, our brains trick us. (msd)

It is wise to remember that while all paragraphs have a topic, not all paragraphs have main ideas. Some background or descriptive paragraphs, which are meant to set the tone or mood of a piece of writing, may not have any main idea at all.

Exercise 1: Locating Topics in Textbook Material

Locate the topic of each paragraph. Remember to ask the question "Who or what is the paragraph about?"

1. Tickets for athletic events and musical concerts sometimes get resold for much greater amounts than the original price—a market transaction known as "scalping." For example, an original buyer may resell a $75 ticket to a concert for $200, $250 or more. Reporters sometimes denounce scalpers for "ripping off" buyers by charging "exorbitant" prices. But is ticket scalping really undesirable? Not on economic grounds! We must first recognize that such ticket resales are voluntary transactions. If both buyer and seller did not expect to gain from the exchange, it would not occur! There are no losers or victims here. Both buyer and seller benefit from the transaction. The scalping market simply redistributes assets (game or concert tickets) from those who would rather have the money to those who would rather have the tickets.

(Campbell R. McConnell, *Economics*, 17/e, 2008)

Topic: _____

[handwritten margin notes at top: Main Idea / Topic / alcohol consumption]

2. Alcohol consumption exacts an alarming toll on college students. Students who drink more frequently die in traffic accidents, receive citations for driving under the influence/driving while intoxicated (DUI/DWI), damage personal or public property, argue or fight, attempt suicide, experience or commit sexual abuse, miss classes, receive failing grades, suffer academic probation, or drop out of college more often than do those who are not drinkers. Most campus rapes occur when the victim, the assailant, or both have been drinking.

(Clinton Benjamin, et al., *Human Biology*, 1997)

Topic: _alcohol consumption_

[handwritten margin note: Main Idea / • Noise can raise once stress level.]

3. Anyone who has roomed with a noisy person, worked in a noisy office, or tried to study with a party going on in the next room can attest to the effect of noise on one's level of stress. Noise can raise blood pressure, increase heart rate, and lead to muscle tension. Noise has been found to be related to job dissatisfaction and to result in irritation and anxiety. Most disturbing is noise that constantly changes in pitch, intensity, or frequency. We may become used to more common and stable noise and almost ignore it. People who live near airports, for example, seem to not even hear the planes after a while. However, just because you become accustomed to the noise or are able to tune it out doesn't mean you are not being affected by it.

(Jerrold Greenberg, *Comprehensive Stress Management*, 9/e, 2006)

Topic: _Effects of noise_

[handwritten margin note: Main Idea / • Arranged marriages use to be big in asia, but now are decreasing due to western influences]

4. In the traditional cultures of Asia, arranged marriages were the rule. Marriages were designed to further the well-being of families, not of the individuals involved. Marriage was traditionally seen as a matter of ancestors, descendants, and property. Supporters of these traditions point out that love is a fleeting emotion and not a sensible basis for such an important decision. Today, arranged marriages are still very common in India, in many Muslim nations, and in sub-Saharan Africa. However, it appears that this tradition is rapidly deteriorating, often in proportion to the degree of Western influence.

(Curtis Byer, et al., *Dimensions of Human Sexuality*, 5/e, 1999)

Topic: _Arranged marriages_

5. If you are like most people, you have indulged in fake listening many times. You go to history class, sit in the third row, and look squarely at the instructor as she speaks. But your mind is far away, floating in the clouds of a pleasant daydream. Occasionally you come back to earth: the instructor writes an important term on the chalkboard, and you dutifully copy it in your notebook. Every once in a while the instructor makes a witty remark, causing others in the class to laugh. You smile politely, pretending that you have heard the remark and found it mildly humorous. You have a vague sense of guilt that you are not paying close attention, but you tell yourself that any material you miss can be picked up from a friend's notes. Besides, the instructor is talking about road construction in ancient Rome and nothing could be more boring. So, back you go into your private little world. Unfortunately, fake listening has two drawbacks: (1) You miss a lot of information, and (2) you can botch a personal or business relationship.

(Hamilton Gregory, *Public Speaking for College and Career*, 4/e, 1996)

Topic: _Fake listening_

6. There has been a significant increase in childlessness in the United States. According to census data, about 16 to 17 percent of women will now complete their childbearing years without having borne any children, compared to 10 percent in 1980. As many as 20 percent of women in their 30s expect to remain childless. Economic considerations have contributed to this shift in attitudes; having children has become quite expensive. According to a government estimate made for 2007, the average middle-class family will spend $204,060 to feed, clothe, and shelter a child from birth to age 18.

Main Idea

(John Witt, *SOC 2010*, rev. 1/e, 2010)

Topic: *Childlessness in the United States*

Exercise 2: Locating Main Ideas in Textbook Material

Locate the main idea sentence of each paragraph. The main idea can be identified by asking the question "What key point does the author want me to know about the topic?"

(Paragraphs in items 1–5 from David G. Myers, *Social Psychology*, 9/e, 2008)

"Anxiety is fear of one's self."

—Wilhem Stekel

1. We infer our emotions by observing our bodies and our behaviors. For example, a stimulus such as a growling bear confronts a woman in the forest. She tenses, her heartbeat increases, adrenaline flows, and she runs away. Observing all this, she then experiences fear. At a college where I am to lecture, I awake before dawn and am unable to get back to sleep. Noting my wakefulness, I conclude that I must be anxious.

   Main idea: _____

2. James Laird instructed college students to pull their brows together and frown while experimenters attached electrodes to their faces. The act of maintaining a frown caused students to report feeling angry. Those students induced to make a smiling face reported feeling happier and found cartoons more humorous. We have all experienced this phenomenon. We're feeling crabby, but then the phone rings or someone comes to the door and elicits from us warm, polite behavior. "How's everything?" "Just fine, thanks. How are things with you?" "Oh, not bad. . . ." If our feelings are not too intense, this warm behavior may change our whole attitude. It's tough to smile and feel grouchy. When Miss Universe parades her smile, she may, after all, be helping herself feel happy. Going through the motions can trigger the emotions.

   Main idea: _____

3. Your gait can affect how you feel. When you get up from reading this chapter, walk for a minute taking short, shuffling steps with eyes downcast. It's a great way to feel depressed. Want to feel better? Walk for a minute taking long strides with your arms swinging and your eyes straight ahead. Can you feel the difference?

   Main idea: _____

4. It appears that unnecessary rewards sometimes have a hidden cost. Rewarding people for doing what they already enjoy may lead them to attribute their doing

it to the reward. This undermines their self-perception that they do it because they like it. If you pay people for playing with puzzles, they will later play with the puzzles less than those who play without being paid. If you promise children a reward for doing what they intrinsically enjoy (for example playing with magic markers) then you will turn their play into work.

Main idea: ___1st Sentence_____

"Take away the cause and the effect ceases."

—Miguel de Cervantes

5. An old man lived alone on a street where boys played noisily every afternoon. The din annoyed him, so one day he called the boys to his door. He told them he loved the cheerful sound of children's voices and promised them each 50 cents if they would return the next day. Next afternoon the youngsters raced back and played more lustily than ever. The old man paid them and promised another reward the next day. Again they returned, whooping it up, and the man again paid them; this time 25 cents. The following day they got only 15 cents, and the man explained that his meager resources were being exhausted. "Please, though, would you come to play for 10 cents tomorrow?" The disappointed boys told the man they would not be back. It wasn't worth the effort, they said, to play all afternoon at his house for only 10 cents. This folk tale illustrates the result of bribing people to do what they already like doing; they may then see their action as externally controlled rather than intrinsically appealing.

Main idea: _____

Exercise 3: Locating Supporting Details in Textbook Material

In previous exercises, we have seen that the main idea in a paragraph is frequently located at either the beginning or end of the paragraph. However, the main idea may also appear in other locations within a paragraph, such as in the middle or at both the beginning and the end. Wherever the main idea is located, it must be supported by details. Most authors provide examples, illustrations, major points, reasons, or facts and statistics to develop their main idea. While a main idea can be either directly stated somewhere in the paragraph or implied, supporting details are always directly stated. The ability to recognize supporting details is of crucial importance in the reading process. Locating supporting details will tell you whether you have correctly identified the main idea.

For those of you who are visual learners, diagrams showing the development of a paragraph and the position of the main idea and supporting details might be helpful. The topic of each of the following paragraphs is perceptual organization.

After reading the explanation for each type of paragraph, write several key supporting details on the line provided.

(Paragraphs 1–4, 6–8 from Richard Schaefer, *Sociology*, 3/e, 2000; Paragraph 5 from Wayne Weiten, *Psychology Applied to Modern Life*, 6/e, 2000)

Main idea sentence

Details

1. *Much of perception is based on prior experience.* For instance, Colin Turnbull tells of the time he took a Pygmy from the dense rain forests of Africa to the vast African plains. The Pygmy had never before seen objects at a great distance. Hence, the first time he saw a herd of buffalo in the distance, he thought it was a swarm of insects. Imagine his confusion when he was driven toward the animals. He concluded that he was being fooled by witchcraft because the "insects" seemed to grow into buffalo before his eyes.

In paragraph 1, the main idea is stated in the first sentence. The author states the main idea and then provides an example to illustrate it. A diagram of this type of paragraph would be a triangle with the point aiming downward. The main idea is represented by the horizontal line at the top.

Supporting details: _____

_____

Details

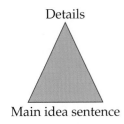

Main idea sentence

2. A college professor was attacked by an actor in a staged assault. Immediately after the event, 141 witnesses were questioned in detail. Their descriptions were then compared to a videotape of the staged "crime." The total accuracy score for the group (on features such as appearance, age, weight, and height of the assailant) was only *25 percent* of the maximum possible. This incident dramatically demonstrates why witnesses to crimes so often disagree. *As you can see, impressions formed when a person is surprised, threatened, or under stress are especially prone to distortion.*

In paragraph 2, the author gives an example at the beginning and uses the main point to draw a conclusion. A diagram for this type of paragraph places the main idea at the bottom of the triangle.

Supporting details: _____

_____

Details

Main idea sentence

Details

3. Harness yourself to a hang glider, step off a cliff, and soar. No matter how exhilarating, your flight still wouldn't provide a true "bird's eye" view. *Many birds see the world in ways that would seem strange to a human.* For example, pigeons, ducks, and humming-birds can see ultraviolet light, which adds an extra color to their visual palette. Homing pigeons and many migrating birds perceive polarized light, which aids them in navigation. The American woodcock can survey a 360-degree panorama without moving its eyes or head.

In paragraph 3, the author begins with an example, states the main idea, and then concludes with additional examples. Because the main idea is in the middle, the diagram resembles a diamond.

Supporting details: _____

_____

Main idea sentence

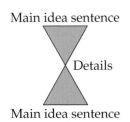

Details

Main idea sentence

4. *Psychologists are gradually convincing lawyers, judges, and police officers of the fallibility of eyewitness testimony.* In one typical court case, a police officer testified that he saw the defendant shoot the victim as both stood in a doorway 120 feet away. Measurements made by a psychologist showed that at that distance light from the dimly lit doorway was extremely weak—less than a fifth of that from a candle. To further show that identification was improbable, a juror stood in the doorway under identical lighting conditions. None of the other jurors could identify him. The defendant was acquitted. Even in broad daylight, eyewitness testimony is untrustworthy. After a horrible DC-10 airliner crash in Chicago 84 pilots who saw the accident were interviewed. Forty-two said the DC-10's landing gear was up, and 42 said it was down! As one investigator commented, the best witness may be a "kid under 12 years old who doesn't have his parents around." *These and other incidents are being used by psychologists to demonstrate to legal professionals the unpredictability of eyewitness testimony.*

In paragraph 4, the author begins with the main idea, provides detailed illustrations of it, and concludes with a restatement of the main idea. A diagram of this type of paragraph would have an hourglass shape.

Supporting details: _____

_____

Main idea not directly stated

5. Remember Evan, that bully from your elementary school? He made your nine-year-old life a total misery—constantly looking for opportunities to poke fun at you and beat you up. Now, when you meet someone named Evan, you notice that your initial reaction is negative and that it takes a while before you warm up to him. Why?

In paragraph 5, the main idea is not stated in any specific sentence. Instead, all of the sentences are working together to create a word picture in your mind. Because no one sentence is clearly the main idea, a diagram of this paragraph might resemble a square or a rectangle.

Exercise 4: Identifying Main Ideas and Supporting Details and Diagramming Paragraphs in Textbook Material

The main idea sentence appears at different locations in the following paragraphs. Write the number of the main idea sentence on the line. Then draw a diagram of the paragraph and list numbers of the supporting detail sentences.

(Information from Ronald B. Adler and Neil Towne, *Looking Out/Looking In*, 10/e, 2002)

"To love others, we must first learn to love ourselves."

—Anonymous

A. (1) A person with high self-esteem is more likely to think well of others. (2) Someone with low self-esteem is more likely to have a poor opinion of others. (3) Your own experience may bear this out: Persons with low self-esteem are often cynical and quick to ascribe the worst possible motives to others, whereas those who feel good about themselves are disposed to think favorably about the people they encounter. (4) As one writer put it, "What we find 'out there' is what we put there with our unconscious projections. (5) When we think we are looking out a window, it may be, more often than we realize, that we are really gazing into a looking glass." (6) Our self concepts influence how we think about ourselves and interact with others.

Main idea sentence: _____ Diagram: _____

Supporting details: _____

B. (1) We often judge ourselves more charitably than we do others. (2) When others suffer, we often blame the problem on their personal qualities. (3) On the other hand, when we're the victims, we find explanations outside ourselves. (4) Consider a few examples. (5) When *they* botch a job, we might think they weren't listening well or trying hard enough; when *we* make the mistake, the problem was unclear directions or not enough time. (6) When *he* lashes out angrily, we say he's being moody or too sensitive; when *we* blow off steam, it's because of the pressure we've been under. (7) When *she* gets caught speeding, we say she should have been more careful;

when *we* get the ticket, we deny we were driving too fast or say, "Everybody does it."

Main idea sentence: _____ Diagram: _____

Supporting details: _____

C. (1) At one time or another you've probably seen photos of sights invisible to the unaided eye: perhaps an infrared photo of a familiar area or the vastly enlarged image of a minute object taken by an electron microscope. (2) You've also noticed how certain animals are able to hear sounds and smell odors that are not apparent to humans. (3) Experiences like these remind us that there is much more going on in the world than we are able to experience with our limited senses; in fact, we're only aware of a small part of what is going on around us. (4) For instance, most people who live in large cities find that the noises of traffic, people, and construction soon fade out of their awareness. (5) Others can take a walk through the forest without distinguishing one bird's call from another or noticing the differences among various types of vegetation. (6) On a personal level, we've all had the experience of failing to notice something unusual about a friend—perhaps a new hairstyle or a sad expression—until it's called to our attention.

Main idea sentence: _____ Diagram: _____

Supporting details: _____

D. (1) The kind of work we do often influences our view of the world. (2) Imagine five people taking a walk through the park. (3) One, a botanist, is fascinated by the variety of trees and plants. (4) The zoologist is looking for interesting animals. (5) The third, a meteorologist, keeps an eye on the sky, noticing changes in the weather. (6) The fourth companion, a psychologist, is totally unaware of nature, instead concentrating on the interaction among the people in the park. (7) The fifth person, being a pickpocket, quickly takes advantage of the others' absorption to make some money. (8) Our occupational roles shape our perceptions.

Main idea sentence: _____ Diagram: _____

Supporting details: _____

E. (1) Even within the same occupational setting, the different roles that participants have can affect their perceptions. (2) Consider a typical college classroom, for example. (3) The experiences of the instructor and students often are quite dissimilar. (4) Having dedicated a large part of their lives to their work, most professors see their subject matter—whether French literature, physics, or speech communication—as vitally important. (5) Students who are taking the course to satisfy a general education requirement may view the subject quite differently: maybe as one of many obstacles that stand between them and a degree, maybe as a chance to meet new people.

Main idea sentence: _____ Diagram: _____

Supporting details: _____

F. (1) Because we're exposed to more input than we can possibly manage, the first step in perception is the selection of which data we will attend to and which we will ignore. (2) Something that is louder, larger, or brighter stands out. (3) This explains why—other things being equal—we're more likely to remember extremely tall or short people and why someone who laughs or talks loudly at a party attracts more attention (not always favorable) than do quiet guests. (4) *Repetitious stimuli, repetitious stimuli, repetitious stimuli*—also attract attention. (5) *ATTENTION IS ALSO FREQUENTLY RELATED to* contrast *or* change *in STIMULATION.* (6) Put differently, unchanging people or things become less noticeable. (7) Selection isn't just a matter of attending to some stimuli; it also involves ignoring other cues.

Main idea sentence: _____ Diagram: _____

Supporting details: _____

SELECTION

*"Over the years, I learned to smother the rage I felt
at so often being taken for a criminal."*

GETTING THE PICTURE

The first paragraph of the essay "Black Men and Public Space" by Brent Staples illustrates how perception affects behavior. By providing the reader with a riveting description, it serves as an introduction to the author's key ideas. In the paragraphs that follow, Staples discusses the effects of being a victim of stereotyping. At the end of the essay, he describes his creative solution to signaling his safe intentions to others.

BIO-SKETCH

Brent Staples, born in 1951, grew up in a family with an alcoholic father. He had little hope of attending college, but a special program gave him extra academic help. After graduating from Widener College (now Widener University) with a BA in 1973, he went on to earn his PhD in psychology from the University of Chicago in 1982. Staples is currently a journalist who writes about political and cultural issues for the *New York Times*. His book *Parallel Time: Growing Up in Black and White* won the Anisfield Wolff Book Award.

BRUSHING UP ON VOCABULARY

warren a mazelike place containing many passageways; a building or area containing many inhabitants in crowded quarters. The word originally referred to a game park.

wee very early; small or tiny

Black Men and Public Space

By Brent Staples

1 MY FIRST VICTIM WAS A WOMAN—white, well-dressed, probably in her early twenties. I came upon her late one evening on a deserted street in Hyde Park, a relatively affluent neighborhood in an otherwise mean, impoverished section of Chicago. As I swung onto the avenue behind her, there seemed to be a discreet, uninflammatory distance between us. Not so. She cast back a worried glance. To her, the youngish black man—a broad six feet two inches with a beard and billowing hair, both hands shoved into the pockets of a bulky military jacket—seemed menacingly close. After a few more

quick glimpses, she picked up her pace and was soon running in earnest. Within seconds she disappeared into a cross street.

2   That first encounter, and those that followed, signified that a vast, unnerving gulf lay between nighttime pedestrians—particularly women—and me.

3   After dark, on the warrenlike streets of Brooklyn where I live, I often see women who fear the worst from me. They seem to have set their faces on neutral, and with their purse straps strung across their chests bandolier-style, they forge ahead as though bracing themselves against being tackled. I understand, of course, that the danger they perceive is not a hallucination. Women are particularly vulnerable to street violence, and young black males are drastically overrepresented among the perpetrators of that violence. Yet these truths are no solace against the kind of alienation that comes of being ever the suspect, a fearsome entity with whom pedestrians avoid making eye contact.

4   Over the years, I learned to smother the rage I felt at so often being taken for a criminal. Not to do so would surely have led to madness. I now take precautions to make myself less threatening. I move about with care, particularly late in the evening. I give a wide berth to nervous people on subway platforms during the wee hours, particularly when I have exchanged business clothes for jeans. If I happen to be entering a building behind some people who appear skittish, I may walk by, letting them clear the lobby before I return, so as not to seem to be following them. I have been calm and extremely congenial on those rare occasions when I've been pulled over by the police.

5   And on late-evening constitutionals I employ what has proved to be an excellent tension-reducing measure. I whistle melodies from Beethoven and Vivaldi and the more popular classical composers. Even steely New Yorkers hunching toward nighttime destinations seem to relax, and occasionally they even join in the tune. Virtually everybody seems to sense that a mugger wouldn't be warbling bright, sunny selections from Vivaldi's *Four Seasons.* It is my equivalent of the cowbell that hikers wear when they know they are in bear country.

(Brent Staples, "Black Men and Public Space" in *Ms. Magazine,* 1986)

✓ COMPREHENSION CHECKUP

Short Answer

1. The topic of the selection is _____

2. The main idea of the selection is stated in the first sentence of paragraph

   _____

3. The following sentence states the main idea of paragraph 3 ⁴.

   I now take precautions to make myself less threatening.

List some specific details from paragraph 3 ⁴ that back up and support the main idea.

   a. _____

   b. _____

c. _____

d. _____

4. What specific words in the first paragraph suggest Staples is a criminal?

_____

True or False

Indicate whether the statement is true or false by writing **T** or **F** in the blank provided.

____T____ 5. In the essay, Brent Staples describes the intimidating effect he has on nighttime pedestrians.

____T____ 6. The first woman described in the essay perceived Staples as a threat to her safety.

____T____ 7. It does not bother Staples to be alienated from those he encounters on the streets.

____T____ 8. Staples has learned to stifle the anger he feels at being taken for a criminal because of his race.

____T____ 9. Staples monitors his movements to make himself appear less threatening to others.

____F____ 10. Staples behaves in the same manner whether dressed in casual clothes or business wear.

____T____ 11. Staples does not want to appear as though he is following someone when he enters a building.

____F____ 12. When pulled over by a policeman, Staples is quick to express his anger and indignation.

____T____ 13. Staples whistles classical music selections to indicate to others that he is unlikely to be a mugger.

____T____ 14. Whistling classical music provides a measure of safety for Staples.

Vocabulary in Context

Each item below includes a sentence from the selection. Using the context clues from this sentence, determine the best meaning of the italicized words.

1. I came upon her late one evening on a deserted street in Hyde Park, a relatively *affluent* neighborhood in an otherwise mean, *impoverished* section of Chicago.

   affluent: _____

   impoverished: _____

2. As I swung onto the avenue behind her, there seemed to be a *discreet*, uninflammatory distance between us.

   discreet: _____

3. To her, the youngish black man—a broad six feet two inches with a beard and billowing hair, both hands shoved into the pockets of a bulky military jacket— seemed *menacingly* close.

   menacingly: _____

4. After a few more quick *glimpses*, she picked up her pace and was soon running in *earnest*.

   glimpses: _____

   earnest: _____

5. That first *encounter*, and those that followed, signified that a *vast*, unnerving gulf lay between nighttime pedestrians—particularly women—and me.

   encounter: _____

   vast: _____

6. They seem to have set their faces on *neutral*, and with their purse straps strung across their chests *bandolier-style*, they *forge* ahead as though bracing themselves against being tackled.

   neutral: _____

   bandolier-style: _____

   _____

   forge: _____

Vocabulary Practice

Using the context clues from each sentence below, choose the best definition for the italicized word, and write the appropriate answer letter in the blank.

_____ 1. The danger they perceive is not a *hallucination*. (paragraph 3)
      a. an illusion
      b. an aggravation
      c. an outrage

_____ 2. Women are particularly *vulnerable* to street violence. (3)
      a. hardened
      b. susceptible
      c. oblivious

_____ 3. Yet these truths are no *solace*. (3)
      a. comfort
      b. criticism
      c. contempt

_____ 4. The kind of *alienation* that comes of being ever the suspect (3)
      a. detraction
      b. correction
      c. separation

_____ 5. A fearsome *entity* (3)
      a. demonstrator
      b. being
      c. worker

_____ 6. Learned to *smother* the rage (4)
      a. instigate
      b. stifle
      c. create

_____ 7. Give a wide *berth* to nervous people (4)
      a. follow
      b. reality
      c. space

_____ 8. Calm and extremely *congenial* (4)
      a. angry
      b. sarcastic
      c. friendly

_____ 9. On late-evening *constitutionals* (5)
      a. demonstrations
      b. initiations
      c. walks

In Your Own Words

1. What kinds of things do you look for when you are trying to decide whether a stranger is threatening?

2. What steps do you take to make yourself less threatening to others when you are out late at night?

3. Respond to the following: "Being perceived as dangerous is a hazard in itself."

The Art of Writing

Write a brief essay discussing the following.

> Have you ever felt that the police treated you unfairly because of your race? Did they ever treat you unfairly because of your age or gender? If so, please briefly describe the experience. Do you think discrimination by the police is a serious issue? What do you think can be done to reduce police discrimination? What role could education and the community play?

Internet Activity

Racial profiling occurs when people are treated differently because of characteristics that are associated with race, most prominently skin color. In the last few years, many discussions of racial profiling have appeared in the media, especially about racial profiling by law-enforcement agencies. Using an Internet search engine like Google <www.google.com> or Yahoo! <www.yahoo.com>, explore the Internet to find discussions or articles about racial profiling. Write a paragraph describing what you learned about racial profiling. Based on what you learned, do you have an opinion about whether law-enforcement agencies should be allowed to engage in racial profiling?

SELECTION

"Little Red Riding Hood set herself up to be mugged."

GETTING THE PICTURE

Did you know that some people are more likely to get mugged than others because of their body language? To assess your "muggability rating," read the article below.

BIO-SKETCH

Dr. Loretta Malandro is a communication expert who has been a professor at both Florida State University and Arizona State University. She is the author of *Say It Right the First Time* and *Fearless Leadership.* Dr. Larry Barker, a social science researcher, is the co-author of *Listen Up.*

BRUSHING UP ON VOCABULARY

perceptively   having or showing keenness of perception, insight, intuition, or understanding

Excerpt from
LOOKING OUT/LOOKING IN

by Loretta Malandro and Larry Barker

THE LOOK OF A VICTIM

Little Red Riding Hood set herself up to be mugged. Her first mistake was skip- 1
ping through the forest to grandma's house. Her second mistake was stopping to pick flowers. At this point, as you might remember in the story, the mean, heavy wolf comes along and begins to check her out. He observes, quite perceptively, that she is happy, outgoing, and basically unaware of any dangers in her surrounding environment. The big bad wolf catches these nonverbal cues and splits to grandma's house. He knows that Red is an easy mark. From this point we all know what happens.

Body movements and gestures reveal a lot of information about a person. Like 2
Little Red Riding Hood, pedestrians may signal to criminals that they are easy targets for mugging by the way they walk. When was the last time you assessed your "muggability rating"? In a recent study two psychologists set out to identify those body movements that characterized easy victims. They assembled "muggability ratings" of sixty New York pedestrians from the people who may have been the most qualified to judge—prison inmates who had been convicted of assault.

The researchers unobtrusively videotaped pedestrians on weekdays between 3
10:00 A.M. and 12 P.M. Each pedestrian was taped for six to eight seconds, the approximate time it takes a mugger to size up an approaching person. The judges (prison inmates) rated the "assault potential" of the sixty pedestrians on a ten-point scale. A rating of one indicated someone was "a very easy rip-off," of two, "an easy dude to corner." Toward the other end of the scale, nine meant a person "would be heavy; would give you a hard time," and ten indicated that the mugger "would avoid it, too big a situation, too heavy."

The results revealed several body movements that characterized easy victims: 4
"Their strides were either very long or very short; they moved awkwardly, raising their left legs with their left arms (instead of alternating them); on each step they tended to lift their whole foot up and then place it down (less muggable sorts took steps in which their feet rocked from heel to toe). Overall the people rated most

muggable walked as if they were in conflict with themselves; they seemed to make each move in the most difficult way possible."

_____

(Dr. Loretta Malandro and Dr. Larry Barker, "The Look of a Victim," in *Nonverbal Communication*, 1988.)

✓ COMPREHENSION CHECKUP

Multiple Choice

Write the letter of the correct answer in the blank provided.

__A__ 1. The main idea of paragraph 1 is expressed in the
   a. first sentence of the paragraph
   b. second sentence of the paragraph
   c. third sentence of the paragraph

__B__ 2. The wolf is aware that Little Red will be easy to mug because
   a. she is an observant person
   b. she is oblivious to her surroundings
   c. she is a nature lover

__A__ 3. The main idea of paragraph 2 is expressed in the
   a. first sentence of the paragraph
   b. third sentence of the paragraph
   c. fourth sentence of the paragraph

__C__ 4. Persons convicted of assault were chosen to participate in the study because
   a. they were readily available
   b. they were not in a position to say no
   c. they knew what characteristics they had looked for in a potential victim

__C__ 5. The body movements of the subjects most likely to be mugged indicate that
   a. they were well-coordinated
   b. they walked with a heel-to-toe motion
   c. they walked awkwardly

__B__ 6. If someone is *unobtrusively* videotaping, they are
   a. paying little attention to their subjects
   b. observing without calling attention to themselves
   c. interacting with those they are observing

In Your Own Words

Here are some tips on how to avoid being a victim. After reading the list of suggestions, determine which of the people depicted in the following picture are potential victims. Give specific reasons for each of your selections.

When visiting entertainment districts, particularly those near high crime areas, dress down if possible. Fine clothes, flashy jewelry, and expensive cars attract attention. Also, be sure to park in an attended garage.

Be alert. Look at your surroundings and notice the people nearby. Robbers like to sneak up on their victims. Stay *off* your cell phone. Talking on a cell phone or texting is a distraction, and robbers are casting about for inattentive victims.

Walk with purpose. Look like you know where you're going and how to get there. Walk fast and fluidly. Just like predators in the wild, armed robbers often attack the slowest in the herd.

Don't let people stop you. If someone tries to ask you for something (the time, directions, bus fare), keep moving. Don't follow strangers.

If you can't avoid walking alone after dark, at least stay in well-lit areas.

When approaching your car, carry your keys in your hand. Be sure to check the passenger seats before you get in.

Don't flash money even when inside a business establishment. Some robbers hang out in stores to spot victims carrying a lot of cash.

When leaving your home, tell someone your exact route and your estimated time of arrival. That way, if something happens to you, the police will know exactly where to look for you.

(Information from Chuck Hustmyre and Jay Dixit, "Marked for Mayhem," in *Psychology Today*, 2009)

The Art of Writing

What is your opinion of each of these suggestions? Can you think of additional suggestions?

Are You a Victim? (2009) *BY KAGAN MCLEOD*

Internet Activity

Consult the Health section of the *Seattle Times* (August 20, 2007) to gain additional tips to help you avoid being a victim of a crime. After reading the tips provided, list the ones that seem most relevant to your life and explain why you consider them to be beneficial. In addition, you can use any search engine to obtain information about ways to avoid being a victim of consumer fraud.

Review Test: *Main Ideas and Details in Textbook Material*

Each of the following groups contains a series of related statements: One of the statements gives a main topic, another statement gives a main idea, and two or more statements give supporting details. Identify the role of each statement in the space provided using the following abbreviations:

> **T** for topic
>
> **MI** for main idea
>
> **SD** for supporting detail

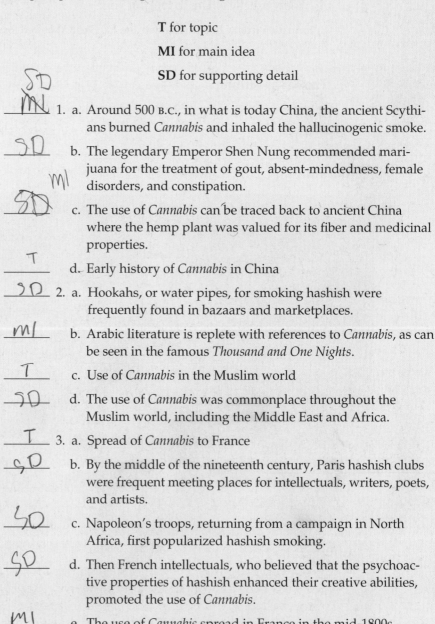

[handwritten: SD / MI] 1. a. Around 500 B.C., in what is today China, the ancient Scythians burned *Cannabis* and inhaled the hallucinogenic smoke.

[handwritten: SD] b. The legendary Emperor Shen Nung recommended marijuana for the treatment of gout, absent-mindedness, female disorders, and constipation.

[handwritten: SD / MI] c. The use of *Cannabis* can be traced back to ancient China where the hemp plant was valued for its fiber and medicinal properties.

[handwritten: T] d. Early history of *Cannabis* in China

[handwritten: SD] 2. a. Hookahs, or water pipes, for smoking hashish were frequently found in bazaars and marketplaces.

[handwritten: MI] b. Arabic literature is replete with references to *Cannabis*, as can be seen in the famous *Thousand and One Nights*.

[handwritten: T] c. Use of *Cannabis* in the Muslim world

[handwritten: SD] d. The use of *Cannabis* was commonplace throughout the Muslim world, including the Middle East and Africa.

[handwritten: T] 3. a. Spread of *Cannabis* to France

[handwritten: SD] b. By the middle of the nineteenth century, Paris hashish clubs were frequent meeting places for intellectuals, writers, poets, and artists.

[handwritten: SD] c. Napoleon's troops, returning from a campaign in North Africa, first popularized hashish smoking.

[handwritten: SD] d. Then French intellectuals, who believed that the psychoactive properties of hashish enhanced their creative abilities, promoted the use of *Cannabis*.

[handwritten: MI] e. The use of *Cannabis* spread in France in the mid-1800s.

_MI_   4. a. During the 1930s, American society began to turn against the use of *Cannabis* by passing laws and launching educational campaigns.

_SD_   b. The U.S. Congress enacted the Federal Marijuana Tax Act of 1937, which regulated the sale of *Cannabis* and resulted in its virtual elimination from the nation's pharmacopoeia.

_SD_   c. The Federal Bureau of Narcotics undertook an "educational campaign" to make the public aware of the dangers of marijuana use.

_T_   d. The crackdown

_SD_   5. a. *Cannabis* can damage lung tissue, much like nicotine.

_SD_   b. The effects of marijuana on the male reproductive system show decreased sperm production and decreased testosterone levels.

_SD_   c. Even moderate use of marijuana impairs learning, short-term memory, and reaction time.

_T_   d. Adverse effects of marijuana use

_MI_   e. Studies have discovered harmful side effects of *Cannabis* use.

_T_   6. a. Medical uses in chemotherapy and glaucoma

_MI_   b. While over the centuries marijuana has been employed to treat numerous ailments, today it is used in contemporary medicine for the treatment of glaucoma and as an aid to chemotherapy.

_SD_   c. Marijuana can significantly reduce ocular pressure in patients with glaucoma.

_SD_   d. The side effects of chemotherapy, which include nausea, vomiting, and loss of appetite, are reduced by the use of marijuana cigarettes.

_SD_   7. a. Perception of time and space may be distorted, and minutes may seem like hours.

_MI_   b. *Cannabis* has significant mind-altering effects.

_T_   c. Marijuana and psychoactive effects.

_SD_   d. For instance, marijuana is associated with a sense of euphoria and calmness.

(Estelle Levetin, *Plants and Society*, 5/e, 2008)

Paraphrasing

When you **paraphrase** something, you express the author's meaning in your own words. Often, you will substitute synonyms for some words (but you may have to leave the key words the same), and you will need to change the phrasing of the original passage. Usually, a paraphrase is shorter than the original passage, but it can also be the same length as the original or even longer.

The ability to paraphrase is important when you review ideas and also when you formulate an implied main idea. Here's an example with two possible paraphrases:

Original: "The man who most vividly realizes a difficulty is the man most likely to overcome it." (Joseph Farrell)

Paraphrase 1: The man who clearly recognizes a problem is the one likely to solve it.

Paraphrase 2: You are more likely to solve a problem if you first recognize clearly that a problem exists.

The first paraphrase replaces key words with synonyms so it is very like the original, and some teachers might consider this plagiarism. The second paraphrase is original because it not only replaces key words with synonyms but also conveys the ideas without using the phrasing of the original.

Now try to paraphrase the passages below. Be sure you use your own words, and do not rely on the phrasing of the original. When you finish, check to make sure that you have captured the meaning of the original.

Exercise 5: Paraphrasing Quotations

Working in a group, paraphrase the following quotations. When you finish, check to make sure the meaning of both statements is the same.

1. Even if you're on the right track, you'll get run over if you just sit there. (Will Rogers)

   _____

   _____

2. One man's justice is another's injustice; one man's beauty another's ugliness; one man's wisdom another's folly. (Ralph Waldo Emerson)

   _____

   _____

3. A toe of the stargazer is often stubbed. (Russian proverb)

   _____

   _____

4. If we could read the secret history of our enemies, we should find in each man's life sorrow and suffering enough to disarm all hostility. (Henry Wadsworth Longfellow)

   _____

   _____

5. You are only what you are when no one is looking. (Robert C. Edwards)

   _____

   _____

6. I have always thought the actions of men the best interpreters of their thoughts. (John Locke)

_____

_____

7. Do not use a hatchet to remove a fly from a friend's forehead. (Chinese proverb)

_____

_____

8. The things which hurt, instruct. (Benjamin Franklin)

_____

_____

9. If a man deceives me once, shame on him; if he deceives me twice, shame on me. (Anonymous)

_____

_____

Formulating Implied Main Ideas

Not all main ideas are directly stated. Sometimes we have to look closely at the details the author has provided in order to determine the main idea.

Implied Main Ideas in Textbook Material

Although textbook material frequently includes directly stated main ideas, it also may contain main ideas that are implied. In the paragraphs below, the main idea is implied rather than stated. Read the paragraphs and try to identify the main idea. Then check the explanation to see whether you have identified it correctly.

> 1. What do you look for in a potential date? Sincerity? Good looks? Character? Conversational ability? Sophisticated, intelligent people are unconcerned with such superficial qualities as good looks; they know "beauty is only skin deep" and "you can't judge a book by its cover." At least they know that's how they _ought_ to feel. As Cicero counseled, "Resist appearance." However, there is now a cabinet full of research studies showing that appearance _does_ matter. The consistency and pervasiveness of this effect is disconcerting. Good looks are a great asset.

"He had but one eye, and the pocket of prejudice runs in favor of two."

—Charles Dickens

The topic of this paragraph is appearance or looks. The implied main idea is: Looks matter, and people who believe that they do not are probably deceiving themselves.

In the next example, the topic is attractiveness and dating. To formulate the main idea, we must pay attention to the attitudes of both young men and young women as described in the paragraph.

> 2. Like it or not, a young woman's physical attractiveness is a moderately good predictor of how frequently she dates. A young man's attractiveness is slightly less a predictor of how frequently he dates. Does this imply, as many have surmised, that women are better at following Cicero's advice? Or does it merely reflect the fact that men more often do the inviting? If women were to indicate their preferences among various men, would looks be as important to them as

they are to men? Philosopher Bertrand Russell thought not: "On the whole women tend to love men for their character while men tend to love women for their appearance." To see whether indeed men are more influenced by looks, researchers conducted a series of experiments. The result: The more attractive a woman was, the more the man liked her and wanted to date her again. And the more attractive the man was, the more she liked him and wanted to date him again.

From the details presented, we can conclude that both men and women put value on opposite-sex physical attractiveness. Our implied main idea should be stated something like this:

Main idea: When it comes to dating, looks appear to matter as much to young women as to young men.

You can see that determining an implied main idea requires you to reduce all of the key information contained in the paragraph to one sentence.

In order to formulate the main idea, it is sometimes helpful, first, to identify the topic and then to ask *who, what, where, when, why,* and *how* about the topic. Read the following paragraph, and try to determine the main idea for yourself before checking the main idea provided.

3. Not everyone can end up paired with someone stunningly attractive. So how do people pair off? Judging from research by Bernard Murstein and others, they pair off with people who are about as attractive as they are. Several studies have found a strong correspondence between the attractiveness of husbands and wives, of dating partners, and even of those within particular fraternities. Experiments confirm this matching phenomenon. When choosing whom to approach in social settings, knowing the other is free to say yes or no, people usually approach someone whose attractiveness roughly matches their own.

Who: men and women

What: pair off

Where: in social settings

When: during interactions with each other

Why: attempting to seek a good physical match

How: by picking people as attractive as they are

The topic of this paragraph is the matching phenomenon. If we look at all the key details, our main idea will look something like this:

Main idea: People tend to pair themselves with others who are similarly attractive.

The next paragraph provides an explanation for couples who are not similarly attractive.

4. Perhaps this research prompts you to think of happy couples who are not equally attractive. In such cases, the less attractive person often has compensating qualities. Each partner brings assets to the social marketplace. The value of the respective assets creates an equitable match. Personal advertisements exhibit this exchange of assets. Men typically offer wealth or status and seek youth and

attractiveness; women more often do the reverse: "Attractive, bright woman, 26, slender, seeks warm, professional male." Moreover, men who advertise their income and education, and women who advertise their youth and looks, receive more responses to their ads. The asset-matching process helps explain why beautiful young women often marry older men of higher social status.

Who: men/women

What: offer compensating qualities

Where: in the social marketplace

When: in relationships

Why: to achieve an equitable match

How: by bartering youth and beauty for wealth and status

When you put together these key details, you should arrive at a main idea that looks something like this:

Main idea: Everyone brings assets to the social marketplace, and people choose partners who have similarly valuable assets.

Now look closely at these paragraphs discussing the social significance of physical attractiveness.

5. In an experiment, Missouri fifth-grade teachers were given identical information about a boy or girl but with the photograph of an attractive or unattractive child attached. The teachers perceived the attractive child as more intelligent and successful in school. Think of yourself as a playground supervisor having to discipline an unruly child. Might you show less warmth and tact to an unattractive child? The sad truth is that most of us assume what we might call a "Bart Simpson effect"—that homely children are less able and socially competent than their beautiful peers.

The main idea of this paragraph is directly stated in the last sentence because the "Bart Simpson effect" is illustrated by the remaining sentences.

In the next paragraph, the main idea is implied because no one sentence is broad enough to cover all of the key details. Try formulating the main idea by expanding the first sentence.

6. What is more, we assume that beautiful people possess certain desirable traits. Other things being equal, we guess beautiful people are happier, sexually warmer, and more outgoing, intelligent, and successful, though not more honest or concerned with others. Added together, the findings define a physical-attractiveness stereotype: *What is beautiful is good.* Children learn the stereotype quite easily. Snow White and Cinderella are beautiful—and kind. The witch and the stepsisters are ugly—and wicked. As one kindergarten girl put it when asked what it means to be pretty, "It's like to be a princess. Everybody loves you."

Main idea: We assume that beautiful people possess certain desirable traits, and we also assume that what is beautiful is good.

In the next few paragraphs, the topic and part of the main idea are provided for you. Use the *who, what, where, when, why,* and *how* strategy to complete the main idea.

7. Undoubtedly, there are numerous advantages to being beautiful. However, attraction researchers report there is also an ugly truth about beauty. Exceptionally attractive people may suffer resentment from those of their own sex. They may be unsure whether others are responding to their inner qualities or just to their looks, which in time will fade. Moreover, if they can coast on their looks, they may be less motivated to develop themselves in other ways.

Topic: The negatives of attractiveness

Main idea: While there are many advantages to being beautiful, there are also

_____

8. To say that attractiveness is important, other things being equal, is not to say that physical appearance always outranks other qualities. Attractiveness probably most affects first impressions. But first impressions are important—and are becoming more so as societies become increasingly mobile and urbanized and as contacts with people become more fleeting. Though interviewers may deny it, attractiveness and grooming affect first impressions in job interviews. This helps explain why attractive people have more prestigious jobs and make more money.

"Clothes and manners do not make the man; but when he is made, they greatly improve his appearance."

—Henry Ward Beecher

Topic: First impressions

Main idea: Physical appearance doesn't always outrank other qualities, but it does affect _____

(David Myers, *Social Psychology, 9/e,* 2008)

Exercise 6: Formulating Implied Main Ideas in Textbook Material

Each of the following paragraphs are concerned with attractiveness. Formulate the implied main idea for each paragraph.

1. Attraction has been described as if it were an objective quality like height, which some people have more of, some less. Strictly speaking, attractiveness is whatever the people of any given place and time find attractive. This, of course, varies. Even in a given place and time, people (fortunately) disagree about who's attractive.

Implied main idea: _____

_____

_____

2. What makes an attractive face depends somewhat on the person's sex. Consistent with men historically having greater social power, people judge women more attractive if they have "baby-faced" features, such as large eyes, that suggest nondominance. Men seem more attractive when their faces—and their behaviors—suggest maturity and dominance. People across the world show remarkable agreement about the features of an ideal male face and female face when judging any ethnic group. For example, "attractive" facial and bodily

features do not deviate too drastically from average. People perceive noses, legs, or statures that are not unusually large or small as relatively attractive. Perfectly symmetrical faces are another characteristic of strikingly attractive people. So in many respects, perfectly average is quite attractive.

Implied main idea: _____

_____

3. Women favor male traits that signify an ability to provide and protect resources. Males prefer female characteristics that signify reproductive capacity. Judging from yesterday's Stone Age figurines to today's centerfolds and beauty pageant winners, men everywhere have felt most attracted to women whose waists are 30 percent narrower than their hips—a shape associated with peak sexual fertility. When judging males as potential marriage partners, women, too, prefer a waist-to-hip ratio suggesting health and vigor. This makes evolutionary sense because a muscular hunk was more likely than a scrawny fellow to gather food, build houses, and defeat rivals. But today's women prefer even more those with high incomes.

Implied main idea: _____

_____

4. Let's conclude this discussion of attractiveness on an upbeat note. First, a 17-year-old girl's facial attractiveness is a surprisingly weak predictor of her attractiveness at ages 30 and 50. Sometimes an average-looking adolescent becomes a quite attractive middle-aged adult. Second, not only do we perceive attractive people as likable, we also perceive likable people as attractive. Perhaps you can recall individuals who, as you grew to like them, became more attractive. Their physical imperfections were no longer so noticeable. When people are warm, helpful, and considerate, they *look* more attractive. Discovering someone's similarities to us also makes the person seem more attractive.

Implied main idea: _____

_____

5. Moreover, love sees loveliness. The more in love a woman is with a man, the more physically attractive she finds him. And the more in love people are, the *less* attractive they find all others of the opposite sex. "The grass may be greener on the other side, but happy gardeners are less likely to notice." To paraphrase Benjamin Franklin, when Jill is in love, she finds Jack more handsome than his friends.

Implied main idea: _____

_____

(David Myers, *Social Psychology, 9/e,* 2008)

Implied Main Ideas in Other Materials

All kinds of written material may include main ideas that are implied rather than directly stated. In fact, you are more likely to encounter a directly stated main idea in textbook material. In other written material, the main idea is often unstated or implied. In the next section, you are going to be formulating the implied main ideas of fables.

> **Exercise 7: Formulating Main Ideas of Fables**

Islamic Folk Stories

BY NASREDDIN HODJA

Nasreddin Hodja was born in Turkey in the early thirteenth century. He served as a religious leader (*imam*) and judge in his village. His folk stories are famous throughout the Middle East, Turkey, Hungary, Russia, and parts of Africa. All of his stories use humor to teach a fundamental lesson about human relationships and are designed to sharpen our perceptions of human failings.

After reading each fable, write the lesson or moral. Identify the implied main idea by reducing the important information in the fable to one sentence.

1. One day the Hodja and his son went on a short journey, the boy seated on a donkey. On the way they met some people coming in the opposite direction.   1

"That's modern youth for you," they said. "The son rides on a donkey and lets his poor old father walk!"   2

When they had gone, the boy insisted that his father take his place on the donkey. The Hodja mounted the donkey, and his son walked at his side. They met some more people.   3

"Just look at that!" they said. "There is a full-grown man riding on the donkey, while his poor little son has to walk!"   4

So, Hodja pulled his son on the donkey, too. After awhile, they saw a few more people coming down the road.   5

"Poor animal!" they said. "Both of them are riding on it and it is about to pass out."   6

"The best thing to do," said Nasreddin, when they had disappeared from sight, "is for both of us to walk. Then there can be no such arguments."   7

So they continued their way walking beside the donkey. It was not long before they met another group.   8

"Just look at those fools," they said pointing to the Hodja and his son. "They plod along in the heat of the sun, and their donkey takes it easy!"   9

"You will have learned, my boy," said the Hodja, when they had gone, "just how difficult it is to escape the criticism of wagging tongues!"   10

"Don't judge any man until you have walked two moons in his moccasins."

—Native American saying

Moral: _____

_____

Main idea sentence: _____

_____

2. The Hodja was invited to an important banquet, and he went in his everyday clothes. No one paid any attention to him whatsoever, and he remained   1

hungry and thirsty, and very bored. Eventually he slipped out of the house unobserved and made his way home. Here he changed into his best clothes, putting on a magnificent turban, a fine silk robe, and a large fur coat over all. Then he made his way back to the banquet.

This time he was welcomed with open arms. The host bade him sit beside   2
him, and offered him a plate covered with the choicest delicacies.

The Hodja took off his fur coat and held it to the plate.   3

"Eat, my beauty!" he said.   4

"Sir, what are you doing?" exclaimed his astonished host.   5

"It was the fur coat, not the man inside, which conjured up these delica-   6
cies," replied the Hodja. "Let it then eat them!"

Moral: _____

_____

Main idea sentence: _____

_____

3. A poor man was passing through Ak-Shehir with only a piece of dry   1
bread between himself and starvation. As he passed by an eating house,
he saw some very appetizing meatballs frying in a pan over the charcoal
fire, and carried away by the delicious smell, he held his piece of dry bread
over the pan in the hope of capturing some of it. Then he ate his bread,
which seemed to taste better. The restaurant owner, however, had seen
what was going on, and seizing the man by the scruff of his neck, dragged
him off before the magistrate, who at this time happened to be Nasreddin
Hodja, and demanded that he be compelled to pay the price of the pan of
meatballs.

The Hodja listened attentively, then drew two coins from his pocket.   2

"Come here a minute," he said to the restaurant owner.   3

The latter obeyed, and the Hodja enclosed the coins in his fist and rattled   4
them in the man's ear.

"What is the meaning of this?" said the restaurant owner.   5

"I have just paid you your damages," said the Hodja. "The sound of money   6
is fair payment for the smell of food."

Moral: _____

_____

Main idea sentence: _____

_____

(Charles Downing, *Tales of Hodja,* 2002)

SELECTION

*"In this particular circumstance, the people for whom
the art was intended chose to reject the art."*

GETTING THE PICTURE

The proverb "Beauty is in the eye of the beholder" implies that beauty is highly relative and that people will have varied opinions about what is actually beautiful. What

is pleasing to the eye of one of us is an eyesore to another. So too with art. People will have varied opinions about what constitutes art. In the selection below, taken from a popular art history textbook, the author Rita Gilbert describes a controversy over a work of modern art.

BIO-SKETCH

Rita Gilbert wrote her first edition of *Living with Art* in 1985. Her fourth edition of the book won a first-place award for outstanding design and production at the 1995 New York Book Show. Mark Getlein has taken over as author of this textbook. Getlein has written a variety of textbooks including *A History of Art in Africa* and *The Longman Anthology of World Literature.* As a painter, he is able to help students understand both the intellectual and practical processes of creating art.

BRUSHING UP ON VOCABULARY

dismantle to take apart. *Dismantle* in Old French literally meant "to divest of a mantle or cloak." *Dismantle* derives from the French word part *des,* meaning "off," and *mantler,* meaning "to cloak." In Middle French, *demanteler* meant to tear down the walls of a fortress.

integrity the state of being whole or entire; honesty. *Integrity* derives from the Latin word *integer,* which refers to a whole number in mathematics.

Excerpt from

GILBERT'S LIVING WITH ART

by Mark Getlein

PUBLIC ART

Rarely has the question "What is art?" caused such a public uproar as in a controversy 1 that erupted in New York City in the early 1980s. At the center of the drama was a monumental sculpture by Richard Serra, entitled *Tilted Arc,* a 12-foot-high, 120-foot-long steel wall installed in a plaza fronting a government building in lower Manhattan.

Commissioned by the Art-in-Architecture division of the General Services 2 Administration, *Tilted Arc* was part of a program that allocates 0.5 percent of the cost of federal buildings to the purchase and installation of public art. Soon after the sculpture's installation, however, the public for whom it was intended spoke out, and their message was a resounding *"That's* not art!" More than 7,000 workers in surrounding buildings signed petitions demanding the sculpture's removal. Opponents of the work had numerous complaints. *Tilted Arc,* they maintained, was ugly, rusty, and a target for graffiti. It blocked the view. It disrupted pedestrian traffic, since one had to walk all the way around it rather than straight across the plaza. It ruined the plaza for concerts and outdoor ceremonies. At a public hearing, one man summed up the opposition view: "I am here today to recommend its relocation to a better site—a metal salvage yard."

Artists, dealers, and critics rushed to the sculpture's defense. The sculptor 3 himself argued vehemently against any attempt to move *Tilted Arc,* maintaining that it had been commissioned specifically for that site and any new location would destroy its artistic integrity.

The battle raged for many months, and while there were dissenting voices 4 from all sides, it shaped up principally as a struggle between the art establishment (pro) and the general public (con). At last, in an unusual editorial, *The New York Times*—a newspaper that heavily supports the arts—took a stand. "One cannot choose to see or ignore *Tilted Arc,* as if it were in a museum or a less conspicuous public place. To the complaining workers in Federal Plaza, it is, quite simply, unavoidable. . . . The public has to live with *Tilted Arc;* therefore the public has a right to say no, not here."

This time the public won, and the question "What is art?" was answered by 5 a kind of popular referendum, a majority decision. *Tilted Arc* was dismantled and removed in March of 1989.

Does this outcome mean that *Tilted Arc* is not art, or that it isn't good art? No, 6 it does not mean either of those things. It means simply that, in this particular circumstance, the people for whom the art was intended chose to reject the art. And similar circumstances have, very likely, occurred since the earliest artists of prehistory began painting on the walls of their caves.

(Mark Getlein, *Gilbert's Living with Art,* 8/e, 2008)

✓ COMPREHENSION CHECKUP

Multiple Choice

Write the letter of the correct answer in the blank provided.

_____ 1. Which sentence best states the main idea of the selection?
- a. *Tilted Arc* was a waste of the taxpayers' money.
- b. If there is a disagreement over public art, the art establishment should have the deciding vote.
- c. The general public of New York City chose to reject a sculpture entitled *Tilted Arc.*
- d. Richard Serra is overrated as a sculptor.

_____ 2. In paragraph 1, *Tilted Arc* is described as being a *monumental* sculpture. This description implies that it is
- a. large in size
- b. refined
- c. ordinary
- d. famous around the world

_____ 3. By choosing to use the words *uproar, controversy,* and *erupted* in the first paragraph, the author implies that
- a. the public was moderately interested
- b. the sculpture provoked a swift and strong reaction
- c. unhappiness with the sculpture developed slowly

_____ 4. From the context of paragraph 2, it can be determined that the word *resounding* most nearly means
- a. cheerfully expressed
- b. quietly voiced
- c. loudly uttered

5. The public expressed all of the following misgivings about *Tilted Arc* *except*
   a. it disrupted vehicular traffic
   b. it was ugly and a target for graffiti
   c. outdoor ceremonies and concerts were no longer feasible

6. A synonym for the word *vehemently* as used in paragraph 3 is
   a. ardently
   b. compassionately
   c. silently

7. *The New York Times* took the following basic position in its editorial:
   a. Because the public and the federal workers could not avoid the sculpture, their opinion about whether it should stay counted for a lot.
   b. Because the sculpture could be disassembled and relocated elsewhere, it should be moved to a more welcoming location.
   c. Because it was commissioned specifically for the site and the sculptor opposed its removal, it should stay.

True or False

Indicate whether the statement is true or false by writing **T** or **F** in the blanks provided.

"The monument sticks like a fishbone in the city's throat."

—Robert Cowell

8. The author suggests that similar rejections of public art have occurred in the past.

9. A *dissenting* opinion expresses an opposing viewpoint.

10. A *conspicuous* place is one that is hard to find or see.

11. We can assume that *The New York Times* cast the deciding vote in the tiebreaker between the art establishment and the general public.

12. The sculptor felt that it was in the public's best interest to relocate the sculpture to a place where it would be enjoyed and appreciated.

In Your Own Words

All of the following are paraphrases of testimony given at a hearing on the proposal to remove *Tilted Arc* from the plaza in front of a federal office building.

First determine whether the statement is pro (in favor of keeping *Tilted Arc* at its original site) or con (dismantling it). Then state whether the reasons given are helpful or unhelpful to the position taken (pro or con).

1. Richard Serra is one of our leading artists, and his work commands very high prices. The government has a responsibility to the financial community. It is bad business to destroy this work because you would be destroying property.

2. *Tilted Arc's* very tilt and rust remind us that the gleaming and heartless steel and glass structures of the state apparatus can one day pass away. It therefore creates an unconscious sense of freedom and hope.

3. *Tilted Arc* looks like a discarded piece of crooked or bent metal; there's no more meaning in having it in the middle of the plaza than in putting an old bicycle that got run over by a car there.

Tilted Arc (1981) *BY RICHARD SERRA*

© Art on File/Corbis

4. *Tilted Arc* launches through space in a thrilling and powerful acutely arched curve.

5. *Tilted Arc* is big and rusty and ugly.

6. Because of its size, thrusting shape, and implacably uniform rusting surface, *Tilted Arc* makes us feel hopeless, trapped, and sad. This sculpture would be interesting if we could visit it when we had time to explore these feelings, but it is too depressing to face every day on our way to work.

The Art of Writing

In a brief essay, respond to one of the items below.

1. Do you agree with the conclusion drawn by the *New York Times* that the sculpture should be removed? Explain why.

2. Do you think that the public should always have the final say on whether a work of public art should be displayed or should remain on display? Why or why not?

3. Is there any public art in your area that became controversial? Why did it become controversial? Was it because of the cost, its appearance, or a combination of factors? Was the controversy resolved? How?

Internet Activity

1. Richard Serra is featured in the Arts section of *Time* (June 4, 2007, pp. 65–67). (Go to www.time.com/serra.) Read the profile of the artist and write a brief summary. What is your impression of the two sculptures presented in the profile?

2. Read an online biography of Richard Serra, and view some of his other sculptures. You might consult one of the following:

www.pbs.org/art21/artists/serra/index.html

www.artcyclopedia.com/artists/serra_richard.html

Does the information provided give you a different perspective on Serra from that of the reading selection? What is your opinion of his work?

Vocabulary Puzzle

Directions: Use the vocabulary words to complete the puzzle.

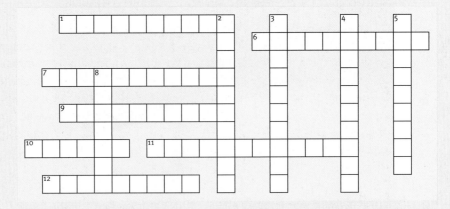

allocates	dismantled	referendum	salvage
commissioned	dissenting	relocation	uproar
conspicuous	integrity	resounding	vehemently

ACROSS CLUES

1. Taken apart
6. Angrily; ardently
7. Easily seen or noticed
9. Movement to a different place
10. A state of noisy disturbance or excitement
11. Gave an official order for
12. The state of being whole, entire, complete

DOWN CLUES

2. Disagreeing
3. Loudly uttered
4. Submission of a proposed public measure to a direct popular vote
5. Sets apart for a particular use
8. Something saved from destruction or waste

Summarizing

Summarizing, or restating main ideas in your own words, is a skill you will be called upon to use both in your college classes and at work. In literature classes, for example, you may have to provide a brief summary of a story to show you've read and understood it or to provide your reader with the main points before you offer an analysis. In biology classes, you may have to provide a brief summary of an experiment before describing the process and equipment you used. Later in life, you may also need to provide summaries. For instance, if you become a nurse, you may need to summarize a patient's condition; if you become a sportswriter, you may need to summarize the action in a basketball game; if you become a police officer, you may need to summarize the events leading up to an accident.

STUDY TECHNIQUE 3

Summarizing Short Articles

When you write a summary, you need to present only the main idea and key supporting details in order of importance. Because it omits minor supporting details, a summary is much shorter than the original on which it is based. A good rule of thumb is that a summary should be one-fourth of the length of the original. A good way to identify key supporting details is to answer as many of the *who, what, where, when, why,* and *how* questions about the selection as apply. (Not all these questions will apply to every selection.) Remember, too, that the goal of a summary is brevity; in other words, always make sure that your summary contains only the main idea and key supporting details and does not include information more than once. Omit all trivia and repetition!

Also keep in mind that you are reporting the author's viewpoints and not your own. When writing a summary, never write something like "I feel" or "I think" or "It seems to me." What matters in a summary is what the author thinks. When reading over your summary, make sure you delete all expressions of your own thoughts and opinions.

Exercise 8: Writing a Summary

Directions: You just read an excerpt from Mark Getlein's "Public Art." Try to write a summary of this excerpt. Begin by identifying the main idea.

Main Idea: _____

_____

_____

Now locate the main supporting details by answering as many of the question words as possible:

Who: _____

What: _____

Where: _____

When: _____

Why: _____

How: _____

Next, list five to six of the main supporting details in your own words.

1. _____

   _____

2. _____

   _____

3. _____

   _____

4. _____

   _____

5. _____

   _____

6. _____

   _____

You are now ready to draft your summary.

_____

_____

_____

_____

_____

_____

_____

_____

_____

_____

After writing your summary, read it over. Delete any information that is not crucial to supporting the main idea. Delete any trivia or repetition and any expressions of your own opinion. Is your presentation of information logical? If not, reorganize the information in a more logical way. Now revise your summary.

Brain Teasers

Solve the logic problems.

1. Two men play five games of checkers, and each wins the same number of games. There are no draws. How can this be? _____

2. How many times can you subtract five from twenty-five? _____

3. I have five sisters, and each of my sisters has a brother. How many children did my parents have? _____

Each formula below represents a basic fact. How many can you decipher? The first letter of each word is provided.

1. 13 S and 50 S = the A F _____

2. 7D = I W _____

3. 26 L = the A _____

4. A + E + I + O + U = V _____

5. 50 S = USA _____

6. S + M + T + W + T + F + S = D of W _____

   _____

7. 24 H = I D _____

8. 12 M = I Y _____

9. 60 M = I H _____

10. 12 I = I F _____

VOCABULARY   ## Unit 1: Homonyms and Other Confusing Words

"The difference between the right word and the almost right word is the difference between lightning and the lightning bug."

—Mark Twain

As you learned in the introduction, *homonyms* are words or phrases that sound the same but have different spellings or meanings. The short poem below illustrates the importance of recognizing homonyms and choosing the correct one. Your computer spell checker won't be much help, because it can't tell the difference between wanting to eat a *desert* or a *dessert*. Can you spot the mistakes in the poem?

> English spelling can seam like a maize,
> And put won strait into a hays,
> Butt now never fear,
> The spell-checker is hear,
> And its sew well-deserving of prays.
>
> —*Anonymous*

In addition to homonyms, we have included in this section other troublesome words that you need to know about. An awareness of these words and the ability to use them correctly will make you a better writer.

allusion	A noun meaning "a casual or passing reference to something." *The author made an* allusion *to Aphrodite, the Greek goddess of love and beauty.*
illusion	A noun meaning "something that deceives by producing a false or misleading impression of reality." *The hikers, exhausted and suffering from dehydration, saw a lake up ahead of them. But as they got closer, they realized it was just a cruel* illusion.
alot	A mistake for *a lot. There is no such word as* alot.
a lot	"Many, much." *Peggy felt* a lot *better after getting a good night's sleep.*
allot	A verb meaning "to assign a portion." *Each heir to the family fortune was* allotted *an equal share of the estate.*
already	An adverb meaning "previously." *With just a few minutes left in the game, the Cardinals thought they had* already *won.*
all ready	"Completely prepared." *After gathering her supplies and buying her textbooks, Antoinette felt* all ready *to start school.*

Think about this sentence: She is *all ready* to go to the game because she is *already* dressed.

altogether	An adverb meaning "wholly, entirely." *"There is* altogether *too much violence in public schools," complained the president of the Parent Teacher Association.*
all together	"All at the same place or time." *The family reunion brought the family* all together.
censure	A verb meaning "to strongly disapprove of or officially reprimand." *The senator was* censured *because he had accepted campaign contributions from foreign countries.*
censor	A verb meaning "to examine for the purpose of suppressing or deleting." *The Harry Potter books by J. K. Rawling are* censored *by school libraries across the country.*
cite	A verb meaning "to quote or mention in support." *You may need to* cite *your sources in your English term paper.*
site	A noun meaning "position or location." *The* site *of the Vietnam War Memorial is in Washington D.C.*
desert	A noun meaning "a dry sandy region with little or no plant life." *The Sahara Desert is the largest* desert *in the world.*
desert	A verb meaning "to leave without intending to return." *Marcia wanted to know how Jan could* desert *her husband after fourteen years of marriage.* (The pronunciation is the same as dessert.) Also, a noun meaning "deserved reward or punishment." *The attorney who had cheated many of his elderly clients out of their retirement funds received his just* deserts *when he was disbarred.* (The pronunciation is the same as desserts.)
dessert	A noun meaning "something sweet served at the end of a meal." *Is your favorite* dessert *cake, ice cream, or something else?*

Think about this sentence: Cactus candy is a delectable *dessert* that comes from *desert* cacti.

die	A verb meaning "to cease to live." *Most of our past presidents have already* died.
dye	A noun meaning "a coloring substance." *Did you use* dye *to change the color of your hair?*
	Also, a verb meaning "to color with a dye." *She* dyed *her hair shocking pink to go with her dress.*
emigrate	A verb meaning "to leave one country or region and settle in another." *Many people in the United States have ancestors who* emigrated *from Ireland.*
immigrate	A verb meaning "to come to a new country to settle." *Millions of people have* immigrated *to the United States in search of a better life for themselves and their families.*

Think about this sentence: Oksana's parents *emigrated* from Russia in 1944, *immigrating* first to France and then later to the United States.

fewer	An adjective meaning "not many," refers to number. *Fewer is used before a plural noun. There are* fewer *words in a paperback dictionary than in a hardbound one.*
less	An adverb meaning "not as much or as many." *Less is used to refer to things that cannot be counted. Many people feel that they should be spending* less *time at work and more time at home with their families.*
formally	An adverb meaning "marked by form or ceremony." *The young couple* formally *announced their engagement at a special dinner party.*
formerly	An adverb meaning "at an earlier time; in the past." *The candidate running for president was* formerly *a U.S. senator.*
its	A possessive pronoun meaning "the one or ones that belong to it." *The dog always knew where to find* its *bowl when it was time to eat.*
it's	A contraction for "it is or it has." *The dark clouds indicate that* it's *about to rain.*
later	An adverb or adjective meaning "coming after the usual or proper time." *Later is the comparative form of late. The students wanted to postpone the test until a* later *date.*
latter	An adjective meaning "being the second of two mentioned things." *Matt's parents said he could play only one sport in high school; when they gave him a choice between playing football or being on the track team, he chose the* latter. *Also, an adjective meaning "near to the end." The use of the Internet became very popular during the* latter *part of the 1990s.*

Think about this sentence: Of the first two versions of his story, I prefer the *latter*, but the version he came up with *later* is the best of all.

lie	A noun meaning "something said that is not true." *Mary did not want to go to Cara's birthday party, so she told a little white* lie *and said she had to babysit that night.*
lie	A verb meaning "to say what is not true." *Perjury is* lying *under oath.* Also, a verb meaning "to rest or recline; to exist in a horizontal

position." *Lie* is an intransitive verb; that is, it cannot take a direct object. *The dog often* lies *on the couch even though she knows she is supposed to stay off the furniture.* The past tense of the verb *lie* is *lay*: *Despite having scolded her, she* lay *down there again yesterday.* The present participle of *lie* is *lying*: *I knew when she had been* lying *on the furniture, because it was covered with hair.* The past participle of *lie* is *lain*: *She had* lain *on the couch every day without reproach while my mother was visiting.*

lay   A verb meaning "to put down so as to rest on, in, or against something." *Lay* is a transitive verb; that is, it requires a direct object. *If I* lay *any more books there, the table will break.* The past tense of *lay* is *laid*: *I* laid *a book down on the table last week, and now I can't find it.* The present participle of *lay* is *laying*: *I have been* laying *my books on the table all week.* The past participle of *lay* is *laid*: *In fact, I had* laid *my books down in the same spot for weeks.*

LIE VS. *LAY* CHART

	Present	Past	Past Participle (used with forms of *have*)
To recline	lie, lying	lay	has/have/had lain
To put or place	lay, laying	laid	has/have/had laid something
To tell a falsehood	lie, lying	lied	has/have/had lied

Important Tips

1. When you aren't absolutely sure whether to use *lie* or *lay*, substitute *place* or *put* for *lay*. *Put* it there—*lay* it there.

2. Use the conjugation for *pay* as a substitute for *lay*. For some reason, it's easier to remember *pay, paid, have been paying, had paid* than it is to remember *lay, laid, have been laying, had laid*.

3. Connect the word pair lie and lay with the word pair sit and set to help keep straight which is intransitive and which is transitive. One way to do this is to remember that the two words that contain the letter "i," *lie* and *sit*, go together and are intransitive, which starts with an *i*.

Now that you have studied the vocabulary in Unit 1, practice your new knowledge by completing the crossword puzzle.

Vocabulary Unit 1 Puzzle

Directions: Use words from Homonyms Unit 1 to complete the puzzle.

ACROSS CLUES

3. The student was _____ his backpack on the wrong desk.

5. Tim went to bed much _____ than he should have.

6. Mr. Tang _____ in the hospital after a lengthy illness.

7. The senator was _____ because he made false statements to members of Congress while under oath.

8. _____ John Grisham has written eight successful novels.

10. Was the husband _____ to his wife about where he had been last night? Or, was he telling the truth?

11. Tina added a large mirror to her dining room to give the _____ of more space.

15. Sue and Anna are softball players. The former plays catcher and the _____ plays shortstop.

17. Too many children _____ by drowning in unsupervised swimming pools.

18. We usually eat a low-cal _____ after a fattening meal.

19. The _____ is an area with an arid climate.

21. The workers were going to _____ the foundation for the house next week.

22. The cow gave birth to _____ first calf.

23. The movie was _____ before it was shown on TV.

26. Patty was _____ her hair to match her school colors.

27. Thailand was _____ called Siam.

DOWN CLUES

1. They were dressed _____ in tux and tails to go to the Winter Ball.

2. Some students would do better in college by taking _____ classes.

4. The author made an _____ to a character in *Romeo and Juliet*.

5. The woman was _____ on the ground when the paramedics arrived.

9. Juan _____ (d) from Mexico three years ago.

11. Many people now residing in other countries would like to _____ to the United States.

12. The officer told the suspect to _____ the gun down and put his hands in the air.

13. Every four years the Olympics are held at a different _____. In 2000, they were held in Australia.

14. The members of the class of 1980 will not be _____ again until the next reunion.

16. I should have eaten a lot _____ at our Thanksgiving dinner.

19. Should euthanasia be available for the _____?

20. Steve did not need to take college algebra because he had _____ taken it in high school.

23. Always make sure you _____ your references properly.

24. When he missed work, he _____ to his boss about being sick.

25. On St. Patrick's Day, some people _____ their beer green.

The Author's Purpose and the Rhetorical Modes

The Oath of the Horatii (1784) *BY JACQUES-LOUIS DAVID*

Photo: G. Blot/C. Jean. Louvre, Paris. Réunion des Musées Nationaux/Art Resource, NY.

View and Reflect

In the painting, three brothers are swearing an oath to their father to defeat their enemies or die for Rome.

1. What are the brothers receiving from their father?
2. Compare the postures and attitudes of the men to those of the women. How do the hands of the men and women express their respective attitudes?
3. What does the woman in black in the background of the painting appear to be doing?
4. Notice the three arches in the background of the painting. Where else does the artist repeat this theme of a group of three?
5. What do you think the artist's purpose was in creating this painting?
6. How does the painting illustrate risk-taking behavior?
7. What is the dominant color in the male grouping? What might that color represent?

Determining the Author's Purpose

Highlight or underline the definitions of the key terms. Then write a paraphrase of each definition in the margin.

Most writers create a story, essay, article, or poem with at least one **general purpose** in mind. Because most writers do not directly state their general purpose, the reader must use indirect clues to determine it. We can identify the general purpose by asking the question "Why did the author write this?" Usually, this purpose will fall into one of three broad categories: to inform, to entertain, or to persuade.

Three Broad Categories

Inform
_____
_____

- An author whose purpose is **to inform** will provide readers with knowledge or information. Ordinarily, the material will be presented in an objective, neutral fashion. Authors who write textbooks presenting factual material often have this purpose in mind. Articles in newspapers are also usually meant to inform.

Entertain
_____
_____

- An author whose purpose is **to entertain** will tell a story or describe someone or something in an interesting way. A piece of writing meant to entertain will often make an appeal to the reader's imagination, sense of humor, or emotions. Such writing may be either fiction or nonfiction. Witty, unusual, dramatic, or exciting stories usually have entertainment as their purpose.

Persuade
_____
_____

- Finally, the author's purpose may be **to persuade.** Persuasion goes beyond merely entertaining or providing information. This kind of writing tries to change the reader's opinions by appealing to emotions or intellect. If making an emotional argument, the author may use vividly descriptive passages designed to manipulate the reader's feelings. If making an appeal to intelligence, the author will employ logic and reasoning. Political literature is a common form of writing meant to persuade. Newspaper editorials ordinarily have persuasion as their purpose also.

How Authors Choose Purposes

Audience
_____
_____

Authors take into account their **audience** (those they are writing for) when they choose their **general purpose.** Writers of fiction usually want to entertain readers by creating interesting characters and stories. If an author writes an article for a wellness magazine, the general purpose will probably be to provide information promoting good health. If an author writes a letter to solicit campaign contributions for a political candidate, the general purpose will be to persuade people to give money.

Specific purpose
_____
_____
_____
_____

In addition to a general purpose, authors also usually have a **specific purpose,** which reveals more detailed information about the article than the general purpose. Take the wellness example above. The general purpose is to inform. The specific purpose might be "to inform people about foods that protect against cancer."

Sometimes an author may have more than one purpose in mind. For instance, an author might want both to entertain and to persuade. Or the author might write an entertaining article that also provides information about something important. In these instances, usually one of the author's purposes will be primary. To determine the general and primary purpose, first identify the main idea and the key details that support that idea. Then note the author's choice of words. Is the vocabulary neutral and unbiased? Is it meant to influence our judgment in some way? Finally, note the source of the article or passage. Often the publication that the article or passage comes from will help you identify the author's primary purpose.

Read the paragraph below, and identify the writer's topic, main idea, and general and specific purposes.

The viewpoint, now gaining momentum, that would allow individuals to "make up their own minds" about smoking, air bags, safety helmets, and the like ignores some elementary social realities. The ill-informed nature of this viewpoint is camouflaged by the appeal to values that are dear to most Americans. The essence of the argument is that what individuals do with their lives and limbs, foolhardy though it might be, is their own business, and that any interference would abridge their rights. However, no civil society can survive if it permits each person to maximize his or her freedoms without concern for the consequences of one's act on others. If I choose to drive without a seat belt or air bag, I am greatly increasing my chances, in case of an accident, of being impaled on the steering wheel or exiting via the windshield. It is not just my body that is jeopardized; my careening auto which I cannot get back under control, will be more likely to injure people in other autos, pedestrians, or riders in my car. The individual who chooses to act irresponsibly is playing a game of heads I win, tails the public loses. All too often, the unbelted drivers, the smokers, the unvaccinated, the users of quack remedies, draw on public funds to pay for the consequences of their unrestrained freedom of choice. Their rugged individualism rapidly becomes dependency when cancer strikes, or when the car overturns, sending the occupants to hospitals for treatment paid for at least in part by the public, through subsidies for hospitals and medical training. But the public till is not bottomless, and paying for these irresponsible acts leaves other public needs without funds.

(Amitai Etzioni, "When Rights Collide," in *Psychology Today,* 1977)

Topic:	Individual liberty vs. social responsibility
Main idea:	No civil society can survive if it permits each person to maximize his or her freedom without concern for the consequence of one's act on others.
General purpose:	To persuade
Specific purpose:	To persuade us that there needs to be a balance between individual liberty and social responsibility

The following exercises will give you some practice in determining an author's general purpose.

Exercise 1: Determining the Author's Purpose

Label each sentence according to its general purpose: to inform (I), to entertain (E), or to persuade (P).

_____ 1. Did you ever wonder how all the best athletes make sports seem so easy? The behind the back passes, the triple lutzes, the holes in one; on TV it looks so easy. We sit in our armchairs and say, "I could do that. How hard could it be?" The truth is, if we could do that, we'd be out there doing it. I think that if I had the talent, right now I'd be doing some triple lutzes. What is a lutz anyway? Are three of them a good thing? Do you have to do it in tights? Because if you have to do it in tights, I may have a problem with it.

(Tom Mather, *Voyages in the Toilet Dimension*, 1999)

_____ 2. Stealing goods from retail merchants is a very common crime; it constitutes about 15 percent of all larcenies. A survey in Spokane, Washington, revealed that every twelfth shopper is a shoplifter, and that men and women are equally likely to be offenders. Perhaps shoplifting is so frequent because it is a low-risk offense, with a detection rate of less than 1 percent. Shoppers are extremely reluctant to report shoplifters to the store management. According to one study, of those apprehended for shoplifting, approximately 45.5 percent are actually prosecuted. It is also estimated that men are slightly more likely than women to be shoplifters, and that 41 percent of offenders are white, 29 percent are black, and 16 percent are Hispanic. More than half of shoplifting events occur between the hours of 12:00 P.M. and 6:00 P.M. Interviews with 740 shoplifters in 50 Minneapolis stores revealed that almost half of those who expressed motivation for stealing said that they stole the merchandise because they liked it and did not have enough money to pay for it.

(Frieda Adler et al., *Criminology and the Criminal Justice System*, 7/e, 2010)

_____ 3. The Sound of Music: Enough Already

There was a time when music knew its place. No longer. Possibly this is not music's fault. It may be that music fell in with a bad crowd and lost its sense of common decency. I am willing to consider this. I am willing even to try and help. I would like to do my bit to set music straight in order that it might shape up and leave the main stream of society. The first thing that music must understand is that there are two kinds of music— good music and bad music. Good music is music that *I* want to hear. Bad music is music that *I* don't want to hear. I do not under any circumstances enjoy hold buttons. But I am a woman of reason. I can accept reality. I can face the facts. What I cannot face is the music. Just as there are two kinds of music—good and bad—so there are two kinds of hold buttons—good and bad. Good hold buttons are hold buttons that hold one silently. Bad hold buttons are hold buttons that hold one musically. When I hold I want to hold silently. That is the way it was meant to be.

(Fran Leibowitz, *The Leibowitz Reader*, 1994)

_____ 4. Cheating jeopardizes the basic fairness of the grading process. Widespread cheating causes honest students to become cynical and resentful, especially when grades are curved and the cheating directly affects other students. Cheating may also have long-term effects. Taking the easy way in college may become a habit that can spill over into graduate school, jobs, and relationships. And consider this: would you want a doctor, lawyer, or accountant who had cheated on exams handling your affairs? Cheating sabotages your own academic and personal growth. Don't cheat!

(John Gardener, *Your College Experience*)

> **Exercise 2: Identifying the Clues That Indicate the Author's Purpose and Main Idea**

Read each of the following paragraphs to determine whether the author's primary purpose is (1) to entertain, (2) to persuade, or (3) to inform. Indicate the clues that enabled you to make your decision. Then, in the space provided, write the stated or implied main idea.

1. Today, 40 percent of all youths in the United States, are children of color, yet few of the faces they see on television reflect their race or cultural heritage. As of spring 2009, the only network show centered on minority performers was *Ugly Betty*, with America Ferrera. A handful of others, like *CSI* and *Grey's Anatomy*, included minority actors in an ensemble cast. In that year American Indians were completely absent from network TV, except for one actress with a recurring role in *Terminator: Sarah Connor Chronicles*. What is more, the programs shown earlier in the evening, when young people are most likely to watch television, were the least diverse. However, unscripted reality shows do reflect the audience's racial and ethnic composition, so that Latinos, African Americans, and Asian Americans appear quite regularly.

   (Richard Schaefer, *Sociology*, 12/e, 2010)

   Purpose: _____   Clues: _____

   Main idea: _____

   _____

2. Good manners are back, and for a good reason. As the world becomes increasingly competitive, the gold goes to the team that shows off an extra bit of polish. The person who makes a good impression will be the one who gets the job, wins the promotion, or clinches the deal. Manners and professionalism must become second nature to anyone who wants to achieve and maintain a competitive edge. The lesson is this: You can have good credentials, but a good presentation is everything. You can't neglect etiquette, or somewhere in your career you will be at a competitive disadvantage because of your inability to use good manners or to maintain your composure in tense situations.

   (William G. Nickels et al., *Understanding Business*, 8/e, 2008)

   Purpose: _____   Clues: _____

   _____

   Main idea: _____

   _____

3. If there's one thing this nation needs, it's bigger cars. That's why I'm excited that Ford is coming out with a new mound o' metal that will offer consumers even more total road-squatting mass than the current leader in the humongous-car category, the popular Chevrolet Suburban Subdivision—the first passenger automobile designed to be, right off the assembly line, visible from the Moon. I don't know what the new Ford will be called. Probably something like the "Ford Untamed Wilderness Adventure." In the TV commercials, it will be shown splashing through rivers, charging up rocky mountainsides, swinging on vines, diving off cliffs, racing through the surf, and fighting giant sharks hundreds of feet beneath the ocean surface—all the daredevil things that cars

do in Sport Utility Vehicle Commercial World, where nobody ever drives on an actual road. Anyway, now we have the new Ford, which will be *even larger* than the Subdivision, which I imagine means it will have separate decks for the various classes of passengers. And it will not stop there. This is America, darn it, and Chevrolet is not about to just sit by and watch Ford walk away with the coveted title of Least Sane Motor Vehicle. No, cars will keep getting bigger. I see a time, not too far from now, when people will haul their overdue movies back to the video-rental store in full-size, 18-wheel tractor-trailers with names like The Vagabond. It will be a proud time for all Americans, a time for us to cheer for our country.

(Dave Barry, *Dave Barry Is Not Taking This Sitting Down,* 2000)

Purpose: _____   Clues: _____

_____

Main idea: _____

4. In the traditional cultures of Asia, arranged marriages were the rule. Marriages were designed to further the well-being of families, not of the individuals involved. Marriage was traditionally seen as a matter of ancestors, descendants, and property. Supporters of these traditions point out that love is a fleeting emotion and not a sensible basis for such an important decision. However, most of these traditional cultures have a literature as well as a history full of love-smitten couples who chose death rather than marriage to the person selected by their respective families.

(Curtis Byer et al., *Dimensions of Human Sexuality,* 5/e, 1999)

Purpose: _____   Clues: _____

Main idea: _____

An Introduction to the Rhetorical Modes

Highlight or underline the definitions of the key terms. Then write a paraphrase of each definition in the margin.

In longer reading selections, the main idea is often called the **thesis.** The thesis of an essay, just like the main idea of a paragraph, expresses the most important point the writer is trying to make. The thesis is sometimes called the *controlling idea,* because its primary purpose is to hold the essay or story together.

Four Primary Modes

In the process of creating written work, most writers select a **rhetorical mode of writing** that helps them achieve their purpose. There are four primary rhetorical modes: narration, description, exposition, and persuasion.

Narrative

_____

- Material written in a **narrative mode** tells a story, either true or fictional. In narrative writing, the events of a story are usually ordered chronologically (by time).

Descriptive

_____

_____

- With material written in a **descriptive mode,** the emphasis is on providing details that describe a person, place, or object. The writing may use figurative language and include material that appeals to one or more of the five senses. Descriptive writing most commonly deals with visual perceptions.

Expository

- An author who is trying to explain something will likely use an **expository mode.** Expository writing explains ideas and how things work. It is more likely to be logical and factual. Much of the material that you read in your textbooks follows an expository mode.

Persuasive

- Material written in a **persuasive mode** is meant to convince you of something. Persuasive writing tends to be about controversial topics. It presents an argument and offers evidence. It is writing that is considered to be biased.

Mixed

Sometimes an author will use more than one mode of writing. For example, the author might choose to write a piece that is both descriptive and narrative. This is called a **mixed mode** of writing, and the organization may also be mixed.

Expository Writing with Purpose to Inform

The following selection by Daniel Goleman discusses the topic of emotional intelligence or EQ. Typically people with high EQs are aware of their impulses and have the ability to control and manage them. Also, they are able to keep their focus on a goal and persevere until they achieve it. Goleman's purpose in this selection is to inform and his mode of writing is expository. Notice the use of factual details to inform the reader.

SELECTION

"There is perhaps no psychological skill more fundamental than resisting impulse."

GETTING THE PICTURE

In the excerpt that follows, Daniel Goleman explains how a child's ability to control impulses can have far-reaching consequences.

Read the first paragraph of the excerpt. What choice do you think you would have made at that age? Have there been times in your life when you wanted the immediate short-term reward when you knew that waiting would guarantee a bigger "payoff"? Do you think you can teach people to control their impulses?

BIO-SKETCH

In 1995, Daniel Goleman, former editor of *Psychology Today,* lecturer at Harvard University, and writer for the *New York Times,* published the bestseller *Emotional Intelligence: Why It Can Matter More Than IQ.* In 1998, he wrote *Working with Emotional Intelligence,* which describes how the ability to handle ourselves and others is the key to a successful career. Goleman's latest book is *Ecological Intelligence: How Knowing the Hidden Impacts of What We Buy Can Change Everything.*

BRUSHING UP ON VOCABULARY

inhibition a mental or psychological process that holds back an action, emotion, or thought.

limbic system primitive part of the brain, located near the brain stem, thought to control emotions and behavior.

Excerpt from
EMOTIONAL INTELLIGENCE
by Daniel Goleman

IMPULSE CONTROL: THE MARSHMALLOW TEST

Just imagine you're four years old, and someone makes the following proposal: If you wait until after he runs an errand, you can have two marshmallows for a treat. If you can't wait until then, you can have only one—but you can have it right now. It is a challenge sure to try the soul of any four-year-old, a microcosm of the eternal battle between impulse and restraint, id and ego, desire and self-control, gratification and delay. Which of these choices a child makes is a telling test; it offers a quick reading not just of character, but of the trajectory the child will probably take through life. [1]

There is perhaps no psychological skill more fundamental than resisting impulse. It is the root of all emotional self-control, since all emotions, by their nature, lead to one or another impulse to act. The root meaning of the word *emotion,* remember, is "to move." The capacity to resist the impulse to act, to squelch the incipient movement, most likely translates at the level of brain function into inhibition of limbic signals to the motor cortex, though such an interpretation must remain speculative for now. [2]

At any rate, a remarkable study in which the marshmallow challenge was posed to four-year-olds shows just how fundamental is the ability to restrain the emotions and so delay impulse. Begun by psychologist Walter Mischel during the 1960s at a preschool on the Stanford University campus and involving mainly children of Stanford faculty, graduate students, and other employees, the study tracked down the four-year-olds as they were graduating from high school. [3]

Some four-year-olds were able to wait what must surely have seemed an endless 15 to 20 minutes for the experimenter to return. To sustain themselves in their struggle they covered their eyes so they wouldn't have to stare at temptation, or rested their heads in their arms, talked to themselves, sang, played games with their hands and feet, even tried to go to sleep. These plucky preschoolers got the two-marshmallow reward. But others, more impulsive, grabbed the one marshmallow, almost within seconds of the experimenter's leaving the room on his "errand." [4]

The diagnostic power of how this moment of impulse was handled became clear some 12 to 14 years later, when these same children were tracked down as adolescents. The emotional and social differences between the grab-the-marshmallow preschoolers and their gratification-delaying peers was dramatic. Those who had resisted temptation at four were now, as adolescents, more socially competent: personally effective, self-assertive, and better able to cope with the frustrations of life. They were less likely to go to pieces, freeze, or regress under stress, or become rattled and disorganized when pressured; they embraced challenges and pursued them instead of giving up even in the face of difficulties; they were self-reliant and confident, trustworthy and dependable; and they took initiative and plunged into projects. And more than a decade later, they were still able to delay gratification in pursuit of their goals. [5]

The third or so who grabbed for the marshmallow, however, tended to have fewer of these qualities, and shared instead a relatively more troubled psychological portrait. In adolescence they were more likely to be seen as shying away from social contacts; to be stubborn and indecisive; to be easily upset by frustrations; to think [6] of themselves as "bad" or unworthy; to regress or become immobilized by stress; to be mistrustful and resentful about not "getting enough"; to be prone to jealousy and envy; to overreact to irritations with a sharp temper, so provoking arguments and fights. And, after all those years, they were still unable to put off gratification.

What shows up in a small way early in life blossoms into a wide range of social 7 and emotional competencies as life goes on. The capacity to impose a delay on impulse is at the root of a plethora of efforts, from staying on a diet to pursuing a medical degree. Some children, even at four, had mastered the basics: They were able to read the social situation as one where delay was beneficial, to pry their attention from focusing on the temptation at hand, and to distract themselves while maintaining the necessary perseverance toward their goal—the two marshmallows.

What Walter Mischel, who did the study, describes is perhaps the essence of 8 emotional self-regulation: the ability to deny impulse in the service of a goal, whether it be building a business, solving an algebraic equation, or pursuing the Stanley Cup. His finding underscores the role of emotional intelligence in determining how well or how poorly people are able to use their other mental capacities.

(Daniel Goleman, *Emotional Intelligence*, 1995)

✓ COMPREHENSION CHECKUP

Short Answer

Directions: Answer the following questions briefly, in no more than a sentence or two.

1. What is the overall main idea, or thesis, of this excerpt?

   _____

   _____

2. What is the main idea of paragraph 2?

   _____

3. What words in paragraph 4 demonstrate that it was not easy for the four-year-olds to resist temptation?

   _____

4. What is the main idea of paragraph 5?

   _____

   _____

5. The story discusses children who gave in to temptation and grabbed marshmallows. What consequences did this lack of impulse control have for them when they became adolescents?

   _____

6. List some details from the selection that indicate that the author's purpose was to inform the reader.

   _____

   _____

   _____

   _____

Multiple Choice

Directions: Write the letter of the correct answer in the blank provided.

_____ 7. *Microcosm* as used in paragraph 1 means which of the following?
   a. something regarded as a world in miniature
   b. a small, inexpensive computer
   c. a small organism causing disease
   d. so small as to be invisible except through a microscope

_____ 8. *Trajectory* as used in paragraph 1 means which of the following?
   a. the curve that a body (as a planet or comet) makes in space
   b. a path, progression, or line of development
   c. to throw over

_____ 9. Here are some word pairs from paragraph 1: *impulse/restraint, id/ego, desire/self-control, gratification/delay.* These word pairs are all
   a. homonyms
   b. antonyms
   c. synonyms

_____ 10. In paragraph 2, *to squelch the incipient movement* means
   a. to stop that which is just beginning to appear
   b. to lead from movement to movement
   c. to stop something from reappearing

_____ 11. *Speculative* as used in paragraph 2 means which of the following?
   a. taking part in a risky venture on the chance of making huge profits
   b. buying or selling certain stocks
   c. leading to no definite result

_____ 12. In paragraph 7, a *plethora* of efforts means
   a. a fullness
   b. an abundance
   c. a delighted feeling

In Your Own Words

1. Why do you think being able to wait for a marshmallow at age four correlates with the ability to successfully pursue an academic goal?

2. This excerpt by Daniel Goleman discusses the concept of delayed gratification. How important to a successful life are the skills of being able to focus and exercise self-control? Do you think it is possible to teach focus and self-control to children?

The Art of Writing

In a recent interview, Daniel Goleman said that the best way to raise our EQ levels is to place a high priority on personal interactions with others. He believes that increased reliance on e-mails, texting, and social networking sites hinders full emotional interactions. He speculates that because so much personal communication now takes place through electronic gadgets, today's children are likely to have lower EQs than their parents. He thinks it's important for children to cultivate empathy and compassion and a good way to do that is to "have face to-face interactions and make eye contact with others." Write a short essay giving your opinion on how to help children develop emotional intelligence skills. Do you think the prevalence of communication through electronic devices makes it more difficult for children to develop empathy and compassion?

Internet Activity

Do a web search of Daniel Goleman. What additional information did you find out about him? Give a short list of new information.

Narrative Writing with Purpose to Entertain

The following fable by Aesop has entertainment as its primary purpose. It is an example of the *narrative* mode of writing. Notice that the significant events of the story are told in chronological order.

SELECTION

"Gradually, when things seemed quiet, the country mouse crept out from his hiding place and whispered good-bye to his elegant friend."

GETTING THE PICTURE

Do you think that people who live in cities have a different perspective on life than people who live in rural areas? If you think this, what are some of the differences you see?

BIO-SKETCH

Aesop, a Greek slave, lived from about 620 to 560 B.C.E. According to legend, Aesop was eventually freed because the fables he told exhibited such great wisdom. As a free man, he traveled to Athens, Greece, where he quickly made an enemy of the ruler and was condemned to death.

Many of Aesop's best fables draw parallels between animals and humans in order to illustrate key moral principles and universal lessons. Aesop is responsible for many familiar expressions that have survived to this day, such as "sour grapes," "don't cry over spilt milk," "actions speak louder than words," and "look before you leap."

BRUSHING UP ON VOCABULARY

morsel a little bite. *Morsel* is derived from the Latin word *morsum,* meaning "bitten."

condescend This word is derived from the Latin prefix *de,* meaning "down," "down from," and "away." The meaning of "stoop to the level of inferiors" was first recorded in 1435. The fable states that "the town mouse *condescended* to nibble a little here and there." This means that the town mouse was "politely willing to do something that he thought was beneath his dignity."

rustic The English language is almost always uncomplimentary to the "country cousin." *Rustic* is derived from the Latin word *rus,* meaning "open land, country." In 1585, it acquired the meaning "rough, awkward," and then in 1594, that of "simple and plain."

The Country Mouse and the Town Mouse
BY AESOP

O NCE UPON A TIME A COUNTRY MOUSE, who had a friend in town, invited him to pay 1
a visit in the country for old acquaintance's sake. After the invitation was accepted, the country mouse, though plain, coarse, and somewhat frugal, opened his heart and pantry to honor his old friend and to show him the proper hospitality. There was not a morsel which he had carefully stored that he did not bring forth out of its larder—peas and barley, cheese parings and nuts—with the hope that the quantity would make up for what he feared was wanting in quality to suit the taste of his elegant guest. In turn, the town mouse condescended to nibble a little here and there in a dainty manner while the host sat munching a blade of barley straw.

"The man who suggests his own tediousness has yet to be born."

—Thomas Bailey Aldrich

In their after-dinner chat the town mouse said to the country mouse, "How is 2
it, my good friend, that you can endure this boring and crude life? You live like a toad in a hole. You can't really prefer these solitary rocks and woods to streets teeming with carriages and people. Upon my word of honor, you're wasting your time in such a miserable existence. You must make the most of your life while it lasts. As you know, a mouse does not live forever. So, come with me this very night, and I'll show you all around the town and what life's about."

Overcome by his friend's fine words and polished manner, the country mouse 3
agreed, and they set out together on their journey to the town. It was late in the evening when they crept stealthily into the city and midnight before they reached the large house, which was the town mouse's residence. There were couches of crimson velvet, ivory carvings, and everything one could imagine that indicated wealth and luxury. On the table were the remains of a splendid banquet from all the choicest shops ransacked the day before to make sure that the guests, already departed, would be satisfied.

It was now the town mouse's turn to play host, and he placed his country friend 4
on a purple cushion, ran back and forth to supply all his needs, and pressed dish upon dish on him and delicacy upon delicacy. Of course, the town mouse tasted each and every course before he ventured to place it before his rustic cousin, as though he were waiting on a king. In turn, the country mouse made himself quite at home and blessed the good fortune that had brought about such a change in his way of life.

In the middle of his enjoyment, however, just as he was thinking contemptu- 5
ously of the poor meals that he had been accustomed to eating, the door suddenly flew open, and a group of revelers, who were returning from a late party, burst into the room. The frightened friends jumped from the table and hid themselves in the very first corner they could reach. No sooner did they dare creep out again than the barking of dogs drove them back with even greater terror than before. Gradually, when things seemed quiet, the country mouse crept out from his hiding place and whispered good-bye to his elegant friend.

"To be happy we must not be too concerned with others."

—Albert Camus

"This fine mode of living may be all right for those who like it," he said. "But I'd 6
rather have a crust in peace and safety than all your fine things in the midst of such alarm and terror."

(The Country Mouse and the Town Mouse, Aesop)

✓ COMPREHENSION CHECKUP

Short Answer

Directions: Answer the following questions briefly, in no more than a sentence or two.

1. What clues helped you determine that the author's purpose was to entertain the reader?

_____

_____

_____

_____

_____

2. For what particular audience has the author written the fable?

_____

True or False

Indicate whether the statement is true or false by writing **T** or **F** in the blank provided.

_____ 3. The country mouse did not strive to be a good host to his old friend.

_____ 4. The country mouse did not take part in the feast he set before the town mouse.

_____ 5. In paragraph 4, *rustic* is a synonym for "country."

_____ 6. The late-night revelers entered the room quietly.

_____ 7. The town mouse's residence was lavishly decorated.

Multiple Choice

Write the letter of the correct answer in the blank provided.

_____ 8. What do the words *coarse, plain,* and *frugal* suggest about the country mouse?
   a. He is very lazy.
   b. He has a magnificent lifestyle.
   c. He lives a simple, thrifty life.
   d. He is likely to use obscenities.

_____ 9. A proverb is a traditional saying that offers advice or presents a moral. Which of the following proverbs best describes the attitude of the town mouse?
   a. You win a few, you lose a few.
   b. Absence makes the heart grow fonder.
   c. If you can't beat 'em, join 'em.
   d. Curiosity killed the cat.

_____ 10. Which of the following proverbs best describes the attitude of the country mouse at the end of the fable?
   a. Adventures are for the adventurous.
   b. It's best to be on the safe side.
   c. The early bird catches the worm.
   d. Both a and b.

_____ 11. Which of the following best describes the town mouse's attitude toward the country mouse before their departure to the city?
   a. The country mouse is living his life to the fullest.
   b. The country mouse needs to have new experiences.
   c. The country mouse is very adventurous.
   d. The country mouse should stay right where he is because there's no place like home.

_____ 12. The town mouse and the country mouse crept stealthily into the city. The most likely meaning of the word *stealthily* is
   a. sneakily
   b. loudly
   c. obviously
   d. both a and b

Vocabulary in Context

Look through the paragraph indicated in parentheses to find a word that matches the definition below.

1. thrifty (paragraph 1) _____

2. place where food is kept or stored; pantry (1) _____

3. very full; swarming; abounding (2) _____

4. searched thoroughly; plundered (3) _____

5. urged upon (4) _____

6. scornfully (5) _____

7. merrymakers (5) _____

8. method; way of acting or behaving (6) _____

In Your Own Words

1. What is the main idea of the fable?

2. Working with a partner, paraphrase one of the paragraphs of the fable. Be sure to keep the characters and setting the same.

3. What is the significance of the ending of the fable? What is meant by the last sentence? Explain.

4. Determine which of the following proverbs is more likely to express the attitude of the country mouse. Explain your choice.

   "A life lived in fear is a life half-lived."
   "Better safe than sorry."
   "Nothing ventured, nothing gained."
   "Variety is the spice of life."
   "Acorns were good till bread was found."

The Art of Writing

In a brief essay, respond to the question below.

Are you more like the country mouse or the town mouse? Why?

Internet Activity

The following Web site has a collection of more than 665 of Aesop's fables:

www.Aesopfables.com.

Select three fables you find interesting, and print them. Think about the meaning of the fables and how the moral might apply to your own life. Describe your conclusions in a short paragraph.

Persuasive Writing with Purpose to Persuade

The following is a poem by Judith Ortiz Cofer. The poem's purpose is to persuade, and it is written in a persuasive mode.

SELECTION

*"Finally, you must choose between standing still
in the one solid spot you have found, or you keep moving
and take the risk."*

GETTING THE PICTURE

What idea is Ortiz Cofer trying to convince us to accept? How does she feel life should be lived?

BIO-SKETCH

Judith Ortiz Cofer was born in Puerto Rico in 1952 and is currently a professor of English and creative writing at the University of Georgia. A recipient of the O. Henry Award for a short story, she has also published two volumes of poetry: *Peregrina* in 1986 and *Triple Crown* in 1987. *The Meaning of Consuelo* was published in 2003.

BRUSHING UP ON VOCABULARY

step on a crack, break your mother's back a rhyme children say while they avoid stepping on cracks in a sidewalk. Stepping on a crack is supposed to bring bad luck.

Crossings

BY JUDITH ORTIZ COFER

Step on a crack.
In a city of concrete it is impossible
to avoid disaster indefinitely.
You spend your life peering
downward, looking for flaws,
but each day more and more fissures
 crisscross your path, and like the lines
on your palms, they mean something
 you cannot decipher.
Finally, you must choose between
standing still in the one solid spot you
 have found, or you keep moving
and take the risk:
Break your mother's back.

*"To be alive at all
involves some risk."*
—Harold MacMillan

(Judith Ortiz Cofer, "Crossings," *Reaching for the Mainland and Selected New Poems,* 1987)

✓ COMPREHENSION CHECKUP

In Your Own Words

1. What course of action is Cofer persuading the reader to accept?

2. Explain the meaning of the poem in your own words.

Identifying Mode and Author's Purpose

Many people seek out high levels of stimulation. Complete the questionnaire on page 125 to determine your own level of stimulation. The next article discusses extreme sports—an activity that involves a high level of stimulation. Read the article and think about its purpose and the rhetorical mode the author uses. Then answer the questions that follow.

Do You Seek Out Sensation?

How much stimulation do you crave in your everyday life? You will have an idea after you complete the following questionnaire, which lists some items from a scale designed to assess your sensation-seeking tendencies. Circle either *A* or *B* in each pair of statements.

1. A. I would like a job that requires a lot of traveling.
   B. I would prefer a job in one location.

2. A. I am invigorated by a brisk, cold day.
   B. I can't wait to get indoors on a cold day.

3. A. I get bored seeing the same old faces.
   B. I like the comfortable familiarity of old friends.

4. A. I would prefer living in an ideal society in which everyone was safe, secure, and happy.
   B. I would have preferred living in the unsettled days of our history.

5. A. I sometimes like to do things that are a little frightening.
   B. A sensible person avoids activities that are dangerous.

6. A. I would not like to be hypnotized.
   B. I would like to have the experience of being hypnotized.

7. A. The most important goal of life is to live it to the fullest and to experience as much as possible.
   B. The most important goal of life is to find peace and happiness.

8. A. I would like to try parachute jumping.
   B. I would never want to try jumping out of a plane, with or without a parachute.

9. A. I enter cold water gradually, giving myself time to get used to it.
   B. I like to dive or jump right into the ocean or a cold pool.

10. A. When I go on a vacation, I prefer the comfort of a good room and bed.
    B. When I go on a vacation, I prefer the change of camping out.

11. A. I prefer people who are emotionally expressive, even if they are a bit unstable.
    B. I prefer people who are calm and even-tempered.

12. A. A good painting should shock or jolt the senses.
    B. A good painting should give me a feeling of peace and security.

13. A. People who ride motorcycles must have some kind of unconscious need to hurt themselves.
    B. I would like to drive or ride a motorcycle.

Scoring Give yourself one point for each of the following responses: 1A, 2A, 3A, 4B, 5A, 6B, 7A, 8A, 9B, 10B, 11A, 12A, 13B. Find your total score by adding up the number of points and then use the following scoring key:

    0–3 very low sensation seeking
    4–5 low
    6–9 average
    10–11 high
    12–13 very high

Keep in mind, of course, that this short questionnaire, for which the scoring is based on the results of college students who have taken it, provides only a rough estimate of your sensation-seeking tendencies. Moreover, as people get older, their sensation-seeking scores tend to decrease. Still, the questionnaire will at least give you an indication of how your sensation-seeking tendencies compare with those of others.

(Robert S. Feldman, *Understanding Psychology,* 5/e, 1999)

> *"America has always been defined by risk; it may be our predominant national characteristic."*

GETTING THE PICTURE

In recent years, the young and the fit have been besieged with invitations to participate in man-made "life tests." They are asked, "Do you have what it takes?" And told, "Just do it." Increasingly, reality movies and TV programs like *Survivor* occupy our national attention. As you are reading the article below, try to determine what's behind this preoccupation with testing the limits.

BIO-SKETCH

Karl Taro Greenfeld is a Japanese-American writer—author of *Speed Tribes: Days and Nights with Japan's Next Generation* (1994)—and editor for *Time* magazine's Asian edition.

BRUSHING UP ON VOCABULARY

acronym a word formed by combining the initial letters or syllables of a series of words. It comes from the Greek *akros*, meaning "tip," and *onym*, meaning "name." Large numbers of *acronyms* first began to appear during World War I when WAAC (Women's Army Auxiliary Corps) and similar words were formed. The trend accelerated during World War II with terms such as RADAR (radio detecting and ranging). Some common acronyms are AIDS (acquired immunodeficiency syndrome), NAFTA (North American Free Trade Agreement), and MADD (Mothers Against Drunk Driving).

orgy the word came to us from the Greek word *orgia*, meaning "secret ceremonies." The Greeks held nighttime religious rituals in honor of Dionysius, the Greek god of wine. These *orgia* involved drinking, singing, dancing, and acts of sex. The current meaning is much the same except that the religious element has been eliminated.

bespeak a British term meaning "to speak for or order in advance."

pandemic an epidemic that spreads over a large area, possibly even worldwide. The term comes from the Greek word *pandemos*, meaning "disease of all the people."

perilous involving grave risk; hazardous; dangerous. A long time ago, travel was a highly dangerous undertaking. The word *perilous* comes from the Latin *periculum*, which means, "the danger of going forth to travel."

manifestation clearly evident; an outward indication. From the Latin *manus*, which means "hand," and *festus*, which means "struck." Something that is *manifest* to the senses is something that can be touched or struck by the hand.

pansy a dainty flower with velvety petals and a "thoughtful face." The word is derived from the French *penser*, meaning "to think." The word is also a slang term for an effeminate man.

contemplate to consider thoughtfully. The ancient Roman priests carefully considered various signs or omens that were revealed to them inside the temples of their gods. *Contemplate* is derived from *con*, meaning "with," and *templum*, meaning "temple."

Life on the Edge

By Karl Taro Greenfeld

1 FIVE . . . FOUR . . . THREE . . . TWO . . . ONE . . . SEE YA!" And Chance McGuire, 25, is airborne off a 650-foot concrete dam in Northern California. In one second he falls 16 feet, in two seconds 63 feet, and after three seconds and 137 feet he is flying at 65 m.p.h. He prays that his parachute will open facing away from the dam, that his canopy won't collapse, that his toggles will be handy, and that no ill wind will slam him back into the cold concrete. The chute snaps open, the sound ricocheting through the gorge like a gunshot, and McGuire is soaring, carving S turns into the air, swooping over a winding creek. When he lands, he is a speck on a path along the creek. He hurriedly packs his chute and then, clearly audible above the rushing water, lets out a war whoop that rises past those mortals still perched on the dam, past the commuters puttering by on the roadway, past even the hawks who circle the ravine. It is a cry of defiance, thanks, and victory; he has survived another BASE jump.

"Life has no romance without risk."

—Sarah Doherty, first one-legged person to scale Mount McKinley

2 McGuire is a practitioner of what he calls the king of all extreme sports. BASE is an acronym for building, antenna, span (bridge), and earth (cliffs). BASE jumping has one of the sporting world's highest fatality rates: in its 18-year history, 46 participants have been killed. Yet the sport has never been more popular, with more than a thousand jumpers in the U.S. and more seeking to get into it every day.

3 It is an activity without margin for error. If your chute malfunctions, don't bother reaching for a reserve—there isn't time. There are no second chances.

Still, the sport's stark metaphor—a 4 human leaving safety behind to leap into the void—may be perfect with our times. As extreme a risk-taker as McGuire seems, we may all have more in common with him than we know or care to admit. America has embarked on a national orgy of thrill seeking and risk taking. Extreme sports like BASE jumping, snowboarding, ice climbing, skateboarding and paragliding are merely the most vivid manifestation of this new national behavior.

The rising popularity of extreme 5 sports bespeaks an eagerness on the part of millions of Americans to participate in activities closer to the metaphorical edge, where danger, skill, and fear combine to give weekend warriors and professional athletes alike a sense of pushing out personal boundaries. According to American Sports Data, a consulting firm, participation in so-called extreme sports is way up. Snowboarding has grown 113 percent in five years and now boasts nearly 5.5 million participants. Mountain biking, skateboarding, scuba diving, you name the adventure sport—the growth curves reveal a nation that loves to play with danger. Contrast that with activities like baseball, touch football, and aerobics, all of which have been in steady decline throughout the '90s.

The pursuits that are becoming 6 more popular have one thing in common: the perception that they are somehow more challenging than a game of touch football. "Every human being with two legs, two arms, is going to wonder how fast, how strong, how enduring he or she is," says Eric Perlman, a mountaineer and filmmaker specializing in extreme sports. "We are designed to experiment or die."

7   And to get hurt. More Americans than ever are injuring themselves while pushing their personal limits. In 1997, the U.S. Consumer Safety Commission reported that 48,000 Americans were admitted to hospital emergency rooms with skateboarding-related injuries. That's 33 percent more than the previous year. Snowboarding E.R. visits were up 31 percent; mountain climbing up 20 percent. By every statistical measure available, Americans are participating in, and injuring themselves through, adventure sports at an unprecedented rate.

8   Consider Mike Carr, an environmental engineer and paraglider pilot from Denver who last year survived a bad landing that smashed 10 ribs and collapsed his lung. Paraglider pilots use feathery nylon wings to take off from mountaintops and float on thermal wind currents—a completely unpredictable ride. Carr also mountain bikes and climbs rock faces. He walked away from a 1,500-foot fall in Peru in 1988. After his recovery, he returned to paragliding. "This has taken over many of our lives," he explains. "You float like a bird out there. You can go as high as 18,000 feet and go for 200 miles. That's magic."

9   America has always been defined by risk; it may be our predominant national characteristic. It's a country founded by risk-takers fed up with the English Crown and expanded by pioneers—a word that seems utterly American. Our heritage throws up heroes—Lewis and Clark, Thomas Edison, Frederick Douglass, Teddy Roosevelt, Henry Ford, Amelia Earhart—who bucked the odds, taking perilous chances.

10   Previous generations didn't need to seek out risk; it showed up unin-

"The greater the difficulty, the more glory in surmounting it."

—Epicurus

vited and regularly: global wars, childbirth complications, diseases and pandemics from the flu to polio, dangerous products, and even the omnipresent cold-war threat of mutually assured destruction. "I just don't think extreme sports would have been popular in a ground-war era," says Dan Cady, professor of popular culture at California State University at Fullerton. "Coming back from a war and getting onto a skateboard would not seem so extreme."

But for recent generations, many of these traditional risks have been reduced by science, government, or legions of personal-injury lawyers, leaving Boomers and Generations X and Y to face less real risk. Life expectancy has increased. Violent crime is down. You are 57 percent less likely to die of heart disease than your parents; smallpox, measles, and polio have virtually been eradicated.

Combat survivors speak of the terror and the excitement of playing in a death match. Are we somehow incomplete as people if we do not taste that terror and excitement on the brink? "People are [taking risks] because everyday risk is minimized and people want to be challenged," says Joy Marr, 43, an adventure racer who was the only woman member of a five-person team that finished the 1998 Raid Gauloises, the grandaddy of all adventure races. This is a sport that requires several days of nonstop slogging, climbing, rappelling, rafting, and surviving through some of the roughest terrain in the world. Says fellow adventure racer and former Army Ranger Jonathan Senk, 35: "Our society is so surgically sterile. It's almost like our socialization just desensitizes us. Every time I'm out doing this I'm searching my soul. It's the Lewis and Clark gene, to venture out, to find what your limitations are."

13   Psychologist Frank Farley of Temple University believes that taking conscious risk involves overcoming our instincts. He points out that no other animal intentionally puts itself in peril. "The human race is particularly risk-taking compared with other species," he says. He describes risk-takers as the Type T personality, and the U.S. as a Type T nation. He breaks it down further, into Type T physical (extreme athletes) and Type T intellectual (Albert Einstein, Galileo). He warns there is also Type T negative, that is, those who are drawn to delinquency, crime, experimentation with drugs, unprotected sex, and a whole litany of destructive behaviors.

14   All these Type Ts are related, and perhaps even different aspects of the same character trait. There is, says Farley, a direct link between Einstein and BASE jumper Chance McGuire. They are different manifestations of the thrill-seeking component of our characters: Einstein was thrilled by his mental life, and McGuire—well, Chance jumps off buildings.

15   McGuire, at the moment, is driving from Hollister to another California town, Auburn, where he is planning another BASE jump from a bridge. Riding with him is Adam Fillipino, president of Consolidated Rigging, a company that manufactures parachutes and gear for BASE jumpers. McGuire talks about the leap ahead, about his feelings when he is at the exit point, and how at that moment, looking down at the ground, what goes through his mind is that this is not something a human being should be doing. But that's exactly what makes him take the leap: that sense of overcoming his inhibitions and winning what he calls the gravity game. "Football is for pansies," says McGuire. "What do you need all those

"Who does nothing need hope for nothing."

—J. C. F. von Schiller

pads for? This sport [BASE jumping] is pushing all the limits. I have a friend who calls it suicide with a kick."

16   When a BASE jumper dies, other BASE jumpers say he has "gone in," as gone into the ground or gone into a wall. "I'm sick of people going in," says Fillipino. "In the past year, a friend went in on a skydive, another drowned as a result of a BASE jump, another friend went in on a jump, another died in a skydiving plane crash. You can't escape death, but you don't want to flirt with it either." It may be the need to flirt with death, or at least take extreme chances, that has his business growing at the rate of 50 percent a year.

17   Without some expression of risk, we may never know our limits and therefore who we are as individuals. "If you don't assume a certain amount of risk," says paraglider pilot Wade Ellet, 51, "you're missing a certain amount of life." And it is by taking risks that we may flirt with greatness. "We create technologies, we make new discoveries, but in order to do that, we have to push beyond the set of rules that are governing us at that time," says psychologist Farley.

18   That's certainly what's driving McGuire and Fillipino as they position themselves on the Auburn bridge. It's dawn again, barely light, and they appear as shadows moving on the catwalk beneath the roadway. As they survey the drop zone, they compute a series of risk assessments. "It's a matter of weighing the variables," Fillipino says, pointing out that the wind, about 15 m.p.h. out of the northwest, has picked up a little more than he would like. Still, it's a clear morning, and they've climbed all the way up here. McGuire is eager to jump. But Fillipino continues to scan the valley below them, the Sacramento River rushing through the gorge.

19   Then a white parks-department SUV pulls up on an access road that winds alongside the river. Park Rangers are a notorious scourge of BASE jumpers, confiscating equipment and prosecuting for trespassing. Fillipino contemplates what would happen if the president of a BASE rig company were busted for an illegal jump. He foresees trouble with his bankers, he imagines the bad publicity his business would garner, and he says he's not going. There are some risks he is simply not willing to take.

(Karl Taro Greenfield, "Life on the Edge," *Time*, 1999)

✓ COMPREHENSION CHECKUP

Short Answer

Directions: Drawing on what you learned from the selection, fill in the blanks with an appropriate word, phrase, or sentence.

1. What is the selection about? _____

2. Give an example of each of the following. Your example should be of someone well-known or famous.
   a. Type T physical _____
   b. Type T intellectual _____
   c. Type T negative _____

3. In what ways do we face fewer risks today than previous generations did? Give some specific examples mentioned in the selection.

   a _____

   b. _____

   c. _____

   d. _____

True or False

Indicate whether the statement is true or false by writing **T** or **F** in the blank provided.

_____ 4. BASE jumping has an extremely low fatality rate.

_____ 5. Park Rangers are generally supportive of BASE jumping.

_____ 6. The BASE jumpers described in the article weigh many variables before deciding to perform a BASE jump.

_____ 7. Fillipino was reluctant to endanger his business interests with a jump off the Auburn bridge.

_____ 8. People who are Type T negative are attracted to unlawful activities.

Multiple Choice

Write the letter of the correct answer in the blank provided.

_____ 9. The author's primary purpose in writing this article was to
   a. entertain the reader with a good story about Chance McGuire and friends
   b. persuade people to try extreme sports

    c. provide information about BASE jumping and other extreme sports
    d. convince the reader that extreme sports should be outlawed

_____ 10. It is suggested in the article that
    a. extreme sports will eventually be replaced by regular sports
    b. extreme sports are responsible for many physical injuries
    c. our national heritage is replete with stories of heroic individuals who took risks
    d. both b and c

_____ 11. It is suggested in the article that
    a. our ancestors faced real adversity in the form of disease and war
    b. persons with Type T personalities especially enjoy challenges
    c. some persons who do not face real adversity in their lives turn to extreme sports to fill this void
    d. all of the above

_____ 12. What is the most likely meaning of _weekend warrior_ as used in paragraph 5?
    a. a person who likes to take chances in the summer months
    b. a person who encounters physical challenge and adversity on a daily basis
    c. a person who works hard during the week and relaxes on the weekend
    d. a person who engages in rigorous physical activity primarily on the weekend

_____ 13. Chance McGuire disparages those who
    a. have "gone in"
    b. participate in conventional sports
    c. believe paragliding is superior to BASE jumping
    d. take unwarranted risks

_____ 14. Which sentence best expresses the main idea of the selection?
    a. McGuire is a practitioner of what he calls the king of all extreme sports.
    b. It is an activity without margin for error.
    c. Still, the sport's stark metaphor—a human leaving safety behind to leap into the void—may be perfect with our times.
    d. The rising popularity of extreme sports bespeaks an eagerness on the part of millions of Americans to participate in activities closer to the metaphorical edge, where danger, skill, and fear combine to give weekend warriors and professional athletes alike a sense of pushing out personal boundaries.

Vocabulary in Context

Using the context clues provided, define the following words. Then consult your dictionary to see how accurate your definition is.

1. clearly _audible_ above the rushing water, lets out a war whoop (paragraph 1)

    Definition:_____

2. If your chute _malfunctions,_ don't bother reaching for a reserve (3)

    Definition:_____

3. a human leaving safety behind to leap into the _void_ (4)

    Definition:_____

4. smallpox, measles, and polio have virtually been *eradicated* (11)

   Definition:_____

5. experimentation with drugs, unprotected sex, and a whole *litany* of destructive behaviors (13)

   Definition:_____

Missing Letters

Fill in the missing letter for each word below. Then place that letter on the line of the quote following to complete General Patton's statement.

prac ____ itioner

confisc ____ ting

star ____

p ____ ril

s ____ ourge

vari ____ bles

steri ____ e

per ____ hed

____ nprecedented

contemp ____ ate

predomin ____ nt

ricoche ____ ing

manif ____ station

boun ____ aries

omnip ____ esent

inh ____ bitions

pan ____ y

bespea ____

____ peck

"_____.That is quite different from being rash."

—*General George S. Patton*

In Your Own Words

1. Have you ever tried an extreme sport? Do you think the benefits of participating in an extreme sport outweigh the risks? Based on the article, can you identify some common characteristics of those who participate in extreme sports?

2. Should the law place restrictions on extreme sports? What sorts of restrictions should apply?

3. Do you think that life is more risky today than it was 50 years ago? In what ways might contemporary life be more risky? In what ways might it be less risky?

4. What is the author's primary mode of writing? Give evidence to support your answer.

The Art of Writing

In a brief essay, respond to the item below.

> "Extreme athletes put not only themselves in danger by their activity; rescue workers who rescue extreme skiers from avalanches and medical workers called on to helicopter-lift athletes in trouble out of the rugged terrain are also put at risk." Is this fair?

Internet Activity

To learn more about extreme sports, consult one of the following Web sites:

http://expn.go.com

www.extreme.com

Summarize your findings.

Dean Dunbar, an extreme-sports enthusiast, has been an active participant in a variety of extreme sports despite a degenerative eye condition.

To read about Dunbar, go to www.awezome.com and click on Extreme Dreams. Summarize your findings.

Review Test: Context Clue Practice Using Textbook Material

This is a challenging test, so it might be a good idea to review the discussion of context clues given in Chapter 1. Use the context to determine the meaning of the italicized word(s).

1. What are the odds that you'll be involved in some kind of violent act within the next seven days? 1 out of 10? 1 out of 100? 1 out of 1,000? 1 out of 10,000? According to George Gerbner, the answer you give may have more to do with how much TV you watch than with the actual risk you face in the week to come. Gerbner, former dean of the Annenberg School of Communication at the University of Pennsylvania, claims that heavy television users develop an exaggerated belief in "a mean and scary world." The violence they see on the screen *cultivates* a social *paranoia* that resists notions of trustworthy people or safe environments. (p. 385)

   cultivates: _____

   paranoia: _____

2. On any given week, two-thirds of the major characters in prime-time programs are caught up in some kind of violence. Heroes are just as involved as villains, yet there is great inequality as to age, race, and gender of those on the receiving end of physical force. Old people and children are harmed at a much greater rate than young or middle-aged adults. In the pecking order of "victimage," blacks and Hispanics are killed or beaten more than their Caucasian counterparts. Gerbner notes that it's risky to be "other than clearly white." It's also dangerous to be female. The opening

lady-in-distress scene is a favorite dramatic device to *galvanize* the hero into action. And finally, blue-collar workers "get it in the neck" more often than white-collar executives. (p. 387)

galvanize: _____

3. Not surprisingly, more women than men are afraid of dark streets. But for both sexes the fear of victimization *correlates* with time spent in front of the tube. People with heavy viewing habits tend to overestimate criminal activity, believing it to be ten times worse than it really is. In actuality, muggers on the street *pose* less bodily threat than injury from cars. (p. 389)

correlates: _____

pose: _____

4. Those with heavy viewing habits are suspicious of other people's motives. They subscribe to statements that warn people to expect the worst:

"Most people are just looking out for themselves."

"In dealing with others, you can't be too careful."

"Do unto others before they do unto you."

Gerbner calls this *cynical* mind-set the "mean world syndrome."

The Annenberg evidence suggests that the minds of heavy TV viewers become *fertile* ground for *sowing* thoughts of danger. (p. 389)

cynical: _____

fertile: _____

sowing: _____

5. Gerbner also explains the constant viewer's greater *apprehension* by the process of *resonance*. Many viewers have had at least one firsthand experience with physical violence—armed robbery, rape, bar fight, mugging, auto crash, military combat, or a lover's quarrel that became vicious. The actual *trauma* was bad enough. But he thinks that a repeated symbolic portrayal on the TV screen can cause the viewer to replay the real-life experience over and over in his or her mind. Constant viewers who have experienced physical violence get a double dose. (p. 391)

apprehension: _____

resonance: _____

trauma: _____

6. Because advertising rates are tied directly to a program's share of the market, television professionals are experts at gaining and holding attention. Social critics *decry* the *gratuitous* violence on television, but Stanford psychologist Albert Bandura denies that aggression is unrelated to the story line. The scenes of physical violence are especially compelling because they suggest that violence is a preferred solution to human problems. Violence is presented as a strategy for life. (p. 369)

decry: _____

gratuitous: _____

7. On every type of program, television draws in viewers by placing attractive people in front of the camera. There are very few overweight bodies or pimply faces on TV. When the *winsome* star roughs up a few hoods to help the lovely young woman, aggression is given a positive cast.

   winsome: _____

8. Using violence in the race for ratings not only draws an attentive audience, it transmits responses that we, as viewers, might never have considered before. The media expand our repertoire of behavioral options far beyond what we would discover by trial and error and in ways more varied than we would observe in people we know. Bandura says it's fortunate that people learn from *vicarious* observation, since mistakes could prove costly or fatal. Without putting himself at risk, Tyler Richie, a 10-year-old boy, is able to discover that a knife fighter holds a switchblade at an inclined angle of forty-five degrees and that he jabs up rather than lunging down. We hope that Ty will never have an occasion to put his knowledge into practice. (p. 370)

   vicarious: _____

9. We observe many forms of behavior in others that we never perform ourselves. Without sufficient motivation, Ty may never imitate the violence he sees on TV. Bandura says that the effects of TV violence will be greatly *diminished* if a youngster's parents punish or disapprove of aggression. Yet Ty also shares responsibility for his own actions. (p. 371)

   diminished: _____

(Em Griffen, *A First Look at Communication Theory*, 6/e, 2006)

SELECTION

"All clues, however far-fetched, were followed up, but no trace of Mona Lisa *could be found."*

GETTING THE PICTURE

The article below describes the theft of Leonardo da Vinci's *Mona Lisa*, one of the most famous paintings in the world. Da Vinci (1452–1519) was an Italian artist, scientist, and inventor. Because of his widely varied interests, he created few paintings in his lifetime. The *Mona Lisa* was probably commissioned by a local merchant who wanted a portrait of his young wife. By portraying the young woman in a relaxed, informal way, the painting broke many of the stylistic barriers of the time. Da Vinci, who studied anatomy, created especially lifelike hands. But the eyes of the *Mona Lisa* and the enigmatic half-smile are the painting's best-known features. The *Mona Lisa* hung in Napoleon's bedroom until it was transferred to the Louvre in 1804.

Mona Lisa (1503–1506) *by Leonardo di ser Piero da Vinci*

BRUSHING UP ON VOCABULARY

enigmatic perplexing or mysterious. It is derived from the Greek words *ainigma* and *ainissesthai,* meaning "to speak in riddles." To the ancient Greeks, riddles were a serious business: If you were unable to answer one correctly, you might be handed over to the poser of the riddle for a lifetime of servitude.

patriotism devoted love, and support for and defense of one's country. This word comes from the Greek words *pater,* meaning "father," and *patrios,* meaning "founded by the forefathers." The word *patriotism* referred to someone who was so devoted to his family that he would defend them and the land that his "fathers" founded at great cost.

Excerpt from

GILBERT'S LIVING WITH ART

by Mark Getlein

VINCENZO PERUGIA

At 7:20 on the morning of August 21, 1911, three members of the maintenance 1 staff at the Louvre paused briefly in front of the *Mona Lisa*. The chief of maintenance remarked to his workers, "This is the most valuable picture in the world." Just over an hour later the three men again passed through the Salon Carré, where Leonardo's masterpiece hung, and saw that the painting was no longer in its place. The maintenance chief joked that museum officials had removed the picture for fear he and his crew would steal it. The joke soon proved to be an uncomfortably hollow one. *Mona Lisa* was gone.

Thus begins the story of the most famous art theft in history, of the most fa- 2 mous painting in the world, and of the man who would inevitably become the most famous art thief of all time: Vincenzo Perugia.

French newspapers announced the catastrophe under the banner headline 3 "Unimaginable!" All during the weeks that followed, rumors abounded. A man carrying a blanket-covered parcel had been seen jumping onto the train for Bordeaux. A mysterious draped package had been spotted on a ship to New York, a ship to South America, a ship to Italy. The painting had been scarred with acid, had been dumped in the sea. All clues, however far-fetched, were followed up, but no trace of the *Mona Lisa* could be found.

More than two years would pass before the thief surfaced. Then, in November of 4 1913, an art dealer in Italy received a letter from a man who signed himself "Leonard." Would the dealer like to have the *Mona Lisa?* Would he. Of course it was a joke. But was it? The dealer arranged to meet "Leonard" in a hotel room in Florence. "Leonard" produced a wooden box filled with junk. The junk was removed, a false bottom came out of the box, and there, wrapped in red silk and perfectly preserved, was the smiling face of *Mona Lisa.* The dealer swallowed his shock and phoned for the police.

"Leonard" was actually an Italian named Vincenzo Perugia—a house painter 5 who had once done some contract work in the Louvre. As he told the story of the theft, it was amazingly simple. On the morning in question Perugia, dressed in a workman's smock, walked into the museum, nodded to several of the other workers, and chose a moment when no one else was in the Salon Carré to unhook the painting from the wall. Then he slipped into a stairwell, removed the picture from its frame, stuck it under his smock, and walked out. Stories that Perugia had accomplices have never been proved.

What were the thief's motives? And why, after pulling off what can only be de- 6 scribed as the heist of the century, did he so naively offer the painting to the Italian dealer? Perugia claimed he was motivated by patriotism. *Mona Lisa* was an Italian painting by an Italian artist. Believing (mistakenly) that it had been stolen by Napoleon to hang in France, he wanted to restore it to its rightful home. At the same time, however, he expected to be "rewarded" by the Italian government for his heroic act and thought $100,000 would be a good amount. No one shared this point of view.

Perugia was tried, convicted, and sentenced to a year in prison. After his re- 7 lease he served in the army, married, settled in Paris, and operated a paint store. Soon Perugia, who had so briefly captured the world's headlines, settled back into the obscurity from which he had emerged.

And *Mona Lisa.* After a triumphal tour of several Italian museums, she was 8 returned to France. She hangs—at least as of this writing—safely in the Louvre. Romantics say her smile is even more enigmatic than before.

———————————

(Mark Getlein, *Gilbert's Living with Art,* 6/e, 2002)

✓ COMPREHENSION CHECKUP

Short Answer

1. The topic of this selection is _____ Mona lisa _____

2. The main idea is found in paragraph ____ 2 _____

3. The author's purpose in writing this selection is to _____

4. The mode of rhetoric is _____

True or False

Indicate whether the statement is true or false by writing **T** or **F** in the blank provided.

_____ 5. The man calling himself "Leonard" was actually Vincenzo Perugia.

_____ 6. The author implies that Perugia was not motivated solely by patriotism.

_____ 7. A *naive* individual is sophisticated and worldly.

_____ 8. The French police immediately settled on Perugia as the most likely culprit.

_____ 9. The painting was finally recovered in Rome, Italy.

Multiple Choice

Write the letter of the correct answer in the blank provided.

_____ 10. Perugia was able to steal the *Mona Lisa* successfully because
  a. he had previously worked at the Louvre and thus did not seem out of place
  b. he was wearing clothing that was loose enough to conceal a painting
  c. he was able to steal the painting when no one was looking
  d. all of the above

_____ 11. Perugia was under the impression that
  a. he was engaging in a patriotic gesture
  b. he would be richly rewarded for his services by the Italian government
  c. he would easily be able to sell the painting for millions of dollars
  d. both a and b

_____ 12. We can assume that
  a. Perugia was no longer welcome in his native Italy
  b. the government of France forgave Perugia once his debt to society had been paid
  c. Perugia continued to enjoy his status as a celebrity
  d. the *Mona Lisa* is back in Italy where it belongs

_____ 13. The reader can conclude that
  a. the *Mona Lisa* was seriously damaged by Perugia's theft
  b. Perugia had thought about how to conceal the *Mona Lisa*
  c. Perugia had no intention of parting with the *Mona Lisa*
  d. the chief of maintenance was behind the scheme to steal the painting

_____ 14. The reader can conclude that
  a. the *Mona Lisa* is more carefully protected today
  b. the Italian government determined that the *Mona Lisa* belongs in Italy
  c. the rumors that the painting had been defaced proved to be correct
  d. many hours went by before the painting was discovered to be missing

Vocabulary Matching

Match the vocabulary words in Column A with their synonyms in Column B. Place the correct letter in the space provided.

Column A

_____ 1. inevitably

_____ 2. hollow

_____ 3. famous

_____ 4. catastrophe

_____ 5. far-fetched

_____ 6. surfaced

Column B

a. fiasco; disaster

b. improbable; unlikely

c. protected; unchanged

d. renowned; celebrated

e. empty; false

f. robbery; burglary

Column A   Column B

_____ 7. preserved   g. being unknown

_____ 8. naively   h. joyful; celebratory

_____ 9. heist   i. certainly; unavoidably

_____ 10. obscurity   j. appeared; emerged

_____ 11. triumphal   k. puzzling; mysterious

_____ 12. enigmatic   l. artlessly; credulously

In Your Own Words

1. Perugia was sentenced to a year and two weeks in prison for the theft of the *Mona Lisa,* a surprisingly brief term considering the magnitude of the crime. Why do you suppose he got such a light sentence?

2. Do you think Perugia's sentence was lengthy enough to serve as a deterrent to future art thieves?

3. Have you noticed that many art museums appear to have relatively lax security measures in place? What steps do the museums you have visited take to safeguard their paintings from theft or vandalism?

4. Many museums safeguard valuable paintings by putting them inside glass or plastic viewing boxes. In fact, Perugia himself built *Mona Lisa's* viewing box. How do you feel about viewing paintings through "glass"?

5. In this case, do the ends justify the means?

The Art of Writing

1. Perugia claims he stole the *Mona Lisa* because she was so beautiful and had bewitched him. How do you account for the painting's universal appeal? Write a short essay giving your opinion.

2. Initially, Perugia was a hero to Italians because of his desire to relocate the *Mona Lisa* to Italy. How do you feel about turning a thief into a hero? Are we still likely to do that today? Can you think of any recent instances?

Internet Activity

1. Consult the following Web site to learn more about other famous art thefts including Sweden's National Museum heist, the stolen *Scream,* the Manchester robbery, the Van Gogh Museum robbery, and the biggest U.S. art theft. Briefly summarize your findings.

   www.crimelibrary.com/gangsters_outlaws/outlaws/major_art_thefts/index.html

2. Art theft continues to be a worldwide problem. In 1986, a gang of Irish thieves broke into an estate in Ireland and made off with eleven paintings, including works by Goya, Rubens, Gainsborough, and Vermeer. So far, none have been recovered. To find out about works of art stolen recently, go to the following Web site and click on "Update."

   www.saztv.com

3. Find an article about a recent art theft, and write a description of a stolen painting. What is the overall tone of the painting that was stolen?

Vocabulary Puzzle

Directions: Use the vocabulary words to complete the puzzle.

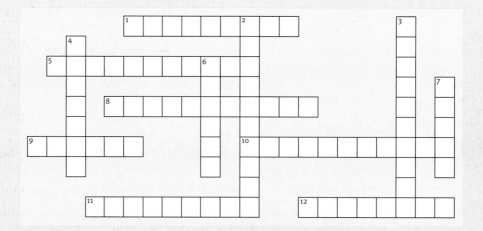

abounded   far-fetched   inevitably   obscurity
accomplices   heist   masterpiece   parcel
catastrophe   hollow   naively   romantics

ACROSS CLUES

1. people preoccupied with love
5. a momentous tragic event
8. a supreme artistic achievement
9. false or meaningless
10. people who knowingly help another in a crime or wrongdoing
11. having little or no prominence or distinction
12. occurred in great quantities

DOWN CLUES

2. has to be expected
3. improbable (omit hyphen)
4. showing a lack of judgment or information
6. package
7. robbery or hold-up

MASTERY TEST: Vincenzo Perugia

Main Idea

_____ 1. Which of the following statements from this selection represents the main idea of paragraph 3?
   a. A man carrying a blanket-covered parcel had been seen jumping onto the train for Bordeaux.
   b. French newspapers announced the catastrophe under the banner headline "Unimaginable!"
   c. All clues, however far-fetched, were followed up, but no trace of the *Mona Lisa* could be found.
   d. The painting had been scarred with acid, had been dumped in the sea.

_____ 2. Which of the following best states the implied main idea of paragraph 6?
   a. Perugia managed to pull off the heist of the century.
   b. Perugia claims he was motivated by patriotism to steal the *Mona Lisa* and return it to Italy; still he wanted the Italian government to reward him.
   c. Perugia acted naively in trying to rid himself of the *Mona Lisa*.
   d. Perugia stole a painting he loved for his own pleasure and satisfaction.

Supporting Details

_____ 3. All of the following were given as rumors for the whereabouts of the *Mona Lisa* **except**
   a. she was headed to Bordeaux
   b. she was headed back to Italy
   c. she had been dumped in the sea after being damaged
   d. she was hidden in a seldom-opened annex at the Louvre

_____ 4. All of the following were given as steps in Perugia's successful attempt to steal the *Mona Lisa* **except**
   a. unhooked the painting from the wall
   b. slipped into a stairwell
   c. signaled the maintenance chief to assist him
   d. stuck the painting under his smock

_____ 5. All of the following occurred after Perugia stole the *Mona Lisa* **except**
   a. he contacted an art dealer and met him in a hotel room
   b. he returned to Italy and became a painter
   c. he served in the army and married
   d. he served a year in prison

_____ 6. All of the following events occurred in the *Mona Lisa*'s history **except**
   a. the *Mona Lisa* was stolen by Vincenzo Perugia in 1911
   b. the *Mona Lisa* toured several Italian museums
   c. Napoleon stole the *Mona Lisa* from Italy so that France would have it
   d. the *Mona Lisa* was recovered in 1913

MASTERY TEST: Vincenzo Perugia *(continued)*

Context

_____ 7. Use the context clues to select the best definition of the italicized word. ". . . no *trace* of the *Mona Lisa* could be found." (paragraph 3)
  a. visible sign
  b. route
  c. touch
  d. mark

_____ 8. Use context clues to select the best meaning of the sentence. "The joke soon proved to be an uncomfortably hollow one." (paragraph 1)
  a. The joke wasn't funny anymore.
  b. It turned out that no one understood the joke.
  c. The workmen needed to stop joking around and get busy.
  d. It took a moment, but then the workmen got the joke and laughed.

_____ 9. Use the context clues to select the best definition of the italicized word. ". . . settled back into the *obscurity* from which he had emerged." (paragraph 7)
  a. prominence
  b. anonymity
  c. poverty
  d. turmoil

Purpose

_____ 10. Which of the following describes the author's purpose in writing this selection?
  a. The author wants to emphasize the evils of art theft.
  b. The author wants to explain some of the mystery surrounding the *Mona Lisa*'s smile.
  c. The author wishes to encourage museums to take proper security measures to protect valuable paintings.
  d. The author wishes to describe an unusual theft by an unlikely thief.

Brain Teasers

Formulas

Decipher the following teasers. The first letter of each word is provided.

1. 2 Ps in a P _____

2. 4Q in a G _____

3. I H a D by MLK _____

4. 3 S to a T _____

5. 100 P in a D _____

6. 9 I in a B G (related to a sport) _____

7. 4 W on a C _____

8. 12 S of the Z _____

9. SW and the 7D (characters in a Disney movie) _____

10. HDD –TMRUTC (nursery rhyme) _____

Kinship Riddles

1. Your grandmother has four daughters. Three of them are your aunts. Who is the fourth one?

   _____

2. If Mark's father is Tom's son, how is Mark related to Tom?

   _____

3. Who is your mother's brother's brother-in-law?

   _____

VOCABULARY   Unit 2: More Homonyms and Other Confusing Words

This unit extends the coverage of homonyms and other confusing words that we began in Chapter 2.

loose	An adverb or adjective meaning "free or released from fastening or attachment." *The dog was running* loose *in the neighborhood instead of being on a leash.*
lose	A verb meaning "to come to be without." *If G.E. and Honeywell merge, Carol will probably* lose *her job.*
passed	A verb, the past tense of the verb *pass. The quarterback* passed *the ball to the tight end, who ran for a touchdown. The E.S.L. student* passed *the TOEFL exam. My grandfather* passed *away last year.* Each of these sentences uses the word passed as a verb expressing action.

past   A noun meaning "former time." *In the* past, *students used typewriters instead of computers.*

Also, an adjective meaning "former." *One of our* past *presidents was Harry Truman.*

Also, an adverb meaning "going beyond something." *Motel 6 is just* past *the Fashion Square shopping center.*

Think about this sentence: This *past* week has *passed* by quickly.

peace   A noun meaning "freedom from dissension or hostilities." *The United States would like Israelis and Palestinians to agree on terms for* peace.

piece   A noun meaning "a limited portion or quantity of something." *Do you want a big* piece *of pumpkin pie or a small one?*

personal   An adjective meaning "concerning a particular person." *Our* personal *lives are often quite different from our public lives.*

personnel   A noun meaning "the body of persons employed in an organization." *The airline employed a wide variety of* personnel, *including pilots, baggage handlers, and ticketing agents.*

Think about this sentence: Sometimes it is not a good idea to share too much *personal* information with other *personnel* in your office.

rain   A noun meaning "water that falls to earth in drops formed from moisture in the air." *It often seems like we have either too much or too little* rain.

rein   A noun meaning "a leather strap fastened to each end of a bit for guiding or controlling an animal." *The stagecoach driver held on tightly to the horses'* reins.

reign   A noun meaning "period of rule or government by a monarch." *The thousand-year* reign *of kings in France came to an end with the execution of King Louis the XVI.*

right   An adjective meaning "in accordance with what is good, proper, just." *The student circled the* right *answer on the quiz. After two years working as a waitress, Emily made the* right *decision to return to college.*

Also, an adjective meaning "opposite of left." *At 18 months, Zachary uses his* right *hand to throw a ball.*

Also, a noun meaning "something that is due to anyone by just claim." *The court gave Carl the* right *to see his daughter on weekends and holidays.*

rite   A noun meaning "a formal ceremony." *Fraternities have increasingly fallen into trouble with school authorities for having initiation* rites *that include hazing.*

write   A verb meaning "to form words or letters; to send a message in writing." *When did you first learn how to* write *your name?*

wright   A combining form meaning "a person who makes or builds something." *William Shakespeare is one of the most famous play*wrights.

Think about this sentence: It is *right* that we should attend the last *rites* of the well-known play*wright.*

stationary	An adjective meaning "not moving." *The cyclist bought a* stationary *bike so that he could practice riding indoors during the winter.*
stationery	A noun meaning "writing paper." *The new bride bought special* stationery *to use for her thank-you notes.*
their	An adjective meaning "possession." Their *apartment was located near the college.*
there	An adverb meaning "direction." *Notice how the word* here *appears in the word* there. *The student union is over* there. Also, a pronoun used to begin a sentence or phrase. There *is an e-mail message waiting for you.*
they're	A contraction for "they are." They're *all packed and ready to go on their trip.*

Think about this sentence: *They're* supposed to be in class, so why do I see them over *there* talking with *their* friends.

tortuous	An adjective meaning "full of twists and turns." *Although it can be a grand adventure, rafting the* tortuous *Colorado River can also be dangerous.*
torturous	An adjective meaning "involving great pain or agony." *Prior to the use of local anesthetics, extracting a tooth was a* torturous *business.*
vain	An adjective meaning "having an excessively high opinion of oneself." *Carly Simon wrote a well-known song titled "You're So* Vain." *Supposedly it's about Mick Jagger of* The Rolling Stones. Also, an adjective meaning "futile." *The joint rescue effort was a* vain *attempt to free the sailors trapped in the submarine.*
vein	A noun meaning "any blood vessel that carries blood back to the heart from some part of the body." *Surface* veins *are often visible just under the skin.*
vane	A noun, a short form of weather *vane. The weather* vane *indicated the direction the wind was blowing.* (weather instrument that goes on top of barns)
weather	A noun meaning "the state of the atmosphere with respect to wind, temperature, cloudiness, etc." *The dry* weather *during the summer led to many forest fires.*
whether	A conjunction used to introduce two or more alternatives. *It makes no difference to me* whether *or not he comes to the party.*
who	A subjective pronoun meaning "what person or persons or which person or persons." *I don't believe you did that paper all by yourself.* Who *helped you?* (Here *who* is the subject of the sentence.)
whom	A pronoun used as the object of a verb or preposition. *To* whom *do you want to give the money?* (Here *whom* is an object of the preposition

to.) *Whom will you meet after the game?* (Here *you* is the subject of the sentence and *whom* is the direct object of the verb *meet*.)

who's   A contraction of "who is." *Who's going with me to the movie tonight?*

whose   A possessive adjective meaning "done by whom or which or having to do with whom or which." *Whose car is this? Your lights are on! The Ford F-150 is a truck* whose *popularity is never in doubt.*

your   A possessive adjective meaning "belonging to you or done by you." *Your classes have been scheduled for mornings only, so that you can work in the afternoons.*

you're   A contraction for "you are." *You're on the list to receive tickets to the rock concert.*

Vocabulary Unit 2 Puzzle

ACROSS CLUES

1. _____ car are we going to take?
2. Juan and Luz Garza purchased _____ new home in December.
3. Boot Camp is considered a _____ of passage for soldiers.
8. Objects are _____ unless moved.
9. The bus passengers were scared when the bus began its descent down the _____ mountain road.
11. The _____ treaty ending World War II was signed aboard the U.S.S. *Missouri*.
13. The _____ manager at Hewlett-Packard hired several new computer technicians.
16. Some people don't believe it matters _____ we have a Republican or a Democrat in the White House.
17. Is _____ going to be a test on homonyms tomorrow?
21. The cowboy saw a snake and pulled on his horse's _____.
23. _____ going to win the World Series this year?
24. What are you going to do if you _____ your cleaning deposit on the apartment?
25. Some people think that "might makes _____."

DOWN CLUES

1. Arthur Miller, who wrote *Death of a Salesman*, is a famous play _____.
4. Before the invention of the Aqua-Lung, diving was _____.
5. Jacob's uncle _____ away at the age of 90.
6. You might want to go to a _____ store to buy school supplies.
7. Katie hoped her _____ tooth would fall out quickly because she wanted money from the tooth fairy.
10. Queen Elizabeth II has had a long _____.
12. The _____ outside was unbearably hot and humid.
14. The candidate admitted that he had made mistakes in the _____.
15. You need to supply a list of _____ references when you apply for a job.
18. *Did Rosa's mother _____ from Peru or Colombia?
19. _____s carry blood back to the heart.
20. The weather _____ indicated a strong wind from the north.
22. _____ chances of doing well in college are better if you attend class regularly.
23. _____ was our most intelligent president?

*Answer found in Homonyms (Vocabulary Unit 1).

Transition Words and Patterns of Organization

The Cardsharps (1594) BY *MICHELANGELO MERISI DA CARAVAGGIO*

Kimbell Art Museum, Fort Worth, TX. Photo: Erich Lessing/Art Resource, NY.

View and Reflect

1. What is the man in the background doing with his right hand?
2. What is the man to the right side of the picture doing behind his back?
3. What is the person to the left of the picture doing? Is he aware of what the other two people are doing?
4. What are your feelings about what's happening in the painting?

Transition Words

When you are reading, it is important to pay close attention to **transition words.** These special words show the relationships between ideas within sentences and within paragraphs. Just as good drivers learn to watch the road ahead closely, using signposts or markers to make their trips easier and safer, good readers learn to pay attention to the author's transition words, making the writing clearer and more comprehensible.

Look at the sentences below. The addition of a transition word signaling a contrast makes a big difference in our ability to understand Juan's situation.

1. Juan was very eager to buy a new home. The thought of leaving the familiar surroundings of his apartment filled him with dread.

2. Juan was very eager to buy a new home. *However,* the thought of leaving the familiar surroundings of his apartment filled him with dread.

The first example doesn't really make a lot of sense. If Juan is so eager to buy a home, why is he filled with dread? The addition of the transition word in the second sentence makes the situation clear. Although Juan wants to buy a home, he is understandably reluctant to give up his safe and comfortable surroundings.

Now look at these two sentences:

1. Trent did poorly in his math classes. He decided to switch his major to economics.

2. *Because* Trent did poorly in his math classes, he decided to switch his major to economics.

The first example makes us guess at the relationship between the two sentences. The addition of the transition word clarifies this relationship.

It's important to note that while lists of transition words are helpful, the groupings of the words given in this chart and in the one on page 170 are not perfect. Many of these words may be used in more than one category. The only reliable way to determine the function of a transition word is by studying the context of the sentence and the paragraph.

Following is a list of transition words, divided into groups by the information they convey. Review this list and then complete the exercises that follow.

4. (example) _____, football players explain a win as being due to their athletic skills but blame the condition of the field for a loss.

5. (comparison) _____, in games that combine skill and chance, winners easily attribute their successes to their skill while losers attribute their losses to chance.

6. When I win at Scrabble, it's (cause and effect) _____ of my verbal dexterity; when I lose, it's (cause and effect) _____ "Who could get anywhere with a Q without a U?"

7. Politicians attribute their success to (steps in a process) _____ their hard work, _____ their reputation, and _____ their strategy. They attribute their losses to factors beyond their control.

Some Common Patterns of Organization

Writers organize their supporting sentences and ideas using **patterns of organization.** Some common patterns of organization are:

1. Classification or division
2. Cause and effect
3. Examples and illustrations
4. Comparison and contrast
5. Listing
6. Steps in a process
7. Definition
8. Chronological order
9. Spatial organization

A writer's chosen pattern of organization will affect the transition words that are used. In the sections that follow, we will discuss patterns of organization and the relationships between patterns of organization and transition words.

The reading selections in this chapter, dealing with ethical and unethical behavior, will give you an opportunity to study some of these patterns of organization and their associated transition words.

Classification or Division

Classification is the process of organizing information into categories. A category is created by noticing and defining group characteristics. The categories we create make it easier to analyze, discuss, and draw conclusions.

Often paragraphs are organized using classification. In the paragraphs below, the author organizes lying into three specific categories. This makes it easier for us to understand and remember the information being presented. Read the paragraphs and then look at the explanation of outlining that follows in Study Technique 4.

Ways to Categorize Lies

"No one means all he says and yet very few say all they mean."

—Henry Adams

This five-part scheme is one way to **categorize** lies.

1. *Lies to save face.* Many lies are committed as a way to prevent embarrassment. Lying to protect another from embarrassment could be called "tact."

2. *Lies to avoid tension or conflict.* Sometimes it seems worthwhile to tell a small lie to avoid conflict. It may be easier to explain our behavior in dishonest terms than to tell the truth and make matters worse.

3. *Lies to guide social interaction.* Sometimes we lie to keep everyday relationships running smoothly.

4. *Lies to expand or reduce relationships.* Some lies are designed to make relationships grow. In one study, a majority of college students (both men and women) willingly lied about themselves to improve their chances of getting a date with an attractive partner. At other times, people lie to end a relationship entirely.

5. *Lies to gain power.* Sometimes we tell lies to show that we're in control of a situation. Lying to gather confidential information—even for a good cause—also falls into the **category** of lying to gain power.

Ronald B. Adler and Russell F. Proctor II, *Looking Out Looking In,* 13th edition, Boston: Wadsworth Cengage, 2011, p. 326–327.

STUDY TECHNIQUE 4

Outlining

An outline is an orderly arrangement of ideas going from the general to the specific. An outline shows the relationship and importance of ideas by using a system of Roman numerals for main headings (I, II, III, etc.), capital letters for subheadings (A, B, C, etc.), and numbers for sub-subheadings (1, 2, 3, etc.). Whether you are using outlining to organize class notes or a reading selection, only the most important points should be included.

A partial outline of the previous selection follows. Notice how the outline highlights the paragraphs' main ideas and major and minor supporting details. It also illustrates classification and division.

I. There are five basic categories of lies (MI)
  A. Lies to save face (MSD)
    1. Prevent embarrassment (msd)
    2. Often called "tact" (msd)
  B. Lies to avoid tension or conflict (MSD)
    1. Prevent a conflict (msd)
    2. Matters aren't made worse (msd)
  C. Lies to guide social interaction (MSD)
  D. Lies to expand or reduce relationships (MSD)
    1. People lie to get a date (msd)
    2. People lie to end a relationship (msd)
  E. Lies to gain power (MSD)
    1. People lie to control a situation (msd)
    2. People lie to gain confidential information

Cause and Effect

In a cause-and-effect relationship, one thing causes another thing to happen. The second event is the effect or result of the first event. Try reading the following anecdote to locate cause-and-effect relationships.

It's Saturday morning. Bob is just about to set off on a round of golf when he realizes that he forgot to tell his wife that the guy who fixes the washing machine is coming around at noon. **So** Bob heads back to the clubhouse and phones home.

"Hello," says a little girl's voice.

"Hi, honey, it's Daddy," says Bob. "Is Mommy near the phone?"

"No, Daddy. She's upstairs in the bedroom with Uncle Frank."

After a brief pause, Bob says, "But you haven't got an Uncle Frank, honey!"

"Yes, I do, and he's upstairs in the bedroom with Mommy!"

"Okay, **then**. Here's what I want you to do. Put down the phone, run upstairs and knock on the bedroom door and shout to Mommy and Uncle Frank that my car has just pulled up outside the house."

"Okay, Daddy!"

A few minutes later, the little girl comes back to the phone.

"Well, I did what you said, Daddy."

"And what was the **result?**"

"Well, Mommy jumped out of bed with no clothes on and ran around screaming; **then** she tripped over the rug and fell down the front steps and she's just lying there. I think she's dead."

"Oh my God! And what was the **reaction** of Uncle Frank?"

"He jumped out of bed with no clothes on, and **then** he was all scared and **so** he jumped out the back window into the swimming pool. He must have forgotten that last week you took out all the water to clean it, **so** he hit the bottom of the swimming pool and is just lying there, not moving. He may be dead, too."

There is a long pause, **then** Bob says, "Swimming pool? Is this 854-7039?"

Now complete the followings sentences, inserting the effect of the given cause.

1. Because Bob forgot to tell his wife about the repairman, he _____.

2. Because the little girl informed Mommy and Uncle Frank that Daddy was home, they _____.

3. Because Bob called the wrong number, he _____.

Exercise 2: Practice with Classification and Division and Cause and Effect Transition Words

Directions: Fill in the blank with an appropriate transition word from the list below. Make sure the sentence makes sense with the transition word you choose.

as a result   because   cause   classified   combine   divide

1. According to criminologist Albert Cohen, young urban males can be _____classified_____ into three general categories: corner boy, delinquent boy, and college boy.

2. We can _____Divide_____ delinquent boys into two groups: those who eventually become law-abiding citizens and those who do not.

3. According to Cohen, we can ___Combine___ all three groups to form a
(classification) subculture that has its own norms, beliefs, and values that are distinct from those of the dominant culture.

(Information from Freda Adler, et al., *Criminology and the Criminal Justice System*, 6/e, 2008)

4. Repeatedly, lie detectors have been proved to be unreliable indicators of lying. ___As a result___, the American Psychological Association has adopted a resolution stating that the evidence for the effectiveness of polygraphs "is still unsatisfactory."
(Cause and Effect)

5. ___Because___ of skepticism about the validity of lie detector tests, many employers have turned instead to written "integrity" tests.
(Cause and Effect)

6. The many sources of possible error in the use of lie detectors ___Cause___ operators to make mistakes when trying to judge another person's honesty.
(Cause and Effect)

(Robert S. Feldman, *Understanding Psychology*, 5/e, 1999)

Examples and Illustration

A paragraph of examples usually gives a general statement of the main idea and then presents one or more concrete examples or illustrations to provide support for this idea. The terms *example* and *illustration* are often used interchangeably, but an illustration can be thought of as an example that is longer and more involved. A main idea might be supported by only one "illustration." Many writers place the most important or convincing example or illustration either first, as an attention-getter, or last, as a dramatic climax.

The following paragraphs provide an illustration of the main idea that most people are basically trustworthy.

"I think that we may safely trust a good deal more than we do."

—Henry David Thoreau

How about some good news for a change? Something to consider when you are in a people-are-no-darn-good mood?

Here's a phrase we hear a lot: "You can't trust anybody anymore." Doctors and politicians and merchants and salesman. They're all out to rip you off, right?

It ain't necessarily so.

To **demonstrate**, a man named Steven Brill tested the theory, in New York City, with taxicab drivers. Brill posed as a well-to-do foreigner with little knowledge of English. He got into several dozen taxis around New York City to see how many drivers would cheat him. His friends predicted in advance that most would take advantage of him in some way.

One driver out of thirty-seven cheated him. The rest took him directly to his destination and charged him correctly. Several refused to take him when his destination was only a block or two away, even getting out of their cabs to show him how close he already was. The greatest irony of all was that several drivers warned him that New York City was full of crooks and to be careful.

You will continue to read stories of crookedness and corruption—of policemen who lie and steal, doctors who reap where they do not sew, politicians on the take. Don't be misled. They are news because they are the exceptions. The evidence suggests that you can trust a lot more people than you think. The evidence suggests that a lot of people believe that. A recent survey by Gallup indicates that 70 percent of the people believe that most people can be trusted most of the time.

Who says people are no darn good? What kind of talk is that?

(Robert L. Fulghum, *All I Really Need to Know I Learned in Kindergarten*, 1988)

Comparison-Contrast

A comparison shows similarities, while a contrast shows differences. Sometimes a writer both compares and contrasts at the same time. In the paragraphs that follow, the author compares and contrasts amateur and professional burglars and burglaries. After you've read the excerpt and done the exercise, look at Study Technique 5, which shows you how to make a comparison-contrast chart.

"The study of crime begins with the knowledge of oneself."

—Henry Miller

George Rengert and John Wasilchick conducted extensive interviews with suburban burglars in an effort to understand their techniques. They found significant **differences** with respect to several factors.

1. *The amount of planning that precedes a burglary.* **Unlike** amateurs, professional burglars plan more.
2. *The extent to which a burglar engages in systematic selection of a home.* Most burglars examine the obvious clues, such as presence of a burglar alarm, a watchdog, mail piled up in the mailbox, and newspapers on a doorstep. **On the other hand,** more experienced burglars look for subtle clues such as closed windows coupled with air conditioners that are turned off.

In addition, Rengert and Wasilchick examined the use of time and place in burglary, and they discovered that time is a critical factor to all burglars, for three reasons.

Both amateur and professional burglars must minimize the time spent in targeted places so as not to reveal an intent to burglarize.

Also, opportunities for burglary occur only when a dwelling is unguarded or unoccupied, usually during daytime. (Many burglars would call in sick so often that they would be fired from their legitimate jobs, **while** others simply quit their jobs because they interfered with their burglaries.)

Further, burglars have "working hours." Many have time available only during a limited number of hours, particularly if they have a legitimate job. One experienced burglar stated that "the best time to do crime is between 8:00 and 9:00 A.M. when mothers are taking the kids to school." **In contrast,** another stated that the best time is in the middle of the afternoon when people are at work.

(Freda Adler, et al., *Criminology*, 5/e, 2004)

Exercise 3: Practice with Comparison-Contrast and Example Transition Words

Directions: Fill in the blank with an appropriate transition word from the list below. Make sure the sentence makes sense with the transition word you choose.

but   despite   example   for example   particular   specifically

Example/illustration

1. A variety of strategies are used to steal vehicles for financial gain. _____ *for Example* _____, the "strip and run" strategy occurs when a thief steals a car, strips it for its parts, and then abandons the vehicle.

2. Another _____ *Example* _____ is the "scissors job," which occurs when scissors are jammed into certain ignition locks in mostly American-made cars, allowing the thief to start the car easily.

3. The "insurance fraud scheme," which occurs when an owner reports his or her car stolen and hides the car for approximately 30 days, or until after the claim is paid, is another _____ *particular* _____ strategy that involves deceit.

4. A combination of motor vehicle theft and robbery is _____ *Specifically* _____ known as "carjacking."

(Information from Freda Adler, et al., *Criminology and the Criminal Justice System,* 6/e, 2008)

Contrast

5. _____ *Despite* _____ the fact that we condemn lying, politicians who tell the truth are rejected by voters.

Contrast

6. We profess to be a country that cherishes our constitution and due process rights; _____ *But* _____ we clap and cheer in movie theaters when "Dirty Harry" types kill the "bad guys."

(Jocelyn M. Polluck, *Ethics in Crime and Justice,* 3/e, 1998)

STUDY TECHNIQUE 5

Creating a Comparison–Contrast Chart

A comparison-contrast chart, like the one here, shows similarities, differences, or similarities and differences between two or more things. When studying closely related topics or reading texts that use the comparison-contrast pattern of development, consider creating a comparison-contrast chart to help you sort out and remember similarities and differences.

The comparison-contrast chart at right lists the differences and similarities discussed in the excerpt on suburban burglars on page 157. Completing this chart will help you learn the main supporting details discussed in the excerpt.

SUBURBAN BURGLARS

Differences

AMATEURS	PROFESSIONALS
1. Plan less	1. Plan more
2. Examine obvious clues	2. _____

Similarities

1. Both must minimize time spent in targeted places.

2. Opportunities are usually best in the daytime.

3. _____

Listing

When an author simply lists information without regard to order, the pattern of organization is referred to as listing or enumeration. Sometimes, authors use numbers (1, 2, 3), letters (a, b, c), or bullets (•) to point out the individual items in the list. Other times, they say *first, second, third*, etc. or *in addition, next*, or *finally*. Often, a colon will be used as punctuation at the start of a list. A variation of the word *follow* may indicate that a list is about to begin. In the excerpt below, the late columnist Ann Landers lists a series of "lies."

And the Third Biggest Lie Is . . .

By Ann Landers

Dear Readers:
A while back, I was asked to print the three biggest lies in the world. I was able to come up with only two: "I'm from the government and I'm here to help you," and "The check is in the mail."

I asked my readers if they could supply the third biggest lie. Thousands rose to the occasion. The mail was simply wonderful. Here's a sampling:

From Lebanon, Pa.: It's a good thing you came in today. We have only two more in stock.

Sparta, Wis.: I promise to pay you back out of my next paycheck.

Woodbridge, N.J.: Five pounds is nothing on a person with your height.

Harrisburg, Pa.: But officer, I only had two beers.

Hammond, Ind.: You made it yourself? I never would have guessed.

Eau Claire, Wis.: It's delicious, but I can't eat another bite.

Charlotte, N.C.: Your hair looks just fine.

Philadelphia: It's nothing to worry about—just a cold sore.

Mechanicsburg, Pa.: It's a terrific high and I swear you won't get hooked.

Dallas: The river never gets high enough to flood this property.

Manassas, Va.: The delivery is on the truck.

Tacoma, Wash.: Go ahead and tell me. I promise I won't get mad.

Billings, Mont.: You have nothing to worry about, honey. I've had a vasectomy.

Philadelphia: The three biggest lies: I did it. I didn't do it. I can't remember.

Chicago: This car is like brand new. It was owned by two retired schoolteachers who never went anywhere.

Boston: The doctor will call you right back.

Montreal: So glad you dropped by. I wasn't doing a thing.

U.S. Stars and Stripes: You don't look a day over 40.

Washington, D.C.: Dad, I need to move out of the dorm into an apartment of my own so I can have some peace and quiet when I study.

Windsor, Ont.: It's a very small spot. Nobody will notice.

Cleveland: The baby is just beautiful!

New York: The new ownership won't affect you. The company will remain the same.

Holiday, Fla.: I gave at the office.

Lansing, Mich.: You can tell me. I won't breathe a word to a soul.

Huntsville, Ala.: The puppy won't be any trouble, Mom. I promise I'll take care of it myself.

Minneapolis: I'm a social drinker, and I can quit anytime I want to.

Barrington, Ill.: Put the map away. I know exactly how to get there.

Troy, Mich.: You don't need it in writing. You have my personal guarantee.

Scarsdale, N.Y.: Our children never caused us a minute's trouble.

Greenwich, Conn.: Sorry, the work isn't ready. The computer broke down.

Detroit: This is a very safe building. No way will you ever be burglarized.

Phoenix: I'll do it in a minute.

Glendale, Calif.: Having a great time. Wish you were here.

Elkhart, Ind.: The reason I'm so late is we ran out of gas.

(Esther P. Lederer and Creators Syndicate, "And the Third Biggest Lie Is . . . ")

Now add to Ann Landers' readers' list. Can you come up with three original "lies" of your own?
List them below.

1. _____

2. _____

3. _____

Steps in a Process

In the steps-in-a-process pattern, something is explained or described in a step-by-step manner. A transition word often introduces each step. Scientific writing commonly follows this pattern. In addition, anyone demonstrating how to make or do something will probably use this pattern.

In the paragraphs that follow, the author gives a step-by-step account of psychologist Lawrence Kohlberg's theory of moral development. The first two paragraphs are outlined for you as an example. Complete the outline of the third paragraph. If you need help with outlining, refer to Study Technique 4 on page 154.

According to Lawrence Kohlberg, moral reasoning develops in **three stages.** In the **first stage,** the preconventional level, children's moral rules and moral values consist of do's and don'ts to avoid punishment. A desire to avoid punishment and a belief in the superior power of authorities are the two central reasons for doing what is right. According to the theory, until the ages of 9 to 11, children usually reason at this level. They think, in effect, "If I steal, what are my chances of getting caught and being punished?" According to Kohlberg, most delinquents and criminals reason at the preconventional level.

Most adolescents reason at **stage two,** the conventional **stage. At this stage,** individuals believe in and have adopted the values and rules of society. Moreover, they seek to uphold these rules. They think, in effect, "It is illegal to steal and therefore I should not steal, under any circumstances."

At the postconventional **level, the final stage,** individuals examine customs and social rules according to their own sense of moral principles and duties. They think, in effect, "One must live within the law, but certain ethical principles, such as respect for human rights, supersede the written

"Those who are too lazy and comfortable to think for themselves and be their own judges obey the laws. Others sense their own laws from within."

—Hermann Hesse

law when the two conflict." This **level** of moral reasoning is generally seen in adults after the age of 20.

(Freda Adler et al., *Criminology*, 6/e, 2007)

I. There are three stages of moral reasoning.
  A. Stage one: the preconventional level
    1. Moral code of do's and don'ts
    2. Two reasons for doing what is right
      a. Avoid punishment
      b. Superior power of authority
    3. Ages 9–11
    4. Delinquents and criminals reason at this level.
  B. Stage two: the conventional stage
    1. Individuals have adopted society's moral code.
    2. Adolescents

  C. _____
    1. Individuals examine customs according to their own sense of moral values.
    2. Personal and ethical principles supersede _____.
    3. Adults after _____.

Definition

A paragraph that uses definition will clarify or explain a key term. Definitions can be developed by providing dictionary meanings or personal meanings. They can also be developed through examples or by comparing and contrasting the key term with other terms.

In the paragraphs below, the authors of *Criminology* attempt to clarify the meaning of *burglary* by providing concrete illustrations, describing distinguishing characteristics, and comparing and contrasting this word to other, similar words. Read the paragraphs and then look at Study Technique 6, which explains mapping.

Burglary

A "burg," in Anglo-Saxon terminology, was a secure place for the protection of one-self, one's family, and one's property. If the burg protects a person from larceny and assault, what protects the burg? The burghers, perhaps. But there had to be a law behind the burghers. And that was the law of burglary, which made it a crime to break and enter the dwelling of another person at night with the intention of committing a crime therein. (Of course it had to be at night, because during the day the inhabitants could defend themselves, or so it was thought.) The common law defined "burglary" as:

> The breaking and entering of the dwelling house of another person at night with the intention to commit a felony or larceny inside

By "breaking," the law **meant** any trespass (unauthorized entry), but usually one accompanied by a forceful act, such as cracking the lock, breaking a windowpane, or scaling the roof and entering through the chimney. The "entering" was complete as soon as the perpetrator extended any part of his or her body into the house in pursuit of the objective of committing a crime in the house. The house had to be a "dwelling," but that **concept** was extended to cover the "curtilage," the attached servants' quarters, carriage houses, and barns. The dwelling also had to be that of "another." And as we mentioned, the event had to occur at "night," which was **defined** as between sundown and sunup.

The most troublesome **term** has always been the "intention to commit a felony or larceny" (even a petty or misdemeanor larceny) inside the premises. How can we know what a burglar intends to do? The best evidence of intent is what the burglar actually does inside the premises. Any crime the burglar commits inside is considered evidence of criminal intention at the moment the burglar broke and entered the dwelling.

(Freda Adler, et al., *Criminology*, 6/e, 2008)

> *"The home of everyone is to him his castle and fortress, as well as his defence against injury and violence, as for his repose."*
>
> —Edward Coke

Exercise 4: Practice with Steps in a Process and Definition Transition Words

Directions: Fill in the blank with an appropriate transition word from the list below. Make sure the sentence makes sense with the transition word you choose.

describe   final   is called   process   step   subsequently   term

1. As a first _____, the study, conducted by psychologist Robert Feldman, looked at the behavior of 32 teenagers who were individually videotaped both lying and telling the truth about whether they liked a drink they had been given.

2. As a final step in the _____, 58 college students were asked to watch the videotapes and judge how much each teenager really liked the drink.

3. _____, researchers concluded that girls were better at lying than boys.

4. The _____ analysis showed a strong link between the most socially adept teenagers and the best deceivers.

(Study Links Proficiency. . . *The Arizona Republic*, 10/28/00)

5. A person _____ a "professional thief" when he or she makes a career of stealing.

6. The term "professional thief" also is used to _____ persons who take pride in their profession, are imaginative, and creative in their work, and accept its risks.

7. The _____ "larceny" refers to theft or stealing and is the most prevalent crime in our society.

(Freda Adler, et al., *Criminology*, 6/e, 2008)

Mapping

Mapping is a technique you can use to organize material you are studying. Similar to outlining, it shows how the main points relate to each other. Unlike outlining, however, it is more visual and less formal. Visual learners may find this a more helpful technique than outlining.

The map below shows the major points and how they relate to one another for the excerpt on burglary (pages 161–162).

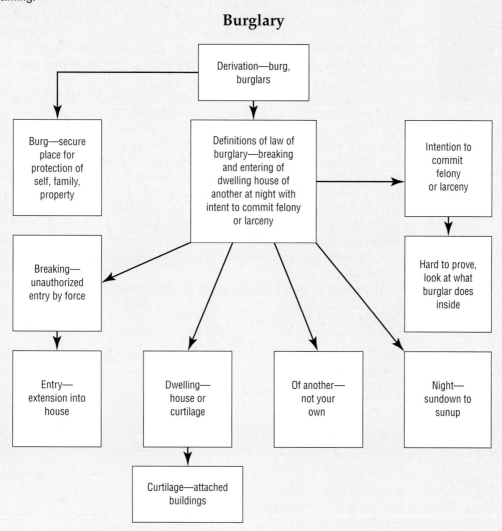

Burglary

Derivation—burg, burglars

Burg—secure place for protection of self, family, property

Definitions of law of burglary—breaking and entering of dwelling house of another at night with intent to commit felony or larceny

Intention to commit felony or larceny

Hard to prove, look at what burglar does inside

Breaking— unauthorized entry by force

Entry— extension into house

Dwelling— house or curtilage

Of another— not your own

Night— sundown to sunup

Curtilage—attached buildings

Chronological Order

The word *chronological* comes from the Greek root *chron,* which means "time." The chronological pattern of organization involves arranging events in the order in which they actually happened. For this reason, historical essays and other articles that are date-oriented are usually organized by this method. Paragraphs written with this pattern are usually very easy to recognize.

The following excerpt is told in chronological order. Read it and then look at Study Technique 7 on time lines.

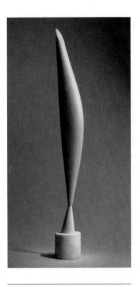

Bird in Space (1923),
CONSTANTIN BRANCUSI

© The Metropolitan Museum of
Art/Art Resource, NY/© 2011
Artists Rights Society (ARS),
New York/ADAGP, Paris.

Brancusi's Bird: Manufactured Metal or Work of Art

A trial held in New York City in **1928** demonstrated just how hard it can be to agree on what constitutes "art." Edward Steichen, a prominent American photographer, purchased a bronze sculpture entitled *Bird in Space* from the Romanian artist Constantin Brancusi, who was living in France. In **1926,** Steichen imported the sculpture to the United States, whose laws do not require payment of customs duty on original works of art as long as they are declared to customs on entering the country. But when the customs official saw the *Bird,* he balked. It was not art he said: it was "manufactured metal." Steichen's protests fell on deaf ears. The sculpture was admitted into the United States under the category of "Kitchen Utensils and Hospital Supplies," which meant that Steichen had to pay $600 in import duty.

In **1927,** with the financial backing of Gertrude Vanderbilt Whitney, an American sculptor and patron of the arts, Steichen appealed the ruling of the customs official. The ensuing trial received a great deal of publicity. Witnesses discussed whether the *Bird* was a bird at all, whether the artist could make it a bird by calling it one, whether it could be said to have characteristics of "birdness," and so on. The conservative witnesses refused to accept the work as a bird because it lacked certain biological attributes, such as wings and tail feathers. The more progressive witnesses pointed out that it had birdlike qualities: upward movement and a sense of spatial freedom. The court decided in favor of the plaintiff. The *Bird* was declared a work of art, and Steichen finally got his money back.

In **today's** market a Brancusi *Bird* would sell for millions of dollars.

(Laurie S. Adams, *Art Across Time*, 3/e, 2007)

STUDY TECHNIQUE 7

Time Lines

A time line is a specialized way of organizing information. Time lines are useful when material needs to be organized chronologically by dates, such as in a history class, although they could also be useful in almost any other class.

All that a time line does is list dates in chronological order along a line and then assign information to the dates. You can make a time line vertically (up and down) or horizontally (across). How specific you want to make a time line (that is, the number of dates and the amount of information you assign to each date) depends on the reading material and your needs.

Complete the time line with information from "Brancusi's Bird." Additional historical dates have been added to put the information in perspective.

1876	Birth date of Constantin Brancusi
1904	Brancusi moves to Paris
1926	_____
1927	_____
1928	_____
1957	Brancusi dies
1973	Steichen dies

The Persistence of Memory *BY SALVADOR DALI*

© The Museum of Modern Art/Licensed by SCALA/Art Resource, NY/© Salvador Dalí,
Fundació Gala-Salvador Dalí/Artists Rights Society (ARS), New York 2011.

Spatial Order

The spatial order pattern is used to describe the location or placement of something. Many of the spatial order transition words are prepositions. The following description of *The Persistence of Memory* by Salvador Dali illustrates spatial order. The transition words are in bold.

The Persistence of Memory

The Persistence of Memory, by Spanish artist Salvador Dali, is one of the most recognizable paintings in the world. At the **top** of the painting, in the **background**, is a realistic sandy beach modeled after Port Lligat in Dali's native Catalonia, Spain. The body of water meets the horizon line, and the sky **above** the horizon contains no clouds, sun, or birds. In the **upper-left** portion of the painting, there's some kind of rectangular slab at the **edge** of the water. On the painting's **upper-right** side, there are jagged rocky cliffs extending down to the water. In the **middle-left**, a clock appears to be hanging from the branch of a dead tree. According to Dali, the image of "soft watches" came to him as he was contemplating Camembert cheese left out too long on a warm sunny day. In the **foreground** of the painting, one watch is drooping over the side of a hard, desk-like surface, while the face of an orange-colored watch is covered with flies. At the **bottom** of the painting appears to be some sort of creature with a distorted version of Dali's own profile, **encircled** by a melted watch. One long-lashed eye is completely shut. We can recognize a nose, a tongue, and a mouth. The creature's head is on our **left**, and its tail is on our **right**. It appears to be lying on **top** of a rock. Stretching **horizontally across** the sand, it shows no sign of life. The painting, only 9 1/2 inches by 13 inches, earned Dali considerable fame by the age of 27. Many art critics suggest that it conveys a dream-like atmosphere because the viewer must pass through the sinister **foreground** and **middle ground** to reach the serene **background**. Is the painting meant to represent our obsession with time and our passage to an inevitable death? We return to the painting again and again to try to decipher the puzzle because Dali himself offered no solution.

Exercise 5: Practice with Chronological Order and Spatial Order Transition Words

Directions: Fill in the blank with an appropriate transition word from the list below. Make sure the sentence makes sense with the transition word you choose.

1769	1963	adjacent	middle	outward	today

1. San Francisco's Alcatraz penitentiary, the "Rock," lies in the _____ of San Francisco Bay.

2. Discovered by early Spanish explorers in _____ , the island was named the Isla de Alcatraces because of the large number of pelicans.

3. The Warden lived in a large house _____ to the prison and actually used inmates with good conduct records for cooking and cleaning.

4. On December 16, 1937, Theodore Cole and Ralph Roe attempted to escape from Alcatraz. Shortly after entering the icy waters of the bay, they were grabbed by the swiftly moving current and swept _____ toward the ocean never to be seen again.

5. The last prisoner left the island in March _____ , when Attorney General Robert F. Kennedy announced the closing of Alcatraz Federal Penitentiary.

6. _____ the island is a historic site operated by the National Park Service and is open to tours.

Review Test: Identifying Patterns of Organization in Textbook Material

Identify the pattern of organization by noting the transitional words.

1. Over the years, television has changed many sports. For example, the World Series is now played in chilly October temperatures at night on the East Coast and in late afternoon on the West Coast, thereby ensuring that the games will be shown on television during prime time in the eastern and central time zones. In another instance, professional basketball playoffs now include 16 of the 27 NBA teams, and the season stretches into June, providing TV with more high-rated games. And the National Hockey League has expanded the pauses in play following certain penalties to more than 30 seconds to allow time for commercials.

   Pattern: _____

   Clues: _____

2. For years, the National Association of Broadcasting (NAB) enforced restrictions on liquor advertising. First, NAB decreed that no hard liquor could be advertised on radio or television. Next, broadcasters were prohibited from showing anyone drinking beer or wine in a commercial; glasses could be hoisted, but no sipping was allowed. Finally, it was decided that currently active sports figures could not appear in beer or wine commercials.

Pattern: _____

Clues: _____

3. The tendency to blame the media for society's woes seems to be escalating. The general public seems convinced that media influences are creating and fostering antisocial behavior and are the reason for all that is wrong with society. These arguments are supported by members of Congress who have tried to curtail the violence on television, blaming it for the increase in violence in our cities. The end result was the introduction of the V-chip in television sets to allow parents to control the types of programs their children watch.

(James R. Wilson, *Mass Media, Mass Culture*, 5/e, 2001)

Pattern: _____

Clues: _____

4. We can divide readers into three types. The most enthusiastic readers are known as bibliophiles—book lovers who consume 50 or more books a year. Bibliophiles started the phenomenon of neighborhood book groups, in which friends and acquaintances gather to discuss a book that they've all read. The second category is the casual reader—those who enjoy reading but find the time to read only a few books a year. The last category, required readers, might read extensively, but they read only what they have to for their job or studies. Many students at both the high school and college levels are required readers. Textbook sales would be nonexistent without students, and the sales of classic literature are highly dependent on college students.

(George Rodman, *Mass Media in a Changing World*, 2/e, 2008)

Pattern: _____

Clues: _____

5. The largest circulating newspaper in the United States happens to be the *National Enquirer*. This popular publication's success can be traced back to 1952, when Generoso (Gene) Pope purchased the *New York Enquirer*. He immediately began filling the newspaper with stories about crime, sex, and violence. In 1958, Pope expanded the *Enquirer* into a national publication and began selling it in supermarkets. He toned down the sex and violence to appeal to a broader audience and began focusing on stories about celebrity gossip, government waste, psychic predictions, life-threatening accidents, and medical advice. At the conclusion of the O. J. Simpson murder trial in 1995, many news reporters conceded that the *Enquirer* had probably covered the story better than anyone else.

Much of that credibility was lost in the final years of the 1990s as the *Enquirer* continued to print weekly stories accusing numerous people of being responsible for the death of JonBenet Ramsey of Colorado. Today, *National Enquirer* reporters are among the highest paid in the nation, and the paper covers major news events with teams of journalists and photographers.

(James R. Wilson, *Mass Media, Mass Culture*, 5/e, 2001)

Pattern: _____

Clues: _____

6. People are defined as illiterate if they can't read because they never learned how. Some experts suggest that as many as one in five Americans are functionally illiterate. This term refers to those who may have some basic skills but cannot read even a simple children's story with comprehension. Alliterates are defined as those who can read but don't. They include people who dislike the act of reading and people who just never picked up the habit. Some experts estimate that as many as 15 percent of Americans are alliterates. According to Gallup polls, fewer books are read in the United States, per capita, than in any other English-speaking country.

(George Rodman, *Mass Media in a Changing World*, 2/e, 2008)

Pattern: _____

Clues: _____

7. Getting a person to buy or rebuy a product involves far more than simply running an ad in a newspaper or a commercial on television. There are three main steps in the selling process: awareness, trial, and reinforcement. *Awareness* is the easiest step. Through repetition and other advertising techniques, consumers are made aware that a product exists. *Trial*, the second step, involves getting people to try the product by sending free samples through the mail, handing them out in stores, giving away discount coupons, and offering price reductions. *Reinforcement* is the necessary third step to persuade users to buy the product again.

Pattern: _____

Clues: _____

8. Buffalo herds played a crucial role in most Plains Indians' culture—providing almost all the basic necessities. Indians ate the buffalo meat, made clothing and teepees out of the hides, used the fats for cosmetics, fashioned the bones into tools, made thread from the sinews, and even burned dried buffalo droppings as fuel. To settlers, however, the buffalo were barriers to western expansion. The herds interfered with construction, knocked over telegraph poles and fences, and could derail trains during stampedes.

Other cultural differences caused misunderstandings between settlers and Native Americans. Among Anglo-Americans, capitalism fostered

Exercise 6: Relationships Within and Between Sentences

Directions: Read the passage below and answer the questions that follow.

Early Methods of Determining Guilt or Innocence

[1]Today, persons charged with criminal offenses are presumed innocent until proven guilty. [2]But the rights we enjoy today did not always exist. [3]It's important to remember that these rights developed slowly over the centuries. [4]At the time the Normans conquered England in 1066, the use of ordeals to determine guilt or innocence was a common practice. [5]For instance, a titled person or one of noble birth could demand trial by battle to determine his guilt or innocence. [6]Winning a sword fight would prove innocence, but losing would show guilt. [7]Because the loser would often be killed or seriously injured, the case would ordinarily be disposed of by the outcome of the battle.

[8]On the other hand, the guilt or innocence of a common person was determined by other types of ordeals. [9]For instance, the accused might be required to walk barefoot over hot coals, hold a piece of red-hot iron, or walk through fire. [10]Because there was no visible sign of any injury, it was believed to be a sign from God that the person was innocent. [11]To conclude, we may now wonder how such a distorted and simplistic belief could have been taken as fact and used to determine a person's guilt or innocence. [12]Obviously, people did not consider the belief a myth during the time that it was official practice.

(Thomas J. Gardner and Terry M. Anderson, *Criminal Evidence,* 7/e, 2010; Robert M. Bohm, *Introduction to Criminal Justice,* 5/e, 2009)

_____ 1. What is the relationship between sentence 1 and sentence 2?
  a. contrast
  b. addition
  c. example
  d. spatial order

_____ 2. What is the relationship between sentence 2 and sentence 3?
  a. cause and effect
  b. emphasis
  c. spatial order
  d. chronological order

_____ 3. What is the relationship between sentence 4 and sentence 5?
  a. cause and effect
  b. steps in a process
  c. contrast
  d. example

_____ 4. The relationship between the first part of sentence 6 and the second part is one of
  a. example
  b. contrast
  c. chronological order
  d. listing

_____ 5. The relationship between the first part of sentence 7 and the second part is one of
   a. comparison
   b. contrast
   c. cause and effect
   d. example

_____ 6. The relationship between the first part of sentence 8 and the second part is one of
   a. contrast
   b. comparison
   c. definition
   d. example

_____ 7. The relationship between the first part of sentence 9 and the second part is one of
   a. comparison
   b. steps in a process
   c. listing
   d. example

_____ 8. The relationship between the first part of sentence 10 and the second part is one of
   a. definition
   b. cause and effect
   c. contrast
   d. comparison

_____ 9. The relationship between the first part of sentence 11 and the second is one of
   a. example
   b. definition
   c. contrast
   d. summary and conclusion

_____ 10. The relationship between the first part of sentence 12 and the second is one of
   a. clarification
   b. definition
   c. contrast
   d. summary and conclusion

Cheating

Top 4 Reasons College Students Cheat

1. It's Not My Fault

2. Everyone Does It

3. It's So Easy to Cheat

4. Gotta Keep Up My GPA

Top 4 Reasons College Students Cheat, HigherEdMorning.com.
www.higheredmorning.com/top-4-reasons-college-students-cheat

Study the Calvin and Hobbes cartoon and answer these questions before reading the selection about cheating.

1. What attitude about cheating does Calvin express?

_____

_____

continued

Cheating *(continued)*

2. What key point is being made in the cartoon? What is being criticized?

_____

_____

3. To *rationalize* means to justify behavior using reasons that appear to be good or valid but that do not reflect the true motivations. Explain how Calvin rationalizes cheating on a test.

_____

_____

SELECTION

"It began in December with a teacher's finding that 28 of 118 Piper High sophomores had stolen sections of their botany project off the Internet."

GETTING THE PICTURE

The article that follows describes what happened when a teacher gave high school students a zero on an assignment after discovering that they had plagiarized. Many educators believe that cheating has become rampant on American campuses. According to a survey of 40,000 U.S. high school students by the Josephson Institute of Ethics, more than half of teenagers say that they have cheated on a test during the last year. In addition, one in three students admitted they used the Internet to plagiarize an assignment. In 2011, Professor Donald McCabe at Rutgers University reported that two-thirds of college students admitted to cheating on tests, homework, and assignments. Fifty-two percent of the students admitted to "copying sentences from websites without citing the source."

BIO-SKETCH

Jodi Wilgoren graduated from Yale University in 1992 with a major in history. After writing for the *Los Angeles Times,* she became a national education correspondent and general assignment reporter for the *New York Times.* Wilgoren is the Midwest bureau chief for the *Times,* responsible for the coverage of 11 states, and also covered the 2004 presidential campaign.

BRUSHING UP ON VOCABULARY

tight-knit well-organized or closely integrated.

clamped became stricter or more repressive; put a stop to. The word *clamp* dates from the mid-1900s and was originally a noun that referred to a device with opposite sides or parts that could be brought closer together to compress something.

empty nester a parent whose children have grown up and moved out. The expression alludes to a nest from which baby birds have flown.

flourishes decorations or embellishments. The word *flourishes* derives from the Latin word *florere*, meaning "to bloom."

School Cheating Scandal Tests a Town's Values

By Jodi Wilgoren

1 PIPER, KANSAS, FEBRUARY 13—The Piper school board normally meets in a cozy conference room at district headquarters, but on Tuesday, folding chairs filled the purple-and-white elementary school gym to accommodate the overflow crowd.

2 More than 100 parents, students, and teachers skipped the basketball game at the high school next door to talk about the plagiarism scandal that has riven this tight-knit community 20 miles west of downtown Kansas City, Kansas, and become talk-show fodder as far away as Guam as a symbol of the decline in American values.

"Let the punishment fit 3 *the crime."*

—Gilbert and Sullivan

It began in December with a teacher's finding that 28 of 118 Piper High sophomores had stolen sections of their botany project off the Internet. The students received zeroes and faced failing the semester. But after parents complained to the school board, the teacher, Christine Pelton, was ordered to raise the grades, prompting her resignation. Now, the community is angrily pointing fingers as they debate right and wrong, crimes and consequences, citizenship and democracy.

4 At Tuesday's meeting, Kay Miesner, who graduated from Piper High School in 1962—28 years after her father, 23 years before her son—

told the board members who overruled Mrs. Pelton, "I know each and every one of you; I think you're all good people." But she said, "I think you made a mistake."

5 Someone yelled, "Yup," and the audience erupted. But Chris McCord, the board president, clamped the emotion, saying, "We'll have none of that."

6 Such tension is unusual here in Piper, a blue-collar bedroom community, in part because of young families drawn by the small school district.

7 Several teachers said that nearly half the high school's 31-member faculty plus its brand new principal planned to resign at year's end over the case, while parents fretted that the school's dwindling reputation might result in a decline in property values and disappearance of scholarship opportunities.

8 Mrs. Pelton, meanwhile, has become a kind of folk hero, with dozens of calls a day offering support—and jobs.

9 "It's not just biology, you're teaching them a lot more than that," Mrs. Pelton, 27, who had planned to resign this spring anyway to start a home-based day care center, said between television appearances the other day. "You're teaching them to

be honest people, to have integrity, to listen, to be good citizens.

10   "We've got rules, and they've got to follow the rules," she added. "I'm not expecting more than what would be expected of them either at home or down the road."

11   Students, plagiarizers and nonplagiarizers alike, have already begun to feel the backlash.

12   A sign posted in a nearby high school read, "If you want your grade changed, go to Piper." The proctor at a college entrance exam last weekend warned a girl wearing a Piper sweatshirt not to cheat. A company in Florida faxed the school asking for a list of students—so it would know whom never to hire. At Tuesday's board meeting, as five television news crews rolled tape, a woman worried that the community had been "stamped with a large purple P on their foreheads for plagiarism."

13   The sophomore leaf project, an elaborate exercise in which students spend months collecting leaves and researching their origins, dates back a decade.

14   Mrs. Pelton, who came to Piper High in the fall of 2000 after a five-year program at the University of Kansas, sent an outline of the assignment home on the first day of school, along with her classroom rules (No. 7: "Cheating and plagiarism will result in failure of the assignment and parent notification. It is expected that all work turned in by the student is completely their own."), which students and parents had to sign.

15   Mrs. Pelton said she began to worry in October, when students' oral presentations, filled with big, unfamiliar words, sounded strangely similar. As she flipped through their projects a month later, she found the writing far more sophisticated than previous assignments. A plagiarism-detection website, turnitin.com, showed one in four were laced with lifted material.

16   The principal, Michael Adams, who declined to be interviewed, backed Mrs. Pelton's decision to give students zeroes, as did the superintendent. But after parents protested at the December 11 school board meeting, the superintendent, Dr. Michael O. Rooney, sent a memorandum home saying he had "reluctantly" directed Mrs. Pelton to deduct just 600 of 1,500 points from the plagiarizers' projects, and to cut its value in the overall grade from 50 percent to 30 percent.

17   Mrs. Pelton said a student told her, "We won."

18   Though teachers here say they begin discussing source citation in the fourth grade, some parents, of students with zeroes and those with A pluses, insist the students did not realize what they were doing was wrong (some say they thought the admonition was against copying from previous students' papers, not taking simple descriptions from research material). Failing a whole semester, they say, is too harsh.

19   "If your boss said to you, 'You were late one day this month so we're not going to pay you for the whole month,' is that fair?" asked Mary Myer, whose son, Mitchell, was not accused of cheating.

20   "Plagiarism is not a cut-and-dried issue," she added. "Somebody who gets in their car and hurts someone, we punish them differently than someone who goes out and shoots someone. Intent matters."

21   It is just the latest plagiarism revelation afflicting American high schools and colleges, aggravated by

*"Honesty's praised
then left to freeze."*

—Juvenal

an Internet age in which research papers—as well as programs to detect cheating—can be downloaded by the dollar. A Rutgers University professors' survey of 4,471 high school students last year found that more than half had stolen sentences and paragraphs from websites, 15 percent handed in papers completely copied from the Internet, and 74 percent had cheated on a test.

22   On talk shows and the Internet, Piper's problems have been linked to recent admissions by the popular historian Stephen Ambrose that he failed to properly attribute passages; the resignation of George O'Leary, Notre Dame's football coach, after revelations that he falsified his résumé; and even alleged lying by executives at Enron.

23   Piper, a farming community founded in 1888 and annexed by the city of Kansas City, Kansas, in 1992, is defined by the four-school district of 1,300 students. Its headquarters doubles as the post office in an enclave without town hall or tavern; even empty nesters wear Piper purple to Pirates athletic events.

24   Many parents have expressed sympathy for the 75 percent of students who did not cheat, some of whom received lower semester grades in biology when the project they had slaved over suddenly counted less than they had anticipated. Some parents have even sent homemade cookies and nut bread to school in quiet solidarity with teachers.

25   "You can stand up for your kids when it's right, but when it's wrong, you can't bail your child out," said Diane Smith, who has a son in the freshman class and a daughter in middle school. "I don't think the board should have that much power; they really outstepped their boundaries."

26   Teachers, ever protective of the sanctity of their grade books, say the board has robbed their independence and professionalism. Instead of a lesson about the importance of honesty and originality, they say, students learned that complaining to higher powers mitigates punishment.

27   "If I make a decision, I don't know if it's going to be backed up," said Angel Carney, a business teacher who submitted her resignation this week. "I had a disagreement with a parent the other day; right away she wanted to go over my head."

28   Even if no one ended up failing, students say they are paying the price. "Whatever you do will always come back to you," Amy Kolich, an 18-year-old senior, said when asked what she had learned from the situation. "In a way, to them, it didn't, but it came back to our school."

29   Piper High's handbook does not mention plagiarism specifically, but says the penalty for cheating, even a first offense, is no credit on the assignment. Administrators are now setting up a committee to handle conflicts over grades and collecting plagiarism policies from other schools.

30   Matthew Mosier, 16, spent hours on his botany project, gathering leaves from neighbors' farms, looking them up on the Web. His grandmother, a quilter, covered his three-ring binder in leaf fabric and embroidered his name on the cover. He bought fancy leaf paper at the Hobby Lobby to print out his reports.

31   Matt ended up with a D, the extra credit for his artistic flourishes washed out by the sentences Mrs. Pelton said he copied.

32   "Am I saying my son's perfect? No and hell no," said Kim Mosier, Matthew's mom, who was not among

those who complained to the board but was pleased by the result. "We sat down with him and said, 'Did you plagiarize?' He said, 'No, Mom, I didn't.' I have to support him until they can prove him different.

"We hire that board, those teachers, that school, that principal—they work for us," she added. "Everybody has that opportunity that they should be questioned on a decision that they make."

(Jodi Wilgoren, "School Cheating Scandal Tests a Town's Values," *New York Times*, 2002)

✓ COMPREHENSION CHECKUP

Matching

Scan the previous selection so that you can match the quotation with the speaker. (Some speakers will be used more than once.)

a. Angel Carney
b. Kay Miesner
c. Chris McCord
d. Christine Pelton

e. Diane Smith
f. Amy Kolich
g. Mary Myer
h. Kim Mosier

_____ 1. "I had a disagreement with a parent the other day; right away she wanted to go over my head."

_____ 2. "I'm not expecting more than what would be expected of them either at home or down the road."

_____ 3. "I don't think the board should have that much power; they really overstepped their boundaries."

_____ 4. "Whatever you do will always come back to you."

_____ 5. "I know each and every one of you; I think you're all good people. . . . I think you made a mistake."

_____ 6. "Everybody has that opportunity that they should be questioned on a decision that they make."

_____ 7. "Somebody who gets in their car and hurts someone, we punish them differently than someone who goes out and shoots someone."

_____ 8. "We'll have none of that."

_____ 9. "You're teaching them to be honest people, to have integrity, to listen, to be good citizens."

_____ 10. "Plagiarism is not a cut-and-dried issue."

Multiple Choice

Write the letter of the correct answer in the blank provided.

_____ 1. Which of the following best expresses the main idea of the selection?
  a. After being ordered to raise the grades of some students accused of cheating, Christine Pelton resigned her position.
  b. Some parents have begun to worry about declining property values.

       c. The plagiarism scandal has engendered divisions in the once close-knit community of Piper.

       d. Christine Pelton is experiencing a great deal of negative publicity because of the cheating incident.

_____ 2. The writer's main purpose in writing this selection is to

       a. entertain the reader with an illustration of the old adage that cheating doesn't pay.

       b. persuade the reader that cheating is morally wrong

       c. explain the cheating incident at Piper and its repercussions

       d. describe the moral values of Christine Pelton

_____ 3. The author's use of the words "on Tuesday," "it began in December," and "at the December 11 school board meeting" is meant to demonstrate

       a. cause and effect

       b. chronological order

       c. compare and contrast

       d. simple listing

_____ 4. Which detail listed below from the selection is least relevant to the author's main idea?

       a. Teachers say the board's decision has robbed them of independence.

       b. Students complain that Piper High now carries a stigma of cheating that affects all of them.

       c. Some parents feel that the board and the teachers work for them.

       d. Matthew Mosier took advantage of his grandmother's skills as a quilter and seamstress to bolster his chances for a good grade on the project.

_____ 5. Which of the following best defines the word *fretted* as it is used in paragraph 7?

       a. worried

       b. kidded

       c. suggested

       d. stipulated

_____ 6. The organizational pattern of paragraph 22 is primarily

       a. examples

       b. definition

       c. spatial order

       d. concession

_____ 7. In paragraph 5, the transition word *but* indicates

       a. addition

       b. reversal

       c. spatial order

       d. contrast

_____ 8. In paragraph 26, the transition word *instead* indicates

       a. example

       b. classification/division

       c. reversal

       d. emphasis

True or False

Indicate whether the statement is true or false by writing **T** or **F** in the blank provided.

_____ 9. According to the selection, the Piper school board normally meets at district headquarters.

_____ 10. Even before the incident, Mrs. Pelton was planning to leave Piper High.

_____ 11. One in four of the student projects submitted to Mrs. Pelton contained material that was not the student's own work.

_____ 12. Mrs. Pelton failed to make students aware of the consequences of cheating in her classroom.

_____ 13. The superintendent, after initially backing Mrs. Pelton, changed his mind.

Vocabulary in Context

Look through the paragraph indicated in parentheses to find a word that matches the definition below.

1. comfortable (paragraph 1)   _____

2. split apart (2)   _____

3. diminishing (7)   _____

4. negative reaction (11)   _____

5. warning (18)   _____

6. settled in advance (20)   _____

7. disclosures (22)   _____

8. condition of being strongly united (24) _____

9. sacredness (26)   _____

10. lessens in force or severity (26)   _____

In Your Own Words

1. Most parents are naturally protective of their children, but they also want to teach them about taking responsibility for their actions. Do you think the parents described in the article were right to intervene?

2. Donald McCabe feels that many teachers are reluctant to address cheating directly in their classrooms. For McCabe, the Piper incident goes a long way toward explaining why teachers are so reluctant to follow through on punishment. McCabe says that "parents are going to complain to principals and the school board, and teachers feel there's no reason to believe they'll get support." Do you think that teachers should crack down on cheating? Has a similar incident occurred in a school system near you? Was the incident decided in the teacher's or the students' favor?

3. The Internet provides students with vast resources. In your opinion, where does using the Internet as a reference end and plagiarism begin?

4. Sue Bigg, a college consultant outside Chicago, says, "I'm afraid that a lot of this cheating comes from home, where the parents' modus operandi is success at any cost." What role do you think parental example plays in a child's decision to cheat?

5. Studies show that students who cheat are likely to make it a way of life. So it's no surprise that today's workplace is full of adults who lie about everything from job experience to company earnings. Nearly three-quarters of job seekers admitted to lying on their résumés in a recent survey by SelectJOBS.com, a high-tech industry employment site. Offenses ranged from omitting past jobs (40 percent) to padding education credentials (12 percent). Is there anything employers might do to discourage cheating by job seekers?

The Art of Writing

In a brief essay, respond to one of the items below. Practice using transition words in your essay.

1. Have you ever cheated on something? If so, did you feel that your cheating was justified at the time the incident took place? Do you still feel that what you did was acceptable? Was your cheating similar to any incidents described in the article?

2. In the Piper incident, many students claimed they copied only a sentence or two and that they didn't know that this amounted to plagiarism. In fact, many students felt there were only so many ways to describe the characteristics of leaves. How would you have decided this case?

Internet Activity

Consult either of the following Web sites to get updated information on the ethical beliefs and practices of high school and college students.

www.academicintegrity.org (Center for Academic Integrity)

www.josephsoninstitute.org (Josephson Institute of Ethics)

If available, print a recent ethics survey or report card.

Summarizing Longer Articles

In Chapter 2, you learned how to summarize a short article. Now you are going to apply the same principles to a longer article and summarize the article you just read about cheating at Piper High School. Summarizing is an important study skill. It forces you to identify the important points of what you have read and reduces the amount of material you have to review for a class discussion or exam. Summarizing simply means restating the main ideas and significant details of a reading selection in your own words. Remember that a summary should include only the author's opinions and not your beliefs.

To summarize, begin by identifying the main idea or thesis of the article. What is the most important point the author is trying to make?

Main Idea or Thesis: _____

_____

_____

Next, identify the main supporting ideas found in the article. Begin by answering as many of the who, what, where, when, why, and how questions as apply to the article. Remember to list important dates, events, and people involved. You may not be able to answer all of the questions.

Who? _____

_____

What? _____

Where? _____

When? _____

Why? _____

_____

How? _____

Now identify three to four main ideas with at least two details for each important point. Some of your information may be the same as what you wrote above. Each of these supporting main ideas may be discussed either in a particular section of the article or at various points throughout the article.

Main Idea 1: _____

_____

Detail 1: _____

Detail 2: _____

_____

Main Idea 2: _____

Detail 1: _____

_____

Detail 2: _____

Main Idea 3: _____

_____

Detail 1: _____

_____

Detail 2: _____

_____

Main Idea 4: _____

_____

Detail 1: _____

_____

Detail 2: _____

_____

You now have placed the important points of the article down on paper. Check what you have written down with a classmate to make sure you have covered the most important information from the article.

After writing your summary, ask yourself whether you have put the ideas in your own words. Then make sure you have included the significant main ideas and details you have listed above. Have you included any expressions of your own opinions? If so, delete them.

Give your summary a title so you will be able to locate it when you are ready to prepare for your exam, and keep it in your class notebook where you will know where to look for it.

As a final step, compare your version to the sample given in the Appendix.

Brain Teasers

Directions: Identify these dynamic "duos" as quickly as you can.

1. Batman and _____

2. Dr. Jekyl and _____

3. Romeo and _____

4. Bert and _____

5. The tortoise and the _____

6. Beauty and the _____

7. Hansel and _____

8. Lady and the _____

9. Frodo and _____

10. Barbie and _____

Directions: Using the clues provided, identify the famous "trios."

1. Three characters created by Dumas who have the motto "all for one and one for all"

   _____

2. The names of Donald Duck's three nephews

   _____

3. The three best friends in the Harry Potter books

   _____

4. Their houses were made of straw, wood, and brick.

   _____

5. Three animated musical chipmunks famous for a Christmas song

   _____

6. Three verb tenses

   _____

7. A simple fire safety technique taught to children

   _____

8. Three characters in Kellogg's Rice Krispies advertisements

   _____

Can you complete the following well-known trios?

1. reading, writing, and _____

2. knife, fork, and _____

3. planes, trains, and _____

4. ready, willing, and _____

5. person, place, or _____

6. sun, moon, and _____

VOCABULARY   Unit 3: Number Prefixes

"All for one, one for all."

—Alexandre Dumas

This is the first of eight vocabulary units designed to expand your vocabulary by means of Latin and Greek prefixes, suffixes, and root words. It is said that more than fifty percent of all the vocabulary in English is directly or indirectly derived from Latin. And Greek and Latin prefixes and roots have had a big impact on the fields of health, science, and technology. Even today new words are created using Latin or Greek word parts. For example, perhaps you are unfamiliar with the following modern terms: bipolar disorder, germicide, and hypertension. If you knew that *bi* means two, *cide* means kill or destroy, and *hyper* means over or above, you could probably figure each of these words out without consulting a dictionary. By learning the word parts presented in the following units, you can unlock the meaning of these and thousands of other useful words.

Many words have "families." A word family is a group of words that are related because they all come from the same source, usually Latin or Greek. The words in the vocabulary units in this book are organized into families to help you learn and remember them more easily. We hope these units prove to be both practical in everyday life and useful to your goal of acquiring a college-level vocabulary.

The following prefixes all indicate numbers:

uni—one	qua(d)—four	sept—seven
mono—one	tetra—four	hept—seven
bi—two	quint—five	oct—eight
di—two	pent—five	
du(o)—two		nov—nine
	hex—six	
tri—three	sex—six	dec, dek—ten

Words made from these word parts, along with their definitions, follow. Supplemental words with these word parts are located in the left margin.

Unitarian universe	**unify**	to make or become a single unit
	unicameral	*-cam-* means "chamber." *Unicameral* refers to a legislative body made up of only one house or chamber.
	bicameral	having two groups in the lawmaking body. The *bicameral* U.S. Congress is made up of the Senate and the House of Representatives.
	univalve	having a shell composed of a single piece, such as a snail
	bivalve	having a shell composed of two parts hinged together, such as a clam or oyster
monograph monotheism	**monochromatic**	of or pertaining to only one color, as in *monochromatic* pottery. It was obvious that Regis, who wore a gray tie, gray shirt, and gray slacks, preferred a *monochromatic* style of dress.
	monogram	initials of a person's name in a design, such as are used on articles of clothing or stationery
	monolith	*-lith* means "stone," so a monolith is a single block or piece of stone of considerable size, sometimes carved into a column or large statue. The sphinx of Egypt is a *monolith*.

	monotonous	sounded or uttered in one unvarying tone; lacking in variety. At the graduation ceremony, many were displeased with the keynote speaker because of his *monotonous* speaking style.
	monocle	an eyeglass for one eye
	monorail	a single rail serving as a track for cars. Taking the *monorail* at Disneyland adds to the excitement.
	monosyllabic	having only one syllable, like *what* or *how*
binoculars binary bipolar	**biracial**	consisting of or representing members of two separate races. Tiger Woods, whose mother is Asian and father is black, is *biracial*.
	bipartisan	made up of or supported by two political parties. Support for education is *bipartisan*.
	bifocals	eyeglasses in which each lens has two parts, one for reading and seeing nearby objects and the other for seeing things further away. Benjamin Franklin invented *bifocals* in 1784.
	bisect	*-sect* means "to cut," so *bisect* means to cut or divide into two equal parts
	bigamy	the act of marrying one person while already legally married to another
	dichotomy	division into two parts or kinds. *-tomy* is derived from the Latin word *temnien*, meaning "to cut." In the United States, there is a *dichotomy* of viewpoints on the issue of the death penalty.
deuce	**duplex**	a house having separate apartments side by side
	duplicate	to make an exact copy of; to double
triage trigonometry troika	**triplicate**	to make three copies of; to triple
	triple	made up of three. He ordered a *triple* cone with vanilla, strawberry, and chocolate. A hit in baseball that lets the batter get to third base.
triumvirate triceratops tricolor trident trimester trinity triad	**triannual**	done, occurring, or issued three times a year, as in a *triannual* magazine
	trilogy	a set of three plays, novels, or other creative works, which form a group, although each is a complete work on its own. *Star Wars*, *The Empire Strikes Back*, and *The Return of the Jedi* make up a *trilogy*.
	quadrangle	an open area surrounded by buildings on all four sides, such as is often seen on college campuses; a plane having four sides
	quatrain	a stanza or poem of four lines, such as in this example by Emily Dickinson:

"Hope" is the thing with feathers

That perches in the soul

And sings the tune without the words

And never stops—at all.

(Thomas H. Johnson, ed., *The Poems of Emily Dickinson*, 1983)

quadrille quadriplegic	**quadriceps**	a large, four-part muscle at the front of the thigh

	quadricentennial	*cen-* means "100" and *-enn-* means "year," so a *quadricentennial* is a 400th anniversary. The United States will celebrate its *quadricentennial* in 2176.
	tetrapod	*-pod* means "foot," so a *tetrapod* is a vertebrate having four legs or one that is descended from a four-legged ancestor
quintessential	**quintessence**	the fifth element; a perfect type or example of something. Works by Picasso are the *quintessence* of modern art.
	pentathlon	an athletic contest with five different track and field events
	hexagram	a six-pointed starlike figure. The Star of David is a *hexagram*.
	sextet	a group of six singers or players
	heptagon	a seven-sided figure
	octet	a group or stanza of eight lines; a company of eight singers or musicians
decalogue	**decimate**	to destroy or kill a large part of. Florida was *decimated* by the hurricane. In the sixteenth century, the word *decimate* meant to kill every tenth man arbitrarily as punishment for mutiny.
	September	originally the seventh month. Our calendar evolved from the original Roman calendar, which began in March instead of January. You can see that making March the first month makes *September* the seventh month.
	October	originally the eighth month
	November	originally the ninth month
	December	originally the tenth month

Now that you have studied the vocabulary in Unit 3, practice your new knowledge by completing the crossword puzzle.

Vocabulary Unit 3 Puzzle

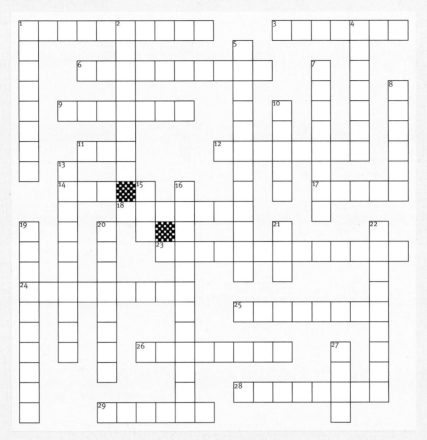

ACROSS CLUES

1. A one-house legislature.
3. Was once the eighth month.
6. At work he does the same thing every day. His job is _____.
9. Tolkien's *The Fellowship of the Ring*, *The Two Towers*, and *The Return of the King* make up the _____ of *The Lord of the Rings*.
11. A word part meaning "eight."
12. An earthquake can _____ an entire city.
14. A word part meaning "one."
17. A group of eight musicians.
18. Agatha Christie's murder mysteries feature a detective who uses a _____ to inspect for clues.
23. Maria Martinez is famous for her black-on-black _____ pottery.
24. There is a _____ of viewpoints on the issue of cloning.
25. The Star of David is a _____.
26. The poet Emily Dickinson is famous for her four-line _____.
28. When you're at Disneyland, be sure to ride on the _____.
29. You will _____ a circle if you draw a line through the middle.

DOWN CLUES

1. A snail has a _____ shell.
2. Each of the stone figures on Easter Island is a _____.
4. Oysters have _____ shells.
5. Michelangelo's statue of David is considered to be the _____ of sculpture.
7. The four-legged horse is an example of a _____.
8. A group of six musicians is a _____.
10. On the reality show *Survivor*, first the two teams are pitted against each other and then they _____ and become one tribe.
13. Too much running and jumping caused him to injure his _____.
15. An abbreviation for what was once the ninth month.
16. There are no _____ vocabulary words in this unit. All of the words have more than one syllable.
19. Figure having four angles or sides.
20. Many people begin wearing _____ to see better after the age of 50.
21. A word part meaning "three."
22. Congress is a _____ legislature.
27. A word part meaning "four."

Interpreting What We Read

Chapters In Part 3

Seasons (1999)
by Gil Mayers

Inference

Relativity (1953) BY *MAURITS CORNELIS ESCHER*

© Topham/The Image Works.

View and Reflect

1. Do the people in the painting appear to be aware of each other's existence?
2. What is the staircase meant to represent?
3. Is there a reason why the figures do not have facial characteristics?
4. What does the painting illustrate about perception?
5. What does the word *relativity* mean?

Introduction to Inference Skills

An inference is an educated guess based upon observable details. We use our intuition and experiences to create a likely interpretation of what is happening, while being careful that our interpretation is logical and realistic. We all draw inferences from observations in our everyday lives. From observable details, we may conclude that a friend is angry or upset, that it is going to rain, that a motorist is driving recklessly, or that a pet is sick.

Readers draw on the evidence presented to them to make reasonable deductions or conclusions about the material. A good reader should always use common sense and knowledge of everyday life in the reasoning process.

Cartoons and jokes require you to read between the lines in order to get the point being made. Study the Randy Glasbergen cartoon below. The cartoon is humorous because the student thinks his term paper is almost finished and yet the reader knows he has most of the work still ahead of him.

© Randy Glasbergen
www.glasbergen.com

"My term paper is almost finished. I updated my software,
defragmented my hard drive, bookmarked an online dictionary, and
installed new ink cartridges. Now all I need are some words and a topic!"

Now try to infer the point of the following joke.

JOKE: MONEY NEEDED

After graduating from high school, David moved away from home to study at a university. One of his letters home reads:

Dear Dad,

The University i$ really great. I am making lot$ of friend$ and $tudying really hard. I $imply can't think of anything I need right now. But, if you like, you can $end me a card, a$ I would love to hear from you.

Love, Your $on

After receiving his son's letter, the father replied by immediately sending a letter back to him.

Dear David,

I kNOw that astroNOmy, ecoNOmics, and oceaNOgraphy are eNOugh to keep even an hoNOr student busy. Do NOt forget that the pursuit of kNOwledge is a NOble task, and you can never study eNOugh.

Love, Dad

Inference: _____

Drawing Inferences from Different Kinds of Material

In many different types of readings, the authors do not state their messages directly, making it necessary for you to infer them. The following are readings from a number of different sources that will challenge you to draw inferences.

Drawing Inferences from Science Fiction

In this section, you will be drawing inferences from a science fiction story.

SELECTION

"Poor Barney is dead an soon I shell be the same."

GETTING THE PICTURE

Most critical readers make inferences as they go along and then, as they are provided more clues by the author, either reject these inferences or subject them to further analysis. At the conclusion of the story, they assemble all of these valid inferences, just as you must do in the following science fiction tale.

BIO-SKETCH

Will Stanton is a widely respected author of science fiction. Some of his novels and short stories include *The Golden Evening of Summer*, *Never in This World*, *The Last Present*, *Once Upon a Time Is Enough*, and *The Old Familiar Booby Traps*. Stanton also wrote for magazines such as *The Magazine of Fantasy and Science Fiction*, *The New Yorker*, and *The Saturday Evening Post*. Even though Stanton's stories were published primarily in the sixties and seventies, they have remained popular not only because of the quality of his writing and storytelling, but also because of his subtle, ironic humor.

BRUSHING UP ON VOCABULARY

jolt a shock or setback

sack slang for *dismissal* as from a job

flimsiest not effective or convincing; weak

BARNEY

by Will Stanton

August 30th. We are alone on the island now, Barney and I. It was something 1 of a jolt to have to sack Tayloe after all these years, but I had no alternative. The petty vandalisms I could have forgiven, but when he tried to poison Barney out of simple malice, he was standing in the way of scientific progress. That I cannot condone.

I can only believe the attempt was made while under the influence of alcohol, 2 it was so clumsy. The poison container was overturned and a trail of powder led to Barney's dish. Tayloe's defense was of the flimsiest. He denied it. Who else then?

September 2nd. I am taking a calmer view of the Tayloe affair. The lonely life 3 here must have become too much for him. That, and the abandonment of his precious guinea pigs. He insisted to the last that they were better suited than Barney to my experiments. They were more his speed, I'm afraid. He was an earnest and willing worker, but something of a clod, poor fellow.

At last I have complete freedom to carry on my work without the mute 4 reproaches of Tayloe. I can only ascribe his violent antagonism toward Barney to jealousy. And now that he has gone, how much happier Barney appears to be! I have given him complete run of the place, and what sport it is to observe how his newly awakened intellectual curiosity carries him about. After only two weeks of glutamic acid treatments, he has become interested in my library, dragging the books from the shelves, and going over them page by page. I am certain he knows there is some knowledge to be gained from them had he but the key.

1. What kind of animal do you think Barney is? _____.
2. What does the narrator infer about Tayloe's relationship to Barney? _____

    _____

3. What has Barney gained since Tayloe's dismissal? _____

    _____

4. What can we infer is the likely intent of the scientific experiments? _____

    _____

September 8th. For the past two days I have had to keep Barney confined and 5 how he hates it. I am afraid that when my experiments are completed I shall have to do away with Barney. Ridiculous as it may sound there is still the possibility that he might be able to communicate his intelligence to others of his kind. However small the chance may be, the risk is too great to ignore. Fortunately there is, in the basement, a vault built with the idea of keeping pests out, and it will serve equally well to keep Barney in.

September 9th. Apparently I have spoken too soon. This morning I let him out 6 to frisk around a bit before commencing a new series of tests. After a quick survey of the room he returned to his cage, sprang up on the door handle, removed the key with his teeth, and before I could stop him, he was out the window. By the time I reached the yard I spied him on the rim of the well, and I arrived on the spot only in time to hear the key splash into the water below.

I own I am somewhat embarrassed. It is the only key. The door is locked. 7 Some valuable papers are in separate compartments inside the vault. Fortunately, although the well is over forty feet deep, there are only a few feet of water in the bottom, so the retrieving of the key does not present an impossible problem. But I must admit Barney has won the first round.

1. Why does Barney dispose of the key in this manner? _____

_____

2. What has Barney accomplished by getting rid of the key? _____

_____

3. Do you think Barney is aware of the writer's intentions toward him? _____

September 10th. I have had a rather shaking experience, and once more in a 8 minor clash with Barney I have come off second best. In this instance I will admit he played the hero's role and may even have saved my life.

In order to facilitate my descent into the well I knotted a length of three- 9 quarter-inch rope at one-foot intervals to make a rude ladder. I reached the bottom easily enough, but after only a few minutes of groping for the key, my flashlight gave out and I returned to the surface. A few feet from the top I heard excited squeaks from Barney, and upon obtaining ground level I observed that the rope was almost completely severed. Apparently it had chafed against the edge of the masonry and the little fellow perceiving my danger had been doing his utmost to warn me.

I have now replaced that section of rope and arranged some old sacking be- 1 neath it to prevent a recurrence of the accident. I have replenished the batteries in my flashlight and am now prepared for the final descent. These few moments I have taken off to give myself a breathing spell and to bring my journal up to date. Perhaps I should fix myself a sandwich as I may be down there longer than seems likely at the moment.

1. What conclusion does the scientist make about the probable cause of the accident?

_____

_____

2. Why does he assume Barney is a hero? _____

_____

September 11th. Poor Barney is dead an soon I shell be the same. He was a 1 wonderful ratt and life without him is knot worth livving. If anybody reeds this please do not disturb anything on the island but leeve it like it is as a shryn to Barney, espechilly the old well. Do not look for my body as I will caste myself into the see. You mite bring a couple of young ratts and leeve them as a living memorial to Barney. Females—no males. I sprayned my wrist is why this is written so bad. This is my laste will. Do what I say an don't come back or disturb anything after you bring the young ratts like I said. Just females.

Goodby

_____

(Will Stanton, "Barney," 1951)

1. Who is the likely writer of this last journal entry? _____

2. What specific requests does this writer make? _____

_____

3. Why does the writer want everyone to stay away? _____

_____

4. Would a sprained wrist account for the sudden grammatical and spelling errors?

_____

5. How did Tayloe's dismissal benefit the final author? Why was it essential for him
to remove Tayloe from the scene? _____

_____

6. What parts of this story are the opposite of what you expected them to be? _____

_____

7. Which group is the author poking fun of in this story? _____

8. In what ways do you think Stanton would like to see this group be more
responsible? _____

_____

Vocabulary in Context

Using the context clues below and in the reading selection, choose the best definition
for the italicized word, and write the appropriate answer letter in the blank. You may
use your dictionary if necessary.

_____ 1. *petty* vandalisms (paragraph 1)
   a. subordinate
   b. small, minor
   c. peevish

_____ 2. simple *malice* (1)
   a. spite
   b. charity
   c. sickliness

_____ 3. cannot *condone* (1)
   a. amplify
   b. make dense
   c. excuse

_____ 4. something of a *clod* (3)
   a. lump of clay
   b. large heavy shoe
   c. oaf

_____ 5. *mute* reproaches (4)
   a. muffle the sound
   b. silent
   c. shared

_____ 6. only *ascribe* (4)
    a. attribute
    b. restrain
    c. occupy

_____ 7. violent *antagonism* (4)
    a. unknown
    b. anxiety
    c. hostility

_____ 8. *frisk* around (6)
    a. search for concealed weapon
    b. romp
    c. dive

_____ 9. *commencing* a new series of tests (6)
    a. starting
    b. assuming
    c. preserving

_____ 10. *facilitate* my descent (9)
    a. make superficial
    b. make easier
    c. make worthy

_____ 11. a *rude* ladder (9)
    a. elemental
    b. ignorant
    c. crude

_____ 12. *chafed* against (9)
    a. irritated
    b. fretted
    c. rubbed

_____ 13. prevent a *recurrence* (10)
    a. repercussion
    b. repetition
    c. restoration

_____ 14. *replenished* the batteries (10)
    a. stocked
    b. perfected
    c. replaced

_____ 15. final *descent* (10)
    a. birth, lineage
    b. step downward
    c. devalue

Drawing Inferences from Newspaper Articles

In this section, you will be drawing inferences from a newspaper article.

SELECTION

"Unlike robots, animals can quickly adapt to
a new terrain."

GETTING THE PICTURE

The previous selection described a very intelligent rat who in the end was able to best a scientist. The selection below describes an ongoing experiment with rats, to harness their native abilities.

BIO-SKETCH

Kenneth Chang is a science writer for the *New York Times*. Prior to joining the *Times* in 2000, he worked as a science reporter for ABCNEWS.com.

BRUSHING UP ON VOCABULARY

terrain a piece of land

commandeer to seize arbitrarily

zombielike mindless, will-less; acting mechanically

A Remote-Controlled Rat:

Using Robotics, Researchers Give Upgrade to Lowly Rats; Study Sees Job for Rodents at Disaster Sites

By Kenneth Chang

1   PROVIDING A BIOLOGICAL TWIST to robotics, scientists have fitted live rats with remote controls to guide them through mazes, past obstacles, and even up trees by typing commands on a laptop computer up to half a mile away.

2   The approach, which takes advantage of an animal's innate ability to do things like climb over rocks, could ultimately be applied to inspecting a disaster area, said the scientists, who report their findings in May's issue of the journal *Nature*.

3   "An animal, especially a rat, has much greater facility for getting around a difficult terrain" than would a robot engineered from scratch, said the senior author of the paper, Dr. John K. Chapin, a professor at the State University of New York's Downstate Medical Center in Brooklyn.

4   The researchers do not commandeer the rat's brains and directly command the animals, zombielike, where to go. Rather, they take advantage of well-worn techniques of training animals by providing rewards.

5   The difference is that in the rats, both the stimuli and the reward are piped directly into the brain, and both can be sent by radio signals from some distance away.

6   Three wires were implanted into the brain of each rat. A pulse of current along one wire stimulated a region of the brain that made the rat feel as if its left whiskers had been touched.

7   A second wire led to the sensing region of the right whiskers. The third was connected to the part of the brain's pleasure center, the medial forebrain bundle.

8   The researchers trained the rats to turn left or right when they felt a stimulus in the corresponding whiskers, rewarding them with a pulse of euphoria in the pleasure center.

9   Strapped on the rat is a tiny backpack containing the antenna for receiving radio signals and a small microprocessor that dispenses the electrical pulses to the rat's brain. The researchers also attached tiny video cameras to get a rat's eye view.

10   Pressing the keys on the researchers' laptop computer sent the radio commands to the rat: the J key to steer the rat left, L to turn it to the right, and K to provide the reward.

11   The researchers also used a joystick like that used in video games to guide the rats up ladders, down stairs, and across narrow ledges.

12   Unlike robots, animals can quickly adapt to a new terrain. The researchers were able to take the rats, which had never been outdoors, and make them climb trees, scurry along branches, turn around and come back down.

13   "Our robot friend was astounded," Dr. Chapin said. "He knew what it would take to have a machine climb a tree having never seen a tree, having never come close to solving that physical problem."

That versatility could find use in search-and-rescue operations, Dr. Chapin said.

While robots can survive high temperatures, toxic chemicals, and even tumbles of several stories in height, remote-controlled animals might be able to penetrate through tiny spaces that robots cannot.

Dr. Robin R. Murphy, director of the Center for Robot-Assisted Search and Rescue who helped coordinate the use of robots at the World Trade Center wreckage, described the research as "very interesting," but added, "I don't think it's appropriate for search and rescue."

The rats would be easily distracted by blood or remains, Dr. Murphy said, adding, "Unfortunately, a lot of this is what rats usually treat as food." Human rescuers and victims would be disconcerted by the sight of rats scurrying around.

"The rats could scare weakened victims to death," Dr. Murphy said.

But she added that remote-controlled animals might be of use in less chaotic environments, like searches for land mines.

Dr. Chapin said he thought many of the problems could be solved.

A wireless computer network could ferry data between a pack of rats so that if one rat were out of direct radio contact with the operator, its signal could still be transmitted through the network, Dr. Chapin said.

And over time, perhaps people could learn to like rats.

"Maybe if it becomes widely known there are these rescue rats," Dr. Chapin said, "people wouldn't be scared."

(Kenneth Chang, "A Remote-Controlled Rat," *New York Times*, 2002)

✓ **COMPREHENSION CHECKUP**

True or False

Indicate whether each statement is true or false by writing **T** or **F** in the space provided.

_____ 1. Dr. Chapin believes that a robot can be better than a rat at climbing over rocks.

_____ 2. The experiment with rats operated under the principle of rewarding good behavior.

_____ 3. Rats can quickly adapt to a new terrain even if they have had no previous experience with it.

_____ 4. Three wires deliver electrical cues to the rat.

_____ 5. If the rat turns in the desired direction, it receives a sensation of pain.

Completion

List three advantages of using a rat at a disaster site.

1. _____

2. _____

3. _____

List three disadvantages of using a rat at a disaster site.

1. _____

2. _____

3. _____

Drawing Inferences from the Selection

1. Pouched rats are currently being used to detect mines in war-torn areas such as Mozambique, where after a 17-year civil war, millions of difficult-to-locate mines are buried. Both of the doctors mentioned in the selection are likely to be in favor of using rats in this way. What specific statement by Dr. Murphy indicates that this is true for her?

   _____

   _____

2. Rats are also being used to locate buried victims in earthquakes. Which of the two doctors mentioned in the selection is more likely to be in favor of the use of rats in this specific situation? _____

Vocabulary Practice

Write the letter of the word that is not related in meaning to the other words in the set.

1. _____ a. innate   b. extrinsic   c. inherent   d. inborn

2. _____ a. facility   b. capability   c. difficulty   d. ease

3. _____ a. euphoria   b. elation   c. gloom   d. well-being

4. _____	a. dispensed	b. apportioned	c. provided	d. hoarded
5. _____	a. scurry	b. creep	c. hasten	d. scoot
6. _____	a. versatility	b. adaptability	c. flexibility	d. rigidity
7. _____	a. disconcerted	b. perplexed	c. composed	d. confused
8. _____	a. chaotic	b. disordered	c. harmonious	d. disorganized

In Your Own Words

1. What can you infer about Dr. Chapin's feelings about the experiment? Does he think it likely that it will be practical to use rats in search-and-rescue missions?

2. What does Dr. Murphy believe about the feasibility of using rats in rescue operations? Cite specific details from the selection to support your conclusions.

3. How do you feel about controlling animals by means of remote-control devices?

4. Do you think that rats should be employed by the U.S. military to sniff out explosives? By law enforcement to sniff out illegal drugs or other contraband?

5. Some people are comfortable using animals such as rats in experiments of this sort, but not animals such as dogs, cats, or monkeys. How do you feel about this issue? Do you have concerns about turning animals into robots serving humans? Explain your reasoning.

Internet Activity

Use a search engine such as Google <www.google.com> or Yahoo! <www.yahoo.com> to locate information about recent developments in animal experimentation. Summarize your findings.

The Art of Writing

In a brief essay, respond to the item below.

Other scientists weighed in with their opinions when this study was first published. One scientist concluded that "rat-patrols" were certainly feasible and that it was "better them than us." Howard Eichenbaum, professor of psychology at Boston University, said that while it was certainly cheaper to turn a rat into a robot than attempt to build a robot to function like a rat, he worried about the ethics of the situation. "We're talking about making animals behave like machines," he said. Finally, some scientists worried that this new "rat technology" could fall into enemy hands. If so, these so-called robo-rats could be guided into government buildings where they could act as suicide bombers. Respond to each of these opinions by the experts, and give your own opinion.

Drawing Inferences from Textbook Material

In this section, you will be drawing inferences from different textbook materials.

Exercise 1: Drawing Inferences from Textbook Excerpts

After reading the following excerpts from college textbooks, choose the statement that can be directly inferred from the material, and write the appropriate letter in the blank.

Ethical Issues

As a graduate student in sociology at Washington State University, Rik Scarce studied radical environmental and animal-rights activists who sometimes break the law to dramatize their cause. When a group calling itself the Animal Liberation Front claimed responsibility for a raid on a university laboratory, in which 23 mink, mice, and coyotes were released and hydrochloric acid was poured on computers (causing an estimated $150,000 in damage), Scarce was subpoenaed to appear before a grand jury. Scarce acknowledged that he knew a prime suspect in the case quite well, but refused to answer any further questions. He argued that testifying about his sources not only would cause environmental activists to refuse to speak with him, curtailing his own research, but also would affect the sociological research effort as a whole. Sources would be less likely to trust other social scientists, and social scientists might shy away from controversial research that required confidentiality. Scarce went to jail rather than violate his commitment to confidentiality.

"You are remembered for the rules you break."

—Douglas MacArthur

(Craig Calhoun, *Sociology,* 7/e, 1997)

_____ 1. We can infer that
   a. the judge in this case was not persuaded by Scarce's argument
   b. the courts agree that information collected during sociological research is confidential
   c. Scarce actually knew nothing about who had raided the laboratory
   d. just as journalists are allowed to protect their sources, so are sociologists

---

A Friend Named Bo

Any of us would be lucky to have a friend such as Bo. Bo is a wonderful companion, loyal and giving unselfishly of time and affection. He is ever-ready to help, and in return, he asks for little.   1

But Bo was trained to be this way.   2

Bo is a 5-year-old golden retriever and labrador mix, a dog trained to be a helpmate to his owner, Brad Gabrielson. Gabrielson has cerebral palsy, and he has little control over his muscles. Yet with the help of Bo, Gabrielson can lead a life of independence.   3

Bo's abilities are many. If the doorbell rings, he answers the door. If Gabrielson drops something, Bo will pick it up. If Gabrielson is thirsty, Bo brings him a drink. One time, when Gabrielson fell, Bo left the apartment, went across the hall to a neighbor's door, where he scratched and barked. When the neighbor proved not to be home. Bo went upstairs to another neighbor's apartment.   4

When that neighbor—who had never encountered Bo before—came to the door, Bo led him downstairs, carefully tugging his hand. As the neighbor helped Gabrielson, Bo stood careful watch at his side. Said Gabrielson later, "On my own, I would have had to lie there . . . until my fiancée got home six hours later." But, he continued, "Bo came over and licked my face, to make sure I was all right, that I responded. Then he went to look for help." And Gabrielson stopped worrying.   5

(Robert S. Feldman, *Understanding Psychology,* 5/e, 1999)

_____ 2. We can infer that
    a. Gabrielson fell as a result of his own carelessness
    b. Gabrielson stopped worrying because he knew that his fiancée would turn up shortly and take care of him
    c. Gabrielson stopped worrying because he trusted that Bo would find help
    d. Gabrielson stopped worrying because his cell phone was nearby

Fiddler on the Mud

What lives in mud, feeds on mud, and finds mates by calling and waving across the mud? But, of course—fiddler crabs, creatures remarkable in many ways but best known as the ultimate experts in mud.   1

The many species of fiddler crabs (Uca) are inhabitants of mud and sand flats in estuaries and other sheltered coasts. Fiddlers are deposit feeders. They feed at low tide, using their pincers to scoop mud up into the mouth. The detritus in the mud is extracted with the help of brushlike mouth parts. Water is pumped from the gill chambers into the mouth to make the lighter detritus float and thus help separate it from the mud. The detritus is swallowed, and the clean mud is spat out on the substrate in neat little balls.   2

Fiddlers are active at low tide and retreat into their burrows at high tide. Each burrow has an entrance (revealed by the neat little balls of mud around it) that the occupant can plug when the tide comes in. At the next low tide, crabs emerge from home to feed and do whatever healthy, active fiddlers like to do.   3

Fiddlers have an interesting sex life. Males feature one tremendously enlarged claw, either right or left. It is brightly colored or highlighted with markings in many species. Females have a much smaller pair, which are used in feeding, as in the case of the males' small pincer. Males use their claw to advertise their sex—to tell females they mean business and to threaten any other males that may be in their way. They wave the claw at low tide on territories established around their burrows. Males entice any interested females into their burrows, and a female may visit a few pads before deciding on a particular one. Males often fight for prospective mates. They fight very carefully: A lost claw means disaster. It takes many molts to regenerate one that is big enough to get the crab back in action, and crabs whose claws are too small or that don't have the right moves can get pretty lonely!   4

In those areas coinhabited by several species of fiddlers, waving is used to prevent a male from attracting females of the wrong species. Some species wave up and down, others sideways. The angle and frequency of waving also vary, and bowing, fancy steps, and other body movements may form part of the ritual. Some beat the claw on the ground, and males of many species even produce sound by vibrating a joint of the large claw. It pays to advertise!   5

(Peter Castro, *Marine Biology*, 8/e, 2010)

_____ 3. We can infer that
    a. the small pincer is useful to female fiddler crabs, but not to males
    b. both sexes of fiddler crabs use the small pincer for feeding
    c. male fiddler crabs use the small pincer to attract female fiddler crabs
    d. a male fiddler crab can quickly regenerate a large claw

_____ 4. We can infer that

    a. the male crab makes use of his large claw to attract female crabs of the right species

    b. male fiddler crabs threaten other male fiddler crabs with their large claw

    c. you can tell the species of a male fiddler crab by how it waves its large claw

    d. all of the above

_____ 5. We can infer that

    a. the fiddler crab's diet consists of mud

    b. the fiddler crab's diet consists of the detritus that is extracted from mud

    c. larger, stronger fiddler crabs eat smaller, weaker ones

    d. fiddler crabs extract nutrition from sea water

Devotion to Animals

"I consider myself a Hindu, Christian, Moslem, Jew, Buddhist, and Confucian."

    —Gandhi

Hinduism is distinctive among world religions for its kindness to animals. A devout Hindu does not kill or eat animals. Cows often wander along Indian streets, and cars and taxis take care to drive around them. Furthermore, visitors to some Hindu temples may find monkeys and even mice well fed and running free. Several extremely popular gods, such as Ganesha and Hanuman, have animal features; and gods such as Shiva and Vishnu are regularly portrayed in the company of their animal companions. A Shiva temple would often be thought incomplete without a statue of Nandi, the bull who is Shiva's vehicle. 1

This devotion to animals in Hinduism has several possible origins: an ancient deification of certain animals, such as the elephant and tiger; the desire to neutralize dangerous or mischievous animals, such as the snake, rat, and monkey; and even a sense that human beings and animals have the same origin (a belief also common in oral religions). Belief in reincarnation has undoubtedly also played a role. When they see animals and insects, many Hindus see prehuman beings who in their spiritual evolution will eventually become human themselves. This brings a feeling of closeness to nonhuman forms of animal life. 2

Among the animals, cows receive special veneration. In rural India, to have a cow is to have milk and butter, fuel (dried dung), and the warmth and comfort associated with household pets. With a cow, one is never utterly destitute. Affection for the cow may represent a vestige of earlier matriarchal society—hinted at by the commonly used term *gau mata,* "mother cow." (The fact that Muslims butcher cows is a source of terrible friction between the Hindus and Muslims in India.) 3

(Michael Molloy, *Experiencing the World's Religions: Tradition, Challenge and Change,* 5/e, 2010)

_____ 6. We can infer that

    a. Hindus generally view animals as evil

    b. Hindus are ordinarily protective of animals

    c. a Muslim is unlikely to eat cow meat

    d. ownership of a cow in Hindu society is a terrible burden

No Cattle, No Dignity

Along with the rest of their country, the Dinka of Sudan have been involved in a war that has torn apart the nation since 1955. Before the war caused institutions to collapse in southern Sudan, the Dinka were the south's richest and proudest tribe. They were high court judges, civil administrators, and doctors, as well as farmers and cowherds. But the loss of cattle changed all that. Cattle stood at the heart of virtually every important tradition and ceremony in Dinka life. Cattle have always been the Dinka's highest form of wealth, but the war caused the loss of many herds. The loss has caused the Dinka to change their myths and adopt new sources of food. The loss of cattle has also changed marriage. An offering of cattle to the bride's family was traditionally the central transaction at a dowry celebration. Nowadays the negotiations are still held, but they are about handshakes and pledges. There is no livestock available to change hands. Despite the loss of life and land caused by war, the loss of cattle may represent the biggest impact of the war on the Dinka. A change in this single part of culture has caused changes throughout the culture.

"There is nothing permanent except change."

—Heraclitus

(Michael Hughes, *Sociology: The Core,* 7/e, 2005)

———— 7. We can infer that
   a. sheep serve an important ceremonial function in Dinka society
   b. the destruction of war has not touched the Dinka's cattle herds
   c. the loss of cattle has had a devastating impact on Dinka society
   d. dowry exchanges in Dinka culture still feature an exchange of cattle

Venomous Snakes are Few

Modern snakes and lizards make up 95 percent of living reptiles. Snakes evolved from lizards during the Cretaceous period and became adapted to burrowing. They lack limbs, so their prey must be subdued and swallowed without the benefit of appendages for manipulating food. Most snakes, like the boas and pythons, are powerful constrictors, suffocating their struggling prey with strong coils. Smaller snakes, such as the familiar garter snakes and water snakes, frequently swallow their food while it is still alive. Still others use toxic saliva to subdue their prey, usually lizards. It is likely that snake venom evolved as a way to obtain food and is used only secondarily in defense.

There are two major groups of venomous snakes. Elapids are represented in the United States by the coral snakes, which inhabit the southern states and display bright bands of red, yellow (or white), and black that completely encircle the body. In these snakes, the fangs, which are modified teeth, are short and permanently erect. The venom is a powerful neurotoxin that usually paralyzes the nervous system. Actually, coral snakes are responsible for very few bites—probably because of their secretive nature, small size, and relatively mild manner.

Vipers, represented in the United States by pit vipers such as the copperhead and cottonmouth and about 15 species of rattlesnakes, make up the remaining venomous snakes of the United States. They have a sophisticated venom delivery system terminating in two large, hollow, needlelike fangs that can be folded against the roof of the mouth when not in use. The venom destroys the victim's red blood cells and causes extensive local tissue damage. These snakes are readily identified by the combination of heat-sensing facial pits, elliptical pupils in the eyes, and a single row of scales on the underside of the tail. None of our harmless snakes has any combination of these characteristics.

First aid for snakebite is not advised if medical attention is less than a few hours away; application of a tourniquet, incising the wound to promote bleeding, and other radical treatments often cause more harm than good. The best method of treating snakebite is through the use of prescribed anti-venin, a serum containing antibodies to the venom. A hospital stay is required because some people are allergic to the serum.

4

Most people are not aware that snakes are perhaps the greatest controllers of disease-carrying, crop-destroying rodents because they are well adapted to following such prey into their hiding places. Also, snakes are important food items in the diets of many other carnivores, particularly birds of prey such as hawks and owls. Their presence in an ecosystem demonstrates the overall health of the environment.

5

(Sylvia Mader, *Biology,* 8/e, 2004)

_____ 8. We can infer that
   a. it is difficult to distinguish elapids from vipers
   b. coral snakes are responsible for the majority of poisonous snake bites in the United States
   c. snakes perform an important function in their ecosystems
   d. a tourniquet should always be applied to a snakebite to keep venom from reaching the heart and causing cardiac arrest

Drawing Inferences from Short Stories

In this section, you will be drawing inferences from a short story.

SELECTION

"When autumn came the men decided to look for the
rattler's den and execute mass slaughter."

GETTING THE PICTURE

The story that follows is a classic. Charles Finney describes the life-and-death cycle of the western diamondback rattlesnake. Pay particular attention to how well suited the diamondback was to the environment before the arrival of man.

BIO-SKETCH

Charles Finney (1905–1984) was born in Sedalia, Missouri. He attended the University of Missouri and worked for the *Arizona Daily Star* in Tucson, Arizona, in various writing capacities from 1930 to 1970. His most famous book, *The Circus of Dr. Lao,* earned the 1935 National Booksellers Award for the most original novel. In addition to his other novels, he contributed short stories to various magazines such as *The New Yorker* and *Harper's.* This short story, "The Gladiator," has been selected for publication in numerous literature anthology textbooks.

BRUSHING UP ON VOCABULARY

nemesis an unconquerable opponent or rival. The word is derived from the ancient Greek goddess of divine retribution. The goddess Nemesis punished the pretentious with her mighty sword.

chaparral cock-roadrunner a large (two-foot-long) terrestrial cuckoo residing in the arid regions of the western United States, Mexico, and Central America.

to homestead to acquire or settle on unclaimed land. A law was passed in the 1860s that offered up to 160 acres of land to any man who paid a registration fee, lived on the land for five years, and cultivated or built on it.

flank the side of an animal or person, between the ribs and the hip.

rendezvous an agreement to meet at a certain time or place. The word is borrowed from Middle French and literally means "to present yourself."

THE LIFE AND DEATH OF A WESTERN GLADIATOR

by Charles Finney

He was born on a summer morning in the shady mouth of a cave. Three others 1 were born with him, another male and two females. Each was about five inches long and slimmer than a lead pencil.

Their mother left them a few hours after they were born. A day after that his 2 brothers and sisters left him also. He was all alone. Nobody cared whether he lived or died. His tiny brain was very dull. He had no arms or legs. His skin was delicate. Nearly everything that walked on the ground or burrowed in it, that flew in the air or swam in the water or climbed trees was his enemy. But he didn't know that. He knew nothing at all. He was aware of his own existence, and that was the sum of his knowledge.

The direct rays of the sun could, in a short time, kill him. If the temperature 3 dropped too low he would freeze. Without food he would starve. Without moisture he would die of dehydration. If a man or a horse stepped on him he would be crushed. If anything chased him he could run neither very far nor very fast.

Thus it was at the hour of his birth. Thus it would be, with modifications, all 4 his life.

But against these drawbacks he had certain qualifications that fitted him to 5 be a competitive creature of this world and equipped him for its warfare. He could exist a long time without food or water. His very smallness at birth protected him when he most needed protection. Instinct provided him with what he lacked in experience. In order to eat he first had to kill; and he was eminently adapted for killing. In sacs in his jaws he secreted a virulent poison. To inject that poison he had two fangs, hollow and pointed. Without that poison and those fangs he would have been among the most helpless creatures on earth. With them he was among the deadliest.

He was, of course, a baby rattlesnake, a desert diamondback, named Crotalus 6 atrox by the herpetologists Baird and Girard and so listed in the *Catalogue of North American Reptiles* in its issue of 1853. He was grayish brown in color with a series of large dark diamond-shaped blotches on his back. His tail was white with five black crossbands. It had a button on the end of it.

Little Crotalus lay in the dust in the mouth of his cave. Some of his kinfolk lay 7 there too. It was their home. That particular tribe of rattlers had lived there for scores of years.

The cave had never been seen by a white man.   8

Sometimes as many as two hundred rattlers occupied the den. Sometimes 9 the numbers shrunk to as few as forty or fifty.

The tribe members did nothing at all for each other except breed. They 10 hunted singly; they never shared their food. They derived some automatic degree of safety from their numbers, but their actions were never concerted toward using their numbers to any end. If an enemy attacked one of them, the others did nothing about it.

Young Crotalus's brother was the first of the litter to go out into the world 11 and the first to die. He achieved a distance of fifty feet from the den when a Sonoran racer, four feet long and hungry, came upon him. The little rattler, despite his poison fangs, was a tidbit. The racer, long skilled in such arts, snatched him up by the head and swallowed him down. Powerful digestive juices in the racer's stomach did the rest. Then the racer, appetite whetted, prowled around until it found one of Crotalus's little sisters. She went the way of the brother.

Nemesis of the second sister was a chaparral cock. This cuckoo, or roadrun- 12 ner as it is called, found the baby amid some rocks, uttered a cry of delight, scissored it by the neck, shook it until it was almost lifeless, banged and pounded it upon a rock until life had indeed left it, and then gulped it down.

Crotalus, somnolent in a cranny of the cave's mouth, neither knew nor cared. 13 Even if he had, there was nothing he could have done about it.

On fourth day of his life he decided to go out into the world himself. He rip- 14 pled forth uncertainly, the transverse plates on his belly serving him as legs.

He could see things well enough within his limited range, but a five-inch-long 15 snake can command no great field of vision. He had an excellent sense of smell. But having no ears, he was stone deaf. On the other hand, he had a pit, a deep pockmark between eye and nostril. Unique, this organ was sensitive to animal heat. In pitch blackness, Crotalus, by means of the heat messages recorded in his pit, could tell whether another animal was near and could also judge its size. That was better than an ear.

The single button on his tail could not, of course, yet rattle. Crotalus wouldn't 16 be able to rattle until that button had grown into three segments. Then he would be able to buzz.

He had a wonderful tongue. It looked like an exposed nerve and probably 17 was exactly that. It was forked, and Crotalus thrust it in and out as he traveled. It told him things that neither his eyes nor his nose nor his pit told him.

Snake fashion, Crotalus went forth, not knowing where he was going, for 18 he had never been anywhere before. Hunger was probably his prime mover. In order to satisfy that hunger, he had to find something smaller than himself and kill it.

He came upon a baby lizard sitting in the sand. Eyes, nose, pit, and tongue told Crotalus it was there. Instinct told him what it was and what to do. Crotalus gave a tiny one-inch strike and bit the lizard. His poison killed it. He took it by the head and swallowed it. Thus was his first meal.

During his first two years Crotalus grew rapidly. He attained a length of two feet; his tail had five rattles on it and its button. He rarely bothered with lizards anymore, preferring baby rabbits, chipmunks, and round-tailed ground squirrels. Because of his slow locomotion he could not run down these agile little things. He had to contrive instead to be where they were when they would pass. Then he struck swiftly, injected his poison, and ate them after they died.

At two he was formidable. He had grown past the stage where a racer or a roadrunner could safely tackle him. He had grown to the size where other desert dwellers—coyotes, foxes, coatis, wildcats—knew it was better to leave him alone.

He found "her" on a rainy morning. Of that physical union six new rattle-snakes were born. Thus Crotalus, at two, had carried out his major primary function: he had reproduced his kind. In two years he had experienced everything that was reasonably possible for desert diamondback rattlesnakes to experience except death.

He had not experienced death for the simple reason that there had never been an opportunity for anything bigger and stronger than himself to kill him. Now, at two, because he was so formidable, that opportunity became more and more unlikely.

He grew more slowly in the years following his initial spurt. At the age of twelve he was five feet long. Few of the other rattlers in his den were older or larger than he.

He had a castanet of fourteen segments. It had been broken off occasionally in the past, but with each new molting a new segment appeared.

His first skin-shedding back in his babyhood had been a bewildering experience. He did not know what was happening. His eyes clouded over until he could not see. His skin thickened and dried until it cracked in places. His pit and his nostrils ceased to function. There was only one thing to do and that was to get out of that skin.

Crotalus managed it by nosing against the bark of a shrub until he forced the old skin down over his head, bunching it like the rolled top of a stocking around his neck. Then he pushed around among rocks and sticks and branches, literally crawling out of his skin by slow degrees. Wriggling free at last, he looked like a brand new snake. His skin was bright and satiny, his eyes and nostrils were clear, his pit sang with sensation.

For the rest of his life he was to molt three or four times a year. Each time he did it he felt as if he had been born again.

At twelve he was a magnificent reptile. Not a single scar defaced his rippling symmetry. He was diabolically beautiful and deadly poison.

His venom was his only weapon, for he had no power of constriction. Yellow-ish in color, his poison was odorless and tasteless. It was a highly complex mixture of proteids, each in itself direly toxic. His venom worked on the blood. The more poison he injected with a bite, the more dangerous the wound. The pain rendered by his bite was instantaneous, and the shock accompanying it was profound. Swelling began immediately, to be followed by a ghastly oozing. Injected directly into a large vein, his poison brought death quickly, for the victim died when it reached his heart.

At the age of twenty Crotalus was the oldest and largest rattler in his den. He 31 was in the golden age of his viperhood.

He was six feet long and weighed thirteen pounds. His whole world was only 32 about a mile in radius. He had fixed places where he avoided the sun when it was hot and he was away from his cave. He knew his hunting grounds thoroughly, every game trail, every animal burrow.

He was a fine old machine, perfectly adapted to his surroundings, accus- 33 tomed to a life of leisure and comfort. He dominated his little world.

But men were approaching. Spilling out of their cities, men were settling in 34 that part of the desert where Crotalus lived. They built roads and houses, set up fences, dug for water, planted crops.

They homesteaded the land. They brought new animals with them—cows, 35 horses, dogs, cats, barnyard fowl.

The roads they built were death traps for the desert dwellers. Every morning 36 new dead bodies lay on the roads, the bodies of the things the men had run over and crushed in their vehicles.

That summer Crotalus met his first dog. It was a German shepherd which had 37 been reared on a farm in the Midwest and there had gained the reputation of being a snake-killer. Black snakes, garter snakes, pilots, water snakes; it delighted in killing them all. It would seize them by the middle, heedless of their tiny teeth, and shake them violently until they died.

This dog met Crotalus face to face in the desert at dusk. Crotalus had seen 38 coyotes aplenty and feared them not. Neither did the dog fear Crotalus, although Crotalus then was six feet long, as thick in the middle as a motorcycle tire, and had a head the size of a man's clenched fist. Also this snake buzzed and buzzed and buzzed.

The dog was brave and a snake was a snake. The German shepherd snarled 39 and attacked. Crotalus struck him in the underjaw; his fangs sank in almost half an inch and squirted big blobs of poison into the tissues of the dog's flesh.

The shepherd bellowed with pain, backed off, groveled with his jaws in the 40 desert sand, and attacked again. He seized Crotalus somewhere by the middle of his body and tried to flip him in the air and shake him as, in the past, he had shaken slender black snakes to their death. In return, he received another poison-blurting stab in his flank and a third in the belly and a fourth in the eye as the terrible, writhing snake bit wherever it could sink his fangs.

The German shepherd had enough. He dropped the big snake and in sick, 41 agonizing bewilderment crawled somehow back to his master's homestead and died.

The homesteader looked at his dead dog and became alarmed. If there was 42 a snake around big enough to kill a dog that size, it could also kill a child and probably a man. It was something that had to be eliminated.

The homesteader told his fellow farmers, and they agreed to initiate a war of 43 extermination against the snakes.

The campaign during the summer was sporadic. The snakes were scattered 44 over the desert, and it was only by chance that the men came upon them. Even so, at summer's end, twenty-six of the vipers had been killed.

"The greatest joy in nature is the absence of man."

—Bliss Carman

"Nature thrives on patience; man on impatience."

—Paul Boese

When autumn came the men decided to look for the rattler's den and exe- cute mass slaughter. The homesteaders had become desert-wise and knew what to look for.

They found Crotalus's lair, without too much trouble—a rock outcropping on a slope that faced south. Cast-off skins were in evidence in the bushes. Bees flew idly in and out of the den's mouth. Convenient benches and shelves of rock were at hand where the snakes might lie for a final sunning in the autumn air.

They killed the three rattlers they found at the den when they first discovered it. They made plans to return in a few more days when more of the snakes had congregated. They decided to bring along dynamite with them and blow up the mouth of the den so that the snakes within would be sealed there forever and the snakes without would have no place to find refuge.

On the day the men chose to return nearly fifty desert diamondbacks were gathered at the portals of the cave. The men shot them, clubbed them, smashed them with rocks. Some of the rattlers escaped the attack and crawled into the den.

Crotalus had not yet arrived for the autumn rendezvous. He came that night. The den's mouth was a shattered mass of rock, for the men had done their dyna- miting well. Dead members of his tribe lay everywhere. Crotalus nosed among them, tongue flicking as he slid slowly along.

There was no access to the cave anymore. He spent the night outside among the dead. The morning sun warmed him and awakened him. He lay there at full length. He had no place to go.

The sun grew hotter upon him and instinctively he began to slide toward some dark shade. Then his senses warned him of some animal presence near by; he stopped, half coiled, raised his head and began to rattle. He saw two upright figures. He did not know what they were because he had never seen men before.

"That's the granddaddy of them all," said one of the homesteaders. "It's a good thing we came back." He raised his shotgun.

_____

(Charles Finney, "The Life and Death of a Western Gladiator")

✓ **COMPREHENSION CHECKUP**

Main Ideas, Supporting Details, and Purpose

Drawing on what you learned from the selection, answer the questions or fill in the blanks appropriately.

1. What is the author's main idea? _____

_____

2. What was the author's purpose in writing the story? _____

_____

_____

3. How does the author want the reader to feel about rattlesnakes at the end of the story? _____

_____

4. The rattlesnake "senses" the presence of other animals by using its _____.

5. The group of rattlesnakes described in the story lived in a _____.

6. The story of Crotalus is told in _____ (pattern of organization).

True or False

Indicate whether each statement is true or false by writing **T** or **F** in the blank provided.

_____ 7. Crotalus' only weapon is his venom.

_____ 8. Rattlesnakes molt three or four times a year.

_____ 9. When part of a rattlesnake's tail breaks off, it is never replaced.

_____ 10. Rattlesnakes work in concert to kill their prey.

_____ 11. Crotalus had his first meal when he was only five inches long.

_____ 12. A rattlesnake can't make a buzzing sound until the button on the end of the tail is at least three segments long.

Drawing Inferences from the Selection

For each of the statements write **Y** on the line if the inference can be logically inferred or **N** if the inference can't be logically inferred.

_____ 13. The author suggests that Crotalus did not survive his encounter with the homesteaders.

_____ 14. On the basis of the information in paragraphs 11 and 12, we can infer that baby rattlesnakes have a high survival rate.

_____ 15. The baby rattlesnake is taught by older snakes how to fend for itself.

_____ 16. The spreading of human settlements is in direct conflict with the lifestyle of the rattlesnake.

_____ 17. The homesteaders were likely aware that snakes are an important part of an ecosystem.

_____ 18. The reader can assume that it is easier to kill a rattlesnake before the age of two than it is to kill it after the age of two.

Vocabulary in Context

Look through the paragraph indicated in parentheses to find a word that matches the definition below.

1. actively poisonous (paragraph 5) _____

2. sleepy (13) _____

3. to plan with ingenuity; devise (20) _____

4. confusing or completely puzzling (26) _____

5. fiendishly; wickedly (29) _____

6. occurring at irregular intervals (44) _____

7. assembled (47) _____

8. shelter or protection from danger (47) _____

Vocabulary Puzzle

Directions: Use the vocabulary words below to complete the crossword puzzle.

agile	dehydration	fang	symmetry
cave	delicate	litter	tidbit
ceased	den	sac	whet
concerted	eminently	slim	writhe
defaced			

ACROSS CLUES

2. a cave used as a place of shelter
3. fragile; easily damaged
4. stimulate
6. quick; nimble
7. abnormal loss of water from the body (or tissue)
10. planned or devised together
11. the means by which poison is injected
13. excellence of proportion
14. a hollow in the earth

DOWN CLUES

1. number of young brought forth at one birth
2. marred

5. a small morsel of food
8. highly; very
9. baglike structure containing fluid
10. stopped; discontinued
12. twist
13. slender

In Your Own Words

1. Some people are very fearful of snakes, even harmless ones. What do you think causes this irrational fear?

2. What are some things people can do to avoid being bitten by a rattlesnake while hiking or camping in the wilderness?

3. How did the snake come to be so vilified in Western culture? Do you think movies help or harm the snake's reputation?

4. Have you ever been bitten by a snake? Do you know anyone who has been bitten? Did you know that the strength of a snake's venom varies depending on how old the snake is, when it last ate, and what time of day the strike occurs? How much it affects a person also depends on how deeply the fangs penetrate and how much venom is injected. How should a person be treated after a snake bite?

The Art of Writing

Explore your own feelings about snakes. Are you fearful of them or respectful? Does your particular culture view snakes in a specific way? Write a few paragraphs giving your opinion of humans' treatment of snakes.

Internet Activities

1. Consult the following Web site to research the history of snakes and the mythology associated with them. Write a few paragraphs discussing what you learn.

   www.umass.edu/nrec/snake_pit/pages/begin.html

2. There are many different kinds of rattlesnakes. To learn more about rattlesnakes, including one that is an albino, visit the Web site sponsored by the American International Rattlesnake Museum in Albuquerque, New Mexico:

   www.rattlesnakes.com

   First, read about two different kinds of rattlesnakes, and then make a list of their similarities and differences. What can you infer about the rattlesnake's ability to survive? Is it well equipped to survive in the modern world or is it in danger of extinction?

Drawing Inferences from Cartoons

Study the cartoon by Gary Larson below and then write an appropriate caption or main idea sentence for it.

"Freeze, Earl! Freeze! ... Something rattled!"

Drawing Inferences from Fables

While many people see the wolf as a symbol of untamed wilderness, others view the wolf as a vicious animal. Fables and fairy tales such as "Little Red Riding Hood" and "The Three Little Pigs" have emphasized the negative traits of "The Big Bad Wolf."

What inferences can you draw from the following fable about the characteristics of the wolf?

The Wolf and the Crane

A wolf devoured his prey so ravenously that a bone got stuck in his throat, and in extreme agony, he ran and howled throughout the forest, beseeching every animal he met to pull out the bone. He even offered a generous reward to anyone who succeeded in pulling it out. Moved by his pleas as well as the prospect of the money, a crane ventured her long neck down the wolf's throat and drew out the bone. She then modestly asked for the promised reward, but the wolf just grinned and bared his teeth.

"Ungrateful creature!" he replied with seeming indignation. "How dare you ask for any other reward than your life? After all, you're among the very few who can say that you've put your head into the jaws of a wolf and were permitted to draw it out safely."

   Moral: *Expect no reward when you serve the wicked, and be thankful if you escape injury for your pains.*

(Jack Zipes, ed., *Aesop's Fables*)

Drawing on what you learned from this fable, list two characteristics of the wolf.

1. _____

2. _____

Based on what you already know and what you learned from this fable, explain the following sayings in your own words.

1. It's important to keep the wolf from one's door.

   _____

2. Beware a wolf in sheep's clothing.

   _____

3. He is as hungry as a wolf.

   _____

4. It's bad manners to wolf your food down.

   _____

5. He has many girlfriends and is such a wolf.

   _____

6. What inferences can you draw about the wolf from these sayings?

   _____

Drawing Inferences from Journals

In this section you will be drawing inferences from journal writing.

SELECTION

"Once I had become aware of the strong feeling of property rights which existed amongst the wolves, I decided to use this knowledge to make them at least recognize my existence."

GETTING THE PICTURE

The following selection was written in the early 1960s by Farley Mowat, a noted conservationist. Mowat was hired by the Canadian government to investigate the claim that hordes of wolves were slaughtering arctic caribou. He was sent to live alone in the arctic tundra where he was supposed to establish contact with the wolves so he could better understand their behavior. This brief excerpt describes his initial contact with the wolf he came to call "George."

BIO-SKETCH

Farley Mowat, born and raised in Canada, considers himself to be a "Northern Man." He says that he likes to think he is a "reincarnation of the Norse saga men and, like them, [his] chief concern is with the tales of men, and other animals, living under conditions of natural adversity." The recipient of numerous awards, Mowat's two best-known works, *A Whale for the Killing* (1984) and *Never Cry Wolf* (1963), were made into popular movies.

BRUSHING UP ON VOCABULARY

cognizance perception or knowledge. To take *cognizance* of something is to notice or recognize it. *Cognizance* comes from the Latin *cogni*, which means "to come to know."

baleful harmful or threatening harm; ominous, deadly.

inviolate kept sacred or unbroken, intact.

diurnal done or happening in the daytime. The first part of the word does not come from *di*, meaning "two," but from *dies* meaning "day."

nocturnal the opposite of *diurnal*—means "done or happening at night."

cache a place in which stores of food are hidden.

austerely very plainly or simply, with no ornamentation or luxury.

epitome a good example that shows all the typical qualities.

WOLF SONGS

by Farley Mowat

GEORGE

Quite by accident I had pitched my tent within ten yards of one of the major paths 1 used by the wolves when they were going to, or coming from their hunting grounds to the westward; and only a few hours after I had taken up residence one of the wolves came back from a trip and discovered me and my tent. He was at the end of a hard night's work and was clearly tired and anxious to go home to bed. He came over a small rise fifty yards from me with his head down, his eyes half-closed and a preoccupied air about him. Far from being the preternaturally alert and suspicious beast of fiction, this wolf was so self-engrossed that he came straight on to within fifty yards of me, and might have gone right past the tent without seeing it at all, had I not banged my elbow against the teakettle, making a resounding clang. The wolf's head came up and his eyes opened wide, but he did not stop or falter in his pace. One brief, sidelong glance was all he vouchsafed to me as he continued on his way.

It was true that I wanted to be inconspicuous, but I felt uncomfortable at 2 being so totally ignored. Nevertheless, during the two weeks which followed, one or more wolves used the track past my tent almost every night—and never, except on one memorable occasion, did they evince the slightest interest in me.

By the time this happened I had learned a good deal about my wolfish neigh- 3
bors, and one of the facts which had emerged was that they were not nomadic
roamers, as is almost universally believed, but were settled beasts and the pos-
sessors of a large permanent estate with very definite boundaries.

The territory owned by my wolf family comprised more than a hundred square 4
miles, bounded on one side by a river but otherwise not delimited by geographical
features. Nevertheless there *were* boundaries, clearly indicated in wolfish fashion.

Anyone who has observed a dog doing his neighborhood rounds and leaving 5
his personal mark on each convenient post will have already guessed how the
wolves marked out *their* property. Once a week, more or less, the clan made the
rounds of the family lands and freshened up the boundary markers—a sort of
lupine beating of the bounds. This careful attention to property rights was perhaps made necessary by the presence of two other wolf families whose lands
abutted on ours, although I never discovered any evidence of bickering or disagreements between the owners of the various adjoining estates. I suspect, therefore, that it was more of a ritual activity.

In any event, once I had become aware of the strong feeling of property 6
rights which existed amongst the wolves, I decided to use this knowledge to
make them at least recognize my existence. One evening, after they had gone off
for their regular nightly hunt, I staked out a property claim of my own, embracing perhaps three acres, with the tent at the middle, and *including a hundred-
yard-long section of the wolves' path.*

Staking the land turned out to be rather more difficult than I had anticipated. 7
In order to ensure that my claim would not be overlooked, I felt obliged to make
a property mark on stones, clumps of moss, and patches of vegetation at intervals of not more than fifteen feet around the circumference of my claim. This
took most of the night and required frequent returns to the tent to consume
copious quantities of tea; but before dawn brought the hunters home the task
was done, and I retired, somewhat exhausted, to observe results.

I had not long to wait. At 0814 hours, according to my wolf log, the leading 8
male of the clan appeared over the ridge behind me, padding homeward with
his usual air of preoccupation. As usual he did not deign to glance at the tent; but
when he reached the point where my property line intersected the trail, he
stopped as abruptly as if he had run into an invisible wall. He was only fifty yards
from me and with my binoculars I could see his expression very clearly.

His attitude of fatigue vanished and was replaced by a look of bewilderment. 9
Cautiously he extended his nose and sniffed at one of my marked bushes. He did not
seem to know what to make of it or what to do about it. After a minute of complete
indecision he backed away a few yards and sat down. And then, finally, he looked
directly at the tent and at me. It was a long, thoughtful, considering sort of look.

Having achieved my object—that of forcing at least one of the wolves to take 10
cognizance of my existence—I now began to wonder if, in my ignorance, I had
transgressed some unknown wolf law of major importance and would have to
pay for my temerity. I found myself regretting the absence of a weapon as the
look I was getting became longer, yet more thoughtful, and still more intent.

I began to grow decidedly fidgety, for I dislike staring matches, and in this 11
particular case I was up against a master, whose yellow glare seemed to become
more baleful as I attempted to stare him down.

The situation was becoming intolerable. In an effort to break the impasse I
loudly cleared my throat and turned my back on the wolf (for a tenth of a second) to indicate as clearly as possible that I found his continued scrutiny impolite, if not actually offensive.

He appeared to take the hint. Getting to his feet he had another sniff at my
marker, and then he seemed to make up his mind. Briskly, and with an air of decision, he turned his attention away from me and began a systematic tour of the area I had staked out as my own. As he came to each boundary marker he sniffed it once or twice, then carefully placed *his* mark on the outside of each clump of grass or stone. As I watched I saw where I, in my ignorance, had erred. He made his mark with such economy that he was able to complete the entire circuit without having to reload once, or to change the simile slightly, he did it all on one tank of fuel.

The task completed—and it had taken him no longer than fifteen minutes—
he rejoined the path at the point where it left my property and trotted off towards his home—leaving me with a good deal to occupy my thoughts.

Once it had been formally established, and its existence ratified by the wolves
themselves, my little enclave in that territory remained inviolate. Never again did a wolf trespass on my domain. Occasionally, one in passing would stop to freshen up some of the boundary marks on his side of the line, and, not to be outdone in ceremony, I followed suit to the best of my ability. Any lingering doubts I might have had as to my personal safety dissolved, and I was free to devote all my attention to a study of the beasts themselves.

Very early in my observations I discovered that they led a well-regulated life,
although they were not slavish adherents to fixed schedules. Early in the evenings the males went off to work. They might depart at four o'clock or they might delay until six or seven, but sooner or later off they went on the nightly hunt. During this hunt they ranged far afield, although always—as far as I could tell—staying within the limits of the family territory. I estimated that during a normal hunt they covered thirty or forty miles before dawn. When times were hard they probably covered even greater distances, since on some occasions they did not get home until the afternoon. During the balance of the daylight hours they slept—but in their own peculiarly wolfish way, which consisted of curling up for short wolf-naps of from five to ten minutes' duration; after each of which they would take a quick look about, and then turn round once or twice before dozing off again.

The females and the pups led a more diurnal life. Once the males had departed in the evening, the female usually went into the den and stayed there, emerging only occasionally for a breath of air, a drink, or sometimes for a visit to the meat cache for a snack.

This cache deserves special mention. No food was ever stored or left close to
the den; and only enough was brought in at one time for immediate consumption. Any surplus from a hunt was carried to the cache, which was located in a jumble of boulders half-a-mile from the den, and stuffed into crevices, primarily for the use of the nursing female who, of course, could not join the male wolves on extended hunting trips.

The cache was also used surreptitiously by a pair of foxes who had their own
den close by. The wolves must have known of the location of the foxes' home, and probably knew perfectly well that there was a certain amount of pilfering from their cache; but they did nothing about it even though it would have been a simple

matter for them to dig out and destroy the litter of fox pups. The foxes, on their side, seemed to have no fear of the wolves, and several times I saw one flit like a shadow across the esker within a few yards of a wolf without eliciting any response.

Later I concluded that almost all the dens used by the Barren Land wolves 20 were abandoned fox burrows which had been taken over and enlarged by the wolves. It is possible that the usefulness of the foxes as preliminary excavators may have guaranteed them immunity; but it seems more likely that the wolves' tolerance simply reflected their general amiability.

During the day, while the male wolves took it easy, the female would be reason- 21 ably active about her household chores. Emerging boisterously from the close confines of the den, the pups also became active—to the point of total exhaustion. Thus throughout the entire twenty-four-hour period there was usually something going on, or at least the expectation of something, to keep me glued to the telescope.

After the first two days and nights of nearly continuous observing I had about 22 reached the limits of my endurance. It was a most frustrating situation. I did not dare to go to sleep for fear of missing something vital. On the other hand, I became so sleepy that I was seeing double, if not triple, on occasion; although this effect may have been associated with the quantities of wolf-juice which I consumed in an effort to stay awake.

I saw that something drastic would have to be done or my whole study pro- 23 gram would founder. I could think of nothing adequate until, watching one of the males dozing comfortably on a hillock near the den, I recognized the solution to my problem. It was simple. I had only to learn to nap like a wolf.

It took some time to get the knack of it. I experimented by closing my eyes 24 and trying to wake up again five minutes later, but it didn't work. After the first two or three naps I failed to wake up at all until several hours had passed.

The fault was mine, for I had failed to imitate *all* the actions of a dozing wolf, 25 and, as I eventually discovered, the business of curling up to start with, and spinning about after each nap, was vital to success. I don't know why this is so. Perhaps changing the position of the body helps to keep the circulation stimulated. I *do* know, however, that a series of properly conducted wolf-naps is infinitely more refreshing than the unconscious coma of seven or eight hours' duration which represents the human answer to the need for rest.

Unfortunately, the wolf-nap does not readily lend itself to adaptation into our 26 society, as I discovered after my return to civilization when a young lady of whom I was enamored at the time parted company with me. She had rather, she told me vehemently, spend her life with a grasshopper who had rickets, than spend one more night in bed with me.

As I grew more completely attuned to their daily round of family life I found 27 it increasingly difficult to maintain an impersonal attitude toward the wolves. No matter how hard I tried to regard them with scientific objectivity, I could not resist the impact of their individual personalities. Because he reminded me irresistibly of a Royal Gentleman for whom I worked as a simple soldier during the war, I found myself calling the father of the family George, even though in my notebooks, he was austerely identified only as Wolf "A."

George was a massive and eminently regal beast whose coat was silver-white. 28 He was about a third larger than his mate, but he hardly needed this extra bulk to emphasize his air of masterful certainty. George had presence. His dignity was unassailable, yet he was by no means aloof. Conscientious to a fault, thoughtful of others, and affectionate within reasonable bounds, he was the kind of father whose idealized image appears in many wistful books of human family reminiscences, but whose real prototype has seldom paced the earth upon two legs. George was, in brief, the kind of father every son longs to acknowledge as his own.

His wife was equally memorable. A slim, almost pure-white wolf with a thick ruff around her face, and wide-spaced, slightly slanted eyes, she seemed the picture of a minx. Beautiful, ebullient, passionate to a degree, and devilish when the mood was on her, she hardly looked like the epitome of motherhood; yet there could have been no better mother anywhere. I found myself calling her Angeline, although I have never been able to trace the origin of her name in the murky depths of my own subconscious. I respected and liked George very much, but I became deeply fond of Angeline, and still live in hopes that I can somewhere find a human female who embodies all her virtues.

Angeline and George seemed as devoted a mated pair as one could hope to find. As far as I could tell they never quarreled, and the delight with which they greeted each other after even a short absence was obviously unfeigned. They were extremely affectionate with one another, but, alas, the many pages in my notebook which had been hopefully reserved for detailed comments on the sexual behavior and activities of wolves remained obstinately blank as far as George and Angeline were concerned.

Distressing as it was to my expectations, I discovered that physical lovemaking enters into the lives of a pair of mated wolves only during a period of two or three weeks early in the Spring, usually in March. Virgin females (and they are all virginal until their second year) then mate; but unlike dogs, who have adopted many of the habits of their human owners, wolf bitches mate with only a single male, and mate for life.

Whereas the phrase "till death us do part" is one of the more amusing mockeries in the nuptial arrangements of a large proportion of the human race, with wolves it is a simple fact. Wolves are also strict monogamists, and although I do not necessarily consider this an admirable trait, it does make the reputation for unbridled promiscuity which we have bestowed on the wolf somewhat hypocritical.

(Farley Mowat, "George," *Wolf Songs*)

✓ **COMPREHENSION CHECKUP**

Multiple Choice

Write the letter of the correct answer in the blank provided.

_____ 1. If the author were reading this selection out loud, he would most likely sound
   a. solemn
   b. admiring
   c. angry
   d. perplexed

_A_　　2. From this article, you could conclude that the author
a. has a genuine affection for animals
b. considers hunting a favorite pastime
c. is a rancher who is afraid that wolves will kill his cattle
d. dislikes outdoor life

_B_　　3. The word *offensive* in the last line of paragraph 12 means
a. illegal
b. insulting
c. damaging
d. aggressive

_C_　　4. From paragraph 22, you could infer that the "wolf-juice" the author consumed is most likely
a. coffee
b. beer
c. tea
d. milk

_A_　　5. All of the following are examples of how male and female wolves behave *except*
a. male and female wolves are promiscuous
b. the males hunt for food while the females stay close to the den
c. the males rest during the day while the females do household chores
d. male and female wolves are likely to mate for life

_B_　　6. The writer's main purpose in writing this selection is to
a. relate humorous anecdotes about the wolf
b. describe the wolf's behavior and habitat
c. explain why wolves are disappearing from the wild
d. persuade hunters to treat the wolf with more respect

_D_　　7. The information presented in paragraphs 25–26 supports which of the following statements?
a. Mowat discovered that a wolf-nap is far less refreshing than seven hours of sound sleep.
b. Mowat discovered that all of the actions of a dozing wolf must be enacted to have a successful wolf-nap.
c. Mowat discovered that by taking wolf-naps, he was not endearing himself to a particular lady friend.
d. both b and c

_A_　　8. Paragraphs 28–29 provide details that primarily
a. describe the physical and personality characteristics of George and Angeline
b. demonstrate the superiority of wolf characteristics in contrast to humans
c. describe the paternal and maternal characteristics of the wolf
d. all of the above

_B_　　9. Which of the following occurred first?
a. The lead wolf backed away and sat down.
b. The author marked "his" property.
c. The author turned his back on the wolf.
d. The lead wolf made his mark and then trotted off toward home.

_____ 10. Which of the following observations best support the author's contention that the wolves led a well-regulated life?
   a. While the males were gone, the females and pups retreated to the den.
   b. During the balance of daylight hours, they slept.
   c. Early in the evenings the wolves went off to hunt.
   d. All of the above

_____ 11. We can infer that the author of this selection
   a. is happily married
   b. is looking for a partner who embodies characteristics similar to that of Angeline
   c. feels competitive toward George
   d. feels that a wolf's reputation for promiscuity is well-deserved

_____ 12. All of the following is given as evidence of the wolves' amiability *except*
   a. the wolves did not trespass on the author's territory
   b. the wolves let nearby foxes pilfer from their meat cache without retaliating
   c. if properly executed, wolf naps are more refreshing than seven hours of continuous sleep
   d. Angeline and George were extremely affectionate with one another and appeared never to quarrel

Vocabulary in Context

Each item below includes a sentence from the selection. Using the context clues provided, write a preliminary definition for the italicized word. Then look up the word in a dictionary and write the appropriate definition.

   1. "Far from being the *preternaturally* alert and suspicious beast of fiction, this wolf was so self-engrossed that he came straight on to within fifty yards of me." (paragraph 1)

      Your definition: _____

      Dictionary definition: _____

   2. "The wolf's head came up and his eyes opened wide, but he did not stop or *falter* in his pace." (1)

      Your definition: _____

      Dictionary definition: _____

   3. "One brief, sidelong glance was all he *vouchsafed* to me as he continued on his way." (1)

      Your definition: _____

      Dictionary definition: _____

   4. "It was true that I wanted to be *inconspicuous*, but I felt uncomfortable at being so totally ignored." (2)

      Your definition: _____

      Dictionary definition: _____

   5. "Nevertheless, during the two weeks which followed, one or more wolves used the track past my tent almost every night—and never, except on one memorable occasion, did they *evince* the slightest interest in me." (2)

Your definition: _____

Dictionary definition: _____

6. "In order to ensure that my claim would not be overlooked, I felt obliged to make a property mark on stones, clumps of moss, and patches of vegetation at intervals of not more than fifteen feet around the *circumference* of my claim." (7)

Your definition: _____

Dictionary definition: _____

7. This took most of the night and required frequent returns to the tent to consume *copious* quantities of tea." (7)

Your definition: _____

Dictionary definition: _____

8. As usual he did not *deign* to glance at the tent; but when he reached the point where my property line *intersected* the trail, he stopped as abruptly as if he had run into an invisible wall." (8)

Your definition: _____

Dictionary definition: _____

Your definition: _____

Dictionary definition: _____

Vocabulary Practice

Complete the sentences with one of the following vocabulary words.

abutted	embodies	monogamist	temerity
adherent	enamored	murky	transgressed
aloof	enclave	nomadic	unassailable
bestowed	hypocritical	pilfering	unbridled
ebullient	immunity	surreptitiously	vehemently

1. Having lived in ten homes in the last two years, he led a _____ existence.

2. Her property directly _____ mine.

3. By the time he was 18, he had _____ most laws.

4. For his vacation, he wanted to find a quiet _____ far off the beaten path.

5. Don't bother offering her dessert because she is a strong _____ of the Atkins diet.

6. After missing his 12:30 curfew, Danny _____ crept through the house while hoping his parents wouldn't awaken.

7. Susan was caught _____ small items from the store.

8. He was granted _____ in exchange for his testimony.

9. Joe is so _____ with Rosa that I think a wedding will occur shortly.

10. Despite unrelenting pressure from the prosecutor, the defendant _____ proclaimed his innocence.

11. He is a man of such integrity that his word is considered _____.

12. At the funeral, Mark stood _____ from the rest of the family.

13. Her _____ personality helps to explain why so many people choose to be around her.

14. Sara searched through the _____ water trying in vain to find her diamond ring.

15. She _____ all the traits of an excellent student.

16. Several players had the _____ to criticize the coach for conducting extended practices.

17. He was a committed _____ who had been married for over forty years to the same wife.

18. Regis _____ the $1,000,000 prize on the winning contestant.

19. It's _____ for Karen to lecture about healthy life choices when she continues to smoke.

20. Nothing can beat a young child's _____ enthusiasm for summer vacation.

In Your Own Words

1. Mowat discovered that in many instances the myths of wolf behavior are not the same as the reality. List as many discrepancies between the two as you can find.

2. Mowat asserted his property rights by "marking" the boundaries of his territory. How is the lead wolf's response contrary to what we might typically expect?

3. Mowat comes to admire the wolves in many respects and in some instances feels that their lifestyle is superior to ours. What specific aspects of wolf behavior does Mowat admire?

4. An artist could probably paint a picture using Mowat's descriptions of George and Angeline. Give a brief synopsis of each one, including character traits. What key details does Mowat use in order to portray the wolves in human terms?

5. Explain the symbiotic relationship between the wolves and foxes.

The Art of Writing

In a brief essay, respond to the item below.

In the United States, one of the most controversial conservation issues is the reintroduction of wolves into areas where they have long been extinct. One group feels that parks such as Yellowstone need wolves to preserve an ecological balance. These groups note that an overabundance of deer is currently overgrazing vast areas of the park. Because wolves are a natural predator of deer, they would help control the deer population. On the other hand, many feel that the wolf is detrimental to human beings, and the loudest opposition to reintroduction comes from the ranching community, which is fearful of massive livestock loss.

Come up with several suggestions for resolving the dispute between the two groups. If necessary, go to the library or the Internet and do additional research.

Internet Activity

One of the best Web sites about wolves is sponsored by *Nova* of the Public Broadcasting System. Check out its website at

> www.pbs.org/wgbh/nova/wolves

Then take a short quiz to see how much you know about the relationship between the domestic dog and the wolf. Finally, print an article of interest to you, and list some inferences that can be drawn from it.

Brain Teasers

Each of the clues below contains a number and some letters that symbolize commonly recognized phrases. Figure out the phrase paying particular attention to the number in each one. The first one has been done for you.

Example: <u>3 S and Y O three strikes and you're out.</u>

1. a P is W 1000 W _____

2. T for 2 _____

3. Y the 1 for M _____

4. playing 20 Q _____

A car license plate can give information about the owner. Can you name each owner's career?

1. LUV2SNG _____

2. FOTOGR4 _____

3. IPNTPIX _____

4. ALLRIZ _____

5. LIFSAVR _____

6. STORKDR _____

7. CARETKR _____

8. SAYAHH _____

9. 2N2R4 _____

10. REALTR _____

11. 10SPRO _____

12. APR 15 _____

13. 24KT _____

14. 2THDR _____

15. 4CASTR _____

16. IFYTFYR _____

17. W8LFTR _____

18. LITIG8 _____

VOCABULARY | **Unit 4: Word Parts Featuring Polar Opposites**

"For there is nothing either good or bad, thinking makes it so."
—William Shakespeare

In this unit, we will be working with words having opposite meanings, such as "love" and "hate." We will also introduce you to the word parts *meter*, *equi*, and *a(n)*. Words made from these word parts, along with their definitions, follow. Supplemental words with these word parts are located in the left margin.

phil(o)—love

oenophile

bibliophile	Since *biblio-* means "book," a *bibliophile* is a person who loves or collects books.
philanderer	a man who makes love to a woman he can't or won't marry. *Ander* means "male."
philanthropist	a person who shows love for others by donating money or services to help them. Bill and Melinda Gates are both *philanthropists*.
philosopher	a person who offers views and theories on profound questions; "a lover of wisdom." Socrates, Plato, and Aristotle were ancient Greek *philosophers*.
philharmonic	loving music; a symphony or orchestra. The *Philharmonic* Orchestra performs once a month.
philately	the collection and study of postage stamps and postmarks

mis—hate; bad(ly)

misadvised
misappropriate
miscast
mischaracterize
miscommunication
mishandled
mispronunciation

misanthrope	a person who hates or distrusts people. Ebenezer Scrooge, a character in *A Christmas Carol* by Charles Dickens, was the town *misanthrope*.
misogynist	Since *-gyn-* means "woman," a *misogynist* is a person who hates or is hostile toward women.
miscreant	a vicious or depraved person
misconstrue	to think of in a wrong way, to misunderstand. Taryn *misconstrued* Brad's response because to her a grunt indicates a sign of displeasure.
misnomer	a wrong name; an error in naming a person or thing. It is a *misnomer* to call a whale a fish.

eu—good or well; dys—bad, abnormal, difficult

eugenic
euphonious

eulogy	a speech or composition praising a person or thing, especially a person who has just died
euphemism	a word or phrase that is used in place of another that is considered to be offensive. "Adult entertainment" is a *euphemism* for "pornography."
euphoria	a feeling of great joy or excitement

	euthanasia	the act of putting someone to death painlessly or allowing him or her to die by withholding medical assistance. *To euthanize* means to subject to *euthanasia*.
dysfunctional dyspeptic dystrophy	**dysentery**	infectious disease of the large intestine marked by diarrhea. *Dysentery* literally means "bad bowel."
	dyslexia	any of a variety of reading disorders

meter—measure

speedometer	an instrument to measure the rate of travel in miles or kilometers
odometer	an instrument for measuring distance traveled, as in a car
pedometer	an instrument that measures the distance walked or run by recording the number of steps taken
barometer	an instrument that measures atmospheric pressure

macro—large or long; micro—small

macrocosm	the universe considered as a whole. *Cosmo* means "universe."
microcosm	a little world, a world in miniature; a group thought of as representing a larger group. The 100 representatives to Boys' State were a *microcosm* of the U.S. high school population.
microbe	a disease-causing bacterium; a small bit of life
microfilm	film bearing a miniature photographic copy of graphic or textual material

equi—equal

Don't confuse *equi* with *equus*, which means "horse." (An *equestrian* competition involves horse riding.)

equity	fairness; justice. Also the value of a piece of property after subtracting the amount owed on it in mortgages and liens. How much *equity* do you have in your home?
equitable	fair or just. Maria's will made sure that her assets were distributed in an *equitable* fashion among her three sons.
equivalent	equal in value, measure, force, or significance. Eat five servings of fresh fruits and vegetables or their *equivalent* every day.

a(n)—not, without

atypical	not typical; irregular; abnormal
amoral	without a sense of moral responsibility
aseptic	free from the living germs of disease
atrophy	a wasting away or a shrinking up of a part of the body. Muscles can *atrophy* from lack of use. Can the mind also *atrophy* from lack of use?
anomaly	not following the usual rule or pattern; abnormal. The penguin, which cannot fly, is an *anomaly* among birds.

amorphous   without a definite shape or form. When Carlos examined the amoeba through the microscope, he discovered that it had an *amorphous* shape.

anemia   a condition in which a person's blood does not have enough red blood cells

asymmetrical having or showing a lack of symmetry; not balanced. Because the design in the painting was *asymmetrical*, it was not pleasing to the eye.

poly—many

polyandry
polytheism

polychromatic having or exhibiting many colors

polysyllabic consisting of four or more syllables. *Pol-y-syl-lab-ic* has five syllables.

polytechnic   pertaining to or offering instruction in a variety of industrial arts, applied sciences, or technical subjects

Now that you have studied the vocabulary in Unit 4, practice your new knowledge by completing the crossword puzzle.

Vocabulary Unit 4 Puzzle

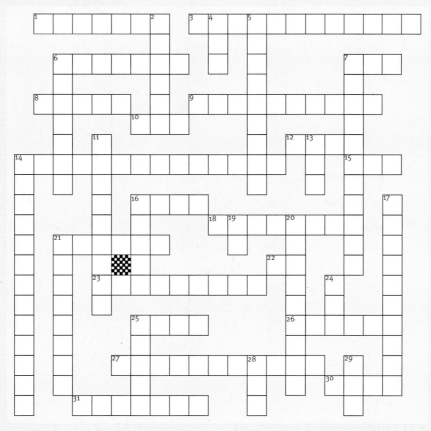

ACROSS CLUES

1. Pneumonia and strep throat are caused by a _____.
3. Her features were not perfectly aligned. Instead they were _____.
6. The roadrunner is an _____ among birds because it rarely flies.
7. A word part meaning "hate or bad."
8. A word part meaning "measure."
9. A confirmed _____ will probably not enjoy the company of women.
10. A word part meaning "bad or difficult."
12. A word part meaning "one."*
14. The _____ made a large monetary contribution to the new science building.
15. The abbreviation for what was once the ninth month.*
16. A word part meaning "four."*
18. An instrument measuring how many miles you have traveled in your car.
21. Condition when a person is lacking sufficient red blood cells.
22. A word part meaning "good or well."
23. The vet said that our dog Bandit was so sick that we should _____ him.
25. A word part meaning "many."
26. A person who lacks moral standards is _____.
27. Thomas Jefferson, a true _____, had over 6,000 volumes of books in his private collection.
30. A word part meaning "five."*
31. A muscle can _____ from lack of use.

DOWN CLUES

2. After Pat's mother died, he delivered a stirring _____ at her memorial service.
4. A word part meaning "six."*
5. A world in miniature is a _____.
6. Surgical instruments must be maintained in _____ condition.
7. Did the reporter _____ the president's remarks or did he quote him accurately?
11. A _____ is used to f orecast changes in the weather.
13. The abbreviation for what was once the eighth month.*
14. According to the Bible, Jacob gave his son Joseph a coat of many colors, or a _____ garment.
16. A word part meaning "five."*
17. A liter is almost _____ to a quart.
19. A word part meaning "two."*
20. The judge rendered a decision considered to be _____ by both parties to the dispute.
21. It would be _____ for an *A* student to fail a test.
24. A word part for two.*
25. A word part meaning "love."
28. A word part meaning "six."*
29. An abbreviation for what was once the tenth month.*

*From a previous unit.

Figurative Language

The Figure 5 in Gold (1928) *BY CHARLES DEMUTH*
© The Metropolitan Museum of Art/Art Resource, NY.

The Great Figure

BY WILLIAM CARLOS WILLIAMS

Among the rain
and lights
I saw the figure 5
in gold
on a red
firetruck
moving
tense
unheeded
to gong clangs
siren howls
and wheels rumbling
through the dark city.
—*Sour Grapes: A Book
of Poems,* 1921

View and Reflect

1. What is the relationship between this painting and William Carlos William's poem "The Great Figure"?
2. What figurative comparisons are used in the poem?
3. How many times do you see the number 5 repeated in the painting?
4. The red shape represents the fire truck. Does the repetition of the number 5 help to give the fire truck a feeling of moving quickly down a city street? What other elements in the painting add to the feeling of movement?
5. How closely did the artist come to interpreting the description of the fire truck in the poem?

Figures of Speech

THE FAR SIDE®   BY GARY LARSON

© 1983 FarWorks, Inc. All Rights Reserved/Dist. by Creators Syndicate

The Far Side® by Gary Larson © 1983 FarWorks, Inc. All Rights Reserved. The Far Side® and the Larson® signature are registered trademarks of FarWorks, Inc. Used with permission.

"Hang him, you idiots! Hang him! ... 'String him up' is a figure of speech!"

Figurative language (or figures of speech) compares two or more unlike things. **Similes** use *like, as,* or *as if* to make the comparison. Look at the following example and see if you can identify the simile:

> Silence fell while we both cooled down. I knew we would, we always did. Coming apart and coming together, like pigeons fussing on a street corner. It had been like this for as long as I could remember. He had raised me himself, in this shop.
> (Lisa Scottoline, *Running from the Law,* 1996)

In this example, the settling of disagreements is compared to the actions of a flock of pigeons. The differences between the two things are readily apparent, but the similarities between the two enable the reader to come to a better understanding of the situation being described. Most of us have seen how pigeons interact. While they may separate momentarily, they soon come back together again. With a little imagination, the reader now better understands how the two individuals in the example respond to each other.

A **metaphor** compares two unlike things without using *like, as,* or *as if.* In a metaphor, one thing is spoken of as though it were something else. Look at the following example of a metaphor:

> At 81, he is a prune—old, dried up, and wrinkly, but still sweet in the middle.

In this case, an old man is being directly compared to a prune.

Personification is figurative language that assigns human attributes or feelings to a nonhuman object. Authors use personification to make their writing clearer or more vivid. Look at the following example:

> In a hurry to get to California, Marcus set his speedometer at 85, and the car *gobbled* up the road before him.

A car is incapable of gobbling. This use of personification tells us that the car is moving very quickly.

Read the following example and locate the figures of speech:

> [W]hen I spotted the Hamiltons, they struck me as the king, queen, and jack of diamonds. Satisfied and privileged, face cards all, nestled in a corner of this exclusive Main Line restaurant.
> (Lisa Scottoline, *Running from the Law,* 1996)

    1. In the sentences above, what are the Hamiltons being compared to?

    2. What are the similarities between the two things being compared?

    3. What implications can be drawn about the Hamiltons from this comparison?

    4. What are the author's likely feelings toward the Hamiltons?

Exercise 1: Identifying Similes, Metaphors, and Personification

Directions: Indicate whether the comparison being made uses a simile, metaphor, or personification by writing **S**, **M**, or **P** in the blank provided.

_____ 1. "My life is like a broken bowl." (Christina Rossetti)

_____ 2. "'Hope' is the thing with feathers that perches in the soul." (Emily Dickinson)

__M__ 3. "I'm a riddle in nine syllables." (Sylvia Plath)

__D__ 4. "A's had once come running." (William Goldman)

__P__ 5. "To the north is the Gila River, small and timid most of the year." (Sandra Day O'Connor)

__M__ 6. "The world is a glass overflowing with water." (Pablo Neruda)

__P__ 7. "The sea awoke at midnight from its sleep." (Henry Wadsworth Longfellow)

__S__ 8. "Oh my love is like the melody that's sweetly played in tune." (Robert Burns)

_____ 9. "The rain plays a little sleep-song on our roof at night." (Langston Hughes)

_____ 10. "The alarm clock meddling in somebody's sleep." (Gwendolyn Brooks)

__S__ 11. "Papa's hair is like a broom, all up in the air." (Sandra Cisneros)

__P__ 12. "But when the trees bow down their heads, the wind is passing by." (Christina Rossetti)

__S__ 13. "They don't walk like ordinary dogs, but leap and somersault like an apostrophe and comma." (Sandra Cisneros)

__M__ 14. "As my mother taught me, life is a marathon." (Maria Shriver)

__S__ 15. "The car as he drives, drifts from lane to lane like a raft on a river." (Joan Aleshire)

__P__ 16. "When the stars threw down their spears and water'd heaven with their tears." (William Blake)

Exercise 2: Interpreting Figurative Language

Directions: Read the passages below, and answer the questions that follow. (The similes and metaphors are set in italics.)

The fog spread over the forest *like a soft veil* shrouding everything. The air was *as dense as chocolate cake,* and Mike's breathing sounded laborious to his ears. He had been walking the serpentine path for what seemed like hours caught *like a rat in a maze.* He prayed he was still headed in the right direction. Pictures of food filled his mind, and he was as ravenous *as a bear awakening after the long winter's hibernation.* He knew he could sleep for a week.

In the fog, the trees loomed above him *as shadowy monsters ready to pounce.* Tree roots *like hidden traps* clutched and clawed at his feet as he stumbled along. *As frightening as a muffled scream,* a night owl's sudden cry pierced the air, causing him to tremble uncontrollably. The forest *was a labyrinth* from which he might never escape.

Suddenly, a light beckoned to him from afar. It shimmered in the distance *like the beams from a lighthouse on a dark sea.* The light flickered closer and closer until Monica emerged out of the blackness *like some ghostly apparition.* "Hi," she said. "When Monty came back alone I thought you might be in some sort of trouble."

1. If the fog covering the forest is like a veil, how good is the visibility? _____

2. What might the air have in common with chocolate cake? _____

3. What does being caught *like a rat in a maze* indicate about his ability to escape? _____ Think of a more original comparison of your own. _____

_____

4. In what way is the forest a labyrinth? Why is Mike afraid of parts of the forest?

_____

5. How do we know the beams of the flashlight were a welcome sight to Mike?

_____

6. Monty is most probably a _____

Exercise 3: Identifying and Interpreting Figurative Comparisons

Directions: Each of the sentences below contains a figurative comparison. In the space provided, identify the real subject, indicate what it is being compared to, and explain the meaning of the sentence. Number 1 has been completed as an example.

1. Flattery is like cologne water, to be smelt of, not swallowed.

Subject: flattery _____

Compared to: cologne water _____

Meaning: Flattery is not to be taken seriously. _____

2. "In matters of style, swim with the current; in matters of principle, stand like a rock." (Thomas Jefferson)

   Subject: _____

   Compared to: _____

   Meaning: _____

   _____

3. A good laugh is sunshine in a house.

   Subject: _____

   Compared to: _____

   Meaning: _____

4. "Wealth is like seawater; the more we drink, the thirstier we become." (Arthur Schopenhauer)

   Subject: _____

   Compared to: _____

   Meaning: _____

5. "Life is a great big canvas, and you should throw all the paint on it you can." (Danny Kaye)

   Subject: _____

   Compared to: _____

   Meaning: _____

6. "Some books are to be tasted; others to be swallowed; and some few to be chewed and digested." (Francis Bacon)

   Subject: _____

   Compared to: _____

   Meaning: _____

7. "How sharper than a serpent's tooth it is to have a thankless child!" (Shakespeare)

   Subject: _____

   Compared to: _____

   Meaning: _____

8. Success is a ladder that cannot be climbed with your hands in your pockets.

   Subject: _____

   Compared to: _____

   Meaning: _____

9. "Marriage is like life in this—that it is a field of battle, and not a bed of roses." (Robert Louis Stevenson)

   Subject: _____

   Compared to: _____

   Meaning: _____

10. Friendship is like a bank account. You can't continue to draw on it without making deposits.

Subject: _____

Compared to: _____

Meaning: _____

Imagery

In addition to the figures of speech discussed earlier, writers use **imagery** to create word pictures. Imagery is language that has a sensory quality. It can appeal to any of the five senses—sight, sound, taste, touch, and smell. A good reader must not only be able to recognize imagery but also understand the author's intent in presenting it.

Figurative Language and Imagery in Poetry

In this section, you will read two poems and explore their use of figurative language and imagery.

Exercise 4: Analyzing Figurative Language and Imagery in Poetry

Directions: Read this poem by Billy Collins, the U.S. poet laureate for 2001–2003 and answer the questions that follow.

Introduction to Poetry
BY BILLY COLLINS

I ask them to take a poem
and hold it up to the light
like a color slide
or press an ear against its hive.
I say drop a mouse into a poem
and watch him probe his way out,
or walk inside the poem's room
and feel the walls for a light switch.
I want them to water ski
across the surface of a poem
waving at the author's name on the shore.
But all they want to do
is tie the poem to a chair with a rope
and torture a confession out of it.
They begin beating it with a hose
to find out what it really means.

(Billy Collins, *The Apple that Astonished Paris*, 1988)

1. Who is the speaker referring to when he says "they" and "them"?

   _____

2. According to the first four stanzas, which ones of the five senses (sight, hearing, touch, taste, smell) are necessary to read a poem?

   _____

3. What does the speaker mean when he says, "I want them to water ski across the surface of a poem waving at the author's name on the shore"?

   _____

   _____

4. According to the speaker, those looking at a poem "tie the poem to a chair with a rope," "torture a confession out of it," and "begin beating it with a hose." What do these images suggest to you? How do they contrast to the other images the speaker has already described?

   _____

5. How does the speaker feel a poem should be read?

   _____

6. How do you think a poem should be read?

   _____

7. What is the main idea of the poem? What is the author's purpose in writing the poem?

   _____

   _____

   _____

SELECTION

*"I love people who harness themselves, an ox to a heavy
cart, who pull like water buffalo."*

GETTING THE PICTURE

Piercy wrote the poem as an expression of gratitude to those who do physical labor such as growing the food that we eat. As you are reading the poem, think about what work means to you.

BIO-SKETCH

Marge Piercy was born in Detroit, Michigan, to a family she characterizes as working class. She was the first member of her family to attend college. Piercy has published fifteen volumes of poetry, including *Colors Passing Through Us*. In addition, she has published several novels and a play.

To Be of Use

BY MARGE PIERCY

The people I love the best
jump into work head first
without dallying in the shallows
and swim off with sure strokes almost out of sight.
They seem to become natives of that element,
the black sleek heads of seals
bouncing like half-submerged balls.
I love people who harness themselves, an ox to a heavy cart,

"If a man will not
work, he will not eat."

—2 Thessalonians 3:10

who pull like water buffalo, with massive patience,
who strain in the mud and the muck to move things forward,
who do what has to be done, again and again.

I want to be with people who submerge
in the task, who go into the fields to harvest
and work in a row and pass the bags along,
who are not parlor generals and field deserters
but move in a common rhythm
when the food must come in or the fire be put out.

The work of the world is common as mud.
Botched, it smears the hands, crumbles to dust.
But the thing worth doing well done
has a shape that satisfies, clean and evident.
Greek amphoras for wine or oil,
Hopi vases that held corn, are put in museums
but you know they were made to be used.
The pitcher cries for water to carry
and a person for work that is real.

(Marge Piercy, *Circles on the Water*, 1982)

✓ **COMPREHENSION CHECKUP**

Multiple Choice

Write the letter of the correct answer in the blank provided.

_____ 1. This poem implies that
     a. a life of leisure is better than a life of work
     b. work that is worth doing has its own intrinsic value
     c. strenuous labor should be avoided
     d. people should begin working when they are young

_____ 2. The speaker of the poem has little respect for people who
   a. direct others from the sidelines
   b. escape doing their fair share
   c. are above doing menial labor
   d. all of the above

_____ 3. A person who "jumps in head first"
   a. avoids difficult labor
   b. is ready and willing to go to work
   c. is reckless
   d. is a slow starter

_____ 4. The phrase "natives of that element" refers to people who
   a. are experiencing something foreign to them
   b. are in their natural environment
   c. make things seem easy
   d. both b and c

_____ 5. The phrase "dallying in the shallows" refers to people who are
   a. unable to swim
   b. prompt and courteous
   c. making only a half effort
   d. having fun

_____ 6. The ox image is used to describe
   a. people who avoid heavy labor
   b. people who need a lot of personal freedom
   c. people who are willing to exert themselves to accomplish something
   d. people who are so slow they can't accomplish anything

_____ 7. The harvest image is used to describe
   a. people who hold back hoping someone else will do it
   b. people who are willing to work for others
   c. people who like to work by themselves
   d. people who are natural leaders

_____ 8. In "To Be of Use" the speaker is describing
   a. a philosophy about the importance of useful work
   b. a close friend
   c. an imaginary world
   d. the importance of taking it easy

_____ 9. The expression "common as mud" means
   a. rare
   b. everywhere
   c. disgusting
   d. lacking in value

_____ 10. The overall feeling of the poem is one of
   a. alarm
   b. high spirits
   c. seriousness
   d. sadness

_____ 11. "The black sleek heads of seals bouncing like half-submerged balls" is an example of
   a. simile
   b. metaphor
   c. personification
   d. antonym

_____ 12. "The pitcher cries for water to carry" is an example of
   a. simile
   b. metaphor
   c. literary allusion
   d. personification

Vocabulary Practice

Write a sentence responding to each question.

1. dallying (verb) Do you think it is a good idea to *dally*? Why or why not? _____
   _____

2. shallows (noun) When would you be better off in the *shallows*? _____
   _____

3. natives (noun) What region are you a *native* of? _____
   _____

4. element (noun) What is your natural *element*? _____
   _____

5. sleek (adjective) What animal has *sleek* fur? _____
   _____

6. submerged (verb) A whale can be *submerged* for a half hour. How long can you be *submerged*? _____
   _____

7. botched (verb) Can you think of a time when you *botched* a job? _____
   _____

In Your Own Words

1. In the poem, what do the references to Greek amphoras and Hopi vases tell us about work?

2. What is the meaning of the last two lines of the poem?

3. What does the author mean when she says, "The work of the world is common as mud"?

The Art of Writing

In a brief essay, discuss what this poem has to say about people and work. Describe a time when you were involved in work that you found very satisfying. When are you willing to do hard work?

Internet Activity

Do you have a career goal? Have you met with a career counselor to explore possible careers? Pull up your college's Web site and click on career services or counseling. Find out what services are available to you. Does the Web site contain an interest inventory? If so, take it to help you decide what sorts of careers match your interests and talents.

Check out the Web site below, and print a want ad for a job that looks appealing to you.

www.careerpath.com

Imagery in Nonfiction

In this section, you will read a nonfiction excerpt and explore its use of imagery.

SELECTION

"What would I do if four bears came into my camp?
Why, I would die, of course."

GETTING THE PICTURE

In the excerpt from *A Walk in the Woods*, Bill Bryson gives a descriptive account of his attempt to hike the 2,100-mile Appalachian Trail. As you read the excerpt, notice how the sensory images involve the reader. These images were carefully chosen by the author to heighten the sense of excitement and danger.

BIO-SKETCH

Bill Bryson is the best-selling author of *A Short History of Nearly Everything* and *A Walk in the Woods*. Born in Des Moines, Iowa, Bryson lived in England for over 20 years while writing for *The Times*. He is noted for witty, entertaining writing that accurately describes life in the United States from the perspective of one who has been away long enough to see things clearly.

BRUSHING UP ON VOCABULARY

plundered stole goods from a place or person. The word is derived from the German *plundern*, which means "to rob of household goods." Early use of the word implied using force in time of war or civil disorder.

voluminous having ample folds or fullness. The word is derived from the Latin word *volumen*, meaning "a roll of sheets." In ancient times, people wrote on sheets of parchment that were then tightly rolled onto sticks, making scrolls. As one read the scroll, it was unwound on one stick and rewound on the other. The parchment that was rolled was known as *volumen*. When scrolls were no longer in wide use, the term *volume* was substituted for a book of considerable size. *Volume* came to mean "any large amount or quantity."

soberly seriously, solemnly, gravely. The word comes from the Latin word *sobrius*, meaning "not drunk."

vivid full of life, bright, clearly perceived. The word is derived from the Latin word *vivo*, meaning "live." At the time of the Roman Empire, if something was *vivid*, it was thought to be lively.

Excerpt from

A Walk in the Woods

BY BILL BRYSON

On the afternoon of July 4, 1983, three adult supervisors and a group of youngsters 1
set up camp at a popular spot beside Lake Canimina in the fragrant pine forests
of western Quebec, about eighty miles north of Ottawa, in a park called La Verendrye
Provincial Reserve. They cooked dinner and, afterwards, in the correct fashion, se-
cured their food in a bag and carried it a hundred or so feet into the woods, where they
suspended it above the ground between two trees, out of reach of the bears.

About midnight, a black bear came prowling around the margins of the camp, 2
spied the bag, and brought it down by climbing one of the trees and breaking a branch.
He plundered the food and departed, but an hour later he was back, this time entering
the camp itself, drawn by the lingering smell of cooked meat in the campers' clothes
and hair, in their sleeping bags and tent fabric. It was to be a long night for the Canimina party. Three times between midnight and 3:30 A.M. the bear came to the camp.

Imagine, if you will, lying in the dark alone in a little tent, nothing but a few mi- 3
crons of trembling nylon between you and the chill night air, listening to a 400-pound
bear move around your campsite. Imagine its quiet grunts and mysterious snufflings,
the clatter of upended cookware and sounds of moist gnawings, the pad of its feet and
the heaviness of its breath, the singing brush of its haunch along your tent side. Imagine the hot flood of adrenaline, that unwelcome tingling in the back of your arms, at
the sudden rough bump of its snout against the foot of your tent, the alarming wild
wobble of your frail shell as it roots through the backpack that you left casually
propped by the entrance—with, you suddenly recall, a Snickers in the pouch. Bears
adore Snickers, you've heard.

And then the dull thought—oh, God—that perhaps you brought the Snickers in 4
here with you, that it's somewhere in here, down by your feet or underneath you
or—wait, *shhhhh* . . . yes!—the unutterable relief of realizing that the bear has withdrawn to the other side of the camp or shambled back into the woods. I tell you right
now I couldn't stand it.

So imagine what it must have been like for poor little David Anderson, aged twelve, 5
when at 3:30 A.M. on the third foray, his tent was abruptly rent with a swipe of claw and
the bear, driven to distraction by the rich, unfixable, everywhere aroma of hamburger,
bit hard into a flinching limb and dragged him shouting and flailing through the camp
and into the woods. In the few moments it took the boy's fellow campers to unzip themselves from their accoutrements—and imagine, if you will, trying to swim out of suddenly voluminous sleeping bags, take up flashlights and makeshift cudgels, undo tent
zips with helplessly fumbling fingers, and give chase—in those few moments, poor little
David Anderson was dead.

Now imagine reading a nonfiction book packed with stories such as this—true 6
tales soberly related—just before setting off alone on a camping trip of your own into
the North American wilderness. Through long winter nights in New Hampshire, while
snow piled up outdoors and my wife slumbered peacefully beside me, I lay saucer-eyed
in bed reading clinically precise accounts of people gnawed pulpy in their sleeping bags,
plucked wimpering from trees, even noiselessly stalked as they sauntered unawares
down leafy paths or cooled their feet in mountain streams. People whose one fatal

mistake was to smooth their hair with a dab of aromatic gel, or eat juicy meat, or tuck a Snickers in their shirt pocket for later, or in some small, inadvertent way pique the olfactory properties of the hungry bear.

My particular dread—the vivid possibility that left me staring at tree shadows on   7 the bedroom ceiling night after night—was having to lie in a small tent, alone in an inky wilderness, listening to a foraging bear outside and wondering what its intentions were. I was especially riveted by a photograph taken late at night by a camper with a flash at a campground in the West. The photograph caught four black bears as they puzzled over a suspended food bag. The bears were clearly startled but not remotely alarmed by the flash. It was not the size or demeanor of the bears that troubled me—they looked almost comically unaggressive, like four guys who had gotten a Frisbee caught up in a tree—but their numbers. Up to that moment it had not occurred to me that bears might prowl in parties. What on earth would I do if *four* bears came into my camp? Why, I would die, of course.

(Bill Bryson, *A Walk in the Woods*, 1997)

✓ COMPREHENSION CHECKUP

Multiple Choice

Directions: For each item, circle the letter corresponding to the best answer.

_____ 1. The main idea expressed in this excerpt is that
   a. you never know when something unfortunate is going to happen to you
   b. reading a frightening book late at night is not a good idea
   c. David Anderson would be alive today if the adults in his party had exercised more caution
   d. those drawn to camping in the wilderness should be aware of the dangers from bears

_____ 2. The author's primary purpose is to
   a. entertain the reader with scary bear stories
   b. persuade readers to join him on a camping trip
   c. persuade readers that bears should be eliminated from the North American wilderness
   d. describe the habitat of the black bear

_____ 3. The author suggests that
   a. the Canimina party followed correct camping procedures in disposing of their excess food
   b. the Canimina party's lack of experience in camping was responsible for young David's death
   c. although food was hung out of the reach of bears, one managed to get hold of it anyway
   d. both a and c

_____ 4. David Anderson's abduction was used to illustrate
   a. the friendliness of large, furry mammals
   b. the ever-present danger from hungry bears
   c. the contempt some campers feel for the wilderness
   d. the joys of camping

_____ 5. From this excerpt you could conclude that
   a. danger lurks in the woods
   b. bears do not always forage by themselves
   c. bears have a very keen sense of smell
   d. all of the above

_____ 6. The quiet grunts, mysterious snufflings, and clatter of upended cook-ware are all images that appeal to our sense of
   a. smell
   b. taste
   c. touch
   d. hearing

Vocabulary in Context

Directions: In the paragraphs indicated in parentheses, find a word that correctly matches the definition given, and write it in the space provided.

1. having a pleasant scent (paragraph 1) _____

2. searching stealthily (2) _____

3. borders; edges (2) _____

4. staying on in a place longer than expected (2) _____

5. hindquarters (3) _____

6. unspeakable; beyond expression (4) _____

7. shuffled (4) _____

8. raid, attack (5) _____

9. personal clothing or equipment (5) _____

10. temporary; expedient (5) _____

11. weapons; club (5) _____

12. slept (6) _____

13. unintentional (6) _____

14. excite; arouse; provoke (6) _____

15. sense of smell (6) _____

16. to hold the eyes (7) _____

17. conduct; behavior (7) _____

In Your Own Words

1. What is it about camping that many people find so compelling?

2. How can we help protect campers from both human and animal predators?

The Art of Writing

Make a chart with each of the five senses as a category. In your chart, place each relevant detail from the excerpt under the appropriate category.

Internet Activity

To learn more about the black bear, use any search engine and type in "black bear facts." Or visit one of the following Web sites:

www.bear.org

www.animals.nationalgeographic.com/animals/.../black-bear.html

www.americanbear.org/blackbearfacts.htm

Did you learn anything about black bears that surprises you?

The Use of Symbols

A **symbol** is a person, object, or event that stands for something beyond its literal meaning. A good symbol captures in a simple form a more complicated reality. For example, a white dove symbolizes peace, a skull symbolizes death, a flag symbolizes a country's values and aspirations, and a black cat crossing our path symbolizes bad luck. Writers use symbols to create a mood, to reinforce a theme, or to communicate an idea.

Exercise 5: Identifying Symbols

See if you can identify the following symbols or icons. What does each icon symbolize?

1. _____

2. _____

3. _____

4. _____

5. _____

6. _____

7. _____

8. _____

9. _____

10. _____

11. _____

12. _____

Exercise 6: Analyzing Signs and Symbols

Directions: Read this excerpt. Then complete the activity that follows.

Symbols convey information or embody ideas. Some are so common that we find it difficult to believe they didn't always exist. Who, for example, first used arrows to indicate directions? We follow them instinctively now, but at some point they were new and had to be explained. Other symbols embody more complex ideas and associations. Two well-known and ancient symbols are the yin-yang symbol and the swastika.

The yin-yang symbol, also known as the taiji (or tai chi) diagram, embodies the worldview expressed in ancient Chinese philosophy. It gives elegant visual forms to ideas about the dynamic balance of opposites that are believed to make up the universe and explain existence: male (yang) and female (yin), being and nonbeing, light and dark, action and inaction, and so on. The symbol makes it clear that these opposites are mutually interdependent, that as one increases the other decreases, that a portion of each is in the other, that they are defined by each other, that both are necessary to make the whole.

The swastika has an important lesson to teach about symbols, which is that they have no meaning in themselves but are given a meaning by a society or culture. The swastika was first used as a symbol in India and Central Asia, possibly as early as 3000 B.C.E. It takes its name from the Sanskrit word *svastika*, meaning "good luck" or "good fortune." (Sanskrit was the most important language of ancient India.) In Asia, the swastika is still widely used as an auspicious symbol, even on commercial products. Until the 1930s, the swastika was a popular good-luck symbol in the West as well. Today, however, it is so thoroughly associated with the Nazis, who adopted it as their emblem, that it has become for us a symbol of fascism, racial hatred, and the unspeakable atrocities of the concentration camps. Our instinctive recoil from the swastika underscores not only the power of symbols to serve as repositories for ideas and associations, but also the ability of those ideas and associations to change, sometimes radically.

Among the most pervasive symbols in our visual environment today are logos and trademarks, which are symbols of an organization or product. An impressive number of these are the work of Paul Rand, one of the most influential of all American graphic designers. Simple, clear, distinctive, and memorable, each of these corporate logos has become familiar to millions of people around the world, instantly calling to mind the company and its products or services. As with any symbol, a logo means nothing in itself. It is up to an organization to make its logo familiar and to convince people through sound business practices to associate it with such virtues as service, quality, and dependability.

(Mark Getlein, *Living with Art*, 7/e)

Can you identify these well-known corporate symbols from their descriptions?

1. golden arches _____

2. a bull's eye _____

3. an apple with a bite taken out of its right side _____

4. a black swoosh _____

5. Sleeping Beauty's castle _____

6. the head of an eagle in flight _____

Exercise 7: Identifying the Appropriate Color Word

Directions: Read this excerpt. Then complete the activity that follows.

Symbolic Use of Color

When you're in debt, you speak of being "in the red"; when you make a profit, you're "in the black." When you're sad, you're "blue"; when you're healthy, you're "in the pink"; and when you're jealous, you're "green with envy." To be a coward is to be "yellow" and to be inexperienced is to be "green." When you talk a great deal, you talk "a blue streak"; and when you are angry, you "see red." As revealed through these timeworn clichés, language abounds in color symbolism.

(Joseph DeVito, *Essentials of Human Communication, 3/e,* 1999)

See how many of the following phrases you can complete with the appropriate color word below. (Some color words will be used more than once.)

black	brown	gray	pink	rose
blue	gold	green	red	silver

1. He is in a _____ mood.

2. The little boy was good as _____.

3. Mike is true _____.

4. The movie star got the _____ carpet treatment.

5. Every cloud has a _____ lining.

6. People who drink too much are said to see _____ elephants.

7. He looks at the world through _____ -colored glasses.

8. Nora is a good gardener. She has a _____ thumb.

9. Silence is _____ en.

10. I'm going to _____ -bag my lunch.

11. The police caught him _____ -handed.

12. Jeff is the _____ sheep of the family.

13. He was beaten _____ and _____.

14. Play some more of those _____ en oldies.

15. He's very smart. He has lots of _____ matter.

16. There's too much _____ tape involved.

Exercise 8: Cultural Meanings of Colors

Directions: **Study** the chart below. Does it surprise you that the meanings of colors vary so much from culture to culture? Then complete the activity that follows.

Color	Cultural Meanings and Comments
Red	In China, red symbolizes prosperity and rebirth and is used for festive and joyous occasions; in France and the United Kingdom, masculinity; in many African countries, blasphemy or death; and in Japan, anger and danger. Red ink, especially among Korean Buddhists, is used only to write a person's name at the time of death or on the anniversary of the person's death, and so problems result when American teachers use red ink to mark the homework of Korean Buddhists.
Green	In Ireland, green symbolizes patriotism; among some Native Americans, femininity; to the Egyptians, fertility and strength; and to the Japanese, youth and energy.
Black	In Thailand, black symbolizes old age; in parts of Malaysia, courage; and in much of Europe and North America, death.
White	In Thailand, white symbolizes purity; in many Muslim and Hindu cultures, purity and peace; and in Japan and other Asian countries, death and mourning.
Blue	In Iran, blue symbolizes something negative; in Egypt, virtue and truth; in Ghana, joy; among the Cherokee, defeat.
Yellow	In China, yellow symbolizes wealth and authority; in Egypt, happiness and prosperity, and in many countries throughout the world, femininity.
Purple	In Latin America, purple symbolizes death; in Europe, royalty; in Egypt, virtue and faith; in Japan, grace and nobility; and in China, barbarism.

(Adapted from Joseph DeVito, *Essentials of Human Communication, 3/e,* 1999)

What do each of these colors symbolize in the United States?

1. red _____

2. green _____

3. black _____

4. white _____

5. blue _____

6. yellow _____

7. purple _____

*"Our favorite publication as new immigrants was the
Sears Catalog."*

GETTING THE PICTURE

The excerpt below is taken from Rose Castillo Guilbault's memoir, *Farmworker's Daughter—Growing Up Mexican in America*. In it, Guilbault describes growing up as a Mexican immigrant in a farming community during the 1960s. She shares a memory of the importance of the Sears Roebuck Catalog to her family. In what way does the catalog serve as a symbol of the American dream?

BIO-SKETCH

At the age of five, Rose Castillo Guilbault and her mother left Mexico for California's Salinas Valley. Rose, with a great deal of hard work and help from mentors, gradually perfected her English and began writing for her school newspaper. After graduating from college, she became a writer for the *San Francisco Chronicle*. She entered broadcasting and has worked with both CBS and ABC, winning an EMMY for outstanding children's programming. She was appointed to serve on the California Community College Board of Governors.

BRUSHING UP ON VOCABULARY

Sears Catalog Sears, Roebuck, and Company, commonly called Sears, is a chain of American department stores. Its mail order catalogs, first published in 1896, were famous for the wide variety of items available, but were discontinued in 1993. At its height in popularity, the catalog was referred to as the "Consumers' Bible." The Sears Wish Book was a very popular Christmas-themed catalog.

homesteaders those who settled and farmed land

materialism concerned with money and material possessions rather than with spiritual or ethical values

Excerpt from

Farmworker's Daughter—Growing up Mexican in America

BY ROSE CASTILLO GUILBAULT

Book of Dreams

Our favorite publication as new immigrants was the Sears Catalog. This "wish book" 1
was a symbol for America's bounty and what could be had with hard work. It was a
book that came to our home and from which we could leisurely, conveniently, choose

anything we could possibly want and have it delivered to our doorstep. The concept was amazing to us. This wasn't about accumulating goods but about obtaining a piece of the American pie.

Many of today's immigrants are easily caught in this country's web of overcon- 2 sumption, easy credit, and easy debt. But in the early sixties, the values in rural areas were different.

Every new catalog was savored. We all had our own favorite sections. Papá, eyes 3 sparkling, would ease himself into his chair after dinner and examine the tools, hunting rifles, and cameras. Then he'd pass the catalog to Mamá, who—for what seemed to be hours—studied the pretty dresses, household appliances, dishes, and linens.

By the time the catalog made its way into my hands, my palms itched with desire. 4 At Easter, I would lose myself in pages of frilly pastel dresses with matching hats and purses. In the Christmas season, which brought my favorite edition of the year—the thickest one—I would sit for hours staring glassy-eyed at the pages and pages of toys, dolls, and games.

But we never ordered anything frivolous. The inside of our farmhouse was sparsely 5 furnished with hand-me-down furniture from the boss, except for the TV and a cheap, nylon forest green sofa set my father had bought my mother as a wedding gift.

Extravagances were unaffordable. Only the most practical and necessary items 6 could be bought, like my mother's first washing machine, a school coat for me, and thick dark-denim overalls to keep Papá warm in the frostiest of dawns.

The Sears catalog also had other uses. I'd cut out the models and use them as 7 paper dolls, and my mother would match English words with pictures: "¿Estas ollas, serán 'pots' en inglés?"

Many years later I acquired a 1941 Sears catalog. I enjoyed looking at the old 8 clothing styles and reading and rereading the two stories it had on typical Sears customers. One profiled the Browns of Washington State, who arrived as homesteaders, lived in a tent with their children until their farm produced enough for them to build a two-room shack, and eventually built a comfortable farmhouse on their land. Photos showed Mr. and Mrs. Brown with their new cream separator, daughter Evelyn with her new Elgin bicycle, and the whole family listening to their Silvertone radio phonograph—all from Sears, of course.

The second story described the Yeamens of Glendale, in Los Angeles County. Mr. 9 Yeamen worked at Lockheed Aviation, a mile and a half commute from the family's "modern, five-room bungalow . . . with a barbecue grill in the backyard and a view of the mountains from every window." Photographs showed the various family members with their Sears products: Dad relaxing on a slider swing in the backyard, Mom putting avocado sandwiches in lunch boxes, and the kids romping in their stylish clothes.

The Browns and the Yeamens, the catalog summarized, are what all of us want to 10 be—"good, solid, dependable Americans."

As corny and blatantly commercial as those stories were, I enjoyed reading them. 1 I thought it modeled what Americans were really like. These were, after all, real people, not TV characters. Even though my family of Mexican immigrants probably didn't have a whole lot in common with the Browns and the Yeamens, we too shopped from the Sears catalog—a book that made us believe everything was reachable and ours to have, just as it was for every other family in America.

And just like the people in the catalog, my family prospered too. Not in great leaps 1 and bounds like the Browns of Washington State, but little by little. Our progress was marked, of course, by the occasional splurge from the Sears catalog.

When I got to the point where I had to own my own clarinet or drop out of elemen- 1 tary school band (there was a limit to how long we could borrow from the music department) my family had to make a choice. I was not a great musician, we all knew that, but the band was a wholesome activity that integrated me into school life—into America—and so it was important for me. One evening after dinner, my parents called me into the living room. I searched their faces for a clue, but they remained mysteriously impassive until my father revealed a wrinkled brown package hidden behind his back.

My heart began pounding when I saw the Sears return address. Then, out of the 14 bag came a compact gray and white case, and inside, lying on an elegant bed of royal blue rayon velvet, were the ebony pieces of a brand new clarinet. Never in my stolen afternoons with the Sears catalog had I imagined possessing something so fine!

A newspaper article would later describe the Sears catalog as "the best record of 15 American material culture." But to many of us, the catalog transcended materialism. It was about making dreams come true.

(Rose Castillo Guilbault, *Farmworker's Daughter*, 2005)

✓ **COMPREHENSION CHECKUP**

Multiple Choice

Directions: For each item, write the letter corresponding to the best answer.

_____   1. The author received a _____ from the Sears catalog.
   a. a clarinet
   b. a set of paper dolls
   c. a school coat
   d. both a and c

_____   2. As mentioned in the excerpt, the author's family was interested in all of the following in the Sears catalog *except*
   a. household appliances
   b. lawn furniture
   c. clothing
   d. tools

_____   3. The Sears catalog made the author's family believe all of the following *except*
   a. everything is reachable and possible with hard work
   b. dreams can come true
   c. desired items can be conveniently delivered to one's doorstep
   d. possessing luxury items makes life worthwhile

_____   4. From the selection we can infer that
   a. the author was a very materialistic person
   b. the author liked watching TV
   c. the author was thrilled to receive a clarinet from the Sears catalog
   d. the author disliked reading about people from other walks of life

_____   5. Guilbault's mother enjoyed the catalog for all of the following reasons *except*
   a. to look at toys for her daughter
   b. to look at household items
   c. to look at beautiful clothing
   d. to practice English

_____ 6. The author's main idea is
   a. anybody can afford to buy something from Sears
   b. people have a good life if they can afford lots of possessions
   c. the Sears Catalog stood as a symbol for what could be achieved in America
   d. the values in rural America are different from those in the cities

_____ 7. In paragraph 2, the pattern of organization is
   a. comparison
   b. contrast
   c. cause and effect
   d. steps in a process

True or False

Directions: Indicate whether each statement is true or false by writing **T** or **F** in the space provided.

_____ 8. The 1941 Sears catalog featured typical Sears customers.

_____ 9. The author always got to look at the catalog before anyone else in her family.

_____ 10. Being in the band helped the author feel like she was a part of her school community.

_____ 11. The author's family became less and less affluent the longer they lived in the U.S.

_____ 12. The author felt that her family had a lot in common with the Browns and the Yeamens.

Vocabulary in Context

Directions: Without consulting a dictionary, write a definition in the blank provided for each of the following phrases.

1. obtaining a piece of the American pie (paragraph 1)

   _____

2. caught in the country's web (2)

   _____

3. palms itched with desire (4)

   _____

4. staring glassy-eyed at the pages (4)

   _____

5. furnished with hand-me-down furniture (5)

   _____

6. in great leaps and bounds (12)

_____

Directions: Give a synonym for each of the following vocabulary words.

7. rural (paragraph 2) _____

8. frilly (4) _____

9. frivolous (5) _____

10. romping (9) _____

11. corny (11) _____

12. blatantly (11) _____

Understanding the Words in the Selection

Directions: In the blanks below, write the word from the list that best completes the sentence. Use each word only once.

bounty	pastel	sparsely	wholesome
compact	profiled	splurge	
impassive	savored	transcended	

1. Because of the ruler's _____, people in his country were saved from starvation.

2. The proud quarterback _____ his success on the football field.

3. While the bride wore white, each of her bridesmaids wore _____ shades.

4. The concert, to the disappointment of the promoters, was _____ attended.

5. The governor of California was _____ in the latest issue of *Newsweek.*

6. I'm going to _____ on a brand-new expensive car next year.

7. The nutritionist emphasizes eating only _____ foods.

8. Her _____ face hid her anger from her son.

9. Mark didn't have a lot of room in his new apartment so he purchased a _____ stereo system.

10. The supermodel's beauty _____ that of all the other contestants.

In Your Own Words

1. Do you know any recent immigrants? If so, what was the reason they came to the United States? How difficult are they finding it to make their way in America? To adjust to U.S. culture?

2. The Sears Roebuck Catalog is featured prominently in this selection. Can you think of any catalogs that are influential in today's society? How do these catalogs affect our values? What do these catalogs symbolize?

3. In paragraph 2 of the selection, Guilbault criticizes the materialism of recent immigrants. Do you agree with her assessment? What do you think recent immigrants value?

The Art of Writing

Rose Guilbault's mother had a dream of purchasing her own home. For Rose, the dream was to perfect her English and obtain a college education. Describe your American Dream in a short essay.

Internet Activity

1. Do some research on Justice Sonia Sotomayor, the first Hispanic appointed to the U.S. Supreme Court. What is her background? How did she get to this lofty position?

2. Mexican immigrants and their descendants have a unique place in the story of U.S. immigration. To find out more about this important cultural group, consult the following Web site and then write a few paragraphs describing what you have learned.

www.memory.loc.gov/learn//features/immig/mexican.html

Brain Teasers

Head Wordplay
What is the meaning of the following?

1. She was *head over heels* in love. _____

2. The *headmaster* makes all decisions about what classes will be offered.
   _____

3. The generals are meeting right now at their *headquarters*.
   _____

4. Ever since the news announcement, she's been *out of her head* with worry. _____

5. People will be asked who the *head of the household* is on the census forms.
   _____

6. This class is *way over my head*. _____

7. The babysitter says the little boy is way too *headstrong* for his own good.
   _____

8. He's been trying to find a job, but he's just *knocking his head against a wall.* _____
   _____

| VOCABULARY | **Unit 5: Word Parts Featuring Direction and Motion** |

"Turn about is fair play."

In Unit 5, you will be introduced to word parts related to direction and motion. Words made from these word parts, along with their definitions, follow. Supplemental words with these word parts are located in the left margin.

vert—turn; con—with; in—not, opposite, into, within

avert
a- means "from," and *-vert* means "turn," so the literal meaning of *avert* is "to turn from." Martha *averted* her eyes during the violent parts of the movie. *Avert* also means "prevent," as in she narrowly *averted* an accident.

invert
Here *in-* means "opposite," so when you *invert* something you are turning it upside down. She could tell that Marco did not know how to read because he had the newspaper *inverted*.

vertigo
a dizzy feeling, especially the feeling that everything is spinning around. After Katrinka got off the merry-go-round, she experienced a bout of *vertigo*.

subvert
to overturn or undermine something established. In the 1950s and 1960s, rock 'n' roll was thought likely to *subvert* the wholesome values of American teenagers.

convert
to turn from one form, use, or belief to another. Missionaries around the world try to *convert* people to Christianity. As a noun, *convert* (pronounced con-vert, with the stress on the first syllable) means a person who has changed from one belief or religion to another.

divert
to turn aside. Trapped by the Doberman, Alicia tried to *divert* the dog's attention by throwing a bone across the yard.

perverse **versatile**
able to turn with ease from one thing to another. The basketball player was very *versatile* in that he could play many positions.

vertebra(e)
any one of the bones that make up the spinal column, or backbone. The backbone enables us to turn our bodies.

mis, mit—send; re—back, again; dis—apart, away; ad—toward

missionary **mission**
missile
missive
a special duty or errand that a person or group is sent to do by a church, government, or other entity. Also, a place where a group of missionaries or diplomats live and work. The diplomatic *mission's* goal was to facilitate peace in the Middle East. *Mission* Santa Clara is marked by a California state historical marker.

admit
ad- means "toward," so the literal meaning of *admit* is "to send toward, or to let go." When you buy a ticket to a movie, you are *admitted* to the theater. Carol *admitted* that she had not told the truth to Rob.

submissive
willing to give in or obey another; humble or obedient. For years, Shawna had been *submissive* to her husband; finally, after too much abuse, she decided to file for divorce.

	remit **(remission)**	*Re-* means "back" or "again." *Remit* means "to send back," or "to let go." Mark needs to *remit* his car payment by the first of each month. Cerise's breast cancer is currently in *remission*.
	intermission	stopping for a time; an interruption. There is a twenty-minute *intermission* between Act I and Act II of the play. The original meaning of the word was "to send between."
	intermittent	stopping and starting again from time to time. During a baby's first year of life, pediatricians recommend *intermittent* checkups or well-baby visits.
	dismiss	*Dis-* means "away," so the literal meaning of *dismiss* is "to send away," or "to tell or allow to leave." He was *dismissed* from the army after failing to report for duty.
	emissary	A person sent on a special mission. The *emissary* was sent to Cuba to arrange a meeting with the president.
	emit	to send out or give forth. The owl *emitted* a shrill screech before attacking its prey. Motor vehicles *emit* toxic fumes that contribute to air pollution.

ven—come; circum—around

venue	**prevent**	to keep from happening, to stop. The literal meaning is "to come before" or "to act in anticipation of." Vaccinations *prevent* the spread of disease.
	convention	a meeting of members or delegates from various places. The literal meaning is "coming with." The Republican Party held its *convention* in New York in 2004.
	circumvent	to get around, often by using sly or tricky methods. Warren thought we should deal with the problem directly; Sylvia thought we should try to *circumvent* it.

se—apart, away from

	separate	to keep or put apart. Tina's job at the cannery required her to *separate* the good peaches from the bad ones.
	seclude	to keep away from others; to remove from social contact. *-clude* is derived from *claudere*, meaning "to shut, or close." The literal meaning of *seclude* is "to close away from."
	segregation	the practice of keeping people of different religious, racial, or ethnic groups apart from each other.

sequ (secut)—following

sequential non sequitur consequential obsequious	**consecutive**	following in a regular order without a break. In Phoenix, Arizona, it is unusual to have rain for two *consecutive* days.

	sequence	one thing following after another. A bizarre *sequence* of events led to his apprehension and arrest.
	sequel	a literary or film work that takes up and continues the narrative of a preceding work. The *sequel* to the movie *Star Wars* is *The Empire Strikes Back*.
	consequence	the effect, result, or outcome of something occurring earlier. When you are under oath in a court of law, you must tell the truth or face the *consequences*.

dia—through, across, apart, thoroughly; pro—forward; log(ue)—speech, word

	diagonal	*-gonia* means "angle," so *diagonal* means "connecting two nonadjacent angles." It also means "slanting." Martina's dress had *diagonal* stripes.
	dialect	a form of language that is used only in a certain place or with a certain group. *-lect* means "to speak," so the literal meaning is "to speak across." Because of television, regional *dialects* in the United States are in danger of disappearing.
epilogue neologism	**dialog(ue)**	conversation between two or more persons; an exchange of ideas or opinions on a particular issue with a view to reaching a friendly agreement.
	diagnosis	*-gnosis* means "to know," so a *diagnosis* means "a thorough examination or learning of all the facts in order to determine the nature of a disease." The doctor's *diagnosis* was that the patient suffered from heat exhaustion.
	prognosis	*pro-* is a prefix meaning "forward," so a *prognosis* is a forecast or prediction of how a disease will develop in a person and what the chances are that the person will get well. After undergoing radiation treatments for prostate cancer, his *prognosis* for a full recovery was excellent.
	progressive	moving forward. His *progressive* improvement in math is impressive.

duc—lead; in—into

	reduce	to lead back; to decrease. Kristin wanted to *reduce* her intake of caffeinated drinks.
	abduct	to take someone away forceably; to kidnap. The literal meaning is "to lead away." Most missing children are *abducted* by a parent in a custody dispute.
	conduct	to lead or guide. The meeting was *conducted* by the vice president.
	conducive	helping to bring about; contributing. The quiet in the library is *conducive* to studying.
seduction deduction	**seduce**	to lead away, lead astray. In the *Star Wars* movies, Darth Vader was *seduced* by the dark side of the Force.

deduct   to lead away; subtract. If I save my receipt, the store will *deduct* 10 percent from the price of a new pair of shoes.

induce   to lead or move by persuasion or influence; to bring about or cause. Can't I *induce* you to stay a little longer?

Now that you have studied the vocabulary in Unit 5, practice your new knowledge by completing the crossword puzzle on page 259.

Vocabulary Unit 5 Puzzle

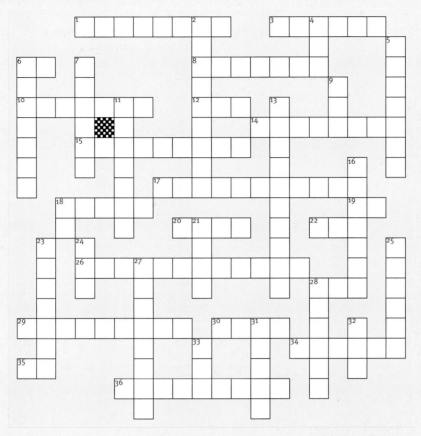

ACROSS CLUES

1. A line slanting from one corner to the opposite corner of a rectangle is a _____ line.

3. If I trade in my old camera, the store will _____ $25 from the price of a new one.

6. A word part meaning "away from."

8. The power failure at the college caused instructors to _____ classes early.

10. It had been his lifelong dream to _____ an orchestra.

12. A word part meaning "with."

14. The two parties were brought together in the hope that they could resolve the dispute with a civil _____.

15. For many students, talking by other students is not _____ to taking a quiz.

17. The _____ of taking drugs could be addiction.

18. A peace agreement was signed between the two countries to _____ further hostilities.

19. A word part meaning "back or again."

20. A word part meaning "following."

22. A word part meaning "send."

26. There was _____ rainfall every few hours all afternoon.

28. A word part for two.*

29. The doctor's _____ was that Ray had chicken pox.

30. A word part meaning "turn."

34. Should you _____ the number of hours that you work so that you can concentrate on your classes?

35. A word part meaning "into."

36. The doctor said that Anna had a good _____ for a complete recovery.

DOWN CLUES

2. The _____ and murder of Charles Lindbergh's son in 1932 led to stronger federal laws against kidnapping.

4. A word part meaning "apart or away."

5. The actress Reese Witherspoon had to speak in a southern _____ for her role in *Sweet Home Alabama*.

6. If you have a contagious disease, it might be necessary to _____ you from others.

7. After her child swallowed a strange pill, the doctor told the mother to _____ vomiting immediately.

9. A word part meaning "forward."

11. When Taryn married Mike, she agreed to _____ to his religion.

13. Have you ever tried to _____ a rule by finding a way to get around it?

16. Christina's ear infection caused her to lose her balance and experience feelings of _____.

18. A word part meaning "toward."

21. Cars _____ carbon monoxide and other harmful gases.

23. A group of doctors were sent on a humanitarian _____ to help with a medical crisis.

24. A word part meaning "across."

25. In *The Lord of the Rings*, the Hobbit Frodo must fight against the power of the "one ring" to _____ him.

27. Former president Jimmy Carter has been an active _____ for peace around the globe.

28. The police were trying to _____ traffic away from the scene of the accident.

31. Please _____ your payment no later than the fifteenth of each month.

32. A word part meaning "lead."

33. A word part meaning "come."

*From a previous unit.

Tone

American Gothic (1930) *BY GRANT WOOD*

© Hulton Archive/Apic/Getty Images/Art © Figge Art Museum,
successors to the Estate of Nan Wood Graham/Licensed
by VAGA, New York, NY.

View and Reflect

1. Notice how the lines of the pitchfork are repeated in the man's shirt front and on the front of his overalls. What might the upright tines of the pitchfork symbolize?
2. The man looks the viewer straight in the eye, while the woman averts her eyes and looks at something in the distance. Why might the artist have depicted the woman in this fashion?
3. The painting is frequently caricaturized. What qualities might make it a favorite subject of caricaturists?
4. What is the overall tone of the painting?

Tone

Tone refers to the emotional quality of a piece of writing. Just as a speaker's voice can convey a wide range of tones, so can a writer's voice. We infer a speaker's tone by paying attention to such things as word choice, voice volume, and facial expressions. The available clues are more limited when we are trying to infer the tone of a writer's voice. An essay does not speak loudly or softly; it can't frown or smile. If we want to identify the tone of a written work, we can only look at what the author has written. Word choice, phrasing, and subject matter all contribute to the tone of a piece of writing. When you're reading something, it's important for you to be aware of the author's tone. Is the author being humorous or argumentative, or both? Is the author expressing outrage or giving praise? Is the author being ironic or earnest? Understanding the tone of a piece of writing is important to understanding its meaning.

A piece of writing can express one or more of a great variety of possible tones. You need to be familiar with some of the more common possibilities. We will begin by identifying the tones of particular statements taken from pieces of writing. These exercises will help you understand tone and will familiarize you with some of the many ways of describing tone. Then we will work on identifying and describing the overall tone of a piece of writing.

The words mentioned in the chart below are useful for describing tone. Words on the same line have the same or a similar meaning.

Useful Words for Describing Tone

- excited, stirred up, impassioned
- loving, affectionate, fond
- surprised, astonished, amazed, incredulous
- mournful, sorrowful
- cruel, brutal, vicious
- angry, outraged, offended
- bitter, resentful
- formal, stiff
- patronizing, condescending, supercilious
- cheerful, glad, joyful, ecstatic, elated
- humorous, funny, amusing, comical, entertaining
- arrogant, haughty, contemptuous
- cynical, negative, pessimistic
- optimistic, positive, encouraging
- whining, complaining, querulous
- witty, clever

- peevish, cross, irritable
- charming, pleasing, attractive, delightful
- flattering, fawning, obsequious
- skeptical, doubtful, questioning
- scolding, chiding
- sad, glum
- dictatorial, domineering, overbearing, tyrannical
- rude, churlish, boorish
- compassionate, caring, solicitous
- self-pitying, self-indulgent
- alarmed, fearful, anxious
- critical, disapproving
- depressed, gloomy, discouraged
- solemn, grave, somber
- informal, casual, relaxed
- objective, neutral, matter-of-fact

Useful Words for Describing Tone *(continued)*

- evasive, secretive, furtive
- remorseful, regretful
- scornful, derisive, contemptuous
- vindictive, vengeful
- serious, earnest, sober
- befuddled, confused
- sarcastic, mocking, sneering
- admiring, appreciative
- playful, lively
- irreverent, disrespectful, impertinent

- disgusted, offended
- appreciative, thankful, grateful
- nostalgic, sentimental, wistful
- perplexed, puzzled, bewildered
- contemptuous, disdainful, scornful
- ambivalent, conflicted, wavering
- informative, instructive
- sincere, honest, frank
- satiric, mocking
- ironic, tongue-in-cheek

Exercise 1: Identifying Tone

Directions: Read the following dialog between a police officer and a speeding motorist. After reading each statement, indicate which word best describes the speaker's tone by writing the appropriate letter in the blank provided.

The Traffic Ticket

___B___ 1. Officer: "Lady, what's the matter with you? What took you so long to stop?"
   a. casual   b. cross   c. pessimistic

___C___ 2. Driver: "Officer, I didn't hear the siren. What's your problem? I know I didn't do anything wrong."
   a. sincere   b. vicious   c. disdainful

___B___ 3. Officer: "You were speeding."
   a. clever   b. matter-of-fact   c. appreciative

___C___ 4. Driver: "Me? Speeding? Are you sure?"
   a. chiding   b. charming   c. doubting

___A___ 5. Officer: "Ma'am, what's wrong with you? Do you have any idea at all how fast you were going?"
   a. annoyed   b. vicious   c. appreciative

___B___ 6. Driver: "Oh my goodness! How fast *was* I going?"
   a. ambivalent   b. alarmed   c. vengeful

___C___ 7. Officer: "I have you on the radar gun going 50 miles an hour in a 15-mile-an-hour school zone."
   a. admiring   b. playful   c. informative

___B___ 8. Driver: "Are you sure, Officer? How can that be? I was watching my
speedometer."
   a. thankful   b. perplexed   c. sneering

___A___ 9. Officer: "No doubt about it, lady! Our radar is very accurate."
   a. assertive   b. sentimental   c. wavering

___C___ 10. Driver: "I'm so sorry, Officer I'm really sorry. I'll be more careful next
time."
   a. wistful   b. contemptuous   c. remorseful

___B___ 11. Officer: "Hand me your driver's license and your registration."
   a. ambivalent   b. demanding   c. fawning

___C___ 12. Driver: "Yes. Oh my! I can't believe it. I can't find them. I was in such a
hurry I must have left them at home."
   a. bored   b. cruel   c. bewildered

Traffic School: Some random comments by the officer teaching traffic school two
weeks later.

___B___ 13. Officer: "Good morning class. Apparently you all couldn't think of
anything else to do today, right?"
   a. angry   b. humorous   c. elated

___B___ 14. Officer: "I want to give you some sobering statistics. Every year traffic
accidents kill 43,000 people, injure 2.6 million, and cause 130 billion
dollars in damage."
   a. self-indulgent   b. grave   c. churlish

___A___ 15. Officer: "We *can't* control other drivers, but we *can* control our own
behavior."
   a. impassioned   b. witty   c. haughty

___C___ 16. Officer: "For your safety and the safety of other motorists, *please* think
about the consequences of your actions."
   a. boorish   b. disapproving   c. imploring

Exercise 2: Identifying Tone in Textbook Material

Directions: Read the passages below and choose the word that best describes the
speaker's tone by writing the appropriate letter in the blank provided.

*"Hurt not the earth,
neither the sea, nor the
trees."*

—Revelations 7:3

_____ 1. Our impact on the health of the oceans is much more profound than we
often assume. You can do a lot to help save the oceans. First of all, take
care of the environment. If you go to the seashore or go snorkeling or
diving, do not disturb in any way the environment. Return any overturned rocks to their original positions. Leave all forms of life where
they are. If you go fishing, know the regulations and take only what
you really need for food. Return undersized fish. Corals and shells
should be left alone, and alive, in their natural home. Be sure to tell
merchants you object to their sale of shells, corals, sand dollars, and
other marine life, which were most probably collected alive and killed

for sale. Don't buy the yellowfin tuna that is caught in nets that trap dolphins. Look for the "dolphin-safe" seal on the label.

(Peter Castro, *Marine Biology*, 6/e, 2003)

a. cynical
b. serious
c. arrogant
d. outraged

_____C_____ 2. Remember the *Leave It to Beaver* reruns on television? Mother would spend the day whisking around the house in a stylish outfit protected by an apron, tidying and scrubbing and fixing a delicious dinner, and greet Father warmly when he returned from his day at work. Well, times have changed. Or have they? More than 61 percent of married American women are part of the workforce today. But guess who is still tidying and scrubbing and fixing delicious dinners in American homes? Women. And—here's the kicker—*most women seem to think this is fair!*

"The battle for women's rights has been largely won."

—Margaret Thatcher

(Michael Hughes, *Sociology: The Core*, 7/e, 2005)

a. rueful
b. nostalgic
c. amazed
d. scolding

_____A_____ 3. We have seen that anorexia is a serious disease with deep-seated causes and devastating, potentially fatal effects. Julie was one of those who couldn't beat anorexia. She died when she was only 17. We will never go to college together and share a dorm room. She will never fulfill her dream of becoming a nurse. And we will never grow old living beside each other and watching our kids grow up together. Anorexia killed my beautiful vibrant friend.

(Stephen E. Lucas, *The Art of Public Speaking*, 7/e, 2001)

a. sorrowful
b. angry
c. loving
d. whining

_____A_____ 4. Our math classroom is on the third floor of a building that overlooks the top floor of a parking ramp. At most three or four cars are parked up there, although it contains enough space for at least fifty cars. The lower levels of the ramp are also fairly empty. The ramp is only for the use of faculty. We students have to park some distance from campus and even then we have to get to school by 7:30 in the morning if we are to find a parking space. . . . I think the current situation is disgusting. The faculty already enjoy many privileges, including "faculty restrooms," which are distinctive from those simply labeled "restroom." Enough is enough!

(Michael Hughes, *Sociology: The Core*, 7/e, 2005)

a. outraged
b. vindictive
c. pessimistic
d. alarmed

_____ 5. If you are beginning to think that being computer illiterate may be occupational suicide, you are getting the point. Workers in every industry come in contact with computers to some degree. Even fast-food workers read orders on computer screens. Nearly 80 percent of the respondents to a survey said that they believe it is impossible to succeed in the job market without a working knowledge of technology. Respondents who earned $45,000 a year or more were three times more likely to use a computer than those who earned less. As information technology eliminates old jobs while creating new ones, it is up to you to learn the skills you need to be certain you aren't left behind.

(William G. Nickels, *Understanding Business*, 8/e, 2008)

a. excited
b. bitter
c. cautious
d. serious

___C___ 6. I honestly feel Robert can contribute more than I can. He's better educated. He's just plain smarter. He's genuinely gifted, and when he's able to apply himself, he can really accomplish something, can make a name for himself.

(Gloria Bird, *Families and Intimate Relationships*, 1994)

a. critical
b. sympathetic
c. candid
d. sentimental

_____ 7. "Anna, I told you to stop talking. If I've told you once, I've told you 100 times. I told you yesterday and the day before that. The way things are going, I'll be telling it to you all year, and, believe me, I'm getting pretty tired of it. And another thing, young lady . . ."

(Myra Pollack Sadker and David Miller Sadker, *Teachers, Schools, and Society*, 5/e, 2000)

a. ironic
b. sorrowful
c. scolding
d. playful

_____ 8. Ever wonder how schools get their names—and which names are the most popular? The National Education Resource Center researched the most popular proper names for U.S. high schools: Washington, Lincoln, Kennedy, Jefferson, Roosevelt (both Franklin and Teddy), and Wilson. (Presidents do well.) (To date, no school has chosen Richard M. Nixon as a namesake.) But proper names are not the most common high school names. Directions dominate: Northeastern, South, and Central High School are right up there. While creativity obviously is not a criterion, politics is. Citizens fight over whether schools should be named after George Washington and Thomas Jefferson—who, after all, were slaveholders. And, considering how many women are educators, it is amazing that so few schools are named to honor women. Some schools have honored writers or reflect local leaders and culture. In Las

Vegas, you will find schools named Durango, Silverado, and Bonanza, which some complain sound more like casinos than western culture.

(Myra Pollack Sadker and David Miller Sadker, *Teachers, Schools, and Society,* 5/e, 2000)

    a. affectionate
    b. flippant
    c. optimistic
    d. outraged

_____ 9. It's Saturday morning, and you are helping clean out your grandmother's attic. After working a while, you stumble upon a trunk, open it, and discover inside hundreds of old postcards. Thinking about getting to the football game on time, you start tossing the cards into the trash can. Congratulations! You have just thrown away a year's tuition.

(Stephen E. Lucas, *The Art of Public Speaking,* 7/e, 2001)

    a. elated
    b. regretful
    c. sarcastic
    d. demanding

__B__ 10. When the expectant mother drinks, alcohol is absorbed into her bloodstream and distributed throughout her entire body. . . . The fetus is surrounded by the same alcoholic content as its mother had. After being drowned in alcohol, the fetus begins to feel the effect. But it can't sober up. It can't grab a cup of coffee. It can't grab a couple of aspirin. For the fetus's liver, the key organ in removing alcohol from the blood, is just not developed. The fetus is literally pickled in alcohol.

(Stephen E. Lucas, *The Art of Public Speaking,* 7/e, 2001)

    a. carefree
    b. aghast
    c. casual
    d. congratulatory

Exercise 3: Determining Tone in Literature

Directions: Read the following excerpts and indicate the tone of the passage. (You may refer to the list of words at the beginning of the chapter.)

1. I could've been somebody, you know? my mother says and sighs. She has lived in this city her whole life. She can speak two languages. She can sing an opera. She knows how to fix a TV. But she doesn't know which subway train to take to get downtown. I hold her hand very tight while we wait for the right train to arrive.

    She used to draw when she had time. Now she draws with a needle and thread, little knotted rosebuds, tulips made of silk thread. Someday she would like to go to the ballet. Someday she would like to see a play. She borrows opera records from the public library and sings with velvety lungs powerful as morning glories.

    Today while cooking oatmeal she is Madame Butterfly until she sighs and points the wooden spoon at me. I could've been somebody, you know? Esperanza, you go to school. Study hard. That Madame Butterfly was a fool. She stirs the oatmeal. Look at my *comadres*. She means Izaura, whose husband left, and Yolanda, whose husband is dead. Got to take care all your own, she says shaking her head.

Then out of nowhere:

Shame is a bad thing, you know. It keeps you down. You want to know why I quit school? Because I didn't have nice clothes. No clothes, but I had brains.

Yup, she says disgusted, stirring again. I was a smart cookie then.

(Sandra Cisneros, *The House on Mango Street*, 1984)

The tone is ____ Regretfel / Rumorsfel ____

What clues did you use to determine the tone? ____ I could of been ____

2. My Rules

If you want to marry me, here's what you'll have to do
You must learn how to make a perfect chicken dumpling stew
And you must sew my holey socks and you must soothe my troubled mind
And develop the knack for scratching my back
And keep my shoes spotlessly shined
And while I rest you must rake up the leaves
And when it is hailing and snowing
You must shovel the walk, and be still when I talk
And—hey, where are you going?

(Shel Silverstein, *Where the Sidewalk Ends*, 2003)

The tone is ____ Humorous ____

What clues did you use to determine the tone? _____

3. I was glad enough when I reached my room and locked out the mold and the darkness. A cheery fire was burning in the grate, and I sat down before it with a comforting sense of relief. For two hours I sat there, thinking of bygone times; recalling old scenes, and summoning half-forgotten faces out of the mists of the past; listening, in fancy, to voices that long ago grew silent for all time, and to once familiar songs that nobody sings now.

I slept profoundly, but how long I do not know. All at once I found myself awake, and filled with a shuddering expectancy. All was still. All but my own heart—I could hear it beat. Presently the bedclothes began to slip away slowly toward the foot of the bed, as if someone were pulling them! I could not stir; I could not speak.

(Mark Twain, "A Ghost Story")

The tone is _____

What clues did you use to determine the tone? _____

"There is only one way to degrade mankind permanently and that is to destroy language."

—David Hare

4. Attention, techno-weenies. Stop littering the info highway. Don't call a grammatical time-out when you log on. English is English, whether it comes over the phone, via the Postal Service (excuse me, "snail mail"), or on the Internet.

Let's clean up cyberspace, gang. You wouldn't use *pls* for *please*, *yr* for *your*, or *thnx* for *thanks* in a courteous letter. So why do it on the Net? You don't shout or whisper on the telephone. So why use ALL CAPITAL or all lowercase letters in your e-mail? Making yourself hard to read is bad "netiquette."

And another thing. IMHO (in my humble opinion), those abbreviations like CUL (see you later) and BTW (by the way) are overused. You're too busy for full sentences? So what are you doing with the time you're saving by using cute shortcuts? Volunteering at your local hospital? Sure. I'm ROFL (rolling on floor laughing).

You digerati can speak E-lingo among yourselves, but try real English if you want the cyber-impaired to get it. Next time you log on, remember there's a person at the other end, not a motherboard. Use appropriate grammar and punctuation. Be clear and to the point. And consider phoning once in a while.

(Patricia T. O'Connor, *Woe Is I*, 1996)

The tone is _____

What clues did you use to determine the tone? _____

_____

5. There is no egg in eggplant nor ham in hamburger. And neither pine nor apple in pineapple. English muffins were not invented in England nor French fries in France. If we examine some paradoxes in English we find: that quicksand takes you down slowly; boxing rings are square; and a guinea pig is neither from Guinea nor is it a pig. And why is it that writers write, but fingers don't fing, grocers don't groce, and hammers don't ham? If the plural of tooth is teeth, why isn't the plural of booth beeth? One goose, 2 geese. So, one moose, 2 meese? If the teacher taught, why didn't the preacher praught? If a vegetarian eats vegetables, what does a humanitarian eat? Why do people recite at a play yet play at a recital? Park on driveways and drive on parkways? You have to marvel at a language whereby a house can burn up as it burns down. You fill in a form by filling it out. And why, when I wind up a watch, do I start it, but when I wind up an essay, do I end it?

(Richard Lederer, *Crazy English*, 1989)

The tone is _____ confused/puzzled/humorous _____

What clues did you use to determine the tone? _____

6.   To manage to keep up a brain
       Is no easy job, it is plain;
       That's why a great many
       Don't ever use any,
       Thus avoiding the care and the strain!

The tone is _____

What clues did you use to determine the tone? _____

7. At precisely 5:30 in the morning, a bearded man in khaki trousers, a flannel shirt, and a string tie strode to the end of the dock and announced through a megaphone: "Bass anglers, prepare for the blast-off!" In unison, the fishermen turned their ignitions, and Lake Maurepas boiled and rumbled and swelled. Blue smoke from the big outboards curled skyward and collected in an acrid foreign cloud over the marsh. The boats inched away from the crowded ramp

and crept out toward where the pass opened its mouth to the lake. The procession came to a stop at a lighted buoy.

"Now the fun starts," said a young woman standing next to R.J. Decker. She was holding two sleeping babies.

The starter raised a pistol and fired into the air. Instantly a wall of noise rose off Maurepas: the race was on. The bass boats hiccuped and growled and then whined, pushing for more speed. With the throttles hammered down, the sterns dug ferociously and the bows popped up at such alarming angles that Decker was certain some of the boats would flip over in midair. Yet somehow they planed off perfectly, gliding flat and barely creasing the crystal texture of the lake. The song of the big engines was that of a million furious bees; it tore the dawn all to hell.

It was one of the most remarkable moments Decker had ever seen, almost military in its high-tech absurdity: forty boats rocketing the same direction at sixty miles per hour. In darkness.

Most of the spectators applauded heartily.

"Doesn't anyone ever get hurt?" Decker asked the woman with the two babies, who were now yowling.

"Hurt?" she said. "No, sir. At that speed you just flat-out die."

(Carl Hiaasen, *Double Whammy*, 1987)

In the passage above, the term *blast-off* is used to convey the seriousness of this sport. Normally, the term is associated with what Florida activity? _____

_____

What kind of figurative language is the author using when he says the boats "hiccuped, growled, and whined"? _____

What kind of figurative language is the author using when he likens the sound of the boats to bees? _____

Why does the start of the race seem like a military operation? _____

_____

What can you infer about the author's feelings toward this sport? _____

_____

SELECTION

"These last ten years of coming to terms with my disease would turn out to be the best ten years of my life—not in spite of the illness, but because of it."

GETTING THE PICTURE

The following excerpt from Michael J. Fox's book, titled *Lucky Man*, expresses Fox's optimistic spirit after being diagnosed with Parkinson's disease. The book, published in 2002, describes how he learned to cope with Parkinson's disease and how he accepted the illness as a challenge and a positive factor in his life. Fox is an example of a person who sees a glass as being half-full rather than as half-empty.

BIO-SKETCH

Born Michael Andrew Fox in 1961 in Edmonton, Canada, Fox later added the "J" to his name in honor of actor Michael J. Pollard. Fox grew up loving hockey and even had dreams of one day playing in the National Hockey League. Later, though, after experimenting with writing, art, and playing guitar in rock-and-roll bands, he came to realize that he loved acting.

His first paid acting job was costarring in a sit-com for the Canadian Broadcasting Corporation. At 18, he moved to Los Angeles and took a series of bit parts before winning the role of Alex P. Keaton on *Family Ties* in 1981. He earned three Emmy Awards and a Golden Globe for his performances in that role. Although diagnosed with Parkinson's disease in 1991, Fox continued his acting career, starring in the TV show *Spin City* as well as in several films, including *Back to the Future, Doc Hollywood*, and *The American President*. He disclosed his condition in 1998 and retired from *Spin City* in 2000.

Although still strongly committed to acting, Fox has shifted most of his energies to the Michael J. Fox Foundation for Parkinson's Research, which he founded in 2000. He hopes the foundation can discover the cause and find a cure for Parkinson's disease.

BRUSHING UP ON VOCABULARY

Parkinson's disease According to the Michael J. Fox Foundation's Web site, Parkinson's is a "chronic, progressive disorder of the central nervous system. . . . Parkinson's disease has been known since ancient times. An English doctor, James Parkinson, first described it extensively in 1817. Symptoms of Parkinson's may include tremors or trembling, difficulty maintaining balance and gait, rigidity or stiffness of the limbs and trunk, and general slowness of movement." The cause of the disease is still unknown, as is the ability to predict who will get it.

missive a written message or letter, originally from the Latin *missus*, meaning "send."

geek a strange or eccentric person, probably from the Scottish word *geck*, meaning "fool."

Excerpt from

Lucky Man

BY MICHAEL J. FOX

A Wake Up Call

Gainesville, Florida—November 1990

I woke up to find the message in my left hand. It had me trembling. It wasn't a fax, 1 telegram, memo, or the usual sort of missive bringing disturbing news. In fact, my hand held nothing at all. The trembling was the message.

I was feeling a little disoriented. I'd only been shooting the movie in Florida for a 2 week or so, and the massive, pink-lacquered, four-poster bed surrounded by the pastel hues of the University Center Hotel's Presidential Suite still came as a bit of a shock each morning. Oh yeah: and I had a ferocious hangover. That was less shocking.

Even with the lights off, blinds down, and drapes pulled, an offensive amount of 3 light still filtered into the room. Eyes clenched shut, I placed the palm of my left hand across the bridge of my nose in a weak attempt to block the glare. A moth's wing—or so I thought—fluttered against my right cheek. I opened my eyes, keeping my hand suspended an inch or two in front of my face so I could finger-flick the little beastie across the room. That's when I noticed my pinkie. It was trembling, twitching, auto-animated. How long this had been going on I wasn't exactly sure. But now that I noticed it, I was surprised to discover that I couldn't stop it.

Weird—maybe I slept on it funny. Five or six times in rapid succession I pumped 4 my left hand into a fist, followed by a vigorous shaking out. Interlocking the fingers of each hand steeple-style with their opposite number, I lifted them up and over behind my head and pinned them to the pillow.

Tap. Tap. Tap. Like a moisture-free Chinese water torture, I could feel a gentle 5 drumming at the back of my skull. If it was trying to get my attention, it had succeeded. I withdrew my left hand from behind my head and held it in front of my face, steadily, with fingers splayed—like the bespectacled X-ray glasses geek in the old comic book ad. I didn't have to see the underlying skeletal structure; the information I was looking for was right there in the flesh: a thumb, three stock-still fingers, and out there on the lunatic fringe, a spastic pinkie.

It occurred to me that this might have something to do with my hangover, or 6 more precisely with alcohol. I'd put away a lot of beers in my time, but had never woken up with the shakes; maybe this was what they called delirium tremens? I was pretty sure they would manifest themselves in a more impressive way—I mean, who gets the d.t.'s in one finger? Whatever this was, it wasn't alcoholic deterioration.

Now I did a little experimentation. I found that if I grabbed my finger with my 7 right hand, it would stop moving. Released, it would keep still for four or five seconds, and then, like a cheap wind-up toy, it would whir back to life again. *Hmmm.* What had begun as a curiosity was now blossoming into full-fledge worry. The trembling had been going on for a few minutes with no sign of quitting and my brain, fuzzy as it was, scrambled to come up with an explanation. Had I hit my head, injured myself in some way? The tape of the previous night's events was grainy at best. But I didn't feel any bumps. Any pain in my head was from boozing, not bruising.

Irreconcilable Differences

Throughout the course of the morning, the twitching would intensify, as would my 8 search for a cause—not just for the rest of that day, but for months to follow. The true answer was elusive, and in fact wouldn't reveal itself for another full year. The trembling was indeed the message, and this is what it was telling me:

> That morning—November 13, 1990—my brain was serving notice: it had 9 initiated a divorce from my mind. Efforts to contest or reconcile would be futile; eighty percent of the process, I would later learn, was already complete. No grounds were given, and the petition was irrevocable. Further, my brain was demanding, and incrementally seizing, custody of my body, beginning with the baby: the outermost finger of my left hand.

Ten years later, knowing what I do now, this mind-body divorce strikes me as a 10 serviceable metaphor—though at the time it was a concept well beyond my grasp. I had no idea there were even problems in the relationship—just assumed things were pretty good between the old gray matter and me. This was a false assumption. Unbeknownst to me, things had been deteriorating long before the morning of the pinkie rebellion. But by declaring its dysfunction in such an arresting manner, my brain now had my mind's full attention.

It would be a year of questions and false answers that would satisfy me for a time, 11 fueling my denial and forestalling the sort of determined investigation that would ultimately provide the answer. That answer came from a doctor who would inform me that I had a progressive, degenerative, and incurable neurological disorder; one that I may have been living with for as long as a decade before suspecting there might be anything wrong. This doctor would also tell me that I could probably continue acting for another "ten good years," and he would be right about that, almost to the day. What he did not tell me—what no one could—is that these last ten years of coming to terms with my disease would turn out to be the best ten years of my life—not in spite of my illness, but because of it.

I have referred to it in interviews as a *gift*—something for which others with this 12 affliction have taken me to task. I was only speaking from my own experience, of course, but I stand partially corrected: if it is a gift, it's the gift that just keeps on taking.

Coping with this relentless assault and the accumulating damage is not easy. No- 13 body would ever choose to have this visited upon them. Still, this unexpected crisis forced a fundamental life decision: adopt a siege mentality—or embark upon a journey. Whatever it was—courage? acceptance? wisdom?—that finally allowed me to go down the second road (after spending a few disastrous years on the first) was unquestionably a gift—and absent this neurophysiological catastrophe, I would never have opened it, or been so profoundly enriched. That's why I consider myself a lucky man.

(Michael J. Fox, *Lucky Man,* 2002)

> *"Be willing to have it so; acceptance of what has happened is the first step in overcoming the consequences of any misfortune."*
>
> —William James

✓ COMPREHENSION CHECKUP

Multiple-Choice

Write the letter of the correct answer in the blank.

_____ 1. The reader may conclude that Michael J. Fox
  a. knew immediately that he had Parkinson's disease
  b. initially thought that he might have slept on his finger in an awkward position
  c. thought that his finger was trembling because he had been drinking alcohol to excess
  d. both b and c

_____ 2. Which of the following is true about what doctors told Fox?
  a. He would only be able to continue acting for a few more months.
  b. He had just ten years to live.
  c. He had an incurable neurological disorder.
  d. None of the above

_____ 3. Which of the following is true about Fox's reaction to his disease?
   a. He quickly adopted a siege mentality that has stayed with him for ten years.
   b. He has always been cheerful about his disease.
   c. He now views his disease as a complete catastrophe.
   d. He now sees his disease as a special sort of gift.

_____ 4. What does Fox mean when he says, "I woke up to find the message in my left hand"?
   a. A friend had placed a letter in his left hand while he was sleeping.
   b. He awoke to find his left hand clutching a beer bottle.
   c. The trembling finger of his left hand was telling him something.
   d. His left hand was swollen from an unknown trauma that must have happened the night before.

_____ 5. What does Fox mean when he says, "my brain was demanding and incrementally seizing custody of my body"?
   a. His brain was starting to do things to his body that he could not stop.
   b. His brain was no longer obeying his wishes and demands.
   c. His condition was gradually getting worse.
   d. All of the above.

_____ 6. When Fox states that "efforts to contest or reconcile would be futile," he means that
   a. there is nothing he can do about the situation
   b. the situation is shocking
   c. given time and work the situation can be ameliorated
   d. Both a and b

_____ 7. The overall tone expressed in this selection could best be described as
   a. acceptance
   b. puzzlement
   c. bitterness
   d. despair

_____ 8. Which of the following proverbs best expresses the main idea of the selection?
   a. The bigger they are the harder they fall.
   b. Blood is thicker than water.
   c. When the cat's away the mice will play.
   d. Every cloud has a silver lining.

_____ 9. What does Fox do directly after he discovers his twitching little finger?
   a. makes a fist and then shakes out his fingers
   b. places his fingers behind his head
   c. spreads his fingers out in front of his face
   d. grabs his left finger with his right hand

_____ 10. Which of the following expresses how the author feels?
   a. Other people are responsible for your happiness.
   b. A catastrophe can lead to an even richer life.
   c. Coming to terms with his disease has been a positive in his life.
   d. Both b and c

_____ 11. What implications does the phrase "mind-brain divorce" have for Fox?
     a. The mind is something different from the brain.
     b. His mind and brain had once cooperated well, but now were no longer doing so.
     c. When his mind tells his brain to make his body stop shaking, his brain does not obey.
     d. All of the above.

_____ 12. What are some of the things that Fox means when he calls his disease a "gift"?
     a. He means that it has brought only happiness in his life.
     b. He means that from his personal perspective it has been a gift.
     c. He means that it gave him the opportunity to begin a journey that has enriched his life.
     d. Both b and c

True or False

Indicate whether the statement is true or false by writing **T** or **F** in the blank provided.

_____ 13. A doctor felt that Fox may have had Parkinson's disease for ten years prior to its discovery.

_____ 14. Fox discovered his trembling when he was in the University Center Hospital.

_____ 15. Fox's finger kept moving when he held it.

_____ 16. Fox often woke up shaking after drinking.

_____ 17. Fox searched for a cause for his dysfunction for many months.

Vocabulary in Context

Determine the meaning of the following words from the context without using a dictionary. (The paragraph in which the word appears in the reading selection is indicated in parentheses.) Write your answers in your own words in the space provided.

1. offensive (paragraph 3) _____

2. pinkie (3) _____

3. auto-animated (3) _____

4. fuzzy (7) _____

5. dysfunction (10) _____

6. arresting (10) _____

7. affliction (12) _____

Vocabulary Puzzle

Directions: Look through the paragraphs indicated in parentheses to find words that match the definitions below. Then write these words in the puzzle.

ACROSS CLUES

8. unyielding; severe, strict, or harsh (paragraph 13)
9. hard to comprehend (8)
10. any prolonged effort to overcome resistance (13)
13. gradations or varieties of colors; tints (2)
14. to cause a person to accept something not desired (9)
16. spread out (5)
17. the act of making worse (6)
18. lying under or beneath (5)
19. extreme or intense (2)

DOWN CLUES

1. closed tightly (paragraph 3)
2. written message; letter (1)
3. not to be recalled; unalterable (9)
4. a great, often sudden calamity (13)
5. preventing or hindering by action in advance (11)
6. declining in physical qualities (11)
7. flapped about (3)
11. not successful; useless (9)
12. to make clear or evident to the eye (6)
15. to start on a trip (13)

In Your Own Words

Psychotherapist Alan McGinnis, author of *Power of Optimism*, says that optimists see themselves as "problem solvers and trouble shooters." According to McGinnis, the following qualities help optimists maintain a positive attitude while still being realistic:

- They look for partial solutions.

- They believe they have control over their future.

- They interrupt their negative trains of thought.

- They heighten their powers of appreciation.

- They are cheerful even when they can't be happy.

- They accept what cannot be changed.

In what ways has Michael J. Fox demonstrated an optimistic tone?

The Art of Writing

In a brief essay, respond to one of the following quotes:

1. "Courage is resistance to fear, mastery of fear—not absence of fear." (Mark Twain)

2. "Courage is the price that life exacts for granting peace. The soul that knows it not, knows no release." (Amelia Earhart)

What do you think the author means? Do you agree? Why or why not? How does the quote apply to the situation that Michael J. Fox faced?

Internet Activity

1. For information about Parkinson's disease and the Michael J. Fox Foundation for Parkinson's Research, go to its Web site:

   www.michaeljfox.org

   Based on what you read there, write a paragraph about what's new in Parkinson's research.

2. Two other organizations dealing with Parkinson's are

   • The Parkinson's Disease Foundation, www.pdf.org

   • The National Parkinson Foundation, www.parkinson.org

   Go to the Web site of one of these organizations, and write a paragraph about its mission and activities.

Irony and Satire

Irony refers to a contrast between what people say and what they actually mean. An ironic comment intends a meaning that is contrary to its stated meaning. The intended meaning is often the opposite of the stated meaning. For instance, if someone backs into your car, you might say, "That's just great!" Your intended meaning is that something bad just happened, but your words say that something good just happened. Since the meaning of an ironic statement is often expressed indirectly, you must use inference to discover it.

Satire refers to comments that exaggerate flaws or failings for the purpose of making them seem ridiculous. Because satire relies on distortion, it is often humorous. Almost anything can be satirized, including people, institutions, and ideas.

Exercise 4: Identifying Irony and Satire

Directions: The Polish poet Wislawa Szymborska (1923–) won the Nobel Prize for Literature in 1996. The Nobel committee praised her for the "ironic precision" of her poetry. Read the following poem on bodybuilders and then answer the questions that follow.

Bodybuilders' Contest

BY WISLAWA SZYMBORSKA

From scalp to sole, all muscles in slow motion.
The ocean of his torso drips with lotion.
The king of all is he who preens and wrestles
with sinews twisted into monstrous pretzels.
Onstage he grapples with a grizzly bear
the deadlier for not really being there.
Three unseen panthers are in turn laid low,
each with one smoothly choreographed blow.

He grunts while showing his poses and paces.
His back alone has twenty different faces.
The mammoth fist he raises as he wins
is tribute to the force of vitamins.

(Wislawa Szymborska, *View with a Grain of Sand*, 1993)

1. What is the tone of this poem?

2. How can we tell that the poet is making fun of bodybuilders? Exactly what in the poem makes her feelings clear?

3. How many of the senses are represented in this poem? What is the overall image of the bodybuilder?

4. What metaphors does Szymborska use? What is she trying to convey with each of these metaphors?

SELECTION

"Standing in line is so important, it's the first thing they teach you how to do at school."

GETTING THE PICTURE

In the following satire, Tom Mather humorously talks about standing in line.

BIO-SKETCH

Tom Mather is a former humor columnist for the *BGNews* at Bowling Green State University in Bowling Green, Ohio. He published his first book, *The Cheeseburger Philosophy,* at the age of 21. Below is an excerpt from his second book, *Voyages in the Toilet Dimension,* which was published in 1999.

BRUSHING UP ON VOCABULARY

admonish to reprove or scold in a mild-mannered way. The word *admonish* derives from the Latin *ad,* meaning "to," and *monere,* meaning "advise or warn."

out of line behaving improperly.

Waiting in Life's Long Lines
BY TOM MATHER

It's time to discuss The Great American Pastime. And I'm not talking about baseball. 1

No, America's new pastime is standing in line. 2

Standing in line is so important, it's the first thing they teach you how to do at school: 3

"As soon as you're finished, everyone get in line." 4

"We're not leaving until everyone gets in line." 5

They continually admonish bad kids by telling them that they are "out of line." 6

It seems that for practically everything we do today, we have to wait in line. Whether it's to see the new baby, or pay our respects to the dead, we wait in line. 7

We stand in line so much, we even wait when we're not working. What happens when you get fired? You go wait in the unemployment line. The government figures, "They don't have anything else to do. They might as well stand in line." 8

To be fair, people in other countries stand in line too. It's just a little different when they do it. For example, you probably have heard how in many countries the people wait hours in long lines for food. You might not realize that Americans wait hours in long lines for fun. 9

Yes, that's right. It's gotten so bad there are even parks designed specifically for standing in line. Some of the more famous ones are Disneyland, Disney World, and Six Flags. Have you been to any of these? Whoever said, "The shortest distance between two points is a line," never went to an amusement park. They have designed rides that allow you to stand in line for up to three hours, so that you can go down hills and through turns at 70 miles per hour. Never mind that most people did that on the trip there, because they wanted to get there as early as possible, to avoid the lines. 10

So if being in a line can be so much "fun," then how come we hate it so much? I think it's not so much the actual standing in line that we hate. The problem is that one line always moves faster than the other. And it's always the line you're not in. If you get 11

"When you sit with a nice girl for two hours, you think it's only a minute. But when you sit on a hot stove for a minute, you think it's two hours."

—Albert Einstein

in the short line, there is inevitably some crazy event that holds up the line. You know you're going to be in trouble when you hear one of the following:

"Price check on lane fourteen, price check on lane fourteen."

"What do you mean you don't take VISA?" or

"I could've *sworn* I brought my checkbook."

And no place is more annoying about lines than banks. There will be 30 people in line, and one teller. But that kind of thing you're used to. What the banks like to do, in addition, is to have five other tellers working at the same time on other projects. They each sit at their own window, watching to see how long the line can get, counting pennies. This in turn leads to a lot of bank robberies, because some people get so mad at those holding up the line, they decide it's just easier and quicker to hold up the line.

Lines aren't simply long, they can be confusing too. There's the line to get tickets, the line to get food, the line to get in, and the line to get out. Half of the problem is figuring out which line is the one you want to be in.

"Is this the line to buy tickets?"

"Tickets? I thought this was the line for the women's bathroom."

(Tom Mather, *The BG News*, 1997)

✓ COMPREHENSION CHECKUP

Multiple Choice

Write the letter of the correct answer in the blank provided.

_____ 1. The topic of this article is
   a. baseball
   b. standing in line at banks
   c. standing in line
   d. waiting in line at theme parks

_____ 2. The author mentions that Americans stand in line for all of the following *except*
   a. to visit a new baby
   b. to pay our respects to the dead
   c. to see a teller at a bank
   d. to visit Santa Claus and his elves

_____ 3. The author's purpose in writing this selection is to
   a. inform us of ways to foil bank robberies
   b. entertain us with examples of where and when Americans stand in line
   c. persuade us to abandon the time-wasting custom of standing in line
   d. explain how the custom of standing in line differs in the United States from other countries

_____ 4. The tone of this article could best be described as
   a. sentimental and sad
   b. humorous and ironic
   c. angry and vindictive
   d. cautious and logical

_____ 5. You can infer from the article that the author believes that
   a. standing in line has gotten out of hand
   b. people had better learn to cope with the irritation of standing in line
   c. standing in line is fun
   d. people should learn to talk to each other while standing in line to relieve the boredom

_____ 6. The statement "some people get so mad at those holding up the line, they decide it's just easier and quicker to hold up the line" is an example of
   a. a play on words
   b. a literary allusion
   c. an ironic exaggeration
   d. both a and c

_____ 7. The main intention of the writer is to
   a. describe rude persons who hold up lines
   b. expose the rudeness of bank tellers
   c. comment on the problems inherent in standing in lines
   d. extol the virtues of a system in which lines don't exist and it's every person for her- or himself

_____ 8. The author of this selection says that schools
   a. encourage students to stand in line
   b. disparage students by telling them that they are out of line
   c. both a and b
   d. none of the above

_____ 9. The author would agree that
   a. Americans wait hours in lines for food
   b. children should not be forced to stand in line
   c. lines are lots of fun if you have the right attitude
   d. lines can be confusing at times

_____ 10. The author ends the selection with an illustration of
   a. the difficulty in figuring out the correct line to stand in
   b. the irritation people feel when standing in a lengthy line
   c. the differences between the employed and the unemployed
   d. the differences between U.S. citizens and Europeans

SELECTION

"My definition of a good sculpture is 'a sculpture that looks at least vaguely like something.'"

GETTING THE PICTURE

In this selection, Dave Barry is poking fun at modern art. Like much of the viewing public, he is not sure that nonrepresentational art is actually art at all.

BIO-SKETCH

Dave Barry is best known for writing his syndicated column for the *Miami Herald*. He is also a best-selling author. The *New York Times* called Mr. Barry the funniest man in America.

BRUSHING UP ON VOCABULARY

velveteen a cotton fabric with soft velvet pile.

Pomodoro Arnaldo Pomodoro was born in Italy in 1926. He has had many exhibitions in Italy, other European countries, and the United States. He is best known for his artistic stage designs and his modern sculptures located near public buildings.

Excerpt from

Dave Barry Is Not Taking This Sitting Down

BY DAVE BARRY

"Perpetual modernness is the measure of merit in every work of art."

—Ralph Waldo Emerson

Like many members of the uncultured, Cheez-It–consuming public, I am not good 1 at grasping modern art. I'm the type of person who will stand in front of a certified modern masterpiece painting that looks, to the layperson, like a big black square, and quietly think: "Maybe the actual painting is on the other side."

I especially have a problem with modernistic sculptures, the kind where you, the 2 layperson, cannot be sure whether you're looking at a work of art or a crashed alien spacecraft. My definition of a good sculpture is "a sculpture that looks at least vaguely like something." I'm talking about a sculpture like Michelangelo's *David*. You look at that, and there is no doubt about what the artist's message is. It is: "Here's a naked man the size of an oil derrick."

I bring this topic up because of an interesting incident that occurred recently in 3 Miami. . . . Miami tends to have these interesting incidents, and one of them occurred a little while ago when Dade County purchased an office building from the city of Miami. The problem was that, squatting in an area that the county wanted to convert into office space, there was a large ugly wad of metal, set into the concrete. So the county sent construction workers with heavy equipment to rip out the wad, which was then going to be destroyed.

But guess what? Correct! It turns out that this was NOT an ugly wad. It was art! 4 Specifically, it was Public Art, defined as "art that was purchased by experts who are not spending their own personal money." The money of course comes from the taxpayers, who are not allowed to spend this money themselves because (1) they probably wouldn't buy art, and (2) if they did, there is no way they would buy the crashed-spaceship style of art that the experts usually select for them.

The Miami wad is in fact a sculpture by the famous Italian sculptor Pomodoro 5 (like most famous artists, he is not referred to by his first name, although I like to think it's "Bud"). This sculpture cost the taxpayers $80,000, which makes it an important work of art. In dollar terms, it is 3,200 times as important as a painting of dogs playing poker, and more than 5,000 times as important as a velveteen Elvis.

"Art is the expression of an enormous preference."

—Wyndham Lewis

Fortunately, before the sculpture was destroyed, the error was discovered, and the 6 Pomodoro was moved to another city office building, where it sits next to the parking garage, providing great pleasure to the many taxpayers who come to admire it.

I am kidding, of course. On the day I went to see it, the sculpture was, like so 7 many pieces of modern taxpayer-purchased public art, being totally ignored by the actual taxpaying public, possibly because it looks—and I say this with all due artistic respect for Bud—like an abandoned air compressor.

So here's what I think: I think there should be a law requiring that all public art 8 be marked with a large sign stating something like: "NOTICE! THIS IS A PIECE OF ART! THE PUBLIC SHOULD ENJOY IT TO THE TUNE OF 80,000 CLAMS!"

Also, if there happens to be an abandoned air compressor nearby, it should have 9 a sign that says: "NOTICE! THIS IS NOT ART!" so the public does not waste time enjoying the wrong thing. The public should enjoy what the experts have decided the public should enjoy. That's the system we use in this country, and we're going to stick with it. . . .

(Dave Barry, *Dave Barry Is Not Taking This Sitting Down*, 2000)

✓ COMPREHENSION CHECKUP

The Main Idea

What is the main idea of this selection? _____

_____

_____

True or False

Indicate whether the statement is true of false by writing **T** or **F** in the blank provided.

_____ 1. By calling Pomodoro "Bud," Barry is expressing respect for Pomodoro.

_____ 2. Barry has an appreciation for realistic sculpture such as Michelangelo's *David*.

_____ 3. When Barry refers to himself as a member of the "Cheez-It–consuming public," he means that his tastes are simple and unrefined.

_____ 4. The Pomodoro sculpture was almost destroyed by construction workers.

_____ 5. According to Barry, the Pomodoro sculpture is very popular with the general public.

Agree or Disagree

Indicate whether Dave Barry is likely to agree or disagree by writing **A** or **D** in the blank provided.

_____ 6. Modern art is worthy of our respect.

_____ 7. Taxpayers rather than "experts" are better judges of art.

_____ 8. The more expensive a piece of art is, the more merit it has.

_____ 9. It is often difficult to tell the difference between modern art and junk.

_____ 10. The public, given a choice, would probably not select the modern art that is often on display outside public buildings.

Multiple Choice

_____ 11. The topic of this selection is
  a. public art
  b. sculpture
  c. Pomodoro
  d. abandoned air compressors

_____ 12. The tone of this selection is
  a. serious
  b. nostalgic
  c. satiric
  d. dictatorial

_____ 13. Dave Barry's reason for writing this selection was to
  a. encourage more spending of taxpayer dollars on public art
  b. poke fun at modern art
  c. persuade Dade County to stop purchasing expensive sculptures
  d. explain his theory of good sculpture

_____ 14. When Dave Barry says, "The public should enjoy what the experts have decided the public should enjoy," he is being
  a. irreverent
  b. ironic
  c. sarcastic
  d. all of the above

Vocabulary in Context

Match the vocabulary word from the selection (on the left) with the most appropriate definition (on the right), and write the letter in the space provided. Refer to the paragraph in the selection for context clues.

_____ grasping (paragraph 1)   a. dollars

_____ certified (1)   b. extraterrestrial

_____ layperson (1)   c. nonexpert

_____ alien (2)   d. sitting

_____ squatting (3)   e. large quantity

_____ wad (3)   f. comprehending; understanding

_____ convert (3)   g. change

_____ clams (8)   h. guaranteed; confirmed

In Your Own Words

Why does Barry mention that Dade County placed the sculpture next to a parking garage? Do you think that Barry considers a parking garage an appropriate location for the sculpture? Why or why not?

The Art of Writing

1. In a brief essay, respond to the questions below.

   Is there any public art in your area that became controversial? Why did it become controversial? Was it because of the cost? Was it because of the appearance of the artwork? Was it a combination of factors? How was the controversy resolved?

2. Study the cartoon "Eye of the Beholder." How does this cartoon illustrate Dave Barry's main idea?

   _____

   _____

   _____

Eye of the Beholder

Cartoon: Eye of the Beholder, Jeff MacNelly. Copyright © 1997 Tribune Media, Services. All rights reserved. Reprinted with permission.

Internet Activity

Go to the *Miami Herald* Web site:

   www.miamiherald.com/living/columnists/dave_barry/

Select a column by Barry and print it. After reading the column, state Barry's main idea in your own words. List the details that Barry gives to support his main idea.

*"But among the iron rods of the train, the handrail broke
and went through Frida from one side to the other at the
level of the pelvis."*

GETTING THE PICTURE

This excerpt from Hayden Herrera's biography of the artist Frida Kahlo gives both
Kahlo's and her friend Alejandro Gomez Arias's accounts of the accident that changed
her life. She spent over a month in the hospital and endured many operations. Doctors were amazed that she survived. As Kahlo told Arias, "Death dances over my bed
at night." Bedridden for over three months, she learned to paint when her mother
attached a portable easel and a mirror to her bed so that she could be her own model.

BIO-SKETCH

Biographer/historian Hayden Herrera has lectured widely, curated several exhibitions of art, taught Latin American art at New York University, and been awarded a
Guggenheim Fellowship. She is the author of numerous articles and reviews for such
publications as the *New York Times*. In addition to *Frida,* her books include *Frida
Kahlo: The Paintings, Mary Frank,* and *Matisse: A Portrait.* Frida Kahlo's life story is
depicted in the movie *Frida,* starring Salma Hayek as the artist and Alfred Molina as
her husband, the renowned Mexican muralist Diego Rivera. The movie, released in
2002, is based on Hayden Herrera's biography of Frida Kahlo.

BRUSHING UP ON VOCABULARY

toreador a term for a bullfighter or matador; the term *toreador* (from the Spanish *torear,*
"to bait a bull") was first used by the French composer Georges Bizet in his opera *Carmen.*

lesion an injury to the body tending to result in impairment or loss of function.

contusion a bruise; an injury to the underlying tissue without the skin being broken.

Excerpt from

Frida

BY HAYDEN HERRERA

Accident and Aftermath

It was one of those accidents that make a person, even one separated by years from 1
the actual fact, wince with horror. It involved a trolley car that plowed into a flimsy
wooden bus, and it transformed Frida Kahlo's life.

   Far from being a unique piece of bad luck, such accidents were common enough 2
in those days in Mexico City to be depicted in numerous *retablos* (small votive paintings offering thanks to a holy being, usually the Virgin, for misfortunes escaped).

Buses were relatively new to the city, and because of their novelty they were jammed with people while trolley cars went empty. Then, as now, they were driven with toreador bravado, as if the image of the Virgin of Guadalupe dangling near the front window made the driver invincible. The bus in which Frida was riding was new, and its fresh coat of paint made it look especially jaunty.

The accident occurred late in the afternoon on September 17, 1925, the day after 3 Mexico had celebrated the anniversary of its independence from Spain. A light rain had just stopped; the grand gray government buildings that border the Zocalo looked even grayer and more severe than usual. The bus to Coyoacan was nearly full, but Alejandro and Frida found seats together in the back. When they reached the corner of Cuahutemotzin and 5 de Mayo and were about to turn onto Calzada de Tlalpan, a trolley from Xochimilco approached. It was moving slowly but kept coming as if it had no brakes, as if it were purposely aiming at a crash. Frida remembered:

> A little while after we got on the bus the collision began. Before that we had 4 taken another bus, but since I had lost a little parasol, we got off to look for it and that was how we happened to get on the bus that destroyed me. The accident took place on a corner in front of the San Juan market, exactly in front. The streetcar went slowly, but our bus driver was a very nervous young man. When the trolley went around the corner the bus was pushed against the wall.
>
> I was an intelligent young girl, but impractical, in spite of all the freedom 5 I had won. Perhaps for this reason, I did not assess the situation nor did I guess the kind of wounds I had. The first thing I thought of was a *ballero* [Mexican toy] with pretty colors that I had bought that day and that I was carrying with me. I tried to look for it, thinking that what had happened would not have major consequences.
>
> It is a lie that one is aware of the crash, a lie that one cries. In me there were 6 no tears. The crash bounced us forward and a handrail pierced me the way a sword pierces a bull. A man saw me having a tremendous hemorrhage. He carried me and put me on a billiard table until the Red Cross came for me.

When Alejandro Gomez Arias describes the accident, his voice constricts to an 7 almost inaudible monotone, as if he could avoid reliving the memory by speaking of it quietly:

> The electric train with two cars approached the bus slowly. It hit the bus in 8 the middle. Slowly the train pushed the bus. The bus had a strange elasticity. It bent more and more, but for a time it did not break. It was a bus with long benches on either side. I remember that at one moment my knees touched the knees of the person sitting opposite me, I was sitting next to Frida. When the bus reached its maximal flexibility it burst into a thousand pieces, and the train kept moving. It ran over many people.
>
> I remained under the train. Not Frida. But among the iron rods of the 9 train, the handrail broke and went through Frida from one side to the other at the level of the pelvis. When I was able to stand up I got out from under the train. I had no lesions, only contusions. Naturally the first thing I did was to look for Frida.
>
> Something strange had happened. Frida was totally nude. The collision 10 had unfastened her clothes. Someone in the bus, probably a house painter, had been carrying a packet of powdered gold. This package broke, and the gold fell all over the bleeding body of Frida. When people saw her they cried, '*La bailarina, la bailarina!*' With the gold on her red, bloody body, they thought she was a dancer.

"Although the world is full of suffering, it is full also of overcoming it."

—Helen Keller

I picked her up—in those days I was a strong boy—and then I noticed with horror that Frida had a piece of iron in her body. A man said, 'We have to take it out!' He put his knee on Frida's body, and said 'Let's take it out.' When he pulled it out, Frida screamed so loud that when the ambulance from the Red Cross arrived, her screaming was louder than the siren. Before the ambulance came, I picked up Frida and put her in the display window of a billiard room. I took off my coat and put it over her. I thought she was going to die. Two or three people did die at the scene of the accident, others died later.

The ambulance came and took her to the Red Cross Hospital, which in those days was on San Jeronimo Street, a few blocks from where the accident took place. Frida's condition was so grave that the doctors did not think they could save her. They thought she would die on the operating table.

Frida was operated on for the first time. During the first month it was not certain that she would live.

The girl whose wild dash through school corridors resembled a bird's flight, who jumped on and off streetcars and buses, preferably when they were moving, was now immobilized and enclosed in a series of plaster casts and other contraptions. "It was a strange collision," Frida said. "It was not violent but rather silent, slow, and it harmed everybody. And me most of all."

Her spinal column was broken in three places in the lumbar region. Her collarbone was broken, and her third and fourth ribs. Her right leg had eleven fractures and her right foot was dislocated and crushed. Her left shoulder was out of joint, her pelvis broken in three places. The steel handrail had literally skewered her body at the level of the abdomen.

(Hayden Herrera, *Frida: A Biography of Frida Kahlo*, 1983)

✓ COMPREHENSION CHECKUP

Multiple Choice

Write the letter of the correct answer in the blank provided.

_____ 1. Which of the following statements best expresses the main idea of the selection?
  a. Frida rode a bus.
  b. A handrail broke and went through the pelvis of Frida.
  c. Frida sustained severe injuries in a terrible bus accident but survived.
  d. Frida's spinal column was broken.

_____ 2. The author's main purpose is to
  a. inform
  b. entertain
  c. persuade

_____ 3. The main pattern of organization of paragraph 3 is
  a. example
  b. listing
  c. cause and effect
  d. chronological order

_____ 4. All of the following statements about the bus are true *except*
   a. the bus was new
   b. the bus was fairly empty
   c. the bus was made of wood
   d. the bus was headed to Cayoacan

_____ 5. In paragraph 2, Frida describes the bus as being driven with "toreador bravery." With this image, she means to imply all of the following about the bus driver *except*
   a. he was driving safely and cautiously
   b. he was driving as though he were invincible
   c. he was driving with great daring
   d. he was taking risks

_____ 6. In paragraph 3, the author describes the government buildings as "more severe than usual." This is an example of
   a. simile
   b. metaphor
   c. personification
   d. symbol

_____ 7. The first two sentences in paragraph 14 bring to mind the image of someone who is
   a. calm and careful
   b. a young risk-taker
   c. fun-loving
   d. both b and c

_____ 8. What is Frida's tone in the last two sentences of paragraph 14?
   a. grave
   b. self-pitying
   c. regretful
   d. all of the above

True or False

Indicate whether the statement is true or false by writing **T** or **F** in the blank provided.

_____ 9. Mexican Independence Day is September 17.

_____ 10. The bus driver was an anxious older man.

_____ 11. The trolley was electric with two cars.

_____ 12. The doctors were confident that they could save Frida's life.

_____ 13. Frida's right leg and right foot were injured in the accident.

_____ 14. The rods that pierced Frida were part of the bus.

Sequence

Number the events in the order in which they occurred in the reading selection.

_____ a. Frida gets off a bus to look for her parasol.

_____ b. The trolley car plows into Frida's bus.

_____ c. Frida is operated on.

_____ d. Frida begins to hemorrhage.

_____ e. The ambulance comes and picks up Frida.

_____ f. The handrail pierces Frida.

_____ g. Frida is laid out on the billiard table.

Vocabulary in Context

Each item below includes a sentence from the selection. Using the context clues provided, write a preliminary definition for the italicized word. Then look up the word in a dictionary and write the appropriate definition.

1. "It was one of those accidents that make a person, even one separated by years from the actual fact, *wince* with horror." (paragraph 1)

   Your definition: _____

   Dictionary definition: _____

2. "Far from being a *unique* piece of bad luck, such accidents were common enough in those days in Mexico City to be *depicted* in numerous retablos (small votive paintings offering thanks to a holy being, usually the Virgin, for misfortunes escaped)." (2)

   Your definition: _____

   Dictionary definition: _____

   Your definition: _____

   Dictionary definition: _____

3. "The bus in which Frida was riding was new, and its fresh coat of paint made it look especially *jaunty*." (2)

   Your definition: _____

   Dictionary definition: _____

4. "When Alejandro Gomez Arias describes the accident, his voice *constricts* to an almost *inaudible monotone,* as if he could avoid reliving the memory by speaking of it quietly:" (7)

   Your definition: _____

   Dictionary definition: _____

   Your definition: _____

   Dictionary definition: _____

5. "The bus had a strange *elasticity*." (8)

   Your definition: _____

   Dictionary definition: _____

6. "Frida's condition was so *grave* that the doctors did not think they could save her." (12)

   Your definition: _____

   Dictionary definition: _____

In Your Own Words

1. What is the overall tone created by this excerpt? What specific images contribute to the tone?

2. What details of the accident scene are clearly depicted? Why are these images particularly sharp or vivid?

The Art of Writing

Write a short essay discussing one of the following quotations attributed to Frida Kahlo. Be sure to describe the tone of the quotation.

1. "In this hospital, death dances around my bed at night." (said shortly after her accident)

2. "I was a child who went about in a world of colors. My friends, my companions, became women slowly. I became old in instants." (said during her long recovery at home)

Internet Activity

For additional information about Frida Kahlo, explore the following Web sites:

www.sfmoma.org/

www.robinurton.com/history/frida-y-diego.htm

The first is a Web site sponsored by the San Francisco Museum of Modern Art. The painting *Frida and Diego Rivera* (1931) is in the museum's permanent collection. Study the painting carefully. What do you think Kahlo was trying to express about the couple's relationship in the painting? Did she use any symbols?

The second Web site shows many pictures and self-portraits by Kahlo. Summarize what you learn from the Web site about Kahlo.

MASTERY TEST: Frida—Accident and Aftermath

Main Idea

_____ 1. Which of the following would be the best title for the selection?
   a. The Accident that Transformed Frida's Kahlo's Life
   b. Frida—The Early Years
   c. A Famous Painter Takes Shape
   d. A Long Journey of Healing

_____ 2. The implied main idea of paragraph 2 is
   a. in Mexico City at that time, pedestrians had to be extremely careful
   b. trolleys became less popular as people switched to buses
   c. Frida was riding in a brand new bus when the accident occurred
   d. accidents similar to what happened to Frida were not uncommon in Mexico City

MASTERY TEST: Frida—Accident and Aftermath   *(continued)*

_____ 3. The implied main idea of paragraph 15 is
- a. Frida had a broken collarbone and broken ribs
- b. the handrail had penetrated Frida's body
- c. Frida sustained numerous severe injuries in the accident
- d. Alejandro's injuries were less severe than Frida's

Supporting Detail

_____ 4. All of the following were key factors contributing to the accident *except*
- a. the bus was not sturdily built
- b. the trip took place the day after the anniversary of Mexico's independence from Spain
- c. the trolley was unable to stop in time
- d. the bus driver was a nervous young man

Context

_____ 5. A *flimsy* wooden bus could be all of the following *except*
- a. sturdily built
- b. light
- c. easily damaged
- d. insubstantial

Purpose

_____ 6. The author wrote the selection to
- a. describe how Frida chose the subject matter of her paintings
- b. inform the reader of a transformative event in Frida's life
- c. demonstrate how one event can have lifelong repercussions
- d. explain how no one is immune to hardship and suffering in life

Pattern of Organization

_____ 7. Alejandro Gomez Arias describes the accident using time order and
- a. contrast
- b. spatial order
- c. classification
- d. listing

_____ 8. The pattern of organization for paragraph 15 is
- a. definition and example
- b. listing
- c. comparison
- d. contrast

Sentence Relationships

_____ 9. What is the relationship expressed in the sentence below? "Buses were relatively new to the city, and because of their novelty they were jammed with people while trolley cars went empty."
- a. time order
- b. classification
- c. cause and effect
- d. steps in a process

MASTERY TEST: Frida—Accident and Aftermath   (*continued*)

Inference

_____ 10. We can infer that Frida was in shock because of all of the following *except*
a. she tried to look for her lost toy
b. she did not recognize the significance of her injuries
c. she was incapable of tears
d. she looked like a dancer covered with gold powder

_____ 11. We can assume Frida possessed all of the following attributes before the accident *except*
a. she was physically active
b. she was cautious
c. she was full of energy and high spirits
d. she sometimes acted impetuously

Tone

_____ 12. How would you describe Alejandro Gomez Arias's tone in paragraphs 8–13 as he recounts the accident?
a. condescending
b. light-hearted and casual
c. skeptical
d. somber and grave

Brain Teasers

Animal Wordplay

Write the meaning of the italicized words.

1. The actress Betty White is no *spring chicken*. _____

2. We need to *beef up* our defense budget. _____

3. The crowd went *hog wild* when their team won the Super Bowl. _____

4. She's a *mousy* little thing, isn't she? _____

5. Our teacher is such a *shrimp*. _____

6. Even at formal dinners, she *wolfs down* her food. _____

7. My former friend was a real *snake in the grass*. _____

8. *Battering rams* were some of the first big weapons. _____
_____

9. There is something *fishy* about his insurance claim. _____

10. She's such a *chameleon* that you can't count on what she says. _____

VOCABULARY	# Unit 6: Word Parts Featuring "Blood" Relations

"He that flies from his own family has far to travel."
—Latin proverb

This unit begins with the word parts *inter-* and *intra-*, *-medius*, *ped-*, *-capt* and *-cept*, and *cap-* and *corp-*. It concludes with word parts for blood relations and the suffix *-cide*. Words made from these word parts, along with their definitions, follow. Supplemental words with these word parts are located in the left margin.

inter—between, among; intra—within, inside; medius—middle

interpersonal	between persons. In hopes of bettering his relationships with his peers, he is taking a class called *Interpersonal Communication*.
intrapersonal	self-knowledge, as in *intrapersonal* intelligence
interloper	a person who intrudes into the affairs or business of others
interlude	an intervening episode; an interval in the course of action. There was a brief *interlude* of good weather between the two storms.
interject	to interrupt with; to insert. Class is much more interesting when students *interject* questions or comments during the lecture.
intercede	to come between or plead on another's behalf. Because the mother was unable to refrain from taking drugs, the state *interceded* and placed the young child in foster care.
intervene	to come between. When the two boys got into a fight, the teacher *intervened* to settle the dispute.
intermediate	coming between two other things or events; in the middle. Adolescence is an *intermediate* stage that comes between childhood and adulthood.
intermediary	*medius* means "middle." An *intermediary* is a go-between or mediator. The airline hired an *intermediary* to write a contract acceptable to both labor and management.

Left margin notes:
intraspecies
intravenously

interlibrary
intermarry

ped—child

The Latin prefix *ped-* also means "foot," as in *pedal* and *pedestrian*. Don't get the two meanings confused.

pediatrician	a doctor who takes care of babies and children
pedagogy	comes from the Greek word *paidos*, meaning "child," and *agogos*, meaning "leader." In Latin, a *pedagogue* was a slave who escorted children to school and then was responsible for supervising them. Later the term came to refer to a teacher. Today, the word refers to teaching or the study of teaching.

	pedophile	an adult who has a sexual desire for a child. In California, a suspected *pedophile* was charged in the rape and murder of a five-year-old girl.
	pedantic	showing off learning in a boring way or attending too closely to the minute details of a subject. The term originally referred to a schoolmaster.

capt, cept—hold, seize, take

captivate reception perceptible susceptible	**captivity**	the condition of being held by force. There are very few giant pandas held in *captivity*.
	capability	the power to do something
	capacious	able to hold much. The best features of the house were the *capacious* walk-in closets.
	deception	If we practice *deception*, we are "taking" something from someone by fraud.
	intercept	to take or seize on the way (between). He *intercepted* the quarterback's pass and ran 30 yards for the touchdown.

cap—head; corp—body

capitalism capitulate recapitulate	**decapitate**	to cut off the head. During the French Revolution, people were *decapitated* by the guillotine.
	caption	a title at the head of an article or below a photo in a newspaper or magazine. Sonia quickly scanned the *captions* to determine whether the articles were relevant to her research paper.
	capital punishment	the killing of someone by law as punishment for a crime
	corporal punishment	physical punishment (of the body), as in whipping or spanking
corporeal incorporate	**corpulent**	fat and fleshy; stout body build
	corporation	a business, city, college, or other body of persons having a government charter, which gives it some of the legal powers and rights of a person.
	corps	a group of people joined together in some work; a section or special branch of the military. *Corps* has the same pronunciation as apple "core." After graduation from college, Jeremy joined the Peace *Corps*. At age fifty-five, Kirk retired from the Marine *Corps*.
	corpse	the dead body of a person

mater, matri—mother; pater, patri—father; soror—sister; frater, fratri—brother; homo—man; genus—birth, begin, race; cide—kill

matron matrimony matriculate matrilineal	This section discusses "blood" relations and the suffix *-cide*, which means "kill."	
	maternal	relating to a mother. The *maternal* instincts of a lioness make it dangerous to get caught playing with the cubs.

	maternity	the state of being a mother. The new mothers were in the *maternity* ward of the hospital.
	matricide	The suffix *-cide,* as in insecti*cide* and pesti*cide,* means "kill," so *matricide* means murdering one's mother.
expatriate patron patriarchy paternalistic patrician patrimony	**paternal**	relating to a father. Your father's father is your *paternal* grandfather.
	paternity	the state of being a father. The mother brought a *paternity* suit against her child's father.
	patricide	murdering one's father
	fraternity	a brotherhood. College *fraternities* are groups of young men who live together like brothers.
	fratricide	murdering one's brother
	sorority	a sisterhood. College *sororities* are groups of young women who live together like sisters.
	sororicide	murdering one's sister
	homicide	the murder of one human being by another. *Homo-* means "same," but *homo-* also has a second meaning of "man," which is the meaning that applies to the word *homicide* and other words. The *homo-* meaning "same" has a different derivation than the *homo-* meaning "man."
	Homo sapiens	mankind; human beings. *Sapiens* means "wisdom," so *Homo sapiens* are humans with wisdom. This is the scientific term for all human beings.
carcinogenic congenial generic indigenous	**genius**	A *genius* is a person with very high intelligence. The word *genius* has an interesting etymology. It comes from *genus,* meaning "birth." The ancient Romans believed that each person was assigned a guardian spirit at birth.
	genocide	the systematic killing of a national or ethnic group. The word *genocide* was first applied to the attempted extermination of the Jews by the Nazis.
	genesis	the beginning; the origin. The first book of the Bible is called *Genesis* because it gives an account of the Creation.
	genealogy	a history of a person's descent from ancestors. Your "family tree" or birth history shows your *genealogy.*

Now that you have studied the vocabulary in Unit 6, practice your new knowledge by completing the crossword puzzle on the next page.

Vocabulary Unit 6 Puzzle

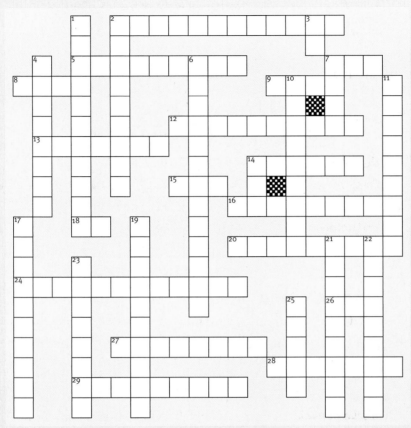

ACROSS CLUES

2. Roberta's _____ advises going easy in toilet-training toddlers.
5. An act of _____ has a mother as a victim.
7. A word part meaning "head."
8. A word part meaning "man."
9. A word part meaning "kill."
12. Kill by beheading.
13. The newspaper issued a re-traction because the _____ had mistakenly identified the wrong person as the arsonist.
14. A dead body.
15. A word part meaning "child."
16. There was a brief musical _____ between the first and second acts of the play.
18. A word part meaning "apart."*
20. The defensive back tried to _____ the pass.
24. The school board hired an _____ to work on conflicts between parents and faculty.

26. A word part meaning "forward."*
27. I was pleased to receive stationery with my _____.*
28. The first book of the Bible.
29. Virginia, who traces her fam-ily history back to the May-flower, is an expert in _____.

DOWN CLUES

1. "Humans with wisdom." (Don't leave a space between the two words.)
2. DNA tests were conducted to determine the child's _____.
3. A word part meaning "toward."*
4. If his victim dies, he will be charged with _____.
6. Conflict management and as-sertiveness are _____ skills that can help you become a more effective person.
7. A word part meaning "seize."
10. The U.S. decided to _____ in the dispute between the two

nations in the hope of pre-venting a war.
11. Bob raised his hand to _____ a question, but the teacher ignored him.
14. A word part meaning "with."*
17. A 3-ounce bourbon and soda and a 12-ounce light beer have an _____ amount of alcohol.*
19. Is Marie Barone on *Everybody Loves Raymond* an _____ because she meddles in Ray and Debra's life without being asked?
21. The doctor told the _____ man that he needed to go on a diet.
22. The _____ was sentenced to life in prison for the rape and murder of the young child.
23. Students who major in edu-cation take classes in _____.
25. A word part meaning "between."

*From a previous unit.

Reading Critically

Chapters in Part 4

The Peaceable Kingdom (c. 1834)

by Edward Hicks (1780–1849)
Oil on canvas, 30 × 35 ½" (76.2 × 90.2 cm).
National Gallery of Art, Washington, D.C.

Fact and Opinion

The Starry Night (1889) *BY VINCENT VAN GOGH*

Digital Image © The Museum of Modern Art/
Licensed by SCALA/Art Resource, NY.

View and Reflect

1. How many stars are in the painting?
2. What is the structure on the left side of the painting?

   The topic of this chapter is fact and opinion. The answer to the first question is factual because it can be verified. The answer to the second question is an opinion. Many people have different ideas about the structure on the left—some think it's a mountain or a bush, and others think it represents van Gogh's inner turmoil because it was completed while van Gogh was in a mental asylum.
3. What is the tallest building in the town? Is your answer fact or opinion?

Introduction to Fact and Opinion

In order to be a critical reader, you must be able to tell the difference between fact and opinion. Writers sometimes present opinions as though they were facts. You need to be able to know when this is happening.

A **fact** is a statement whose truth or falsity can be proved in some objective way. Statements of fact can be verified or disproved by records, tests, historical or scientific documents, or personal experience. A statement of fact offers neither judgment nor evaluation. Factual statements present information without interpreting it. Statements of fact often rely on concrete data or measurements. Here are some examples of statements of fact and how they can be proved.

Statement	Type of Proof
George Washington was our first president.	Historical records
I have seven french fries left on my plate.	Counting
It's sunny outside.	Observation
He's six feet tall.	Measurement

An **opinion** expresses a personal preference or value judgment. Statements of opinion cannot be proved to be true or false. Here are some examples of opinions. The words that express a preference or value judgment are underlined.

George Washington was a <u>great</u> president.

These french fries are <u>delicious</u>.

It is a <u>lovely</u>, sunny day.

He is <u>very</u> tall.

Statements of future events or probabilities are often opinions no matter how reasonable or likely they seem.

By the year 2020, 90 percent of Americans will be online.

In 2020, water will be rationed.

Statements of fact can sometimes be false. Both of the following statements are factual, but only one of them is correct.

George Washington was 67 years old when he died.

George Washington was 66 years old when he died.

Exercise 1: Identifying Facts and Opinions

Directions: Study the painting of the *Mona Lisa* on page 136. Indicate whether each statement below contains a fact or an opinion by writing **F** or **O** in the space provided. (Note that not all factual statements will be true.)

_F_ 1. The *Mona Lisa* measures 30 × 21 inches (or approximately 77 × 53 centimeters).

_f_ 2. The *Mona Lisa* has been a part of France's royal collection since the early sixteenth century.

_O_ 3. The painting of the polite lady with the self-satisfied expression is perhaps the most recognized work of art in the world.

_O_ 4. The otherworldly landscape in the background seems at odds with *Mona Lisa*'s maternal image in the foreground.

_F_ 5. Leonardo painted the *Mona Lisa* with oils on a poplar wooden panel.

_f_ 6. The *Mona Lisa* is encased in a 157 × 98-inch box of triplex glass, a gift from the Japanese on the occasion of the painting's 1974 trip to Japan—the last time it left the Louvre.

_f_ 7. This bullet-proof box is kept at a constant 68 degrees Fahrenheit and 55 percent humidity, which is maintained by a built-in air conditioner and nine pounds of silica gel.

_O_ 8. *Mona Lisa* seems like a goddess or a saint.

_O_ 9. The painting's magic might derive from our desire to know whether the lady is smiling, and if she is, why?

_f_ 10. In 2003, the *Mona Lisa* received a checkup in which the box surrounding it was opened and the climatic conditions as well as the painting's condition were examined.

Exercise 2: Identifying Facts and Opinions

Directions: First, study the illustrations on the following page. Then indicate whether each statement contains a fact or an opinion by writing **F** or **O** in the space provided. (Remember that a statement may state a fact, even if it is false.)

_____ 1. Your future life depends on the position of the stars and planets on the date of your birth.

_____ 2. The Western system of astrology is based on month and day of birth.

_____ 3. The Eastern system of astrology is based on year of birth.

_____ 4. A child born on March 15, 2003, is a "Pisces" in Western astrology.

_____ 5. In the Eastern system, a child born in 2003 is a "goat."

_____ 6. In the Western system of astrology, the symbol for Capricorn is a goat.

_____ 7. In the Eastern system, a "rabbit" seeks tranquility.

_____ 8. Except for the scales of Libra, the twelve signs of the zodiac are symbolized by living creatures.

Eastern (Chinese)

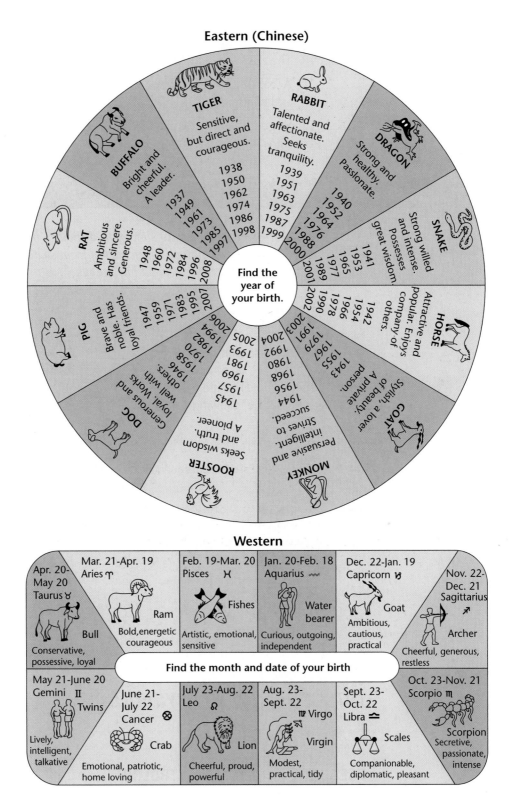

Western

Eastern and Western Astrological charts from Jon Peterson and Stacey A. Hagen in *Better Writing Through Editing,*
New York: McGraw-Hill, 1999, p. 56. Copyright © 1999 McGraw-Hill. Reprinted by permission of
The McGraw-Hill Companies, Inc.

_____ 9. The symbols of the Eastern zodiac are all animals.

_____ 10. The zodiac has an amazing influence on our lives.

_____ 11. According to the Western zodiac, a Libra is compassionate, diplomatic, and pleasant.

_____ 12. Virgo is the only female in the Western zodiac; the other three human signs are all male.

SELECTION

"Astrology's popularity shows the difficulty many people have separating valid psychology from systems that seem valid but are not."

GETTING THE PICTURE

Many newspapers and magazines around the country carry daily horoscopes, and millions of readers consult them. Some consult their horoscopes just "for the fun of it." Others, however, take horoscopes very seriously, using them to guide their daily activities and plan their futures. How do you feel about horoscopes? If you take them seriously, perhaps the following selection will change your mind.

BRUSHING UP ON VOCABULARY

nitpicking being critical of inconsequential information or data.

horoscopes predictions or advice based on the position of the planets and signs of the zodiac at the time of your birth. *Horoscope* comes from the Greek words *hora,* meaning "hour," and *skopos,* meaning "watching." Most newspapers publish daily horoscopes that attempt to predict what is going to happen to you on a particular day and to advise you how to act according to those predictions.

Excerpt from

INTRODUCTION TO PSYCHOLOGY

by Dennis Coon

PSEUDOPSYCHOLOGY—ASTROLOGY

A **pseudopsychology** *is any unfounded system that resembles psychology.* [1] Many pseudopsychologies offer elaborate schemes that give the appearance of science, but are actually false. (*Pseudo* means "false.") Pseudopsychologies change little over time because their followers do not seek new data. In fact, pseudopsychologists often go to great lengths to avoid evidence that contradicts their beliefs. Scientists, in contrast, actively look for contradictions as a way to advance knowledge. They must be skeptical critics of their own theories.

If pseudopsychologies have no scientific basis, how do they survive and why 2 are they so popular? There are several reasons, all of which can be demonstrated by a critique of astrology.

Problems in the Stars Astrology is probably the most popular pseudopsy- 3 chology. Astrology *holds that the position of the stars and planets at the time of one's birth determines personality traits and affect behavior.* Like other pseudopsychologies, astrology has repeatedly been shown to have no scientific validity.

The objections to astrology are numerous and devastating: 4

1. The zodiac has shifted by one full constellation since astrology was first set up. 5 However, most astrologers simply ignore this shift. (In other words, if astrology calls you a Scorpio you are really a Libra and so forth.)

2. There is no connection between the "compatibility" of couples' astrological 6 signs and their marriage and divorce rates.

3. Studies have found no connection between astrological signs and leadership, 7 physical characteristics, career choices, or personality traits.

4. The force of gravity exerted by the physician's body at the moment of birth 8 is greater than that exerted by the stars. Also, astrologers have failed to explain why the moment of birth should be more important than the moment of conception.

5. A study of over 3,000 predictions by famous astrologers found that only a small 9 percentage were fulfilled. These "successful" predictions tended to be vague ("There will be a tragedy somewhere in the east in the spring.") or easily guessed from current events.

6. If astrologers are asked to match people with their horoscopes, they do no 10 better than would be expected by chance.

7. A few astrologers have tried to test astrology. Their results have been just as 11 negative as those obtained by critics.

In short, astrology doesn't work. 12
Then why does astrology often seem to work? 13
The following discussion tells why. 14

Uncritical Acceptance If you have ever had your astrological chart done, 15 you may have been impressed with its apparent accuracy. However, such perceptions are typically based on **uncritical acceptance** (*the tendency to believe positive or flattering descriptions of yourself*). Many astrological charts are made up of mostly flattering traits. Naturally, when your personality is described in *desirable* terms, it is hard to deny that the description has the "ring of truth." How much acceptance would astrology receive if the characteristics of a birth sign read like this:

> **Virgo:** You are the logical type and hate disorder. Your nitpicking is unbear- 16 able to your friends. You are cold, unemotional, and usually fall asleep while making love. Virgos make good doorstops.

Positive Instances Even when an astrological description contains a mix- 17 ture of good and bad traits, it may seem accurate. To find out why, read the following personality description.

"When I want your opinion, I'll give it to you."

—Lawrence J. Peter

YOUR PERSONALITY PROFILE

You have a strong need for other people to like you and for them to ad- 18
mire you. You have a tendency to be critical of yourself. You have a great
deal of unused energy which you have not turned to your advantage.
While you have some personality weaknesses, you are generally able to
compensate for them. Your sexual adjustment has presented some problems for you. Disciplined and controlled on the outside, you tend to be
worrisome and insecure inside. At times you have serious doubts as to
whether you have made the right decision or done the right thing. You
prefer a certain amount of change and variety and become dissatisfied
when hemmed in by restrictions and limitations. You pride yourself on being an independent thinker and do not accept other opinions without
satisfactory proof. You have found it unwise to be too frank in revealing
yourself to others. At times you are extroverted, affable, sociable, while at
other times you are introverted, wary, and reserved. Some of your aspirations tend to be pretty unrealistic.

*"Too often we enjoy the
comfort of opinion
without the discomfort
of thought."*

—John F. Kennedy

Does this describe your personality? A psychologist read this summary indi- 19
vidually to college students who had taken a personality test. Only 5 students
out of 79 felt that the description failed to capture their personalities. Another
study found that people rated this "personality profile" as more accurate than
their actual horoscopes.

Reread the description and you will see that it contains both sides of several 20
personality dimensions ("At times you are extroverted . . . while at other times you
are introverted . . ."). Its apparent accuracy is an illusion based on the **fallacy of
positive instances,** *in which we remember or notice things that confirm our expectations and forget the rest.* The pseudopsychologies thrive on this effect. For example,
you can always find "Leo characteristics" in a Leo. If you looked, however, you
could also find "Gemini characteristics," "Scorpio characteristics," or whatever.

The fallacy of positive instances is used by various "psychic mediums" who 21
pretend to communicate with the deceased friends and relatives of audience
members. An analysis of their performances shows that the number of "hits"
(correct statements) made by these fakes tends to be very low. Nevertheless,
many viewers are impressed because of the natural tendency to remember apparent hits and ignore misses. Also, embarrassing misses are edited out before
the shows appear on television.

The Barnum Effect   Pseudopsychologies also take advantage of the **Barnum** 22
effect, *which is a tendency to consider personal descriptions accurate if they are
stated in very general terms.* P. T. Barnum, the famed circus showman, had a formula for success: "Always have a little something for everybody." Like the all-
purpose personality profile, palm readings, fortunes, horoscopes, and other
products of pseudopsychology are stated in such general terms that they can
hardly miss. There is always "a little something for everybody." To observe the
Barnum effect, read *all* 12 of the daily horoscopes found in newspapers for several days. You will find that predictions for other signs fit events as well as those
for your own sign do.

Astrology's popularity shows the difficulty many people have separating valid 23
psychology from systems that seem valid but are not. The goal of this discussion,
then, has been to make you a more critical observer of human behavior and to

clarify what is, and what is not, psychology. In the meantime, here is what the "stars" say about your future:

> Emphasis now on education and personal improvement. A learning experi- 24
> ence of lasting value awaits you. Take care of scholastic responsibilities before
> engaging in recreation. The word *reading* figures prominently in your future.

Pseudopsychologies may seem like no more than a nuisance, but they can do 25 harm. For instance, people seeking treatment for psychological disorders may become the victims of self-appointed "experts" who offer ineffective, pseudoscientific "therapies." Valid psychological principles are based on observation and evidence, not fads, opinions, or wishful thinking.

(Dennis Coon, *Introduction to Psychology: A Modular Approach to Mind and Behavior*, 10/e, 2006)

✓ COMPREHENSION CHECKUP

True or False

Indicate whether the statement is true or false by writing **T** or **F** in the blank provided.

_____ 1. Pseudopsychologists look for examples that contradict their beliefs.

_____ 2. Pseudopsychologies are always changing and improving.

_____ 3. Astrology has been shown to have scientific validity.

_____ 4. A person who *aspires* to be a doctor seeks to become one.

_____ 5. Scorpios always display Scorpio characteristics.

Multiple Choice

Write the letter of the correct answer in the blank provided.

_____ 6. A pseudopsychology is a _____ system that purports to be a valid psychology.
  a. valid
  b. current
  c. false
  d. common sense

_____ 7. Pseudopsychologies state personality descriptions in general terms and so provide "a little something for everybody." They do this to take advantage of
  a. the force of gravity
  b. uncritical acceptance
  c. the fallacy of positive instances
  d. the Barnum effect

_____ 8. So-called psychic hotlines typically dispense lots of flattering information to callers. The "psychics" are relying on _____ to create an illusion of accuracy.
  a. analysis of the zodiac
  b. uncritical acceptance
  c. the Barnum effect
  d. the fallacy of positive instances

_____ 9. Each New Year's Day, "psychics" make predictions about events that will occur during the coming year. The vast majority of these predictions are wrong, but the practice continues each year. The _____ helps to explain why people only remember predictions that seemed to come true and forget all of the errors.
   a. pattern of uncritical acceptance
   b. fallacy of positive instances
   c. Barnum effect
   d. Virgo effect

_____ 10. Other kinds of pseudopsychology mentioned in the essay are
   a. palm readings
   b. personality profiles
   c. fortunes
   d. all of the above

Fact or Opinion

Indicate whether the statement is a fact or an opinion by writing **F** or **O** in the blank provided.

_____ 1. The zodiac has shifted by one full constellation since astrology was first set up.

_____ 2. Many astrological charts are made up of mostly flattering traits.

_____ 3. Only 5 students out of 79 felt that the description failed to capture their personalities.

_____ 4. Studies have found no connection between astrological signs and leadership. . . .

_____ 5. _Pseudo_ means "false."

Vocabulary

Answer each of the following questions with a complete sentence.

1. elaborate (adjective) Have you ever created anything _elaborate_? _____

   _____

2. devastating (adjective) Have you recently heard about a _devastating_ event? _____

   _____

3. exert (verb) What subject do you have to _exert_ yourself the most in? _____

   _____

4. hemmed in (verb) What makes you feel _hemmed in_ or surrounded? _____

   _____

5. affable (adjective) Is there somebody you know who is especially _affable_ and pleasant? _____

   _____

6. reserved (adjective) Are there certain people you tend to be *reserved* around?

_____

7. valid (adjective) Under the law, what needs to be *valid* or binding? _____

_____

In Your Own Words

1. Why do you think the author includes the warning paragraph at the end of the selection?

2. Do you know anybody who has been duped by unscrupulous astrologers? Why were they willing to consult them in the first place?

3. Allison DuBois is a Phoenix resident who states on her Web site: "I can contact the deceased, I can profile the living, and I predict future events. Readings can be conducted on the phone and by e-mail." The *Arizona Republic* reported that the charge for such a reading was $250 per hour. Is this a legitimate business enterprise? Or do you think DuBois should have to prove her credibility before she takes people's money? Do you think that the law should do anything about people who make these kinds of claims?

The Art of Writing

1. Read the daily horoscope in your local newspaper. Does the horoscope for your astrological sign seem to apply to you? Read what is written for people with other astrological signs. Does this information seem to apply equally as well to you as to them? Does this lead you to any conclusions about astrological forecasts? Write a few paragraphs summarizing your findings.

2. In what way does the following cartoon reinforce the author's main ideas in the reading selection?

Internet Activity

Consult the Web site below. Scroll down to DuBois's professed abilities and criticism. Assuming that the information is accurate, which viewpoint do you find most persuasive?

www.answers.com/topic/Allison-dubois

*"Artists working in Paleolithic caves used a wide
variety of techniques . . ."*

GETTING THE PICTURE

Altamira, the cave described in the following selection, was shut down in 2002 as a preventive measure after nearby Lascaux (in southwestern France) was devastated by a fungal infection. Instead of viewing the actual cave, most visitors to Altamira can tour a replica of part of the cave. Such restrictions are necessary because visitors introduce fungi and bacteria to the cave. With the high humidity inside the cave, mold-like conditions develop rapidly, threatening the wall paintings within.

BIO-SKETCH

Penelope J. E. Davies is an associate professor of Roman art and architecture at the University of Texas at Austin. She is a recent winner of the Vasari Award, given annually for the outstanding publication by an art historian.

BRUSHING UP ON VOCABULARY

flint a chunk of hard stone.

bison a buffalo.

radiocarbon dating determination of the age of objects of organic origin by measurement of their radiocarbon content.

Directions: First, skim the reading selection. Read the first and last paragraph, the first and last sentence of subsequent paragraphs, the subheadings, and study the illustration. (This is similar to the survey step of SQ3R.) After skimming the selection, answer the true or false and multiple-choice questions that follow the selection.

Then scan the selection to locate specific pieces of information to fill in the blanks.

Excerpt from

JANSON'S HISTORY OF ART

by Penelope J. E. Davies

PREHISTORIC ART

Prehistoric paintings were first recognized in 1878 in a cave named Altamira, in 1 the village of Santillana del Mar in northern Spain. Accompanying her father, Count Don Marcelino Sanz de Sautuola, as he scoured the ground for flints and animal bones, 12-year-old Maria looked up to spy bison, painted in bold black outline and filled with bright earth colors on the ceiling of the cave. There, and in other more recently discovered caves, the painted and engraved images depict animals as the dominant subject.

Upper Paleolithic Prehistoric cave painting, Altamira, Spain.

© Melba Photo Agency/Punchstock.

"Art is a delayed echo."

—George Santayana

When they first assessed the Altamira paintings toward the end of the nine- 2 teenth century, experts declared them too advanced to be authentic and dismissed them as a hoax. Indeed, though cave art represents the dawn of art as we know it, it is often highly sophisticated. The bison of Altamira were painted from memory, yet their forms demonstrate the painters' acute powers of observation, and an equal skill in translating memory into image. Standing at rest, or bellowing, or rolling on the ground, the bison behave in these paintings as they do in the wild.

Initially, scholars assigned relative dates to cave paintings by dating them ac- 3 cording to the degree of naturalism they displayed, that is, how closely the image resembled the actual subject in nature. As naturalism was considered at that time the most advanced form of representation, the more naturalistic the image, the more evolved and, therefore, the more recent it was considered to be. Radiocarbon dating exposed the flaws in this approach.

CAVE PAINTING

Artists working in Paleolithic caves used a wide variety of techniques to achieve 4 the images that have survived. Often working far from cave entrances, they

Illuminated the darkness using lamps carved out of stone and filled with fat or marrow. Archaeologists have found several of these lamps at a cave in Lascaux, France, and elsewhere. Sometimes, when the area of rock to be painted was high above ground level, they may have built scaffolds of wood, stabilized against the wall by driving the poles into the limestone surface.

They prepared the surface by scraping the limestone with stone tools, bring- 5 ing out its chalky whiteness as a background. Some images were then engraved on the wall, with a finger if the limestone was soft enough, or, where it was harder, with a sharp flint. Sometimes they combined this technique with the application of color. Black was created using vegetal charcoal and perhaps charred bones. Ochre, a natural iron ore, provided a range of vivid reds, browns, and yellows. For drawing—outlines of animals, for instance—the charcoal and ochre were deployed in chunks, like a crayon; to generate paint, they ground the minerals into powder on a large flat stone. By heating them to extremely high temperatures, they could also vary the shades of red and yellow.

To fill in animal or human outlines with paint, they mixed the powders with 6 blenders, which consisted of cave water, saliva, egg white, vegetal or animal fat, or blood; they then applied the colors to the limestone surface, using pads of moss or fur, and brushes made of fur, feather, or chewed stick. Pigment was also often chewed up in the mouth and then blown through animal bones or reeds, or spit directly onto the walls to form images. In some cases, paint was applied in dots. An analysis of the paintings indicates that women and adolescents were painters as well as men.

INTERPRETING PREHISTORIC PAINTING

As majestic as these paintings can be, they are also profoundly enigmatic: what 7 purpose do they serve? The simplest view, that they were merely decorative— "art for art's sake"—is highly unlikely. Most of the existing paintings and engravings are readily accessible, and many more that once embellished caves that open directly to the outside have probably perished. But some lie deep inside extended cave systems, remote from habitation areas and difficult to reach. In these cases, the power of the image may have resided in its making, rather than in its viewing. According to some historians who have attempted to interpret these images, the act of painting or incising the image may have served some ritual or religious purpose.

"The object of art is to give life a shape."

—Jean Anouilh

Perhaps early humans perceived an image as equivalent to the animal it 8 represented, and therefore, to create or perceive the image was to exert power over what it portrayed. Image making could have been considered as a force of sympathetic magic, which might improve the success of a hunt. Gouge marks on cave walls indicate that in some cases spears were cast at the images. Similarly, artists may have hoped to stimulate fertility in the wild—ensuring a continuous food supply—by depicting pregnant animals. A magical-religious interpretation might explain the choice to make animals appear lifelike. Some scholars have cast the paintings in a central role in early religion, as images for worship. Most important, recent interpretations have acknowledged that one explanation may not suffice for all times and places.

(Penelope J. E. Davies, et al., *Janson's History of Art: Western Tradition*, 7/e, 2007)

✓ COMPREHENSION CHECKUP

Skimming Exercise

Directions: After skimming the selection, answer the true or false and multiple-choice questions.

True or False

_____ 1. Artists prepared their "canvas" by first scraping the walls of the cave.

_____ 2. In prehistoric times, cave painting was solely a masculine activity.

_____ 3. The paintings may have been produced as part of a magic ritual to ensure a good hunt.

_____ 4. The cave paintings in Altamira, Spain, were the first to be recognized.

_____ 5. The cave paintings were always thought to be genuine.

Multiple Choice

_____ 6. The cave painters might have drawn the paintings to
   a. ensure a successful hunt
   b. ensure the successful propagation of the animals they hunted
   c. serve as a form of ritualistic magic
   d. all of the above

_____ 7. Cave paintings were initially believed to be hoaxes because
   a. they appeared to be an advanced form of art
   b. they were painted from photographs
   c. they had a modern color palette
   d. they were created with oil-based pigments

_____ 8. According to the selection, cave paintings depicted animals as all of the following *except*
   a. the way they are in the wild
   b. the dominant subject matter
   c. domesticated animals
   d. pregnant

_____ 9. To create a painting on the ceiling of a cave, the artist would likely have needed
   a. light from a torch or lamp
   b. some form of scaffolding
   c. neither a nor b
   d. both a and b

_____ 10. According to the selection, paint was applied to the walls by all of the following means *except*
   a. pads of moss or fur
   b. trowel
   c. brushes made of feathers
   d. hollow animal bones used as blowing straws

Scanning Exercise

Directions: Scan the selection to find the following information:

11. What animal did twelve-year-old Maria discover painted on the ceiling of the cave in Altamira? _____

12. What method is used to determine the relative age of cave paintings?

_____

13. What is the name of the iron ore that provided material for red, brown, and yellow paint? _____

14. What weapons were sometimes thrown at the animals on the cave walls?

_____

15. Lamps carved from stone were discovered in a cave in _____, France.

Vocabulary in Context

Fill in the blanks using words from the following list. Not all words will be used.

accessible	embellished	profoundly	suffice
acute	enigmatic	remote	vivid
depicted	equivalent	resided	
deployed	hoax	scoured	
dominant	perished	stabilized	

1. Volunteers _____ the mountains for the missing climbers.

2. Rembrandt _____ many of his subjects in drab colors.

3. The United States is the _____ power in the world today.

4. Many of van Gogh's paintings featured _____ colors.

5. More troops were recently _____ to Iraq.

6. *Mona Lisa's* _____ smile has fascinated millions of visitors to the Louvre in Paris.

7. Many colleges across the country are trying to make the campus more _____ to the disabled.

8. Entire families _____ in the latest tornado.

9. I don't think I'll be seeing much of my friend Ann since she and her husband relocated to a _____ part of the world.

10. His hearing was so _____ that he could almost hear a pin drop in the next room.

11. The seamstress _____ the wedding dress with seed pearls, sequins, and lace.

12. Albert Einstein, having a genius-level IQ, was considered to be _____ intelligent.

Fact or Opinion

Indicate whether the statement is fact or opinion by writing **F** or **O** in the blank provided.

_____ 1. Prehistoric paintings were first recognized in 1878 in a cave named Altamira, in the village of Santillana del Mar in northern Spain.

_____ 2. When they first assessed the Altamira paintings toward the end of the nineteenth century, experts declared them too advanced to be authentic and dismissed them as a hoax.

_____ 3. Archaeologists have found several of these lamps at a cave in Lascaux, France, and elsewhere.

_____ 4. In some cases, paint was applied in dots.

_____ 5. An analysis of the paintings indicates that women and adolescents were painters as well as men.

_____ 6. As majestic as these paintings can be, they are also profoundly enigmatic: what purpose do they serve?

_____ 7. The simplest view, that they were merely decorative—"art for art's sake"—is highly unlikely.

_____ 8. In these cases, the power of the image may have resided in its making, rather than in its viewing.

In Your Own Words

1. Most art today is created to be viewed by relatively large numbers of people. Cave art, on the other hand, is not readily accessible. Why do you think it was created in the deep recesses of caves?

2. It appears that both men and women were cave artists. However, as time progressed, women were excluded from creating art. Why do you think that happened?

3. Why do you think cave painters primarily painted large animals such as bison and bears, rather than the smaller animals that must have existed at the same time?

4. Do you think the desire to produce art is universal?

5. Do you think cave art has some hidden meaning? Or is it just "art for art's sake"?

The Art of Writing

What do you think the cave paintings mean? Do you think the selection of caves' relatively permanent places, was deliberate? Why do you think early humans painted primarily animal images rather than human images? Write a short essay giving your interpretation.

Internet Activity

Visit the Altamira, Lascaux, or Chauvet Web site. Choose a cave painting and write a few paragraphs describing it. What kind of feeling does it evoke in you?

Mastery Test: Prehistoric Art

Main Idea

_____ 1. Which of the following statements best represents the overall main idea of the selection?
- a. Long ago artists created cave paintings of animals that are both majestic and enigmatic.
- b. In many cases, cave art consisted of sophisticated drawings of animals.
- c. Cave artists made their paints from natural elements.
- d. Both adults and adolescents participated in creating prehistoric cave paintings.

Supporting Detail

_____ 2. Which of the following is *not* an accurate detail?
- a. The cave artists used chunks of charcoal and ochre for drawing.
- b. Experts were convinced the paintings were authentic as soon as they saw them.
- c. Artists sometimes spit pigment directly on the walls.
- d. The paintings depict bison doing the sorts of things that they do in the real world.

Context

_____ 3. What is the meaning of the italicized word in the context of the following sentence?
"Indeed, though cave art represents the *dawn* of art as we know it, it is often highly sophisticated."
- a. the fullest expression
- b. a period lacking in technical accomplishment
- c. the earliest period; the beginning
- d. a middle stage of development

Purpose

_____ 4. Which of the following describes the author's purpose in writing this selection?
- a. to entertain
- b. to persuade
- c. to inform

Pattern of Organization

_____ 5. Identify the pattern of organization of paragraph 6.
- a. steps in a process
- b. classification or division
- c. definition
- d. cause and effect

Mastery Test: Prehistoric Art (*continued*)

Transitions

_____ 6. The transition words *for instance* in paragraph 5 indicate
    a. comparison and contrast
    b. example
    c. definition
    d. cause and effect

_____ 7. The transition word *also* in paragraph 6 indicates
    a. reversal
    b. concession
    c. contrast
    d. addition

_____ 8. The transition word *similarly* in paragraph 8 indicates
    a. spatial order
    b. reversal
    c. comparison
    d. summary and conclusion

Inference

_____ 9. The selection implies which of the following?
    a. The author admires the cave paintings and their creators.
    b. Not all of the paintings are very sophisticated.
    c. Radiocarbon dating is a more accurate tool for dating the cave paintings than evaluating their naturalism.
    d. All of the above

Tone

_____ 10. The overall tone of this selection is
    a. pessimistic
    b. objective
    c. subjective
    d. ironic

Fact and Opinion

_____ 11. "Images of animals were incised or painted on the surfaces of cave walls."
This is a statement of
    a. fact
    b. opinion

_____ 12. "One explanation of the meaning of the cave paintings may not be sufficient for all times and places."
This is a statement of
    a. fact
    b. opinion

The next two selections on fact and opinion focus on the topic of food and health. What these selections have to say about food may surprise you.

"What do these insects that we are eating every day taste like?"

GETTING THE PICTURE

Do you know how many insect body parts are allowed in your Fig Newton? Quite a lot, actually. The FDA has published a booklet titled *Food Defect Action Levels* that specifies exactly how many are allowed. According to a University of Ohio study, we eat one to two pounds of insects each year without knowing it. Is this necessarily bad for us? Apparently not. In fact, in many cultures, insects are deliberately consumed as either a staple to the diet (they're high in protein) or as a delicacy. To find out more about detecting "filth" in food, read the following selection by Mary Roach.

BIO-SKETCH

Mary Roach's humorous science articles have appeared in *Salon, Discover, Vogue,* the *New York Times Magazine,* and *Outside.* She has a monthly column titled "My Planet" in *Reader's Digest* and is a contributing editor at *Health* magazine. Recent books include *Stiff: The Curious Life of Human Cadavers* and *Spook: Science Tackles the Afterlife.*

BRUSHING UP ON VOCABULARY

thrip tiny sucking insects.

aesthetic pertaining to a sense of beauty.

esoteric understood by only a select few who have special knowledge.

entomophagous feeding on insects.

angora yarn or fabric made from the hair of an Angora rabbit or an Angora goat.

Bug Heads, Rat Hairs—Bon App*tit!

By Mary Roach

1 IF YOU MADE FIG NEWTONS for a living and you wanted to know how many insects could get into your Newtons without your getting into hot water with the FDA, you could look it up on the U.S. Food and Drug Administration's Food Defect Action Levels Web site. Here you would learn that fig paste is allowed to have up to 13 insect heads per 100 grams.

You would then become side-tracked and further learn that approximately four rodent hairs are allowed in a jar of peanut butter, that an average of 60 thrips are allowed in 100 grams of frozen broccoli, that 10 grams of

"Reason, observation, and experience—the Holy Trinity of Science."

—Robert G. Ingersoll

hops are allowed to contain 2,500 aphids, and that 5 milligrams of rat excreta in a pound of sesame seeds is A-OK with the FDA.

3   What you would not learn is why the FDA might put a limit on insects' heads and not other parts of their anatomy, what rat excreta tastes like, and what sort of person takes a job that entails searching for insect heads in fig cookie innards. To find these things out, you would have to pay a visit to one of the FDA's regional filth labs. You would, but now you don't have to, because I'm doing it for you.

4   I have arranged to meet with an entomologist named Dana Ludwig, who works in the FDA's Alameda, Calif., Filth Lab, which analyzes thousands of samples of foods, most imported from the Pacific Rim, each year. In a moment of social ineptitude, I have asked Ludwig if the ludwig is a relative of the earwig. Straight off the bat, I have my foot in my mouth. I should be used to having feet in my mouth, for humans are eating insect parts all the time without knowing it. According to an Ohio State University Extension fact sheet, most Americans unintentionally swallow 1 to 2 pounds of insects and insect pieces each year. Insects are very lightweight. If you think about how many of them it would take to make 2 pounds (and I advise you not to), you will begin to appreciate the somewhat shocking dimensions of our entomophagous intake.

5   The Alameda Filth Lab employs several analytical entomologists. Ludwig refers to them collectively as "filth people." Just inside the lab doorway, we stop to go over our clothing with a lint roller. A sign on the wall says, "Pet-Hair Free Zone." Ludwig is looking at my shirt. The look says that there's a name for me too, somewhere in the neighborhood of "filth person."

6   "There's a lot of hair on your shirt," says Ludwig as nicely as she can. The problem turns out to be my pet angora sweater. Ludwig covers me up with a lab coat. If my sweater were to shed into a food sample, some hapless Third World manufacturer might be cited for an infestation of lavender angora rabbits.

7   For demonstration purposes, Ludwig has set aside a bag of imported black bean wafers. Earlier in the morning, she measured out a sample of the wafers and put them in a beaker with boiling hydrochloric acid. Two hours later, the acid has digested the black bean wafer ingredients, leaving nothing solid behind but "the filth." Ludwig sieves the liquid to isolate the filth, which looks but probably does not taste like a teaspoon of melted coffee ice cream. She then scrapes it onto a "filth plate," which she slides under her microscope.

8   Ludwig shows me the head of a book louse, a mite fragment, a confused flour beetle underwing fragment, assorted hairs, and an ant head. The magnified ant head is beautiful, a fragment of translucent amber, like what's left on your tongue in the morning when you fall asleep with a Ricola in your mouth. I ask Ludwig why there are so many more heads than bodies. I am trying to imagine the scenario that would result in an ant's head winding up in the flour sack while the rest of its body continues along its merry way. I am one confused flour beetle.

9   Ludwig explains that insects' "head capsules" are often more durable than their bodies. "This is especially common with larvae and caterpillars, where the body parts are soft and really get messed up" in the

milling process. In other words, the bodies are in the food too; they're just not countable.

10   What do these insects that we are eating every day taste like? FDA entomologist Steve Anghold told me that if you have enough aphids ground up in a batch of hops, it might conceivably make the beer taste sweeter, because aphids secrete a sweet fluid. In fact, he went on to say, ants "herd aphids like cattle and milk 'em," feeding the sweet fluid to their ant infants. "That's why aphids are called ant cows," he said. It was one of those unsettling journalistic moments where you wonder whether your source has been having an especially dull afternoon and is having you on for the fun of it.

11   I ask Ludwig if a couple dozen beetle larvae would change the taste of a food. She says the insects she typically deals with wouldn't impart much flavor, but that "their metabolic byproducts probably don't taste very good." I ask her what exactly she means by "metabolic byproducts." She says, "Their waste materials." She isn't talking about coffee grounds and recyclables. Not only do you have to put up with thrips in your broccoli, you have to put up with thrip excreta.

12   If it makes you feel any better, none of this filth is bad for you. With the exception of the dermested beetle larvae, which have hook-shaped hairs that become embedded in your intestines and prompt all manner of gastroenterological sturm und drang, the insects encompassed in the FDA's Food Defect Action Levels are objectionable either on a purely aesthetic level, or as an indicator of unsanitary warehouse conditions.

13   On the contrary, meals made from "microlivestock," as edible insects are called by those who enjoy eating them, are good for you. According to the Ohio State fact sheet, caterpillars have as much protein as beef, a fraction of the fat, 10 times the iron and way more riboflavin and thiamine. Plus the ranches take up much less room and can be staffed by cowboy ants hired away from low-paying aphid-herding jobs.

14   Ludwig's area of expertise is filth hair identification. On her desk between the copy of "World of Moths" and an 8-by-10 color photograph of Colorado potato beetles mating, is a diploma in hair and fiber microscopy. The more common filth hairs—rats, dogs, cats, mice—she can identify under the microscope by sight. For less common specimens she consults highly esoteric reference books and a cabinet of "authentics": sample animal hairs culled from zoos.

15   She opens a drawer and shows me a glass slide with a mongoose hair fixed to it, and another from a ring-tailed cat. While Ludwig is off attending to a sample of chili paste, I pull open another drawer. This one contains human hairs of various ethnicities. "Japanese arm hair," says one label. There are Chinese hairs, Caucasian hairs, Filipino hairs, knuckle hairs, eyelashes, eyebrow hairs. Without saying a word, Ludwig reaches in front of me and slides the drawer shut, leading me to wonder whether somewhere in that collection is an authentic human pubic hair.

16   Ludwig and her colleagues also make use of excreta "authentics," glass vials of teeny tiny sample turds. I notice one labeled "caterpillar excreta." Each unit in the vial is as small as a cake crumb.

17   One more reason to ranch caterpillars and not cows.

(Mary Roach, "Bug Heads, Rat Hairs—Bon App*tit," 1/14/00)

✓ COMPREHENSION CHECKUP

Fact or Opinion

Underline the factual part of each statement.

1. In a moment of social ineptitude, I have asked Ludwig if the ludwig is a relative of the earwig.

2. Ludwig sieves the liquid to isolate the filth, which looks but probably does not taste like a teaspoon of melted coffee ice cream.

3. A sign on the wall says, "Pet-Hair Free Zone."

Indicate whether the statement is fact or opinion by writing **F** or **O** in the blank provided.

_____ 4. Straight off the bat, I have my foot in my mouth.

_____ 5. According to an Ohio State University Extension fact sheet, most Americans unintentionally swallow 1 to 2 pounds of insects and insect pieces each year.

_____ 6. The Alameda Filth Lab employs several analytical entomologists.

_____ 7. Ludwig refers to them collectively as "filth people."

_____ 8. If my sweater were to shed into a food sample, some hapless Third World manufacturer might be cited for an infestation of lavender angora rabbits.

Multiple Choice

Write the letter of the correct answer in the blank provided.

_____ 1. The topic of this selection is
a. Fig Newtons
b. laboratory conditions
c. insect parts in food
d. the nutritional value of insects

_____ 2. The author's purpose in writing this selection is to
a. entertain the reader with an amusing account of a visit to a "filth" lab
b. persuade the reader to lobby the FDA for more stringent food safety guidelines
c. inform the public about insect parts in food
d. both a and c

_____ 3. The tone of this selection could best be described as
a. sentimental and somber
b. mean-spirited and critical
c. lightly humorous and witty
d. respectful and thoughtful

_____ 4. When the author speculates that "some hapless Third World manufacturer might be cited for an infestation of lavender angora rabbits," she is being
a. maudlin
b. serious
c. facetious
d. compassionate

_____ 5. The statement "the ranches take up much less room and can be staffed by cowboy ants hired away from the low-paying aphid-herding jobs," is an example of
   a. humor by exaggeration
   b. literary allusion
   c. figurative language
   d. transition words

_____ 6. The use of the word *microlivestock* (paragraph 13) to refer to edible insects is a(n)
   a. understatement
   b. euphemism
   c. simile
   d. inference

_____ 7. From the selection as a whole, we can infer that the author
   a. no longer eats foods imported from the Pacific Rim
   b. is amazed at how many bug parts are consumed unintentionally in the American diet
   c. believes that insect by-products in food are bad for us
   d. wishes everyone could visit a "filth" lab

_____ 8. The term *metabolic byproducts* (paragraph 11) is a
   a. figurative expression
   b. reference to waste material
   c. joke
   d. scientific term referring to photosynthesis

_____ 9. Synonyms for *sturm and drang* (paragraph 12) are all of the following *except*
   a. storm and stress
   b. turmoil and upheaval
   c. calmness and placidity
   d. tumultuousness

_____ 10. "As small as a cake crumb" is a
   a. simile
   b. metaphor
   c. personification
   d. literary allusion

_____ 11. Throughout the selection, the author uses the pronoun *you*, which makes her style
   a. formal and serious
   b. informal and chatty
   c. objective and neutral
   d. serious and somber

_____ 12. When the author writes in the last sentence of paragraph 8, "I am one confused flour beetle," she is being
   a. formal
   b. humorous
   c. charming
   d. flattering

True or False

Indicate whether the statement is true or false by writing **T** or **F** in the blank provided.

_____ 13. Under FDA guidelines, a certain amount of insect parts are permissible in food products.

_____ 14. The dermested beetle larvae can cause intestinal distress.

_____ 15. The average American unknowingly ingests at least six pounds of insects or insect parts yearly.

_____ 16. A caterpillar head capsule is more durable than its body.

_____ 17. Aphids secrete a sour fluid.

_____ 18. Caterpillars have as much protein as chicken.

_____ 19. Ludwig is an expert in identifying filth hair.

_____ 20. "Authentics" are sample hairs gathered from zoos.

_____ 21. Excreta "authentics" are waste products.

_____ 22. An entomologist studies insects.

Vocabulary Practice

Write the meanings of the following words or phrases.

1. getting into hot water (paragraph 1) _____

2. sidetracked (2) _____

3. A-OK (2) _____

4. straight off the bat (4) _____

5. foot in my mouth (4) _____

Vocabulary in Context

Choose one of the following words to complete each of the sentences below. Use each word only once. Be sure to pay close attention to the context clues provided.

durable	impart
embedded	ineptitude
encompasses	infestation
fragments	innards
hapless	translucent

1. The _____ student couldn't seem to remember to bring all of his supplies to class each day.

2. After Wanda broke the pitcher, tiny _____ of glass were found for days.

3. The stained glass window in the church was _____.

4. That dress has proved to be especially _____; I have worn it for over ten years.

5. _____ in the limestone were several valuable pieces of pottery.

6. For most home owners, an _____ of termites is cause for alarm.

7. I like to eat freshly caught fish, but I don't like to clean out the _____.

8. His _____ as a mechanic is well known; as a result, he should probably choose another profession.

9. I'd like to _____ some advice: Most people are about as happy as they make up their minds to be.

10. An unabridged dictionary _____ far more information than an abridged one.

In Your Own Words

1. What does the title of the selection mean? How does the title indicate the author's point of view?

2. Do you think food products should be more carefully regulated by the FDA?

3. Would you be willing to pay more for food that is certified as "pure"?

4. Recent research indicates that dirt might actually be good for us. For instance, children who are allowed to play in dirt and mud appear to have stronger immune systems than children who are kept scrupulously clean. Do you think the same thing is true about food? The FDA assures us that a small amount of contamination causes no harm, but do you think there is also a benefit to eating food that contains a small amount of insect parts?

5. In your opinion, what are the best kinds of food for good health? How much of each of these foods should a person eat every day?

6. Are you an "eat to live" or "live to eat" kind of person? Explain the difference between the two "food" philosophies.

The Art of Writing

Would you be willing to adapt your diet to include bugs if they were proven to be both nutritious and environmentally friendly? After studying the chart below, write a few paragraphs giving your opinion.

NUTRITIONAL VALUE OF INSECTS
(per 100 grams)

	Protein (g)	Fat (g)	Carbohydrate (mg)	Calcium (mg)	Iron (mg)
Crickets	12.9	5.5	5.1	75.8	9.5
Grasshoppers (large)	14.3	3.3	2.2	27.5	3.0
Red ants	13.9	3.5	2.9	47.8	5.7
Termites	14.2	N/A	N/A	0.050	35.5
Weevils	6.7	N/A	N/A	0.186	13.1
For comparison: Ground Beef (lean)	24.0	18.3	0.00	9.00	2.09
Fish—cod (broiled)	22.95	0.86	0.00	0.031	1.0

(from data collected by Jared Ostrem and John VanDyk for the Entomology Department of Iowa State University)

Internet Activity

Read the following interview with Mary Roach:

www.identitytheory.com/interviews/roach_interview.html

Summarize what you learned about her former and present jobs and how she got her start as a writer. What advice for others does she share?

SELECTION

> *"The heart of the flavor industry lies between Exit 4
> and Exit 19 of the New Jersey Turnpike."*

GETTING THE PICTURE

The following excerpt from *Fast Food Nation* was included in *Best Science Writing* of 2001. In it, author Eric Schlosser describes how fast-food products acquire their particular tastes.

BIO-SKETCH

Eric Schlosser has received numerous awards for his investigative journalism, including a National Magazine Award. His first book, *Fast Food Nation,* has been a national best-seller since its initial publication in 2001. A correspondent for the *Atlantic Monthly,* Schlosser set out to explore "the dark side of the American meal."

BRUSHING UP ON VOCABULARY

barrage a sudden outpouring. The original *barrage* was a dam designed to contain large amounts of water. It comes from the French *barrage*, meaning "barrier," and had an opposite meaning from its present one.

innocuous not harmful or injurious; harmless. Derived from the Latin word part *in*, meaning "not," and *nocuus*, meaning "hurtful."

palatable acceptable or agreeable to the palette or taste; appetizing. Comes directly from the Latin word *palatum*, meaning "roof of the mouth."

Excerpt from
FAST FOOD NATION

by Eric Schlosser

"It requires a certain kind of mind to see beauty in a hamburger bun."

—Ray Kroc

FOOD PRODUCT DESIGN

The taste of McDonald's French fries has long been praised by customers, competitors, and even food critics. Their distinctive taste does not stem from the type of potatoes that McDonald's buys, the technology that processes them, or the restaurant equipment that fries them. Other chains buy their French fries from the same large processing companies, use Russet Burbanks, and have similar fryers in their restaurant kitchens. The taste of a fast food fry is largely determined by the cooking oil. For decades, McDonald's cooked its French fries in a mixture of about 7 percent soy oil and 93 percent beef fat. The mix gave the fries their unique flavor—and more saturated beef fat per ounce than a McDonald's hamburger.

Amid a barrage of criticism over the amount of cholesterol in their fries, 2 McDonald's switched to pure vegetable oil in 1990. The switch presented the company with an enormous challenge: how to make fries that subtly taste like beef without cooking them in beef fat. A look at the ingredients now used in the preparation of French fries suggests how the problem was solved. At the end of the list is a seemingly innocuous, yet oddly mysterious phrase "natural flavor." The frozen potatoes and the cooking oil at McDonald's both contain "natural flavor." That fact helps to explain not only why the fries taste so good, but also why most fast food—indeed, most of the food Americans eat today—tastes the way it does.

Open your refrigerator, your freezer, your kitchen cupboards, and look at the 3 labels on your food. You'll find "natural flavor" or "artificial flavor" in just about every list of ingredients. The similarities between these two broad categories of flavor are far more significant than their differences. Both are man-made additives that give most processed food its taste. The initial purchase of a food item may be driven by its packaging or appearance, but subsequent purchases are determined mainly by its taste. Americans now spend more than $1 trillion on food every year—and more than 90 percent of that money is spent on processed food. But the canning, freezing, and dehydrating techniques used to process food destroy most of its flavor. Since the end of World War II, a vast industry has arisen in the United States to make processed food palatable. Without this flavor industry, today's fast food industry could not exist. The names of the leading American fast food chains and their best-selling menu items have become famous worldwide, embedded in our popular culture. Few people, however, can name the companies that manufacture fast food's taste.

The flavor industry is highly secretive. Its leading companies will not divulge 4 the precise formulas of flavor compounds or the identities of clients. The secrecy is deemed essential for protecting the reputation of beloved brands. The fast food chains, understandably, would like the public to believe that the flavors of their food somehow originate in their restaurant kitchens, not in distant factories run by other firms.

The heart of the flavor industry lies between Exit 4 and Exit 19 of the New 5 Jersey Turnpike. More than fifty companies manufacture flavors along that stretch of the Turnpike. Indeed, the state produces about two thirds of the flavor additives sold in the United States.

International Flavors & Fragrances (IFF), the world's largest flavor company, 6 has a manufacturing facility off Exit 8A in Dayton, New Jersey. A tour of the IFF plant is the closest thing in real life to visiting Willy Wonka's chocolate factory. Wonderful smells drift through the hallways, men and women in neat white lab coats cheerfully go about their work, and hundreds of little glass bottles sit on laboratory tables and shelves. The bottles contain powerful but fragile flavor chemicals. The long chemical names on the little white labels seem like a strange foreign language. The chemicals are mixed and poured and turned into new substances, just like magic potions.

IFF's snack and savory lab is responsible for the flavor of potato chips, corn 7
chips, breads, crackers, breakfast cereals, and pet food. The confectionary lab
devises the flavor for ice cream, cookies, candies, toothpastes, mouthwashes, and
antacids. The beverage lab creates the flavors for popular soft drinks, sports
drinks, bottled teas, wine coolers, and for all-natural juice drinks, organic soy
drinks, and malt liquors.

In addition to being the world's largest flavor company, IFF makes the smell 8
of household products such as deodorant, dishwashing detergent, bath soap,
shampoo, furniture polish, and floor wax. All of these aromas are made through
the same basic process: mixing different chemicals to create a particular smell.
The basic science behind the scent of your shaving cream is the same as that
governing the flavor of your TV dinner.

The aroma of the food can be responsible for as much as 90 percent of its 9
flavor. Scientists now believe that human beings acquired the sense of taste as a
way to avoid being poisoned. Edible plants generally taste sweet; deadly ones,
bitter. Taste is supposed to help us differentiate food that's good for us from food
that's not. The taste buds on our tongues can detect the presence of half a dozen
or so basic tastes, including sweet, sour, bitter, salty, and astringent. Taste buds
offer a relatively limited means of detection, however, compared to the human
olfactory system, which can perceive thousands of different chemical aromas.
Indeed "flavor" is primarily the smell of gases being released by the chemicals
you've just put in your mouth.

The act of drinking, sucking, or chewing a substance releases its volatile 10
gases. They flow out of your mouth and up your nostrils, or up the passageway
in the back of your mouth, to a thin layer of nerve cells called the olfactory epithelium, located at the base of your nose, right between the eyes. The brain
combines the complex smell signals from the epithelium with the simple taste
signals from the tongue, assigns a flavor to what's in your mouth, and decides if
it's something you want to eat.

The Food and Drug Administration does not require flavor companies to dis- 11
close the ingredients of their additives, so long as all the chemicals are considered
by the agency to be GRAS (Generally Regarded As Safe). This lack of public dis-
closure enables the companies to maintain the secrecy of their formulas. It also
hides the fact that flavor compounds sometimes contain more ingredients than
the foods being given their taste. The ubiquitous phrase "artificial strawberry
flavor" gives little hint of the chemical wizardry and manufacturing skill that can
make a highly processed food taste like a strawberry.

"Chemicals—noxious
substances from which
modern food is made."

—Unknown

A typical artificial strawberry flavor, like the kind found in a Burger King 12
strawberry milk shake, contains the following ingredients: amyl acetate, amyl
butyrate, amyl valerate, anethol, anisyl formate, benzyl acetate, benzyl isobutyrate, butyric acid, cinnamyl isobutyrate, cinnamyl valerate, cognac essential oil,
diacetyl, dipropyl ketone, ethyl butyrate, ethyl cinnamate, ethyl heptanoate,
ethyl heptylate, ethyl lactate, ethyl methylphenylglycidate, ethyl nitrate, ethyl
propionate, ethyl valerate, heliotropin, hydroxyphrenyl-2-butanone (10 percent
solution in alcohol), a-ionone, isobutyl anthranilate, isobutyl butyrate, lemon
essential oil, maltol, 4-methylacetopphenone, methyl anthranilate, methyl ben-
zoate, methyl cinnamate, methyl heptine carbonate, methyl naphthyl ketone,
methyl salicylate, mint essential oil, neroli essential oil, nerolin, neryl isobutyrate,

orris butter, phenethyl alcohol, rose, rum ether, y-undecalactone, vanillin, and solvent.

The 1960s were the heyday of artificial flavors. For the past twenty years 13 food processors have tried hard to use only "natural flavors" in their products. However, natural flavors and artificial flavors sometimes contain exactly the same chemicals, produced through different methods. A natural flavor is not necessarily purer or healthier than an artificial one. Natural and artificial flavors are now manufactured at the same chemical plants, places that few people would associate with Mother Nature. Calling any of these flavors "natural" requires a flexible attitude toward the English language and a fair amount of irony.

In addition to flavor additives, most processed food has color additives, 14 which are used to make processed foods look good. Food coloring serves much the same purpose as women's makeup, and it's often made from the same basic ingredients. Titanium dioxide, for example, is a mineral with many different uses. It can give candies, frosting, and icing their bright white colors. It is used as a coloring in makeup. And it is also commonly used in white house paints. So you can use titanium dioxide to ice your cake—or paint your house. At Burger King, Wendy's, and McDonald's, color additives can be found in many of the sodas, salad dressings, cookies, chicken dishes, and even sandwich buns.

One of the most widely used color additives comes from an unexpected 15 source. Cochineal extract (also known as carmine or carminic acid) is made from the dead bodies of small bugs harvested mainly in Peru and the Canary Islands. The little bugs are collected, dried, and ground into a coloring additive. It takes about 70,000 of the insects to make a pound of carmine, which is used to make processed foods look pink, red, or purple. Dannon strawberry yogurt gets its color from carmine, as do many candies, frozen fruit bars, fruit fillings, and Ocean Spray pink grapefruit juice drink.

The U.S. government claims that the color and flavor additives widely used in 16 processed foods are safe. That may not always be the case. Carmine can cause allergic reactions in some people. Tartrazine, a yellow food coloring, can cause hyperactivity, headaches, rashes, and an increased risk of asthma in some children. It has been banned in Norway, Finland, and Austria, but is still used by food companies in the United States and Great Britain. Tartrazine can be found in British and American sodas, candies, chewing gum, Jell-O, and butterscotch pudding mixes, among other things.

A number of scientists now worry that eating so many different chemicals in 17 processed foods may not be good for young children. While each of the widely used chemical additives may be safe to eat by itself, the safety of eating a large combination of additives at every meal remains unknown. "We assume that because these things do not make us drop dead, they're safe," says Dr. Vyvyan Howard, a leading expert on toxic substances at the University of Liverpool in England. "It's not true. In my opinion, I would recommend that kids just stay away from them."

(Eric Schlosser, *Fast Food Nation*, 2001)

✓ COMPREHENSION CHECKUP

Multiple Choice

Write the letter of the correct answer in the blank provided.

_____ 1. The main idea of the selection is that
  a. the fast food we eat every day contains many interesting ingredients
  b. the production of McDonald's French fries is a complicated process
  c. if teenagers really knew what was in fast food, they'd stop eating it
  d. flavor and color additives have transformed the foods Americans eat

_____ 2. The author's purpose in writing this selection is to
  a. criticize the flavor industry
  b. inform the public about what fast food is made of
  c. describe how a strawberry milkshake is made
  d. persuade readers to abandon McDonald's take-out

_____ 3. According to Schlosser, the ingredient that makes McDonald's French fries taste so good is
  a. salt
  b. monosodium glutamate
  c. natural flavor
  d. peanut oil

_____ 4. Titanium dioxide is used in all of the following *except*
  a. dishwashing detergent
  b. cake frosting
  c. house paint
  d. makeup

_____ 5. All of the following get their color from carmine *except*
  a. Dannon strawberry yogurt
  b. Ocean spray pink grapefruit juice drink
  c. orange marmalade
  d. raspberry fruit fillings

_____ 6. From paragraph 13, we can infer that a natural flavor
  a. comes directly from nature
  b. has little to do with nature
  c. is very fattening
  d. is extremely expensive

_____ 7. Tartrazine, a yellow food coloring
  a. has been banned in Norway and Finland
  b. can cause headaches and rashes
  c. is found in Jell-O and butterscotch pudding mixes
  d. all of the above

_____ 8. All of the following conclusions can be drawn from the selection *except*
  a. McDonald's bowed to pressure and changed the cooking method of its French fries
  b. the author of the selection does not believe that color additives in processed food are always safe
  c. brightly colored foods taste better than bland-looking ones
  d. color additives are important in making processed food look good

_____ 9. After reading the selection, we can conclude that
   a. a strawberry milkshake made at home is likely to contain fewer flavor additives than one purchased at Burger King
   b. companies are willing to share their flavor formulas
   c. Pop-Tarts are unlikely to contain color and flavor additives
   d. both a and c

_____ 10. In paragraph 3, the transition word *both* is used to show
   a. chronological order
   b. comparison
   c. steps in a process
   d. none of the above

_____ 11. In paragraph 1, the words *distinctive* and *unique* are
   a. antonyms
   b. homonyms
   c. synonyms
   d. similes

_____ 12. The author of the selection concludes with
   a. a warning about the dangers of chemical additives for children
   b. an opinion from an expert in toxic substances
   c. U.S. government facts and statistics
   d. both a and b

Fact or Opinion

For each of the following statements, write **F** if the statement is primarily factual or **O** if the statement represents an opinion.

_____ 1. For decades, McDonald's cooked its French fries in a mixture of about 7 percent soy oil and 93 percent beef fat.

_____ 2. The frozen potatoes and the cooking oil at McDonald's both contain "natural flavor."

_____ 3. The similarities between natural and artificial flavors are far more significant than their differences.

_____ 4. Americans now spend more than $1 trillion on food every year—and more than 90 percent of that money is spent on processed food.

_____ 5. Indeed, New Jersey produces about two thirds of the flavor additives sold in the United States.

_____ 6. International Flavors & Fragrances (IFF), the world's largest flavor company, has a manufacturing facility off Exit 8A in Dayton, New Jersey.

_____ 7. A tour of the IFF plant is the closest thing in real life to visiting Willy Wonka's chocolate factory.

_____ 8. The long chemical names on the little white labels seem like a strange foreign language.

_____ 9. Edible plants generally taste sweet; deadly ones, bitter.

_____ 10. The Food and Drug Administration does not require flavor companies to disclose the ingredients of their additives, so long as all the chemicals are classified as GRAS (Generally Regarded As Safe).

Vocabulary in Context

Look through the paragraphs listed below to find a word that matches each of the definitions. Write the words on the lines provided.

1. not harmful or injurious; harmless (paragraph 2) _____

2. pleasing to the taste (3) _____

3. disclose; reveal (4) _____

4. the innermost or central part (5) _____

5. easily damaged (6) _____

6. omnipresent (11) _____

7. prime; period of greatest success (13) _____

8. prohibited; forbidden (16) _____

In Your Own Words

1. For some people, McDonald's and other fast-food restaurants represent "comfort food." They associate cheeseburgers, French fries, and milkshakes with fond childhood memories. And, of course, some people just like the taste of foods such as the Big Mac. Former president Bill Clinton was a notorious example. What can nutritionists and other concerned individuals do to get children and adults to eat fewer highly processed foods?

2. Part of the appeal of a "Happy Meal" is the free toy. Do you think pressure should be exerted to get fast-food restaurants to stop making direct appeals to children?

3. Did the selection change your mind about eating highly processed foods? Or do you still think they can be part of an overall healthy diet?

4. Throughout the United States, meals in school cafeterias have come to resemble the meals at fast-food restaurants. Indeed, some schools have gone so far as to allow Subway or Pizza Hut to sell their products *in* the school cafeteria. Is this a good idea? Why or why not?

5. Many children badger their parents to take them to fast-food restaurants because they see these places advertised on TV. Do you think Congress should limit food advertisements aimed specifically at children?

The Art of Writing

1. What does your current diet look like? Keep track of the foods you eat for one week. If you are eating highly processed foods, what can you do to substitute more nutritious food products? Can you think of two dietary changes you should be making?

2. Healthy eating can be a real challenge today with all of the fast foods available and the cautions expressed about other food choices (beef, tuna, lettuce, peanut butter). How do you personally cope with all of the dietary guidelines and warnings?

Internet Activities

1. The United States Department of Agriculture (USDA) has determined that diet should no longer be a "one size fits all" concept. As a result, there is a new approach to the traditional food pyramid. A healthy diet is now based on age, sex, and level of activity. To determine your appropriate food choices, log on to

   www.choosemyplate.gov

   Write a paragraph or two about the dietary selections that are appropriate for you.

2. To learn more about food safety and preventing food-borne illnesses, visit one of the following Web sites:

   www.cfsan.fda.gov/

   www.foodsafety.gov

   Make a list of the prevention tips most valuable to you.

Review Test: Fact and Opinion

Directions: Identify each numbered sentence in the following paragraphs as either a fact (**F**) or an opinion (**O**).

A Culture of Cheating

(1) Recent studies demonstrate that the majority of college students do their research online. (2) Apparently, the temptation to cut and paste passages from Web site postings and pass them off as one's own is irresistible to many. (3) Surveys done by the Center for Academic Integrity show that from 1999 to 2005, the percentage of students who approved of this type of plagiarism rose from 10 percent to 41 percent. (4) At the same time, the percentage who considered cutting and pasting from the Internet to be a serious form of cheating fell from 68 percent to 23 percent. (5) Perhaps the worst form of Internet plagiarism is the purchase of entire papers from other writers. (6) Increasingly, the Web sites that sell essays to students are based in other countries, including India, Ukraine, Nigeria, and the Philippines.

Sentence 1 _____

Sentence 2 _____

Sentence 3 _____

Sentence 4 _____

Sentence 5 _____

Sentence 6 _____

(1) A cross-cultural study compared cheating by students in Lebanon and the United States. (2) Researchers found a high willingness to cheat among students in both countries: 54 percent of the U.S. students and 80 percent of the Lebanese students reported having cheated in some way during the past year.

(3) The study determined that in both cultures, students were more willing to cheat if they perceived their peers to be dishonest and if they thought their cheating was unlikely to be reported.

Sentence 1 _____

Sentence 2 _____

Sentence 3 _____

(1) The center for Academic Integrity estimates that at most schools, more than 75 percent of the students engage in some form of cheating. (2) Students have been caught not only cutting passages from the Internet and pasting them into their papers without citing the source, but also sharing questions and answers on exams, collaborating on assignments they are supposed to do independently, and even falsifying the results of their laboratory experiments. (3) Worse, many professors have become inured to the problem and have ceased to report it.

Sentence 1 _____

Sentence 2 _____

Sentence 3 _____

(1) Perhaps the increase in student cheating reflects widely publicized instances of cheating in public life, thereby creating an alternative set of values in which the end justifies the means. (2) When young people see sports heroes, authors, entertainers, and corporate executives exposed for cheating in one form or another, the message seems to be "Cheating is OK, as long as you don't get caught."

Sentence 1 _____

Sentence 2 _____

(Richard T. Schaefer, *Sociology*, 12/e, 2007)

Brain Teasers

Explain the meaning of the following "plant" words or phrases.

1. She keeps *beating around the bush* whenever I try to discuss her vacation plans.

   _____

2. His hard work in the campaign *bore unexpected fruit.* _____

3. She is always *going out on a limb* for her son. _____

4. As soon as she got away from her family, she *blossomed* into a beautiful person.

   _____

5. Apple has *branched out* into many areas of the media. _____

   _____

6. Campaign signs *sprouted* on all the lawns in our neighborhood. _____

7. The attorney managed to *plant* doubts in the jury's mind over the guilt of his client.

   _____

8. She needs to *prune* her expenses or she won't have enough money to get through the
   rest of the year. _____

9. Our plans to rent a house on the beach for a month were *nipped in the bud.*

   _____

10. Even though she and I don't really get along, we had a *fruitful* discussion. _____

Point of View

Christina's World (1948) *BY ANDREW WYETH*

Digital Image © The Museum of Modern Art/Licensed by
SCALA/Art Resource, NY.

View and Reflect

1. How would you describe the landscape depicted in the painting?
2. How does the artist convey the model's inability to walk?
3. Why do you think the artist chose not to show the model's face?
4. What is the model focused on? What is her point of view?
5. What is the overall tone of the painting?

Introduction to Point of View

Point of view is defined as a mental attitude from which a person views or judges something. Other terms for point of view are *perspective* and *standpoint*. A point of view can be favorable, unfavorable, or neutral. A writer's point of view leads to opinions and beliefs.

View I

View II

View III

In the best-selling book *The 7 Habits of Highly Effective People*, Stephen R. Covey describes an experiment that took place at Harvard University. Professors showed one group of students the drawing in View I of a toothless old woman with a large nose and chin buried in her dark collar. Another group of students was shown the drawing in View III of a profile of a young woman. Each group studied their assigned drawing for about ten seconds. When ten seconds had elapsed, both groups were shown the third picture, in View II. When the groups were asked to describe what they now saw, each group strongly tended to describe the picture it had previously studied for ten seconds. But when particular features of either the old woman or the young lady were pointed out to the group as a whole, the students momentarily saw the other point of view expressed in the other picture. However, when they looked away for a brief interval, they again immediately saw the picture they had been conditioned to see.

All of us have points of view on many topics. Our particular backgrounds and experiences shape our points of view. It took the Harvard students only ten seconds to become conditioned to see only one image. Our family, friends, school experiences, religion, and the media among other influences have conditioned us over a lifetime to have particular points of view and to see things in certain ways.

The cartoon on the next page illustrates how point of view is relative to our experiences.

A critical reader must be able to recognize and understand an author's point of view. While you may not agree with the author on a particular subject, it is important to maintain an open and questioning attitude.

"It's all according to your point of view. To me, you're a monster."

Exercise 1: Identifying Point of View

Directions: To better understand point of view, select one of the following fairy tales, and retell it from the point of view of the character mentioned.

1. *Cinderella* from the point of view of one of her stepsisters
2. *Little Red Riding Hood* from the point of view of the wolf
3. *Snow White and the Seven Dwarfs* from the point of view of the queen

Exercise 2: Identifying an Author's Point of View in Textbook Material

Directions: Read each of the following selections from textbooks, and indicate the author's point of view in your own words.

EXAMPLE

Many people are concerned that art be "pretty." These people often remark, for example, "I only want to look at pleasant things" or "There's already too much ugliness in this world" or "Isn't that cute! It's darling!" They want only happy endings at the movies; they want only to be entertained. The problem with insisting that all art be pretty is that doing so limits art to one kind of expression.

Because human experience is much richer than the cute and pleasant, art should be free to reflect life in all its richness. It would be nice if everything in life were pleasing, but some of the most important things are not so nice. Birth and death can be rather painful; so can falling in or out of love. Who is to stop an artist from saying something truthful about these or any other aspects of life that she or he finds meaningful?

(Thomas Buser, *Experiencing Art Around Us*, 1995)

Author's point of view: <u>Art should be free to reflect all facets of life.</u>

_____

1. Stress is not always harmful. In fact, a lack of stress, sometimes called "rust out," can lead to boredom, apathy, and less than optimal health. Moderate stress may enhance behavioral adaptation and is necessary for maturation and health. Stress stimulates psychological growth. It has been said that "freedom from stress is death" and "stress is the spice of life."

(Charles B. Corbin, *Concepts of Fitness and Wellness*, 4/e 2002)

Author's point of view: _____

_____

2. If you want to get ahead in an organization, it is important to do a good job. But it is also important that people like you. If people like you, they will forgive just about anything you do wrong. If they don't like you, you can do everything right and it will not matter. Many hardworking talented people have been by-passed for promotion and fired simply because their boss or some other high-level manager didn't like them. In fact, when Henry Ford fired Lee Iacocca, he used only four words to explain his decision: "I don't like you."

(Robert N. Lussier, *Human Relations in Organizations*, 4/e, 1999)

Author's point of view: _____

_____

3. Smoking interferes with your studying and your concentration: It's a disaster for your lungs, all of your body systems, your skin and your other organs, your immune system, and your brain. It's an insult you commit against yourself. (You already know the specific health risks, so I won't bore you with those. And I won't even mention chewing tobacco and its carcinogenic effects on the mouth, the throat, and the rest of the body.) If you don't smoke, that's terrific. Keep on *not* smoking. If you do smoke, make the decision to quit. I know it's a tough habit to break. Cigarette smoking is considered more addictive than co-caine, but if you want to quit, you can. Do you really want to go through life with cigarettes controlling you?

(Janet Elder, *Exercise Your College Reading Skills*, 1/e, 2004)

Author's point of view: _____

_____

4. The educational practice known as *tracking*, or grouping students by abilities, may contribute to failure. Students placed in low-track classes lack the stimula-tion of higher-ability peers and often get poorer teaching. They rarely move up to higher tracks, and many lose interest in trying to do better. Furthermore, since

school failure and contact with antisocial peers are often related to antisocial behavior, grouping poor achievers together may solidify problem behaviors.

(Diane E. Papalia, *Human Development*, 8/e, 2001)

Author's point of view: _____

_____

5. Jennifer unlocked her door quickly, raced inside, and shut it loudly behind her. She fastened the lock, threw the bolt, dropped her books on the floor, and made her way to the kitchen for her usual snack. Within a few minutes Jennifer was ensconced on the sofa, the television on and her stuffed animals clutched firmly in her hand. She decided to do her homework later. Her parents would be home then, and she tried not to spend too much time thinking about being lonely. She turned her attention to the television, to spend the next few hours watching talk shows. Jennifer is a latchkey kid. More than one in five children between 5 and 13, like Jennifer, are left to care for themselves after school. Although the average latchkey child is left alone two and a half hours per day, a significant number are alone much longer, more than thirty-six hours per week. Some latchkey children adjust to their situations. But, for others, problems do develop, and sad to say there are few educational or social agencies to respond to their needs.

(Myra P. Sadker and David Sadker, *Teachers, Schools, and Society*, 8/e, 2008)

Author's point of view: _____

_____

6. Lamar was finishing junior high school with resignation and despair. He had just managed to squeak through Beaton Junior High with poor grades and no understanding of how this frustrating experience would help him. He wasn't good at schoolwork and felt that the classes he had to sit through were a waste of time. Lamar's father had left school after eighth grade to go to work. Although he did not make much money, he had a car and seemed to be getting along okay. Lamar's mother had left high school when she became pregnant and had never returned. Neither of Lamar's parents thought school was critical, although both wanted Lamar to finish. But Lamar's patience was wearing thin. He wanted to end these long, boring days, get a job, and get a car. He'd had enough of school. Unfortunately, Lamar is a good candidate to join the nation's dropouts. Today, roughly one out of every nine students does not graduate from high school. This represents not only a loss of human potential but also increased costs in welfare, unemployment benefits, and potential criminal activity. And that is a national tragedy.

(Myra P. Sadker and David Sadker, *Teachers, Schools, and Society*, 8/e, 2008)

Author's point of view: _____

_____

7. The first step to improvement is always self-awareness. Analyze your shortcomings as a listener and commit yourself to overcoming them. Good listeners are not born that way. They have *worked* at learning how to listen effectively. Good listening does not go hand in hand with intelligence, education, or social standing. Like any other skill, it comes from practice and self-discipline. Begin to think of listening as an active process. So many aspects of modern life encourage us to listen passively. We "listen" to the CD while studying or "listen" to the

television while moving about from room to room. This type of passive listening is a habit—but so is active listening. We can learn to identify those situations in which active listening is important. If you work seriously at becoming a more efficient listener, you will reap rewards in your schoolwork, in your personal and family relations, and in your career.

(Stephen E. Lucas, *The Art of Public Speaking*, 9/e, 2007)

Author's point of view: _____

_____

8. Littleton, Colorado; Jonesboro, Arkansas; West Paducah, Kentucky; Peal, Mississippi; Edinboro, Pennsylvania; Springfield, Oregon—these are now more than just names of small and medium-size cities. They resonate with the sound of gunshots of kids killing other kids on school grounds. Each town was the scene of schoolhouse murders. As a result, people no longer perceive schools as safe havens but as another extension of the harsh reality of violence in society. But how accurate is that impression? Statistics demonstrate that a child has a one in a million chance of being killed at school. According to the Center for Disease Control, 99 percent of violent deaths of school-aged children occurred *outside* school grounds. Twenty-three times more children are killed in gun *accidents* than in school killings. Schools, then, are *safer* than their neighborhoods, but people still are unnerved by a perception of an alarming rise in schoolyard violence, perhaps generated by heavy media coverage of the recent incidents.

(Richard Schaefer, *Sociology*, 10/e, 2007)

Author's point of view: _____

_____

SELECTION

> *"He crowded her into the wall then, trying to break her grip.*
> *He held on to the baby and pushed with all his weight."*

GETTING THE PICTURE

As you are reading "Popular Mechanics" by Raymond Carver, think about the point of view of each character. Where should your sympathies lie—with the wife, the husband, or the baby?

BIO-SKETCH

Raymond Carver is considered by many to be one of the great short story writers of the twentieth century. The language of his stories is deceptively simple and, as in this short story, is meant to mirror the language used by the working poor. Carver based his realistic portrayals on what he knew best. Married at 19, and a father soon afterward, Carver, with no marketable skills, was forced to work at a series of odd jobs to support his family. Unfortunately, the strains proved to be too much, and his first marriage ended in divorce. Eventually, he received his B.A. from what is now California State University–Humboldt and began a career as an English and creative writing instructor.

In his over twenty-year career, his writings have received many honors, including nominations for a Pulitzer Prize, three O' Henry Awards, two grants from the National Endowment for the Arts, and a Guggenheim Fellowship. Mr. Carver died in 1988 of lung cancer, and his second wife, the poet Tess Gallagher, collaborated with director Robert Altman to create the critically acclaimed movie *Short Cuts,* based on a collection of Carver short stories. Interestingly, the short story below has also been published under the title "Little Things." What do you suppose, given Carver's personal history, he meant to imply by the change in the title?

Popular Mechanics
BY RAYMOND CARVER

Early that day the weather turned and the snow was melting into dirty water. 1 Streaks of it ran down from the little shoulder-high window that faced the backyard. Cars slushed by on the street outside, where it was getting dark. But it was getting dark on the inside too.

He was in the bedroom pushing clothes into a suitcase when she came to the door.   2

"I'm glad you're leaving! I'm glad you're leaving!" she said. "Do you hear?"   3

He kept on putting his things into the suitcase.   4

"I'm so glad you're leaving!" She began to cry. "You can't even look me in the face, 5 can you?"

Then she noticed the baby's picture on the bed and picked it up.   6

He looked at her and she wiped her eyes and stared at him before turning and 7 going back to the living room.

"Bring that back," he said.   8

"Just get your things and get out," she said.   9

He did not answer. He fastened the suitcase, put on his coat, looked around the 10 bedroom before turning off the light. Then he went out to the living room.

She stood in the doorway of the little kitchen, holding the baby.   11

"I want the baby," he said.   12

"Are you crazy?"   13

"No, but I want the baby. I'll get someone to come by for his things."   14

"You're not touching this baby," she said.   15

The baby had begun to cry and she uncovered the blanket from around his 16 head.

"Oh, oh," she said, looking at the baby.   17

He moved toward her.   18

"For God's sake!" she said. She took a step back into the kitchen.   19

"I want the baby."   20

"Get out of here!"   21

She turned and tried to hold the baby over in a corner behind the stove.   22

But he came up. He reached across the stove and tightened his hands on the baby.   23
"Let go of him," he said.   24
"Get away, get away!" she cried.   25
The baby was red-faced and screaming. In the scuffle they knocked down a flow-   26
erpot that hung behind the stove.

He crowded her into the wall then, trying to break her grip. He held on to the   27
baby and pushed with all his weight.

"Let go of him," he said.   28
"Don't," she said. "You're hurting the baby," she said.   29
"I'm not hurting the baby," he said.   30
The kitchen window gave no light. In the near-dark he worked on her fisted fin-   31
gers with one hand and with the other hand he gripped the screaming baby up under
an arm near the shoulder.

She felt her fingers being forced open. She felt the baby going from her.   32
"No!" she screamed just as her hands came loose.   33
She would have it, this baby. She grabbed for the baby's other arm. She caught the   34
baby around the wrist and leaned back.

But he would not let go. He felt the baby slipping out of his hands and he pulled   35
back very hard.

In this manner, the issue was decided.   36

(Raymond Carver, *What We Talk About When We Talk about Love*, 1981)

✓ COMPREHENSION CHECKUP

Fact Check

Answer the following factual questions.

1. At what time of day does the story occur? _____

2. Where is the baby's picture? _____

3. Is the baby a boy or a girl? _____

4. Where was the flowerpot hanging? _____

5. What is the baby wrapped in? _____

Vocabulary Practice

1. How many times is the word *little* used? _____ To what does it refer?

   _____

2. In the story, where does the author refer to "light" and "dark"? What does he
   mean to imply by each of these references?

   _____

   _____

   _____

   _____

   _____

In Your Own Words

1. In the beginning of the story, concrete details set the scene for the reader. What is the overall tone of the first paragraph?

2. When did the man decide he wanted the baby? What is the man's likely reason for wanting the baby?

3. Is the baby in any actual physical danger? What is meant by the last line of the story? What has been decided? What has happened to the baby?

4. In what way is the baby symbolic of the couple's relationship?

5. Why don't the characters have names? Why are they only referred to as *he, she,* and *baby*?

6. The story illustrates how parents can harm their children. In what ways can parents psychologically damage their children? Do you think psychological abuse of children can be as destructive as physical abuse of children?

7. In the story, the parents are behaving in an immature manner, like children fighting over a toy. What attributes do adults need to possess to be able to rear a child successfully? What attributes should they possess in order to have a healthy marriage?

8. Do you think *Popular Mechanics* is true to the way most relationships end today? What can people do to end a relationship on a positive note?

9. Whose point of view do you support—the wife's, the husband's, or the baby's?

The Art of Writing

Read the *The Judgment of Solomon* and then answer the questions that follow.

The Judgment of Solomon

Once two women came before Solomon. "My lord," the first woman said, "this woman and I were living alone in the same house when I gave birth to a baby boy. Three days later she also had a baby boy. That night both of us went to sleep holding our babies. But this woman fell asleep on top of her baby, and the poor child died. At midnight she woke up and saw that her baby was not breathing. She crept into my room, quietly took my baby away from me, and put her dead baby in my bed."

"You are lying!" cried the second woman.

"Let the woman finish her story," Solomon ordered.

"When I woke up," the first woman went on, "I discovered the dead baby in my bed, but I saw that it was not my baby. Now I want my baby back."

"Nonsense!" answered the second woman, and the two women argued back and forth while King Solomon looked on. Finally he said, "Bring me a sword."

The king's servants brought him a sword. "Now," ordered the king, "cut the baby in two, and give half to each woman. That way both of them will be satisfied."

"No!" cried the first woman, weeping. "Let her have the child. Anything, as long as you do not harm him."

"It is a good judgment," the second woman said. "If I cannot have the baby, at least she will not have him."

For a moment everyone was silent. Then King Solomon spoke. "Give the first woman the child," he said. "She is the mother. She loves the baby so much that she would rather part with him than see him hurt."

When the people heard this judgment, they marveled at Solomon, for they knew the wisdom of God was in him.

Source: I Kings iii

1. In a few paragraphs compare and contrast "The Judgment of Solomon" with "Popular Mechanics." How are the endings of the two stories different? What aspects of the two stories are the same? How similar are the characters?

2. What is the significance of "The Judgment" of Solomon to "Popular Mechanics"?

Internet Activity

Use a search engine such as Google (www.google.com) to find out more information about the magazine *Popular Mechanics*. Why do you suppose Carver chose the name of the magazine for the title of his short story?

SELECTION

"Now the point of the story is this: Did the tiger come out of the door, or did the lady?"

GETTING THE PICTURE

Ralph Waldo Emerson once wrote: "As a man thinketh so is he, and as a man chooseth so is he." The princess described in this classic short story faces a clear dilemma. She must choose the fate of her lover and in the process reveal what sort of person she is. As you are reading the story, keep the quotation in mind. When you finish, explain the meaning of the quotation as it applies to the princess.

BIO-SKETCH

Frank Stockton (1834–1902) was born in Philadelphia. He was a wood engraver by trade but spent much of his time writing stories. His earliest stories were for children, but later he began writing for adults. Stockton's most famous story, "The Lady or the Tiger?" appeared in 1882 in the *Century Magazine*. It caused a great outcry, and debates were held all over the country to decide the ending.

BRUSHING UP ON VOCABULARY

epithalamic measure marriage dance.

barbaric lacking civilizing influences; primitive. It comes from the Latin word *barbaricus*, meaning "foreign or rude." It is often used to describe someone who is uncultured and ignorant.

The Lady or the Tiger?

BY FRANK R. STOCKTON

In the very olden time, there lived a semibarbaric king, whose ideas, though some- 1
what polished and sharpened by the progressiveness of distant Latin neighbors,
were still large, florid, and untrammeled, as became the half of him which was barbaric. He was a man of exuberant fancy, and, withal, of an authority so irresistible
that, at his will, he turned his varied fancies into facts. He was greatly given to self-
communing; and when he and himself agreed upon any thing, the thing was done.
When every member of his domestic and political systems moved smoothly in its appointed course, his nature was bland and genial; but whenever there was a little hitch,
and some of his orbs got out of their orbits, he was blander and more genial still, for
nothing pleased him so much as to make the crooked straight and crush down un-
even places.

Among the borrowed notions by which his barbarism had become semified was 2
that of the public arena, in which, by exhibitions of manly and beastly valor, the
minds of his subjects were refined and cultured.

But even here the exuberant and barbaric fancy exerted itself. The arena of the 3
king was built, not to give the people an opportunity of hearing the rhapsodies of dying gladiators, nor to enable them to view the inevitable conclusion of a conflict between religious opinions and hungry jaws, but for purposes far better adapted to
widen and develop the mental energies of the people. This vast amphitheater, with its
encircling galleries, its mysterious vaults, and its unseen passages, was an agent of
poetic justice, in which crime was punished, or virtue rewarded, by the decrees of an
impartial and incorruptible chance.

When a subject was accused of a crime of sufficient importance to interest the 4
king, public notice was given that on an appointed day the fate of the accused person
would be decided in the king's arena—a structure which well deserved its name; for
although its form and plan were borrowed from afar, its purpose emanated solely
from the brain of this man, who, every barleycorn a king, knew no tradition to which
he owed more allegiance than pleased his fancy, and who ingrafted on every adopted
form of human thought and action the rich growth of his barbaric idealism.

When all the people had assembled in the galleries, and the king, surrounded by 5
his court, sat high up on his throne of royal state on one side of the arena, he gave a
signal, a door beneath him opened, and the accused subject stepped out into the
amphitheater. Directly opposite him, on the other side of the enclosed space, were
two doors, exactly alike and side by side. It was the duty and the privilege of the person on trial to walk directly to these doors and open one of them. He could open either door he pleased. He was subject to no guidance or influence but that of the
aforementioned impartial and incorruptible chance. If he opened the one, there came
out of it a hungry tiger, the fiercest and most cruel that could be procured, which immediately sprang upon him and tore him to pieces as a punishment for his guilt. The
moment that the case of the criminal was thus decided, doleful iron bells were
clanged, great wails went up from the hired mourners posted on the outer rim of the
arena, and the vast audience, with bowed heads and downcast hearts, wended slowly
their homeward way, mourning greatly that one so young and fair, or so old and respected, should have merited so dire a fate.

But if the accused person opened the other door, there came forth from it a lady, 6 the most suitable to his years and station that his majesty could select among his fair subjects, and to this lady he was immediately married as a reward of his innocence. It mattered not that he might already possess a wife and family, or that his affections might be engaged upon an object of his own selection. The king allowed no such subordinate arrangements to interfere with his great scheme of retribution and reward. The exercises, as in the other instance, took place immediately, and in the arena. Another door opened beneath the king, and a priest, followed by a band of choristers and dancing maidens blowing joyous airs on golden horns and treading an epithalamic measure, advanced to where the pair stood, side by side; and the wedding was promptly and cheerily solemnized. Then the brass bells rang forth their merry peals, the people shouted glad hurrahs, and the innocent man, preceded by children strewing flowers on his path, led his bride to his home.

This was the king's semibarbaric method of administering justice. Its perfect 7 fairness is obvious. The criminal could not know out of which door would come the lady. He opened either he pleased, without having the slightest idea whether, in the next instant, he was to be devoured or married. On some occasions the tiger came out of one door, and on some out of the other. The decisions of this tribunal were not only fair, they were positively determinate. The accused person was instantly punished if he found himself guilty; and if innocent, he was rewarded on the spot, whether he liked it or not. There was no escape from the judgments of the king's arena.

The institution was a very popular one. When the people gathered together on one 8 of the great trial days, they never knew whether they were to witness a bloody slaughter or a hilarious wedding. This element of uncertainty lent an interest to the occasion which it could not otherwise have attained. Thus, the masses were entertained and pleased, and the thinking part of the community could bring no charge of unfairness against this plan; for did not the accused person have the whole matter in his own hands?

This semibarbaric king had a daughter as blooming as his most florid fancies and 9 with a soul as fervent and imperious as his own. As is usual in such cases, she was the apple of his eye and was loved by him above all humanity. Among his courtiers was a young man of that fineness of blood and lowness of station common to the conventional heroes of romance who love royal maidens. This royal maiden was well satisfied with her lover, for he was handsome and brave to a degree unsurpassed in all this kingdom; and she loved him with an ardor that had enough of barbarism in it to make it exceedingly warm and strong. This love affair moved on happily for many months until one day the king happened to discover its existence. He did not hesitate nor waver in regard to his duty in the premises. The youth was immediately cast into prison, and a day was appointed for his trial in the king's arena. This, of course, was an especially important occasion; and his majesty, as well as all the people, was greatly interested in the workings and development of this trial. Never before had such a case occurred; never before had a subject dared to love the daughter of a king. In afteryears such things became commonplace enough; but then they were, in no slight degree, novel and startling.

The tiger cages of the kingdom were searched for the most savage and relentless 10 beasts, from which the fiercest monster might be selected for the arena; and the ranks of maiden youth and beauty throughout the land were carefully surveyed by competent judges in order that the young man might have a fitting bride in case fate did not determine for him a different destiny. Of course, everybody knew that the deed with which the accused was charged had been done. He had loved the princess, and neither he, nor she, nor anyone else thought of denying the fact; but the king would not think of allowing any fact of this kind to interfere with the workings of the tribunal, in which he took such delight and satisfaction. No matter how the affair turned out, the youth would be disposed of; and the king would take an aesthetic pleasure in watching the course of events which would determine whether or not the young man had done wrong in allowing himself to love the princess.

The appointed day arrived. From far and near the people gathered and thronged 11 the great galleries of the arena; and crowds, unable to gain admittance, massed themselves against its outside walls. The king and his court were in their places, opposite the twin doors—those fateful portals, so terrible in their similarity!

All was ready. The signal was given. A door beneath the royal party opened, and 12 the lover of the princess walked into the arena. Tall, beautiful, fair, his appearance was greeted with a low hum of admiration and anxiety. Half the audience had not known so grand a youth had lived among them. No wonder the princess loved him! What a terrible thing for him to be there!

As the youth advanced into the arena, he turned, as the custom was, to bow to 13 the king. But he did not think at all of that royal personage; his eyes were fixed upon the princess, who sat to the right of her father. Had it not been for the moiety of barbarism in her nature, it is probable that lady would not have been there; but her intense and fervid soul would not allow her to be absent on an occasion in which she was so terribly interested. From the moment that the decree had gone forth that her lover should decide his fate in the king's arena, she had thought of nothing, night or day, but this great event and the various subjects connected with it. Possessed of more power, influence, and force of character than anyone who had ever before been interested in such a case, she had done what no other person had done—she had possessed herself of the secret of the doors. She knew in which of the two rooms that lay behind those doors stood the cage of the tiger, with its open front, and in which waited the lady. Through these thick doors, heavily curtained with skins on the inside, it was impossible that any noise or suggestion should come from within to the person who should approach to raise the latch of one of them. But gold—and the power of a woman's will—had brought the secret to the princess.

And not only did she know in which room stood the lady ready to emerge, all 14 blushing and radiant, should her door be opened, but she knew who the lady was. It was one of the fairest and loveliest of the damsels of the court who had been selected as the reward of the accused youth, should he be proved innocent of the crime of aspiring to one so far above him; and the princess hated her. Often had she seen, or imagined that she had seen, this fair creature throwing glances of admiration upon the person of her lover, and sometimes she thought these glances were perceived and even returned. Now and then she had seen them talking together; it was but for a moment or two, but much can be said in a brief space. It may have been on most unimportant topics, but how could she know that? The girl was lovely, but she had dared to raise her eyes to the loved one of the princess; and with all the intensity of the savage blood transmitted to her through long lines of wholly barbaric ancestors, she hated the woman who blushed and trembled behind that silent door.

When her lover turned and looked at her, and his eye met hers as she sat there 15 paler and whiter than anyone in the vast ocean of anxious faces about her, he saw, by the power of quick perception which is given to those whose souls are one, that she knew behind which door crouched the tiger, and behind which stood the lady. He had expected her to know it. He understood her nature, and his soul was assured that she would never rest until she had made plain to herself this thing, hidden to all other lookers-on, even to the king. The only hope for the youth in which there was any element of certainty was based upon the success of the princess in discovering this mystery; and the moment he looked upon her, he saw she had succeeded, as in his soul he knew she would succeed.

Then it was that his quick and anxious glance asked the question: "Which?" It was as plain to her as if he shouted it from where he stood. There was not an instant to be lost. The question was asked in a flash; it must be answered in another.

Her right arm lay on the cushioned parapet before her. She raised her hand and made a slight, quick movement toward the right. No one but her lover saw her. Every eye but his was fixed on the man in the arena.

He turned, and with a firm and rapid step he walked across the empty space. Every heart stopped beating, every breath was held, every eye was fixed immovably upon that man. Without the slightest hesitation he went to the door on the right and opened it.

*   *   *   *

Now, the point of the story is this: Did the tiger come out of the door, or did the lady?

The more we reflect upon this question, the harder it is to answer. It involves a study of the human heart which leads us through devious mazes of passion, out of which it is difficult to find our way. Think of it, fair reader, not as if the decision of the question depended upon yourself, but upon that hot-blooded semibarbaric princess, her soul at white heat beneath the combined fires of despair and jealousy. She had lost him, but who should have him?

How often, in her waking hours and in her dreams, had she started in wild horror and covered her face with her hands as she thought of her lover opening the door on the other side of which waited the cruel fangs of the tiger!

But how much oftener had she seen him at the other door! How in her grievous reveries had she gnashed her teeth and torn her hair when she saw his start of rapturous delight as he opened the door of the lady! How her soul had burned in agony when she had seen him rush to meet that woman, with her flushing cheek and sparkling eye of triumph; when she had seen him lead her forth, his whole frame kindled with the joy of recovered life; when she had heard the glad shouts from the multitude and the wild ringing of the happy bells; when she had seen the priest, with his joyous followers, advance to the couple and make them man and wife before her very eyes; and when she had seen them walk away together upon their path of flowers, followed by the tremendous shouts of the hilarious multitude, in which her one despairing shriek was lost and drowned!

Would it not be better for him to die at once and go to wait for her in the blessed regions of semibarbaric futurity?

And yet, that awful tiger, those shrieks, that blood!

Her decision had been indicated in an instant, but it had been made after days and nights of anguished deliberation. She had known she would be asked, she had decided what she would answer, and without the slightest hesitation she had moved her hand to the right.

The question of her decision is one not to be lightly considered, and it is not for me to presume to set myself up as the one person able to answer it. And so I leave it with all of you: Which came out of the opened door—the lady or the tiger?

(Frank R. Stockton, "The Lady or the Tiger?," 1882)

"He who reflects too much will achieve little."

—J.C.F. von Schiller

✓ COMPREHENSION CHECKUP

Multiple Choice

Write the letter of the correct answer in the blank provided.

_____ 1. The king is described as possessing all of the following character traits except that of being
   a. semibarbaric
   b. tyrannical
   c. generous and forgiving
   d. self-absorbed

_____ 2. Given the similarity of the princess to her father, we can assume that she is
   a. timid
   b. semibarbaric
   c. fervid
   d. both b and c

_____ 3. The narrator calls the king's system of deciding the fate of the accused "poetic justice." This is an example of
   a. literary allusion
   b. irony
   c. patterns of organization
   d. summary

_____ 4. The princess's lover is lacking
   a. good looks
   b. high social standing
   c. bravery
   d. height

_____ 5. The tiger chosen for the trial of the princess's lover is all of the following _except_
   a. savage
   b. relentless
   c. meek
   d. fierce

_____ 6. The maiden chosen for the princess's lover is
   a. fair and lovely
   b. blushing and radiant
   c. rich and powerful
   d. both a and b

_____ 7. The guilt or innocence of the accused is determined by
   a. a confession
   b. a court of law
   c. the appearance of a tiger or a lady
   d. the king's subjects

_____ 8. "She was the apple of his eye" is a figurative expression meaning that
   a. the king considered the princess to be expendable
   b. the king was very fond of the princess
   c. the princess was the king's favorite person
   d. both b and c

_____ 9. The king's system of dispensing justice is
   a. arbitrary and capricious
   b. fair to all concerned
   c. unpopular with his subjects
   d. civilized

_____ 10. The author states that the reader must look to the character of the princess to determine
   a. whether the princess's lover will live or die
   b. whether love or jealousy will win out
   c. how the story will end
   d. all of the above

True or False

Indicate whether the statement is true or false by writing **T** or **F** in the blank provided.

_____ 11. The king's daughter has a fervent soul.

_____ 12. The king places a high value on human life.

_____ 13. The king approves of his daughter's love affair.

_____ 14. Both the king and the princess are present at the arena.

_____ 15. The princess is fond of the maiden behind the door.

_____ 16. The princess points to the door on the left.

_____ 17. The princess's lover unhesitatingly follows the princess's signal to go to the right.

_____ 18. The princess's lover expects the princess to know the secret of the doors.

_____ 19. When the princess's lover turns toward the king, his attention is focused on the princess.

_____ 20. Of all the onlookers, the king alone knows the secret of what is behind each door.

Vocabulary in Context

Using the context clues below, write a definition for the italicized word.

1. "... by the decrees of an *impartial* and incorruptible chance."

   Definition: _____

2. "... with bowed heads and *downcast* hearts ..."

   Definition: _____

3. "He did not hesitate nor *waver* in regard to his duty in the premises."

   Definition: _____

4. "... opposite the twin doors—those fateful *portals* ..."

   Definition: _____

5. "... but her intense and *fervid* soul would not allow her to be absent ..."

   Definition: _____

6. ". . . which leads us through devious *mazes* of passion, out of which it is difficult to find our way."

   Definition: _____

Vocabulary Practice

Look through the paragraph indicated in parentheses to find a word that matches the definition below.

1. pleasantly gentle or agreeable (paragraph 1) _____

2. ecstatically expressing feelings or enthusiasm (3) _____

3. issued forth; originated (4) _____

4. proceeded or went; traveled (5) _____

5. pertaining to a sense of beauty (10) _____

6. an indefinite portion, part, or share (13) _____

7. daydreams (22) _____

Vocabulary in Context

Match the word in Column A with the definition in Column B.

Column A

_____ 1. florid

_____ 2. untrammeled

_____ 3. barbaric

_____ 4. bland

_____ 5. valor

_____ 6. doleful

_____ 7. dire

_____ 8. retribution

_____ 9. peals

_____ 10. tribunal

_____ 11. damsel

_____ 12. imperious

_____ 13. unsurpassed

_____ 14. ardor

_____ 15. commonplace

_____ 16. competent

_____ 17. thronged

_____ 18. devious

Column B

a. zeal; fervor

b. maiden

c. ordinary

d. ornate; showy

e. shifty; underhand

f. court of justice

g. loud, sustained sound

h. properly qualified

i. unrestrained

j. sorrowful; mournful

k. crowded

l. crude; primitive

m. terrible

n. pleasantly gentle or agreeable

o. punishment for a wrong act

p. not exceeded

q. courage or bravery

r. dictatorial; domineering

In Your Own Words

1. Describe the nature of the princess in your own words. How might these qualities influence her decision?

2. From what you know of the princess, which door do you think she pointed to: the one hiding the lady or the one hiding the tiger? State your reasons.

3. The princess's lover goes to the door on the right "without the slightest hesitation." If you were the young man, would you follow the princess's direction? Explain your answer.

4. The king's form of punishment is obviously unfair because an innocent person could pick the door with the tiger and a guilty one could pick the door with the lady. However, looking at the situation from another point of view, in what way could the king's form of punishment be considered fair?

The Art of Writing

In a brief essay, write your own ending, telling what happens when the young man opens the door. Describe the princess's reaction as the door opens. Describe the young man's reaction to what he finds.

Internet Activity

Do a Google search to find information explaining how Frank R. Stockton came to write "The Lady or the Tiger?" Briefly summarize your findings.

SELECTION

"Sometimes I think it is because instead of feeling that the bear is trespassing on my property, in my heart I believe that I am trespassing on his."

GETTING THE PICTURE

In this selection, Anna Quindlen's brief encounter with a bear serves as a catalyst to explore her feelings about her place in nature.

BIO-SKETCH

Anna Quindlen began her career as a journalist over 30 years ago. The selection below comes from her *New York Times* "Public and Private" column. In addition to writing nonfiction and receiving a Pulitzer Prize for her work, Quindlen successfully made the transition to fiction. Her novels have sold millions of copies and many have been made into movies. She is the first writer to have her work appear on the fiction, nonfiction, and self-help *New York Times* Best Seller lists. Quindlen, a graduate of Barnard College, is married to Gerald Krovatin, an attorney, and is the mother of three children. She currently resides in New York City where she writes the prestigious "The Last Word" column for *Newsweek*.

BRUSHING UP ON VOCABULARY

adenoidal   sounding as if the nose were pinched; nasal.

emphysema   a chronic lung disease characterized by labored breathing and wheezing.

apiaries   a place where bees or bee hives are kept.

Our Animal Rites

By Anna Quindlen

1   The bear had the adenoidal breathing of an elderly man with a passion for cigars and a tendency toward emphysema. My first thought, when I saw him contemplating me through tiny eyes from a rise just beyond the back porch, was that he looked remarkably bearlike, like a close-up shot from a public nature program.

2   I screamed. With heavy tread—pad, pad, pad, harrumph, harrumph—the bear went off into the night, perhaps to search for garbage cans inexpertly closed and apiaries badly lighted. I sat on the porch, shaking. Everyone asks, "Was he big?" My answer is, "Compared to what?"

3   What I leave out when I tell the story is my conviction that the bear is still watching. At night I imagine he is staring down from the hillside into the lighted porch, as though he had a mezzanine seat for a performance on which the curtain had already gone up. "A nice female, but not very furry," I imagine him thinking, "I see the cubs have gone to the den for the night."

4   Sometimes I suspect I think this because the peace and quiet of the country have made me go mad, and if only I could hear a car alarm, an ambulance siren, the sound of a boom box playing "The Power" and its owner arguing with his girlfriend over whether or not he was flirting with Denise at the party, all that would drive the bear clear out of my head.

5   Sometimes I think it is because instead of feeling that the bear is trespassing on my property, in my heart I believe that I am trespassing on his.

6   That feeling is not apparent to city people, although there is something about the sight of a man cleaning up after a sheepdog with a sheet of newspaper that suggests a kind of horrible atonement. The city is a place built by the people, for the people. There we say people are acting like animals when they do things with guns and bats and knives that your ordinary bear would never dream of doing. There we condescend to our animals, with grooming parlors and cat carriers, using them to salve our loneliness and prepare us for parenthood.

7   All of you who lost interest in the dog after the baby was born, you know who you are.

8   But out where the darkness has depth, where there are no street lights and the stars leap out of the sky, condescension, a feeling of supremacy, what the animal-rights types call speciesism, is impossible. Oh, hunters try it, and it is pathetic to consider the firepower they require to bring down one fair-sized deer. They get three bear days in the autumn, and afterward there is at least one picture in the paper of a couple of smiling guys in hats surrounding the carcass of an animal that looks, though dead, more dignified than they do.

9   Each spring, after the denning and the long, cold drowse, we wait to see if the bear that lives on the hill above our house beats the bullets. We discover his triumph through signs: a pile of bear dung on the lawn, impossible to assign to any other animal unless mastodons still roam the earth. A garbage box overturned into the swamp, the cole slaw container licked clean. Symmetrical scratch marks five feet up on a tree.

10   They own this land. Once, long ago, someone put a house on it. That was when we were tentative interlopers, when we put a farmhouse here and a barn there. And then we went nuts, built garden condos with pools and office complexes with parking garages and developments with names that always included the words Park, Acres, or Hills. You can't stop progress, especially if it's traveling 65 miles an hour. You notice that more this time of year, when the possums stiffen by the side of the road.

11   Sometimes the animals fight back. I was tickled by the people who bought a house with a pond and paid a good bit of money for a little dock from which to swim. It did not take long for them to discover that the snapping turtles were opposed to the addition to their ecosystem of humans wearing sunscreen. An exterminator was sent for. The pond was dredged. A guest got bit. The turtles won.

I've read that deer use the same trails all their lives. Someone comes along and puts a neo-Colonial house in the middle of their deer paths, and the deer will use the paths anyway, with a few detours. If you watch, you can see that it is the deer that belong and the house which does not. The bats, the groundhogs, the weasels, the toads—a hundred years from now, while our family will likely be scattered, their descendants might be in this same spot. Somewhere out there the bear is watching, picking his nits and his teeth, breathing his raggedy bear breath, and if he could talk, maybe he'd say, "I wonder when they're going back where they belong."

(Anna Quindlen, "Our Animal Rites" *The New York Times*, 8/05/1990)

✓ COMPREHENSION CHECKUP

Multiple Choice

Write the letter of the correct answer in the blank provided.

_____ 1. We can infer that Quindlen probably feels that
   a. we are not superior to animals
   b. we are justified in treating animals in a condescending manner
   c. children should be careful around hunters during bear season
   d. boom boxes should be outlawed

_____ 2. In paragraph 6, when Quindlen says "we say people are acting like animals when they do things with guns and bats and knives that your ordinary bear would never dream of doing," she is demonstrating support for
   a. the judicial system
   b. the bear
   c. the police officer
   d. teenagers

_____ 3. The dominant tone throughout is
   a. playful
   b. serious
   c. nostalgic
   d. objective

_____ 4. The author's point of view toward grooming parlors and cat carriers is
   a. favorable
   b. unfavorable
   c. neutral

_____ 5. We can infer that Quindlen was frightened by the bear for all of the following reasons *except*
   a. called 911
   b. screamed
   c. sat on the porch shaking
   c. still mentally "sees" the bear

_____ 6. "Stars leap out of the sky" in paragraph 8 is an example of
   a. simile
   b. personification
   c. metaphor
   d. hyperbole

_____ 7. According to Quindlen, all of the following are signs that a bear made it through the winter *except*
   a. bear dung left on the lawn
   b. tracks leading from a den
   c. a garbage box overturned into the swamp
   d. a coleslaw container licked clean

_____ 8. Why does it please Quindlen that the turtles won a victory against a homeowner?
   a. Quindlen is opposed to the use of exterminators to eradicate wildlife.
   b. Quindlen is jealous of rich people who can afford big homes with private docks.
   c. Quindlen feels that animals are in actuality the owners of the land.
   d. Quindlen likes animals more than she likes people.

_____ 9. What is ironic about the builders' use of the words "Park, Acres, or Hills" in the title of their developments?
   a. The developers have harmed nature to put up their buildings.
   b. The developers like to use impressive-sounding names to sell more real estate.
   c. The developers are all staunch conservationists.
   d. The developers have created wildlife refuge centers in those areas.

_____ 10. In the last paragraph of the selection, Quindlen clearly states her point of view about animal "rites." Who is she supportive of?
   a. motorists who travel at the legal speed limit
   b. humans who wear sunscreen
   c. animals
   d. hunters

True or False

Indicate whether the statement is true or false by writing **T** or **F** in the blank provided.

_____ 11. Quindlen believes that with a concerted effort we can halt the incursion by human beings on the animals' lands.

_____ 12. Quindlen believes that hunting is an inherently dignified sport.

_____ 13. Quindlen indicates that "her" bear might have been searching for honey.

_____ 14. Quindlen implies that some people use dogs to prepare for parenthood.

_____ 15. Quindlen implies that she has children at home with her.

_____ 16. Sometimes Quindlen longs for the distractions of city life.

Vocabulary in Context

In the paragraphs indicated, find a word that matches the definition given, and write the word in the space provided.

Paragraph 1

1. looking at attentively and thoughtfully _____

Paragraph 2

2. step _____

Paragraph 3

3. strong belief; certainty _____

4. balcony _____

Paragraph 6

5. reparation; something done to make amends for wrongdoing _____

6. display a superior attitude _____

7. remedy; relieve _____

Paragraph 8

8. the dead body of an animal _____

Paragraph 9

9. similar in size, shape, or position; parallel _____

Paragraph 10

10. uncertain; hesitant _____

11. intruders _____

Paragraph 11

12. scraped out _____

In Your Own Words

1. What is Quindlen's main idea? What is her purpose in writing this selection?

2. What does Quindlen mean to imply by the use of the words "Animal Rites" in the title, rather than "Animal Rights"?

3. Do you think animals have rights? If so, what are some of those rights?

4. In the selection, Quindlen gives a specific example of what happens when humans push back the boundaries of wildlife habitats. What, if anything, should we do about it?

5. What is Quindlen's specific point of view in regard to the topic of "animal rights"?

The Art of Writing

Write a short essay discussing the following: What in your view is our responsibility to animals? How can we successfully co-exist with animals? How can we preserve as much of an animal's habitat as possible?

Internet Activity

1. Use any search engine to find out more about the term "speciesism" as used in paragraph 8 of the selection. Write a paragraph reporting your findings.

2. Consult Anna Quindlen's Web site www.annaquindlen.com to find out more about the books and columns she has written. Write a paragraph discussing what you found to be most interesting about either her personally or her work.

Multiple Points of View: The Vietnam War Memorial

Fought in the 1960s and 1970s, the Vietnam War deeply divided the country. Presidents Eisenhower and Kennedy sent military advisers to aid the noncommunist South Vietnamese in resisting the communist North Vietnamese. Under President Johnson, U.S. involvement deepened to the point at which half a million U.S. troops

Vietnam Veterans Memorial (1981–1983) *BY MAYA YING LIN*

© R. Morley/PhotoLink/Getty Images

became involved in the conflict. In 1973, President Nixon negotiated a cease-fire with North Vietnam, and soon all U.S. troops returned home. In 1982, the Vietnam Veterans Memorial was dedicated to the American soldiers who had been killed or rendered missing in action in Vietnam.

The Vietnam Veterans Memorial, located on the mall in Washington, D.C., receives about 3.5 million visitors annually. Designed to help promote national reconciliation, it has become America's best-known public artwork. Although initial reaction to the memorial design was positive, many veterans came to feel that it had a tone of "defeat." As a result, a flag and *The Face of Honor* sculpture were added.

Presented below are three different points of view about the memorial, one from author Tom Wolfe, another from the designer of the memorial Maya Lin, and the last from the *Congressional Quarterly.*

Vietnam Memorial

In 1982, a group of Vietnam veterans had just obtained Congressional approval for a memorial that would pay long-delayed tribute to those who had fought in Vietnam with honor and courage in a lost and highly unpopular cause. They had chosen a jury of architects and art worldlings to make a blind selection in an open competition; that is, anyone could enter, and no one could put his name on his entry. Every proposal had to include something—a wall, a column—on which a hired engraver could inscribe the names of all 57,000-plus members of the American military who had died in Vietnam. Nine of the top 10 choices were abstract designs that could be executed without resorting to that devious and accursed bit of trickery: skill. Only the No. 3 choice was representational. Up on one end of a semicircular wall bearing the 57,000 names was an infantryman on his knees beside a fallen comrade, looking about for help. At the other end, a third infantryman had begun to run along the top of the wall toward them. The sculptor was Frederick Hart.   1

The winning entry was by a young Yale undergraduate architectural student named Maya Lin. Her proposal was a V-shaped wall, period, a wall of polished black granite inscribed only with the names; no mention of honor, courage, or gratitude; not even a flag. Absolutely skillproof, it was.   2

Many veterans were furious. They regarded her wall as a gigantic pitiless tombstone that said, "Your so-called service was an absolutely pointless disaster." They made so much noise that a compromise was struck. An American flag and statue would be added to the site. Hart was chosen to do the statue. He came up with a group of three soldiers, realistic down to the aglets of their boot strings, who appear to have just emerged from the jungle into a clearing, where they are startled to see Lin's V-shaped black wall bearing the names of their dead comrades.   3

Naturally enough, Lin was miffed at the intrusion, and so a make-peace get-together was arranged in Plainview, New York, where the foundry had just completed casting the soldiers. Doing her best to play the part, Lin asked Hart—as Hart recounted it—if the young men used as models for the three soldiers had complained of any pain when the plaster casts were removed from their faces and arms. Hart couldn't imagine what she was talking about. Then it dawned on him. She assumed that he had covered the model's body in wet plaster and removed it when it began to harden. No artist of her generation (she was 21) could even conceive of a sculptor   4 starting out solely with a picture in his head, a stylus, a brick of moist clay, and some armature wire. No artist of her generation dared even speculate about . . . skill.

(Tom Wolfe, *Hooking Up,* 2000)

Multiple Choice

Write the letter of the correct answer in the blank provided.

_____ B ___ 1. We can assume that a blind selection was used to
    a. allow those who were well known in the art world to have a better chance of being chosen
    b. give each entry an equal chance to be chosen
    c. keep the press from knowing the results too early in the process
    d. keep the public from voicing opinions prematurely

_____ D ___ 2. Which of the following value assumptions does the writer seem to make?
    a. A person as young as Lin could not possibly understand the concept of skill.
    b. A representational design embodying skill is superior to a design that is abstract.
    c. The veterans were justifiably angry about Lin's design.
    d. All of the above

_____ D ___ 3. The expression "miffed at the intrusion" implies
    a. acceptance
    b. displeasure
    c. annoyance
    d. both b and c

_____ C ___ 4. The tone of the writer toward Maya Lin is
    a. indifferent
    b. sympathetic
    c. contemptuous
    d. neutral

Boundaries

I wanted to create a memorial that everyone would be able to respond to, regardless of whether one thought our country should or should not have participated in the war. On a personal level, I wanted to focus on the nature of accepting and coming to terms with a loved one's death. Simple as it may seem, I remember feeling that accepting a person's death is the first step in being able to overcome that loss.

I felt that as a culture we were extremely youth-oriented and not willing or able to accept death or dying as a part of life. The rites of mourning, which in more primitive and older cultures were very much a part of life, have been suppressed in our modern times. In the design of the memorial, a fundamental goal was to be honest about death, since we must accept that loss in order to begin to overcome it. The pain of the loss will always be there, it will always hurt, but we must acknowledge the death in order to move on.

What then would bring back the memory of a person? A specific object or image would be limiting. A realistic sculpture would be only one interpretation of that time. I wanted something that all people could relate to on a personal level. At this time I had as yet no form, no specific artistic image.

Then someone in my class received the design program, which stated the basic philosophy of the memorial's design and also its requirements: all the names of those missing and killed (57,000) must be a part of the memorial; the design must be apolitical, harmonious with the site, and conciliatory.

These were all the thoughts that were in my mind before I went to see the site.

Without having seen it, I couldn't design the memorial, so a few of us traveled to Washington, D.C., and it was at the site that the idea for the design took shape. The site was a beautiful park surrounded by trees, with traffic and noise coming from one side—Constitution Avenue.

I had a sudden impulse to cut into the earth.

I imagined taking a knife and cutting into the earth, opening it up, an initial violence and pain that in time would heal. The grass would grow back, but the initial cut would remain a pure flat surface in the earth with a polished, mirrored surface, much like the surface on a geode when you cut it and polish the edge. The need for the names to be on the memorial would be the memorial; there was no need to embellish the design further. The people and their names would allow everyone to respond and remember.

It would be an interface, between our world and the quieter, darker, more peaceful world beyond. I chose black granite in order to make the surface reflective and peaceful. I never looked at the memorial as a wall, an object, but as an edge to the earth, an opened side. The mirrored effect would double the size of the park, creating two worlds, one we are a part of and one we cannot enter. The two walls were positioned so that one pointed to the Lincoln Memorial and the other pointed to the Washington Monument. By linking these two strong symbols for the country, I wanted to create a unity between the nation's past and present.

On our return to Yale, I quickly sketched my idea up, and it almost seemed too simple, too little. But the image was so simple that anything added to it began to detract from it.

I always wanted the names to be chronological, to make it so that those who served and returned from the war could find their place in the memorial.

As far as all the controversy, I really never wanted to go into it too much. The memorial's starkness, its being below grade, being black, and how my age, gender, and race played a part in the controversy, we'll never quite know. I think it is actually a miracle that the piece ever got built. From the beginning I often wondered, if it had not been an anonymous entry 1026 but rather an entry by Maya Lin, would I have been selected?

(Maya Lin, *Boundaries*, 2000)

Multiple Choice

Write the letter of the correct answer in the blank provided.

____ 1. Which one of the following statements best reveals the writer's attitude toward the memorial?

 a. A memorial is not the place for personal reflection.

 b. A war memorial must include a heroic statue.

 c. A realistic sculpture would have been too limiting.

 d. A black memorial is more appropriate for a losing war effort.

_A_____ 2. A key point the writer makes is that

    a. in light of the many controversies, it's surprising that the memorial was ever built

    b. the site did not influence the design

    c. the reflective property of black granite was an unexpected dividend

    d. it was important that the names of those who died be listed on the memorial in alphabetical order

_B_____ 3. The writer would agree with which of the following statements?

    a. Black granite was chosen to indicate deep sadness and shame.

    b. The names are the memorial; no further embellishment is required.

    c. It was important to link the Vietnam Memorial to the Washington Monument and the Jefferson Memorial.

    d. A memorial should make a political statement.

_D_____ 4. What can we infer about the values of the writer?

    a. She feels that the first step toward overcoming a loved one's death is acceptance of the loss.

    b. She believes that American culture focuses too much on the problems of the elderly.

    c. She feels that death and dying should be a part of life.

    d. Both a and c

A Quiet Place for Personal Reflection

1 Snow and ice carpet the ground, making walking especially hazardous. Yet thousands have come on this cold January day to see the Vietnam Veterans Memorial.

2 Each year, more than 2.5 million people visit the site, located just north of the Lincoln Memorial, ranking it among the most popular tourist attractions in Washington.

3 For many, the monument's shimmering black panels—containing the names of the more than 58,000 American men and women who died in Vietnam—symbolize the nation's effort to come to grips with one of the most divisive chapters in its history.

4 "This place is an important national symbol, like the Statue of Liberty," says John R. Gifford, 43, a Westport, Massachusetts, police officer who was making his second visit to the memorial.

5 But, Gifford says, the "Wall" is more than just a symbol. It has deep personal meaning for those who lived during the Vietnam era—especially those who fought or lost a loved one in the war. "You can see how hard it is when folks who have lost someone near and dear to them in Vietnam come here," he says.

6 The monument contains 140 slabs of black granite quarried in India. The names are inscribed in chronological order, beginning with the first American casualy in 1959 and ending with those who died in 1975, the year South Vietnam fell.

7 The Wall consists of two sections, each 246 feet long, that meet at a 125-degree angle, forming a wide V. The height of the wall rises from just a foot, at each end, to about 10 feet at the point where the sections meet.

8 The design by Maya Lin, a young architecture student, was controversial when she proposed it almost two decades ago. Many veterans wanted a more traditional war monument—with statues of soldiers. But Lin wanted the memorial to be "a quiet place, meant for personal reflection and private reckoning." When submitting her design in 1981, she wrote, "The actual area is wide

and shallow, allowing for a sense of privacy, and the sunlight from the memorial's southern exposure, along with the grassy park surrounding and within its walls, contribute to the serenity of the area. Thus, the memorial is for those who have died, and for us to remember them."

9   To mollify the critics, the Vietnam Veterans Memorial Fund (VVMF) in 1982 commissioned the late Frederick Hart, a noted Washington, D.C., sculptor, to create a traditional statue to accompany Lin's design. Sited just a few feet from the Wall, it depicts three rifle-carrying infantryman—a white, a black, and a Hispanic.

10   Judging by the streams of visitors to the Wall, and the solemnity that envelops it, Lin's concept was sound. "This is such a solemn place," says Mark Yanick, a 37-year-old human resources trainer from Washington, D.C., who had brought an out-of-town friend to see the Wall. "This is the only monument I've ever been to where there is total silence, even when it's crowded."

11   The memorial is the brainchild of Jan C. Scruggs, an infantryman who was wounded in Vietnam. Scruggs conceived of the idea for a memorial after watching Michael Chamino's The Deer Hunter, a troubling 1979 film about the tortured lives of a group of returning Vietnam vets. "After I made the decision that we needed something like this, I became obsessed with it," he says.

12   Along with other veterans from "Nam," Scruggs formed the VVMF in 1979 to raise money and find a location and design for the memorial. The project came together with remarkable speed. Within a few years, they had raised more than $8 million from private sources, including more than 275,000 individuals. In 1980, Congress provided two acres on the Mall for the memorial.

13   That year, the VVMF held a design competition. Lin, then a 21-year-old student at Yale University, bested the 1,421 entries submitted, many by some of the world's leading architects. Construction began in March 1982, and in November the memorial was dedicated.

14   "We figured that a lot of people would come the first year because it would be a novelty, but after that it would just be something for the vets," Scruggs says. "Now it's a symbol to the nation, much like the Eiffel Tower is the symbol of France."

("A Quiet Place for Personal Reflection," *Congressional Quarterly*, 2000)

Multiple Choice

Write the letter of the correct answer in the blank provided.

_____ 1. The phrase *to mollify* as used in paragraph 9 means
      a. to annoy
      b. to appease
      c. to embroil
      d. to mislead

_____ 2. It is amazing that
      a. it took so long to raise enough money to build the monument
      b. visitors to the memorial become so loud and excited
      c. the memorial grounds remain quiet even when they are crowded
      d. such a small number of people submitted design proposals

_____ 3. We can assume that
      a. the Wall has become a national symbol that has little personal meaning for people who visit it
      b. the memorial depicts the passing of time from the first fatality to the last

  c. Lin's design proposal was popular right from the start

  d. the memorial is located far from other monuments in Washington, D.C.

_____ 4. It is ironic that

  a. a wall has come to symbolize a nation's coming to terms with a difficult chapter in its history

  b. the controversial memorial has endured as a popular tourist attraction

  c. the design submitted by a young architecture student was chosen over designs submitted by world famous architects

  d. all of the above

Some Facts About the Vietnam Wall

Directions: Scan the three previous selections to locate the following specific pieces of information about the Vietnam Memorial. Insert the missing information in the blanks.

1. The Vietnam memorial was designed by _____, an architecture student at _____ University.

2. There were _____ entries submitted in the competition to design the Vietnam Memorial.

3. One wall of the memorial points to the _____ Monument and the other wall to the _____ Memorial.

4. The memorial is made up of _____ (number) polished black _____ slabs.

5. In 1982, a sculpture of three infantrymen by _____ was commissioned.

6. The Vietnam Memorial was the idea of _____, an infantryman wounded in Vietnam.

Determining Point of View

Below is a list of the selections you have just read. For each one, indicate whether the author's point of view about the Vietnam Memorial is primarily positive, negative, or neutral.

1. "Vietnam Memorial" _____

2. "Boundaries" _____

3. "A Quiet Place for Personal Reflection" _____

SELECTION

GETTING THE PICTURE

The poem "The Vietnam Wall" is considered to be a picture poem in that the lines vary in length to express how deaths are recorded on the wall. The poem lines start out very short because few American soldiers died in the beginning of the conflict. In the middle of the poem, the lines are much longer as the recorded deaths grew in number. The lines of the poem are short at the end as the conflict was winding down and there were fewer American deaths.

BIO-SKETCH

Albert Rios has been a professor of English at Arizona State University since 1982. He has received fellowships from the Guggenheim Foundation and the National Endowment for the Arts. In addition, he is the recipient of the Western Literature Association's Distinguished Achievement Award and the Arizona Governor's Arts Award. He has been called "the best Latino poet writing in English today."

BRUSHING UP ON VOCABULARY

headlock a wrestling hold in which the body of one wrestler is rendered immobile by the arm and body of the other wrestler.

The Vietnam Wall

BY ALBERTO RÍOS

I
Have seen it
And I like it: The magic,
The way like cutting onions
It brings water out of nowhere.
Invisible from one side, a scar
Into the skin of the ground
From the other, a black winding
Appendix line.
   A dig.
   An archaeologist can explain.
The walk is slow at first,
Easy, a little black marble wall
Of a dollhouse,
A smoothness, a shine
The boys in the street want to give.
One name. And then more
Names, long lines, lines of names until
They are the shape of the U.N. Building
Taller than I am: I have walked
Into a grave.

And everything I expect has been taken away, like that, quick:
> The names are not alphabetized.
> They are in the order of dying,
> > An alphabet of—somewhere—screaming.

I start to walk out. I almost leave
But stop to look up names of friends,
My own name. There is somebody
Severiano Rios.
Little kids do not make the same noise
Here, junior high school boys don't run
Or hold each other in headlocks.
No rules, something just persists
Like pinching on St. Patrick's Day
Every year for no green.
> No one knows why.
Flowers are forced
Into the cracks
Between sections.
Men have cried
At this wall.
I have
Seen them.

———————————

(Alberto Ríos, "The Vietnam Wall," 1988)

✓ COMPREHENSION CHECKUP

Multiple Choice

Write the letter of the correct answer in the blank provided.

_____ 1. When the author refers to the ground as "skin" he is using
  a. hyperbole
  b. synonym
  c. personification
  d. simile

_____ 2. The author alludes to the number of names recorded on the wall by referring to
  a. a scar and an appendix line
  b. a dollhouse and the U.N. Building
  c. an alphabet
  d. the boys in the street

_____ 3. The author's point of view toward the memorial is
    a. positive
    b. negative

_____ 4. The author alludes to the ability of the memorial to cause sadness on the part of the viewer by using the image of
    a. cutting onions
    b. an archaeologist's dig
    c. the smoothness and shininess of the wall
    d. St. Patrick's Day

_____ 5. The poem states that the names on the Vietnam Wall are listed
    a. in order of importance
    b. by branches of the armed services
    c. by order of death
    d. randomly

_____ 6. The author feels as though he has walked into a grave mostly because
    a. the area surrounding the memorial is dense with foliage
    b. the monument is smooth and shiny like a headstone
    c. the monument slopes downward until the wall is taller than he is
    d. the monument site is quiet

_____ 7. At the monument site, people's behavior is characterized by
    a. laughter and camaraderie
    b. tears and subdued behavior
    c. wrestling and horsing around
    d. fear and intimidation

_____ 8. An alphabet "screaming" is an example of
    a. simile
    b. hyperbole
    c. understatement
    d. personification

_____ 9. Before the author leaves the monument he
    a. cries
    b. looks up the names of friends
    c. looks up his own last name
    d. both b and c

_____ 10. The overall tone of the poem is
    a. nostalgic
    b. solemn
    c. bitter
    d. optimistic

In Your Own Words

1. Why does Ríos look up his own name? What is the significance of his finding the name Severiano Rios?

2. What does the author mean by the image "Invisible from one side, a scar/Into the skin of the ground/From the other, a black winding/Appendix line"?

3. Over the last twenty years, the National Park Service has collected more than 65,000 objects left at the Vietnam Memorial by visitors, including service

medals, combat boots, flowers, poems, and photographs. Some visitors to the memorial place a piece of paper over a name and then draw back and forth with a pencil to make a "rubbing" of it. Why do you think many visitors are so expressive when they visit the memorial?

4. Paul Spreiregen, a Washington-based architect who organized the competition and helped select the judging panel, views Lin's design as an effective symbol: "It's a rift in the earth, as the war was a tear in the fabric of the American experience." Stanley Karrow, author of *Vietnam: A History*, says that the monument "stands as a vivid symbol of both unity and redemption." What do you think the memorial symbolizes?

The Art of Writing

1. Compare and contrast the poem by Ríos to "The Mending Wall" by Robert Frost. How do the poems emphasize the purpose of a wall?

2. In a brief essay, respond to the item below:
   The Vietnam Memorial is often referred to as "the Wall." There are many idiomatic expressions that have the word *wall* in them, such as the walls have ears, one's back to the wall, beat one's head against the wall, climb the walls, drive someone up the wall, fly on the wall, go to the wall, handwriting on the wall, hole in the wall, off the wall, and run into a stone wall. Choose one of these expressions, and explain its meaning.

Internet Activity

1. Go to the following Web site and read one of Alberto Ríos's interviews. Write a summary of what you learned about Ríos.

   www.public.asu.edu/~aarios/

2. Investigate the Virtual Wall at

   www.thevirtualwall.org.

   Write a summary of your findings.

3. Using the Internet, investigate one of the following "walls" and write a summary of your findings.

Wall Street	Wailing Wall
Hadrian's Wall	Great Wall of China
Berlin Wall	

An Introduction to Propaganda Techniques

Webster's dictionary defines **propaganda** as "a systematic effort to promote a particular cause or point of view or to damage an opposing one." Propaganda has evolved to suggest that the information being advanced is purposely false and misleading. Propaganda techniques are ordinarily designed to appeal to the emotions rather than the intellect. The techniques frequently appear in politics to appeal to voters and in advertising to persuade consumers to purchase certain products. A critical thinker has the ability to recognize propaganda techniques and avoid being misled by them.

Following are some common propaganda techniques.

Bandwagon

The bandwagon technique encourages people to think that because a lot of people are doing something or supporting some position, they must do it too or risk being left out. This propaganda device appeals to the "follow the crowd" mentality. Beer commercials often rely on the bandwagon technique.

EXAMPLES:

"Come and get it or miss out." "This is a limited time offer." "Apple sold one million iPads in just 28 days."

Plain Folks

The plain folks technique is commonly used by politicians who are striving to demonstrate that they are just like everybody else. Moreover, advertisers often feature actors or actresses in their commercials who look and sound like ordinary people.

EXAMPLES:

A candidate running for office is shown playing basketball, hunting, grocery shopping, or just hanging out with family members.

Testimonial

A testimonial is similar to an endorsement. Famous athletes or stars are paid to "testify" about a particular product. In addition, well-respected people may endorse a politician who is running for office, or they may help promote a certain position or idea.

EXAMPLES:

Ashton Kutcher endorses Nikon digital cameras, Jennifer Aniston endorses Smartwater, Eva Longoria endorses L'Oreal hair products, and both Drew Barrymore and Ellen Degeneres endorse Covergirl makeup.

Name-calling

This technique consists of attaching a negative label to a person or an idea. It is used widely in political campaigns and in advertising.

EXAMPLES:

My opponent is a flip-flopper who can't make up his mind. First he's for

_____ and then he's against it.

My opponent is an "elitist" who simply doesn't understand the problems of everyday hardworking Americans.

Advertisers tend to be more subtle in their attacks.

EXAMPLE:

Our allergy-relief medication will relieve sneezing and runny nose without causing drowsiness.

This implies that the competitor's brand will cause drowsiness.

Glittering Generality

In this technique, "virtuous words" are used to promote a particular point of view. Words with positive emotional overtones such as "truth," "liberty," "honor," "justice," and "the American way" are often exploited to influence others. Also, "glad words," such as "best," "good," "honest," and "fair," are often deployed to promote a particular product. Because glad words mean different things to different people, statements that employ them can't be proved or disproved.

EXAMPLES:

Americans who want to preserve their liberty will vote against a candidate who supports a tax hike.

Zest is the best toothpaste.

Stereotyping

Stereotyping applies generalizations to whole groups of people. It is linked to prejudice and can easily lead to discrimination.

EXAMPLES:

Girls are not as good in math or science as boys. All blondes and athletes are dumb. The homeless are there by choice. Tall men are natural leaders.

Card Stacking

The term refers to stacking the deck (as in cards) in the speaker's favor. Key facts or statistics are selectively omitted and only the information favorable to a particular point of view is included.

EXAMPLES:

Four of five dentists surveyed prefer new and improved Zest toothpaste.

While the statement may be technically correct, the advertiser is under no obligation to disclose the fact that the four who endorsed Zest were all paid to give their approval.

Zest toothpaste fights gingivitis, brightens your smile, visibly whitens yellow, discolored teeth, and stops bad breath.

The advertiser includes only positive attributes and does not mention that the toothpaste contains chemicals that are potentially harmful.

Transfer

This technique uses symbols that most people revere or love to sell a product, candidate, or idea. The hope is that the good feelings engendered by the symbol will spill over or be transferred. Some common symbols are the American flag, Uncle Sam, and the Statue of Liberty. A politician running for office is usually either wearing a flag pin or photographed with the flag as a backdrop.

EXAMPLE:

A cigarette ad features a man on a horse with a background of blue skies and wide-open spaces.

In this example, the advertiser hopes to create an association between the land and the freedom to do as one pleases as embodied by the cigarette.

Sex Appeal

Sex appeal is frequently used in advertising to sell products. For instance, sexual undertones are present in many beer commercials, which are designed to show how drinking a particular brand will make a man more masculine or more sexually desirable. Ads aimed at women often emphasize caring and romance on the part of men. For example, an attractive husband gives his beloved wife a diamond necklace. Or a young woman shows her friends a diamond engagement ring that her fiancé just purchased from a popular jewelry store.

Music

Music is used to influence emotions in both politics and commercials. Bill Clinton played Fleetwood Mac's "Don't Stop" to great effect in his first presidential campaign. A public appearance by the President is accompanied by the song "Hail to the Chief," which evokes feelings of respect and patriotism. "Like a Rock" by Bob Seger has inspired commercials promoting the toughness of Chevrolet trucks. The popular song "I'd Like to Teach the World to Sing" by the New Seekers ties Coca Cola to feelings of peace and love.

Exercise 3: Identifying Propaganda Techniques

Directions: For each statement, identify the propaganda technique being used. Use each technique only once.

bandwagon	name-calling	stereotyping
card stacking	plain folks	testimonial
glittering generalities	sex appeal	transfer
music		

1. Smartnet—the Internet broker with great information, great service, and great people to help you invest your money wisely. _____

2. "I wouldn't think about banking anywhere else than Dollar Bank." —Sarah Brooks, CEO of True Blue Corporation _____

3. Satin Hand Cream is available without a prescription. For pennies a day, it can make your hands beautiful again. Effectively eliminates dryness, scaliness, and embarrassing age spots. _____

4. Janet Hardworker for Governor—just a small-town gal with a big heart. _____

5. A commercial: A driver zooms away in a black Jaguar accompanied by the music "Born to Be Wild." _____

6. All women are bad drivers. _____

7. My opponent is misguided in his support of vouchers for private schools. His foolish, reckless scheme will bankrupt the public schools. Think again before giving him your vote in November. _____

8. A picture of the Statue of Liberty with the following statement below it: Freedom Insurance will protect your family when they need it the most. _____

9. "All trucks on our lot have to go. We need room for the new inventory. Hurry on down. Don't be left out of this once-in-a-lifetime deal. If you don't try us, we both lose." _____

10. Sexy model purrs, "Nothing comes between me and my blue velvet jeans." _____

11. What propaganda technique does the following cartoon illustrate? _____

"Thank goodness all those negative campaigns are over and done with. Now we can concentrate for the next few years on griping about the winners."

© Steve Benson

12. A typical American, whom we'll call Mary, is watching television and sees a commercial for a prescription drug with a name that sounds like a *Star Wars* planet, such as "Lipitor" or "Zoloft." This commercial shows trained actors pretending to be regular humans just like Mary, ruefully telling the camera how foolish they feel because they failed to ask their doctor about the prescription drug—we'll call it "Endor"—that paid millions of dollars to make the commercial. The commercial does not make it entirely clear what Endor does, but it is clear that if you don't ask your doctor about it, you have the IQ of spinach.

At the end of the commercial, an announcer warns Mary about the possible side effects of Endor, including (but not limited to) headache, nausea, spontaneous combustion of the eyeballs, and death of the patient and the patient's entire extended family. But Mary isn't paying attention to the announcer. She's thinking that, although she feels perfectly healthy, she doesn't want to be the kind of idiot loser who fails to ask her doctor about Endor.

(Dave Barry, *I'll Mature When I'm Dead,* 2010)

What specific propaganda techniques does the paragraph above illustrate?

_____

Brain Teasers

Explain what's humorous about each of these newspaper headlines.

1. Include Your Children When Baking Cookies

_____

2. Police Begin Campaign to Run Down Jaywalkers

_____

3. Stolen Painting Found by Tree

_____

4. Deer Kill 17,000

_____

5. Red Tape Holds Up New Bridges

_____

6. Kids Make Nutritious Snacks

_____

7. Local High School Dropouts Cut in Half

_____

8. New Vaccine May Contain Rabies

_____

9. Hospitals Are Sued by 7 Foot Doctors

_____

VOCABULARY   ## Unit 7: Word Parts Featuring Politics and Religion

"Change is the law of life."

—John Fitzgerald Kennedy

This unit begins with word parts relating to law, politics, and power. It then looks at word parts relating to religious beliefs. The last section covers word parts relating to time.

   Words made from these word parts, along with their definitions, follow. Supplemental words with these word parts are located in the left margin.

legation
legatee
delegation   legis—law; demos—people; polis—city; graph—write
legacy   **legal**   of or based on law; lawful. Comes from the Latin *legis* meaning
legate   "law." Cynthia needed to see a lawyer to find out if her marriage to
relegate   Paul was *legal*.

legislature   a group of people who meet together to write and enact laws. The Florida state *legislature* played an active role in the battle for Florida's electoral votes during the presidential race between Al Gore and George W. Bush.

legitimate   allowed by law or custom; being justifiable. He had a *legitimate* claim to ownership of the land.

illegitimate   against the laws or rules

democracy   *Demos* means "the people" in Greek, so *democracy* means "government by the people"

demography   Literally, *demography* means "writing about people." It is the science of vital and social statistics, concerned with such things as the births, deaths, diseases, marriages, and the educational level of a population. A *demographer* gathers data, such as in the census we take every ten years, and then compiles that data into maps and charts. A *demographic* map might show income levels in different areas of a city or county.

The following words come from the Greek word *polis*, which means "city-state." In ancient Greece, each city was a state unto itself because there was no greater political authority.

megalopolis   **political**   In ancient Greece, each city-state was responsible for its own *political* or governmental affairs. Today, the word also refers to *political* parties, such as Libertarian, Republican, Democratic, or Green.
politic
politicize

politician   a person who is active in politics as a career; a seeker or holder of public office

cracy—rule, strength, power; archy—rule; auto—self, by oneself; theo—god

anarchy   the complete absence of government or the rule of law

monarchy   government by one person, usually a king, queen, or emperor. Monaco is an example of a *monarchy*.

aristocracy   **autocracy**   government in which one person has all the power. *auto-* means "self or by one's self." Germany under Adolf Hitler was an *autocracy*. Hitler was an *autocrat*.
bureaucracy

oligarchy   a form of government in which power is vested in a few persons

plutocracy   a government in which the wealthy class rules

patriarchy   an institution or organization in which power is held by males and passed on through males, quite often from father to son

matriarchy   a family, society, or state governed by women or in which a woman is the dominant member of the group. The Navajo nation is a *matriarchy*.

theocracy   *theo-* means "god," so a *theocracy* means "rule by God." A *theocracy* is a government that claims to be based on divine authority.

agogos—lead, bring together, excite; potis—powerful; syn—same

demagog(ue)	according to its word parts, a *demagogue* is a person who leads and excites people, or a person who gains power by arousing people's emotions and prejudices. The word usually has a negative connotation. Hitler was a *demagogue*.
synagogue	a building where Jews gather for worship and religious study. The literal meaning is "a place to which people are brought together or led to." The origin of the word *synagogue* may date back to the sixth century B.C.E. when the Jewish people were in exile in Babylon. Formal worship in a temple was impossible, so the Jewish people began to meet in members' homes. These homes became the first *synagogues*.
potent	having great power; having a strong effect on the body or mind; producing powerful physical or chemical effects. The doctor told the patient that she needed some *potent* medicine.
potential	capable of coming into being but not yet actual. He had the *potential* to become a great swimmer.
potentate	a person having great power; a ruler or monarch. The sultan was a very wealthy *potentate*.

deus—god; sanct—holy; sacri—holy; ology—study of, -ism, doctrine, or theory

theology	the study of God and religious beliefs
atheism	the belief that there is no god
monotheism	the belief that there is only one god. Judaism, Christianity, and Islam are *monotheistic* religions.
polytheism	the belief in more than one god. The ancient Greeks were *polytheists*. Their gods included Zeus, Athena, and Apollo.
deity	a god or goddess. The ancient Greeks and Romans believed in many *deities*.
deify	to make a god of. In ancient Rome, the emperors were often *deified*.
sanctuary	a sacred or holy place; a place of protection, shelter, or refuge. The World Wildlife *Sanctuary* was created to provide a home for animal species in danger of extinction.
sanctify	to make saintly or holy
sanction	approval given by someone in authority. The students formed a club with the *sanction* of the school administration.
sacred	holy or set apart for some religious purpose; not to be broken or ignored. She took a *sacred* vow to become a nun.
sacrament	a sacred ceremony in Christian churches, such as baptism and Holy Communion. A *sacrament* was originally an oath of allegiance taken by a Roman soldier.

chrono—time; temp—time, moderate; ana—back, up, again

chronic	**chronology**	the science or study of measuring time; arranging events in the sequence in which they happened. What was the *chronology* of events for the assassination of President Kennedy?

synchronize According to its word parts, *synchronize* means "at the same time." We need to *synchronize* our watches so that we can meet at the restaurant at the same time. *Synchronized* swimming is an Olympic event.

anachronism The literal meaning is "back in time"; anything that is out of its proper time in history is an *anachronism*. Using a horse and buggy for transportation is an *anachronism* in the United States today.

chronicle to tell or write the story of; a *chronological* record of events; a history. Lewis and Clark *chronicled* their adventures as they made their way to the Pacific Northwest.

chronometer a device for measuring time; a clock or watch. A stop watch is one kind of *chronometer*.

extemporaneous
temporal
temporize

temporary lasting or effective for a short time only. She worked at Macy's as *temporary* help during the Christmas holidays.

contemporary existing or happening in the same period of time; a person living in the same period as another. George W. Bush and Bill Clinton are *contemporaries*.

temper a mood or state of mind; also, to moderate. He was in a foul *temper* after he wrecked his brand-new car. The passing years *tempered* his rashness.

temperate neither very hot nor very cold; moderate. Hawaii has a *temperate* climate.

temperance moderation in one's actions, appetites, or feelings; drinking few, if any, alcoholic beverages. Is a lifestyle that emphasizes *temperance* healthier?

Now that you have studied the vocabulary in Unit 7, practice your new knowledge by completing the crossword puzzle on the next page.

Vocabulary Unit 7 Puzzle

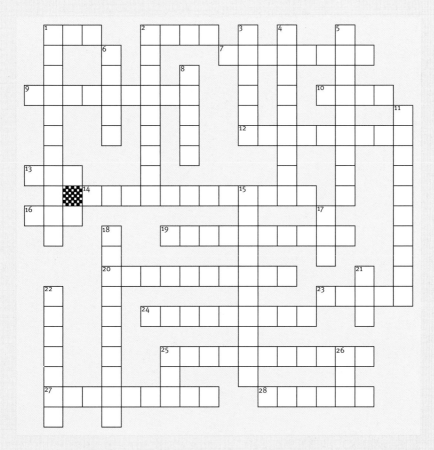

ACROSS CLUES

1. A word part meaning "with."*
2. A word part meaning "god."
7. Rule by one person, usually a king or queen.
9. A person with great power; a ruler.
10. A word part meaning "many."*
12. The climate in Vilcabamba, Ecuador, is a _____ 70 degrees Fahrenheit all year long.
13. A word part meaning "child."*
14. The U.N. considered the dictator's government to be _____ because he seized power from the lawfully elected president.
16. A word part meaning "come."*
19. Alex would like to run for political office. Many people think he would be a good _____.
20. The belief in only one god.
23. To make a god of.
24. A country governed by a few people is an _____.
25. A typewriter is an _____ today.
27. Churches have historically given _____ to those in trouble.
28. A word part meaning "time."

DOWN CLUES

1. A wristwatch is an example of a _____.
2. A person who "leads and excites people."
3. Snow White ate an apple that contained a _____ poison that put her into a deathlike sleep.
4. Zachary received the _____ of baptism when he was two months old.
5. Rule by god.
6. A word part meaning "holy."
8. It is not _____ to park close to a fire hydrant.
11. The literal meaning is "to write about people."
15. Where a woman is the dominant member of the society.
17. A word part meaning "head."*
18. _____ advocates proposed laws that would outlaw the sale of alcohol.
21. A word part meaning "across."*
22. The belief that there is no god.
25. A word part meaning "back."
26. A word part meaning "same."

*From a previous unit.

Bias

The Uprising (L'Emeute) (1848 or later) *BY HONORÉ DAUMIER*

The Phillips Collection, Washington, D.C.

View and Reflect

This painting depicts a scene from a revolution. According to Duncan Phillips, who purchased the painting in 1931, *Uprising* stands as a "symbol for all pent-up human indignation."

1. What emotion is the man with the raised fist expressing? What is the significance of his casual dress?
2. Is the crowd standing still or advancing? How can you tell?
3. Is there anything in this painting that could relate to the war for American independence?

Introduction to Bias

A **bias** is a strong leaning in either a positive or a negative direction. Bias is very similar to prejudice. Good critical readers must be aware of their own biases and the biases of others.

Sometimes writers simply state their biases; however, most biases are implied by the writer. Subjective material generally places more emphasis on opinions than facts, and it is more likely to display a strong bias.

A critical reader will study the author's line of reasoning, notice whether opinions are supported by facts and reasons, and then decide if the author's bias has hindered the making of a good argument.

Look at the following cartoon. Does the person in the first frame express a bias?

Carlson Cartoon, "I'm sick of all these immigrants . . ." (Art, 1e, p. 337) CARLSON © 2000 Milwaukee Sentinel.
Reprinted with permission of Universal Uclick. All rights reserved.

As you are reading textbook material, keep in mind that the authors also have biases. Their biases will influence the way they present the material. Although textbooks primarily deal with factual material, authors must decide what facts to include, omit, and emphasize. Pay attention to the author's tone and choice of words to determine whether he or she is biased. Such caution is especially important when the material deals with a controversial issue.

Two interesting and important personalities in the early history of the United States were John Adams and Alexander Hamilton. In 1789, George Washington was unanimously elected our first president, Adams became our first vice-president, and Hamilton became our first secretary of the treasury. Hamilton resigned from the cabinet in 1795, during Washington's second term. Adams was elected the second president in 1797 and served one term. Adams and Hamilton, both instrumental in the founding of the United States, came to have an increasing dislike for each other.

Read the following two quotes from two different history textbooks, and decide which example gives the reader a more negative view of Alexander Hamilton.

EXAMPLE 1

Hamilton even secretly plotted with certain members of the cabinet against President Adams, who had a conspiracy rather than a cabinet on his hands.

(Thomas A. Bailey, et al., *American Pageant*, 1998)

EXAMPLE 2

Although Hamilton had resigned from the Treasury Department in 1795, key members of Adams's cabinet turned to the former secretary for advice.

(James West Davidson, et al., *Nation of Nations*, 2001)

The first quote appears to portray Hamilton in a far more sinister way. The words *plotted* and *conspiracy* are examples of words with strong negative feelings.

Exercise 1: Predicting Bias from Titles

Directions: The following is a list of actual book titles. Read through the list and place a check mark before the titles that are likely to be biased.

_____ 1. *Just How Stupid Are We? Facing the Truth About the American Voter* by Rick Shenkman

_____ 2. *A Field Guide to Household Bugs* by Joshua Abarbanel

_____ 3. *The Dumbest Generation: How the Digital Age Stupefies Young Americans and Jeopardizes Our Future (Or, Don't Trust Anyone Under 30)* by Mark Bauerlein

_____ 4. *American Sketches* by Walter Isaacson

_____ 5. *Day of Reckoning: How Hubris, Ideology, and Greed Are Tearing America Apart* by Patrick J. Buchanan

_____ 6. *Traffic: Why We Drive the Way We Do* by Tom Vanderbilt

_____ 7. *Let Their Spirits Dance* by Stella Pope Duarte

_____ 8. *The Read-Aloud Handbook* by Jim Trelease

_____ 9. *Signs and Symbols: The Complete Encyclopedia* by Mark O'Connell and Raje Airey

_____ 10. *The Langston Hughes Reader* by George Braziller

_____ 11. *Bright-Sided: How the Relentless Promotion of Positive Thinking Has Undermined America* by Barbara Ehrenreich

_____ 12. *The Trouble with Boys* by Peg Tyre

"Thanks to words we have been able to rise above the brutes; and thanks to words we have often sunk to the level of demons."

—Aldous Huxley

Denotative and Connotative Language

When you look a word up in the dictionary, you are determining its exact meaning, without the suggestions or implications that it may have taken on. This is called the

denotative meaning of a word. In contrast, the **connotative** meaning of a word refers to the ideas or feelings suggested by the word.

Words that have the same denotative meaning can have much different connotative meanings. The words *cautious* and *timorous*, for example, have similar denotative meanings, but their connotative meanings are very different. *Cautious* has a positive ring. It's good to be "cautious," isn't it? The word *timorous*, however, has a more negative connotative meaning. It suggests fearfulness or reluctance. The words *firm*, *resolute*, and *obstinate* all have similar denotative meanings. Which of these words has the more negative connotation?

Not all words have connotative meanings. The words *pen* and *pencil*, for example, do not evoke strong emotions. Words that are heavily connotative are often referred to as "loaded" or "emotionally charged." Writers who have a particular point of view and want to persuade you to accept that view often make use of loaded words or phrases. Thus, subjective material is more likely to rely on heavily connotative language, and it is more likely to display a strong bias. If a writer approves of a city's monetary policy toward libraries, the word *thrifty* might be used. If the writer disagrees with the policy, the word *cheap*, which calls up negative feelings, might be used instead. The connotation of the words used can tell you a lot about the speaker or writer's opinion.

Exercise 2: Recognizing Connotative Meaning

Directions: Which of the following words in each group is the most positive? Write that word on the line.

1. _____ resolute, stubborn, unyielding

2. _____ timid, wary, cautious

3. _____ bizarre, eccentric, nutty

4. _____ old-fashioned, traditional, out-of-date

5. _____ obnoxious, abrasive, self-assertive

6. _____ thin, slim, scrawny

7. _____ miserly, cheap, thrifty

8. _____ foolhardy, courageous, vainglorious

9. _____ curious, nosy, officious

10. _____ solemn, dignified, glum

Exercise 3: Identifying Connotative Language

Directions: What are the three connotative words in the cartoon on page 383? Put these three connotative words in order from the most positive to the most negative.

1. _____

2. _____

3. _____

Exercise 4: Using Connotative Language

Well-known linguist S. I. Hayakawa developed the idea of "conjugating irregular verbs" to demonstrate how connotative language works. With Hayakawa's method, an action or a personality trait is "conjugated" to show how it can be viewed either favorably or unfavorably depending on the "spin" we put on it. Study the examples and then complete activity.

For example:

    I'm casual.

    You're a little careless.

    He's a slob.

Or:

    I'm thrifty.

    You're money conscious.

    She's a cheapskate.

Try a few of these conjugations yourself.

1. I'm tactful. _____

2. I'm conservative. _____

3. I'm relaxed. _____

4. I'm quiet. _____

5. I'm proud. _____

Exercise 5: Identifying Bias in Textbook Material

Directions: Read each paragraph. Then choose the best answer for each item.

A.   Elephants, like humans, grieve, cry from frustration and sadness, and help
     one another. They have a long childhood and remain with their mothers for
     fifteen years. They are sensitive, intelligent, and affectionate, and they long
     for social relationships. Now try to imagine one of these magnificent crea-
     tures in complete isolation, spending its entire life in either a small cage or
     the back of a truck, being moved from city to city. Confined, chained, and
     caged, the elephant quickly learns the futility and brutal repercussion of pro-
     testing. Picture this dignified and social animal responding to this isolation
     and lack of space. Pacing, weaving, rocking, sucking, or chewing on the steel
     bars of the cage are the animals' response to monotony and loneliness. Many,
     of course, simply go mad.

     (Larry A. Samovar, *Oral Communication: Speaking Across Culture,* 10/e, 1998)

     _____ 1. The author is most opposed to which of the following?
               a. depriving an elephant of its mother
               b. moving elephants from city to city
               c. depriving an elephant of companionship and space
               d. depriving an elephant of peanuts

     _____ 2. The choice of the words "futility and brutal repercussion of protest-
               ing" suggest that
               a. the elephant will be sent to a zoo if it causes trouble
               b. the elephant will be dealt with harshly if it protests
               c. the elephant will not be allowed to socialize with other elephants
                   if it does not behave
               d. elephants will not receive treats if they cause trouble

B.   There it was—the ship from New York bobbing down the Atlantic Coast and
     through the Caribbean. It was a 3,100-ton barge loaded with unwanted trash.
     After 41 days and more than 2,000 smelly miles at sea, the barge was still
     searching for a home. With an end to its odious odyssey nowhere in sight, the
     scow raised once again the dilemma of a throwaway society, quickly running
     out of room for all its solid waste.

     (Larry A. Samovar, *Oral Communication: Speaking Across Culture,* 10/e, 1998)

     _____ 1. In this paragraph, the author expresses disgust for
               a. large barges
               b. a society that does not reuse and recycle materials
               c. smelly trash
               d. New Yorkers

     _____ 2. Which phrase best expresses the author's disapproval?
               a. "bobbing down the Atlantic Coast"
               b. "throwaway society, quickly running out of room"
               c. "2,000 smelly miles at sea"
               d. "solid waste"

C.   One of history's most tragic figures, Wolfgang Amadeus Mozart began his per-
     forming career as a child prodigy. He played the piano (still something of a

novelty in his day), harpsichord, organ, and violin beautifully, and was taken by his father on a number of concert tours through several European countries. The young performer delighted his noble audiences, but was rewarded with flattery and pretty gifts rather than fees. Mercilessly prodded by his self-seeking father, upon whom he remained emotionally dependent most of his life, Mozart constantly sought to please his parent (who was never satisfied), his wife (demanding and ungrateful), his public (appreciative but ungenerous), and finally himself (who never doubted his own genius). Though fun-loving, sociable, and generous to a fault, Mozart never learned the art of getting along with people. He could not refrain from offering honest but unsolicited criticism; nor could he bring himself to flatter a potential patron. Fiercely independent, he insisted upon managing his own affairs, although he was quite incapable of doing so. Few besides Mozart's great contemporary Haydn appreciated the true worth of this man who wrote such quantities of beautiful music in such a short time. Mozart lived a short and difficult life, and now lies buried in an unmarked grave.

(Jean Ferris, *Music the Art of Listening*, 7/e, 2008)

_____ 1. Which statement best expresses the main point the author is trying to convey about Mozart's life?
   a. [Mozart] was rewarded with flattery and pretty gifts rather than fees."
   b. "Mozart lived a short and difficult life . . ."
   c. "[Mozart] began his performing career as a child prodigy."
   d. "Mozart constantly sought to please his parent . . ."

_____ 2. In this paragraph, the author expresses disapproval of all the following *except*
   a. Mozart's father
   b. Mozart's wife
   c. Mozart's mother
   d. Mozart's public

D. There are hundreds of fad diets and diet books, but such diets are usually unbalanced and may result in serious illness or even death. Fad diets cannot be maintained for long periods; therefore, the individual usually regains any lost weight. Less than 5 percent of people who lose weight maintain the loss for more than a year. Constant losing and gaining, known as the "yo-yo syndrome," may be as harmful as the original overweight condition.

(Charles B. Corbin, *Concepts of Fitness and Wellness*, 7/e, 2008)

_____ 1. The author is opposed to
   a. fruits and vegetables
   b. fad diets
   c. constant losing and gaining of weight
   d. both b and c

_____ 2. The author would agree that
   a. fad diets are often popularized by celebrities
   b. fad diets are a good way to maintain a healthy weight
   c. fad diets are likely to be unhealthy
   d. if persons lose weight by means of a fad diet, it is likely they will maintain the weight loss for at least several years

E.　You should know that the gap between the earnings of high school graduates and college graduates, which is growing every year, now ranges to more than 80 percent. According to the U.S. Census Bureau, the holders of bachelor's degrees will make an average of $51,206 per year as opposed to just $27,915 for high school graduates. That's a whopping additional $23,291 a year. Thus, what you invest in a college education is likely to pay you back many times. That doesn't mean there aren't good careers available to non-college graduates. It just means that those with an education are more likely to have higher earnings over their lifetime. But the value of a college education is more than just a larger paycheck. Other benefits include increasing your ability to think critically and communicate your ideas to others, improving your ability to use technology, and preparing yourself to live in a diverse world. Knowing you've met your goals and earned a college degree also gives you the self-confidence to continue to strive to meet your future goals.

(William G. Nickels, et al., *Understanding Business*, 8/e, 2008)

_____ 1. The author would agree that
　　　a.　college is a waste of time for many people
　　　b.　college is a good investment
　　　c.　it is unlikely that in the future there will be an earnings gap between those who choose to attend college and those who do not
　　　d.　students are unlikely to recover their original investment in a college education

_____ 2. The author would disagree with which of the following statements?
　　　a.　A college education is unlikely to develop critical thinking skills.
　　　b.　A college degree is unlikely to contribute to a feeling of self-confidence.
　　　c.　A college education is unlikely to prepare a student to live in a diverse, technical world.
　　　d.　All of the above

F.　Let us imagine that you are feeling good as you take a long, deep puff on your cigarette. But let us add a touch of realism to this scene by asking you to also picture what your body is doing with this invisible and sinister chemical as it invades your body. Your gums and teeth are the first recipients of the poisonous chemical. While the smoke pays but a short visit to your mouth it is leaving enough pollution to increase the risk of painful gum diseases and the agony of mouth and throat cancer. But this is just the beginning. As the smoke continues its journey into your unsuspecting lungs, you will soon find that your breathing is shallow and impaired, for now the smoke deposits insidious toxins that, after a period of time, will increase your chances of crippling and deadly cancer. Your stomach too will experience the effects of this corrupt and silent killer. While you cannot see them, small bits of acid are coating your stomach, adding to the chances that you will develop lacerated ulcers. Think about all this the next time you decide that it is okay to take one little puff of this cleverly concealed stick of dynamite.

(Larry A. Samovar, *Oral Communications: Speaking Across Culture*, 10/e, 1998)

_____ 1. Which phrase expresses the author's bias against smoking?
　　　a.　"invisible and sinister chemical"
　　　b.　"agony of mouth and throat cancer"
　　　c.　"corrupt and silent killer"
　　　d.　all of the above

_____ 2. The author would agree that
   a. smoking is on the rise with young teens
   b. young girls smoke to keep from gaining weight
   c. smoking is not a healthful activity
   d. smoking is such a pleasurable activity that it is worth the risk of cancer and other diseases

Exercise 6: Identifying Bias

Directions: Read the following accounts of a confrontation between women faculty members and the administration of a local college. The first description is biased in favor of the women, and the second is biased against them. Circle the biased or loaded words in both accounts, and then write an objective or unbiased account of the event using neutral words.

1.   This past week, 25 female faculty members struck a blow against male dominance and caught the attention of Wellstone College's sexist administration for three hours. The well-justified protest was organized by those hard-working female teachers in the trenches who are forced to cope with degrading working conditions, unfair salary scales, and lack of promotional opportunities. Embarrassed administrators watched in disgrace as the teachers organized a peaceful, orderly picket line in front of the administration building. The teachers carried placards and talked calmly and earnestly to passersby. Many passersby voiced support of the protest. When the media arrived, an apologetic college vice president rushed forward to agree to form a committee to study the group's modest demands and to immediately curtail discriminatory policies. The group's success serves as an inspiration to oppressed female employees everywhere.

2.   An outlandish protest was lodged against the administration of Wellstone College on November 15. A group of irate female faculty disgraced themselves by milling about in front of the administration building. They thrust placards in the faces of passersby and railed against supposed inequities in hiring, wages, working conditions, and promotion of female faculty. It required a great deal of patience and diplomacy on the part of the college vice president to maintain control of the disturbance and to soothe the group's hurt feelings. Speaking in a dignified manner, the vice president promised to evaluate the teachers' claims in a calmer, more appropriate setting. Judging from the chorus of boos that were heard, it appears that the ladies have done a grave disservice to themselves and to the college with their immoderate demands and juvenile, attention-seeking behavior.

_____

_____

_____

_____

_____

_____

SELECTION

> *"(Children) are spoken of as a responsibility, a legal*
> *liability, or an encumbrance."*

GETTING THE PICTURE

The following excerpt is taken from the essay "Somebody's Baby," which appears in the book *High Tides in Tucson* by Barbara Kingsolver. Carefully read the excerpt to determine the author's bias. As you read, think about your own opinion of how we treat children in the United States. Also think about how your opinion might affect your interpretation of this reading selection.

BIO-SKETCH

Barbara Kingsolver, a full-time writer since 1987, was born in Annapolis, Maryland, in 1955 and received her B.A. from Depaux University and her M.S. from the University of Arizona. Her first novel, *Bean Trees*, published in 1988, was a highly acclaimed book portraying relationships among women. Kingsolver has received numerous awards for her books, articles, and poetry. In 2000, she was awarded the National Humanities Medal, honoring her for her service to the arts.

BRUSHING UP ON VOCABULARY

foot the bill pay the bill; settle the accounts

Excerpt from

Somebody's Baby

BY BARBARA KINGSOLVER

In the U.S.A., where it's said that anyone can grow up to be President, we parents are left   1
pretty much on our own when it comes to the Presidents-in-training. Our social programs for children are the hands-down worst in the industrialized world, but apparently
that is just what we want as a nation. It took a move to another country (Spain) to make
me realize how thoroughly I had accepted my nation's creed of every family for itself.
Whenever my daughter crash-landed in the playground, I was startled at first to see a
sanguine, Spanish-speaking stranger pick her up and dust her off. And if a shrieking
bundle landed at *my* feet, I'd furtively look around for the next of kin. But I quickly came
to see this detachment as perverse when applied to children, and am wondering how it
ever caught on in the first place.

My grandfathers on both sides lived in households that were called upon, after   2
tragedy struck close to home, to take in orphaned children and raise them without a
thought. In an era of shortage, this was commonplace. But one generation later that
kind of semi-permeable household had vanished, at least among the white middle
class. It's a horrifying thought, but predictable enough, that the worth of children in

America is tied to their dollar value. Children used to be field hands, household help, even miners and factory workers—extensions of a family's productive potential and so in a sense, the property of an extended family. But *precious* property, valued and coveted. Since the advent of child-labor laws, children have come to hold an increasingly negative position in the economy. They're spoken of as a responsibility, a legal liability, or an encumbrance. The political shuffle seems to be about making sure they cost as little as possible, and that their own parents foot the bill. Virtually every program that benefits children in this county, from *Sesame Street* to free school lunches, has been cut back in the last decade—in many cases, cut to nothing. If it takes a village to raise a child, our kids are knocking on a lot of doors where nobody seems to be home. . . .

If we intend to cleave like stubborn barnacles to our great American ethic of every 3 nuclear family for itself, then each of us had better raise and educate offspring enough to give us each day, in our old age, our daily bread. If we don't wish to live by bread alone, we'll need not only a farmer and a cook in the family, but also a home repair specialist, an auto mechanic, an accountant, an import-export broker, a forest ranger, a therapist, an engineer, a musician, a poet, a tailor, a doctor, and at least threes shifts of nurses. If that seems impractical, then we can accept other people's kids into our lives, starting now.

(Barbara Kingsolver, *High Tide in Tucson*, 1995)

 COMPREHENSION CHECKUP

Short Answer

1. What is Kingsolver's main idea? _____

_____

2. What is Kingsolver's bias about the way the U.S. treats children?

_____

_____

3. To what extent does Kingsolver rely on facts to support her opinions?

_____

4. Give some examples of Kingsolver's use of connotative language to support her

arguments. _____

_____

Vocabulary in Context

Directions: Find the words in paragraph 1 that mean:

1. cheerful; confident _____

2. a state of being aloof; disinterested _____

3. characterized by machine production _____

4. in a stealthy manner; sneaky _____

5. statement of beliefs; principles _____

6. deviating from what is considered right or good _____

Find the words in paragraph 2 that mean:

1. wanted ardently _____

2. ordinary _____

3. an obstruction; a burden _____

4. arrival; coming _____

5. a period of ten years _____

Find the words in paragraph 3 that mean:

1. a system of moral standards _____

2. to bring in goods from another country to sell _____

3. a basic social unit consisting of parents and their children living in one household

_____

4. to adhere; cling to _____

5. to send goods to another country for sale _____

6. a saltwater shellfish that attaches itself to rocks, ship bottoms, etc. _____

In Your Own Words

Considering that Kingsolver's purpose is to persuade the reader to accept her point of view, did she change your opinion on this issue?

The Art of Writing

1. What further information would you like to have to be able to better evaluate Kingsolver's thesis?

2. Create a slogan or bumper sticker that expresses Kingsolver's point of view. Example: "Kids are people too."

Internet Activity

Did you know that Kingsolver wrote her first novel in a closet? Consult her official Web site to find out more about her writing career. To read about her early years, click on: About Barbara: Biography. Then write a short biographical sketch or profile about her.

www.kingsolver.com

Euphemism

The word **euphemism** is derived from the Greek word *euphemos*, meaning "to use a good word for an evil or unfavorable word." The Greek prefix *eu* means "good," and *phemi* means "speak."

When someone substitutes an inoffensive word or phrase for one that could be offensive to someone, they are using a euphemism. Most of the time euphemisms are used to be polite or to avoid controversy. The result is often a more positive connotation, such as when a garbage collector is referred to as a "sanitation engineer" or a clerk is referred to as a "junior executive."

Euphemisms can also be used to mislead or obscure the truth. For example, we could say that a worker was fired, dismissed, terminated, or sacked. Or, as often happens, we could soften the blow by saying that the worker was "furloughed," "discontinued," "out-placed," "made redundant," "uninstalled," or "riffed" (an acronym for reduction in force). With big layoffs, when lots of workers are let go, we could take the responsibility away from the employer or employee, and place it instead on economic or market forces. In such cases, we might refer to "downsizing," "workforce adjustments," and "releasing resources."

Exercise 7: Identifying Euphemisms

Directions: Rewrite the paragraph below by substituting more direct and frank language for the italicized euphemisms.

I was driving down the street in my *preowned vehicle* when I came upon a *pavement deficiency*. As a result I *made contact with* the car in front of me. The other car was being driven by a *senior citizen* who yelled at me angrily. I immediately started to *perspire* because I was afraid I would be late getting to the *memorial park*. When I spoke to the policeman who arrived shortly I *stretched the truth* a little about the speed I was going, but he issued me a ticket anyway. I don't know how I'm going to be able to pay the ticket, because I was recently *terminated* from my job and I am currently *financially embarrassed*. I did, however, arrive in time to see the *deceased,* my pet cat, *laid to rest*. He had *passed on* because a *mixed breed dog* not on a leash had attacked him. I noticed that the *animal control warden* had come to pay his respects. It had been a hard day and so I headed to a *cocktail lounge* to meet friends.

SELECTION

"What, exactly, is adult content?"

GETTING THE PICTURE

What do you think the intent is behind the use of the euphemisms "adult content" and "adult language"? Are they meant to be descriptive? Or are they meant to purposely obscure the truth?

BIO-SKETCH

Bob Greene, a former syndicated columnist for the *Chicago Tribune,* is the best-selling author of *Duty: A Father, His Son, and the Man Who Won the War.*

BRUSHING UP ON VOCABULARY

mayhem random or deliberate violence; rowdy disorder. The word derives from the old French *maim.* In the nineteenth century, the word acquired the meaning of "chaos."

paradoxical a seemingly contradictory statement that expresses a possible truth. The word comes from Greek *paradoxon,* which means "contrary opinion."

sheepish embarrassed or bashful; like a sheep, as in meekness.

Excerpt from

Chevrolet Summers,
Dairy Queen Nights
BY BOB GREENE

Adults Only

It's one of the great untruths of our times, and it is so common that it passes without 1 notice.

You see it—or some variation of it—on television screens, in movie advertise- 2 ments, on the labels of recorded music. The wording goes something like this:

"Adult content." Or: "Contains adult language." 3

Few people ever stop to think about what this means. What, exactly, is adult 4 content? What words constitute adult language?

In our contemporary culture, adult content usually means that people are shown 5 attacking each other with guns, hatchets and blowtorches; that half-naked people are assaulting other people, ripping their clothes off, treating humans like garbage; that people are detonating other people's cars and houses, setting fire to property, blud-geoning and disemboweling and pumping holes in one another. That's adult content; that's how adults behave.

Adult language? Adult language, by our current definition, consists of the foulest 6 synonyms for excrement, for sexual activity, for deviant content. Adult language usu-ally consists of four letters; adult language is the kind of language that civilized people are never supposed to use.

It makes you wonder what lesson we are sending—not only to children, but to 7 ourselves. If a TV show or motion picture concerned itself with responsible adults treating each other and the people around them with kindness, with consideration, with thoughtfulness, that TV show or movie would never be labeled as containing adult content. If a TV show or movie dealt quietly and responsibly with as many choices of conscience and generosity that adults face every day in the world, it would not warrant an "adult content" rating.

Similarly, if a movie featured adults talking with each other civilly, never resorting 8 to gutter language or obscenities, choosing their words with care and precision, no one would ever think to describe the dialogue as "adult." A cable TV show or a music CD in which every word spoken or sung was selected to convey a thought or emotion without resorting to cheap and offensive vulgarities—that TV show or that CD would never be labeled as containing adult language.

We seem to be so sheepish about what our culture has become—so reluctant to 9 concede the debasement of society—that we have decided to declare that darkness is light, that down is up, that wrong is right. We are sending a clear signal to young people: The things in our world that are violent, that are crude, that are dull and mean-spirited are the things that are considered "adult." The words that children are taught not to say because they are ugly and foul are "adult language." As if they are something to strive for, to grow into.

What is the solution? Truth in packaging might be a good idea, although it will 10 never happen. No movie studio that has hired a top-money action star to headline in a film that consists of explosions, bloodshed and gore would ever agree to describe the movie truthfully. The lie of "adult content" is acceptable to Hollywood; the true label of "pathetic, moronic content, suitable for imbeciles" will never see the light of day.

Language? The movie studios, cable channels, and record labels can live with the 11 inaccurate euphemism of "adult language." To phrase it honestly—"infantile, igno-rant, pitiful language"—would remove a certain sheen from a big-budget entertain-ment project.

Ours is becoming a society in which the best ideals of childhood—innocence, 12 kindness, lack of spitefulness, rejection of violence—are qualities toward which adults ought to strive. A paradoxical society in which the things labeled "adult"—lack of restraint, conscienceless mayhem, vulgarity, raw and cynical carnality—are the things that children should be warned against growing up to embrace.

So perhaps we should learn to read the current "adult" warning labels in a differ- 13 ent way. "Adult content" on a movie or television show should be read as a warning against becoming the kind of adult who welcomes such things into his or her life. The "adult language" label on a TV show or CD should be read as a genuine kind of warn-ing to children about becoming the sort of adult who chooses to speak that way.

Then there is "For Mature Audiences Only," but that will have to wait for another 14 day. . . .

(Bob Greene, *Chevrolet Summers, Dairy Queen Nights*, 1997)

✓ COMPREHENSION CHECKUP

Multiple Choice

Write the letter of the correct answer in the space provided.

_____ 1. We can infer that the writer probably feels that
   a. we are sending the wrong message to our children
   b. entertainment today depicts responsible adults
   c. children might as well get used to hearing obscenities

_____ 2. When Greene says, "That's adult content; that's how adults behave" in paragraph 5, he is being
   a. admiring
   b. sarcastic
   c. humorous

_____ 3. The dominant tone throughout is
   a. playful
   b. offended
   c. nostalgic

_____ 4. The author's point of view toward the current use of the term "adult content" in labeling contemporary entertainment is
   a. favorable
   b. unfavorable
   c. neutral

_____ 5. We can infer that Greene is not fond of
   a. entertainment that glorifies violence
   b. entertainment that features human beings treating each other with kindness and consideration.
   c. entertainment that features big-budget stars

_____ 6. The words "pathetic, moronic content, suitable for imbeciles" in paragraph 10 have a
   a. positive connotation
   b. negative connotation
   c. neutral meaning

_____ 7. The phrase "never see the light of day" in paragraph 10 means
   a. it will take place at night
   b. it's not going to happen
   c. it might or might not happen

_____ 8. As used in paragraph 11, _sheen_ most nearly means
   a. beauty
   b. luster
   c. opulence

_____ 9. Greene feels strongly that the word _adult_
   a. should not be used to describe behavior that is immature, destructive, or degrading
   b. is an apt description of violent or vulgar content
   c. has nothing to do with mass entertainment

_____ 10. Greene in the last paragraph implies that
   a. he prefers to see movies that appeal to mature audiences
   b. he likes to see old classics
   c. the word "mature" is also being used euphemistically

Vocabulary in Context

In the space provided, write the letter for the word or phrase that gives the best definition of the italicized word as used in the selection.

_____ 1. "What words _constitute_ adult language?"
   a. restrict
   b. appoint

     c. form; make up

     d. challenge

_____ 2. "In our *contemporary* culture . . ."

     a. simultaneous

     b. recently produced visual art

     c. modern; of the present time

     d. a person at nearly the same age as another

_____ 3. ". . . it would not *warrant* an 'adult content' rating."

     a. defeat

     b. vouch for

     c. hasten

     d. justify

_____ 4. ". . . choosing their words with care and *precision* . . ."

     a. scientific exactness

     b. accuracy

     c. strict observance

     d. mechanical exactness

_____ 5. ". . . was selected to *convey* a thought or emotion . . ."

     a. carry from one place to another

     b. communicate; impart

     c. transport

     d. take away secretly

_____ 6. "The things in our world that are violent, that are *crude* . . ."

     a. in a raw or unrefined state

     b. rudimentary or undeveloped

     c. showing a lack of completeness

     d. vulgar

_____ 7. "As if they are something to *strive for*, to grow into."

     a. make strenuous efforts toward a goal

     b. contend in opposition; compete

     c. struggle vigorously; as in resistance

     d. rival; vie

_____ 8. ". . . the true label of *pathetic*, moronic content . . . "

     a. sad; sorrowful; mournful

     b. causing or evoking pity

     c. pitiful; contemptible

     d. made or liable to suffer

In Your Own Words

1. Do you think adults should have to censor their speech when they are around impressionable children in such public places as stadiums, amusement parks, and schools? Should fines be issued when adults cross the line and utter vulgar words around young kids?

2. Do you think Hollywood has gone too far in its portrayal of "adult" situations? What kind of rating system for movies would you like to see implemented?

3. A proposal has been made to give movies that show actors smoking an "R" rating because smoking in movies is said to encourage children to begin smoking themselves. How do you feel about this proposal?

4. Young children surfing the Internet are sometimes inadvertently exposed to online pornography. Some pornographic Web sites are only one or two letters different from popular children's sites. What do you think should be done about this?

5. If you have young children, how do you keep them from being exposed to inappropriate material either on TV or on the computer?

6. Many people from other countries are confused about what values or standards American society represents. How would you describe American culture today?

The Art of Writing

Choose one of the following and write a few paragraphs stating your opinion.

1. Do you agree or disagree with Greene's central argument? Write a few paragraphs supporting your point of view.

2. Some professors have suggested that media literacy classes designed to teach children the dangers of media should be a required part of grade school and high school curriculums. What do you think about this idea? Would it help?

3. Do you think the media has primarily a positive or a negative impact on people? How would you characterize this impact?

Internet Activity

1. Do research on the rating system for U.S. movies by accessing the Motion Picture Production Code. Do you think this voluntary system goes too far or not far enough? Write a few paragraphs giving your opinion.

2. Go to the Freedom Forum at

   www.freedomforum.org

   Locate a current research report and briefly discuss its results.

REVIEW TEST: Vocabulary in Context, Tone, Fact and Opinion, Bias

Read this passage and answer the questions that follow.

Debt

It may seem like a good idea to buy that cubic zirconia from the Home Shopping Network with your triple-platinum Visa card, but beware. That hasty decision could be the death of you.

Consumer debt has reached an all-time high in many parts of the world. In the United States in the 1990s, households had seventy cents of debt for every dollar they spent in a year. Today, Americans carry almost ninety-nine cents of debt for every dollar they spend. With this has come an increase in bankruptcies, suicides, health problems, and feelings of despair.

If a person finds himself, because of economic hardship, in a position in which he is forced to receive without being able to reciprocate, this state of affairs can be psychologically devastating. He may avoid asking for help. He may withdraw from friends rather than put himself in the position of being unable to pay. Meanwhile, heavy debt can leave an individual with less access to preventative health care, medicine, and medical visits. In a survey of 1,036 Ohioans, researchers found that those who claimed the highest levels of stress about their debt reported worse health than those with lower levels of debt-related stress.   3

This combination of stress, health problems, feeling like a worthless member of society, and social isolation creates the perfect climate for depression and suicide. This is especially true, at least one study has shown, when a person is hounded by debt collectors. Being all alone, except for calls from one's creditors, is enough to push a lot of people over the edge.   4

In Sri Lanka, there has been a rash of suicides in four major paddy-farming districts because of poverty and debt. Farmers there often borrow against their future crop successes. Unfortunately, the yields sometimes cannot be sold for enough to cover the debt. In the period before harvest, traditionally a time of celebration, financially hard-pressed farmers swallow pesticides.   5

But nowhere is this issue more pressing than Japan, where there is a prevailing stigma against asking for help for mental-health issues. This, and an especially strong sense of social obligation, can create an overwhelming burden for a man who finds himself unemployed or in debt. Japan's suicide tally is now more than 30,000 a year, roughly three times the number of people killed in traffic accidents and double the per capita suicide rate in the United States. Most of the victims are men, and nearly a third of the suicide notes cite economic hardship.   6

What You Can Do

Never a borrower or a lender be. On second thought, never a borrower be. The lenders seem to come out okay, especially at 18 percent interest compounded monthly.   7

(Laura Lee, *100 Most Dangerous Things in Everyday Life and What You Can Do About Them*, 2004)

_____ 1. In paragraph 3, the word *reciprocate* most likely means
   a. to take back
   b. to move back
   c. to give in return
   d. to criticize

_____ 2. In paragraph 4, the word *hounded* most likely means
   a. rewarded
   b. pursued relentlessly
   c. harassed
   d. both b and c

———— 3. The tone of the first paragraph is best described as
  a. ironic
  b. angry
  c. peevish
  d. serious

———— 4. The overall tone of the reading is best described as
  a. instructive
  b. admiring
  c. optimistic
  d. sentimental

———— 5. The tone of the final paragraph is best described as
  a. loving
  b. appreciative
  c. rude
  d. clever

———— 6. The sentence below states
  a. a fact
  b. an opinion
  c. both fact and opinion

"In the United States in the 1990s, households had seventy cents of debt for every dollar they spent in a year."

———— 7. The sentence below states
  a. a fact
  b. an opinion
  c. both fact and opinion

"In a survey of 1,036 Ohioans, researchers found that those who claimed the highest levels of stress about their debt reported worse health than those with lower levels of debt-related stress."

———— 8. The sentence below states
  a. a fact
  b. an opinion
  c. both fact and opinion

"Being all alone, except for calls from one's creditors, is enough to push a lot of people over the edge."

———— 9. The author has a strong bias
  a. in favor of accumulating debt
  b. in opposition to accumulating debt

———— 10. Paragraph 6 refers to "a prevailing stigma." A *stigma* has a
  a. positive connotation
  b. negative connotation

SELECTION

"Perhaps the most fundamental form of bias in instructional materials is the complete or relative exclusion of a particular group or groups . . ."

GETTING THE PICTURE

In the United States, the question of bias in textbooks is increasingly becoming a controversial issue. The excerpt by Myra and David Sadker describes various forms of bias that can appear in textbooks.

BIO-SKETCH

Dr. Myra Sadker was professor of education and dean of the school of education at American University (Washington, D.C.) until her death in 1995 from breast cancer. She and her husband, Dr. David Sadker, also a professor at American University, gained a national reputation for their work in confronting gender bias and sexual harassment. The Sadkers' work has been mentioned in hundreds of newspapers and magazines.

BRUSHING UP ON VOCABULARY

suffrage the right to vote. Originally, *suffrage* meant "intercessory prayers." The term evolved to mean a vote given to support a proposal or in favor of the election of a particular person. The Constitution of the United States declares, "No state shall be deprived of its equal *suffrage* in the Senate."

suffragette a woman seeking the right to vote through organized protest. The *suffragettes* were members of the Women's Suffrage Movement, an organization that combined demonstrations and militant action to campaign for the right to vote in the late nineteenth and early twentieth centuries.

bootlegger a smuggler of liquor. The term, which arose in the late nineteenth century, refers to the smugglers' habit of concealing bottles of liquor in their boots.

Excerpt from

TEACHERS, SCHOOLS, AND SOCIETY

by Myra and David Sadker

SEVEN FORMS OF BIAS

Many Americans are passionate about how various groups are portrayed in text-books. In the 1970s and 1980s, textbook companies and professional associations, such as the American Psychological Association, issued guidelines for nonracist and nonsexist books; as a result, textbooks became more balanced in their description of underrepresented groups. Today, educators work to detect underrepresentation of those groups. 1

Following is a description of seven forms of bias, which can be used to assess 2 instructional materials. Although this approach has been used to identify bias against females and various racial and ethnic groups, it can also help identify bias against the elderly, people with disabilities, non-English speakers, gays and lesbians, limited English speakers, and other groups.

Invisibility

Perhaps the most fundamental form of bias in instructional materials is the 3 complete or relative exclusion of a particular group or groups from representation in text narrative or illustrations. Research suggests, for example, that textbooks published prior to the 1960s largely omitted any consideration of African-Americans within contemporary society and, indeed, rendered them relatively invisible in accounts of or references to the United States after Reconstruction. Latinos, Asian-Americans, and Native Americans were largely absent from most resources as well. Many studies indicate that women, who constitute more than 51 percent of the U.S. population, represented approximately 30 percent of the persons or characters referred to throughout the textbooks in most subject areas.

Stereotyping

By assigning rigid roles or characteristics to all members of a group, individual 4 attributes and differences are denied. While stereotypes can be positive, they are more often negative. Some typical stereotypes include

- African-Americans as servants, manual workers, professional athletes, or   5 troublemakers
- Asian-Americans as laundry workers, cooks, or scientists
- Mexican-Americans as non-English speakers or migrant workers
- Middle-class Americans in the dominant culture as successful in their professional and personal lives
- Native Americans as "blood-thirsty savages" or "noble sons and daughters of the earth"
- Men in traditional occupational roles and as strong and assertive
- Women as passive and dependent and defined in terms of their home and family roles

Imbalance and Selectivity

Curriculum may perpetuate bias by presenting only one interpretation of an is- 6 sue, a situation, or a group of people. These imbalanced accounts simplify and distort complex issues by omitting different perspectives. Examples include

- The origins of European settlers in the New World are emphasized, while   7 the origins and heritage of other racial and ethnic groups are omitted.
- The history of the relations between Native Americans and the federal government is described in terms of treaties and "protection," omitting broken treaties and progressive government appropriation of Native American lands.
- Sources refer to the fact that women were "given" the vote but omit the physical abuse and sacrifices suffered by the leaders of the suffrage movement that "won" the vote.
- Literature is drawn primarily from Western male authors.
- Math and science courses reference only European discoveries and formulas.

Unreality

Many researchers have noted the tendency of instructional materials to ignore 8
facts that are unpleasant or that indicate negative positions or actions by individual leaders or the nation as a whole. By ignoring the existence of prejudice,
racism, discrimination, exploitation, oppression, sexism, and intergroup conflict
and bias, we deny children the information they need to recognize, understand,
and perhaps some day conquer the problems that plague society. Examples of
unreality may be found in programs that portray

- People of color and women as having economic and political equality with   9
  white males
- Technology as the resolution of all our persistent social problems

Fragmentation and Isolation

Bias through fragmentation or isolation primarily takes two forms. First, content 10
regarding certain groups may be physically or visually fragmented and delivered
separately (for example, a chapter on "Bootleggers, Suffragettes, and Other Di-
versions"). Second, racial and ethnic group members may be depicted as interacting only with persons like themselves, isolated from other cultural communities.
Fragmentation and isolation ignore dynamic group relationships and suggest
that nondominant groups are peripheral members of society.

Linguistic Bias

Language is a powerful conveyor of bias in instructional materials, in both blatant 11
and subtle forms. Written and verbal communication reflects the discriminatory
nature of the dominant language. Linguistic bias issues include race or ethnicity,
gender, accents, age, disability, and sexual orientation—for example,

- Native Americans are frequently referred to as "roaming," "wandering," or   12
  "roving" across the land. These terms might be used to apply to buffalo or
  wolves; they suggest a merely physical relationship to the land, rather than
  a social or purposeful relation. Such language implicitly justifies the seizure
  of native lands by "more goal-directed" white Americans who "traveled" or
  "settled" their way westward.
- Such words as *forefathers, mankind,* and *businessman* deny the contribution
  and existence of females.

The insistence that we live in an English only, monolingual society creates 13
bias against non-English speakers in this country and abroad. An imbalance of
word order ("boys and girls") and a lack of parallel terms ("girls and young
men") are also forms of linguistic bias.

Cosmetic Bias

Cosmetic bias offers the appearance of an up-to-date, well-balanced curriculum. 14
The problem is that, beyond the superficial appearance, bias persists. Cosmetic
bias emerges in a science textbook that features a glossy pullout of female scientists but includes precious little narrative of the scientific contributions of women.
A music book with an eye-catching, multiethnic cover that projects a world of

diverse songs and symphonies belies the traditional white male composers lurking behind the cover. This "illusion of equity" is really a marketing strategy directed at potential purchasers who *flip* the pages and might be lured into purchasing books that appear to be current, diverse, and balanced.

(Myra Pollack Sadker and David Miller Sadker, *Teachers, Schools, and Society,* 6/e, 2003)

✓ COMPREHENSION CHECKUP

Multiple Choice

Write the letter of the correct answer in the blank provided.

_____ 1. The authors' primary purpose is to
   a. argue that bias against nondominant groups should be eliminated from textbook material
   b. describe the destructive effects of stereotyping
   c. describe seven forms of group bias that often appear in textbooks
   d. explain the history of group bias in textbooks

_____ 2. You could infer from this excerpt that the authors favor
   a. exposing students to multiple viewpoints about particular issues
   b. presenting historical facts regardless of their unpleasantness
   c. minimizing the contributions of nondominant groups in textbook material
   d. both a and b

_____ 3. The last sentence of paragraph 3 ("Many studies indicate that women . . .") is a statement of
   a. fact
   b. opinion

_____ 4. Which of the following best expresses the main idea of paragraph 3?
   a. the first sentence
   b. the second sentence
   c. the last sentence
   d. There is no main idea.

_____ 5. In the last paragraph, the authors express a bias against textbooks that
   a. include the contributions of nondominant groups
   b. devalue Western culture
   c. emphasize female accomplishments over male ones
   d. only appear to take into account the contributions of non-dominant groups

_____ 6. A synonym for the word *blatant* as used in paragraph 11 on linguistic bias is
   a. dominant
   b. obvious
   c. offensive
   d. tasteless

_____ 7. The authors probably feel that stereotyping
   a. cannot be avoided
   b. obscures individual differences

_____ 8. The word *peripheral* as used in "peripheral members of society" most likely means
　　a. dominant
　　b. superficial
　　c. marginal
　　d. essential

_____ 9. As used in the last paragraph, the word *lurking* has a
　　a. negative connotation
　　b. positive connotation

_____ 10. In the last paragraph the phrase *illusion of equity* implies that
　　a. the material is balanced and diverse
　　b. bias still persists in the material
　　c. the material presented is comprehensive and fair
　　d. none of the above

In Your Own Words

The Sadkers provide a justification or rationale for bias and sensitivity committees. What justifications do they provide? Do you agree with their views? Why or why not?

The Art of Writing

In a brief essay, respond to the item below.

> When do you think it is appropriate to censor textbooks for material that could be objectionable to some group? Is it important for children to read textbooks that contain controversial or objectionable thoughts or expressions? When children are exposed to so much objectionable and offensive material by the mass media, does it make sense to censor textbooks?

Internet Activity

Go to the American Library Association's Web site at

www.ala.org

Type in "banned books" to locate a list of the 100 most frequently challenged books. Print a copy of the list, and see which books you recognize. How many have you read? Do you think these books should be banned? Are there ways to respond to objectionable books other than banning them?

SELECTION

"Mass media are very powerful socialization agents."

GETTING THE PICTURE

Television, movies, novels, magazines, and songs all promote the idea of a special soul mate. Do you think the media has an influence on romantic relationships? Has it affected the way you want to look, and what you think a prospective partner should look like? Do you think a special someone is waiting for you out there and fate will eventually bring you together? The following selection analyzes the effects of the media on romance. Some of the author's conclusions may surprise you.

BIO-SKETCH

Dr. Mary-Lou Galician, author of several books about this essay's topic, is head of Media Analysis and Criticism and a professor in the Walter Cronkite School of Journalism and Mass Communication at Arizona State University, where thousands of students of all majors have learned how to be "media literate" in her popular classes. Known internationally by her nickname "Dr. FUN" (because of her musical motivation program *FUN-dynamics!—The FUN-damentals of DYNAMIC Living*), she is the creator of *Realistic Romance—The Thinking Person's Relationship Remedy* and maintains the media literacy Web site www.RealisticRomance.com, where you can take her *Dr. FUN's Mass Media Love Quiz* and get her *Dr. Galician's Prescriptions.*

BRUSHING UP ON VOCABULARY

Prince Charming The fairy tale *Cinderella* by Charles Perrault (1856) featured the hero Prince Charming. The term has come to refer to a man who fulfills all the romantic expectations of a woman.

Snow White The fairy tale was written by the Brothers Grimm and was the basis of a 1937 animated feature by Walt Disney. Snow White, pursued by a jealous queen, hides with the Seven Dwarfs. The queen locates Snow White and feeds her a poisoned apple, but Prince Charming awakens her with a kiss.

Beauty and the Beast The 1991 Walt Disney movie was based on a classic French fairy tale. To break the spell placed upon him and his servants, a beast (in reality, an enchanted prince) must earn the love of Belle or risk remaining a beast forever.

Tarzan and Jane A fictional character created by Edgar Rice Burroughs (1914), Tarzan is the son of an English lord but was raised in the African jungle by apes. Jane Porter, rescued by Tarzan, becomes his wife and the mother of his son.

Pretty Woman This popular 1990 movie starred Richard Gere as Edward Lewis, a successful, wealthy lawyer, who hires the beautiful Vivian Ward, a prostitute played by Julia Roberts. They fall in love, and in the process Edward changes into a better person and Vivian gets a chance to start a new life.

Jerry Maguire Jerry Maguire, a sports agent played by Tom Cruise, wants to lead a more ethical life. His new moral sense isn't welcome at his firm and he is fired. Left with only one client and the love of Dorothy Boyd, played by Renee Zellweger, he discovers what's really important in life.

MEDIA LITERACY: PORTRAYALS OF SEX, LOVE, AND ROMANCE IN THE MASS MEDIA

by Dr. Mary-Lou Galician

Test yourself by taking *DR. FUN's Mass Media Love Quiz*, based on my media literacy teaching and research: 1

> **For each statement, select "TRUE" or "FALSE" to indicate YOUR belief.**

1. Your perfect partner is cosmically predestined for you, so nothing/nobody can ultimately separate you.

2. There's such a thing as "love-at-first-sight."

3. Your true soul mate should KNOW what you're thinking or feeling without your having to tell.

4. If your partner is truly meant for you, sex is easy and wonderful.

5. To attract and keep a man, a woman should look like a model or a centerfold.

6. The man should NOT be shorter, weaker, younger, poorer, or less successful than the woman.

7. The love of a good and faithful true woman can change a man from a "beast" into a "prince."

8. Bickering and fighting a lot mean that a man and a woman really love each other passionately.

9. All you really need is love, so it doesn't matter if you and your lover have very different values.

10. The right mate "completes you" by filling your needs and making your dreams come true.

11. In real life, actors and actresses are often very much like the romantic characters they portray.

12. Since media portrayals of romance aren't "real," they don't really affect you.

Dr. FUN's Mass Media Love Quiz © 1995, 2000 by Dr. Mary-Lou Galician. All Rights Reserved. Used by permission.

YOUR ANSWERS

I hope you answered "FALSE" to ALL 12 statements of my "*Dr. FUN'S Mass Media* 2 *Love Quiz*," based on my research and teaching focused on what we learn about sex, love, and romance from the mass media and how these portrayals affect us. All 12 are myths and stereotypes perpetuated by the mass media.

If you answered "TRUE" to some of them, don't worry: You're like most 3 people who take the quiz. The problem is that while most of us know the right responses, we still believe the unrealistic ones our popular culture presents to us.

Mass media are very powerful socialization agents. From the time we're very 4 young, we're barraged with fairy-tale depictions of romantic love in the popular culture—movies and television, books and magazines, recordings and radio, the Internet, advertising, and even the news—so we shouldn't feel too bad if we wind up with some unrealistic expectations. Remember: Mass media rely on simplification, distortions of reality, dramatic symbols, and myths and stereotypes to communicate their messages.

Unfortunately, false-love images and scripts of courtship put pressure on *both* 5 women and men—to measure up to what I call "media-myth P.C."—Playboy Centerfolds and Prince Charmings. Some media-constructed unrealistic expectations can even lead to depression and other dysfunctions, and several can be downright dangerous. So it's smart to become aware and change our unhealthy views.

With this in mind, let's look more closely at the mass media myths and ste- 6 reotypes in my quiz, for each of which I have a corresponding media literacy "antidote"—the 12 *Dr. Galician's Prescriptions (Rxs),* which the media rarely present:

MYTH 1. While you're seeking your one-and-only Mr. or Ms. "Right" (by the 7 way, I prefer the term "appropriate partner"), your blinders prevent you from seeing a whole spectrum of candidates who could make an excellent match. And a partner who is "perfect" would be less than fully human, even though media myths glorify the unrealistically ideal.

Rx 1. Consider Countless Candidates.

MYTH 2. There's attraction-at-first-sight; real loves takes real time. Too many 8 movies and TV shows give us the opposite idea. But they have only two hours to spin their tales. And advertisers have only 30 seconds. How long have you known each other? Take your time. You have lots more of it in real life.

Rx 2. Consult Your Calendar and Count Carefully.

MYTH 3. Mind-readers function only in circuses—and romance novels, which 9 feed our fantasy of having a perfect relationship without really working at it. Realistically, romantic partners learn about each other by daring to be open and honest (and courteous) about what they want.

Rx 3. Communicate Courteously.

MYTH 4. As with all intimacy, genuinely good sex takes time, trust, and to- 10 getherness. In real life (unlike in the pages of *Playboy* and *Cosmo*), the essential element of love is NOT sex: It's committed long-term relationships.

Rx 4. Concentrate on Commitment and Constancy.

MYTH 5. Real love doesn't superficially turn a person into an object. Neverthe- 11 less, even though they might not realize it, many males subconsciously use actresses, models, and centerfolds as a standard for their own real-life partners, who cannot help disappointing them (unless they, too, have had the surgical and photographic enhancements that pop culture icons get). What's worse is that even women's magazines reinforce unhealthy female body images.

Rx 5. Cherish Completeness In Companions (Not Just The Cover).

MYTH 6. To fit the "Me-Tarzan, You-Jane" cultural stereotypes that mass me- 12 dia perpetuate, many leading men in movies and TV shows have to stand on boxes to appear taller than their leading ladies. Even news anchor "couples" are usually an older male-younger female duo. These images reinforce sexual inequality and block many potentially wonderful relationships from ever getting started. Studies show that peer couples are the happiest.

Rx 6. Create Coequality; Cooperate.

MYTH 7. Children who see "Beauty and the Beast" should be warned that 13 Belle's attempts to reform her captor would be most unwise in real life. We cannot change others—especially not abusive "heroes" (or "heroines"!) who have some good inside if only their partners can be "good enough" to bring it out. This fallacy underlies domestic violence. We *can* see the myth as a metaphor for fixing our own "beastly" side.

Rx 7. Cease Correcting and Controlling; You Can't Change Others (Only Yourself).

MYTH 8. Invariably in mass media, a male and female who take an instant strong dislike to each other will (eventually) discover that they're made for each other—despite their continual bickering. Respectful disagreement is healthy, but these constant combatants need conflict-resolution training. Don't confuse fighting with passion: Love is about peace, not war. [14]

Rx 8. Courtesy Counts; Constant Conflicts Create Chaos.

MYTH 9. Opposites frequently attract—but they don't stay together very long except in mass media mythology. Can you imagine a real-life dinner party mixing the friends of "Pretty Woman" and her stockbroker boyfriend? Though rarely demonstrated by the mass media, shared values (not "interests") form the basis of lasting romantic relationships. [15]

Rx 9. Crave Common Core-Values.

MYTH 10. Although "love" songs cultivate this "Snow White" syndrome (Her big Disney solo was "Someday My Prince Will Come"!), using your partner as a completer, fixer, or rescuer—someone from whom you "take" or "get"—is robbery, not romance. (And that goes for "incomplete" MEN like Jerry Maguire!). But where's the dramatic conflict in well-adjusted, self-sufficient individuals who choose to share their already-full lives? [16]

Rx. 10. Cultivate Your Own Completeness.

MYTH 11. Many men and women are less than satisfied with their real-life romantic partners because they aren't like their idealized image of a celebrity they think they know. When countless adolescent girls wanted *Twilight's* star to "bite them" at publicity events for the film, the actor who portrayed the hero-vampire was amazed. [17]

Rx 11. De-Construct Celebrities.

MYTH 12. Though we might not be aware of the all-pervasive media culture, we subconsciously incorporate its messages and myths into our own lives. In my own studies of Baby Boomers and Generation Xers, I've found that avid consumers of movies and fashion and fitness magazines tend to have more unrealistic and stereotypical expectations about coupleship, and, correspondingly, less satisfaction in their own real romantic relationships. [18]

Rx 12. Calculate the Very Real Consequences of Unreal Media.

Does all this mean we should avoid romantic media entirely? [19]

We can still enjoy the metaphoric meanings and pure "escape" that romantic media myths offer us (though stereotypes are always harmful to us and others), but it's not wise to use media myths—or media celebrities—as models in our real lives. It's much healthier and smarter to make yourself the hero or heroine of your own true love story.

My ultimate advice: "Get real about romance!"

✓ **COMPREHENSION CHECKUP**

Multiple Choice

Write the letter of the correct answer in the space provided.

_____ 1. All of the following are myths about romantic love *except*
   a. true love always happens quickly, even at first sight
   b. true love only happens to women who look like models or centerfolds
   c. couples with similar values have a better chance of staying together
   d. continual fighting and bickering is a sign of true love

_____ 2. According to the selection, all of the following are true *except*
   a. even though we can recognize myths about romantic love portrayed in the media, they still affect us
   b. images about romantic love in the mass media affect only women
   c. the mass media are full of images about romantic love
   d. unrealistic expectations about romantic love in the mass media can sometimes lead to depression

_____ 3. A good title for this selection would be
   a. "Love at First Sight?"
   b. "The Perfect Partner"
   c. "Recognizing Myths of Romantic Love"
   d. "How to Find Your One and Only"

_____ 4. Which statement below best reflects the main idea of the selection?
   a. The way we view ourselves and our expectations for romantic relationships are often shaped by our exposure to the mass media.
   b. Unrealistic beliefs about romantic love cause difficulties in finding a good partner.
   c. There are many potential partners available for everyone.
   d. Romantic love rarely leads to marriage.

_____ 5. The author is likely to agree with which of the following statements?
   a. Love can overcome every obstacle.
   b. Love at first sight is how most good romantic relationships begin.
   c. It is reasonable to expect perfection in a potential mate.
   d. True love is not likely to change an abusive partner.

_____ 6. The author has a strong bias against
   a. media literacy education
   b. scholarly research on the topic of love
   c. the current patterns of courtship in the United States
   d. the media's unrealistic depiction of love and romance

True or False

Indicate whether each statement is true or false by writing **T** or **F** in the space provided.

_____ 1. Everyone has a perfect partner who will appear at the right moment.

_____ 2. The author believes that mass media can influence the way we think and feel about ourselves.

_____ 3. Mass media can communicate messages by means of stereotypes.

_____ 4. Mass media can put pressure on women to measure up to *Playboy* centerfolds.

_____ 5. The author urges us to become aware of the media's power to manipulate our views.

_____ 6. Honesty and openness cause romantic couples to break apart.

_____ 7. Women's magazines, as well as men's magazines, can foster unhealthy body images.

_____ 8. If people are truly opposites, they have a better chance of succeeding in a long-term romantic relationship.

_____ 9. Love has more in common with peace than with war.

_____ 10. It is a good idea to model your romantic relationships on how celebrities behave.

Vocabulary in Context

Match the definition in the second column with the vocabulary word in the first column. Write the letter on the line.

_____ 1. predestined

_____ 2. soul mate

_____ 3. barraged

_____ 4. depictions

_____ 5. dysfunctions

_____ 6. blinders

_____ 7. spectrum

_____ 8. perpetuate

_____ 9. duo

_____ 10. enhancements

_____ 11. icons

_____ 12. abusive

_____ 13. combatants

_____ 14. ultimate

_____ 15. reinforce

a. brawlers; fighters

b. bombarded; attacked

c. foreordained

d. variety; a broad range

e. final; conclusive

f. improvements

g. strengthen

h. objects of devotion

i. something that impedes vision or discernment

j. impairments

k. a person with whom one has a strong affinity or connection

l. portrayals

m. to make continual

n. physically harmful

o. a couple

In Your Own Words

1. Can you think of any recent movies or TV shows in which the "romantic" relationships depicted were unrealistic? In what ways were they unrealistic?

2. At a very young age, many young children start watching Disney classic movies such as *The Little Mermaid, Cinderella, Sleeping Beauty, The Lady and the Tramp,* and *Snow White*. A common theme in these movies is the heroine being rescued by the hero. Do you think this scenario sets the stage for later unrealistic expectations about romance?

3. Do you think that all of the situations listed by the author truly are myths and stereotypes? Or do you think that some of these situations are realistic and true?

4. What do you think about the author's prescriptions to overcome her list of myths? Do you think that all of these prescriptions make sense? Or do you think that some could hinder the growth of a healthy relationship?

The Art of Writing

Many celebrities with surgically enhanced bodies have been blamed for the huge surge in women having plastic surgery. Write a few paragraphs giving your opinion on this subject. Do you think celebrities and the media are mainly responsible for this trend? Or do you think there are other influences?

Internet Activity

Many girls and young women have eating disorders. A recent poll suggests that 40% of first- second- and third-grade girls want to be thinner, and 80% of 10-year-old girls are worried about being fat. Do some research about eating disorders at the National Institute of Mental Health Web site.

www.nimh.nih.gov/

Write a paragraph summarizing your findings.

An Introduction to Logical Fallacies

As we have noted in the introduction to this chapter, bias gets in the way of critical thinking. Most people have a bias of some sort, whether it is racial, sexual, religious, or political. A bias can result in opinions formed without sufficient evidence. Sometimes biases lead people to distort, exaggerate, or even to falsify. At other times, biases are expressed as errors in reasoning. At first glance, a statement or argument may seem reasonable, but a closer look shows it to be faulty. Errors in reasoning can be the result of sloppy thinking, but sometimes they may be motivated by a wish to deceive. Biased reasoning often seeks to convince by appealing to emotion rather than logic.

This section introduces you to logical fallacies (errors in reasoning) that often appear in argumentative material. It will help prepare you for your work with arguments in Chapter 11.

It's important to remember that although logical fallacies may seem to make sense, they actually have a fatal flaw. In the list that follows, the name of each fallacy indicates the particular error in reasoning that has occurred.

Faulty Cause and Effect

In this fallacy, the arguer assumes that because A and B regularly occur together, A must be the cause of B.

> **EXAMPLE:** Every spring we sacrifice a person to the sun god, and every spring the rains come and the crops grow. Therefore, sacrificing a person to the sun god causes the rains to come.

In this example, the arguers have mistakenly assumed that because two events are regularly correlated, there must be a cause-and-effect relationship between them.

> **EXAMPLE:** In the following cartoon, Fred Basett is guilty of faulty cause-and-effect reasoning. He thinks that because the car washing happened before the rain, the car washing caused the rain.

Non Sequitur

In a non sequitur argument, the conclusion does not follow from the evidence.

> **EXAMPLE:** She will make a fine governor because she is an excellent attorney.

> **EXAMPLE:** Thousands of people have seen lights in that sky that they could not identify. It has become obvious that there is life on other planets.

Circular Logic (also called "Begging the Question")

This fallacy is committed when the conclusion restates the information presented as evidence. You assume as true what you are trying to prove.

> **EXAMPLE:** Bungee jumping is dangerous because it's unsafe.

Saying bungee jumping is unsafe is just another way of saying that it's dangerous.

EXAMPLE: The team is in last place because it has lost more games than the other teams.

EXAMPLE: The Dilbert cartoon below is an example of circular reasoning.

Hasty Generalization

We commit the fallacy of hasty generalization when we draw a general conclusion from a sample that is biased or too small. For example, if a small-business owner hired three people from Utopia and none of them were reliable workers, he might say: "The workers from Utopia are unreliable." In this example, a general conclusion is drawn from a sample that is too small to support such a sweeping statement. Had he hired some other people from Utopia, they might have turned out to be good workers. Hasty generalizations can lead to harmful stereotypes.

EXAMPLE: I have two friends who drive BMWs and their cars are always breaking down. They have nothing but trouble from those cars. BMWs are junk.

This judgment is based on only two people. Maybe these two individuals have mistreated their BMWs or not maintained them.

Either/Or (False Dilemma)

This is a fallacy of black-and-white thinking in which only two choices are given; there are no shades of gray. People who exhibit this type of thinking have a "bumper sticker" mentality. They say things like "America—love it or leave it." When we polarize issues, we make it more difficult to find a common ground.

EXAMPLE: Either we elect a Republican as president or crime rates will skyrocket.

EXAMPLE: If we don't elect a Democrat as president, then the economy will falter.

EXAMPLE: In the following cartoon, Hagar's wife is offering only two viewpoints on an issue.

HAGAR: © 1991. Distributed by King Features Syndicate.

False Analogy (Comparing Apples and Oranges)

In this fallacy, two things that are not really similar are portrayed as being alike. In most false analogies, there is not enough evidence to support the comparison.

> **EXAMPLE:** Schools are no different from businesses. They should be run the same way.

> **EXAMPLE:** Children are like dogs. They need to be strongly disciplined.

Ad Hominem (Against the Man)
Personal Attack (Name-calling)

In this fallacy, the arguer attacks the person making the argument rather than the argument or claim. For instance, saying that Jill is a liar does not disprove Jill's argument that free speech is critical in a democracy.

> **EXAMPLE:** Hugh Hefner, founder of *Playboy* magazine, has argued against censorship of pornography. Someone who disagrees with Hefner's position might respond by saying Hefner is an immature man who never outgrew the adolescent fantasies of his youth and that therefore his argument is worthless.

This response makes no attempt to show why Hefner's arguments against the censorship of pornography are flawed. Instead it attacks Hefner's character. The response is reduced to this:

1. Hugh Hefner is an immature person.

2. Therefore, Hugh Hefner's argument must be bad.

Ad Populum (To the People)

This kind of argument seeks to win agreement by making an appeal to common prejudices, values, and emotions. It does not rely on facts or reasoning and is similar to bandwagon in that it is an appeal to numbers. At its extreme, the ad populum argument relies on "mob appeal."

> **EXAMPLE:** The fact that the majority of upstanding Americans support the death penalty proves that it is morally right.

> **EXAMPLE:** Americans are strong, independent, and free, so we need to privatize Social Security.

Red Herring

An uncooked herring has a very strong odor. According to legend, if a herring is dragged across the trail of an animal (or person) that dogs are tracking, the dogs will abandon the original scent and follow the scent of the herring. An arguer commits the red herring fallacy when he seeks to distract his audience by raising an irrelevant issue that he claims settles the original point at issue. Attention is directed away from the debatable point to one that most people will quickly agree with. Red herring fallacies are extremely common in politics.

> **EXAMPLE:** It is pointless to worry about too much violence on TV when thousands are killed by drunk drivers every year.

> **EXAMPLE:** Many people criticize Thomas Jefferson for being an owner of slaves. But Jefferson was one of our greatest presidents, and his Declaration of Independence is one of the most eloquent pleas for freedom and democracy ever written. Clearly, these criticisms against Jefferson are unwarranted.

The issue here is whether Jefferson can be criticized for owning slaves, not whether he was one of America's greatest presidents or whether he deserves credit for writing the Declaration of Independence.

> **EXAMPLE:** Critics have accused my administration of doing too little to save the family farm. These critics forget that I grew up on a farm. I know what it's like to get up at the crack of dawn to milk the cows. I know what it's like to work all day in the field in the blazing sun. Family farms are what made this country great, and those who criticize my farm policies simply don't know what they're talking about.

The issue is whether the speaker's administration is doing enough to save the family farm. The fact that the speaker grew up on a farm is a red herring used to distract attention from this issue.

Slippery Slope

This fallacy assumes that taking a first step down a path will necessarily lead to later steps. We often hear arguments of this type: "We can't allow A, because A will lead to B, and B will lead to C, and we sure don't want C!" The image is of a boulder rolling uncontrollably down a steep hill. When we assume that the first step will inevitably lead to disaster without presenting evidence, we are committing the slippery slope fallacy.

> **EXAMPLE:** Requiring ratings on record labels will lead to censorship and government control of free speech.

> **EXAMPLE:** Dr. Rogers has proposed that we legalize physician-assisted suicide. However, if we allow physician-assisted suicide, eventually there will be no respect for human life.

> **EXAMPLE:** The following cartoon illustrates slippery slope thinking.

...SURE, THIS IS HOW IT STARTS... TODAY A SETTLEMENT, TOMORROW A CITY, NEXT THING YOU KNOW WE'LL BE MOVING TO THE SUBURBS...

SIX CHIX: © Rina Piccolo. Distributed by King Features Syndicate.

Exercise 7: Identifying Logical Fallacies

Directions: Indicate the logical fallacies being used in each of the following items.

_____ 1. Central State University has won its first two basketball games, and therefore it's going to win all of its games.
   a. slippery slope
   b. either/or
   c. hasty generalization

_____ 2. I just washed my car, so I know it's going to rain.
   a. circular logic
   b. faulty cause and effect
   c. ad hominem

_____ 3. The Wildcats are in last place because they lost more games than any other team.
   a. ad populum
   b. ad hominem
   c. circular logic

_____ 4. Senator Wealthy wants to change the inheritance tax laws. But he's a notorious womanizer who has a profligate lifestyle. So let's not waste our time with his proposals.
   a. hasty generalization
   b. ad hominem
   c. non sequitur

_____ 5. Either the Democrats will quickly unite behind Gary Goodfellow, or the Republicans will roll to victory.
   a. faulty cause and effect
   b. red herring
   c. either/or

_____ 6. Don't ever let children have second helpings of dinner. If you do, pretty soon they will be gorging themselves.
   a. red herring
   b. slippery slope
   c. circular logic

_____ 7. Americans are honest, hardworking, and caring. That's why we need to lower taxes.
   a. ad populum
   b. either/or
   c. slippery slope

_____ 8. Phil likes chocolate because he's a caring person.
   a. either/or
   b. non sequitur
   c. ad populum

_____ 9. Araceli did poorly in a bilingual school. Bilingual education must be a failure.
   a. ad hominem
   b. red herring
   c. hasty generalization

_____ 10. To improve education, we can either hire more teachers or build more schools.
   a. either/or
   b. false analogy
   c. slippery slope

_____ 11. All of the following contain fallacies *except:*
   a. We can't adopt Laurie Legislator's proposal. She comes from a long line of chiselers.
   b. The school rules state that after three absences you can be dropped from a class.
   c. I'm going to have bad luck for the rest of the year because a black cat crossed my path on New Year's Day.

_____ 12. All of the following contain fallacies *except:*
   a. Two of my son's friends got in accidents the day after they got their licenses at 16. Sixteen-year-olds should not be allowed to drive.
   b. An Infiniti is a good car because it costs a lot of money.
   c. I didn't study for the final exam, and I failed it.

Brain Teasers

What animal is associated with the statement below?

1. To stretch one's neck for a better view _____

2. To repeat another's words _____

3. To try to attract compliments _____

4. To lower the head quickly _____

5. To annoy _____

6. To eat too much is to be a _____

7. A supporter of war _____

8. An opponent of war _____

9. A coward _____

10. One who stays up late _____

11. Free as a _____

Analyzing and Evaluating Arguments

Trial by Jury (1964) BY THOMAS HART BENTON

The Nelson-Atkins Museum of Art, Kansas City, Missouri. Bequest of
the artist F/75-21/11. Photo by Mel McLean. © T.H. Benton and
R.P. Benton Testamentary Trusts/Licensed by VAGA, New York, NY.
© T.H. Benton and R.P. Benton Testamentary Trusts/UMB Bank.

View and Reflect

1. Which figure in the painting is making an argument? Do you think this person is the prosecutor or the defense attorney?
2. How many jurors appear in the painting? What is the composition of the jury in terms of sex and ethnicity?
3. Who do you think the defendant is?
4. Does this scene accurately depict how a courtroom looks? In what ways does it differ? Have you ever served on a jury?

An Introduction to Argument

The critical reader must be able to evaluate arguments. When you evaluate an **argument** (a claim supported by reasons or evidence), you determine its value or persuasiveness. When an author tries to persuade a reader that something is true or correct by presenting supporting reasons or evidence, an argument is being made. This means that an argument is different from an ordinary assertion, which need not be backed up by reasons or evidence.

Arguments focus on a matter of dispute or a controversial topic. For instance, the question "Do the majority of 18-year-olds drink alcohol?" is not very debatable. We can answer it with research and statistical evidence. However, if we change the question to "Should it be lawful for 18-year-olds to drink alcohol?" we have a good argument. This is because the lawful drinking age is a controversial topic. Some people will support lowering the drinking age to 18 and others will oppose it.

In order to effectively evaluate an argument, a reader must first understand its components. The next section demonstrates how to analyze the structure of an argument.

Analyzing Arguments

An argument has four parts or characteristics: the issue, the claim, the support, and the assumptions.

The Structure of an Argument

- **Issue**: a controversial or debatable topic. It must be something that people disagree about or with.
- **Claim:** (conclusion) the key point. This is what the author is trying to prove.

  All of the following are claims: Smoking should be outlawed. We should do whatever it takes to protect the environment. Illegal immigrants should be given a path to become citizens.

- **Support:** (premises) evidence given for the claim. The support can be made up of facts, statistics, expert opinion, research, personal experience, or experiences of others.
- **Assumption:** something that is believed to be true but has not been proven. When you get together with a friend once a week for lunch, you assume your friend likes your company. If the bank's hours of business are from 9 to 5, we assume it is going to be open if we go there during those hours. Assumptions are assertions the author believes but may leave unsaid.

  Let's examine our previous example about the legal drinking age. However, let's make a contrary claim that the legal drinking age should stay at 21. As an argument it might look something like this:

  Issue: Should the <u>legal drinking age</u> remain at age 21?

  To find the issue, ask: "What is the controversial topic?"

  In the example above, the controversial topic is underlined.

  Claim: To curb alcohol abuse among the young, the legal drinking age should remain at age 21.

  To find the claim, ask: "What is the author's position on the issue?"

Support: In the early 1970s, many states lowered the drinking age to accommodate the returning Vietnam War veterans. Alcohol-related highway deaths rose and states went back to the age 21 cutoff. On average, traffic deaths drop by 16% when the drinking age goes from 18 to 21. Federal highway safety authorities estimate that since 1984, approximately 25,000 lives have been saved.

To find the support, ask: "What reasons or evidence does the author give to back up the claim?"

Assumptions: Right now many 18-year-olds drink alcohol illegally. Lowering the drinking age to 18 would only increase teen drinking, including by younger teens. People at age 21 are more mature than teenagers and are more likely to drink responsibly.

To find the author's assumptions, ask: "What does the author take for granted without bothering to prove?"

Exercise 1: Identifying the Issue and Writing an Opposing Claim

Directions: First, underline the issue in each claim. Then, for each of the claims, write an opposing claim.

1. Capital punishment is inhumane and should be abolished.

   Opposing claim: _____

2. Medical marijuana should be legalized.

   Opposing claim: _____

3. College tuition should be raised significantly to reflect the true costs of education.

   Opposing claim: _____

   _____

4. Nutritional supplements are potentially dangerous and should be regulated by the FDA the same as drugs.

   Opposing claim: _____

5. College football players should be paid to play.

   Opposing claim: _____

Exercise 2: Providing Support

Directions: For each claim listed below, identify reasons that support each side of the argument.

A. It should be permissible to sell beer at college football games.

Yes **Supporting Reasons**	**No** **Supporting Reasons**
1. _____	1. _____
2. _____	2. _____
3. _____	3. _____

B. It should be lawful to use animals to test drugs and cosmetics.

Yes	**No**
Supporting Reasons	**Supporting Reasons**
1. _____	1. _____
2. _____	2. _____
3. _____	3. _____

C. Texting while driving should be outlawed.

Yes	**No**
Supporting Reasons	**Supporting Reasons**
1. _____	1. _____
2. _____	2. _____
3. _____	3. _____

Exercise 3: Identifying the Evidence that Supports the Claim

Directions: Each group of sentences below begins with a claim. Some of the sentences support the claim, and some don't. Write an **S** (for support) on the line next to the sentence that directly supports the claim. Leave the other sentences blank.

EXAMPLE:

Claim: Students should have to attend school year round.

_____ Year-round school doesn't boost learning.

___S___ Students forget too much over long summer breaks.

_____ Year-round schools ruin parents' vacation plans.

___S___ Because most parents work, students are left to hang out in the summer with no one supervising them.

_____ Most large cities also have charter schools.

1. **Claim:** School cafeterias in elementary schools should offer only healthy food choices.

    _____ Fast food isn't bad for the very young.

    ___S___ Many of today's kids are alarmingly overweight.

    ___S___ Obese kids are more likely to become overweight adults with health problems.

    _____ If parents make good food choices, kids will imitate them.

    _____ Some environmentalists condemn drinking water from plastic bottles.

2. **Claim:** Public schools should require students to wear uniforms.

    ___S___ Recent studies show that school uniforms reduce peer pressure.

    _____ Nurses in hospitals wear uniforms.

_S_ Uniforms make it easier to identify those who are not from the school.

____ Uniforms interfere with students' rights of self-expression.

_S_ Having a uniform prevents gang members from displaying their colors.

3. **Claim:** All-day kindergarten should be mandatory for all children.

_S_ With all-day kindergarten, working parents will save on child care.

____ Public schools did not have kindergarten in the 1800s.

_S_ Teachers report greater academic progress by students who attend all-day kindergarten.

____ All-day kindergarten programs are too expensive.

____ All-day kindergarten programs can be very stressful for some children.

4. **Claim:** High school students should be required to learn a foreign language.

_S_ Foreign languages are increasingly needed in this age of globalization.

____ The official language of the Roman Empire was Latin.

____ It's a personal choice whether or not to be bilingual.

____ Students are made to do enough in schools as it is without having to learn a foreign language.

_S_ Studying a foreign language broadens students by acquainting them with the culture, history, and literature of another country.

5. **Claim:** Tattoos and body piercings should be approached with caution.

_S_ There is always a risk of infection with tattoos and body piercings.

____ Tongue rings can damage teeth.

____ Many sports stars have tattoos.

_S_ Tattoos and body piercings should be considered permanent alterations to the body.

____ Tattooing is becoming more popular.

6. **Claim:** Smoking should be banned in privately owned facilities.

____ Business owners have the right to operate their businesses without undue government interference.

____ Bans on smoking can reduce revenue at restaurants and bars and put them out of business.

____ If people don't like to be around smokers, they can go to another restaurant.

____ If government can control the actions of private citizens in restaurants, what's to stop it from extending its reach into private residences?

_S_ The right to smoke should not interfere with the nonsmoker's right to breathe smoke-free air.

_S_ Studies show that secondhand cigarette smoke increases the risk of disease in individuals who do not smoke themselves.

7. **Claim:** The laws should not allow physician-assisted suicide of the terminally ill.

   _S_ Physician-assisted suicide undermines the value of life and could give troubled people who are not ill the idea that suicide is acceptable.

   _S_ Physicians have taken an oath to do no harm.

   ____ Too many medical and financial resources are used to keep people alive who want to die.

   _S_ Sometimes sick individuals are pressured to end their lives sooner by family members eager to inherit money.

   _S_ Many ill people say they want to die, but they are just depressed and need medication to relieve their depression.

   ____ All cultures have funeral practices.

8. **Claim:** People should drink regular tap water rather than buying water in plastic bottles.

   ____ Water keeps people hydrated, which is important when the weather is hot.

   _S_ Bottled water can be as contaminated as tap water.

   _S_ Bottled water is more expensive than tap water.

   _S_ A large percentage of plastic water bottles end up in landfills or the ocean, which harms the environment.

   _S_ Bottled water often lacks fluoride, which is needed to prevent tooth decay.

Now let's look more closely at the assumptions underlying arguments. Although assumptions are usually left unsaid, they are sometimes included. In the following example, the author's assumption is stated explicitly.

   Claim: The driving age should be raised to age 18.

   Evidence: Statistics show 16-year-olds are more likely to cause accidents than drivers 18 years or older.

   Assumption: There would be fewer accidents if the driving age were raised to age 18.

Exercise 4: Identifying the Assumptions

Directions: Identify the assumptions for the following claims from Exercise 3. Write your answers below.

1. **Claim:** Tattoos and body piercings should be approached with caution.

   Assumption: _Approaching with caution can make you see if it's something you really want_

2. **Claim:** Smoking should be banned in privately owned facilities.

   Assumption: _The owners would decide if smoking should be banned at their facilities_

3. **Claim:** The law should not allow physician-assisted suicide of the terminally ill.
   Assumption: _By not allowing more people would have_
   more time to say bye to their families

4. **Claim:** People should drink regular tap water rather than buying water in plastic bottles.
   Assumption: _Tap water won't have all the_
   chemicals bottled water does.

Exercise 5: Understanding Assumptions

Directions: Read this selection and answer the questions that follow.

Brownie

BY ROGER FOUTS

I grew up on a farm where animals were a very important part of our family's life. 1

My closest animal companion was our dog, Brownie. Feisty and fiercely loyal, 2 Brownie was a fixture of our household. She needed us and we needed her. In addition to guarding the house, she baby-sat the youngest kids in the fields during the harvest season.

One day I saw Brownie do something that shaped my view of animals forever. 3 She saved my brother's life. It happened during cucumber-picking season when I was four years old. The whole family—my parents, six brothers, and one sister—had been out in the field all day working. Brownie had been watching over me and my nine-year-old brother, Ed, whenever he got tired of picking. By the time the sun was going down our Chevy flatbed was piled high with boxes of cucumbers. It was time to head home for dinner. Ed wanted to ride back on our older brother's bicycle, a big thing that he could barely control. My parents said OK and Ed headed out on the bike, chaperoned by Brownie. Twenty minutes later, the rest of us clambered onto the truck and left the field with my twenty-year-old brother, Bob, driving.

It was the dry season, six months or so since the last rain, and the dirt road was 4 blanketed with four or five inches of chalky dust. As the truck drove along the well-worn tire ruts in the road, it kicked up a huge cloud of dust that covered us on all sides, making it impossible to see more than two feet ahead or behind. After going along for a while, we suddenly heard Brownie barking very loudly and very persistently. We looked down and we could just make her out next to the front fender. She was sniping at the right front tire. This was very strange behavior. Brownie had come to the fields hundreds of times and had never once barked at the truck. But now she was practically attacking it. My brother Bob thought this was odd but didn't give Brownie much thought as he plowed ahead even as her barking became more frenzied. Then, without further warning, Brownie dove in front of the truck's front tire. I heard her shriek, and I felt a thump as we drove over her body. Bob hit the brakes, and we all got out. Brownie was dead. And right there in front of the truck, not ten feet away, was Ed, struck on his bike in the deep tire rut, unable to escape. Another two seconds and we would have run him down.

Brownie's death was devastating to all of us. I had seen animals die before, but 5 this one was my nearest and dearest friend. My parents tried to explain that Brownie had only done what either of them would have done for us. No one doubted for a second that Brownie had sacrificed her own life to save my brother's. She saw a dangerous situation unfolding, and she did what she had to do to protect the boy she had been baby-sitting for so many years. Had she not acted, the course of our family's life would have been very different.

(Roger Fouts, *Next of Kin*, 1997)

1. Roger Fouts is a strong proponent of animal rights. What assumptions about animals (and dogs in particular) does Fouts make in this excerpt?

   _____

   _____

2. How might this incident transform someone into a crusader for animal rights?

   _____

   _____

3. How does this excerpt appeal to our emotions rather than our reasoning ability?

   _____

   _____

4. In what ways could this excerpt be viewed as a form of propaganda?

   _____

   _____

Evaluating Arguments

Now that we know what an argument is and how it is put together, let's talk about how to evaluate an argument. Here are the key steps for evaluating an argument.

1. Think critically and skeptically about the support (reasons or evidence) that the argument presents and the assumptions that the argument makes. Is the author's support relevant and persuasive? Do the assumptions defeat or weaken the argument?

2. Ask yourself how well the support and assumptions back up the conclusion. If the assumptions are not shared by the reader or if the support is weak or false, then the argument will be unpersuasive, unsound, or invalid.

3. Many good arguments will attempt to directly refute key points in the opposing argument. The absence of such a refutation can be a sign of weakness in an argument. If the author omits the refutation, ask yourself why he or she has done so.

Applying Critical Thinking Skills to Arguments

1. **Question claims that are based solely on anecdotal evidence, opinions, or testimonials.** Instead, pay more attention to those claims that are supported by research studies. For example, many herbal supplements have not been rigorously tested for safety and effectiveness. Yet, they are promoted as being both safe and effective by many enthusiastic users. Many celebrities today are providing questionable or even dangerous medical advice. Some make claims about the effectiveness of alternative cancer "cures" that medical experts would

challenge. Testimonials by themselves do not constitute proof. Be wary of claims that are not substantiated by other evidence. While everyone is entitled to his or her own opinion, opinions are not facts.

2. **Be careful in evaluating poll data.** Remember that not all people respond honestly in surveys or polls. Many people say they are for someone or something when they are not. They may wish to please the pollster or to portray themselves in a more favorable light. Results to particular poll questions also depend on how the question was asked. For instance, if asked, "Are you in favor of welfare?" most people say "no." But if asked, "Are you in favor of helping the poor?" many people will say "yes."

3. **Examine opposing viewpoints carefully.** In evaluating an argument, never rely on just one source. Instead, investigate opposing viewpoints. To come to a balanced conclusion, you need to study the points made by the opposition. Don't assume that what you already believe must be true. And don't become so enamored of a particular argument that you neglect to investigate the opposing viewpoint. The goal should be to discover truth, even it means that you might have to change your original position.

4. **Recognize the fallibility of experts.** Experts provide valuable information about many subjects of interest, but they are not infallible. Just because someone has a PhD or MD does not mean we can automatically assume the argument he or she espouses is correct. As critical thinkers, we must remain skeptical.

Exercise 6: Evaluating Arguments

Directions: Identify the conclusion (or central issue) and the supporting reasons in each of the following excerpts. Where indicated, also list the logical fallacies used.

A. A Fair Share of Resources?

The affluent lifestyle that many of us in the richer countries enjoy consumes an inordinate share of the world's natural resources and produces a shockingly high proportion of pollutants and wastes. The United States, for instance, with less than 5 percent of the total population, consumes about one-quarter of most commercially traded commodities and produces a quarter to half of most industrial wastes.

To get an average American through the day takes about 450 kg (nearly 1,000 lbs) of raw materials, including 18 kg (40 lbs) of fossil fuels, 13 kg (29 lbs) of other minerals, 12 kg (26 lbs) of farm products, 10 kg (22 lbs) of wood and paper, and 450 liters (119 gal) of water. Every year we throw away some 160 million tons of garbage, including 50 million tons of paper, 67 billion cans and bottles, 25 billion styrofoam cups, 18 billion disposable diapers, and 2 billion disposable razors.

This profligate resource consumption and waste disposal strains the life-support system of the Earth on which we depend. If everyone in the world tried to live at consumption levels approaching ours, the results would be disastrous. Unless we find ways to curb our desires and produce the things we truly need in less destructive ways, the sustainability of human life on our planet is questionable.

(William Cunningham & Barbara Saigo, *Environmental Science*, 6/e, 2001)

1. What is the author's claim? _____

_____

2. List the author's support for the argument.

    a. _____

    b. _____

    c. _____

3. Is the author's claim adequately supported by factual evidence or inadequately

    supported? Give reasons for your answer. _____

    _____

4. List some examples of highly connotative language. _____

    _____

5. What is your overall assessment of the author's argument? _____

    _____

B. Just How Stupid Are We?

James Madison famously said that if men were angels, we wouldn't need government. It could as well be said that if politicians were angels, we wouldn't have to
worry about the voters' ignorance. Politicians would simply do the right thing. They
wouldn't play on voters' fears or pander to their irrational biases. Unfortunately,
angelic politicians are rare, so the issue that must absorb our energies is raising the
level of ordinary voters to make them less ignorant.

Schooling by itself is not the answer. More than half of all Americans now have
some college education. Yet they are no more knowledgeable about civics than
Americans a half-century ago, when fewer than half of all citizens even graduated
from high school (six in ten in 1940 never even got past the eighth grade). What's
needed is specifically an emphasis on civics. Studies show that people who know civics are less easily manipulated by politicians. Americans do not pick up civics lessons
by osmosis. They have to be taught it.

The time has arrived when we need to restore civics to the college curriculum.
Studies show that students who take civics courses in high school usually forget
what they learn after a few years. This is an argument in favor of doing more civics,
not less. Students should be required to take civics courses not only in high school
but in college as well. Most colleges have not placed an emphasis on civics. A beguil-
ing but unproven assumption is that by the time students reach college they understand the basic facts about American government. This may once have been the case,
when college was restricted to an elite group. But now that college is open to everybody we need to admit that many students arrive with an inadequate understanding
of civics. Their ignorance of civics should no longer be regarded as somebody else's
problem. College students naturally would resist attending classes in civics. Few college teachers would want to teach the subject. But there is a way to teach civics without being boring or tedious. It is by requiring students to read newspapers and other
news sources. We cannot of course force students to read anything. But if we test
students on current events they will read what they have to in search of the answers.
I recommend giving all freshmen in American colleges weekly current events tests.
Those who pass with flying colors should be eligible for federal tuition subsidies paid
for out of a special fund. Graduation should be made contingent on achieving at least
a passing grade.

(Rick Shenkman, *Just How Stupid Are We?*, 2008)

1. What is the author's claim? _____

_____

_____

_____

2. List the author's support for the argument.

    a. _____

    b. _____

    _____

    c. _____

3. What type of support is offered for the author's claim: primarily facts or primarily opinions? _____

4. What assumptions is the author making?

_____

_____

_____

5. What is your overall assessment of the author's argument?

_____

_____

C. Inside Job

Roughly four or five fast-food workers are now murdered on the job every month, usually during the course of a robbery. Although most fast-food robberies end without bloodshed, the level of violent crime in the industry is surprisingly high. In 1998, more restaurant workers were murdered on the job in the United States than police officers.

America's fast-food restaurants are now more attractive to armed robbers than convenience stores, gas stations, or banks. Other retail businesses increasingly rely upon credit card transactions, but fast-food restaurants still do almost all of their business in cash. While convenience store chains have worked hard to reduce the amount of money in the till (at 7-Eleven stores the average robbery results in a loss of about thirty-seven dollars), fast-food restaurants often have thousands of dollars on the premises. Gas stations and banks now routinely shield employees behind bullet-resistant barriers, a security measure that would be impractical at most fast-food restaurants. And the same features that make these restaurants so convenient—their location near intersections and highway off-ramps, even their drive-through windows—facilitate a speedy getaway.

The same demographic groups widely employed at fast-food restaurants—the young and the poor—are also responsible for much of the nation's violent crime. According to industry studies, about two-thirds of the robberies at fast-food restaurants involve current or former employees. The combination of low pay, high turnover, and ample cash in the restaurant often leads to crime. A 1999 survey by the National Food Service Security Council, a group funded by the large chains, found that about half of all restaurant workers engaged in some form of cash or property theft—not including the theft of food. The typical employee stole about $218 a year; new employees stole almost $100 more.

Studies conducted by Jerald Greenberg, a professor of management at the University of Ohio and an expert on workplace crime, have found that when people are treated with dignity and respect, they're less likely to steal from their employer. "It may be common sense," Greenberg says, "but it's obviously not common practice." The same anger that causes most petty theft, the same desire to strike back at an employer perceived as unfair, can escalate to armed robbery. Restaurant managers are usually, but not always, the victims of fast-food crimes. Not long ago, the day manager of a McDonald's in Moorpark, California, recognized the masked gunman emptying the safe. It was the night manager.

The leading fast-food chains have tried to reduce violent crime by spending millions on new security measures—video cameras, panic buttons, burglar alarms, additional lighting. But even the most heavily guarded fast-food restaurants remain vulnerable. In April of 2000, a Burger King on the grounds of Offut Air Force Base in Nebraska was robbed by two men in ski masks carrying shotguns. They were wearing purple Burger King shirts and got away with more than $7,000. Joseph A. Kinney, the president of the National Safe Workplace Institute, argues that the fast-food industry needs to make fundamental changes in its labor relations. Raising wages and making a real commitment to workers will do more to cut crime than investing in hidden cameras. "No other American industry," Kinney notes, "is robbed so frequently by its own employees."

(Eric Schlosser, *Fast-Food Nation: The Dark Side of the All-American Meal*, 2001)

1. What is the author's claim? _____

   _____

2. List the author's support for the argument.

   a. _____

   b. _____

   c. _____

3. Is Sentence 1 an example of fact or opinion?

   _____

4. Is the following sentence a fact or an opinion?
   "Raising wages and making a real commitment to workers will do more to cut crime than investing in hidden cameras."

   _____

5. What is your overall assessment of the author's argument?

   _____

   _____

D. Come Together . . . Right Now!

Small children play with cyberpets while old women stare out their windows at empty streets. Grandparents feel lonely and useless while, a thousand miles away, their grandchildren do not get the love and attention they desperately need. What's wrong with this picture? A lot.

In our society today, we practice a particularly virulent form of segregation—we separate people by age. We put our 3-year-olds together in preschools or day care centers, our 14-year-olds together in high schools, and our 80-year-olds in nursing homes—institutions that Betty Friedan, in *The Fountain of Age*, vividly labels "play-pens for adults."

Segregating the generations in this way means that people of all ages lose out: Older people are deprived of the energy and joy of children, and our kids end up learning their ideas about the world from each other or from television instead of through that most time-honored of traditions: being socialized by their elders.

But age segregation is more than just one of those regrettable casualties of changing times. It is a dangerous pattern that leads to all sorts of other social breakdowns. When our elders have no regular, everyday contact with young people, they rarely have the same emotional stake in the fate of their communities. They are less likely to care about the environment and to invest in green spaces and playgrounds. An older person who never mingles with children and no longer feels a sense of common cause with the young may not vote in favor of school referendums, child-health laws, or funding for teen programs. To put it bluntly, he may simply fail to see what a good school system has to do with him and his well-being. By the same token, a child who has no contact with old people is more likely to look the other way when one of them needs assistance or to become impatient when they share a joke or story. Age segregation fosters short-term selfish planning by the old and less empathy and respect from the young.

Because they don't get to know each other as people, old and young alike tend to think in negative stereotypes (often, alas, generated by the media). This breeds misunderstanding and fear. How many times do older people freeze up when they see a rambunctious group of young people approaching? Or hold back from nurturing or correcting other people's kids for fear of being misinterpreted? For their part, children often see older people as hopelessly out of it, if not downright weird, with nothing to contribute to their lives.

Yet society cannot hold together when old people are afraid of children and children are afraid of old people. Every culture is just one generation away from anarchy: It is the socialization of the young by the elders that allows the next generation to come of age civilized. A society in which this torch no longer gets passed is a society in trouble.

Each generation has its own wisdom and ways of loving. When we bring them together, we create a kind of social wealth that enriches us all.

(Mary Pipher, "Come Together . . . Right Now!" in *Parents*, December 1999)

1. What is the author's claim? _____

   _____

2. List the author's support for the argument.

   a. _____

   _____

   b. _____

   c. _____

3. Is the author's claim adequately supported by factual evidence or inadequately supported because it depends primarily on personal opinion?

   _____

4. What specific negative stereotypes does the author mention? _____

_____

_____

_____

5. What is your overall assessment of the author's argument?

_____

_____

E. Yes, Let's Pay for Organs

Pennsylvania plans to begin paying the relatives of organ donors $300 toward funeral expenses. Already there are voices opposing the very idea of pricing a kidney.

It is odd that with 62,000 Americans desperately awaiting organ transplantation to save their life, no authority had yet dared to offer money for the organs of the dead in order to increase the supply for the living. If we can do anything to alleviate the catastrophic shortage of donated organs, should we not?

One objection is that Pennsylvania's idea will disproportionately affect the poor. The rich, it is argued, will not be moved by a $300 reward; it will be the poor who will succumb to the incentive and provide organs.

So what? Where is the harm? What is wrong with rewarding people, poor or not, for a dead relative's organ? True, auctioning off organs in the market so that the poor could not afford to get them would be offensive. But this program does not restrict supply to the rich. It seeks to increase supply for all.

Moreover, everything in life that is dangerous, risky, or bad disproportionately affects the poor: slum housing, street crime, small cars, hazardous jobs. By this logic, coal mining should be outlawed because the misery and risk and diseases of coal mining disproportionately fall on people who need the money.

No, the real objection to the Pennsylvania program is this: It crosses a fateful ethical line regarding human beings and their parts. Until now we have upheld the principle that one must not pay for human organs because doing so turns the human body—and human life—into a commodity. Violating this principle, it is said, puts us on the slippery slope to establishing a market for body parts. Auto parts, yes. Body parts, no. Start by paying people for their dead parents' kidneys, and soon we will be paying people for the spare kidneys of the living.

Well, what's wrong with that? the libertarians ask. Why should a destitute person not be allowed to give away a kidney that he may never need so he can live a better life? Why can't a struggling mother give her kidney so her kids can go to college?

The answer is that little thing called human dignity. We have a free society, but freedom stops at the point where you violate the very integrity of the self. We cannot allow live kidneys to be sold at market. It would produce a society in which the lower orders are literally cut up to serve as spare parts for the upper. No decent society can permit that.

But kidneys from the dead are another matter entirely. To be crude about it, whereas a person is not a commodity, a dead body can be. Yes, it is treated with respect. But it is not inviolable. It does not warrant the same reverence as that accorded a living soul.

The Pennsylvania program is not just justified, it is too timid. It seeks clean hands by paying third parties—the funeral homes—rather than giving cash directly to the relatives. Why not pay them directly? And why not $3,000 instead of $300? That might even address the rich/poor concern: after all, $3,000 is real money, even for bankers and lawyers.

The Pennsylvania program does cross a line. But not all slopes are slippery. There is a new line to be drawn, a very logical one: rewards for organs, yes—but not from the living.

The Talmud speaks of establishing a "fence" around the law, making restrictions that may not make sense in and of themselves but that serve to keep one away from more serious violations. The prohibition we have today—no selling of *any* organs, from the living or the dead—is a fence against the commoditization of human parts. Laudable, but a fence too far. We need to move the fence in and permit incentive payments for organs from the dead.

Why? Because there are 62,000 people desperately clinging to life, some of whom will die if we don't have the courage to move the moral line—and hold it.

(Charles Krauthammer, "Yes, Let's Pay for Organs," *Time,* 5/17/99)

1. What is the author's claim? _____

_____

2. List the author's support for the argument.

   a. _____

   b. _____

   c. _____

   _____

3. What logical fallacies or propaganda devices can you identify?

   a. _____

   _____

   b. _____

   _____

   c. _____

4. How does the author respond to the opposing point of view?

   _____

   _____

5. What is your overall assessment of this argument?

   _____

   _____

   _____

   _____

   _____

*"The line between news and entertainment has become
blurred in most media."*

GETTING THE PICTURE

Photographs have always been susceptible to manipulation, and today they can be altered in ways that are virtually undetectable. Examples, of course, abound. Models and movie stars who grace the covers of magazines and billboards really don't look exactly like their media images. Most of us are aware of these "too good to be true" images. But now the public has to be even more wary of manipulation by the media. Too often we read about reporters making up stories, altering information and quotes, and, in general, manipulating the truth. Recently, we learned that our government hired actors to pose as reporters in ads to push a particular agenda. Because not too many of us are going to abandon the quest to be informed, what do you think our rights and responsibilities as viewers are? The selection below discusses this issue and offers some suggestions for citizens to follow.

BIO-SKETCH

William P. Cunningham is professor emeritus at the University of Minnesota. In addition to writing environmental science textbooks, he has written many articles in the field of biology.

BRUSHING UP ON VOCABULARY

deregulation halting or reducing government regulation.

patsy a slang term for a scapegoat or fall guy.

stealth ad any ad that attempts to hide the marketer's identity and fool the consumer.

Excerpt from

ENVIRONMENTAL SCIENCE

by William P. Cunningham

DON'T BELIEVE EVERYTHING YOU SEE OR HEAR ON THE NEWS

In our own everyday lives most of us are inundated by information and misinfor- 1
mation. Competing claims and contradictory ideas battle for our attention. The rapidly growing complexity of our world and our lives intensifies the difficulties in knowing what to believe or how to act. Consider how the communications revolution has brought us computers, e-mail, cell phones, mobile faxes, pagers, the World Wide Web, hundreds of channels of satellite TV, and direct mail or electronic marketing that overwhelm us with conflicting information. We have more choices than we can possibly manage, and know more about the world around us than ever before, but, perhaps, understand less. How can we deal with the barrage of often contradictory news and advice that inundates us?

By now, most of us know not to believe everything we read or hear. "Tastes 2 great . . . Low, low sale price . . . Lose 30 pounds in 3 weeks . . . You may already be a winner . . . Causes no environmental harm . . . I'll never lie to you . . . Two out of three doctors recommend . . ." More and more of the information we use to buy, elect, advise, judge, or heal has been created not to expand our knowledge but to sell a product or advance a cause.

For most of us, access to news is becoming ever more abundant and ubiqui- 3 tous. Internet web logs comment on events even as they're happening. Cable television news is available around the clock. Live images are projected to our homes from all over the world. We watch video coverage of distant wars and disasters as if they are occurring in our living rooms, but how much do we really know about what's going on? At the same time that media is becoming more technically sophisticated, news providers are also becoming more adept at manipulating images and content to convey particular messages.

"The day you write to please everyone you no longer are in journalism. You are in show business."

—Frank Miller, Jr.

Many people watch TV news programs and read newspapers or web logs 4 today not so much to be educated or to get new ideas as to reinforce their existing beliefs. A State of the Media study by the Center for Journalistic Excellence at Columbia University concluded that the news is becoming increasingly partisan and ideological. The line between news and entertainment has become blurred in most media. Disputes and disasters are overdramatized, while too little attention is paid to complex issues. News reports are increasingly shallow and one-sided, with little editing or fact checking. On live media, such as television and radio, attack journalism is becoming ever more common. Participants try to ridicule and demean their opponents rather than listening respectfully and comparing facts and sources. Many shows simply become people shouting at each other. Print media also is moving toward tabloid journalism, featuring many photographs and sensationalistic coverage of events.

According to the State of the Media Report, most television stations have all 5 but abandoned the traditional written and edited news story. Instead, more than two-thirds of all news segments now consist of on-site "stand-up" reports or live interviews in which a single viewpoint is presented as news without any background or perspective. Visual images seem more immediate and are regarded as more believable by most people: after all, pictures don't lie, but they can give a misleading impression of what's really important. Many topics, such as policy issues, don't make good visuals, and therefore never make it into TV coverage. Crime, accidents, disasters, lifestyle stories, sports, and weather make up more than 90 percent of the coverage on a typical television news program. If you watched cable TV news for an entire day, for instance, you'd see on average, only 1 minute each about the environment and health care, 2 minutes each on science and education, and 4 minutes on art and culture. More than 70 percent of the segments are less than 1 minute long, meaning that they convey more emotion than substance. People who get their news primarily from TV are significantly more fearful and pessimistic than those who get news from print media.

Partisan journalism has become much more prevalent since the deregulation 6 of public media. From the birth of the broadcasting industry, the airwaves were regarded and regulated as a public trust. Broadcasters, as a condition of their licenses, were required to operate in the "public interest" by covering important policy issues and providing equal time to both sides of contested issues. In 1988, however, the Federal Communications Commission ruled that the proliferation of mass media gives the public adequate access to diverse sources of information. Media outlets no longer are obliged to provide fair and balanced coverage of issues. Presenting a single perspective or even a deceptive version of events is no longer regarded as a betrayal of public trust.

[1]A practice that further erodes the honesty and truthfulness of media coverage 7 is the use of video news releases that masquerade as news stories. [2]In these videos, actors, hired by public relations firms, pose as reporters or experts to promote a special interest. [3]Businesses have long used this tactic to sell products, but a recent disturbing development is placement of news videos by governmental agencies. [4]For example, in 2004, the federal Department of Health and Human Services sent video stories to TV stations promoting the benefits of the recently passed but controversial Medicare drug law. The actors in these videos appeared to be simply reporting news, but, in fact, were presenting a highly partisan viewpoint. Critics complained that these "stealth ads" undermine the credibility of both journalists and public officials. Kevin W. Keane, a Health Department spokesman, dismissed the criticism, saying this is "a common, routine practice in government and the private sector." In 2004, the federal government paid $88 million to public relations firms and news commentators to represent administration positions on policy issues.

How can you detect bias in a news report? Ask yourself the following questions: 8

1. What political positions are represented in the story?

2. What special interests might be involved here? Who stands to gain presenting a particular viewpoint? Who is paying for the message?

3. What sources are used as evidence in this story? How credible are they?

4. Are statistics cited in the presentation? Are citations provided so you can check the source?

5. Is the story one-sided, or are alternate viewpoints presented? Are both sides represented by credible spokespersons, or is one simply a patsy set up to make the other side look good?

6. Are the arguments presented based on facts and logic, or are they purely emotional appeals?

We need to practice critical thinking to detect bias and make sense out of what 9 we see and hear. Although the immediacy and visual impact of television or the Internet may seem convincing, we have to use caution and judgment to interpret the information they present. Don't depend on a single source for news. Compare what different media outlets say about an issue before making up your mind.

(William P. Cunningham, et al., *Environmental Science*, 9/e, 2007)

✓ COMPREHENSION CHECKUP

True or False

Indicate whether the statement is true or false by writing **T** or **F** in the space provided.

_____T_____ 1. It is possible for a news provider to manipulate images and content.

_____T_____ 2. According to the author, news reports are increasingly one-sided.

_F_____ 3. On live media, attack journalism is a thing of the past.

_F_____ 4. More than three-quarters of all news segments consist of stand-up reports.

_F_____ 5. Policy issues make up more than 90 percent of the coverage on a typical television news program.

_F_____ 6. People who get news primarily from TV tend to be more optimistic than those who get their news from magazines or newspapers.

_T_____ 7. In 2004, the federal government paid $88 million to public relations firms and news commentators to present administration positions on various issues.

_F_____ 8. Kevin Keane apparently believes that stealth ads are common practices in government and the private sector.

Multiple Choice

Write the letter of the correct answer in the space provided.

_____ 9. A key point the author makes is that
   a. complex issues get too much attention from the media
   b. news reports bend over backwards to present multiple points of view
   c. Americans are overwhelmed by conflicting information
   d. news and entertainment are presented as two separate and distinct entities

_____ 10. We can infer that the author of this selection is in favor of
   a. partisan journalism
   b. providing equal time on controversial issues
   c. allowing actors to pose as reporters or experts
   d. using so-called stealth ads

_____ 11. Which sentence among the following from paragraph 7 contains the most emotionally loaded language?
   a. sentence 1
   b. sentence 2
   c. sentence 3
   d. sentence 4

_____ 12. The author would probably agree with which of the following statements?
   a. Access to news is becoming ever more restricted.
   b. Print journalism and tabloid journalism are beginning to resemble each other in some respects.
   c. News reports are scrupulously checked to make sure the facts are accurate.
   d. Attack journalism is a thing of the past in live television.

_____ 13. All of the following are statements of opinion *except*
   a. "by now, most of us know not to believe everything we read or hear"
   b. "we have more choices than we can possibly manage, and know more about the world around us than ever before, but, perhaps, understand less"

c. "a State of the Media study by the Center for Journalistic Excellence at Columbia University concluded that the news is becoming increasingly partisan and ideological"

d. "the line between news and entertainment has become blurred in most media"

_____ 14. Which of the following best describes the author's attitude toward the current state of the news story?
   a. ambivalent
   b. concerned
   c. objective
   d. compassionate

_____ 15. A reasonable inference that can be drawn is that
   a. deregulation of the media has contributed to the rise in partisan journalism
   b. both sides of widely disputed issues continue to be presented
   c. actors posing as reporters are representing the government point of view in advertisements
   d. both a and c

_____ 16. Which of the following best describes the author's main purpose?
   a. to encourage the public to think critically about information presented by the media
   b. to inform the public about possible bias in news reports
   c. to persuade the reader to lobby the government to return regulation to the media industry
   d. both a and b

_____ 17. In paragraph 2 the author gives examples to demonstrate
   a. the stupidity of the public
   b. deceptive advertising techniques
   c. products to help people lose weight
   d. remedies for cancer

_____ 18. As used in paragraph 7, the words _erodes, masquerade, controversial,_ and _disturbing_ have a
   a. negative connotation
   b. positive connotation

_____ 19. The author expresses a negative bias toward all of the following _except_
   a. the Center for Journalistic Excellence at Columbia University
   b. e-mail, cell phones, mobile faxes, and pagers
   c. stealth ads
   d. cable television news

_____ 20. The author concludes the selection with a warning to
   a. practice critical thinking in order to detect bias in the media
   b. rely on only a single source you know and trust for daily news
   c. make up your mind about an issue after comparing different viewpoints
   d. both a and c

Vocabulary in Context

Each question below has a sentence from the selection and another sentence. A word is italicized in both sentences. Use the context clues in the two sentences to determine the meaning of the word.

1. "In our own everyday lives most of us are *inundated* by information and misinformation."

   He is such a dynamic speaker that he is *inundated* with requests to speak at various charitable events.

   Inundated means _____

2. "For most of us, access to news is becoming ever more abundant and *ubiquitous*."

   Commercials are *ubiquitous* on evening TV.

   Ubiquitous means _____

3. "Participants try to ridicule and *demean* their opponents rather than listening respectfully and comparing facts and sources."

   If you lie and cheat to get ahead in your career, you are likely to *demean* yourself.

   Demean means _____

4. "A State of the Media study by the Center for Journalistic Excellence at Columbia University concluded that the news is becoming increasingly *partisan* and ideological."

   His goal was to remain neutral and above *partisan* politics.

   Partisan means _____

5. "At the same time that media is becoming more technically sophisticated, news providers are also becoming more *adept* at manipulating images and content to convey particular messages."

   Karla is an *adept* tennis player; she has won many tournaments.

   Adept means _____

6. "People who get their news primarily from TV are significantly more fearful and *pessimistic* than those who get news from print media."

   With their continual fights, I am very *pessimistic* about their marriage surviving much longer.

   Pessimistic means _____

7. "News reports are increasingly *shallow* and one-sided, with little editing or fact checking."

   I think that she is a *shallow* person because her conversation is limited to discussions about hair and makeup.

   Shallow means _____

8. "A practice that further *erodes* the honesty and truthfulness of media coverage is the use of video news releases that masquerade as news stories."

   When government officials mislead the public, the public's trust in the government *erodes*.

   Erodes means _____

In Your Own Words

1. In a 2003 Gallup poll, 62 percent of the respondents stated that they believed news organizations are often inaccurate in their reporting. What factors do you think have led to the public's loss of confidence in the news media?

2. Do you primarily get your news from cable, local news channels, nightly network news, satirical comedy shows, the Internet, morning TV shows, or radio talk shows? Do you think the source of your news tends to be biased or slanted, or does it tend to be objective?

3. With the Internet, people can select only the news that interests them or that expresses views they already support. Do you think the ability to do this is going to encourage less tolerance and more polarization on the part of the public?

4. Do you think the nightly news has a liberal or a conservative bias? Give reasons for your view.

5. Do you think TV news programmers choose stories for their entertainment value or because they represent serious, important issues?

6. Do you think television has a vested interest in disasters? Does watching TV news make you feel like you are living in a world of perpetual crisis?

7. Media education is a mandatory part of the high school curriculum in Australia, Canada, and Great Britain. Do you think the United States should also make it a school requirement?

The Art of Writing

1. The author of this selection is presenting an argument. Identify the issue, the claim, the support, and the assumptions. Do you think his argument has validity?

2. Keep track of the topics presented on a nightly newscast. Be sure to note how much time is devoted to discussions of crime, accidents, disasters, lifestyle stories, sports, weather, the environment, health care, science, education, art, and culture. How long does each segment last? What can you conclude about the information presented?

Internet Activity

Evaluate the following Web sites. What is the point of view of each? Do the Web sites reflect any biases?

The National Association for Media Literacy Education:

http://namle.net/about

Association for Media Literacy:

www.aml.ca

Media Alliance:

www.media-alliance.org

SELECTION

"There was no member of the Virginia delegation who did not own slaves, and of all members of Congress at least a third owned or had owned slaves."

GETTING THE PICTURE

Both John Adams, the second president, and Thomas Jefferson, the third president, died on the same day—the Fourth of July, 1826. Although both had wished to attend the fiftieth-anniversary celebration of the Declaration of Independence, neither was able to. Congress nevertheless paid tribute to both men, forever linking the two old "patriots"—Adams, the chief advocate of the Declaration, and Jefferson, its author. In his epitaph, Adams chose to say nothing of his political accomplishments, instead extolling the virtues of piety, humility, and industry. Jefferson wished to be remembered for his creative work. The inscription on his tombstone reads as follows:

Here Was Buried
THOMAS JEFFERSON
Author of the Declaration of American Independence,
Of the Statute of Virginia for Religious Freedom,
And Father of the University of Virginia

BIO-SKETCH

Historian David McCullough won the Pulitzer Prize for a biography of President Harry Truman in 1993 and again in 2001 for a biography of John Adams, our second president. He has said that the six years that it took him to write *John Adams* were the best years of his writing career.

BRUSHING UP ON VOCABULARY

redundant wordy or unnecessarily repetitious. Derived from the Latin *unda*, meaning "wave." When speakers or writers are wordy, they are said to have a *redundant* style because their "waves" of words go on and on, repeating themselves.

preamble an introductory statement; a preface. In Latin, *pre* means "before," and *ambular* means "to walk." The introductory portion of an essay or a speech is called a *preamble* because it comes first or "walks before."

mercenary a professional soldier hired to serve in a foreign army. The word can be traced back to the Latin *mercenarius*, meaning "one who works for wages." When Jefferson mentions "mercenaries" in the Declaration of Independence, he is referring to the Hessians who fought under the British flag in the Revolutionary War.

Excerpt from
JOHN ADAMS

by David McCullough

JEFFERSON, ADAMS, AND THE DECLARATION OF INDEPENDENCE

Jefferson was to draft the declaration. But how this was agreed to was never 1 made altogether clear. He and Adams would have differing explanations, each writing long after the fact.

According to Adams, Jefferson proposed that he, Adams, do the writing, but 2
that he declined, telling Jefferson he must do it.

"Why?" Jefferson asked, as Adams would recount. 3

"Reasons enough," Adams said. 4

"What can be your reasons?" 5

"Reason first: you are a Virginian and a Virginian ought to appear at the head 6
of this business. Reason two: I am obnoxious, suspected and unpopular. You are
very much otherwise. Reason third: You can write ten times better than I can."

Jefferson would recall no such exchange. As Jefferson remembered, the com- 7
mittee simply met and unanimously chose him to undertake the draft. "I con-
sented: I drew it [up]."

. . .

Congress had to review and approve the language of the drafted declaration 8
before it could be made official. Deliberations commenced at once, continuing
through the next morning, July 3, when mercifully the temperature had dropped
ten degrees, broken by the storm of the previous day.

For Thomas Jefferson it became a painful ordeal, as change after change was 9
called for and approximately a quarter of what he had written was cut entirely.
Seated beside Benjamin Franklin, the young Virginian looked on in silence. He is
not known to have uttered a word in protest, or in defense of what he had written. Later he would describe the opposition to his draft as being like "the ceaseless action of gravity weighing upon us night and day." At one point Franklin
leaned over to tell him a story that, as a printer and publisher over so many years,
he must have offered before as comfort to a wounded author. He had once
known a hatter who wished to have a sign made saying, JOHN THOMPSON,
HATTER, MAKES AND SELLS HATS FOR READY MONEY, this to be accompanied
by a picture of a hat. But the man had chosen first to ask the opinion of friends,
with the result that one word after another was removed as superfluous or redundant, until at last the sign was reduced to Thompson's name and the picture
of the hat.

Beyond its stirring preamble, most of the document before Congress was 1●
taken up with a list of grievances, specific charges against the King—"He has
plundered our seas, ravaged our coasts, burnt our towns. He is at this time transporting large armies of foreign mercenaries to complete the works of death,
desolation and Tyranny. . . ." And it was the King, "the Christian King of Great
Britain," Jefferson had emphasized, who was responsible for the horrors of the
slave trade. As emphatic a passage as any, this on the slave trade was to have
been the ringing climax of all the charges. Now it was removed in its entirety
because, said Jefferson later, South Carolina and Georgia objected. Some northern delegates, too, were a "little tender" on the subject, "for though their people
have very few slaves themselves yet they had been pretty considerable carriers."

In truth black slavery had long since become an accepted part of life in all of 1
the thirteen colonies. Of a total population in the colonies of nearly 2,500,000
people in 1776, approximately one in five were slaves, some 500,000 men,
women, and children. In Virginia alone, which had the most slaves by far, they
numbered more than 200,000. There was no member of the Virginia delegation
who did not own slaves, and of all members of Congress at least a third owned
or had owned slaves. The total of Thomas Jefferson's slaves in 1776, as near as

can be determined from his personal records, was about 200, which was also the approximate number owned by George Washington.

. . .

In time Jefferson and Adams would each denounce slavery. Jefferson was to 12 write of the degrading effects of the institution on both slave and master. Adams would call slavery a "foul contagion in the human character." But neither [they] nor any other delegate in Congress would have let the issue jeopardize a declaration of independence, however strong their feelings. If Adams was disappointed or downcast over the removal of Jefferson's indictment of the slave trade, he seems to have said nothing at the time. Nor is it possible to know the extent of Jefferson's disappointment or if the opposition of South Carolina and Georgia was truly as decisive as he later claimed. Very possibly there were many delegates, from North and South, happy to see the passage omitted for the reason that it was patently absurd to hold the King responsible for horrors that, everyone knew, Americans—and Christians no less than the King—had brought on themselves. Slavery and the slave trade were hardly the fault of George III, however ardently Jefferson wished to fix the blame on the distant monarch.

Of more than eighty changes made in Jefferson's draft during the time 13 Congress deliberated, most were minor and served to improve it. But one final cut toward the conclusion was as substantial nearly as the excise of the passage on the slave trade, and it appears to have wounded Jefferson deeply.

To the long list of indictments against the King, he had added one assailing the 14 English people, "our British brethren," as a further oppressor, for allowing their Parliament and their King "to send over not only soldiers of our common blood, but Scotch and foreign mercenaries to invade and destroy us." And therein, Jefferson charged, was the heart of the tragedy, the feeling of betrayal, the "common blood" cause of American outrage. "These facts have given the last stab to agonizing affection, and manly spirit bids us renounce forever these unfeeling brethren," he had written. "We must endeavor to forget our former love for them."

This most emotional passage of all was too much for many in Congress, and to 15 it Jefferson had added a final poignant note: "We might have been a free and great people together." Nearly all of this was removed. There was to be no mention of a "last stab," or "love," or of the "free and great people" that might have been.

Finally, to Jefferson's concluding line was added the phrase "with a firm reli- 16 ance on the protection of divine Providence," an addition that John Adams assuredly welcomed. Thus it would read:

> And for the support of this Declaration, with a firm reliance on the protection 17
> of divine Providence, we mutually pledge to each other our lives, our fortunes, and our sacred honor.

But it was to be the eloquent lines of the second paragraph of the Declaration 18 that would stand down the years, affecting the human spirit as neither Jefferson nor anyone could have foreseen. And however much was owed to the writings of others, as Jefferson acknowledged, or to such editorial refinements as those contributed by Franklin or Adams, they were, when all was said and done, his lines. It was Jefferson who had written them for all time:

> We hold these truths to be self-evident, that all men are created equal, that 19
> they are endowed by their Creator with certain unalienable rights, that

among these are life, liberty, and the pursuit of happiness. That to secure these rights, governments are instituted among men, deriving their just powers from the consent of the governed.

. . .

In old age, trying to reconstruct events of that crowded summer, both Thomas 20 Jefferson and John Adams would incorrectly insist that the signing took place July 4.

Apparently there was no fuss or ceremony on August 2. The delegates simply 21 came forward in turn and fixed their signatures. The fact that a signed document now existed, as well as the names of the signatories, was kept secret for the time being, as all were acutely aware that by taking up the pen and writing their names, they had committed treason. Whether Benjamin Franklin quipped "We must all hang together, or most assuredly we shall hang separately" is impossible to know, just as there is no way to confirm the much-repeated story that the diminutive John Hancock wrote his name large so the King might read it without his spectacles. But the stories endured because they were in character, like the remark attributed to Stephen Hopkins of Rhode Island. Hopkins, who suffered from palsy, is said to have observed, on completing his spidery signature, "My hand trembles, but my heart does not."

(David McCullough, *John Adams*, 2001)

✓ COMPREHENSION CHECKUP

Short Answer

1. At the beginning of the selection, Adams makes a claim that Jefferson should be the one to write the Declaration. What support does he provide?

   a. _____

   b. _____

   c. _____

Multiple Choice

Write the letter of the correct answer in the blank provided; you may refer to the reading selection or to other sections of this book if necessary.

_____ 2. The mode of rhetoric in this selection is primarily
   a. narration
   b. description
   c. exposition
   d. persuasion

_____ 3. The overall pattern of organization is primarily
   a. cause and effect
   b. comparison-contrast
   c. example
   d. chronological order

_____ 4. In paragraph 1, Adams portrays himself as
   a. self-congratulatory
   b. defeated
   c. self-deprecatory
   d. gleeful

_____ 5. In the debate over the wording of the Declaration, Jefferson
   a. became angry when changes were suggested
   b. was actively engaged in debating corrections
   c. remained silent
   d. fought vigorously for every word

_____ 6. Jefferson was a proud representative of
   a. Delaware
   b. Virginia
   c. Massachusetts
   d. New York

_____ 7. On his plantation, Jefferson
   a. hired only free men
   b. had only a few slaves
   c. had many slaves
   d. farmed with the aid of family members only

_____ 8. The actual signing of the Declaration of Independence occurred on
   a. July 2
   b. July 4
   c. August 2
   d. December 26

_____ 9. The state with the most recorded slaves was
   a. South Carolina
   b. Georgia
   c. Kentucky
   d. Virginia

_____ 10. Jefferson's Declaration
   a. listed grievances against the king
   b. defended the practice of slavery
   c. criticized the use of foreign mercenaries
   d. both a and c

_____ 11. In his original draft of the Declaration, in addition to his indictment of the king, Jefferson assailed
   a. the British people
   b. John Locke
   c. the Virginia delegation
   d. France

_____ 12. As used in paragraph 10, the words *plundered, ravaged, burnt,* and *desolation* have a
   a. negative connotation
   b. positive connotation

True or False

Indicate whether the statement is true or false by writing **T** or **F** in the blank provided.

_____ 13. Washington and Jefferson owned a comparable number of slaves.

_____ 14. By affixing their signatures to the Declaration, the delegates were committing an act of treason.

_____ 15. John Hancock was large in stature.

_____ 16. Approximately forty changes were made to Jefferson's Declaration.

_____ 17. The most memorable lines in Jefferson's Declaration are contained in the second paragraph.

_____ 18. Paragraph 10 provides a partial list of Jefferson's reasons (support) for creating a new government.

_____ 19. Jefferson is using figurative language when he says that opposition to his draft is like the ceaseless action of gravity.

Vocabulary in Context

Cross out the incorrect word in each sentence, and write the correct word from the following list in the blank provided. (Use each word only once.)

ardent	desolate	eloquent	plundered
commence	diminutive	emphatic	poignant
denounced	downcast	excise	superfluous

_____ 1. Once children turn 5 in the United States they usually end their formal schooling.

_____ 2. Santa's elves are known for their large size.

_____ 3. The audience applauded enthusiastically after the president delivered a stirring and bland speech.

_____ 4. He already had accumulated sufficient credits to graduate; any further credits were purely essential.

_____ 5. After Carolyn failed her final exams, she was especially ecstatic.

_____ 6. In his closing argument, the prosecutor praised the defendant's heinous crime.

_____ 7. Mike professed his love to his sweetheart in a warm, loving, dispassionate manner.

_____ 8. When asked whether she wanted to be given a Lexus as her award, Carmen gave a very tentative nod "yes."

_____ 9. The grave-robbers protected the valuables in the tombs.

_____ 10. Conditions in the country were fertile after the drought destroyed the land.

_____ 11. The movie _Selena_, about the life of the late singer, was heartbreaking and unaffecting in places.

_____ 12. The surgeon's only recourse was to preserve the infected flesh after gangrene had set in.

In Your Own Words

1. The pursuit of happiness is one of the "unalienable rights" written into the Declaration. What do you think Jefferson meant by "the pursuit of happiness"? What do you think most Americans today require for a "happy life"?

2. Oscar Wilde once said, "In this world there are only two tragedies. One is not getting what one wants, and the other is getting it." What do you think he meant? Do you agree or disagree with him?

The Art of Writing

In a brief essay, respond to the item below.

Rabbi Harold Kushner says that an individual doesn't become happy by pursuing happiness. Instead, he says that "happiness is like a butterfly—the more you chase it, the more it flies away from you and hides. But stop chasing it, put away your net and busy yourself with other, more productive things than the pursuit of personal happiness, and it will sneak up on you from behind and perch on your shoulder." Explain Kushner's concept using examples from your own life.

Internet Activity

Visit the following Web site to learn more about John Adams.

www.whitehouse.gov/history/presidents

List several facts that were new to you and were not mentioned in the reading selection.

STUDY TECHNIQUE 9

Venn Diagrams

A Venn diagram is an illustration that shows similarities and differences between topics using a graphic of two overlapping circles. Notice the diagram below. In the circle on the left, characteristics specific only to Jefferson are listed; in the circle on the right, characteristics specific only to Adams are listed; in the overlapping area, characteristics shared by both Adams and Jefferson are listed.

Complete the Venn diagram comparing and contrasting Jefferson and Adams by listing more traits unique to each of these men and more traits they shared. Then write a paragraph comparing and contrasting the two men. You will find that it is much easier to write a comparison-contrast assignment after creating such a Venn diagram.

Jefferson

1. Was from Virginia
2. Wrote Declaration
3.

Both

1. Died on July 4, 1826
2. Denounced slavery
3.
4.
5.

Adams

1. Was from Massachusetts
2. Advocated Declaration
3.

Introduction to Deductive and Inductive Reasoning

In the final step of analyzing a selection, the reader must evaluate the soundness of the author's reasoning. Often our evaluation is based on deductive or inductive reasoning.

Deductive Reasoning

The word *deduction* comes from the Latin *de*, meaning "from," and *duc*, meaning "to lead." In **deductive reasoning,** we move from a general principle and a specific example to reach a conclusion.

Here's an example of a deductive argument:

Major premise (Support): All of Stephen King's books are enjoyable.

Minor premise (Support): *Under the Dome* is a book by Stephen King.

Conclusion: Therefore, *Under the Dome* is enjoyable.

This deductive argument has two premises: First, the general principle (also called the *major premise*): "All of Stephen King's books are enjoyable." Second, the specific instance (or *minor premise*), "*Under the Dome* is a book by Stephen King." Finally, it has a conclusion: "*Under the Dome* is enjoyable." This type of deductive argument—with a major premise, a minor premise, and a conclusion—is called a **syllogism.** If both the major and minor premises are true, and the conclusion follows from the premises, then the conclusion must be true, and we have a *sound* argument. Since the conclusion follows from the premises, the argument is also *valid*.

But not all deductive arguments are valid. Look at this example:

Major premise: All of Stephen King's books are enjoyable.

Minor premise: The book I'm reading now is enjoyable.

Conclusion: Therefore, the book I'm reading now is a Stephen King book.

This argument is *invalid* because, while both premises may well be true, the conclusion does not follow from these premises. The book you're reading now might not be a Stephen King book. It might be an enjoyable book by another author. We can also say this about deductive arguments: You can rely on the conclusion only if the argument is both sound and valid.

Inductive Reasoning

Like *deduction,* the word *induction* comes from the Latin root *duc*, meaning "to lead," and *in*, meaning "into." In **inductive reasoning,** specific examples, evidence, or propositions lead to a more general conclusion.

Here's an example of inductive reasoning:

It's Wednesday, and you're trying to decide what restaurant to go to this weekend. You're thinking about three possibilities: Great Flavors, Hot and Spicy, and

Healthy Stuff. So you start talking to your friends. Bill tells you that Great Flavors is all right, but nothing special. Tanya says that Hot and Spicy is too hot and spicy. Lisa says that she enjoyed Healthy Stuff. You talk to some other people too. They all tell you about the same thing. The food at Great Flavors is mediocre. Hot and Spicy goes overboard. And Healthy Stuff serves food that is nutritious *and* delicious. So you decide that you will probably have a good time at Healthy Stuff, and that's where you will go.

The argument here moves from specific information about three restaurants to a general conclusion about which restaurant would be most enjoyable.

As this example shows, a conclusion reached by inductive reasoning is only as sound as the quality of the information on which it is based. If the information on which you based your conclusion is bad, so will be your conclusion.

So inductive arguments lead to conclusions that are only *probably* true. You couldn't conclude from your survey that you would *certainly* have a good time at Healthy Stuff. You could only conclude that you would *probably* have a good time there. The better your information is, the more probable your conclusion will be true.

You can now see one important difference between deductive and inductive reasoning. Deductive reasoning produces conclusions that are either true or false. But inductive reasoning produces conclusions that are only probably true or false.

Exercise 7: Identifying Inductive and Deductive Arguments

Directions: After studying each example, indicate whether the argument is inductive or deductive by writing I or D in the blank provided. Be prepared to discuss whether the conclusion is valid or invalid.

_____ 1. The only passenger train running between Tucson and Los Angeles is operated by Amtrak. Wynona is taking a passenger train from Tucson to Los Angeles. So Wynona must be traveling on an Amtrak train.

_____ 2. I was at Mall of America this morning, and it was crowded with shoppers carrying shopping bags filled with recent purchases. So the economy must be doing well.

_____ 3. When I don't eat breakfast I start feeling weak around 10:30. I missed breakfast this morning, so I know I'm going to start feeling weak around 10:30.

_____ 4. Frida likes all kinds of jazz music. Marco gave Frida a jazz CD. Frida is going to like her new CD.

_____ 5. When the principal visited Lois Johnson's classroom, the children were running around the classroom talking and playing with each other, while Ms. Johnson yelled at them to take their seats and be quiet. The principal concluded that Ms. Johnson did not know how to maintain discipline.

_____ 6. Yomiko has noticed that many of the speakers at the seminars she attends are dull. Yomiko will be going to a seminar tomorrow. Yomiko expects that some of the speakers at the seminar will be dull.

GETTING THE PICTURE

The following is an annotated version of the Declaration of Independence. The Declaration as a whole is considered a classic deductive argument. If pared down to its basic parts—major premise, minor premise, and conclusion—the syllogism would look like this:

Major premise: When a government becomes tyrannical in its treatment of its people, the people have a right to overthrow it and create a new government.

Minor premise: The government of Great Britain has become tyrannical in its treatment of Americans.

Conclusion: Therefore, Americans have a right to overthrow the British government and create a new government.

If these premises are true, then the conclusion must be true.

THE DECLARATION OF INDEPENDENCE

by Thomas Jefferson

INTRODUCTION

A general statement

When in the course of human events, it becomes <u>necessary</u> for one people to dissolve the political bands which have connected them with another, and to assume among the Powers of the earth, the separate and equal station to which the Laws of Nature and Nature's God entitle them, a decent respect to the opinions of mankind requires that they should <u>declare the causes which impel them to the separation.</u>

1   Key word

Impersonal tone

Purpose stated

PREAMBLE

We hold these truths to be self-evident, that <u>all men are created equal</u>, that <u>they are endowed by their Creator with certain unalienable Rights</u>, that among <u>these are Life, Liberty and the pursuit of Happiness.</u>

2 Five propositions given

General philosophy of government

That <u>to secure these rights, Governments are instituted among Men</u>, deriving their just powers from the consent of the governed.

3

That <u>whenever any Form of Government becomes destructive of these ends, it is the Right of the People to alter or to abolish it</u>, and to institute a new Government laying its foundation on such principles and organizing its powers in such form, as to them shall seem most likely to effect their Safety and Happiness. Prudence, indeed, will dictate that Governments long established should not be changed for light and transient causes; and accordingly all experience hath shown that mankind are more disposed to suffer, while evils are sufferable, than to right themselves by abolishing the forms to which they are

4 Fifth is most crucial—asserts the right of revolution

accustomed. But when a long train of abuses and usurpations pursuing invariably the same Object evinces a design to reduce them under absolute Despotism, it is their right, it is their duty, to throw off such government, and to provide new Guards for their future security.

Such has been the patient sufferance of these Colonies; and such is now the necessity which constrains them to alter their former Systems of Government. The history of the present King of Great Britain is a history of repeated injuries and usurpations, all having in direct object the establishment of an absolute Tyranny over these States. *To prove this, let Facts be submitted to a candid world.*

He has <u>refused his Assent to Laws</u>, the most wholesome and necessary for the public good.

He has forbidden his Governors to pass Laws of immediate and pressing importance, unless <u>suspended in their operation</u> till his Assent should be obtained; and when so suspended, he has utterly neglected to attend to them. He has refused to pass other Laws for the accommodation of large districts of people, unless those people would relinquish the right of Representation in the Legislature, a right inestimable to them and formidable to tyrants only.

He has called together legislative bodies at places unusual, uncomfortable, and distant from the depository of their public Records, for the sole purpose of fatiguing them into compliance with his measures.

He has <u>dissolved Representative Houses repeatedly</u>, for opposing with manly firmness his invasions on the rights of the people.

He has refused for a long time, after such dissolutions, to cause others to be elected; whereby the Legislative powers, incapable of Annihilation, have returned to the People at large for their exercise, the State remaining in the mean time exposed to all the dangers of invasion from without, and convulsions within.

He has endeavoured to prevent the population of these States; for that purpose obstructing the Laws for Naturalization of Foreigners; refusing to pass others to encourage their migrations hither, and raising the conditions of new Appropriations of Lands.

He has <u>obstructed the Administration of Justice</u>, by refusing his Assent to Laws for establishing Judiciary powers.

He has made Judges dependent on his Will alone, for the tenure of their offices, and the amount and payment of their salaries.

He has erected a multitude of New Offices, and sent hither swarms of Officers to harass our People, and eat out their substance.

Margin notes:

INDICTMENT OF GEORGE III
Four groups of facts listed

Proof : 28 grievances

Group I charges 1–12: describe the abuse of king's executive power

Word *candid* implies an appeal to fair and unbiased

5

6

7 Charges are arranged by topics, not chronologically

8 Charges are purposely ambiguous: no names, dates, or places are identified

9

10

11

12

13

14

He has <u>kept among us, in times of peace, standing 15 Armies</u> without the Consent of our legislatures.

He has affected to render the Military independent of 16 and superior to the Civil power.

Group II charges 13–22: subjected America to unconstitutional measures

He has combined with others to subject us to a jurisdic- 17 tion foreign to our constitution, and unacknowledged by our laws; giving his Assent to their Acts of pretended Legislation:

For Quartering large bodies of armed troops among us: 18

For protecting them, by a mock Trial from punish- 19 ment for any Murders which they should commit on the Inhabitants of these States:

<u>For cutting off our Trade with all parts of the world:</u> 20

<u>For imposing Taxes on us without our Consent:</u>   21

<u>For depriving us in many cases of the benefits of Trial 22 by Jury:</u>

For transporting us beyond Seas to be tried for pre- 23 tended offences:

For abolishing the free System of English Laws in a 24 neighboring Province, establishing therein an Arbitrary government, and enlarging its Boundaries so as to render it at once an example and fit instrument for introducing the same absolute rule into these Colonies.

<u>For taking away our Charters</u>, abolishing our most 25 valuable Laws, and altering fundamentally the Forms of our Governments:

For suspending our own Legislatures, and declaring 26 themselves invested with power to legislate for us in all cases whatsoever.

He has abdicated Government here, by declaring us 27 out of his Protection and waging War against us.

Group III charges 23–27: the king is charged with violence and cruelty

He has <u>plundered</u> our seas, <u>ravaged</u> our Coasts, <u>burnt</u> 28 Emotionally charged our towns, and <u>destroyed</u> the Lives of our people.   verbs

He is at this time transporting large Armies of foreign 29 Mercenaries to compleat the works of death, desolation and tyranny, already begun with circumstances of Cruelty & perfidy scarcely paralleled in the most barbarous ages, and totally unworthy of the Head of a civilized nation.

He has constrained our fellow Citizens taken Captive 30 on the high Seas to bear Arms against their Country, to become the executioners of their friends and Brethren, or to fall themselves by their Hands.

He has excited domestic insurrections amongst us, 31 and has endeavoured to bring on the inhabitants of our frontiers, merciless Indian savages, whose known rule of warfare, is an undistinguished destruction of all ages, sexes, and conditions.

Group IV final charge

In every stage of these Oppressions We have Peti- 32 Colonies have tioned for Redress in the most humble terms: <u>Our</u>   appealed in vain repeated <u>Petitions have been answered only by repeated injury</u>. A Prince, whose character is thus marked by every act which may define a Tyrant, is unfit to be the ruler of a free people.

DENUNCIATION OF THE BRITISH PEOPLE

Nor have We been wanting in attentions to our British 33 brethren. We have warned them from time to time of attempts by their legislature to extend an unwarrantable jurisdiction over us. We have reminded them of the circumstances of our emigration and settlement here. We have appealed to their native justice and magnanimity, and we have conjured them by the ties of our common kindred to disavow these usurpations, which would inevitably interrupt our connections and correspondence. <u>They too have been deaf to the voice of Justice and of consanguinity</u>. We must, therefore, acquiesce in the necessity, which denounces our Separation, and hold them, as we hold the rest of mankind, Enemies in War, in Peace Friends.

This section finishes the case for independence

Use of metaphor

CONCLUSION

We, therefore, the representatives of the united States 34 of America, in General Congress, Assembled, appealing to the Supreme Judge of the world for the rectitude of our intentions, do, in the Name, and by Authority of the good People of these Colonies, solemnly publish and declare, That these United Colonies are, and of Right ought to be Free and Independent States; that they are absolved from all Allegiance to the British Crown, and that all political connection between them and the State of Great Britain, is and ought to be totally dissolved; and that as Free and Independent States, they have full Power to levy War, conclude Peace, contract Alliances, establish Commerce, and to do all other Acts and Things which Independent States may of right do. And for the support of this Declaration, with a firm reliance on the protection of divine Providence, <u>we mutually pledge to each other our Lives, our Fortunes and our sacred Honor.</u>

Personal tone

A solemn vow from men of honor

(Stephen E. Lucas, *The Stylistic Artistry of the Declaration of Independence*, 1989.)

✓ COMPREHENSION CHECKUP

Short Answer

In one or two sentences, answer the questions below.

1. In the very first sentence, Jefferson makes a claim that people are entitled by "the Laws of Nature and Nature's God" to separate and equal stations. What does this claim mean?

_____

_____

_____

2. According to Jefferson's reasoning in paragraph 2, what truths does he say are self-evident? What is meant by the term *self-evident*?

_____

_____

_____

3. According to paragraph 3, what is the purpose of governments? From where do governments derive their power?

_____

_____

_____

4. In paragraph 4, Jefferson responds to those who would throw off governments for "light and transient causes." What sort of cause does he say you need to "throw off governments"?

_____

_____

_____

5. Jefferson hopes that a listing of specific acts of tyranny by George III will convince others that the American colonies are justified in separating themselves from England. List some factual evidence given by Jefferson to justify independence. What are the most serious complaints?

_____

_____

_____

6. What is Jefferson referring to in the next-to-the-last paragraph? Do you think the British Parliament accepted Jefferson's claim?

_____

_____

_____

7. What does Jefferson announce in the last paragraph?

_____

_____

_____

8. What is the overall tone of Jefferson's argument?

_____

_____

_____

Vocabulary Practice

From the list below, determine the antonym for each set of the following listed words.

abolish	despotism	endowed	prudence	solemnly
acquiesce	emigration	magnanimous	ravaged	transient

1. stingy; mean; petty; greedy   _____

2. preserved; guarded   _____

3. continuous; perpetual; everlasting   _____

4. foolishness; senselessness; rashness   _____

5. initiate; secure; support   _____

6. democracy; liberalism; liberty   _____

7. silly; jocularly   _____

8. immigration   _____

9. object; resist; dissent; refuse   _____

10. divested; deprived; forfeited   _____

In Your Own Words

1. To whom do you think Jefferson is speaking to in his Declaration?

2. Many reform movements have been inspired by Jefferson's Declaration. Do you think that Jefferson was aware that he was speaking to future generations?

The Art of Writing

In a brief essay, respond to the items below.

1. The phrase "that all men are created equal" has caused considerable controversy. What do you think Jefferson meant by it? What is your interpretation of the phrase?

2. Do you think that the sort of rebellion advocated by Jefferson in the Declaration could ever be justified in today's world? In what circumstances?

Internet Activity

1. To learn more about Thomas Jefferson, go to

   www.monticello.org

   Click on "A Day in the Life of Jefferson" to follow Jefferson through a typical 24 hours during his retirement at Monticello. Then, to learn more about Jefferson's role in the Lewis and Clark Expedition, click on "Jefferson and the Expedition." Peruse this portion of the site to find a page of interest to you; print it and briefly summarize your findings.

2. To learn more about the Declaration of Independence and to view material from the collections of the Library of Congress, go to

   http://lcweb.loc.gov/exhibits/declara/declara1.html

   Click on either "Chronology of Events" or "Objects in the Exhibition." If you select the chronology, create a short time line of the events leading up to the signing of the Declaration. Or select an object in the current exhibition, and briefly describe it.

*"In all criminal prosecutions, the accused shall enjoy the
right to a speedy and public trial . . ."*

GETTING THE PICTURE

Opinion on the ratification of the U.S. Constitution was almost evenly divided between those who favored its passage and those who did not. Many were opposed because they feared that a strong federal government would usurp the power of the states and individual citizens. As a result, a compromise was reached. If the Constitution were approved, amendments would be added at a later date that would safeguard individual liberties. The ten amendments adopted later became the Bill of Rights.

BIO-SKETCH

James Madison is called the "father of the Constitution." His *Federalist Papers* contributed to the constitution's ratification. It was Madison who introduced a series of amendments, ten of which were ratified by the states to become the Bill of Rights. Later, Madison assisted Thomas Jefferson in forming a political party that aimed to promote ordinary citizens as opposed to the rich and powerful. Madison served as secretary of state during Jefferson's presidency and, in 1808 succeeded Jefferson as president.

(Thomas E. Patterson, *The American Democracy*, 8/e, 2008)

BRUSHING UP ON VOCABULARY

abridging curtailing

quartered lodged

THE BILL OF RIGHTS

Articles in Addition to, and Amendment of, the Constitution of the United States of America, Proposed by Congress, and Ratified by the Legislatures of the Several States, Pursuant to the Fifth Article of the Original Constitution.

AMENDMENT I

Congress shall make no law respecting an establishment of religion, or prohibiting the free exercise thereof; or abridging the freedom of speech, or of the press; or the right of the people peaceably to assemble, and to petition the Government for a redress of grievances.

AMENDMENT II

A well-regulated Militia, being necessary to the security of a free State, the right of the people to keep and bear Arms, shall not be infringed.

AMENDMENT III

No soldier shall, in time of peace be quartered in any house, without the consent of the Owner, nor in time of war, but in a manner to be prescribed by law.

AMENDMENT IV

The right of the people to be secure in their persons, houses, papers, and effects, against unreasonable searches and seizures, shall not be violated, and no Warrants shall issue, but upon probable cause, supported by Oath or affirmation, and particularly describing the place to be searched, and the persons or things to be seized.

AMENDMENT V

No person shall be held to answer for a capital, or otherwise infamous crime, unless on a presentment or indictment of a Grand Jury, except in cases arising in the land or naval forces, or in the Militia, when in actual service in time of War or public danger; nor shall any person be subject for the same offence to be twice put in jeopardy of life or limb; nor shall be compelled in any criminal case to be a witness against himself; nor be deprived of life, liberty, or property, without due process of law; nor shall private property be taken for public use, without just compensation.

AMENDMENT VI

In all criminal prosecutions, the accused shall enjoy the right to a speedy and public trial, by an impartial jury of the State and district wherein the crime shall have been committed, which district shall have been previously ascertained by law, and to be informed of the nature and cause of the accusation; to be confronted with the witnesses against him; to have compulsory process for obtaining witnesses in his favor, and to have the Assistance of Counsel for his defence.

AMENDMENT VII

In Suits at common law, where the value in controversy shall exceed twenty dollars, the right of trial by jury shall be preserved, and no fact tried by a jury, shall be otherwise reexamined in any Court of the United States, than according to the rules of the common law.

AMENDMENT VIII

Excessive bail shall not be required, nor excessive fines imposed, nor cruel and unusual punishments inflicted.

AMENDMENT IX

The enumeration in the Constitution, of certain rights, shall not be construed to deny or disparage others retained by the people.

AMENDMENT X

The powers not delegated to the United States by the Constitution, nor prohibited by it to the States, are reserved to the States respectively, or to the people.

✓ **COMPREHENSION CHECKUP**

Fill in the Blank

Identify the correct amendment and fill in the blank provided.

1. Lt. Col. Oliver North frequently cited the _____ Amendment privilege against self-incrimination when he refused to testify about the Iran-Contra scandal.

2. Rap artist Snoop Dogg (real name: Calvin Broadus) believes his lyrics are constitutionally protected by the _____ Amendment.

3. Today's debate over handgun control is based on the _____ Amendment.

4. The constant noise and glare of military planes at an airport interfered with the normal use of adjoining land as a chicken farm. The owner protested and was awarded just compensation because of the _____ Amendment.

5. A Jehovah's Witness feels his child is not required to salute the flag at school because of the _____ Amendment.

6. The _____ Amendment exists to answer the objections of those who thought that naming some rights but not all results in the government's claiming the power to prevent a person from "lying on his left side on a long winter's night."

7. Bail of $200,000 for a person who has robbed a store is prohibited under the _____ Amendment.

8. The Supreme Court let stand a Georgia decision that bans organized prayers before public school football games because of the _____ Amendment.

9. Under the _____ Amendment, a confession cannot be considered voluntary unless preceded by proper warnings (Miranda).

10. Because of Amendment _____ , the national government can't place a soldier in a private citizen's home to live without the owner's permission (during peacetime).

11. Because of Amendment _____ , a person cannot be made to wait years with a charge hanging over his or her head.

12. In 1971, the federal government sought to prohibit the *New York Times* from publishing the "Pentagon Papers." However, the Supreme Court ruled that such a prohibition was a violation under the _____ Amendment.

Vocabulary in Context

Complete each of the following by selecting the two words that make the best sense in the passage as a whole.

ascertained	compensation	disparage	grievances
impartial	infamous	infringed	redress

1. It was cruel of you to _____ me for attempting to get just _____ from my employer. After all, I deserve some money because it's against the law to fire people because of their age.

2. Sue _____ the facts about the _____ outlaw by searching through old newspapers and magazines.

3. You _____ on my right to breathe clean air when you smoked in our office. We have to share the same workspace, and we need to compromise. We need to find someone _____ to help us settle this dispute.

4. Annoyed by random locker searches, the students at Central High petitioned the school board for a _____ of their _____.

In Your Own Words

1. Why do you think these particular rights were considered important by the framers of the Constitution? If you were to write a contemporary Bill of Rights, what other rights would you include?

2. Phrases such as "due process of law" and "cruel and unusual punishment" are always open to interpretation. What are the advantages of such abstract language? Would more specific language have been better? Why or why not?

3. The Second Amendment is complicated and open to multiple interpretations. Do you think this amendment grants today's citizens the right to own guns? Or does it only grant them the right to carry guns in militias?

4. How important is it for people to be aware of the Bill of Rights? Do you think those who apply to be U.S. citizens should have to demonstrate real understanding of the Constitution and the Bill of Rights?

Frank and Ernest

Frank & Ernest used with the permission of Thaves and the Cartoonist Group. All rights reserved.

The Art of Writing

Complete one of the following.

1. The First Amendment states that "Congress shall make no law . . . abridging the freedom of speech." In the beginning, the Founding Fathers wanted to protect political speech. Today, while political speech continues to be protected, the First Amendment has been expanded to cover other sorts of topics, too. Some scholars consider the First Amendment to be the most important amendment to the Constitution. In your opinion, which of the first ten amendments (Bill of Rights) is the most important? In a brief essay, give reasons for your choice.

2. Rewrite the Bill of Rights in modern, colloquial English, and illustrate each with a relevant example.

Internet Activity

Visit the Constitution Center Web site at

www.constitutioncenter.org

You can take a tour of the museum, review Supreme Court cases, or explore the Constitution and the Bill of Rights.

SELECTION

"Peale failed to create a truly grand state-type portrait . . ."

GETTING THE PICTURE

Most of us are accustomed to seeing George Washington on the dollar bill, but what did George Washington really look like? At Arizona State University, digital images were created using a plaster mask and bust of Washington made by French sculptor Jean Antoine Houdon when the president was 53. Computers then adjusted the digital images to represent key ages in his life. The new images, considered the most realistic to date, are available at Washington's Mount Vernon home. And the researchers concluded that he looks nothing like the Gilbert Stuart image on the dollar bill.

BIO-SKETCH

Wayne Craven, a leading historian of American sculpture, is professor emeritus of art history at the University of Delaware. He has written about American art from the Colonial period to the present time. His books include *Colonial American Portraiture, Sculpture in America,* and *American Art,* the textbook from which this excerpt is taken. He currently serves on the editorial board of the Smithsonian in American art.

BRUSHING UP ON VOCABULARY

Hessians German soldiers in the service of King George III of Great Britain during the Revolutionary War. The Hessians numbered about 30,000. On the night of December 25, 1776, General George Washington led his army across the Delaware River at Trenton, New Jersey, and surprised and defeated them.

Excerpt from

AMERICAN ART

by Wayne Craven

GEORGE WASHINGTON PAINTINGS

As a young man, Charles Willson Peale (1741–1827) had been a clocksmith, sil- 1 versmith, and saddler in Annapolis before deciding to become a portrait painter in the mid-1760s. In fact, he traded a newly made saddle for some lessons in painting.

Peale moved to Philadelphia just before the outbreak of the Revolutionary 2 War, in which he served as an officer of the Continental Army, part of the time with General George Washington. The military and political struggles produced

General George Washington before Princeton,
(1779) CHARLES WILLSON PEALE

Library of Congress, Prints and Photographs Division, Detroit Publishing
Company Collection, [LC-D43-T01-50260].

George Washington (The Lansdowne Portrait)
(1796) GILBERT STUART

Library of Congress Prints and Photographs Division [LC-DIG-pga-03226].

something the colonists had few of—American heroes. Late in 1778, Congress, meeting in Philadelphia, summoned its commander-in-chief for strategic planning sessions. During that period, Peale was commissioned by the Executive Council of Pennsylvania to paint a large portrait of the greatest American hero of all.

The full-length portrait was meant to glorify George Washington and incite 3 patriotic pride and fervor in the breast of all who saw it. Peale made studies of the battlefields of Trenton and Princeton, where Washington had inflicted stinging defeats upon the British troops and captured over a thousand Hessians. The artist made specific reference to the battle of Princeton in the background of his portrait by including Princeton College's Nassau Hall on the horizon. Hessian flags are conspicuous among the trophies of war that surround the general.

Despite the opportunity his subject offered, Peale failed to create a truly 4 grand state-type portrait—no American painter yet had experience in making such an heroic image. The military accouterments notwithstanding, Peale's *Washington* does not achieve the heroic grandeur and dignity usually associated

"A work of art cannot be satisfied with being a representation; it should be a presentation."

—Jacques Reverdy

with the great man. George Washington was a tall man, to be sure, but Peale's tendency to attenuate the human figure, and the small size of Washington's head, cause him to appear gangly and lacking in refined proportions. Moreover, the pose in which he placed Washington is so casual, even awkward, that it precludes any feeling of greatness or of a dramatic moment. Even the face of Washington is unheroic. Be they commander-in-chief or merchant, Peale was incapable of idealizing his subjects—this produced an accurate likeness, but not an heroic ideal. Peale's *Washington* gives us a truthful representation of our first national hero, but tells us of his greatness through the collection of objects that surround him, rather than through the man himself.

Another extraordinary talent was Gilbert Stuart (1755–1828), who was born 5 and grew up in Rhode Island. Realizing the need for training that was unavailable in America, Stuart embarked in 1777 for London, where he spent several destitute years before the well-known artist Benjamin West learned of his plight and took him into his own studio. Stuart quickly mastered the style of portrait painting and left West to set up his own studio, which became one of the most successful in London.

Stuart liked painting portraits because they could be completed quickly, and 6 they were lucrative. By then he had developed a taste for elegant high living and was always in need of money. Despite numerous commissions, Stuart's extravagant lifestyle carried him ever deeper into debt, until his only recourse was flight to Ireland. There he worked from 1787 to 1792, achieving considerable success and acclaim, but again accruing such debts that it was once more necessary to flee or go to prison—and so he returned to America in 1793.

There, his portraits brought Stuart all the work he could handle, but ambi- 7 tious to establish a practice among the new governmental leadership of the young republic, he moved to Philadelphia in 1794.

Stuart's first portrait of Washington was painted in Philadelphia in the Spring 8 of 1795. It shows the subject, extremely sober and aloof, turned obliquely to the viewer's right. Dissatisfied, Stuart sought another sitting from the president in 1796. The result was the creation of two portraits that have ever since been the accepted image of the great man. The bust-length (Athenaeum) portrait shows the head turned to our left. The original unfinished portrait, now owned by the National Portrait Gallery, Stuart kept in his studio throughout his life, and from it produced well over one hundred replicas.

"A work of art is an exaggeration."

—André Gide

The third portrait (Lansdowne) is a full-length state portrait for which Stuart 9 used the bust image (Athenaeum) for painting the head. Here, finally, was a portrait of Washington that equaled the adulation and hero-worship that had by then enveloped him. In fact, Stuart's image of Washington has often been criticized, beginning with Martha Washington, for not capturing an accurate likeness of the man. What it did capture, however, was an image that expressed what admirers over the centuries wished to think him—dignified, solemn, and stately, a statesman of international stature. Although Peale's may present a more accurate likeness, Stuart's portrait surpasses Peale's image in its idealization.

(Wayne Craven, *American Art,* 2003)

✓ **COMPREHENSION CHECKUP**

Multiple Choice

Write the letter of the correct answer in the space provided.

_____ 1. Charles Peale's painting of George Washington was criticized for all of the following reasons *except*
   a. Washington was portrayed too realistically
   b. Washington's head was too small for his body
   c. Washington was made to look too heroic
   d. Washington's pose was too casual

_____ 2. Gilbert Stuart moved from England to Ireland and then back to America because
   a. he did not earn much money from his portrait painting
   b. he had to flee from his debts
   c. he failed to complete paintings for which he had received money
   d. his wife was spending too much money

_____ 3. Stuart painted _____ portraits of Washington.
   a. one
   b. two
   c. three
   d. four

_____ 4. Martha Washington wanted Stuart to paint a
   a. more realistic portrait of Washington
   b. more heroic-looking painting
   c. more dignified and stately painting
   d. portrait that future admirers would accept

_____ 5. Peale practiced all of the following vocations *except*
   a. artist
   b. army officer
   c. musician
   d. silversmith

True or False

Indicate whether the statement is true or false by writing **T** or **F** in the space provided.

_____ 6. Peale studied under the artist Benjamin West.

_____ 7. Both Peale and Stuart painted full-length portraits of Washington.

_____ 8. Stuart moved to Washington, D.C., to be closer to governmental leaders.

_____ 9. Peale was well known for idealizing his subjects.

_____ 10. Peale placed a building from Princeton College in the background of his painting of Washington.

Vocabulary in Context

In the paragraphs indicated, find a word that matches the definition given, and write the word in the space provided.

1. to extol; to honor with praise (paragraph 3) _____

2. easily seen or noticed; readily observable (3) _____

3. equipment of a soldier (4) _____

4. to make thin or slender (4) _____

5. makes impossible; prevents (4) _____

6. lacking food, clothing, and shelter (5) _____

7. distressing condition or situation (5) _____

8. profitable; money-making (6) _____

9. spending more than is necessary or wise (6) _____

10. serious; solemn (8) _____

11. reserved; reticent (8) _____

12. excessive admiration (9) _____

13. surrounded (9) _____

Vocabulary Practice

Use each of the following words in a sentence. You may change or add endings. The paragraph number in parentheses tells you where the word is located in the story.

1. summoned (paragraph 2) _____

_____

2. incite (3) _____

_____

3. embarked (5) _____

_____

4. elegant (6) _____

_____

5. surpasses (9) _____

_____

In Your Own Words

1. Take this short true or false quiz (courtesy of the George Washington Mount Vernon Estate) to see how much you know. Circle **T** for true and **F** for false.

George Washington

T F   1. Chopped down a cherry tree.

T F   2. Had wooden teeth.

T F   3. Once threw a silver dollar across the Potomac River.

T F   4. Was the first president to live in the White House.

T F   5. Wore a wig.

T F   6. Had two children with his wife, Martha.

T F   7. Was born on February 11, 1732.

T F   8. Attended college.

T F   9. Was the first man to sign the U.S. Constitution.

T F 10. Introduced the mule to America.

T F 11. Declined the opportunity to be king.

2. Do you think Gilbert Stuart's painting of George Washington created a stereotype of him? How could this painting serve as propaganda for a new nation?

3. Do you think George Washington was "photoshopped" by Stuart?

The Art of Writing

1. Choose one of the following claims and provide support for it.
   a. The Charles Willson Peale portrait should be used to commemorate the first president of the United States.
   b. We should continue to use the Gilbert Stuart painting to commemorate the first president of the United States.

2. Paraphrase the following quotations. When you are finished, check to make sure the meaning of both statements is the same.

George Washington's "Rules of Civility and Decent Behavior in Company and Conversation"

1. Every action done in company ought to be done with some sign of respect to those that are present.

_____

2. Show nothing to your friend that may affright him.

_____

3. Show not yourself glad at the misfortune of another, even though he were your enemy.

_____

4. Be not hasty to believe flying reports to the disparagement of anyone.

_____

5. Play not the peacock, looking everywhere about you to see if you be well decked, if your shoes fit well, if your stockings set neatly and clothes handsomely.

_____

6. Associate yourself with men of quality if you esteem your own reputation, for it is better to be alone than in bad company.

_____

_____

7. Be not apt to relate news if you know not the truth thereof.

_____

8. Be not curious to know the affairs of others.

_____

9. Undertake not what you cannot perform; but be careful to keep your promise.

_____

10. Speak no evil of the absent, for it is unjust.

_____

Internet Activity

Take a virtual tour of Mount Vernon at

www.mountvernon.org

Write a paragraph describing an object you found interesting or something new you learned about George Washington.

MASTERY TEST: George Washington Paintings

Write the letter of the correct answer in the space provided.

Main Idea

_____ 1. The main idea expressed in this selection is that
  a. portraits of famous people should present an accurate likeness
  b. Peale painted a picture of George Washington that presented an accurate likeness, but Stuart's painting depicted how admirers wished to view him
  c. Stuart's portrait helped turn Washington into a heroic, larger-than-life figure
  d. it is very difficult to attain success in the field of portrait painting

Supporting Detail

_____ 2. All of the following are true _except_
  a. Peale's painting of Washington was commissioned by the Executive Council of Pennsylvania
  b. in the Peale painting, Washington is wearing military dress
  c. in the Peale painting, Washington exhibits a cross-legged pose
  d. Peale was a self-taught artist

Context

_____ 3. As used in paragraph 9, the word _stature_ most nearly means
  a. natural height
  b. esteem

c. body build

d. wealth

Purpose

_____ 4. The author's primary purpose is to

    a. persuade the reader that Peale had greater artistic talent than Stuart

    b. inform the reader of the difficulties artists encounter before they become successful

    c. discuss two well-known portrait painters who painted very different portraits of George Washington

    d. inform the reader of the many heroic acts performed by the first president of the United States

Pattern of Organization

_____ 5. Paragraph 5 of the selection is primarily organized by

    a. chronological order

    b. spatial order

    c. definition

    d. comparison and contrast

Sentence Relationships

_____ 6. The transition word *moreover* in paragraph 4, sentence 4, indicates

    a. cause and effect

    b. addition

    c. contrast

    d. comparison

_____ 7. "Stuart liked painting portraits because they could be completed quickly and they were lucrative." This sentence involves

    a. comparison and contrast

    b. classification and division

    c. cause and effect

    d. definition and example

Inference

_____ 8. From this selection you could conclude that

    a. Peale's painting of Washington made him look noble

    b. Stuart was fiscally responsible

    c. Martha Washington believed portraits should not idealize their subjects

    d. Peale was unfamiliar with Washington as a military commander

Tone

_____ 9. If the author were delivering this selection orally, his tone of voice would probably be

    a. humorous

    b. angry

    c. informative

    d. satiric

Fact and Opinion

_____ 10. "Peale's *Washington* does not achieve the heroic grandeur and dignity usually associated with the great man." (paragraph 4) This is a statement of
a. fact
b. opinion

Bias

_____ 11. Which of the following quotations from the selection reveals a biased attitude on the part of the author of this selection?
a. "Despite the opportunity his subject offered, Peale failed to create a truly grand state-type portrait . . ."
b. "There, his portraits brought Stuart all the work he could handle."
c. "In fact, Stuart's image of Washington has often been criticized."
d. "By then he had developed a taste for elegant high living and was always in need of money."

Author's Reasoning

_____ 12. Which statement offers support for the author's claim that the Peale painting failed as propaganda?
a. General Washington is dressed in his military uniform.
b. In the painting, General Washington appears to have a small head perched on a gangly body.
c. The painting makes reference to Washington's victory at Princeton.
d. In the painting, General Washington is surrounded by trophies of war.

Brain Teasers

Literary Insults

Explain the meaning of each of the following insults.

1. "I've just learned about his illness. Let's hope it's nothing trivial."
   —Irvin S. Cobb

2. "He has never been known to use a word that might send a reader to the dictionary."
   —William Faulkner (about Ernest Hemingway)

3. "I've had a perfectly wonderful evening. But this wasn't it."
   —Groucho Marx

4. "They never open their mouths without subtracting from the sum of human knowledge."
   —Thomas Brackett Reed

5. "Some cause happiness wherever they go; others whenever they go."
   —Oscar Wilde

6. "A modest little person, with much to be modest about."
   —Winston Churchill

7. "Thank you for sending me a copy of your book; I'll waste no time reading it."
   —Moses Hadas

8. "He can compress the most words into the smallest idea of any man I know."
   —Abraham Lincoln

9. "He is a self-made man and worships his creator."
   —John Bright

10. "He has the attention span of a lightning bolt."
    —Robert Redford

| VOCABULARY | Unit 8: Word Parts Featuring Study, Feeling, and Faith |

"To acquire knowledge one must study. To acquire wisdom one must observe."
—Marilyn vos Savant

This unit begins with the word parts *-ology, geo-, helio-,* and *terr-;* moves on to *path-, ten-* or *tin-, fid-* and *cred-,* and *tact-* and *tang-;* and concludes with *-ject* and *locut-.* Words made from these word parts, along with their definitions, follow. Supplemental words with these word parts are located in the left margin.

logy—study or science of

astronomy	*astro-* means "pertaining to the stars," so *astronomy* is the science that studies such things as the origins, composition, and motions of the stars and planets.
astrology	the study that assumes and attempts to interpret the influence of the heavenly bodies on human affairs. Horoscopes are based on *astrology*.
seismology	the science and study of earthquakes.
sociology	the science or study of the origin, development, organization, and functioning of human society.
anthropology	*anthro-* means "man," so *anthropology* is the science that studies human beings, especially their origin, development, division, and customs.
paleontology	*paleo-* means "old," so *paleontology* is the science of the forms of life existing in past geological periods.

geo—earth; helio—sun; terr—earth, land

geology	the science that deals with the dynamics and physical history of the earth. A *geologist* studies the earth's crust and the way in which its layers were formed.
geography	the study of the surface of the earth, its division into continents and countries, and the climate, natural resources, and inhabitants of the regions.
geocentric	having or representing the earth as the center, as in the *geocentric* theory of the universe.
heliocentric	having or representing the sun as the center of the universe.
apogee	*apo-* means "off" or "away," so the *apogee* is the point in the orbit of the moon at which it is farthest from the earth; the highest point or most exalted point. Is Tiger Woods at the *apogee* of professional golf?
perigee	*Peri* means "near," so the *perigee* is the point in the orbit of the moon at which it is nearest to the earth; the lowest point.

terrarium
subterranean
parterre

territory	any large stretch of land or region.
terrain	a tract of land with reference to its natural features or military advantages. He purchased a home with five acres of hilly *terrain*.

| | **terra firma** | Latin for firm or solid earth. After the long ocean voyage, Shawn was grateful to be back on *terra firma*. |
| | **terrestrial** | pertaining to, consisting of, or representing the earth. Coyotes are *terrestrial* animals. |

path(o), pathy—feeling, suffering, emotion

apathetic	**antipathy**	an aversion; a strong feeling against. Although Adella liked animals, she had a real *antipathy* toward cats.
empathy		
pathology	**apathy**	lack of strong feeling, interest, or concern. Because of public *apathy*, no real reform was likely to occur.
sociopath		
	pathos	the quality in life or art of evoking a feeling of pity or compassion. As the heroine lay dying, the musical score turned to *pathos*.
	pathetic	causing or evoking pity either sympathetically or contemptibly. The fireman was haunted by the victim's *pathetic* cries for help.
	pathological	characterized by an unhealthy compulsion; habitual; concerned with diseases. Unfortunately, you cannot trust her word because she is a *pathological* liar.

ten(t), tin—hold, cling, keep

abstinence	**tenacious**	gripping firmly; holding fast. Despite their separation, he cannot rid himself of his wife; she has a *tenacious* hold on his feelings.
tenable		
sustenance	**retentive**	able to hold, keep, remember. Calla has an extremely *retentive* mind for facts and figures.
	tenure	the length of time something is held; the status of holding a job permanently. Professors work hard to achieve *tenure*.
	detention	being held back; forced delay or confinement. Because of Mike's behavior, he has a *detention* every day this week.
	tenant	a person who pays rent to use land; to hold, occupy, or dwell in.
	pertinent	relevant; holding to the point. Don't bother me with trivial details; I only want the *pertinent* information.

fid—faith(ful); cred—believe

affidavit	**fidelity**	loyalty. The subjects pledged *fidelity* to their new king.
fiduciary		
perfid**y**	**infidel**	a person who does not believe in a particular religion; an unbeliever; a person who disbelieves a particular theory or belief.
	confident	sure, certain, assured; a strong belief in oneself. Nina was utterly *confident* she would pass the bar exam and become a lawyer.
	diffident	lacking faith in one's own ability, worth, or fitness; timid, shy.
creed		
creditable	**credulous**	willing to believe things even without proof; easily convinced. It is easy to play tricks on Charlotte; she is so *credulous* that she'll believe anything.
credence		
credulity		
credulity		

incredulous   not willing or able to believe; doubtful. Mona gave Sam an *incredulous* look when she found out he'd won the lottery.

tact, tang—touch

contact
tangential

intangible   not able to be touched or grasped; vague, elusive. He has many fine *intangible* qualities like compassion and forthrightness.

tactile   perceptible to the touch.

intact   untouched; remaining sound or whole. When Juan found his wallet, it was still *intact* and held all of his credit cards and money.

ject—throw

adjacent
conjecture
trajectory

dejected   to depress the spirits. The literal meaning of *deject* is "to throw down."

eject   to drive or force out; to throw out.

inject   The literal meaning of *inject* is "to throw in." She *injected* some humor into a dreary situation.

interject   *Inter* means "between," so an *interjection* is a remark "thrown into" a conversation, often abruptly. To interject means "to interrupt."

project   to throw forward; to predict; to cause to be heard clearly. The teacher easily *projected* her voice so that those sitting in the back of the class had no trouble hearing.

locut (loqu)—speak, talk

circumlocution
elocution
colloquial

eloquent   graceful and forceful in speech. *e-* means "out," and *loqu-* means "speak," so the literal meaning is to "speak out." At the trial's end, the defense attorney gave an *eloquent* summation of the evidence favoring his client's innocence.

loquacious   talkative. Some people are more *loquacious* when they are nervous or uncomfortable.

Now that you have studied the vocabulary in Unit 8, practice your new knowledge by completing the crossword puzzle on the next page.

Vocabulary Unit 8 Puzzle

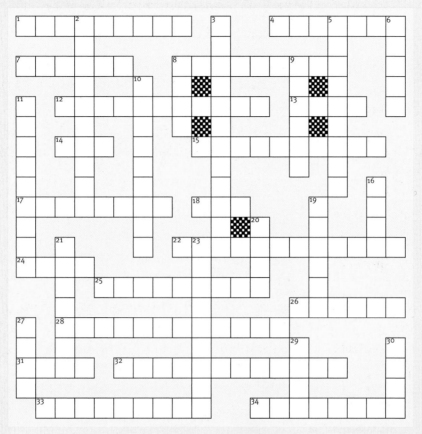

ACROSS CLUES

1. After the bitter custody battle, Sarah had _____ for her ex-husband.
4. She used her _____ sense to read the braille letters with her fingers.
7. Because of public _____, the voter turnout was low.
8. Because Jerry cut classes, he had to serve a _____ after school.
12. Samantha gave Matt an _____ look when she learned he had spent all his hard-earned money gambling in Las Vegas.
13. A word part meaning "throw."
14. A word part meaning "faith."
15. Susie is so _____ that her friends wonder when she pauses to breathe.
17. The Miami Hurricanes became _____ when they lost the college national championship game after the second overtime.
18. Abbreviation for what was once the eighth month.*
22. If you are interested in dinosaurs, you might want to take a course in _____.
24. A word part meaning "god."*

25. Oregon was a _____ before it became a state.
26. The landlord had to evict the _____ because he wasn't paying his rent.
28. Margaret Mead revolutionized the field of _____ with her research on the customs of the people of Samoa.
31. A word part meaning "hold."
32. The theory that regards the sun as the center of the universe.
33. If you are interested in social organization, you might study _____.
34. At the wedding ceremony, the couple pledged their undying _____ to each other.

DOWN CLUES

2. There are many _____ qualities like patience that go into making a successful leader.
3. A _____ liar might be able to pass a polygraph test.
5. Holding her son's head above the water, she maintained a _____ grip until they reached safety.

6. He did not want to _____ the annoying student from the class, but he finally had to tell him to leave.
8. A word part meaning "god."*
9. A baby rattlesnake can sometimes _____ more poison than a full-grown rattlesnake.
10. He wanted a summary report with only the _____ details on his desk by 5:00.
11. She felt _____ that she would do well on the test because she had studied hard.
16. A word part meaning "touch."
19. Was his election as president the _____ of his political career?
20. A word part meaning "science of."
21. The _____ was considered to be too rocky for any crops to grow.
23. The science of _____ is not to be confused with the pseudoscience of astrology.
27. A word part meaning "feeling."
29. A word part meaning "believe."
30. A word part meaning "many."*

*From a previous unit.

Evaluating the Evidence

The Thinker (1902) *BY AUGUSTE RODIN*

Library of Congress Prints and Photographs Division,
Detroit Publishing Company Collection, [LC-D416-591]

View and Reflect

Rodin originally sculpted *The Thinker* as part of his unfinished masterpiece *The Gates of Hell*. From his lofty perch at the top of the gate, *The Thinker* was meant to look down and ponder the sins of humanity. At the request of many patrons, Rodin increased the size of the original sculpture and made it freestanding. Today, it is one of the most widely recognized pieces of art in the world.

1. In this sculpture, Rodin tried to create a man "who did not just think with his head, but thought with his entire body." What do you think Rodin meant by this comment? Do you think he succeeded?
2. In 1970, a bomb was set at the base of an original Rodin *Thinker*, badly damaging the statue's feet. The museum decided against encasing the statue in protective glass or having it repaired. Do you think the museum made the right decision?

Evaluating Persuasive Writing

Instead of sticking with neutral, objective language, authors sometimes use language with strong connotations, language designed to arouse the reader emotionally. This is often a sign of bias on the author's part and serves as a signal that the author is trying to influence you. Authors might exploit any or all of the following persuasive techniques:

1. Emotionally Loaded Language

This type of language is designed to appeal directly to your feelings rather than your reasoning abilities. In the example below, notice Dr. William Nolan's use of loaded words in his description of a severely disabled 90-year-old woman who has developed pneumonia. A decision must be made on whether to treat the pneumonia with penicillin or withhold the medication, which would likely cause death within three or four days.

> On the one hand, you cannot bear to see your **once vivacious** mother living the **painful, limited** life to which the stroke has **condemned** her. On the other hand, you hate to be the one to decide to let nature take its course. Until you are actually faced with such a decision, you probably won't be able to predict which course you would take.
>
> I'll tell you what choice I would make. I'd say, "Don't give her any penicillin. Keep her as comfortable as possible and let's see what happens. Maybe she'll have the resistance to fight off the pneumonia on her own and if she doesn't, she'll die a **peaceful** death. I don't want to be responsible for **condemning** my mother to a **living hell**."

(William Nolen, "Deciding to Let Your Parents Die," 1992)

2. Tear-Jerking Stories or References to People and Causes

In the following paragraph, the author describes the plight of the men and women, many of whom are immigrants making hourly wages one-third lower than other employees, who clean the nation's slaughterhouses and have "arguably the worst job in the United States."

> A brief description of some cleaning-crew accidents over the past decade says more about the work and the danger among slaughterhouse sanitation crews than any set of statistics. At the Monfort plant in Grand Island, Nebraska, Richard Skala was beheaded by a dehiding machine. Carlos Vincente, a twenty-eight-year-old Guatemalan who'd been in the United States for only a week, was pulled into the cogs of a conveyor belt at an Excel plant in Fort Morgan, Colorado, and torn apart. Salvador Hernandez-Gonzalez, an employee of DCS Sanitation, had his head crushed by a pork-loin processing machine at an IBP plant in Madison, Nebraska. The same machine had fatally crushed the head of another worker, Ben Barone, a few years earlier. At a National Beef plant in Liberal, Kansas, Homer Stull climbed into a filthy blood-collection tank to clean it. Stull was overcome by hydrogen sulfide fumes. Two co-workers climbed into the tank and tried to rescue him; all three men died. Eight years earlier, Henry Wolf had been overcome by hydrogen sulfide fumes while cleaning the very same

tank; Gary Sanders had tried to rescue him; both men died; and the Occupational Safety and Health Administration (OSHA) later fined National Beef for its negligence. The fine was $480 for each man's death.

(Eric Schlosser, *Fast-Food Nation: The Dark Side of the All-American Meal*, 2001)

3. Figurative Language

In the example below, the author draws on figurative language to describe what's wrong with popular culture.

> The popular culture, in its hierarchy of values, puts the joys of sex far above the happiness of motherhood. The women's magazines, the soaps, romance novels, and prime-time TV all celebrate career, sex, and the single woman. "Taking care of baby" is for Grandma. **Marriage and monogamy are about as exciting as a mashed potato sandwich.** That old triumvirate "the world, the flesh, and the devil" not only has all the best tunes, but all the best ad agencies.

(Patrick J. Buchanan, *The Death of the West*, 2002)

4. Manipulation of Tone

In the first paragraph, the author assumes an ironic tone when she says the United States has the safest food supply. In the second paragraph, she explains the problems inherent in the food production system by making an analogy.

> One of the most insistent marketing messages we hear, trumpeted by both industry and regulators, is that the United States has the safest food supply in the world. Yet according to the Centers for Disease Control's best calculations, each year 76 million Americans—nearly one in four, and that's a lowball estimate—become infected by what they eat. Most find themselves for a few days dolefully memorizing a pattern of bathroom floor tiles. About 325,000 land in the hospital. Two million suffer drawn-out, sometimes lifelong, medical complications from unwittingly eating a contaminated morsel. More than 5,000—about 14 a day—die from indulging in what should be one of life's great pleasures. The "world's safest food supply" regularly doles out *E. coli* O157:H7 in hamburgers, *Salmonella* in alfalfa sprouts, *Listeria* in hot dogs, *Campylobacter* in Thanksgiving turkeys.
> **The site of modern meat production is akin to a walled medieval city,** where waste is tossed out the window, sewage runs down the street, and feed and drinking water are routinely contaminated by fecal material. Each day, a feed-lot steer deposits 50 pounds of manure, as the animals crowd atop dark mountains composed of their own feces. "Animals are living in medieval conditions and we're living in the twenty-first century," says Robert Tauxe, chief of the CDC's foodborne and diarrheal diseases branch. "Consumers have to be aware that even though they bought their food from a lovely modern deli bar or salad bar, it started out in the sixteen hundreds."

(Madeline Drexler, *Secret Agents: the Menace of Emerging Infections*, 2002)

5. Propaganda Techniques

These techniques include bandwagon, plain folks, name calling, and testimonials. In his final book before his death, noted historian Stephen Ambrose wrote about the

Founding Fathers. He had less than positive feelings about Thomas Jefferson, our third president and author of the Declaration of Independence. He described Jefferson as having "a great mind and a limited character." In the following paragraph, Ambrose "name-calls" Jefferson "an intellectual coward."

> Thomas Jefferson, the genius of politics, could see no way for African Americans to live in society as free people. He embraced the worst forms of racism to justify slavery, to himself and those he instructed. The limitations he displayed in refusing both to acknowledge the truth of his own observations on the institution, and his unwillingness to do something, anything, to weaken and finally destroy it, brand him an intellectual coward. . . .

(Stephen Ambrose, *To America: Personal Reflections of an Historian,* 2002)

6. Psychological Appeals

The media frequently employs this technique to create ads that appeal directly to our desire for safety, power, prestige, sex, or popularity.

Fear induction is one of the most effective persuasive techniques. It is commonly used in advertisements and public service announcements, such as the one in the advertisement below that was commissioned by the U.S. Department of Transportation. For fear tactics to work, (1) the appeal must engender a lot of fear, (2) the audience must believe the message, and (3) specific instructions for avoiding the danger must be presented.

These shoes were found 46 yards from the crash caused by a drunk driver. Carissa Deason was thrown 30 yards and not even her father, a doctor, could save her.

Friends Don't Let Friends Drive Drunk

U.S. Department of Transportation

U.S. Department of Transportation/Ad Council.

7. Moral Appeals

Authors may seek to appeal to your sense of morality or fair play. In his book *Living a Life That Matters*, Rabbi Harold Kushner discusses the views of Kenneth Blanchard and the Reverend Norman Vincent Peale.

> Blanchard and Peale call for integrity in the business world both as a tactical advantage and as a matter of principle. If a company encourages employees to increase sales by dishonest means, that company might find its employees padding expense accounts or taking trade secrets to other companies when they move on. Both Blanchard and Peale urge their readers to ask themselves: "If we have to cheat to win, shouldn't we think twice about what business we're in?"

(Harold S. Kushner, *Living a Life That Matters*, 2001)

8. Appeals to Authority

Authors may call attention to the integrity, intelligence, or knowledge of themselves or others to convince you to trust their judgment and believe them, as the following excerpt by James Steyer illustrates.

> If another adult spent five or six hours a day with your kids, regularly exposing them to sex, violence, and rampantly commercial values, you would probably forbid that person to have further contact with them. Yet most of us passively allow the media to expose our kids routinely to these same behaviors—sometimes worse—and do nothing about it.
>
> If we don't start taking responsibility—as parents first, but also by demanding it from the huge media interests, as well as the government officials who are supposed to regulate them on behalf of the public interest—then we put our children at continued risk. We will raise generations of kids desensitized to violence, overexposed to reckless sex, and commercially exploited from their earliest years. And our culture will pay an ever-increasing price.
>
> As a parent, as a national child advocate, as someone who teaches constitutional law and civil liberties courses at Stanford University, and as the head of one of the few independent children's media companies in the United States, I've had a unique vantage point. And from where I stand, the world of media and children is not a very pretty picture. In fact, I'm convinced that the huge influence of the "other parent" should be a matter of national concern for parents, policymakers, and responsible media executives alike.

(James P. Steyer, *The Other Parent*, 2002)

To evaluate persuasive writing, you want to become better at recognizing the techniques we have just discussed. You should also pay attention to the following:

- *Background:* Learn what you can about the author. What other books or articles has the author written? Is the author known for representing certain viewpoints? Is the author involved in advocacy organizations?

- *Assumptions:* Try to identify the values and principles that form the author's basic outlook. Do you agree with this outlook? Contrast the author's basic outlook to other possibilities. What are the values and principles behind opposing outlooks?

- *Organization:* Pay attention to how a piece of writing is organized. How is the author structuring the argument? Where are the reasons or explanations? Do the reasons support the conclusion?

In summary, authors who are trying to persuade do not usually write material that is entirely objective and meant solely to inform. Instead, they tend to make use of factual material to bolster their opinions and conclusions. By recognizing persuasive techniques and understanding the author's motives and underlying assumptions, you will be better able to avoid emotionalism and manipulation and to evaluate the persuasiveness or worth of the argument the author is making rationally and critically.

Death and Dying

Look at this picture and its title. Answer the questions that follow.

The Death of Socrates (1787) BY JACQUES-LOUIS DAVID

© Hutton Archives/Universal Images Group/Getty Images

1. How does the artist focus the viewer's attention on the central figure of Socrates?
2. In David's painting, what does Socrates appear to be doing?
3. How does David convey the sadness of Socrates' friends and family in this painting?
4. What do you think is the likely setting of the painting?

Arguments About Death and Dying

The next three selections focus on death and dying. You will need to evaluate each author's reasoning to see how valid or persuasive it is.

"Some will eventually be 'weaned' back to their own lung power. Others will never draw an independent breath again."

GETTING THE PICTURE

In the United States today, deciding how to treat the terminally ill or those in chronic pain is harder than ever because of the existence of life-prolonging medical technology. As a result, the whole concept of a "good death" has been called into question. One of the top fears of many Americans is dying in a hospital hooked up to machines. The author of this article, a physician, describes the dilemma of caring for a patient who has no realistic chance of recovery.

BIO-SKETCH

Elissa Ely graduated magna cum laude in 1978 from Wesleyan University and earned her M.D. from Harvard Medical School in 1988. Today she is a psychiatrist at the Massachusetts General Hospital. She is also a regular contributor to the *Boston Globe* and a featured commentator on *All Things Considered*, aired by National Public Radio. In addition, she has been a psychiatrist at Tewksbury Hospital and given lectures in psychiatry at Harvard Medical School.

BRUSHING UP ON VOCABULARY

cardiac pertaining to the heart.

respirator an apparatus to produce artificial breathing. Originally, this word came from the Latin *re*, meaning "again," and *spirare*, meaning "to breathe."

chintz cotton fabric with bright colors; borrowed from Hindi *chint* and Sanskrit *citra-s*, meaning "distinctive, bright, clear." The cheetah also gained its name from these words.

Dreaming of Disconnecting a Respirator

By Elissa Ely

1 LATE ONE NIGHT—in the intensive care unit, one eye on the cardiac monitor and one on the Sunday paper, I read this story:

2 An infant lies in a hospital, hooked to life by a respirator. He exists in a "persistent vegetative state" after swallowing a balloon that blocked the oxygen to his brain. This "vegetative state," I've always thought, is a metaphor inaccurately borrowed from na-ture, since it implies that with only the proper watering and fertilizer, a comatose patient will bloom again.

One day his father comes to visit. 3 He disconnects the respirator and, with a gun in hand, cradles his son until the infant dies. The father is arrested and charged with murder.

In the ICU where I read this, many 4 patients are bound to respirators. I look to my left and see them lined up, like potted plants. Some will eventually be "weaned" back to their own lung power. Others will never draw an independent breath again.

5   In Bed No. 2, there is a woman who has been on the respirator for almost two months. When she was admitted with a simple pneumonia, there were no clues she would come apart so terribly. On her third day, she had a sudden and enigmatic seizure. She rolled rapidly downhill. Her pneumonia is now gone, but her lungs refuse independence: She can't come off the machine.

6   I know little about this patient except that she is elderly and European. (It is the peculiar loss of hospital life that patients often exist here with a medical history, but not a personal one.) I sometimes try to picture her as she might have been: busy in a chintz kitchen smelling of pastries. She might have hummed, rolling dough. Now there is a portable radio by the bed, playing Top Ten, while the respirator hisses and clicks 12 times a minute.

7   The family no longer visits. They have already signed the autopsy request, which is clipped to the front of her thick chart. Yet in their pain, they cannot take the final step and allow us to discontinue her respirator. Instead, they have retired her here, where they hope she is well cared for, and where she exists in a state of perpetual mechanical life.

8   I have dreamed of disconnecting my patient's respirator. Every day I make her death impossible and her life unbearable. Each decision—the blood draws, the rectal temperatures, the oxygen concentration—is one for or against life. No action in the ICU is neutral. Yet many of these decisions are made with an eye toward legal neutrality—and this has little to do with medical truth. The medical truth is that this patient exists without being alive. The legal neutrality is that existence is all that is required.

9   Late at night, reading in the ICU, the story of that father—so dangerous and impassioned—puts me to shame. I would never disconnect my patient from her respirator; it is unthinkable. But this is not because I am a doctor. It is because I feel differently toward her than the father toward his son.

10   I do not love her enough.

(Elissa Ely, "Dreaming of Disconnecting a Respirator," *Boston Globe,* 1989)

✓ COMPREHENSION CHECKUP

Evaluating the Evidence

1. Is the author's primary purpose to inform or to persuade? What evidence do you have to support your conclusion?

_____

_____

_____

_____

2. What is the author's background? Does the author have the qualifications to write seriously about this topic?

_____

3. Does the article contain primarily facts or opinions?

_____

_____

   a. List some facts from the article:

   _____

   _____

   _____

   _____

   b. List some opinions from the article:

   _____

   _____

   _____

   _____

4. If the author has a strong bias, write it below. Can you give some examples of emotionally loaded language or material that has been included to create an emotional response on your part?

_____

_____

_____

_____

_____

5. What is your opinion on the topic of euthanasia (mercy killing, assisted suicide)? Do you think that your opinion is biased? If so, does your bias interfere with your ability to evaluate what the author is saying fairly?

_____

_____

_____

_____

6. Does the author use any specific propaganda devices? List them below. How did you react to these techniques?

_____

_____

_____

_____

7. How would you describe the author's tone? What does the tone tell you about the author's bias?

_____

_____

_____

Vocabulary in Context

Select the word that best completes the phrase.

enigmatic   impassioned   perpetually   vegetative   weaned

1. finally _____ from the bottle

2. *Mona Lisa's* _____ smile

3. delivered an _____ speech in favor of voting rights

4. _____ late to class

5. never went out; led a _____ life

The Art of Writing

Write a brief essay giving your opinion about how society should treat people who are in a "persistent vegetative state."

Internet Activity

Using a search engine like Google, find a Web site that deals with the issue of euthanasia, and analyze the Web site by answering the following questions.

1. *Author's purpose:* Is the author's primary purpose to inform or to persuade? Why do you think so?

2. *Emotional appeals:* Where does the author use language that is intended to arouse the reader emotionally? Give two examples of material that is included for its emotional appeal.

3. *Ethical appeals:* What information does the author include to persuade the reader to consider her or him an authority in this area or to trust his or her judgment on this subject?

4. *Logical appeals:* What logical or reasonable arguments does the author use? Is the author using inductive or deductive reasoning?

5. *Psychological appeals:* Is the author trying to manipulate the reader psychologically by appealing to the need for acceptance, power, prestige, and so on?

6. *Propaganda techniques:* What propaganda techniques does the author use? Are the techniques appropriate to his or her purpose? Cite specific examples.

7. *Tone:* What is the author's tone? Is the tone meant to influence or manipulate the reader? Give specific examples of how the author uses tone to affect the reader.

8. *Bias:* What is the author's specific bias? Where is the bias presented? At the beginning? The middle? The end?

Print one or two pages from the Web site.

"There is no blueprint, however, for a good death. Death can't be neatly packaged with a red bow. It is messy, irrational . . ."

GETTING THE PICTURE

The article below explores some fundamental questions about death and dying in the United States today.

BIO-SKETCH

Sheryl Gay Stolberg, a Washington correspondent for the *New York Times*, spent five years covering science and health policy but now covers Congress. Previously, she worked at the *Los Angeles Times* and the *Providence Journal* in Rhode Island. She graduated from the University of Virginia in 1983 and presently lives in Chevy Chase, Maryland, with her husband and two daughters.

BRUSHING UP ON VOCABULARY

melatonin a hormone important in regulating biorhythms.

hospice a health care facility or series of home visits for the terminally ill. Originally, a hospice was a rest house for travelers.

palliative a way of relieving a person from the symptoms of an illness without necessarily curing the disease.

The Good Death: Embracing a Right to Die Well

By Sheryl Gay Stolberg

"The art of living well and the art of dying well are one."

—Epicurus

1 THE COLD BARE FACTS of Barbara Logan Brown's death are these: on July 17, 1996, Mrs. Logan Brown, a 38-year-old mother of two from Rochester, New York, died of AIDS, another statistic in an epidemic that has killed more than 362,000 Americans. Cancer had seeped into her brain; thrush had clogged her throat, making swallowing impossible. An intravenous diet of morphine had rendered her comatose.

2 Those are the cold bare facts. But there are other facts—achingly poignant, indeed, beautiful, some might argue—about Barbara Logan Brown's death. They are recounted here by Roberta Halter, herself a mother of four who cared for her dying friend and is today the guardian of Mrs. Logan Brown's son and daughter:

3 "The last time Barbara was able to go outside, she sat on the front porch. The girls and I went upstairs and took poster paint and painted a big huge smiley face above her bed. The next day, everyone put hand prints all over the wall. The children called it 'The Hands of Love,' and they started to paint messages on the wall. After the paint had dried, we let visitors come. By the end of the

day, there were messages everywhere. It was kind of a tribute to her while she was still living. And it was wonderful."

4   It was in Mrs. Halter's view, a good death.

5   A good death. It is a provocative phrase.

A MYSTERY PROFANED

6 The Supreme Court has weighed in on one of the most divisive moral, legal, and medical questions of the day: whether the Constitution gives Americans a fundamental right to a physician's help in dying. The justices said it does not, leaving the battle over whether to permit or prohibit assisted suicide to rage on among lawyers and legislators, doctors and ethicists across the country.

7   While the court ruled on the constitutional issue, what remains unsettled—indeed, unsettling—is the idea at the heart of the assisted-suicide question: that for most Americans, modern medicine has made dying worse.

8   America is often called a "death-denying" society; each year the United States spends millions on efforts to conquer death, or at least to postpone it. The self-help shelves of bookstores overflow with such pearls as "Stop Aging Now!" and "Stay Young the Melatonin Way."

9   If Americans don't deny death, they often trivialize it, said Joan Halifax, a Zen Buddhist priest who founded the Project on Being with Dying in Santa Fe, New Mexico. "By the time a kid gets into high school, he has seen 20,000 homicides on television," she said. "Death as a mystery to be embraced, entered into and respected has been profaned in our culture."

10   Courtesy of the assisted-suicide debate, the concept of a good death

"Death, the last voyage, the longest, the best."

—Thomas Wolfe

has now emerged, though many experts reject the phrase as simplistic. Dr. Ira Byock, president of the Academy of Hospice and Palliative Medicine, prefers "dying well." Dr. Timothy Keay, an end-of-life care expert at the University of Maryland, says "the least worst death."

11   There is no blueprint, however, for a good death. Death can't be neatly packaged with a red bow. It is messy, irrational, most often filled with sorrow and pain. More than two million Americans die each year; there are as many ways to die as to live. And so unanswerable questions arise: Not only what constitutes a good death and how can it be achieved, but who, ultimately, it is for—the person dying, or those going on living?

12   "I'm a little cynical about this whole notion of good death," said Dr. David Hilfiker, the founder of Joseph's House in Washington, which cares for homeless men dying of AIDS. "Death is really hard for most people. Why should people who are dying have to have a beautiful death? That's putting the burden on them to have some kind of experience that makes us feel good."

13   Indeed, said Dr. Sherwin B. Nuland, the author of "How We Die," the patient's needs often get lowest priority. "A good death," he said, "is in the eye of the beholder."

14   In centuries past, a good death was celebrated in art and literature as *ars moriendi*, the art of dying. Death marked salvation of the soul, neither an ending nor a beginning but, like birth, part of the cycle of life. "True philosophers," Plato wrote, "are always occupied in the practice of dying."

15   Buddhism is filled with stories of Zen masters who write poems in the moments before death, embracing it as the only time in life when absolute

freedom may be realized. In the Middle Ages, Christian monks greeted one another with the salutation *Momento mori,* remember that you must die.

16   Today, it seems, most Americans would rather forget. Asked their idea of a good death, they say, "quick." Keeling over in the garden, trowel in hand, is one ideal, going to bed and not waking up another.

17   That is a reaction against medical technology; if Americans want anything from death, they want to remain in control, to avoid making their exits tethered to a machine. It is fear of a painful, lonely and protracted high-tech death that has fueled the movement to make assisted suicide legal.

18   "The classic idea of the good death is the sudden death," Dr. Nuland said, "but if you think seriously about it, that isn't what you want." "What you really want is a tranquil, suffering-free last few weeks where you have the opportunity for those near you to express what your life has meant to them."

19   A century ago such opportunities could be elusive. Infectious disease caused most deaths; cholera struck, and there was a burial two days later. Dr. Joanne Lynn, director of George Washington University's Center to Improve Care of the Dying, said: "When people went to bed and said 'If I should die before I wake,' they meant it."

20   Today the leading causes of death are heart disease, cancer, and stroke. For older people, disproportionately affected by these ailments, dying can drag on for months or years. Most women, Dr. Lynn said, have eight years of disability before they die; most men, five or six. It might seem, then, that people have time to plan for their deaths, but many don't take advantage. A study to be published in this week's *Annals of Internal Medicine* found that most seriously ill adults in the hospital do not talk to their doctors about being kept alive on life-support machines. They prefer not to discuss it.

21   Americans have been reticent to talk about death; only recently have doctors and families felt obliged to tell a terminally ill person that he was, in fact, dying. Often the truth simply went unremarked, like an elephant in the dining room.

22   In 1969, Elisabeth Kubler-Ross shattered the silence with "On Death and Dying." In it, she described the progression of a patient's coping mechanisms in five stages of dying: denial, anger, bargaining, depression and finally acceptance.

23   Dr. Byock, the author of "Dying Well," offers what he calls the "developmental model" of dying. When he began caring for the terminally ill 20 years ago, he noticed that when he asked patients how they were feeling, often the reply was something like this: "Despite it all, doctor, I am well."

24   The juxtaposition of wellness and dying seemed a paradox, but he has concluded that the two can exist side by side. "In dying," he said, "there are opportunities to grow even through times of severe difficulty, which we would label suffering."

25   In his view, dying well includes love and reconciliation, a settling of worldly affairs and a life's summing up, as stories are recounted and passed to new generations. By these standards, Barbara Logan Brown most certainly had a good death. "Barbara," Mrs. Halter said, "had an opportunity to put her life here on earth in order."

IN THE END, LIBERATION

26   Conventional wisdom holds that people die as they have lived; a crotchety old man in life will be a crotchety old man in death. Not so, say experts in

end-of-life care: death can be both transforming and liberating.

27   Dr. Halifax, the Buddhist priest, tells of a woman whose daughter was a hospice nurse. Throughout her life, the mother had adhered to strict codes of politeness and propriety. A few days before her death, she began screaming in rage and pain.

28   As a nurse, her daughter knew that narcotics could subdue her mother's pain. But she chose to do nothing; the screaming, she believed, was her mother's way of finally expressing herself. "The screaming went on for four days and four nights," Dr. Halifax said. "And about an hour before she died, she lit up, and became extremely peaceful, and relaxed completely. And then she died."

Was it a good death? Dr. Halifax 2 paused.

"A good death," she finally al- 3 lowed, "sounds a little polite. It's like death with manners. I don't want to adorn death. Death is death."

(Sheryl Gay Stolberg, "The Good Death: Embracing a Right to Die Well," the *New York Times*, 1997)

✓ COMPREHENSION CHECKUP

Content and Structure

Write or circle the best answer for each of the following questions. You may refer back to the article.

1. The mode of rhetoric in this selection is primarily _____.

   (Explain the answer you give.) _____

   _____

2. The pattern of organization in paragraph 3 is primarily
   a. comparison-contrast
   b. example
   c. chronological order
   d. cause and effect

3. In paragraphs 14–16, two types of death are contrasted. Describe the two types below.

   a. _____

   _____

   b. _____

   _____

4. Explain the cause and effect relationship in paragraph 17.

   Cause: _____

   Effect: _____

5. In paragraphs 18–20, Stolberg implies several contrasts. State three things being contrasted.

   a. _____

   _____

   b. _____

   _____

c. _____

_____

6. In paragraph 21, Stolberg uses a figure of speech to describe Americans' reluctance to speak of death. Identify and then explain the meaning of this figure of speech.

_____

_____

7. According to Dr. Byock, what does "dying well" include?

a. _____

b. _____

c. _____

8. Explain the meaning of the phrase "death with manners" in the last paragraph.

_____

9. Write the overall main idea of the selection below.

_____

_____

10. The author's purpose is to _____. (Explain the answer you give.)

_____

11. To support her conclusion, the author primarily relies on
    a. statistics from research studies
    b. expert opinion from health-related fields
    c. her own observations and opinions

12. The author's tone throughout the article is
    a. loving
    b. angry
    c. serious
    d. humorous

Vocabulary in Context

For each italicized word from the article, use your dictionary to find the best definition according to the context.

1. other facts—achingly *poignant* (paragraph 2) _____

2. they often *trivialize* it (9) _____

3. has been *profaned* in our culture (9) _____

4. exits *tethered* to a machine (17) _____

5. lonely and *protracted* high-tech death (17) _____

6. a *tranquil,* suffering-free last few weeks (18) _____

7. such opportunities could be *elusive* (19) _____

8. *reticent* to talk about death (21) _____

9. *juxtaposition* of wellness and dying (24) _____

_____

10. *crotchety* old man (26) _____

11. *adhered* to strict codes (27) _____

12. politeness and *propriety* (27) _____

13. *subdue* her mother's pain (28) _____

14. to *adorn* death (30) _____

In Your Own Words

1. Compare and contrast the experience of dying described at the beginning of the selection to that described at the end. From the perspective of the patient, which one would you call a "good death"? From the perspective of the family? Be sure to provide arguments that support your position.

2. Do you think dying today is more dehumanizing than in the past? Why or why not?

3. Do you have a living will? Why are so many Americans reluctant to make provisions for death?

4. Dr. Jack Kevorkian, the so-called Dr. Death, insisted that those in chronic pain with no chance of recovery have a right to a physician-assisted suicide with the administration of mercy-killing drugs. The Supreme Court has decided that no such general right can be found in the Constitution. Do you think that laws should be passed authorizing physician-assisted suicide? Or do you think that laws should be passed banning it?

What is the main idea of the cartoon below? Is Steve Benson, the cartoonist, in favor of assisted suicide, or not? What logical fallacy is being illustrated?

By permission of Steve Benson and Creators Syndicate.

The Art of Writing

1. The Greek word parts *eu,* meaning "good," and *thanatos,* meaning "death," appear in the word *euthanasia,* so the literal meaning of this term is "good death." Euthanasia is also thought of as "mercy killing." Euthanasia may be either active or passive: in the first case, death is deliberately inflicted, sometimes by a relative; in the second, life-support systems are withdrawn and the patient dies naturally. Controversy surrounding the morality of euthanasia has increased in recent years because of advances in medical technology that make it possible for human beings, both newborn and old, to be kept alive almost indefinitely, even when severely impaired. In a brief essay, explain where you stand on euthanasia. Do you think life is sacred, so that euthanasia is always wrong? Do you think that the patient's ability to continue to enjoy life should influence the decision? Who should make the decision? The patient? The family? The doctor? The courts? Be sure to provide arguments that support your position.

2. Imagine trying to sum up your life in just six words. Julius Caesar described one of his greatest victories with the Latin words "veni, vidi, vici." This translates as "I came, I saw, I conquered." The phrase succinctly captures Caesar's arrogant confidence in his military abilities. What short statement could describe the essence of who you are? Should you select a single memorable occasion, make a silly joke, or describe a daily activity? The following are examples of six-word memoirs:

   > "Never really finished anything, except cake."
   > "I wouldn't change it a bit."
   > "I watched a lot of television."
   > "I traveled each and every highway."
   > "Each day's better than the next."

   In a brief essay, write your own six-word memoir with an explanation of its meaning.

Internet Activity

The Web sites below (with very similar URLs) discuss euthanasia from radically different perspectives. Visit the two sites and browse through their Web pages and links. After determining the point of view of each, list the various persuasive techniques they employ.

   www.euthanasia.com

   www.euthanasia.org

Review Test: Transition Words

This review test on transition words also provides background information for the reading selection that follows. Do the test below and then proceed to the reading selection entitled "Whose Grave Is This Anyway?"

Write the correct word(s) in the blank provided.

1. The actual burial vault of King Tutankhamum was opened in 1923. The coffin was made of 242 pounds of pure gold and was sculpted into a jeweled effigy of the king himself. When the mummy inside was unwrapped, it _____ was covered with jewels.
   a. despite
   b. truly

    c. also

    d. besides

2. _____, the mummy was in a state of extreme decay, possibly from use of excessive amounts of embalming oil. The lengthy embalming process, which took over seventy days to complete, included thoroughly washing the body, removing the internal organs, covering the body with sodium, drying it, coating it with resin, and wrapping it in linen. Finally, the pharaoh was ready to be displayed to the public.

    a. In spite of

    b. However

    c. Again

    d. As well as

3. The media was ecstatic _____ this was the first time that a pharaoh's tomb had been discovered reasonably intact in the Valley of the Kings. They marveled at the precious objects the tomb contained, including gold sandals, rings, necklaces, bracelets, and amulets. And, in case the king wanted to travel, there were even two full-size gold chariots.

    a. because

    b. unlike

    c. to emphasize

    d. overall

4. _____ robbers had tunneled into King Tutankhamum's tomb shortly after he was interred, they had taken very little. About all they accomplished was to desecrate the holy site.

    a. Again

    b. Although

    c. Underneath

    d. Hence

5. _____, priests were called in to purify the site. They quickly resealed the tomb, and then they left behind curses to intimidate those who would attempt to enter the sacred shrine again.

    a. In spite of

    b. As noted

    c. So

    d. Yet

6. Inside the tomb over a hundred *ushabti*, three-foot-high statues of servants, were lined up _____ the king's body, ready to wait on him in death as they had waited on him in life.

    a. as indicated

    b. next to

    c. further

    d. right

7. King Tutankhamum ascended the throne at age 9, died at age 19, and never actually participated in a battle. _____, his tomb is crowded with images of him as a great warrior.
   a. Yet
   b. Finally
   c. Here again
   d. Thus

8. Tutankhamum became pharaoh after his childhood marriage to the daughter of the pharaoh Akhenaten. _____ his father-in-law Akhenaten, King Tutankhamum is not considered to be a great pharaoh.
   a. Overall
   b. Unlike
   c. Furthermore
   d. Without a doubt

9. _____, he was a totally innocuous one.
   a. As well as
   b. Once again
   c. Hence
   d. Instead

10. He has achieved fame solely _____ his tomb was discovered intact. Debris from other nearby tombs had covered the entrance hiding the tomb from view. _____ Carter removed the waste material on November 4, 1922, he discovered one stone step leading downwards. He uncovered fifteen more steps and then a blocked doorway. As Carter slowly worked his way into the tomb, he described it this way: "My eyes grew accustomed to the light, details of the room within emerged slowly, and gold— everywhere the glint of gold."
    a. again; Furthermore
    b. because; After
    c. nevertheless; Despite
    d. still; Once again

SELECTION

*"No matter who opens a tomb and takes away its contents,
that person is violating the intentions of those who sealed
the tomb originally."*

GETTING THE PICTURE

How often does a person's most cherished dream come true? After fifteen years of hard work, it happened to British archaeologist Howard Carter.

BIO-SKETCH

Mark Getlein is a painter and an author of textbooks on art-related subjects.

BRUSHING UP ON VOCABULARY

pillage to rob or plunder. *Pillage* is derived from the Old French word *piller*, meaning "spoils or booty."

propriety fitting or proper. *Propriety* is derived from the Latin *propietatem*, meaning "appropriateness."

perpetrator a person who carries out an evil, criminal, or offensive action. *Perpetrator* derives from the Latin word *perpetratus,* meaning "to bring into existence."

mummy the dead body of a human being preserved by the ancient Egyptian process of embalming. The first step in this process was to remove the deceased's brain through the nostrils by means of a long hook. Next, the liver, lungs, intestines, and stomach were removed. All of the organs were then preserved in separate receptacles. The body was soaked in salt water for a lengthy period and thoroughly dried. Later the body was stuffed and then swaddled in clean strips of linen.

Excerpt from

GILBERT'S LIVING WITH ART

by Mark Getlein

WHOSE GRAVE IS THIS ANYWAY?

When Howard Carter and his party opened the tomb of the Egyptian king Tutankhamum in 1922, there was rejoicing around the world. The tomb was largely intact, not seriously pillaged by ancient grave robbers, so it still contained the wonderful artifacts that had been buried with the young king more than three millennia earlier. Over the next several years Carter and his team systematically photographed and cataloged the objects from the tomb, then transported them to the Cairo Museum. 1

There is a certain irony in this story that raises complex ethical questions. Why are Carter and his party not called grave robbers? Why are their actions in stripping the tomb acceptable—even praiseworthy—when similar behavior by common thieves would be deplored? No matter who opens a tomb and takes away its contents, that person is violating the intentions of those who sealed the tomb originally. No matter what the motivation, a human body that was meant to rest in peace for all time has been disturbed. Should this not make us feel uncomfortable? 2

From the beginning some were uneasy about the propriety of unearthing Tutankhamum's remains. When Lord Carnarvon, Carter's sponsor, died suddenly from a mosquito bite, and several others connected with the project experienced tragedies, rumors arose about the "curse of King Tut." But Carter himself died peacefully many years later, and the talk subsided. 3

Perhaps it is the passage of time that transforms grave robbing into archaeology. Carter would no doubt have been outraged if, say, his grandmother's coffin had been dug up to strip the body of its jewelry. But after three thousand years Tutankhamum has no relatives still around to protest. 4

Howard Carter Examining King Tut (1922)

Library of Congress, Prints and Photographs Division [LC-USZ62-60947 (b&w film copy neg.)]

Perhaps it is a question of the words we use to describe such ancient finds. 5
We speak of Tutankhamum's "mummy," and mummy is a clean, historical-sounding
word. Parents bring their children to museums to see the mummies and mummy
cases. We can almost forget that a mummy is the embalmed body of a dead human being, pulled out of its coffin so that we can marvel at the coffin and sometimes the body itself.

Or, perhaps the difference between grave robbing and archaeology lies in the 6
motives of the perpetrators. Common thieves are motivated by greed, by their
quest for money to be made by selling stolen objects. Carter and his team did not
sell the treasures from Tutankhamum's tomb but stored them safely in the Cairo
Museum, where art lovers from around the world can see them. They were, in effect, making a glorious gift to the people of our century and centuries to come (while
at the same time, one must point out, acquiring significant glory for themselves).

The basic issue is a clash of cultural values. To the Egyptians, it was normal 7
and correct to bury their finest artworks with the exalted dead. To us, the idea of
all that beauty being locked away in the dark forever seems an appalling waste.
We want to bring it into the light, to have it as part of our precious artistic heritage. Almost no one, having seen these magnificent treasures, would seriously
propose they be put back in the tomb and sealed up.

In the end, inevitably, our cultural values will prevail, simply because we are 8
still here and the ancient Egyptians are not. After three thousand years, Tutankhamum's grave really isn't his anymore. Whether rightly or wrongly, it belongs to us.

(Rita Gilbert, "Whose Grave Is This Anyway?," *Gilbert's Living with Art*, 6/e, 2002)

✓ COMPREHENSION CHECKUP

(Answers can be found in the selection or the Review Test on pages 489–491.)

Short Answer

Write an answer to each question on the lines provided.

1. Which of the persuasive techniques mentioned in the beginning of the chapter are employed by the author? Give reasons to support your choice.

   _____

   _____

   _____

   _____

   _____

2. In the selection, the author is exploring the difference between grave robbing and archaeology. What specific points does he make to distinguish the two?

   a. _____

   b. _____

   _____

   c. _____

   _____

True or False

Indicate whether each statement is true or false by writing **T** or **F** in the blank provided.

_____ 3. Several people who were associated with unsealing King Tut's tomb died under mysterious circumstances.

_____ 4. King Tut's tomb was discovered close to its original condition.

_____ 5. Howard Carter was a British geologist.

_____ 6. Gold was featured predominantly inside King Tut's tomb.

_____ 7. The wondrous objects removed from King Tut's tomb were stored in the British Museum of Natural History.

Multiple Choice

Write the letter of the correct answer in the blank provided.

_____ 8. King Tut was a pharaoh who
   a. was relatively unimportant in Egyptian history
   b. died at an early age
   c. caused the death of Howard Carter
   d. both a and b

_____ 9. All of the following are true *except*
   a. the furnishings of King Tut's tomb were discovered largely intact
   b. in ancient Egypt, the burial of royalty was done in accord with elaborate rituals
   c. King Tut's coffin was made of pure gold
   d. Lord Carnarvon died before the discovery of King Tut's tomb

_____ 10. The contents of King Tut's tomb were
   a. resealed by Carter and Lord Carnarvon
   b. placed on display so that the public could view them
   c. sold to the highest bidder
   d. stolen by thieves and vandals

_____ 11. The ancient Egyptians
   a. buried their finest pieces of artwork with their dead
   b. took steps to embalm and preserve corpses
   c. tried to preserve royal tombs for eternity
   d. all of the above

_____ 12. The author of the article suggests all of the following *except*
   a. the passage of time transforms grave robbing into the study of archaeology
   b. archaeologists offer opportunities to experience other cultures
   c. archaeologists should stop invading and disturbing the burial sites of past civilizations
   d. King Tut's grave now belongs to humanity

Vocabulary in Context

Fill in the blanks using words from the following list. Use each word only once.

appalling	deplored	prevailed	sponsor
artifacts	heritage	propose	subsided
clash	marvel	quest	transformed
curse	precious	rejoicing	violating

1. After his anger _____, he was quick to apologize to his wife for his outburst.

2. Michael's mother _____ her son's slovenly ways because he failed to pick up anything in his room.

3. I would like to _____ a toast to the new bride and groom.

4. Having children _____ her life.

5. There was much _____ among the students when our team won the state football championship.

6. To someone who is dehydrated, a drop of water is very _____.

7. To determine whether _____ are genuine or fake without damaging them, scientists often use X-rays.

8. Be careful when you travel in foreign countries. You may be accused of _____ social customs you are unfamiliar with.

9. The amount of man-made debris that is found on beaches around the world is _____.

10. He was on a _____ to identify his son's murderer. Nothing would stop him until he fulfilled his goal of seeing the murderer behind bars.

11. When I failed to pay the fortune-teller for her advice, she placed a _____ on my children and my children's children.

12. Genealogy is important to people who want to trace their family _____.

13. When I look at the Eiffel Tower, I can only _____ at the amount of work that went into its construction.

14. We are looking for a _____ for our softball team. Are there any volunteers?

15. Do you think that a red blouse and an orange skirt _____?

16. She successfully _____ on her teenagers to pass up a vacation with friends and join the family on a car trip.

In Your Own Words

1. Do you think it's appropriate to investigate ancient grave sites for archaeological purposes? Why or why not?

2. Do you think it's appropriate to display the bodies found in ancient graves in museums? Why or why not?

The Art of Writing

Do you think museums should be compelled to return works of art that were taken many years ago from another country? What are some relevant considerations for whether antiquities should be returned to the country of origin? What if that country is politically unstable or near a place of tension and fighting? What about the many people who will no longer be able to visit the exhibits if they are moved a long distance away? How much opportunity will people have to learn about other cultures if countries begin taking back their antiquities?

Internet Activity

1. While the most famous mummies have been found in Egypt, other cultures and societies, such as the ancient Incas, have also engaged in mummification. A modern version of mummification is called cryogenics. Bodies are frozen in liquid nitrogen and then preserved in steel containers. Do an Internet investigation of the mummification or cryogenics process, and then write a short summary of your findings.

2. Do you believe in curses? When Howard Carter was warned that "death comes on wings to he who enters the tomb of a pharoah," he paid no attention. And yet his patron, Lord Carnarvon, died of a mosquito bite within days of unsealing King Tut's tomb. Other deaths quickly followed, including the death of a French scientist who visited the tomb shortly after its discovery, an X-ray specialist on his way to examine the mummy, and an American archaeologist who died of a mysterious virus soon after a visit. Mere coincidences? What do you think? Check out the following Web sites and write a paragraph arguing your position on whether there was a curse.

   http://unmuseum.mus.pa.us/mummy.htm

   www.mummytombs.com/egypt/kingtut.htm

MASTERY TEST: Whose Grave Is This Anyway?

Write the letter of the correct answer in the blank provided.

Main Idea

_____ 1. Which of the following best represents the main idea of the selection?
  a. Howard Carter was a courageous man and we owe him a huge debt of gratitude.
  b. Disturbing a gravesite is always wrong.
  c. The archaeological value of exploring ancient graves outweighs the ethical concerns.
  d. Archaeology is nothing more than sanctioned grave robbing.

Supporting Detail

_____ 2. According to the selection, approximately when was King Tut buried?
  a. three millennia ago
  b. in 1922
  c. 3,000 years ago
  d. both a and c

Context

_____ 3. What is the meaning of the italicized word in the following sentence? "In the end, inevitably, our cultural values will *prevail*, simply because we are still here and the ancient Egyptians are not." (paragraph 8)
  a. go into decline
  b. predominate; win out
  c. cease to exist
  d. none of the above

Purpose

_____ 4. Which of the following describes the author's purpose for writing this selection?
  a. to argue that the tomb of King Tut should not have been opened
  b. to persuade the reader that archaeologists are always justified in exploring graves or tombs
  c. to discuss the issue of whether archaeologists should be able to enter and remove items from an ancient tomb
  d. to entertain the reader by describing a unique expedition

Patterns of Organization

_____ 5. Paragraph 7 is organized by
  a. defining key terms
  b. comparing and contrasting different points of view
  c. illustrating the results of an archaeological dig
  d. describing the process of unearthing a tomb

Sentence Relationships

(2) "When Lord Carnarvon, Carter's sponsor, died suddenly from a mosquito bite, and several others connected with the project experienced tragedies, rumors arose about the 'curse of King Tut.' (3) But Carter himself died peacefully many years later, and the talk subsided."

_____ 6. Identify the relationship between the second and third sentence above.
   a. cause and effect
   b. example
   c. contrast
   d. chronological order

"In the end, inevitably, our cultural values will prevail, simply because we are still here and the ancient Egyptians are not."

_____ 7. What is the relationship expressed in the sentence above?
   a. spatial order
   b. because
   c. contrast
   d. summary

Inference

_____ 8. A conclusion that can be drawn from this selection is that
   a. the ancient Egyptians would be flattered to know that so many people now take an interest in their culture
   b. the ancient Egyptians would view Carter's opening of the tomb as a sacrilege
   c. the author of this selection disapproves of the practice of examining the contents of Egyptian tombs
   d. some archeologists avoid displaying artifacts found in tombs because they fear being cursed

Tone

_____ 9. The author's tone can best be described as
   a. objective
   b. sarcastic
   c. contemptuous
   d. amused

Fact or Opinion

_____ 10. "Whether rightly or wrongly, it [Tutankhamum's grave] belongs to us." This sentence is a statement of
   a. fact
   b. opinion

Bias

_____ 11. The use of the word "mummy" to describe an embalmed body is a euphemism because
a. it is likely to be considered less offensive than "dead human body"
b. it is a clean, historical-sounding word
c. children like to see mummies in museums
d. both a and b

Author's Reasoning

_____ 12. All of the following are cited by the author as reasons showing that disturbing the grave was not morally offensive *except*
a. Carter and his team did not sell the treasures from the tomb but instead stored them safely
b. art lovers from around the world can view the treasures taken from the tomb
c. Carter and his team encountered many hardships and dangers
d. after 3,000 years, no relatives of King Tut's survive to protest the unearthing of his body

Brain Teasers

Death Wordplay

State the meaning of each of the following.

1. Interns and residents in hospitals are put on *murderous* schedules.

   _____

2. You need to take the pictures now because the light is *dying quickly*. _____

3. After twenty years in Congress, it was *political suicide* for him to change from a Republican to a Democrat. _____

4. When the company left the area, it dealt a *death blow* to the surrounding community.

   _____

5. Support for political incumbents seems to be *dying out*. _____

6. My two-year-old is going to *be the death of me*! _____

7. Bears are known to hibernate in the *dead of winter*. _____

8. As a presenter at the awards show, she was *dressed to kill*. _____

   _____

9. Plans for opening new parks are *pretty much dead*. _____

10. Many school systems are trying to clean out *the deadwood* until more money is available.

    _____

VOCABULARY   Unit 9: Word Parts Featuring War and Good and Bad

"To be prepared for war is one of the most effective means of preserving peace."
—George Washington

Unit 9 covers vocabulary with the following word parts: *belli-*, *-cede*, and *-ces*; *-gnostos* and *cogni-*; *cur-*; *bene-* and *mal-*; *pos-* and *pon-*; *-trac(t)*; *viv-*; *voc-*. Words made from these word parts, along with their definitions, follow. Supplemental words with these word parts are located in the left margin.

belli—war

	bellicose	inclined or eager to fight; aggressively hostile. The situation worsened daily as each nation sounded more *bellicose* and less inclined to a peaceful resolution.
	belligerent	engaged in warfare; showing readiness to fight; hostile. Amanda thought that Todd's increasingly *belligerent* behavior must be due to using drugs.
		Bellicose and *belligerent* are synonyms.
rebellion	**rebel**	a person who rises in arms against a ruler or government; a person who resists authority, control, or tradition. During the teenage years, many young people are *rebels:* They just can't tolerate their parents' authority.

cede, ces—go (back), yield, withdraw

concession precedent	**cede**	to yield or formally surrender to another. After the battle, the disputed land was *ceded* to the victorious party.
	accede	to give one's consent or approval; to give up, agree. Mona refused to *accede* to her parents' wishes and give her child up for adoption. Instead, she vowed to raise him all by herself.
	precede	to go or come before. In a traditional wedding ceremony in the United States, the bridesmaids *precede* the bride up the aisle.
	recession	the act of receding or withdrawing; a period of economic decline.
	secede	to stop being a member of a group. During the Civil War, Alabama was one of the states that *seceded* from the Union.

gnostos—know; cogni—know

diagnosis ignoramus prognosis	**agnostic**	a person who believes that it is impossible to know whether or not there is a God.
	cognitive	pertaining to the act or process of knowing; perception.
	incognito	with one's identity hidden or unknown. Many movie stars, not wishing to be recognized by fans, travel *incognito*.
	cognizant	being aware or informed of something. Were the parents *cognizant* that their child was suffering from depression?

cur(r)—run

concurrent   occurring or existing simultaneously or side by side. The literal meaning is "running together." What is the likelihood of an earthquake and a tornado happening *concurrently*?

cursive   handwriting in flowing strokes with the letters joined (running) together. Although I can read his printing, his *cursive* writing is often illegible.

cursory   going rapidly over something without noticing details; hasty; superficial. Eva gave the memo a *cursory* reading; she will review it again later when she has more time.

discursive   passing aimlessly from one subject to another; rambling. Because I hadn't seen Marilyn for a long time, our conversation was *discursive*, ranging from our health and our children to new books and movies.

incursion   an invasion of a place or territory; a raid. Has there been another *incursion* into enemy territory?

precursor   a person or thing that comes before and makes the way ready for what will follow; forerunner. Was the typewriter a *precursor* to the computer?

recur   to occur again. The literal meaning is "to run back." As soon as Sonia finishes her antibiotics, her ear infection *recurs*.

bene—well, good; mal—bad

benefactor   a person who has given money or other help as to a charity or school. An anonymous *benefactor* paid Truman's tuition to a private school.

beneficiary   a person or group that receives benefits. In his mother's will, Marco was named as her primary *beneficiary*.

benediction   a blessing; an utterance of good wishes.

benevolent   characterized by expressing goodwill or kindly feelings; kind; generous. Sascha's *benevolent* uncle paid for her trip to the United States.

malpractice   **malcontent**   not satisfied with current conditions; ready to rebel.
malady
malodorous   **malevolence**   the quality or state of wishing evil or harm on others. In the fairy tale
malefactor   "Snow White and the Seven Dwarfs," the *malevolent* stepmother
malicious   plots Snow White's death.
malnourished

malfeasance   misconduct or wrongdoing committed by someone holding a public office. The congressman was accused of *malfeasance* for accepting expensive gifts from a lobbyist.

malign   to speak harmful untruths about someone; slander. Now that she is no longer around to defend herself, it seems unfair to *malign* her.

pos, pon—put, place

postpone   **imposition**   the laying on of something as a burden or obligation. Would it be too
repository   much of an *imposition* for you to watch Colby every day after school
superimpose   for the next two weeks?

depose to remove from office or position, especially high office. The rebels did not succeed in *deposing* the tyrant.

deposition the written statement of a witness, made under oath, but not in court, to be used later at a trial.

trac(t)—pull, draw

retract to draw back; to withdraw. Threatened by the senator's attorneys, the paper was forced to *retract* a statement that it had made earlier in the week about the senator's extramarital affairs. A turtle can *retract* its head.

detract to take something away, especially something worthwhile or attractive. Josie wanted to get contacts because she believed that her glasses *detracted* from her appearance.

traction the power to grip or hold to a surface; moving without slipping; the act of drawing or pulling. When the tires lost *traction* on the wet road, the car began to skid.

viv—live

revival
survivor
vivacious

vivid strikingly bright or intense; realistic; full of life; lively. The flower paintings of Georgia O'Keeffe are famous for their *vivid* colors.

revive renew; restore to life or consciousness. After pulling the 2-year-old from the swimming pool, the paramedics worked frantically to *revive* her.

convivial enjoying a good time with other people, such as at a party; sociable; friendly; jovial. Her new in-laws were so *convivial* that Kelly looked forward to spending the holidays with them.

vivisection the action of cutting into or dissecting a living body. *Antivivisectionist* groups have caused many university researchers to abandon experiments on rhesus monkeys.

voc—call

evocative
equivocate
irrevocable
provoke
vociferous

vocal having a voice; inclined to express oneself with words. The teacher told the class that she wanted them to be *vocal* and participate.

revoke to call back or withdraw; to cancel. Because Tim failed to come home by midnight, his mother *revoked* his driving privileges for the next two weeks.

advocate to support or urge by argument. *ad-* means "to," and *voc-* means "call," so the literal meaning is "to call to." The financial adviser was a strong *advocate* for staying out of debt.

vocation a person's regular occupation or calling.

avocation something a person does in addition to a principal occupation, especially for pleasure; hobby. His *vocation* is teaching, but his *avocation* is surfing.

Now that you have studied the vocabulary in Unit 9, practice your new knowledge by completing the crossword puzzle on the next page.

Vocabulary Unit 9 Puzzle

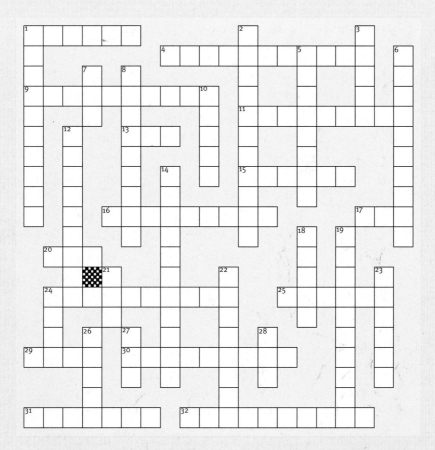

ACROSS CLUES

1. You _____ someone when you spread a false, mean-spirited story about that person.

4. The legislator committed _____ when he accepted a bribe.

9. The judge sentenced the defendant to _____ sentences of three and five years.

11. Prince William, dressed in casual clothes, traveled _____ throughout the United States.

13. A word part meaning "run."

15. Because Sascha had only been underwater for a minute, the paramedics were able to _____ her.

16. The supervisor was _____ of the fact that Carrie and Guillermo were leaving early every Friday.

17. A word part meaning "earth."*

20. A word part meaning "call."

24. An unknown _____ gave Maria enough money to complete her education.

25. Should we _____ a driver's license after only one DUI offense?

29. A word part meaning "yield."

30. His _____ of photography was more important to him than his vocation as a computer programmer.

31. The minute the legislator made the comment, he wished he could _____ it.

32. Kind people are considered to be _____.

DOWN CLUES

1. The employee complained all the time and was known as a _____.

2. The _____ countries were at war with each other.

3. A word part meaning "war."

5. Josh said he was an _____ because he did not know whether God exists.

6. The lawyer took the _____ of the witness to the car accident.

7. The abbreviation for what was once the eighth month.*

8. Was the icebox a _____ to the refrigerator?

10. A word part meaning "pull."

12. He sounded increasingly _____ and less likely to find a peaceful resolution.

14. After the funeral service, the priest delivered a short _____.

18. The army could sense that victory was near.

19. It was a real _____ to have her mother-in-law stay for two months in their tiny house.

21. The abbreviation for what was once the tenth month.*

22. Snow tires have better _____ on snow than regular tires.

23. South Carolina was the first state to _____ from the Union.

24. A word part meaning "good."

26. Darcy's allergies _____ every fall and spring.

27. A word part meaning "bad."

28. A word part meaning "put."

*From a previous unit.

Further Application of Study Techniques

Chapter in Part 5

The Bookworm (c. 1850)

by Carl Spitzweg
© Georg Scháfer Museum/The New York Project
Gesellschaft für Bildarchivierung GmbH

Organizing Textbook Information

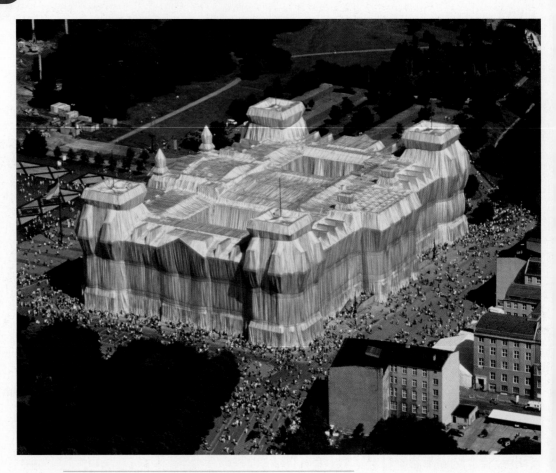

Wrapped Reichstag, Berlin (1971–95) *BY CHRISTO AND JEANNE-CLAUDE*

© Christo 1995. Photo Wolfgang Volz.

View and Reflect

The wrapping of the Reichstag required 1,076,000 square feet of fabric. It took 90 climbers and 120 installation workers to complete the project, which remained in place for only two weeks. All of the projects done by Christo and Jeanne-Claude are temporary, paid for by the artists, and all materials are recycled afterwards. The two have been called "environmental artists" because they work in both rural and urban environments. They force people to view familiar locations in new and different ways.

1. What do you imagine the building here would look like without the wrappings?
2. The Reichstag is Germany's parliament building. Do you think the wrapping of the Reichstag comments on politics? How?
3. Do you consider the wrapping of a large structure like the Reichstag art? Why or why not?

Applying Study Techniques to Textbook Material

In previous chapters of this book, you were introduced to various study techniques. You also practiced applying many of these techniques. In this chapter, we will review those techniques and introduce you to others that will help you study for your college classes. You will also have a chance to practice your newly acquired skills with part of a chapter on the arts from a cultural anthropology textbook.

Skimming

Skimming is a study technique very similar to SQ3R (see page 49). Skimming involves reading material quickly in order to gain a quick overview and identify the main points. As in SQ3R, you read the introduction to the chapter, the summary at the end of the chapter, the section titles and subtitles, and the first sentence of each section and many paragraphs. You also look at the illustrations and read the captions. Once you have skimmed the chapter, you should be able to state its main idea.

Skim through the selection "Art and the Aesthetic" (including the Introduction and Summary, see page 512), and then indicate whether each statement is true or false by writing **T** or **F** in the space provided.

_____   1. People are only interested in things that are practical or useful.

_____   2. It is only in the United States that people are concerned with altering their physical appearance.

_____   3. In some places in Africa, hairstyle indicates that a woman is a widow.

_____   4. Some societies alter body parts other than just hair and beards.

_____   5. Native Americans frequently painted their faces for war.

_____   6. In New Guinea, covering one's face with white clay signifies respect for the deceased.

_____   7. The art of tattooing is practiced in very few places.

_____   8. Tattooing is a modern art form.

_____   9. Tattooing and scarification are more permanent than body paint.

_____ 10. Both Maori men and women had tattoos.

_____ 11. Among the Polynesians, the Marquesa were least likely to cover their bodies with tattoos.

_____ 12. Cutting or creating scars on the body is called scarification.

_____ 13. The aesthetic response is universal.

_____ 14. In a curing ceremony, Navajo singers are using both visual art and performance art.

Scanning

Scanning is the process of quickly searching reading material in order to locate specific bits of information. When you scan, you don't start at the beginning and read until you get to the end. Instead, you run your eyes rapidly over the material to find the information that's important to you. When you go the to the phone book, you scan down through the list of names or businesses until you find the one you are looking for. You don't actually take the time to read every name. Most of us use scanning techniques when we search the TV guide for the time and channel of a favorite show, the dictionary for a specific word, or the newspaper for a particular ad.

Scan through the section "Performance Arts" (see page 517) to find the answers to the following specific questions. Scan titles and subtitles of sections to determine which sections are likely to have the answers. Once you have located the appropriate section, move your eyes rapidly across the information to locate the answers to the questions that follow.

1. In the _____ religious tradition, hymns are sung in unison to draw the congregation together to promote fellowship.

2. In the *voudon* religion, the spirits are called _____.

3. The era of the slave trade began around the _____.

4. _____ may cause illness or death when they possess someone.

5. According to the Tumbuka, a person is cured when he or she is returned to a correct balance between _____ and _____ forces.

6. A Navajo _____ is responsible for performing a curing ritual.

7. The singer creates images of the Holy People out of sand in what are called

_____.

8. The _____ ordered the Navajo not to make permanent images of them.

Annotating

In Study Technique 1 (page 32), you learned how to underline or highlight information and then make notes to yourself in the margins. In the sample material that follows, we have demonstrated these skills for you in the Introduction and part of "Body Arts." Study this example and use it as a guide. Then practice your annotating skills on the sections "Beards," "Head Shaping," and "Altering Other Body Parts"(see page 514).

Outlining

In Study Technique 4 (page 154), we introduced you to outlining, an important study technique for organizing textbook information. Here we will illustrate the proper outlining format by giving you a sample outline for the section "Body Arts." You can then practice outlining the section "Performance Arts."

In a formal outline, main, first-level headings are enumerated with Roman numerals (I, II, III, etc.), second-level headings are enumerated with capital letters (A, B, C, etc.), third-level headings are enumerated with Arabic numbers (1, 2, 3, etc.), and fourth-level headings are enumerated with lowercase letters (a, b, c, etc.). Each level contains information that is more specific than the level above it.

Another rule for making a formal outline is that you cannot have a single subsection; you must have either no subsections or at least two. So, for example, section I cannot have only subsection A; it must have either no subsections or at least subsections A and B.

It takes time to outline textbook material, but the process of outlining helps you to organize and learn the material. If you have done a good job with your outline, you should be able to study from it without having to return to the original textbook material.

Study the outline below for the portion of the textbook chapter "Body Arts." Compare the outline with the text.

I. Body Arts
   A. Physical alterations
      1. Hairstyles
         a. Indicate woman's status (Africa, Hopi)
         b. Indicate clan membership (Omaha)
      2. Beards
         a. Demonstrate religious beliefs (for some)
         b. Denoted social status in ancient times
      3. Head shaping
         a. Universal until 18th century (France)
         b. Tight caps for babies (Netherlands)
         c. Elongation of skull (ancient Andeans and Egyptians)
         d. Headboards (Chinook)
      4. Other body parts
         a. Feet of wealthy girls bound (China)
         b. Holes cut in earlobes (Africa)
         c. Teeth filed to points (African pygmy)
         d. Rings placed on girls' necks (Africa)
         e. Plastic surgery used (Western nations)
   B. Painting of face and body
      1. Face
         a. Used for war (Native Americans)
         b. Used for religious rituals (Native Americans)
         c. Used to enhance social appearance (Native Americans)
      2. Body
         a. May have religious significance
         b. Could be a daily activity
   C. Tattooing and Scarification
      1. Tattooing
         a. Has long history as art form
         b. Practiced by ancient Egyptians, Bretons, Romans
         c. Outlawed by Christians
         d. Rediscovered by sailors in Pacific
         e. Could indicate social status
         f. Most elaborately practiced by Polynesians
         g. Conferred specific privileges
      2. Scarification
         a. Is more limited than tattooing
         b. Can be part of initiation rituals

II. Performance Arts

Mapping

You were introduced to mapping in Study Technique 6 (page 163). Mapping is similar to outlining in that it includes main categories and subcategories. But in contrast to outlining, it is more visual and free-form. Look at the map based on the section "Body Arts." After studying the sample map, try to map the section "Performance Arts." Your goal in mapping is to create a good study guide.

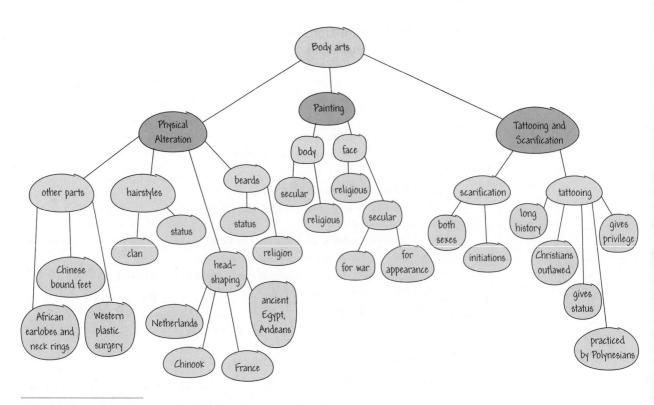

Map of Body Arts

Comparison-Contrast Chart

In Study Technique 5 (page 158), you were introduced to the comparison-contrast chart. Some material lends itself nicely to a comparison-contrast chart, and this is the case with the sections on the Tumbuka and the Navajo. Read these sections, and complete the chart below. In the first column, the categories to be compared and contrasted are listed; in the second and third columns, record the information for the Tumbuka and the Navajo that pertain to that category. We have provided the categories as a sample to help you get started. When you complete the chart, answer the questions that follow.

COMPARISON-CONTRAST CHART		
Category	**Tumbuka**	**Navajo**
Practiced by		
Cause of illness		
Person who performs ceremony		

(Continued)

COMPARISON-CONTRAST CHART (*continued*)		
Category	Tumbuka	Navajo
Role of sick person		
Time of ceremony		
Visual art involved		
Duration of ceremony		

What similarities did you discover about the Timbuka and the Navajo through the process of filling in the chart? What specific examples substantiate your conclusions?

Venn Diagram

In Study Technique 9 (page 445), you learned to make a Venn diagram. Like the comparison-contrast chart, Venn diagrams are helpful for showing similarities and differences. As you will recall, the Venn diagram is made up of two interlocking circles. In the outside parts of the circles, you list the traits that are unique to each subject being discussed, while in the overlapping area you list the traits the two subjects share. The following textbook chapter discusses similarities and differences between tattooing and scarification. Complete the Venn diagram below with information from the textbook chapter. We have given you a few sample items to get you started.

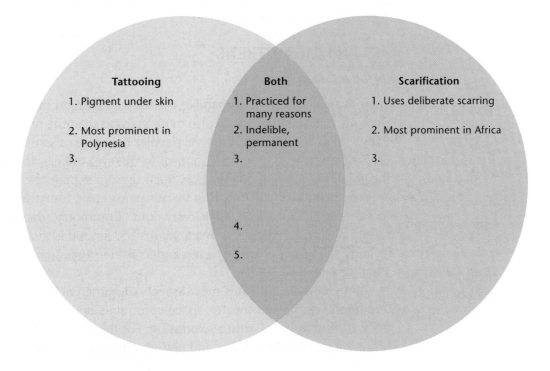

Tattooing

1. Pigment under skin

2. Most prominent in Polynesia

3.

Both

1. Practiced for many reasons

2. Indelible, permanent

3.

4.

5.

Scarification

1. Uses deliberate scarring

2. Most prominent in Africa

3.

SELECTION

*"People around the world are highly creative in altering
their physical appearance."*

GETTING THE PICTURE

Cultural anthropology, the topic of this textbook selection, describes and tries to explain cultural differences.

BIO-SKETCH

James Peoples is currently a professor at Ohio Wesleyan University. His research interests include cultural evolution, human ecology, and cultures of the Pacific. In addition to the textbook *Humanity*, from which this partial chapter is taken, he has published numerous articles in professional journals.

BRUSHING UP ON VOCABULARY

body arts alterations to the physical appearance of the body, including painting, tattooing, and scarification

performance arts art meant to be heard, seen, or personally performed, including music, song, dance, and theater

Excerpt from
HUMANITY

by James Peoples

ART AND THE AESTHETIC
Introduction

Def.—aesthetic
those things
appealing to mind,
senses, emotion

Def.—art is an
expression of the
aesthetic

There is much more to human life than the acquisition of necessities like food, 1 clothing, and shelter. There is also more to living than the production and use of things for their utilitarian value. All peoples have both a sense of and a desire for the *aesthetic: those things that appeal to the eye*, the ear, the taste, the touch, the emotions, and the imagination. Such sensory experiences are important not only for their functional value but because their color, form, design, sound, taste, or feel are pleasurable in their own right. Commonly, these experiences are sought after to stimulate our imaginations and emotions through the creation of feelings of happiness, fear, or even anger. These expressions of the aesthetic are what we generally call *art*.

Although art permeates most aspects of human activity, from clothing and 2 furniture to music and theater, space constraints do not permit us to discuss all these diverse forms of artistic expression. For this reason we limit our discussion to the categories of body arts and performance arts.

Body Arts

MI   <u>People around the world are highly creative in altering their physical appearance</u>. 3 Almost anything that can be done to the body is probably being done or has been done in the past. In Euro-American societies, for example, parts of the body are now being pierced that few people even thought of as pierceable a decade or two ago. For convenience, we focus on the <u>body arts of physical alterations, body painting, and scarification</u>.

3 types of body arts

Physical Alterations

MI   <u>In most societies people attempt to physically alter their bodies</u>. Head and body 4 hair is treated in many different ways. In Western societies hair is styled and often artificially colored. Some people shave their head, their beard, their legs and armpits. Others let their beard and mustache grow and style them in various ways. Still others, particularly middle-aged males, tempt vanity to have replacement hair grown on the top of their head. In most Western societies these actions are mainly a matter of fashion or personal taste; in other societies such actions may have deeper cultural meanings.

Hairstyles   <u>In parts of Africa, a woman's status</u>—for example, whether she is 5 unmarried or married, or is a mother or a widow—<u>is indicated by hairstyle</u>.

Hopi Woman Dressing Hair of Unmarried Girl (1900) *BY HENRY PEABODY*

Among the <u>Hopis</u>, <u>adolescent girls of marriageable age</u> wear their hair in a large whorl on each side of the head, creating the so-called <u>butterfly hairstyle</u>. <u>After marriage</u> they will wear their <u>hair long and parted in the middle</u>. <u>Children among the Omahas</u> had their <u>hair cut in patterns indicating their clan membership</u>.

Beards   Wearing beards is not always a matter of personal taste and fashion. In 6 many societies, such as Hasidic Jews, Mennonites, Amish, some Muslim sects, and Sikhs, wearing a beard is an act of religious belief. In the ancient world social status was frequently associated with beards. In Egypt only the nobility were allowed to wear beards. Not only did noblemen wear beards, but women of the nobility frequently wore artificial beards as well to indicate their social rank. In contrast, in ancient Greece only the nobility were allowed to be clean shaven; men of commoner status had to let their beards grow.

Head Shaping   Hair alterations are usually reversible, for hair will grow back. 7 Other parts of the body are altered on a permanent basis. Cranial deformation or head shaping has been and is still widely practiced among the peoples of the world. The skull of a baby is soft and if the baby's head is bound the shape of the skull can be permanently changed, flattening the back or the forehead or lengthening the head. In parts of France cranial deformation was virtually universal until the eighteenth century. A baby's face was tightly wrapped in linen, resulting in a flattened skull and ears. In the Netherlands, babies once wore tight-fitting caps that depressed the front portion of the skull. The elite classes of the ancient Andean civilizations elongated the skull, as did the ancient Egyptians. For the first year of its life a Chinook baby was wrapped on a hard board, with another board bound against the top and front of the head. This technique resulted in a head with additional breadth. Some peoples of Central Africa bound the heads of female babies to create elongated skulls that came to a point on the back.

Altering Other Body Parts   Some people permanently altered other parts of 8 the body as well. In China the feet of female children of high-status families were bound at the age of 5 or 6 to deform the feet and keep them small. This was not only considered attractive, it was practiced as a visible indication of the fact that the family was sufficiently wealthy that its women did not have to do much physical labor. In parts of Africa and among some Native American peoples holes were cut in earlobes or the lower and upper lips were expanded so that earplugs and large lip plugs could be inserted. Some of these plugs were up to three inches in diameter. Some central African Pygmy peoples file their front teeth into points, which in their culture enhances their attractiveness. In parts of Africa, a series of rings was placed around a girl's neck over a period of time, so that when she reached womanhood her shoulders were pressed down, her neck appeared longer, and she could wear multiple neck rings.

Such alterations continue in modern nations. Much of the lucrative work of 9 plastic surgeons in contemporary Western nations is concerned with altering physical appearance by changing the shapes of the eyes, nose, mouth, and jowls, and increasing or decreasing the size of breasts, lips, thighs, hips, or waistlines.

Painting of Face and Body

Painting is a less drastic and temporary manner of changing an individual's ap- 10 pearance. Some peoples paint only their faces, while others paint almost their entire bodies. Face painting is more common than body painting.

Face Painting   Native American peoples commonly painted their faces for war. 11 Among the Osage, before attacking their enemy, the men would blacken their faces with charcoal, symbolic of the merciless fire and their ferocity. In other Native American groups face painting was individualized, each man using different colors and designs to create a ferocious appearance. Sometimes the manner in which a man painted his face depended on a vision and his spiritual helpers. However, not all face painting was associated with war. Faces were commonly painted for religious rituals as well. In addition, many Native American peoples simply painted their faces to enhance their social appearance. Thus, Native Americans painted their faces for a variety of reasons—warfare, religious rituals, and social appearance—just like other peoples in the world.

Body Painting   Body painting refers to painting the entire body, or most of it. 12 Like face painting, body painting is found all over the world. In some cases, body painting has religious significance and meaning; in other cases, it is purely secular, designed to enhance the person's physical appearance. Many people in Papua, New Guinea, cover their faces and limbs with white clay when a relative or important person dies as a sign of mourning and respect for the deceased. Among the aboriginal peoples of Australia, bodies were painted with red and yellow ocher, white clay, charcoal, and other pigments. During rituals individuals were painted with elaborate designs covering most of the body. The colors and designs were standardized and had symbolic meaning. Ritual specialists who knew these designs did the painting for religious ceremonies. Outside of ritual contexts, for many Australian peoples, body painting was a secular and daily activity, performed by family members on one another. Individuals were free to use whatever colors and designs pleased them, so long as they were not ritual designs.

Tattooing and Scarification

Tattooing and the related practice of scarification are widespread practices. Tat- 13 too designs, achieved by etching and placing a colored pigment under the skin, have been practiced by diverse peoples. When the skin is too dark for tattooing designs to be seen, people may use scarification, the deliberate scarring of the skin to produce designs on the body.

Tattooing   Tattooing has a long history as an art form. Tattooing was practiced 14 in ancient Egypt, as well as by the ancient Scythians, Thracians, and Romans in Europe. The ancient Bretons, at the time of the Roman conquest, were reported to have had their bodies elaborately tattooed with the images of animals. In the fourth century A.D., when Christianity became the official religion of the Roman Empire, tattooing was forbidden on religious grounds. Tattooing virtually disappeared among European peoples until the eighteenth century, when it was discovered in the Pacific and Asia by sailors and reintroduced to Europe as purely secular art.

There is an important difference between body painting and tattooing and 15
scarification: paint is removable; tattooing and scarification are indelible and permanent. As a result, tattooing and scarification are usually associated with societies in which there are permanent differences in social status. In these societies,
the significance and meaning of tattoos varies. However, for the most part, the
more fully tattooed an individual is, the greater the social status.

The adornment of the body by tattoos is most elaborate in the scattered is- 16
lands of Polynesia. In fact, the word *tattoo* itself is Polynesian. The word, like the
practice of tattooing sailors, came into use as the result of the voyages of Western
explorers and whalers in the seventeenth and later centuries. Tongans, Samoans,
Marquesans, Tahitians, the Maori of New Zealand, and most other Polynesian
peoples practiced tattooing, which everywhere was connected to social distinc-
tions such as class or rank, sex, religious roles, and specialization. Polynesian
peoples are all historically related, so it is not surprising that marking the body
with tattoos is found on almost all islands, albeit to different degrees and with
somewhat different styles.

Many Maori had large areas of their bodies covered with tattoos, which could 17
be placed on the torso, thighs, buttocks, calves, and, most notably, the face.
Several instruments were used by skilled tattoo artists to incise the patterns characteristic of most Maori tattoos. One was a small chisel made of bone and etched
into the skin with a hammer. Apparently, no anesthetic was used to relieve the
pain and, in fact, tolerating the pain of the procedure may have been part of its
cultural significance. To make pigment, several kinds of wood were burned for
their ashes. After the artist made the cuts, pigment was rubbed into the wounds
to leave permanent markings. The most skilled tattoo artists were rewarded with
high prestige and chiefly patronage, and their craft was in such high demand
that they traveled widely over New Zealand's two huge islands.

Both Maori men and women wore tattoos, although men's bodies were more 18
thoroughly covered. For both sexes, tattoos were seen not merely as body ornamentation or expression of one's personal identity. Having tattoos brought certain privileges. Men who did not undergo tattooing could not build canoe
houses, carve wood, make weapons, or weave nets. Untattooed women could
not help in the gardens with sweet potatoes, the Maori staple vegetable crop.

In all of Polynesia, it was the people of the Marquesas whose bodies were 19
most covered by tattoos. The highest ranking chiefs even had tattoos on the soles
of their feet. To the Marquesa, a thorough covering of the body was necessary to
protect it from spiritual dangers.

Scarification   Decorating the body by cutting and creating scars, or scarification, 20
is more limited among the world's peoples than tattooing. As in tattooing, scarification is practiced for numerous reasons. Depending on the culture, both men
and women may be scarred. Sometimes the scarred design is on the face; in other
cases, the chest, breast, back, and even the legs and arms may be elaborately
covered with such designs. Sometimes scarification forms part of the puberty rite.
Among the Nuer of the southern Sudan, a series of horizontal cuts is made on the
foreheads of men who have completed male initiation rituals. On young men,
these cuts symbolically mark and communicate their maturity and courage. After
they scarify, these cuts become permanent symbols of Nuer manhood.

Performance Arts

Performance arts encompass music, song, and dance, which use voice, instru- 21 ments, and movement to delight the senses and communicate. Generally, music, song, and dance are closely interrelated, but may differ significantly, depending on whether they are religious or secular in nature. For convenience, we will focus on music in the Judeo-Christian religious tradition, the *voudon* religion of the Caribbean, and in the Navajo curing rituals.

The Judeo-Christian Religious Tradition   People raised in the Judeo-Christian 22 religious tradition are quite familiar with the many functions of music in religious services. The lyrics of familiar hymns sung to praise God are an integral part of worship rituals. Music also helps to create the mood and sense of reverence for the service and is capable of altering the emotional state of the participants. The shared experience of singing in unison may help draw the congregation together, enhancing what many Christian denominations call their fellowship. In these and other ways, music is important in making the congregation receptive to the messages delivered by the sermon and prayers.

Music in the *Voudon* Religion   Music and other forms of performance art are 23 essential to the religious experience for diverse peoples in all parts of the world. The *voudon* (voodoo) religion of the Caribbean heavily incorporates performance arts into religious ceremonies. Followers of *voudon* consider themselves to be people who "serve the spirits" (*loa*). Many *loa* originated and now live in West Africa, where the ancestors of modern Afro-Caribbean peoples were enslaved during the era of slave trade beginning about 1500. *Voudon* temples are elaborately decorated with sacred objects, paintings, and symbolic representations of various *loa*, which show the devotion of the worshippers and make the temple attractive to the spirits. Through drumming, music, and energetic dancing, *voudon* worshippers induce the *loa* to leave their spiritual homes and take over the bodies of those who worship them. When the *loa* possess their human servants, the latter speak with the voices of the *loa*, wear the *loa's* favorite clothing, eat their foods, drink their beverages, and generally assume their identities. Visiting petitioners with problems can ask questions of the worshipper *loa*, who may answer with directions about what course of action to take. *Voudon* drumming, music, and dancing are so totally integrated into temple rituals that the religion is unimaginable without it.

Tumbuka Diviner-Healers   Music is essential to the healing process among 24 many African peoples. The Tumbuka of northern Malawi combine singing, drumming, and dancing in all-night curing sessions. Some kinds of illness are caused by a category of spirits called *vimbuza*. *Vimbuza* cause various kinds of illness and even death when they possess someone. The Tumbuka believe that health requires a balance between bodily cold and hot forces (similar to the bodily "humours" of old Europe). When *vimbuza* enter the body, they create an imbalance between hot and cold forces, leading to the buildup of heat that is culturally interpreted as sickness.

Tumbuka diviner-healers both diagnose illnesses and direct elaborate healing 25 ceremonies that include drumming, music, and dance. The most essential part of the curing ritual is a shared musical experience in the context of a group gathering, with every individual present expected to contribute to the music making. Even patients themselves participate in the total experience by singing, clapping, and dancing. As the sick person dances to the accompanying rhythm of drums and music, the heat inside the person's body increases. This leads the possessing spirit to expend excess energy and cool off. By thus restoring the balance between hot and cold, the individual is cured, at least temporarily.

The Navajo Curing Rituals   For the Navajo of the American Southwest, art is 26 part of curing rituals. In Navajo belief, the most common cause of illness is the loss of harmony with the environment, often caused by the person's violation of a taboo or other transgression. When illness strikes and a diagnosis is made, a Navajo "singer" (curer or medicine man) is called on to organize a complex curing ceremony.

In curing ceremonies, the singer addresses and calls on the Holy People, who 27 are spiritual beings believed by Navajo to have the power to restore sick people to harmony and beauty. Ceremonies usually occur in a hogan (house) at night, and in theory the procedures must be executed perfectly for the cure to work.

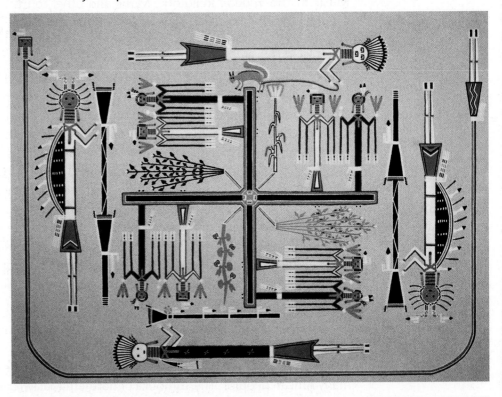

Navajo Sand Painting with Whirling Logs Design (20th Century) *BY Geoffrey Clements*

For the ceremony the singer creates images of the Holy People out of sand, 28 called sandpaintings. Navajo sandpaintings are visual and sacred representations that are created, used in a single ceremony, and then destroyed. Each sandpainting is part of a ceremony that also includes other sacred objects (such as rattles and prayer sticks) and lengthy songs or chants recited by the singer. The song/chants that are recited over the sandpainting and the patient may last for hours. Most song/chants tell of the myths depicted in the specific sandpainting.

There are literally hundreds of sandpaintings. Most ceremonies involve a com- 29 bination of many sandpaintings used in association with particular chants. Because some are quite large and enormously detailed, they often take hours to create. But all must be exact representations of the ideal model of the mythical scene or event depicted. The images are stylized drawings of the Holy People, many of whom are depicted with weapons and armor. Most scenes represented in the sandpaintings are from particular myths familiar to the patient and audience.

Sandpaintings are made for the express purpose of inducing the Holy People 30 to come to the hogan where the ceremony is held. During the ceremony, the patient is usually sitting on the sandpainting itself. The singer completes the transfer of power to the patient when he rubs the patient's body with the sand of the images of the Holy People. After each phase of the ceremony is finished, the sandpainting is destroyed, for the Holy People commanded the Navajo not to make permanent images of them.

Navajo sandpaintings certainly are works of art. Some Anglos who have seen 31 them think it is a shame to destroy such beautiful images that singers and their helpers have worked so hard to create. But in the context of Navajo beliefs, sandpaintings are made for specific curing ceremonials held for particular patients. That purpose—not expressing the singer's creativity, making an artistic statement, celebrating Navajo culture, or publicly displaying the singer's talents—is their objective. For Navajo, fulfilling their purpose requires that the paintings not be permanent.

Summary

1. All cultures have artistic objects, designs, songs, dances, and other ways of ex- 32 pressing their appreciation of the aesthetic. The aesthetic impulse is universal, although cultures vary in their ways of expressing it and the social functions and cultural meanings they attach to it.

2. People raised in the Western tradition are inclined to think of art as something set apart from everyday life—as when we use the phrase "fine arts"—yet we all express ourselves aesthetically in many ways, including how we dress, decorate our houses, and eat our meals.

3. In addition to allowing people to express themselves aesthetically, art serves communicative functions by encoding meanings and messages in symbolic forms.

4. Art takes a multitude of forms, including body art. People around the world change their bodily appearance by such means as physical alterations, application of body paints, tattoos, and scarification. These decorations of the body are used for a variety of purposes, including beautification, expression of individual or group identity, display of privilege or social position, and symbolic indication of social maturity. The tattooing practices of the Maori of New Zealand and other Polynesians exemplify some of these functions.

5. Performance arts include the use of sound and movement for both aesthetic and communicative purposes. Often, performance art is tightly integrated into

a people's spiritual and religious life, from Judeo-Christian worship services to possession trances in the *voudon* religion of the Caribbean.

6. Perhaps many forms of art began as "sacred" in that they were connected to the appeal to or worship of spiritual beings. Certainly, the religious elements of artistic expression are important not only in the history of Western art but also in the artistic traditions of people the world over. In their complex curing ceremonies, Navajo singers use both visual arts (sandpaintings) and performance arts (chants/songs) in appealing to the Holy People. Distinguishing "sacred" and "secular" art seems like a simple thing, but objects with religious significance are often used for practical purposes.

(James Peoples, *Humanity,* 7/e, 2006)

Brain Teasers

What Comes Before?

Examine the three words in each list and determine what single word could come before.

Example: <u>hand</u>   grenade, out, writing

hand grenade, handout, handwriting

1. _____ line, pass, product
2. _____ country, roads, word
3. _____ lands, school, way
4. _____ ball, locker, print
5. _____ hat, liner, nosed
6. _____ boat, letter, seat
7. _____ run, stretch, town
8. _____ storm, plow, shoe
9. _____ cut, net, line

VOCABULARY | **Unit 10: Word Parts Featuring Water, Air, and Life**

"When the well is dry, we know the worth of water."
—Benjamin Franklin

This is the last vocabulary unit. The first group of words in this unit concerns water, air, and life. The second group concerns sleep and light. The final group includes words using the prefix *in-,* but in several variant forms. Words made from these word parts, along with their definitions, follow. Supplemental words with these word parts are located in the left margin.

aqua, hydro—water; pneu—air, breathe, wind

aquatic	**aquarium**	a tank or container filled with water in which collections of animals and plants live; also, the building where these collections are placed on exhibit.
	aqueduct	*–duc* means "to lead," so this word means literally "to lead water." An *aqueduct* can be a pipe for bringing water from a distant place, or it can resemble a canal or tunnel. The Romans built *aqueducts* throughout their empire; many of these are still used today.
	Aquarius	This is the constellation that looks like a man carrying water. If you were born between January 20 and February 18, your zodiac sign would be *Aquarius*.
dehydrate	**hydrant**	a large pipe with a valve for releasing water from a water main
	hydroelectric	electricity generated by the energy of running water, usually water falling over a dam.
	hydrologist	a person who studies water, including the cycle of evaporation and precipitation.
	hydraulic	The literal meaning is "water tube." Today, *hydraulic* is a term used to describe a system operated by the movement of fluid, such as a *hydraulic* jack or *hydraulic* brakes.
	pneumatic	containing wind, air, or gases; filled with or worked by compressed air. The tires on your car are *pneumatic* because they hold pressurized air.
	pneumonia	An inflammation of the lungs that causes difficulty in breathing

nat—birth; bio—life

	nature	the essential character of something; what has always been there from birth.
	native	*Native* has two meanings: First, your *native* state or country is where you were born. Second, *native* plants, animals, and people are the ones that originally came from an area. Eucalyptus trees are not *native* to the United States; they were brought here from Australia.
	nativity	A *nativity* scene is a birth scene, such as you might see at Christmas when the birth of Jesus is celebrated.
	innate	*in-* here means "within," so your *innate* characteristics are those you were born with.
neonatal	**prenatal**	before birth
	postnatal	after birth
biosphere	**biography**	an account of a person's life written by someone else
	autobiography	Because *auto-* means "self," an *autobiography* is the story of one's own life written by oneself.
	biochemistry	the study of the chemistry of life processes in both plants and animals.

	biopsy	the removal of bits of living tissue for analysis
	biodegradable	matter that is capable of breaking down or decomposing so that it can return to the life cycle.
	symbiotic	the living together of two different organisms for mutual benefit

lum, luc—light; photo—light

luminarias	**luminary**	a body or object that gives off light; a person who has attained eminence in a field or is an inspiration to others. Maya Angelou, Rita Dove, and other literary *luminaries* were invited to attend a conference on writing held at Vanderbilt University.
	illuminate	to supply or brighten with light; to enlighten. Sylvia used a flashlight to *illuminate* the boxes in the cellar.
	translucent	permitting light to pass through but not allowing things on the other side to be seen clearly; easily understood; clear. The glass on most shower doors is *translucent*.
elucidate	**lucid**	easily understood; intelligible; sane; glowing with light. After the driver's *lucid* explanation of the events leading to the traffic accident, the police officer had no further questions.
	photography	the art or method of making pictures by means of a camera
	photogenic	forming an appealing subject for photography; producing or emitting light. A *photogenic* politician has an advantage.
	photosynthesis	the process by which green plants form sugars and starches from water and carbon dioxide: This process occurs when sunlight acts upon the chlorophyll in the plant.

hypno(s), dorm, coma—sleep

	hypnosis	an artificially induced trance resembling sleep that is characterized by a heightened susceptibility to suggestion.
	dormitory	a building, as at a college, containing rooms for residents; a large room containing a number of beds and serving as communal sleeping quarters.
	dormant	inactive, as in sleep; undeveloped. Although the volcano has been *dormant* for fifty years, scientists predict an eruption sometime this century.
	coma	a state of prolonged unconsciousness including a lack of response to stimuli
	comatose	lacking vitality or alertness; torpid

Additional meanings of in

As you learned in Unit 5, the Latin prefix *in-* has two distinct meanings: "not" as in the word *inactive*, and "within" or "into" as in the word *incarcerate* (meaning to put in jail or prison). In some English words, *in-* acts as an intensifier, with the meaning "very" or "completely."

infamous	This word does not mean "not famous." Rather, it means "famous but for the wrong reasons." *Infamous* refers to people who have a bad reputation or are notorious, such as Jesse James, Bonnie and Clyde, or Charles Manson.
invaluable	*Invaluable* does not mean "not valuable," but instead means something so valuable that it is priceless. Original copies of the Constitution, your mother's advice, and your grandmother's ring might all be considered *invaluable*.
inflammable	This word means "very flammable." If something is inflammable, it will burn easily. This word is related to the word *inflame*, which means "to catch fire." If something does *not* burn, it would be *non*flammable.
ingenious	*Ingenious* does not mean that a person is not smart. Instead, it means that a person is clever and creative. Inventors such as Thomas Edison and Alexander Graham Bell were *ingenious*.
ingenuous	being naïve about a subject; a childlike candidness. A spy cannot afford to be truly *ingenuous*, although at times she might want to pretend to be *ingenuous*.

Now that you have studied the vocabulary in Unit 10, practice your new knowledge by completing the crossword puzzle on the next page.

Vocabulary Unit 10 Puzzle

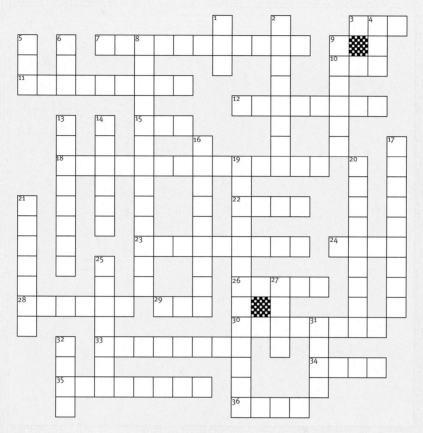

ACROSS CLUES

3. A word part meaning "call."*
7. Bathroom windows are often _____.
10. A word part meaning "born."
11. A relationship of mutual dependency.
12. Picasso, who attained great eminence in the field of art, is an artistic _____.
15. A word part meaning "life."*
18. _____ occurs when sunlight acts upon chlorophyll in a plant.
22. A word part meaning "sleep."
23. Hospital patients who lie in bed too long sometimes develop _____.
24. A word part meaning "air."
26. His writing was very _____ and clear.
28. It is in her _____ to be kind and caring.
29. A word part meaning "put or place."*

30. The driver hit his head on the windshield of the car and became _____.
33. The ancient Romans used an _____ system to move water from one city to another.
34. A word part meaning "water."
35. A birth scene.
36. A word part meaning "believe."*

DOWN CLUES

1. A word part meaning "run."*
2. Jeffrey Dahmer, a serial killer, became _____.
4. An abbreviation for what was once the eighth month.
5. A word part meaning "yield."*
6. A word part meaning "light."
8. The life story of your life written by you.
9. Researchers have concluded that shyness is an _____ characteristic that tends to stay with people throughout their lifetime.

13. A person under the influence of _____ is more susceptible to suggestion.
14. The _____ showed that the growth was benign.
16. Marilyn Monroe often played innocent, childlike, _____ roles.
17. The _____ brakes on your car contain a liquid.
19. The dams along the Colorado River produce _____ power.
20. The iMac computer has an _____ design.
21. In most states, if you park too close to a fire _____, you will get a ticket.
25. The volcano is currently _____, but is expected to erupt within the next decade.
27. A word part meaning "sleep."
31. A word part meaning "pull."*
32. A word part meaning "good."*

*From a previous unit.

Appendices

Sections in Appendices

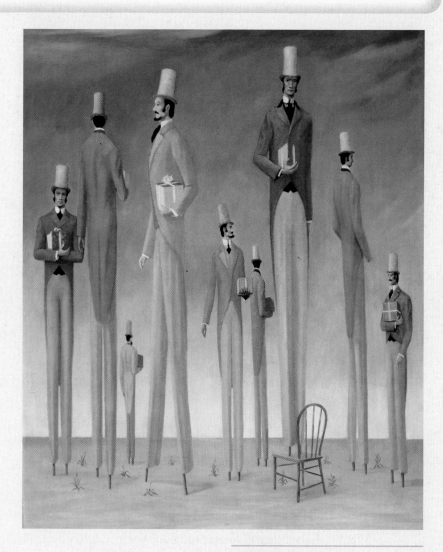

Gift Bearers (1971)

by Philip C. Curtis
Collection of Phoenix Art Museum, Gift of the
Philip C. Curtis Restated Trust U/A/D April 7, 1994

Visual Aids

Bar Graphs

Bar graphs use vertical (top-to-bottom) or horizontal (left-to-right) bars to show comparisons. Usually, longer bars represent larger quantities. The title of the bar graph below is "Annual Earnings and Education." In this graph, the vertical bars represent the average earnings for the U.S. population in 2007 for increasing levels of education. The source of the data is the U.S. Census Bureau, U.S. Department of Commerce.

Annual Earnings and Education

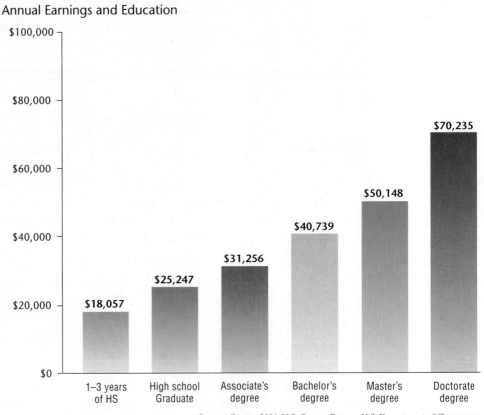

Source: Census 2008. U.S. Census Bureau, U.S. Department of Commerce.

After studying the graph, answer the questions below.

1. What is the average annual income for somebody with a bachelor's degree?

   _____

2. What is the average annual income for somebody with an associate's degree?

   _____

3. What is the average annual income for somebody with a high school diploma?
   _____

4. What is the difference in average annual income between someone with an associate's degree and someone with a high school diploma? _____

5. What is the relationship between level of education and average annual income? _____

6. Would you expect the lifetime earnings of someone with a doctorate degree to be greater on average than for someone with a master's degree? _____

Tables

Tables display information in rows (across) and columns (up and down). The table below demonstrates how two people (Joe and Roscoe) respond differently to the same stressors. Joe encounters a stressor, perceives it as stressful, and winds up with stress. Roscoe, on the other hand, encounters the same stressor, but perceives it in such a way as to avoid stress. Thus, we can see that an event has only potential for eliciting a stress reaction. Whether it actually does elicit a stress reaction depends on how it is perceived.

THE CHRONIC STRESS PATTERN VERSUS THE HEALTHY STRESS PATTERN

Stressor	Joe (Chronic Stress Pattern)	Roscoe (Healthy Stress Pattern)
Oversleeps—awakes at 7:30 instead of 6:30	**Action:** Gulps coffee, skips breakfast, cuts himself shaving, tears button off shirt getting dressed	**Action:** Phones office to let them know he will be late; eats a good breakfast
	Thoughts: I can't be late again! The boss will be furious! I just know this is going to ruin my whole day.	**Thoughts:** No problem. I must have needed the extra sleep.
	Result: Leaves home anxious, worried, and hungry	**Result:** Leaves home calm and relaxed
Stuck behind slow driver	**Action:** Flashes lights, honks, grits teeth, curses, bangs on dashboard with fist; finally passes on blind curve and nearly collides with oncoming car	**Action:** Uses time to do relaxation exercises and to listen to his favorite radio station
	Thoughts: What an idiot! Slow drivers should be put in jail! No consideration of others!	**Thoughts:** Here's a gift of time—how can I use it?

(Continued)

THE CHRONIC STRESS PATTERN VERSUS
THE HEALTHY STRESS PATTERN (*continued*)

Stressor	Joe (Chronic Stress Pattern)	Roscoe (Healthy Stress Pattern)
Staff meeting	**Action:** Sits in back, ignores speakers, and surreptitiously tries to work on monthly report	**Action:** Listens carefully and participates actively
	Thoughts: What a waste of time. Who *cares* what's going on in all those other departments? I have more than I can handle keeping up with my own work.	**Thoughts:** It's really good to hear my coworkers' points of view. I can do my work a lot more effectively if I understand the big picture of what we're all trying to do.
	Results: Misses important input relating to his department; is later reprimanded by superior	**Results:** His supervisor compliments him on his suggestions.
Noon—behind on deskwork	**Action:** Skips lunch; has coffee at desk; spills coffee over important papers	**Action:** Eats light lunch and goes for short walk in park
	Thoughts: That's the last straw! Now I'll have to have this whole report typed over. I'll have to stay and work late.	**Thoughts:** I'll be in better shape for a good afternoon with a little exercise and some time out of the office.
Evening	**Action:** Arrives home 9 P.M., family resentful; ends up sleeping on couch; does not fall asleep until long into the morning	**Action:** Arrives home at usual time; quiet evening with family; to bed by 11 P.M., falls asleep easily
	Thoughts: What a life! If only I could run away and start over! It's just not worth it. I'll never amount to anything.	**Thoughts:** A good day! I felt really effective at work, and it was nice reading to the kids tonight.
	Results: Wakes up late again, feeling awful; decides to call in sick	**Results:** Wakes up early, feeling good

Directions: Indicate whether the statement is true or false by writing **T** or **F** in the blank provided. If you can't tell based on the information provided in the table, write **CT**.

_____ 1. Roscoe, stuck behind a slow driver, listens to the radio.

_____ 2. Joe, stuck behind a slow driver, causes an accident.

_____ 3. Roscoe is chastised by a superior.

_____ 4. Roscoe eats a salad before his walk in the park.

_____ 5. Joe openly tries to work on his monthly report at the staff meeting.

Flowcharts

Flowcharts are often used in textbooks to show cause-and-effect relationships and the sequence of events. The action moves, or flows, in the direction of the arrows. The following flowchart, which appears in a psychology textbook, shows how stress triggers bodily effects, upsetting thoughts, and leading to ineffective behavior. Notice how each element worsens the others in a vicious cycle.

Stress: The Vicious Cycle

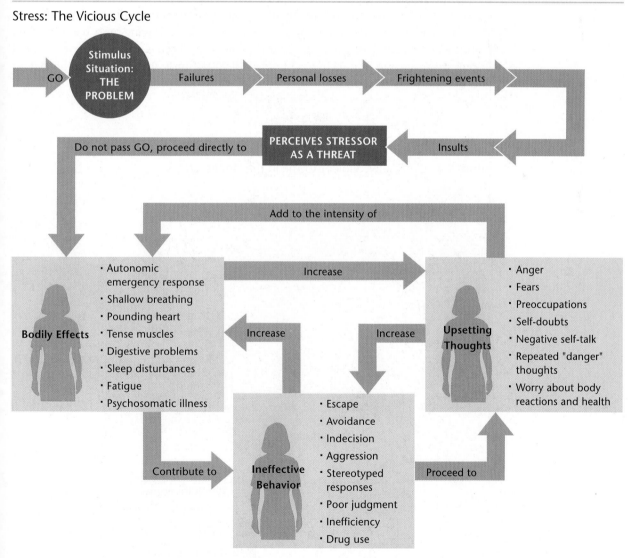

Flowchart, p. 483 from Dennis Coon, *Introduction to Psychology: A Modular Approach to the Mind and Behavior,* 10th ed., 2006, McGraw-Hill. Copyright © 2006 The McGraw-Hill Companies, Inc. Reprinted with permission from The McGraw-Hill Companies, Inc.

Indicate whether the statement is true or false by writing **T** or **F** in the blank provided. If you can't tell based on the flowchart, write **CT**.

_____ 1. Avoidance decreases the bodily effects of stress.

_____ 2. Sleep disturbances contribute to ineffective behavior.

_____ 3. Shallow breathing increases upsetting thoughts like anger.

_____ 4. Poor judgment can lead to negative self-talk.

_____ 5. Anger can intensify digestive problems.

_____ 6. Exercise can reduce the bodily effects of stress.

Maps

Maps are useful for presenting information visually. The legend, which indicates what color or shading represents, is the key to understanding the map. Maps may also have endnotes that explain the specific details. The following map, based on data from the _Statistical Abstract of the United States 2007_, shows the number of violent crimes that occurred in the United States as of 2004. Study the map, using the legend and the endnotes as a guide.

Some States Are Safer: Violent Crime in the United States

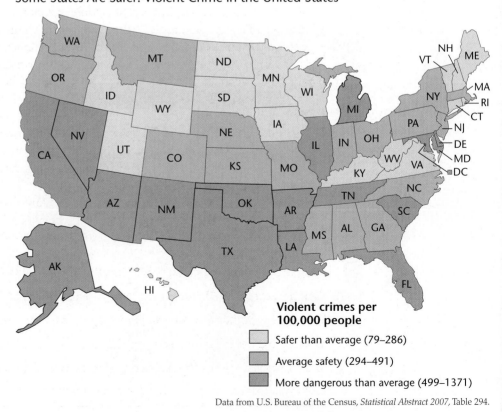

Violent crimes per 100,000 people

Safer than average (79–286)

Average safety (294–491)

More dangerous than average (499–1371)

Data from U.S. Bureau of the Census, _Statistical Abstract 2007_, Table 294.

Violent crimes are murder, rape, robbery, and aggravated assult. The variation of violence among the states is incredible. Some states have a rate that is ten times higher than that of other states. With a rate of 79 per 100,000 people, North Dakota has the lowest rate of violence, while Florida, at 711, has the highest rate. The U.S. average rate is 466 (the total of the states' average rates of violence divided by 50). This total does not include Washington, D.C., whose rate is 1,371, 17 times as high as North Dakota and almost 3 times the national average.

Using the information in the map and legend, answer the following questions.

1. According to the information given, violent crimes are _____, _____, _____, and _____.

2. _____ is the state with the lowest rate of violent crime.

3. The state with the highest rate of violent crime in the United States is _____.

4. How many states are considered to be safer than average? _____.

5. California, Arizona, and Nevada all have _____ rates of violent crime.

6. Hawaii has a safer-than-average rate, but Alaska has a _____ _____ safety rate.

Pie Graphs

Age: 60 and over

Age: under 18 1%

Age: 50s

Age: 18–29

11%

26%

13%

22%

27%

Age: 40s

Age: 30s

Percentage of Individuals Who Have Been Victimized by Identity Theft, by Age

Pie graphs are illustrations that show percentages or proportions as pie-shaped sections of a circle. The whole interior of the circle represents 100 percent. The pie graph illustrates the percentage of people in each age bracket who have been victimized by identity theft, based on information provided by the Federal Trade Commission in April 2005.

According to the FTC, anyone can be a victim of identity theft. The biggest problem is that you may not know your identity has been stolen until something is already amiss. You may get bills for a credit card account you never opened; your credit report may include debts you never knew you had; a billing cycle may pass without your receiving a statement; or you may see charges on your statement that you didn't sign for, didn't authorize, and know nothing about.

Because identity theft is the fastest-growing financial crime, the FTC maintains the Identity Theft Data Clearinghouse and provides information to identify theft victims. You can call toll-free 1-877-ID-THEFT or visit www.consumer.gov/idtheft.

Using the information in the pie graph, answer the following questions.

1. What percentage of victims are in their 30s? _____

2. Which age group has the lowest percentage of identity theft? _____

3. What are the next two lowest groups? _____

4. What reasons do you suppose account for the two highest age groups of identity theft? _____ _____

5. What steps can you take to thwart identity thieves? _____

_____

6. What can you do to protect your social security number? _____

_____

Consumer Labels

Consumer labels are designed to help consumers make wise choices about specific products. Since March 1999, the Food and Drug Administration has required the labels of dietary supplements to carry a "supplements facts" panel. In addition, because most supplements have not been evaluated by the FDA for safety or effectiveness, the label must carry a disclaimer.

What's in a Label?

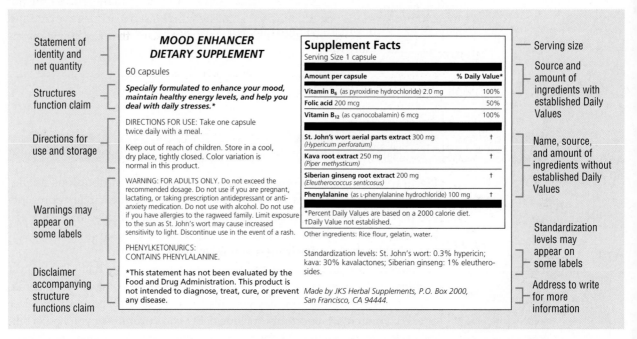

Figure from Paul M. Insel, *Core Concepts in Health,* 11th ed. New York: McGraw-Hill, 2010, p. 363.

Using the information in the dietary supplement label, answer the following questions.

1. What is the meaning of *disclaimer?* _____
   a. a statement that reveals or lays open
   b. a statement that expresses disapproval
   c. a statement that repudiates or denies

2. One capsule of this product contains _____ mg of St. John's wort.

3. Is this product something that should be given to children? _____

4. What is the meaning of *warning?* _____
   a. notification of possible dangers
   b. directions about how much medicine to give
   c. praise of the product

5. What is the recommended dosage for this product? _____

6. Does this product claim to help you if you are suffering from stress? _____

7. Should you take this product if you are going to be in the sun for prolonged periods? _____
   a. Yes, there should be no adverse effect.
   b. No, the product increases the skin's sensitivity to sunlight.

8. Is it safe to take this product with alcohol? _____

Line Graphs

A **line graph,** which takes the form of a line drawn in an L-shaped grid, shows the relationship between two variables. One of these variables is defined along the bottom, on the horizontal (across) axis of the grid. The other variable is defined along the side, on the vertical (up and down) axis of the grid. The line need not be straight; in fact, it is often jagged or curved. Often the bottom scale of the grid measures time (for example, minutes, years, or decades), and so the line graph shows changes over time.

The line graph below depicts the "graying of America," that is, the increasing proportion of elderly people in the U.S. population.

Median Age of U.S. Population

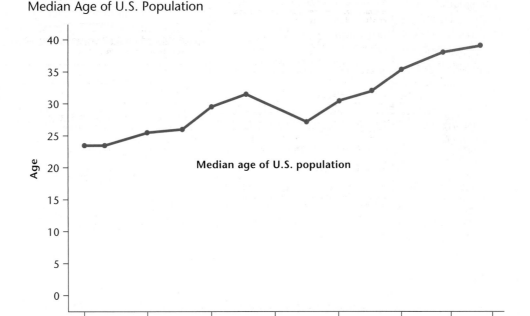

Source: *Statistical Abstracts,* 2007, Table 12.

Using information from the line graph, answer the following questions.

1. In 1900, the median age of the U.S. population was approximately _____.

2. In 1940, the median age of the U.S. population was approximately _____.

3. In 2020, the median age of the U.S. population is projected to be approximately

_____.

Test-Taking Tips

How to Improve Your Performance on Multiple Choice and Essay Exams

General Tips

BEFORE THE TEST

Sometime in the next few weeks you will take a test in one of your classes. Although this advice may seem obvious, you need to prepare for the test. Don't wait until late the night before to begin studying the material. That's too late. Following are some suggestions for preparing for the test.

1. Read the course material before it is discussed in class. Every evening review the day's class notes.

2. Practice the SQ3R method of studying. Annotate and highlight your textbook and class notes.

3. Begin reviewing for a test days in advance. If you learn best by listening, read the material out loud. If you learn best by seeing, make an outline of the material. If you learn best by being physically involved, copy your notes.

4. Find out what the test is going to cover. Your instructor may give you a study guide or sample questions. If not, put together your own study guide and sample questions. What points has the instructor emphasized? What do you think are the most important points?

5. Find out what kind of test it's going to be—multiple choice, true-false, short answer, short essay, or a combination. Knowing what to expect will guide your preparation and ease your anxiety. The most important test-taking tip is—be prepared!

DAY OF THE TEST

The day of the test has arrived. Make sure you have the proper equipment with you—pens, pencils, dictionary, blue books, and so on: Stay calm. By now you should have a good idea what's going to be on the test, and you should be prepared for it.

Now look at the test. Read through the whole test. Look on both sides of all the pages. How many questions are there? Think about how much time you want to devote to each question.

Always save time to check over your answers. Don't lose points because you accidentally skipped a question. And remember to write legibly and put your name on the test paper!

Don't be concerned if some people in the class finish the test much more quickly than you do. You don't know whether those students did well on the test or poorly.

AFTER THE TEST IS RETURNED

After taking a test, think about what happened. Was it what you expected and prepared for? In what ways did it surprise you? Did it cover both lecture and textbook material? Or focus on one or the other? Think about how to change your approach to the course and the next test to take into account what you learned from the format of this test.

At some point, you will get your test back. Or you could ask to see it. This is another opportunity for you. Go

(Continued)

AFTER THE TEST IS RETURNED (continued)

over the test to see where your weaknesses are. What sorts of questions did you have the most trouble with? Many students have trouble with questions phrased in the negative, such as, Which of the following is not a valid conclusion that can be drawn from the evidence below? Did you have trouble with questions of this sort? If so, try to remedy this deficiency in your test preparation before the next test. You also need to go back and learn the material better that gave you trouble, because you may see questions about this material again on future tests, such as a midterm or final exam.

If you did poorly on the test, you may want to make an appointment with your instructor to talk about it. Maybe you need to be working with the instructor or a tutor out of class. Or maybe you should become part of a study group. You might even be taking the course before you're ready for it; maybe you should take some other courses first.

The key point is to treat past tests as learning experiences for what they tell you about your test preparation, how you're doing in the course, and what changes you can make to do better. Above all, maintain a positive attitude.

DEALING WITH TEST-TAKING ANXIETY

While the key to success in test taking is generally adequate preparation, you also need to maintain a positive attitude and stay relaxed. Take the following test to help you determine whether anxiety over test taking may be interfering with your ability to get a good grade.

Test Anxiety Scale

To assess your test-anxiety level, rate yourself from 1 to 5 on each of the following statements.

1—never 2—rarely 3—sometimes
4—often 5—always

1. I have trouble sleeping the night before a test.

_____ _____ _____ _____ _____
 1   2   3   4   5

2. I have visible signs of nervousness right before a test (sweaty palms, shaky hands).

_____ _____ _____ _____ _____
 1   2   3   4   5

3. I have butterflies in my stomach or feel nauseated before a test.

_____ _____ _____ _____ _____
 1   2   3   4   5

4. I am irritable and hard to be around before a test.

_____ _____ _____ _____ _____
 1   2   3   4   5

5. I worry about how others are doing on the test.

_____ _____ _____ _____ _____
 1   2   3   4   5

6. My mind goes blank during the test, or I am unable to recall information.

_____ _____ _____ _____ _____
 1   2   3   4   5

7. I have difficulty choosing answers.

_____ _____ _____ _____ _____
 1   2   3   4   5

8. I make mistakes on easy questions or put answers in the wrong places.

_____ _____ _____ _____ _____
 1   2   3   4   5

9. I am always afraid that I will run out of time.

_____ _____ _____ _____ _____
 1   2   3   4   5

10. I remember the information that I forgot after I have turned in the test.

_____ _____ _____ _____ _____
 1   2   3   4   5

If you gave yourself five or more 4s or 5s, you may be highly anxious about tests. In that case, you should try the following relaxation techniques:

1. Take several long, deep breaths to calm yourself. After a few minutes, close your eyes and imagine a favorite place. Make this mental scene as detailed as you can.

2. Try to relax your whole body, starting with your feet. Work your way up through your body—your legs, torso, chest, arms, neck, head, and face.

3. If permissible, suck on a piece of hard candy.

4. View the test as an opportunity for self-discovery and not as a win/lose proposition.

If you feel that your anxiety is overwhelming, get help from your college counseling center.

CREATING REVIEW TOOLS

Following are some tools you might use to improve your test scores:

1. **To-do lists:** Make a list of the items you need to study for your test. Check each item off as you study it.

2. **Flash cards:** Make 3 × 5 flash cards to test yourself. To learn vocabulary, for example, on one side of the card write the word you need to know, and on the other write the definition Or, to study for a test, on one side write a review question, and on the other write the answer. Carry the cards with you. You will be surprised at the many opportunities you have for studying them, such as when you are standing in line at the bank or a store.

3. **Summary sheets:** Create summary sheets by going through your lecture notes and text underlinings and jotting down the key points on a piece of paper. Quiz yourself on these key points by asking yourself to recall what is on the sheet.

4. **Question-and-answer sheets:** Create question-and-answer sheets by folding a piece of paper in half or using the front and the back of the paper to create tests for yourself. Then test yourself by trying to come up with the right answer to the question or even the right question for the answer.

TAKING MULTIPLE-CHOICE TESTS

On your next multiple-choice test, try applying these tips:

1. Pay close attention to oral and written directions.

2. Don't spend too much time on any one question. Leave a difficult question blank, put a mark beside it, and then come back to it if time permits.

3. For each question, read through all of the answers before choosing one.

4. Don't change an answer unless you are quite sure you have found a better one.

5. If one of your choices is a combination of two or more answers (such as *both A and B*), remember that both parts of the answer must be correct.

6. Be aware that a longer answer is more likely to be correct than a shorter answer. It often takes more words to write a correct answer because it may need qualifying phrases to make it correct.

7. Avoid answers with all-inclusive words like *all, always, everyone, none,* and *nobody* because they are likely to be wrong. Any exception makes the answer wrong.

8. When the question asks you to pick a missing word, look for grammatical clues such as *a* and *an*. *A* goes before words beginning with consonants, and *an* goes before words beginning with vowels.

9. When one of the answers is *all of the above,* and you are pretty sure that two of the three answers are correct but are unsure about the third answer, go with *all of the above*.

10. Be aware that two questions on the test may be similar. Use the correct answer for one question to help you find the correct answer for the other.

11. If there is no penalty for guessing, make an educated guess rather than leaving a question blank.

12. If you are using a computerized scoring sheet, be sure to eliminate any stray marks.

The Essay Test

BEFORE THE TEST

There is no substitute for simply knowing the course material well. But that can be a big task, and realistically, some parts of the material are probably more important, and more likely to appear on an essay test, than others.

One way to give your preparation some focus is to try to think of questions that might appear on the test:

1. Ask yourself what questions you think your teacher might ask.

2. Look at your returned test papers. You can learn a lot by reading the instructor's comments and correcting the answers as needed.

(Continued)

BEFORE THE TEST (continued)

3. Review your class notes and any handouts to see what the teacher emphasized in the course. What topics did the teacher spend the most time on? What topics did the teacher seem to care the most about?

Keep in mind that an essay question may ask for information on a specific topic, or it may be directed at a general understanding of the course material. You need to prepare yourself for both kinds of questions.

General or "big picture" essay questions often deal with relationships among topics or concepts. A good way to prepare for these questions is to:

1. Make an outline or map of the course material.

2. Look at your class notes, handouts, and textbook, and organize this material into an outline. If your teacher has closely followed a textbook, the book's table of contents should give you a good start on making your outline.

3. Prepare answers to your possible questions. You may even want to practice writing out answers.

DURING THE TEST

1. Read the question carefully! You might write a wonderful essay, but if it doesn't answer the question, it will not do you much good. Make sure you know what the question is asking, and make sure you consider all parts of the question.

2. Think about how best to answer the question before you start writing! What material from the course will the answer involve? What do you remember about this material? Think of specific examples that will illustrate your points. Make sure you can answer the six question words: *who, what, where, when, why,* and *how.* If you are prepared well for the test, the more you think about this material, the more of it you will remember.

3. Start writing! Remember to write carefully and legibly. Try to avoid erasures, crossed out words, and words written between lines and in the margins. You might want to consider using a pen with erasable ink. And make sure you answer in complete sentences.

4. Proofread your essay before turning it in! Correct as many grammar, spelling, and punctuation errors as you can. Sloppy writing is likely to produce a bad impression.

If you find you do not have time to answer the questions at the end of the test, write some notes in summary form. These will often earn you at least partial credit.

ORGANIZING YOUR ANSWER

Once you have considered the question and recalled the material you need to answer it, you are ready to think about organizing your answer. Organizing your answer clearly—especially for "big picture" essay questions—will show the teacher how well you understand the relationships among ideas and concepts.

A good answer to an essay question typically includes:

• An introduction, with a clear introductory statement (or thesis)

• Three paragraphs of development, including supporting examples, developed in the same order in which the main ideas are mentioned in the introductory statement (each paragraph should develop only one main idea)

• A conclusion

The introductory statement plays a crucial role in organizing an answer on an essay exam, since it drives the development of the body paragraphs. How can you write an effective introductory statement? One way is to turn the essay question itself into your introductory statement. Imagine you encounter the following item on an exam:

Discuss whether an increase in state financial aid for public education will raise student scores on standardized tests.

You can use this question as the basis of your introductory statement by turning it into a statement and adding reasons. For example, your introductory statement might start:

An increase in state financial aid for public education will raise student scores on standardized tests because . . . [list three reasons]

Or

An increase in state financial aid for public education will not raise student scores on standardized tests because . . . [list three reasons]

(Continued)

ORGANIZING YOUR ANSWER *(continued)*

Once you've devised your introductory statement, you have the outline of your body paragraphs.

Sample Introductory Statement

An increase in state financial aid for public education will raise student scores on standardized tests because *teacher salaries can be increased,* which will attract more talented people into teaching; *more teachers can be hired,* which will reduce class size; and school districts will have *more money available for learning resources and activities.*

Each body paragraph would develop one of the ideas included in the introductory statement:

- Paragraph 1—the role more talented teachers would play in increasing test scores
- Paragraph 2—the role smaller classes would play in increasing test scores
- Paragraph 3—the role more learning resources would play in increasing test scores

KEY WORDS THAT OFTEN APPEAR IN ESSAY QUESTIONS

Following is a list of key words that often appear in essay questions. If you are going to write a good answer to an essay question that uses one of these terms, you need to know what the term means.

analyze — to break down the subject into parts and discuss each part. You will discuss how the parts relate to each other.

comment on — to discuss or explain.

compare — to show differences and similarities, but with the emphasis on similarities.

contrast — to show differences and similarities, but with the emphasis on differences.

criticize — The narrow meaning of *criticize* is to examine something for its weaknesses, limitations, or failings. Does the theory, article, or opinion make sense? If not, why not? In a more general sense, criticize means to find both strengths and weaknesses. In this sense, the meaning of *criticize* is similar to the meaning of *evaluate.*

define — to state the meaning of a term, theory, or concept. You will want to place the subject in a category and explain what makes it different from other subjects in the category.

describe — to explain what something is or how it appears. You will need to draw a picture with words.

diagram — to make a chart, drawing, or graph. You will also want to label the categories or elements, and maybe provide a brief explanation.

discuss — to go over something fully. You will want to cover the main points, give different perspectives, and discuss strengths and weaknesses.

enumerate — to make a list of main ideas by numbering them.

evaluate — to examine for strengths and weaknesses. You will need to give specific evidence and may wish to cite authorities to support your position.

explain — to make clear; to give reasons. An explanation often involves showing cause-and-effect relationships or steps.

illustrate — to use a diagram, chart, figure, or specific examples to explain something further.

interpret — to say what something means. A question that asks for an interpretation usually wants you to state what something means to you. What are your beliefs or feelings about the meaning of the material? Be sure to back up your position with specific examples and details.

justify — to give reasons in support of a conclusion, theory, or opinion.

list — to put down your points one by one. You may want to number each of the points in your list.

outline — to organize information into an outline, using headings and subheadings. Your outline should reflect the main ideas and supporting details.

prove — to demonstrate that something is true by means of factual evidence or logical reasoning.

relate — to discuss how two or more conclusions, theories, or opinions affect each other. You will want to explain how one causes, limits, or develops the other.

(Continued)

KEY WORDS THAT OFTEN APPEAR IN ESSAY QUESTIONS (*continued*)

review   to summarize or sometimes to summarize and then analyze critically.

summarize to put down the main points; to state briefly the key principles, facts, or ideas while avoiding details and personal comments.

trace   to follow the course of development of something in a chronological or logical sequence. You will want to discuss each stage of development from beginning to end.

How to Improve Your Performance on Standardized Tests

PREPARING FOR AND TAKING STANDARDIZED TESTS

At some point, many of you are likely to have to take standardized exams like the SAT, ACT, and GRE. Most standardized exams require you to read passages of varying lengths and then answer questions about the passages. Many of the passages come from literary works, textbooks, essays, news magazines, and documents similar to those you have been reading in *The Art of Critical Reading*. As with most exams, preparation for standardized exams is the key to doing well. Here are some tips:

1. Familiarize yourself with the types of directions and the types of questions that will be on the exam.

2. If possible, take a practice exam or answer sample questions allotting yourself the same amount of time you will have during the actual test.

3. Consider the scoring system. Should you guess? Most experts say that if you can eliminate at least two of the four choices, it's in your best interest to make an educated guess if you don't know the answer.

4. Experiment with the following methods for reading a passage. Determine which method works best for you before taking the big exam.

   • Read the passage carefully and then answer the questions.

   OR

   • Skim the passage, glance at the questions, reread the passage carefully, and then answer the questions.

   OR

   • Read the questions first, then read the passage carefully, and finally answer the questions.

5. Immediately determine the topic and the central theme or main idea of the passage you have read. Read to determine main ideas and to understand concepts. You can go back and look for details later.

6. Make sure you understand the first paragraph of a passage. This paragraph is extremely important. It often gives an overview of the passage, and the main idea is often located there.

7. Mark key parts of the passages or make short notes in the margins if permissible. For instance, you might write *MI* by the main idea and circle key transition words like *in contrast* or *in summary*. But be careful not to overmark.

8. Be sure to read all the possible answers carefully before choosing one. Remember that several answers may be partially correct; the correct answer is the one that most accurately and completely answers the question.

9. If the exam has more than one reading passage, perhaps start with a passage that is about something with which you are already familiar. It is also permissible to tackle the easier questions first.

10. If you must read a passage that you have little interest in, ask yourself what you might learn from the passage.

11. Be aware that your exam is likely to include all of the following:

    • Main idea questions that test your ability to identify the central point.

    • Detail questions that test your ability to locate specific pieces of information.

    • Inference questions that test your ability to understand the implications of the material.

    • Purpose questions that test your ability to understand why the author wrote the passage and who the intended audience is.

    • Vocabulary questions that test your ability to decipher the meaning of words from context clues.

    • Tone questions that test your ability to describe the author's attitude.

Using a Thesaurus

The word *thesaurus* is derived from the Greek *thesauros,* meaning "treasure or treasury." A **thesaurus** is a "treasury" of related words. It is a dictionary of synonyms and antonyms presented alphabetically in categories. Unlike a dictionary, a thesaurus does not give the definition, pronunciation, or etymology of a word.

The purpose of a thesaurus is to enable you to be more precise in the words that you use so that you can express your thoughts exactly. It also enables you to choose alternate words so that you don't just repeat the same word over and over again. Many students find a thesaurus to be an invaluable resource in helping them select just the right word to use in an essay or homework assignment.

As an example, imagine that you have just written the following sentences:

Worn out by evading her pursuers, she now lay prostrate in the desert sand. Trying to conserve her insufficient supply of water, she drank sparingly from her canteen, fully aware that only a few insufficient drops remained.

Notice that the word *insufficient* has been used twice. Replacing the word with a synonym might improve the sentence and help to clarify your meaning. Turning to *Roget's College Thesaurus,* you find the following entry:

INSUFFICIENCY

Nouns—**1,** insufficiency; inadequacy, inadequateness; incompetence, IMPOTENCE; deficiency, INCOMPLETENESS, IMPERFECTION, shortcoming, emptiness, poorness, depletion, vacancy, flaccidity; ebb tide; low water; bankruptcy, insolvency (see DEBT, NONPAYMENT).
2, paucity; stint; scantiness, smallness, none to spare; bare necessities, scarcity, dearth; want, need, deprivation, lack, POVERTY; inanition, starvation, famine, drought; dole, pittance; short allowance *or* rations, half-rations.
Verbs—**1,** not suffice, fall short of (see FAILURE); run dry, run *or* give out, run short; want, lack, need, require; be caught short, be in want, live from hand to mouth; miss by a mile.
2, exhaust, deplete, drain of resources; impoverish (see WASTE); stint, begrudge (see PARSIMONY); cut back, retrench; bleed white.
Adjectives—**1,** insufficient, inadequate; too little, not enough; unequal to; incompetent, impotent; weighed in the balance and found wanting; perfunctory (see NEGLECT); deficient, wanting, lacking, imperfect; ill-furnished, -provided, *or* -stored; badly off.
2, slack, at a low ebb; empty, vacant, bare; out of stock; short (of), out of, destitute (of), devoid (of), denuded (of); dry, drained; in short supply, not to be had for love or money, not to be had at any price; empty-handed; short-handed.
3, meager, poor, thin, sparing, spare, skimpy, stinted; starved, half-starved, famine-stricken, famished; jejune; scant, small, scarce; scurvy, stingy; at the end of one's tether; without resources (see MEANS); in want, poor (see POVERTY); in DEBT. *Slang,* shy of, fresh out of.
Adverbs—insufficiently, *etc.*; in default, for want of; failing.
Antonyms, see SUFFICIENCY.

Notice that the synonyms are presented by parts of speech: nouns, verbs, adjectives, and adverbs. At the end of the entry, antonyms are listed.

Depending on the meaning you are trying to convey, you might choose to replace the word *insufficient* with *inadequate* or *meager*. For instance, your new sentence might now look like this:

Worn out by evading her pursuers, she now lay prostrate in the desert sand. Trying to conserve her insufficient supply of water, she drank sparingly from her canteen, fully aware that only a few meager drops remained.

Exercise 1: Using a Thesaurus

Directions: Use a thesaurus to find two synonyms for each of the words below.

1. insufferable: _____   _____
2. frugal: _____   _____
3. enervate: _____   _____

Exercise 2: Recognizing Synonyms

Directions: Can you recognize the following well-known proverbs? They have been rewritten with synonyms for key words. Rewrite the proverbs to bring them back to their familiar form.

1. Birds of similar plumage assemble.

   _____

2. Sanitation is next to piousness.

   _____

3. An examined kettle does not bubble.

   _____

Now use your thesaurus to rewrite the following proverbs. Find synonyms for at least two words in each proverb.

4. You can't teach an old dog new tricks.

   _____

5. Where there's smoke, there's fire.

   _____

6. Look before you leap.

   _____

7. People who live in glass houses shouldn't throw stones.

   _____

Peter Mark Roget (1779–1869), an English physician, wrote the first thesaurus in 1852 at the age of 73. Since Roget's death, many editions of his thesaurus have been published, including editions that are now on the Internet, such as *Roget's International Thesaurus* www.bartleby.com/110/. Most computer word processing programs, such as MS Word, also feature a thesaurus.

Sample Summary

The following paragraph summarizes the plagiarism scandal described in Jodi Wilgoren's article "School Cheating Scandal Tests a Town's Values" (pages 175–178).

A plagiarism scandal at Piper High School in Kansas caused deep divisions in a once close-knit community. Students in Christine Pelton's sophomore biology class were required to complete a leaf project worth 50 percent of their grade. Upon reviewing the projects, Ms. Pelton discovered with the aid of computer software that 28 of 115 students had plagiarized parts of their reports. Ms. Pelton gave those students zeros on the assignment. Both the principal and the superintendent initially backed Ms. Pelton, but after parental protests, the superintendent intervened and reduced the assignment from 50 percent of the final grade to only 30 percent. He also directed Ms. Pelton to deduct only 600 points instead of 1,500 points from those who were accused of plagiarizing. In protest, Ms. Pelton resigned her position. The resulting scandal pitted parent against parent. Some parents asserted that the leniency unfairly penalized those who did the assignment correctly and that students were being robbed of a valuable lesson in values. Others said that those who plagiarized did not fully understand the meaning of plagiarism. Teachers worried that their authority had been seriously undermined. And because of the media attention focused on Piper, residents feared that the incident made the entire community look bad.

Vocabulary Word Parts

Following is a list of the vocabulary word parts you studied in this text. The prefixes indicating numbers are listed first. The other word parts are listed in alphabetical order.

WORD PART	MEANING	EXAMPLE
uni	one	unify
mono	one	monogram
bi	two	bivalve
di	two	dichotomy
du(o)	two	duplex
tri	three	triplicate
qua(d)	four	quadrangle
tetra	four	tetrapod
quint	five	quintessence
pent	five	pentathlon
hex	six	hexagram
sex	six	sextet
sept	seven	September
hept	seven	heptagon
oct	eight	October
nov	nine	November
dec, dek	ten	December
a(n)	not, without	asymmetrical
ad	toward	admit
agogos	lead; bring together; excite	demagogue
ana	back; up; again	anachronism
aqua	water	aquarium
archy	rule	monarchy
auto	self, by oneself	autocracy
belli	war	belligerent
bene	well	benefactor
bio	life	biography
cap	head	caption
capt, cept	hold; seize; take	captivity
cede, ces	go (back); yield; withdraw	precede
chrono	time	chronology
cide	kill	genocide
circum	around	circumvent
cogni	know	cognitive
coma	sleep	comatose

WORD PART	MEANING	EXAMPLE
con	with	convert
corp	body	corporation
cracy	rule; strength; power	plutocracy
cred	believe	incredulous
cur(r)	run	recur
demos	people	democracy
deus	god	deity
dia	through; across; apart; thoroughly	diagonal
dis	apart; away	dismiss
dorm	sleep	dormant
duc	lead	induce
dys	bad; abnormal; difficult	dysentery
equi	equal	equitable
eu	good; well	eulogy
fid	faith(ful)	fidelity
frater, fratri	brother	fraternity
genus	birth; begin; race	genealogy
geo	earth	geocentric
gnostos	know	agnostic
graph	write	demography
helio	sun	heliocentric
homo	man	homicide
hydro	water	hydroelectric
hypno(s)	sleep	hypnosis
in	not; opposite; into; within	invert
inter	between; among	interpersonal
intra	within; inside	intrapersonal
ism	doctrine; theory	polytheism
ject	throw	inject
legis	law	legislature
locut (loqu)	speak, talk	loquacious
log(ue)	speech; word	dialogue
logy	science of; study of	seismology
lum, luc	light	translucent
macro	large, long	macrocosm
mal	bad	malign
mater, matri	mother	maternity
medius	middle	intermediate
meter	measure	pedometer
micro	small	microfilm
mis	hate; bad(ly)	misconstrue
mis, mit	send	mission
nat	birth	native
pater, patri	father	paternity
path(o), pathy	feeling; suffering; emotion	apathy
ped	child	pediatrician
phil(o)	love	philanthropist
photo	light	photography
pneu	air; breathe; wind	pneumonia

WORD PART	MEANING	EXAMPLE
polis	city	politician
poly	many	polytechnic
pos, pon	put; place	depose
potis	powerful	potent
pro	forward	progressive
re	back; again	remit
sacri	holy	sacred
sanct	holy	sanctuary
se	apart; away from	separate
sequ, secut	following	sequence
soror	sister	sorority
syn	same	synagogue
tact, tang	touch	tactile
temp	time; moderate	temperate
ten(t), tin	hold; cling; keep	detention
terr	earth, land	territory
theo	god	theocracy
trac(t)	pull; draw	traction
ven	come	prevent
vert	turn	divert
viv	live	revive
voc	call	vocal

Text and Art Credit Lines

Introduction

pp. 3–6 Excerpt from *Psychology with In-Psych CD-ROM and Powerweb*, 7th Edition by John Santrock, pp. 408–411. Copyright © 2003 The McGraw-Hill Companies, Inc. Reprinted by permission of The McGraw-Hill Companies, Inc. **pp. 9–10** Excerpt from *Artforms: An Introduction to the Visual Arts*, 7th Edition by Duane Preble, et al., pp. 215–216. Copyright © 2002. Reprinted by permission of Pearson Education Inc., Upper Saddle River, NJ. **pp. 8, 14–16** Excerpt from *Psychology: Approach to Mind and Behavior*, 10th Edition by Dennis Coon, p. 361. Copyright © 2006 Wadsworth, a part of Cengage Learning, Inc. Reproduced by permission. www.cengage.com/permissions. **pp. 20–22** Commencement Address by Marian Wright Edelman: From *The Measure of Our Success*, by Marian Wright Edelman, pp. 76–84. Copyright © 1992 by Marian Wright Edelman. Reprinted by permission of Beacon Press, Boston. **p. 26** "My Uncle Terwilliger on the Art of Eating Popovers" from *Seuss-isms* by Dr. Seuss. Copyright © 1997 by Dr. Seuss Enterprises, L.P. Used by permission of Random House Children's Books, a division of Random House, Inc.

Chapter 1

pp. 33–36 Excerpt from *Core Concepts in Health*, 9th Edition by Paul Insel and Walter T. Roth, pp. 29–31, 43. Copyright © 2002 The McGraw-Hill Companies, Inc. Reprinted by permission of The McGraw-Hill Companies, Inc. **p. 36** Top 20 Stressful Life Events: From "The Social Readjustment Rating Scale" by Thomas H. Holmes and Richard H. Rahe in *Journal of Psychosomatic Research*, Vol. 11, No. 2, August 1967. Copyright © 1967 with permission of Elsevier Ltd. **pp. 45–47** "All-Nighter?" by Sharon LaFraniere in *The New York Times*, June 13, 2009, p. A4. Copyright © 2009, The New York Times Co. All rights reserved. Reprinted with permission. **pp. 51–53** "Overcoming Dyslexia" by Betsy Morris in *Fortune*, May 13, 2002, pp. 55–70. Copyright © 2002 Time Inc. All rights reserved. **p. 56** Excerpt from "The Art of Disappearing" in *Words Under the Words: Selected Poems* by Naomi Shihab Nye. Copyright © 1995 by Naomi Shihab Nye. Reprinted with permission of Far Corner Books, Portland, Oregon. **pp. 58–62** Excerpt adapted from *Public Speaking for College and Career*, 7th Edition by Hamilton Gregory, pp. 130–135, 141. Copyright © 2005. Reprinted by permission of The McGraw-Hill Companies, Inc.

Chapter 2

p. 71 Wavy forms line art: From *Gilbert's Living with Art*, 6th Edition by Mark Getlein, p. 274. Copyright © 2002 The McGraw-Hill Companies, Inc. Reprinted by permission of The McGraw-Hill Companies, Inc. **pp. 73–74** Paragraphs 1–5: Excerpts from *Social Psychology*, 9th Edition by David Myers, pp. 141–142. Copyright © 2008 The McGraw-Hill Companies, Inc. Reprinted by permission of The McGraw-Hill Companies, Inc. **pp. 74–75** Exercise 4, items 1–4: From *Sociology*, 3rd Edition by Richard Schaefer, pp. 54, 56, 158. Copyright © 2000 The McGraw-Hill Companies, Inc. Reprinted by permission of The McGraw-Hill Companies, Inc. **pp. 78–79** "Black Men and Public Space" by Brent Staples in *Ms. Magazine*, 1986. Reprinted by permission of the author. Brent Staples writes editorials for *The New York Times* and is the author of the memoir, *Parallel Time*. **pp. 83–84** Excerpt from Looking Out/Looking In: "The Look of a Victim" from *Nonverbal Communication* by Dr. Loretta Malandro and Dr. Larry Barker. Copyright © 1988 The McGraw-Hill Companies, Inc. Reprinted by permission of The McGraw-Hill Companies, Inc.. **pp. 86–87** Review Test Information: From *Plants and Society*, 5th Edition by Estelle Levetin, pp. 348–351. Copyright © 2008 The McGraw-Hill Companies, Inc. Reprinted by permission of The McGraw-Hill Companies, Inc. **pp. 94–95** Islamic Folk Stories by Nasreddin Hodja: From *Tales of Hodja* by Charles Downing. Copyright © 1964 Charles Downing. New York: Henry Z. Walck, Inc., 1965, pp. 21, 90–91, 44. **pp. 96–97** Excerpt from *Gilbert's Living with Art* by Mark Getlein—Public Art: From *Gilbert's Living with Art*, 8th Edition by Mark Getlin, p. 283. Copyright © 2008 The McGraw-Hill Companies, Inc. Reprinted by permission of The McGraw-Hill Companies, Inc.

Chapter 3

pp. 110–111 Determining the Author's Purpose: From "When Rights Collide" by Amitai Etzioni in *Psychology Today*, October, 1977. Copyright © 1977 Amitai Etzioni. Used by permission of the author. **p. 113** Exercise 2, Identifying the Clues: From *Understanding Business*, 8th Edition by William G. Nickels et al., p. 6. Copyright © 2008 The McGraw-Hill Companies, Inc. Reprinted by permission of The McGraw-Hill Companies, Inc. **pp. 113–114** Excerpt from *Dave Barry is Not Taking This Sitting Down* by Dave Barry. Copyright © 2000 by Dave Barry. Used by permission of Crown Publishers, a division of Random House, Inc. **pp. 116–117** Impulse Control: The Marshmallow Test: From *Emotional Intelligence* by Daniel Goleman. Copyright © 1995 by Daniel Goleman. Used by permission of Bantam Books, a division of Random House, Inc. **p. 124** "Crossings" from *Reaching for the Mainland and Selected New Poems* by Judth Ortiz Cofer. Copyright © 1987 Bilingual Press/Editorial Bilingue, Arizona State University, Tempe, AZ. Reprinted with permission. **pp. 127–130** Excerpt from "Life on the Edge" by Karl Taro Greenfeld in *Time*, September 6, 1999, pp. 29–36. Copyright © 1999, Time Inc. All rights reserved. Reprinted by permission. **pp. 133–135**

Review Test: Context Clue Practice Using Textbook Material, paragraphs 1–9: From *A First Look at Communication Theory*, 6th Edition by Em Griffin. Copyright © 2006 The McGraw-Hill Companies, Inc. Reprinted by permission of The McGraw-Hill Companies, Inc. **pp. 136–137** Vincenzo Perugia: From *Gilbert's Living with Art*, 6th Edition, by Mark Getlin, p. 387. Copyright © 2002 The McGraw-Hill Companies, Inc. Reprinted by permission of The McGraw-Hill Companies, Inc.

Chapter 4

pp. 153–154 Ways to Categorize Lies: Excerpt from *Looking Out Looking In*, 13th Edition, by Ronald B. Adler and Russell F. Proctor II, pp. 326–327. Boston: Wadsworhth Cengage, 2011. **pp. 155–156, 158** Exercise 2, numbers 1–6 & Exercise 3, numbers 1–6: From *Criminology and the Criminal Justice System*, 6th Edition by Freda Adler, et al., p. 295. Copyright © 2007 The McGraw-Hill Companies, Inc. Reprinted by permission of The McGraw-Hill Companies, Inc. **pp. 160–161** Steps in a Process: From *Criminology*, 6th Edition by Freda Adler et al., p. 86. Copyright © 2007 The McGraw-Hill Companies, Inc. Reprinted by permission of The McGraw-Hill Companies, Inc. **pp. 161–162** Burglary: From *Criminology*, 6th Edition by Freda Adler et al., pp. 309–310. Copyright © 2007 The McGraw-Hill Companies, Inc. Reprinted by permission of The McGraw-Hill Companies, Inc. **pp. 156–157** Excerpts from *All I Really Need to Know I Learned in Kindergarten* by Robert L. Fulghum. Copyright © 1986, 1988 by Robert L. Fulghum. Used by permission of Villard Books, a division of Random House, Inc. and the author. **pp. 159–160** "And The Third Biggest Lie is . . ." by Ann Landers: By permission of Esther P. Lederer and Creators Syndicate, Inc. **pp. 167–168** Review Test: Identifying Patterns of Organization in Textbook Material, items 1–3, 5 & 7: From *Mass Media Mass Culture*, 5th Edition by James R. Wilson, pp. 6, 31, 175–176, 217–218, 357. Copyright © 2001 The McGraw-Hill Companies, Inc. Reprinted by permission of The McGraw-Hill Companies, Inc. **pp. 167–168** Review Test: Identifying Patterns of Organization in Textbook Material, items 4 & 6: From *Mass Media in a Changing World*, 2nd Edition by George Rodman, p. 90. Copyright © 2008 The McGraw-Hill Companies, Inc. Reprinted by permission of The McGraw-Hill Companies, Inc. **pp. 175–177** "School Cheating Scandal Tests a Town's Values" by Jodi Wilgoren in *The New York Times*, February 14, 2002, pp. A1, A32. Copyright © 2002 by The New York Times Co. Reprinted with permission. All rights reserved. **p. 185** "Hope is the thing with feathers" reprinted by permission of the publishers and the Trustees of Amherst college from *The Poems of Emily Dickinson*, Thomas H. Johnson, ed., Cambridge, Mass.: The Belknap Press of Harvard University Press. Copyright © 1951, 1955, 1979, 1983 by the President and Fellows of Harvard College.

Chapter 5

pp. 192–194 "Barney" by Will Stanton in *Fifty Short Science Fiction Tales*, pp. 253–255. Copyright © 1963 by Macmillan Publishing Co. Copyright renewed 1993 by Isaac Asimov and Florence A. Conklin. **pp. 197–198** "A Remote-Controlled Rat" by Kenneth Chang in *The New York Times*, May 2, 2002, p. A20. Copyright © 2002 by The New York Times Co. Reprinted with permission. All rights reserved. **p. 201** "A Friend Named Bo" from *Understanding Psychology*, 5th Edition by Robert S. Feldman, p. 184. Copyright © 1999 The McGraw-Hill Companies, Inc. Reprinted by permission of The McGraw-Hill Companies, Inc. **pp. 201–202** Fiddler on the Mud: From *Marine Biology*, 6th Edition by Peter Castro, p. 268. Copyright © 2007 The McGraw-Hill Companies, Inc. Reprinted by permission of The McGraw-Hill Companies, Inc. **pp. 203–204** "No Cattle, No Dignity" from *Sociology: The Core*, 7th Edition by Michael Hughes, p. 53. Copyright © 2005 The McGraw-Hill Companies, Inc. Reprinted by permission of The McGraw-Hill Companies, Inc. **pp. 204–205** Venomous Snakes Are Few: From *Biology*, 8th Edition by Sylvia Mader, p. 569. Copyright © 2004 The McGraw-Hill Companies, Inc. Reprinted by permission of The McGraw-Hill Companies, Inc. **pp. 214–215** The Wolf and the Crane: From *Aesop's Fables*, edited by Jack Zipes. Copyright © 1992 by Jack Zipes. Used by permission of Dutton Signet, a division of Penguin Putnam Group (USA) Inc. **pp. 216–220** Excerpt from *Wolf Songs* by Farley Mowat: From "Good Old Uncle Albert" in *Never Cry Wolf* by Farley Mowat. Reprinted by permission of McClelland and Stewart Ltd., Toronto, Canada, and the author.

Chapter 6

p. 236 "Introduction to Poetry" by Billy Collins from *The Apple that Astonished Paris*. Copyright © 1988, 1996 by Billy Collins. Reprinted with the permission of the University of Arkansas Press, www.uapress.com. **p. 238** "To Be of Use" by Marge Piercy: From *Circles on the Water* by Marge Piercy. Copyright © 1973, 1982 by Marge Piercy and Middlemarsh, Inc. Used by permission of Alfred A. Knopf, a division of Random House, Inc., and Wallace Literary Agency, Inc. **pp. 242–243** Excerpt from *A Walk in the Woods* by Bill Bryson. Copyright © 1997 by Bill Bryson. Used by permission of Broadway Books, a division of Random House, Inc., and Doubleday Canada, a division of Random House of Canada Limited. **p. 246** Analyzing Signs and Symbols: From *Living with Art*, 7th Edition by Mark Getlein, pp. 239–242. Copyright © 2005 The McGraw-Hill Companies, Inc. Reprinted with permission The McGraw-Hill Companies, Inc. **pp. 247, 248** Symbolic Use of Color and Cultural Meaning of Colors: From *Essentials of Human Communication*, 3rd Edition by Joseph A. DeVito. Published by Allyn and Bacon, Boston, MA. Copyright © 1999 by Pearson Education. Reprinted by permission of the publisher. **pp. 249–251** "Book of Dreams" from *Farmworker's Daughter—Growing Up Mexican in America* by Rose Castillo Guilbault. Copyright © 2005 by Rose Castillo Guilbault. Reprinted with permission of the publisher, Heyday Books, c/o Copyright Clearance Center.

Chapter 7

p. 265 Exercise 2: Identifying Tone, Number 2: From *Sociology: The Core*, 7th Edition by Michael Hughes, p. 267. Copyright © 2005 The McGraw-Hill Companies, Inc. Reprinted by permission of The McGraw-Hill Companies, Inc. **p. 265** Exercise 2: Identifying Tone, Number 3: From *The Art of Public Speaking*, 7th Edition by Stephen E. Lucas, p. 358. Copyright © 2001 The McGraw-Hill Companies, Inc. Reprinted by permission of The McGraw-Hill Companies, Inc. **p. 265** Exercise 2: Identifying Tone, Number 4: From *Sociology: The Core*, 7th Edition by Michael Hughes, p. 177. Copyright © 2005 The McGraw-Hill Companies, Inc. Reprinted by permission of The McGraw-Hill Companies, Inc. **p. 266** Exercise 2: Identifying Tone in Textbook Material, Number 5: From *Understanding Business*, 8th Edition by William G. Nickels, p. 613. Copyright © 2008 The McGraw-Hill Companies, Inc. Reprinted by permission of The McGraw-Hill Companies, Inc. **p. 267** Exercise 2: Identifying Tone in Textbook Material, Number 9: From *The Art of Public Speaking*, 7th Edition by Stephen E. Lucas, p. 215. Copyright © 2001 The McGraw-Hill Companies, Inc. Reprinted by permission of The McGraw-Hill Companies, Inc. **p. 267** Exercise 2: Identifying Tone in Textbook Material, Number 10: From *The Art of Public Speaking*, 7th Edition by Stephen E. Lucas, p. 263. Copyright © 2001. Reprinted by permission of The McGraw-Hill Companies, Inc. **pp. 267–268** Excerpt from *The House on Mango Street* by Sandra Cisneros, pp. 90–91. Copyright © 1984 by Sandra Cisneros. Published by Vintage Books, a division of Random House, Inc., and in hardcover by Alfred A. Knopf in 1994. Reprinted by permission of Susan Bergholz Literary Services, New York. All rights reserved. **p. 268** "My Rules" from *Where the Sidewalk Ends* by Shel Silverstein, p. 74. Copyright © 1974, renewed 2002 Evil Eye Music, Inc. Reprinted with permission from the Estate of Shel Silverstein and HarperCollins Publishers. **pp. 269–270** Excerpt from *Double Whammy* by Carl Hiaasen, p. 129. Copyright © 1987 by Carl Hiaasen. Used by permission of G.P. Putnam's Sons, a division of Penguin Group (USA) Inc., and International Creative Management, Inc. **pp. 271–273** Excerpt from *Lucky Man* by Michael J. Fox. Copyright © 2002 by Michael J. Fox. Reprinted by permission of Hyperion. All rights reserved. **p. 278** "Bodybuilders' Contest" in *View with a Grain of Sand* by Wislawa Szymborska, p. 25. Copyright © 1993 by Wislawa Szymborska, English translation by Stanislaw Baranczak and Clare Cavanagh. Copyright © 1995 by Harcourt Inc. Reprinted by permission of the publisher, and Faber & Faber Ltd. **pp. 279–280** "Waiting in Life's Long Lines" by Tom Mather in *The BG News*, Bowling Green State University, August 6, 1997. Reprinted courtesy of The BG News. **pp. 282–283** Excerpt from *Dave Barry is Not Taking This Sitting Down* by Dave Barry. Copyright © 2000 by Dave Barry. Used by permission of Crown Publishers, a division of Random House, Inc. **pp. 286–288** Pages 47–48 from *Frida: A Biography of Frida Kahlo* by Hayden Herrera. Copyright © 1983 by Hayden Herrera. Reprinted by permission of HarperCollins Publishers.

Chapter 8

p. 303 Eastern and Western astrological charts: From *Better Writing Through Editing* by Jon Peterson and Stacey A. Hagen, p. 56. Copyright © 1999 The McGraw-Hill Companies, Inc. Reprinted by permission of The McGraw-Hill Companies, Inc. **pp. 304–307** Excerpt from *Psychology: Approach to Mind and Behavior*, 10th Edition by Dennis Coon, pp. 361. Copyright © 2006 Wadsworth, a part of Cengage Learning, Inc. Reproduced by permission. www.cengage.com/permissions. **pp. 310–312** Excerpt from *Janson's History of Art: Western Tradition*, 7th Edition by Penelope J.E. Davies, et al., pp. 2, 5, 6. Copyright © 2007. Reprinted by permission of Pearson Education, Inc., Upper Saddle River, NJ. **pp. 318–320** "Bug Heads, Rat Hairs—bon app*tit" by Mary Roach, January 14, 2000, salon.com. This article first appeared in Salon.com, at http://www.Salon.com. An online version remains the Salon archives. **pp. 325–328** Excerpt from *Fast Food Nation: The Dark Side of the All-American Meal* by Eric Schlosser. Copyright © 2001 by Eric Schlosser. Reprinted by permission of Houghton Mifflin Harcourt Publishing Company. All rights reserved and from *Chew on This: Everything You Didn't Want to Know about Fast Food* by Eric Schlosser and Charles Wilson. Text copyright © 2006 by Eric Schlosser. Reprinted by permission of Houghton Mifflin Harcourt Publishing Company. All rights reserved. **pp. 332–333** A Culture of Cheating: From *Sociology*, 12th Edition by Richard T. Schaefer, p. 67. Copyright © 2010. Reprinted by permission of The McGraw-Hill Companies, Inc.

Chapter 9

p. 339 Exercise 2: Identifying an Author's Point of View, Numbers 5 & 6: From *Teachers, Schools, and Society*, 8th Edition by Myra Pollack Sadker and David Miller Sadker, pp. 192, 196–197. Copyright © 2008 The McGraw-Hill Companies, Inc. Reprinted by permission of The McGraw-Hill Companies, Inc. **pp. 341–342** Popular Mechanics by Raymond Carver: From *What We Talk About When We Talk about Love* by Raymond Carver. Copyright © 1974, 1976, 1978, 1980, 1981 by Raymond Carver. Used by permission of Alfred A. Knopf, a division of Random House, Inc. **pp. 353–354** "Our Animal Rites" by Anna Quindlen, Op-ed Sunday, August 5, 1990, Section 4, p. 19 in the New York edition of *The New York Times*. Copyright © 1990 by The New York Times Co. All rights reserved. Reprinted with permission. **p. 358** Vietnam Memorial by Tom Wolfe: From "The Invisible Artist" in *Hooking Up* by Tom Wolfe. Copyright © 2000 by Tom Wolfe. Reprinted by permission of Farrar, Straus and Giroux, LLC. **pp. 359–360** Reprinted with the permission of Simon & Schuster Publishing from *Boundaries* by Maya Lin. Copyright © 2000 by Maya Lin Studio, Inc. All rights reserved. **p. 361** "A Quiet Place for Personal Reflection" in *Congressional Quarterly* by Congressional Quarterly on the Web. Copyright © 2000 by Congressional Quarterly Inc. Reproduced with permission of the Congressional Quarterly, Inc. **pp. 364–365** "The Vietnam Wall" by Alberto Rios from *The Lime Orchard*

Subject Index

Index of Artists and Art Works